About the author:

W A Sumner studied theology at Hull University and achieved an M Litt from Oxford University. He has spent many years as a teacher and preacher in schools and churches. He is a reader of the Diocese of Birmingham and is also a hospital chaplain.

THE THEOLOGY OF PARADOX

W.A. Sumner

Book Guild Publishing
Sussex, England

First published in Great Britain in 2015 by
The Book Guild Ltd
The Werks
45 Church Road
Hove, BN3 2BE

Typesetting in Times by
YHY Ltd, London

Printed in Great Britain by
CPI Group (UK) Ltd, Croydon, CR0 4YY

A catalogue record for this book is available from
The British Library.

ISBN 978 1 910298 34 3

Contents

Foreword

Bill Sumner is true to himself in his forthright and challenging style, seen clearly in his Preface, where the reader is warned about what is to come! He speaks self-disparagingly of crankiness in his ideas, but his well-researched book is not as cranky as he hints it might be. In fact, it is remarkably orthodox in most of what he writes. He has much to say that demands serious attention. This is particularly so in his comprehensive and wide-ranging survey of comparative religion, resulting from years of study and his classroom teaching.

I valued his honest and thoughtful discussion throughout the book of the core issues in theology, especially in chapter 2 on Theodicy, chapter 7 on the Incarnation and Apotheosis, and chapter 13 on Miracles. His emphasis on the place of metaphor, parable and allegory as being crucial in any understanding of God is important in today's materialistic climate. It helps to ensure that rationalism is tempered by mystery, that desire for certainty is cautioned by doubt, and that literal interpretation is constrained by scientific knowledge.

His use of allegory on the Atonement in chapter 9 is a novel way of tackling such a complex subject. He does not hold back from sharp criticism of Bultmann's demythologising process in chapter 11 on Mythology. The analysis of Belief, Doubt and Atheism in chapter 18 is thoroughly up-to-date as he tackles the high profile atheistic arguments of Richard Dawkins in a fair and dispassionate way – likewise his comments on Karen Armstrong's chapter on 'Unknowing' in her book *The Case for God.*

Bill Sumner's thorough-going examination of world religions will not please or appeal to everyone, but he is not advocating a syncretistic mish-mash; rather he is attempting to draw out the relevance of continuity in theological study and to help us live with paradox in theology as much as in everyday life.

There are helpful headings to guide the reader through each chapter and these will aid easy reference. It is a book for serious study and a rich source for debate. It will provoke thoughtful and lively discussion – and no doubt disagreement – in lecture room and study group. Bill has tackled a massive task and achieved it successfully in a highly readable manner.

Michael Whinney, Bishop Emeritus, Southwell
June 2014

Acknowledgements

The author wishes to thank Michael Whinney, Peter Turner, Peter Kaye, John Cook and Patrick Morrow.

Preface

The cranks of today are the wise men of tomorrow. The reverse is true: the wise men of today are the cranks of tomorrow. It is a profound truism! How often do we see the bright ideas of today become a little jaded with the passage of time: fashions come and go. This is so often seen in world affairs, politics, philosophy and not least in theology. This work on the subject of paradox in theology may appear to some at first to be decidedly cranky. But this is because it is based on certain assumptions which are not normally accepted in today's world. One such assumption is that people in the ancient world were not all idiots: some were geniuses. Also it assumes that the Bible and other associated ancient writings are not the product of fools: rather they are the considered thoughts of the most highly inspired people of that day and age. That does not mean we have to take them completely literally; what we do need to do is to try to see into their mind-set and work out how it applies to our predicament in the twenty-first century.

There will be many matters in this book which will go against the cosy assumptions of recent scholarship and philosophy. I do not claim to have the answer to every awkward question. But then, neither do they. It is high time that the liberalistic, gratuitous assumptions of today were challenged. The accepted thoughts of the last 200 years need a bomb put under them! A fresh approach to just about everything is urgently needed.

Also what is needed is a 'one-world' mentality. The world is tired of worn-out disputes in politics and religion which lead to nowhere except violence. World peace means finding ways of understanding each other in spite of our differences in religion and culture. I am not talking about compromises or some sort of meaningless syncretism. We need to look at the full range of religious expression and try to find what is at the heart of it and what factors of potential unity can be found. Every time I raise the possibility of an inter-religious analysis, I get a decidedly 'glug' reaction, especially from the academics, who ought to welcome it. But this needs to be done, if only for the urgent need for world unity and cooperation between nations. We all know what the consequences will be if we do not work towards 'one-world-itis'.

It was a big shock when Beethoven burst in on the musical and cultural scene two centuries ago. The classical era had got itself firmly into more than one rut. We too are in various ruts at the moment. He broke all the rules on the subject of musical composition and shocked them all. How about a big shock for theology, and by implication for philosophy, and hence for politics? It is high time we had a complete rethink, and found something positive to lead us forth into this new millennium!

1

A General Introduction to the Theology of Paradox

In a recent TV interview, representatives of four major faiths were asked, 'What does God mean to you?' There was a surprising degree of agreement between the Christian, the Jew, the Muslim and the Hindu. Traditionally, there have been clear-cut boundaries assumed between different religions, but this may be more of an assumption than a reality. Accepting that in the modern world media and communications have had very much a rounding effect on major religions, it becomes progressively more difficult to state with total certainty the core values of any particular faith. It has been the norm for people to take their own faith as absolutely right and other faiths to be completely wrong; this can hardly be maintained. A sympathetic appraisal of any religion will discover its helpful and positive points; also its shortcomings; also its relatedness and dependence on other faiths.

To quote Karl Barth: 'religion is flesh. It shares in the profligacy and essential worldliness of everything ... human religion neither overcomes human worldliness nor transfigures it.'[1] This generalisation covers all forms of Christianity as well as religious behaviour across the spectrum. A study of religions reveals how much they are the product of historical personalities, social circumstances, climate and reaction to other ideas. But faith is something over and above the details of religious expression, and may be seen as the basic link between all manner of religions in their diversity. The common assumption that all religions are really the same is misleading; their very diversity should give the lie to that. And yet there are many underlying assumptions that are the same. The basic needs in human nature are the same the world over; the satisfaction of these needs takes different methods and thought forms.

The basic question for the human race is that there are two

different worlds. One is the world that we see and live in, the physical world. Although some have tried to play down or deny the existence of it, most rational people accept the world as we see it, even with its distortions and uncertainties. At the same time, there has always been (and still is) an awareness of another world of the spirit or divinity which runs parallel to our own and is the end destination at death. How it is pictured and speculations about its nature have been many and various, although many basic assumptions about it have been the same the world over. Jesus in Matthew 22:23–33 is almost certainly saying, in allegorical terms, that we cannot conceive of what the next world is really like. It is on an entirely different dimension and human vocabulary cannot cope with it. So too with attempts at picturing God (or gods): no human imagery comes anywhere near coping with the reality of the divine; it almost always relapses into a projection of human traits and an urge to create God in our own image and control him by our own methods.

This brings us to the first major paradox in life: that the one world can produce or influence the other. If we assume that God is spirit but created the world, how can something uncreated produce something physical? Or even more difficult, how can a perfect agency produce or allow something imperfect? To quote C.S. Lewis: 'to make things which are not itself, and thus to become in a sense, capable of being resisted by its own handiwork is the most astonishing and unimaginable of all the feats we attribute to deity.'[2]

I should begin by defining 'paradox': Barth's idea of 'contrary opinion' is helpful but does not go the whole way. Surprisingly, with Christian theology and that of other religions thoroughly permeated with paradoxes, there is little use or mention of this word until we arrive at the twentieth century, and yet to follow this line of enquiry might help to clarify or resolve all manner of confusions in people's minds on the subject of religion.

The history of the word 'paradox' goes back to Ancient Greece: Zeno appears to be the first to use it. Plato and Aristotle quote him. The purpose of paradox is to arrest attention and stimulate thought. If compressed into two words, such as a 'loud silence', it is termed an oxymoron. The first use of 'paradox' in Christian theology is claimed to be in the works of Boethius, a philosopher of the late Roman Empire. However, he does not develop it in relation to the many contradictions in Christian thought. Many writers have come close to speaking in terms of paradox without actually using the word. Karen Armstrong, for instance, senses that things normally opposed coincide to reveal an underlying unity; she can see no opposition between the 'natural' and the 'supernatural'.[3] Other writers such as Barth and Baillie use the word but do not tease out the full implications of it across the wide spectrum of theology, both Christian and non-Christian.

It is Ronald Hepburn, in the post-war era, who embarks on the 'paradox trail' in a more thorough-going fashion.[4] However, the tone of his book is largely negative on the matter of paradoxes: he would like to resolve them all and speak plainly about the great truths about God and mankind. He does not attempt to draw on any other religious or political ideas; even so, he does raise the possibility of a more thorough realisation of paradox in theological and philosophical debate. One helpful issue raised is the distinction between a contradiction and a paradox. A contradiction is two statements making opposite claims: they can be resolved now or in the future on quite rational grounds and therefore do not form a paradox. An example of this would be light, which has been described by two incompatible models: as wave movements and as particle movements. It would have been a mistake to have rejected one of these ideas in favour of the other, since later it was found that the two statements could be resolved by further scientific research, so there is actually no paradox. But a true paradox is when two contradictory statements, which are true in their own way, cannot be resolved. Neither one can be rejected for fear of losing a certain truth or important process. Paradoxes appear in all forms of knowledge, including literature and mathematics. An example which does not require much mathematical ability is as follows:

$+2 \times +2 = +4$. This is easy and not a problem.
$-2 \times -2 = +4$. Many find this difficult but it is true.

Both these statements are absolutely true and neither of them can be rejected as suspect. They will never be resolved and we have to admit that if line two is denied, then the whole workings of mathematics will collapse asunder. We need both of them and we must recognise that paradoxes are essential in the great workings of things.

An amusing literary paradox comes from Orwell's *Animal Farm*: 'all animals are equal but some are more equal than others'.[5] But paradox is not just a clever literary device used by gifted poets such as Shakespeare. There are various paradoxes emanating from the fact that the solar year is just slightly less than 365.25 days per year. In the *Pirates of Penzance*, Frederick was unfortunately born on 29th February, which meant that in one sense he was 21 years old but in another sense he had had only five birthdays. George Washington was born on 23rd February 1752. His birthday is recorded as 11th February 1752. Both are correct in their own way. This was because in 1752 a calendar correction was done by cutting out eleven days, which meant that they jumped from 2nd September to 14th of September. If the World Calendar were ever to be introduced, then anyone with a birthday on 31st May would be left with no birthdays at all![6]

There is a major paradox emanating from geography with regard to world map-making. It is impossible to render a true drawing of a sphere on a flat piece of paper. There are various devices for doing this, none of which is entirely correct, but all of them contain an important element of truth. There is the Mercator projection which in effect turns the world into a cylinder and leaves it to one's imagination that the two sides join up in the Pacific Ocean. It is correct in that all the compass directions are reliable: however, all the lines of latitude and longitude are straight, which is misleading, and all the land areas towards the poles are exaggerated. It is useful for navigation, but for distances and land areas it is false. Another kind of projection by Gall, which turns the world into segments like portions of orange peel, renders the land areas and distances accurate, but all the compass directions are wrong. There is another projection called the 'conic' one which views the world from a selected 'pole' (not necessarily the North or South Pole). This time the lines of latitude are correct circles, but not the longitude ones. The land areas are proportionately correct but at the edges it all fades out of sight. Whichever projection one uses, there is always a truism but also a false element. It is to no purpose to reject one in favour of another. They all have their part to play and when viewed together they give a fair impression of the world as a sphere. A sphere can be depicted on a flat piece of paper but only with the three-way paradox of three different methods. We shall encounter a three-way paradox when discussing the Trinity and the Atonement. It is impossible to have the full truth without accepting three differing versions of the same thing. It then comes up in three dimensions (3D).

So, in attempting to talk about God, it cannot be done in the flat vocabulary of normal language; it has to be done in an array of contradictory metaphors. The truth then comes up three-dimensionally. We see from this that paradox is more than just a clever literary device for enhancing poetry: it is an important factor found in many areas of life. I have talked about two and three dimensions; there is the possibility of further dimensions available for exploring theological truths.

Returning to Hepburn on the subject of paradox, the impression gained is that he would like to resolve them all and speak plainly about theology. But this cannot be done. The answer is to embrace paradox and contradiction as an inevitable situation in any theological idea, for they help to bring out the richness and mystery of faith. It may be that such matters as Theodicy can receive a solution somewhere in the Wisdom of God, but not in this world, for it is beyond the canons of human logic to cope with it.

From 1 Corinthians 1:19 we can learn that God's logic is not the same as human rationality: 'I will destroy the wisdom of the wise ... where is the wise man ... has not God made foolish the wisdom of the world?'

If we could see that paradox is not a liability but an asset, even a safeguard, that would be a far more constructive approach. Paradox can be seen as a form of 'insulation', like the atmosphere around the world that we breathe: it keeps us alive but also provides a blanket of insulation from destructive intrusions from outer space. The bare and bitter truths about God and humanity are carefully wrapped up in the medium of paradox. Also helpful is the mentality found in Far Eastern religion, that of 'plural belonging' (Hocking).[7] This is the capability of holding two mutually exclusive views simultaneously. Though it is never stated in such terms, it is in fact the ability to cope with paradox; this is something that Western theologians could learn from. All the doctrinal arguments and entrenched positions which have produced dogmas and heresies could be seen in a different light: the truth is often seen in two contradictory statements.[8]

The same is true about contradiction. If we take a positive approach to it, it enriches our understanding of God. Resolving a contradiction is not important. Doubtless some of the contradictory remarks made by Jesus can be harmonised, but what it shows is that God provides for all eventualities, he is not tied down to just one course of action.

Another problem with Hepburn's arguments is the matter of an 'ostensive definition of God'. The assumption here is that God can be defined, yet we know from the Burning Bush incident that God is beyond human definition, even the parameters of human conception.

Exodus 3:14: 'And God said to Moses, "I AM THAT I AM."' The Hebrew of this leaves a very wide range of possibilities of interpretation, since the verb tense is in the present or the future, or even the imperfect. It could mean 'I was what I was' or 'I will be what I will be', or even 'I might be what I might be', and even more elaborate constructions which do not exist in Hebrew. Hebrew has only two verb tenses, and there is no strict demarcation between them. Past, present and future can and often do flow into one another.

What it does not allow for, in this quotation, is philosophical speculations and definitions of God's nature, and any attempt to define it soon becomes an idolater's errand. Also the divine tetragrammaton, YHWH, is clearly related to this. Strictly speaking it is unpronounceable, but is rendered as 'The Lord'. The Jehovah's Witnesses made the mistake of calling God 'Jehovah', but this is an artificial word, being an amalgam of YHWH and the vowels of ADONAI (meaning 'my Lord'). The essential truth is that for him to be God, he is beyond human imagining, and yet paradoxically there is an impression of him in the human mind.

Ecclesiastes 3:11 says, 'God has put eternity into men's minds and yet so that he cannot find out what God has done from the beginning to the end.'

A useful analogy of this could be found in the method of homeopathic medicine: a substance is put into water and then diluted several times to the extent that the original substance is no longer present (or at least cannot be traced by the analyst) and yet there is some sort of impression left in the water, almost a kind of 'memory', which brings about healing.

Hepburn's admission that 'It is very unlikely that God can be ostensively defined or that we can have such sure knowledge by acquaintance of God as the theologian needs to make his case' is a crashing understatement. God is beyond human definition and no vocabulary can be used to describe him. A helpful idea here is the *koan* (something in Zen Buddhism) in which there is a flash of insight, a *satori* which is incommunicable: one can only see it or not see it; it is beyond language. If this idea is applied to Western monotheism, it means that 'knowing God' is either there or not there, and no words can convey this insight. Truths about God are somehow conveyed in the tension between full-blown belief and full-blown atheism. It is a mistake to underestimate atheism: the claim that God does not exist has validity if we assume that existence entails being a part of the physical world, but he is over and above and beyond existence.

Another useful analogy could be as follows. A wet rag needs to be wrung out; it is twisted at both ends and the tension produced causes droplets of water to trickle out. So too with the tension produced between belief and unbelief: deeper truths about God begin to emerge.

Hepburn claims to be a 'linguistic philosopher'. This is fair enough if philosophy is kept to the level of not trying to convey the deepest truths about God. Nowhere in the Bible does it descend to the level of logic, proof, speculation or rationality. Admittedly, language is used to convey the Scriptures, but Hebrew and the mentality that went with it was (and still is) ideally suited to dealing with the deepest encounters between the living God and certain selected persons. The Greek of the New Testament accords well with what the first Christians wished to convey about the incomparable event of the Messiah coming into this world and being a living presence in the life of believers. One might question the use of modern English both in philosophy and theology: the continuing debasement and cultural decline in English, coupled with the plethora of pejorative words which always seem to confuse the issue, make one wonder if another language could not be found. Moreover there is always the possibility of other modes of expression being used: the language of music, mathematics, and pictorial art and symbolism are available for conveying theological truths.

There is some sort of assumption in Hepburn's thoughts that 'logic is logic' not just for humanity but for God too. He does not like 'unsupported statements' about God, which must mean that everything claimed about God has to be supported by human rationality. But how would one support any statement about God if he is on a different dimension to humanity? It is no accident that Jesus spoke of God not in philosophical jargon but in the medium of parables and analogies: 'The Kingdom of God is like ...'. This is a way of saying, 'the intervention of God in this world'. It is no surprise that his teachings do contain contradictions, some of which may amount to paradoxes, for when the eternal God is in contact with the temporal world, there is bound to be some kind of disparity.

Isaiah 55:8: 'for my thoughts are not your thoughts, neither are your ways my ways ... for as the heavens are higher than the earth, so are my ways higher than your ways, and my thoughts than your thoughts.' A positive approach to paradox and contradiction is now seen as a useful course.

Nobody has systematically treated the deep paradoxes of the Christian faith, Theodicy, the Trinity, Atonement, to name but a few, on this sort of basis, let alone drawn comparisons with other religions where similar tensions exist. On a lower level there is the tension over denominationalism and sectarianism in the Christian and other orbits. Reaching for a solution to these matters is almost certainly beyond us in this life, and yet there is the possibility of pondering these matters. Would it be too much to suggest that all these variations in religious faith fulfil some sort of function in the great workings of things?

With regard to contradiction, this too needs to be seen in a positive light and not as some sort of mistake. A helpful analogy would be a pair of scales, with two opposing values which cancel each other out across the fulcrum. Nobody has ever talked about the theology of balance even though the 'balance of nature' is a well-accepted notion and is becoming increasingly more obvious as scientific work proceeds. The same forces and mechanisms can be seen at work in theology. The contrary opinion or contradiction is not an embarrassment but a method for holding things in balance, within one religion or between two or more religions. There is a rich variety of religious expression in human life; God gives the world a degree of stability through the diversity of belief and practice of faith. It is not good enough to say that we can merge all religions together and find a happy medium; that is not what paradox and contradiction are all about. There are times when one idea gains too much weight and tries to blot out other ideas, but the balance comes back in its own way and the net result is that there has been something learnt, perhaps an awareness that was lacking previously. If these mechanisms, paradox and balance, can be seen as God's way of preparing people's minds and leading them to the ultimate truth, then they can be seen in an altogether different light.

It is possible to discern various basic elements in religion. This mostly follows C.S. Lewis's analysis, but with certain additions:[9]

1. The numinous: the feeling of dread, the uncanny, spirits, ghosts, the awareness of another world or state of existence which may seem threatening and unpredictable. It is easy to write this off as pure superstition, but still people go about their lives on this sort of assumption, regardless of how 'logical' or 'advanced' they may claim to be. Also shamanism in many of its basic forms and adaptations is still active in today's world.
2. Some form of morality which stems from some type of law code. Usually this is written and given by the 'god' or the ruler who represents the god. The code may be oral or just a part of one's tradition, and may also be ethical or ritual, or some kind of combination of the two. Either way it brings with it guilt or remorse because of failure to match up to its demands. It is unusual to find anyone who has never experienced guilt; guilt may be rational but may also be augmented by irrational fears.
3. The logical: this is not normally mentioned in this context, but how much of our mathematics, science and philosophy is somehow originally based on some sort of religious assumption? The mathematicians, philosophers and builders of the ancient world did not achieve these matters in some sort of mental vacuum: it was a product of theological speculation. The same is still true to this day for all our theorisings about evolution, creationism and cosmology have basic religious assumptions underpinning them. It is a common assumption in the modern world that science and religion cannot be reconciled. This is a particularly modern fallacy. It is an off-spin of the Papal attempt to control and dogmatise on scientific matters. The truth is that the Reformation gave a new impetus to scientific research because of the way that Papal authority could be questioned with a clear conscience. People tend not to realise that many of our scientists and technologists are people of faith.
4. The coming together of these strands. The numinous and morality are not the same impulse and yet from early times they have been associated. It is God who gives the laws: this pre-dates Moses by a long way. Also the logical versus the numinous has always been a matter for thought since they are not the same thing, and yet logic and laws of nature have become an important attribute of God.

5. The final element is the historical event of Jesus coming as the Messiah of God, something that can hardly have been imagined or fabricated by human nature, and though making an appeal to each of these four strands, transcends all of them and brings them to fulfilment and resolution. All our fears, laws, speculations about the world and their relatedness come to a resolution in his life and ministry. It is true that other faiths have various attempts at a god in human form, and these will be examined later, and yet none of them come anywhere near the distinctive and overwhelming ministry of Jesus.

In these matters we can already see important paradoxes, contradictions and aspects of balance at work. There is the paradox of God coming into the world as a human being: also that religion involves the numinous and the logical. There is the contradiction between perfection in morality and failure and corruption in human nature. With regard to balance, there is the need to balance ritual procedures with logic, two things which do not work on the same level. When considering the full gamut of religious experience and theological claims, these matters become more obvious. This work will attempt to examine a wide range of religious belief and practice in the light of paradox, contradiction, balance and resolution, something which has not been systematically attempted before. But it is important that such a matter is attempted if only for the sake of understanding and cooperation between peoples of different cultures and dogmas. The world is tired of worn-out disputes and empty wrangles often based on entrenched ideas. The world needs unity. That does not mean an interesting list of compromises; still less a plastic kind of religion full of syncretistic ideas. But what we do need is to find the worthwhile elements in any given faith and learn to cope with our differences of opinion.

This work will be done under various headings: Theodicy, legalism, sacred writings, sacrifice, Incarnation, Trinity, Atonement, unity and diversity, mythology, and even more adventurously, calendar calculations.

A paradigm for the logic of humanity as compared with divine

Sam wanted to play at building castles. His Dad gave him a collection of coloured building blocks and gave him a few tips on how to get started. The boy was entranced and began to erect a castle on the nursery floor. He soon learnt how to place one block on another and so build up an ever-growing structure. It occurred to him to build right up to the ceiling. But the higher it got, the less stable it became. Just a thump on the floor or a draught from the door soon had it all come crashing down, especially if it was standing on a wobbly piece of carpet. But this did not stop him starting all over again. He soon realised that there was a limit to how much superstructure he could safely devise. He asked his Dad why this was. Would it be possible to build right up to the ceiling?

His Dad explained that there was a thing called gravity which made the bricks stay down on the ground. If one or two are stacked up carefully, then gravity helps them to stay in place. However, if the building gets too high, or the bricks are not exactly straight on top of each other, then gravity starts to work against it. The building progressively becomes unstable and soon it all comes crashing down.

His Dad then showed him something which did not behave according to gravity. It was a balloon bought from the fair. Sam was intrigued by how it sailed up and hit the ceiling, but the string still dangled so that he could pull it down and then let go again. His Dad warned him not to take the balloon out of doors and let go. Sam did not really understand why not. But he soon found out, for when he took it out into the garden and let go of the string, the balloon sailed off into the sky and refused to come back. He was so upset about how careless he had been not to listen to his Dad's warning. The problem was that he was not really mature enough to understand that there was a gas called helium inside which made the balloon lighter than air. He did not know how to cope with something completely unfamiliar as this was, even though he could see it and handle it: it was still a mystery.

So it is with human logic. God has given us a system of reasoning which is perfectly good as far as it goes. We have the syllogism, something coming from Ancient Greece, in which there are two premises which lead to a conclusion. An example:

All cats have whiskers.

Tiddles is a cat.
Therefore, Tiddles has whiskers.

This is perfectly fair, as long as the two premises are true. However, if one of them is untrue then the conclusion will be wrong or at best unreliable. Take this example:

All women are stupid. (!)
Freda is a woman.
Therefore, Freda is stupid.

This would be perfectly fair, except that the first premise is open to dispute. Doubtless Women's Lib will object strongly. This means that Freda does not have to be stupid. She might be, but this does not follow from these premises.

Another problem with human logic is as follows:

All the rich are wicked exploiters.
Harry is a rich man.
Therefore Harry is a wicked exploiter.

This is a circular argument, often called 'begging the question'. It is only a matter of opinion that all the rich are wicked exploiters. What about the rich benefactors who help out the poor? Furthermore, 'rich' is a value judgement. What do you mean by 'rich'? Is it anyone who has more than £50 in the bank? But circular arguments are abundant in the realms of religion, politics, philosophy and, yes, science too. Perhaps we do not realise how often, inadvertently, we beg the question. Here is another example, not quite so transparent:

The Fascists and the Communists are extremist parties.
Labour, Conservative and Liberal Democrat are moderate parties.
To avoid extremism, vote Tory, Labour or Liberal.[10]

On the face of it this sounds logical enough, and yet there is a hidden problem with the logic of it. The argument includes an unspoken element in the human mind: that extremism is bad and moderation is good, an assumption which is fair enough in most circumstances. It begs the question that moderation is always the right policy. Suppose there was a national crisis which required urgent and extreme measures: moderation would then be an obstacle should martial law need to be declared.

There are many other logical fallacies which are often used, but this goes to show that human logic is not always quite what it appears to be; it has its shortcomings and clever people have ways of swaying public opinion to suit their own policies. Goebbels was a past master at it. So too with the tower of bricks: human logic can only go so far. It can easily become unstable and come crashing down.

Divine logic, however, is not restrained by the parameters of human logic. God gave us the syllogism: he does not have to use it himself. A similar thing applies to the Ten Commandments. God gave us rules to live by, but he does not have to apply them to himself. His logic works on a different basis that we do not understand, even if we see it in action. He shows us such things as Theodicy, Incarnation, Atonement and many other mysteries. We have an awareness of them, but how they work is beyond the capability of the human mind to analyse. Those who do try to rationalise the deep matters of God are like children playing with bricks in the nursery. They have the wrong tools for coping with divine logic. They need something which is not earthbound, but heavenbound, and on that basis we are all dealing with factors that are beyond our comprehension.

God has given us various ways for making a start on conceptualising his deep mysteries. One mode was the parables given to us by Jesus. They speak of eternity and God's intervention in this world. Even though they appear to be easy stories for children, there is a deeper element that defies complete analysis. The other mode God gives us is that of contradiction and paradox. By its very nature, paradox is beyond human analysis and yet eternal truths can be conveyed to the human soul in terms of contradictory statements. This indicates that divine logic is not totally beyond us, but we can never, in this world, take in the full implications and wonder of it all.

A paradigm for the logic of humanity in relation to divine logic

There was a hotel overlooking a wide expanse of the sea. One day, Miriam the chambermaid noticed that the sea appeared to be heaped up at one side of the window, as compared with the other side. She stared at it and could make no sense of it. Why was the water higher at one side of the house than the other? She mentioned it to Charles the hotelier. He was a panicky sort of person; he immediately began to think of some sort of disaster looming. 'You're right,' he gasped, 'does it mean there's a tidal wave or a tsunami building up? Perhaps we had better run for our lives. It could come right up the beach and swamp the whole coastal plain.' They were about to run for their cars when Tom, son of the house, said, 'What's the problem?' He remembered that water always finds its own level, even if the sea has waves. 'That's not a tidal wave: it would be moving along if it were. The sea is perfectly level today, as it always is.' 'So why is the sea not in line with the window frame?' asked Charles.

In reply, Tom went and fetched a spirit level and placed it on the window ledge. 'Look!' he said, 'the window frame is not level.' This was true; in fact the whole building was not quite straight or level. Was it subsidence or just careless work by the builders? It was clearly an optical illusion that the sea was not level. It had to be, if water always finds its own level. But then there are so many things in life that we take as the truth but are actually an optical illusion or a mirage.

A similar and related effect can be seen where a railway runs along beside a canal (or river). There is a place in Oxfordshire where the train takes a bend which means that the track is slightly tilted. But looking at the canal, the water appears to be tilted. This is a very strange effect: it looks as though the canal is sloping. This is impossible; the water has to be dead level. It is the train that is sloping but the passengers are not immediately aware of this. This is another interesting optical illusion or mirage.

What this means is that our patterns of thought are assumed as a matter of habit to be correct. Often they are, but not always. Human logic has its shortcomings, and 'habit of thought' is one of them. We tend to assume that all our logic is on the level. Then by extension we assume that God's logic has to be on the same level, and in agreement with ours. This is our major mistake: to assume that God's mind is the same as that of humanity. It is God's logic that is straight, like the water which finds its own level. It is human logic that is so often tilted out of line, but we usually do not realise it until we are confronted with God's intervention in this world. The supreme example of this was when God's Messiah Jesus appeared and showed us that in many ways human reasoning was out of line. As pointed out by St Paul, Jesus appeared to be weak, foolish and crazy to allow himself to be put to death, but this was the supreme strength, wonder and wisdom; something that humanity has severe difficulties in coping with. The logic of God is the true logic; the logic of humanity is essentially faulty, and confused by illusions and mirages.

Notes

1. Karl Barth, *Commentary on the Epistle to the Romans.*
2. C.S. Lewis, *The Problem of Pain*, Fontana, 1940.
3. Karen Armstrong, *The Case for God*, p. 37.
4. Ronald Hepburn, *Christianity and Paradox.*
5. George Orwell, *Animal Farm*, Penguin, 1945, p. 114.
6. E.G. Richards, *Mapping Time*, Chapter 19.
7. W.E. Hocking, *The Meaning of God in Human Experience.*
8. Bouquet, *Comparative Religion*, 1941.
9. C.S. Lewis, op. cit.
10. R. Thouless, *Straight and Crooked Thinking*, 1956.

2

Theodicy: The Problem of Evil

This is a theme in theology and philosophy which has been a problem since the dawn of time. The word itself comes from Leibniz who coined the term '*La Théodicée*'. Strange as it may seem, the concept of paradox and balance, though implicit in these matters, is never actually stated in these terms. Since the days of Job and well before, this theme has been discussed, but with no convincing solution found. Looking through the various answers that have been offered or implied, there is a lot of negativity involved. It is the atheist's 'magic wand': if there is a God, how is it that there is any evil in the world? We can discern seven main attempts at solving the problem, but not one of them is completely convincing or satisfactory.

Firstly, the multi-deity answer. From the very earliest times mankind has believed in a multiplicity of deities or spirits, and this explains the uncertainties and problems in life. The gods interfere with us and we attempt to influence them by various techniques. Most systems have a notion of a supreme God who produces lower gods whose attitude to us is always somewhat unpredictable. Ancient Greece and Rome are prime examples of this but there are pantheons in virtually every mythological system the world over. All too clear is the projection of human traits up into the heavens, and just as there is no real explanation for evil in human nature, so too the gods are inexplicably badly behaved in their own world. In some systems, a single god is seen as double-faceted, being good and evil, creating and destroying at the same time. Natural disasters and failure in battle are easy to explain, but personal wickedness and guilt are easily offloaded onto another agency, and become a minor issue. This system appears to provide answers on a superficial level, but does not really come to grips with evil in the skies or in the heart of man.

Secondly, the modified pagan multi-god answer. The best example of this is seen in the theorisings of the Gnostics who were prevalent in the Roman Empire, but there are many subtle ideas and permutations on the same sort of lines. It is not just one system of thought, but various schemes which attempt some sort of compromise between monotheism and paganism. It centres on a supreme deity who is perfect but distant from this world, and a world of flesh which is beyond redemption, and yet the soul of man can find salvation, usually through some programme of tough self-discipline. In between God and humanity is a descending order of sub-gods or philosophical entities, the number of which is variable, but they become progressively less perfect than the top god. Leibniz with his 'monads' and various aspects of Eastern religions would come under this heading. Buddhism has been called a form of Gnosticism, although there are many other aspects of it. As an attempt to cope with Theodicy it goes a long way, but not the whole way. There is no real explanation for how the perfect ultimate God can produce something which is less perfect than himself, let alone allowing a world which is beyond redemption.

Thirdly, the denial or deduction of evil. Various systems of thought, including pantheism and monism, seek to say that there is one pervading force in nature (God) in all things. This is not the same as monotheism. The strength in this is that creation is seen in unity including human nature, a view encouraged by recent scientific advances. The idea of evil spirits or forces opposing God is played down or absent. There is a reality transcending all things 'good' or 'bad'. An example of this would be in Shinto, where there is no absolute dichotomy of good and evil. All things have 'rough' and 'gentle' characteristics and there are no inherently evil forces. Confucius, Pelagius, the Ranters and libertines would come under this heading, not to mention many kinds of materialists and antinomialists. But can this be realistic when we see natural disasters, and harm deliberately contrived by human beings, and worse still, certain individuals who can only be described as evil? Also, refusing to admit to the reality of evil can easily result in denial of good. For good to have any meaning, the opposite has to exist as well.[1]

Fourthly, dualism, the use of two gods, good and bad. The clearest example of this appears with Zoroaster and became the prevailing belief of the Persian Empire. This was not to deny the existence of other gods, but the main solution to Theodicy is seen in the cosmic contest between Ahura Mazda the god of light and Angra

Maiynu the god of darkness: good versus evil. A constant struggle is going on not just in the heavens but also in men's hearts. Eventually there will be an apocalypse and the good will finally win through. Traces of this idea can be found in many religions: Shinto, the Hindu festival of Divali, the defeat of Mara at Buddha's Enlightenment.[2]

This system is thought to have worked its way into post-exilic Judaism and hence into the thinking of the early Christians and Jesus himself. It is, however, in an adapted form, for nowhere in Judeao-Christianity is Satan seen as an alternative God. The Devil is a spiritual power to be reckoned with, but in the final analysis he is under the control of the one God. Thus it can be seen that there are various permutations on dualism. The 'yin–yang' configuration in Taoism contains much subtlety. Yang is the masculine, active, warm, bright, fiery, procreative, positive mode in all things. The yin mode is the fertile, feminine, breeding, dark, cold, wet, mysterious, secretive, shadowy aspect of things. They are pictured as white and black, slightly intertwined. There are various versions of it. What is missing is the personal ethical aspect, one's own response to good and evil, even if the *shen* (good spirits) are yang, and the yin are connected with the *kwei* (evil spirits). Taoism has many helpful ideas for peace and harmony in the world, but is not really related to an active God; it is not far from a version of pantheism and does not cope with outright and disastrous evil.[3]

Dualism has pervaded most of Christian theology down to the present but is now being played down by various elements as 'sub-Christian' (C.S. Lewis).[4] There is some sort of embarrassment about mentioning the Devil, but as an answer to Theodicy it is probably the nearest we have come to a solution; and yet the question of how the good God can allow the bad spirit to have any sway in human affairs is not clearly understood. Since it is the basic assumption that Jesus worked under, it has to be taken more seriously than some of these other ideas.

Fifthly, pure monotheism. This may superficially resemble pantheism and yet it is not the same: the one God stands as separate from his creation. It is a popular belief, with at least three major religions being based on it. It brings the question of Theodicy into sharper focus. If God is assumed to be perfect, that throws the question of evil back on to humanity. This is where the classic account of the Garden of Eden is seminal, regardless of whether it is taken as literal or figurative. There was a time in prehistory when there was no evil or pain, but because of wayward humanity, sin, pain and death came in; because of the Fall, all the evils of history ensued from this one act of disobedience. It is interesting that many other systems of thought include a cultural 'recollection' of a Golden Age in the remote past. How and why there came a breakdown in relations with the Creator is not really explained, any more than trying to understand why God created mankind as capable and free to go wrong. Later thinking began to equate the serpent with the Devil, but that is where dualism enters the picture. The Book of Job is the classic attempt at coping with Theodicy on the monotheistic assumption but even here there is no conclusive answer to be found. We can see that a moderated form of dualism has to creep into the equation for any sort of solution to emerge.

Sixthly, materialistic atheism. The denial or reduction of any God or spirit is another avenue for coping with Theodicy. Atheism is mostly associated with the modern world but is actually nothing new. If God is removed from the equation, then there is no final authority supporting the law codes or any other procedures. Authority has to be sought elsewhere. Right and wrong easily become the playground of whoever happens to have snatched political or cultural power. Showbusiness personalities, dictators and self-appointed messiahs begin to redefine ethics to suit their own fancies. In denying an eternal God, a temporal god soon has to emerge as a substitute but since he will not accept responsibility for any evil, he has to point the blame elsewhere. Usually another class of humanity will be found as a scapegoat: the fascists often seek to incriminate so-called 'racial inferiors': the communists blame political 'inferiors' such as the capitalists or the bourgeoisie. It is all about shifting blame: but the guilt still re-emerges regardless. It all goes to show that some sort of substitute for God never carries conviction for very long. As an answer to Theodicy, this idea simply leads us back to the first idea.[5]

Seventhly, 'cartoucheism'. A cartouche, in the sense of an elliptical line drawn round an important issue, like the Pharaoh's name in his tomb, seeks to encapsulate and perhaps in a way to isolate from the main system. In doing so, there is a sense in which the matter is relegated to a secondary position or even forgotten as much as possible. A good example of cartoucheism is the Wheel of Becoming as seen in some types of Buddhism: the good and bad, and all conditions in between, are encapsulated in their own active little system, but the main thrust of Buddhism is something completely other. The yin–yang configuration in Taoism is another. Pandora's Box as an approach to Theodicy is interesting. For many, the Garden of Eden situation has become a cartouche: modern theology has managed to sideline it as 'mythical' and make other matters the main thrust of Judeao-Christianity. Cartoucheism is a form of escapism: we cannot solve the problem, so we try to ignore it, even pretend it does not exist. This too does not work for very long, as the problems of Theodicy reassert themselves all too painfully. It is not possible to stop thinking about Theodicy; the problems of this life will continue to cloud the issue, and yet we are mysteriously driven to trying to find a solution.

A useful analogy to cover all these ideas might be as follows. There was a beetle climbing up a glass vase which had a little water in the bottom. He fell over the edge and into the water. It was not deep enough to drown him but enough to make his life a misery. Because he was wet all over he could not climb up the inside of the vase. He set to pondering why he was stuck in this impasse. He had an awareness that there were humans in the room; perhaps they had tipped the vase on purpose or out of clumsiness but they did not seem to want to help him. He knew the master of the house had a nasty boy who might have done it out of spite. Then it occurred to him to blame himself for being so careless. Of course he could blame another beetle for giving him a push so that he could steal his lunch. And finally, pure escapism, he discovered that he could float on the water and almost forget the problem altogether. Or could he? The fact remains that no matter how we try to rationalise or even ignore the problem, it only takes a major natural disaster, or a drastic problem in one's personal life, for the whole thing to re-emerge painfully.

It would be a mistake to associate any one of these seven ideas with any one particular religion. Elements of them are found working into virtually every system, and that includes political ideologies as well as religions. It would be true to say that every system on earth, ancient or modern, has tried and continues to try to cope with Theodicy in some way or other, in some shape or form. Essentially, there are three sources available for apportioning blame: God(s), Devil(s) and humanity (us). Since in the modern world we have problems with the existence of the first two, that leaves us with looking at ourselves in the mirror. It is interesting that the crisis mentality over global warming and associated matters is being blamed on to the excesses of human consumption. God and the Devil are not being blamed this time! But basically, Theodicy is about finding someone or something to blame. We can see that in the Garden of Eden configuration. But should it be so? Ought not Theodicy to be disentangled from the blame mentality and seen in an entirely different light, without moral or ritual overtones? All this will be unwrapped in the succeeding developments.

The Book of Job in relation to these ideas

There is no certain fixing of a date or authorship of Job. It probably predates Ezekiel. It has been ascribed to Moses or possibly Solomon, but nobody really knows. It would be a mistake to assume that it is the earliest attempt at coping with Theodicy. There are various literary works on this theme stemming from the ancient world, notably *Prometheus Bound* by Aeschylus, *The Dialogue of a Misanthrope* with his own soul (from Egypt), a cuneiform text from Harran, but most notably the 'Babylonian Job', a story about Tabi-Utul-Bel, a good man who fell on misfortune but was finally restored by his god, Marduk. Many of these literary productions probably pre-date Job, but there is no certainty that any of them were dependent on each other. More likely it was an ongoing theme in the soul of mankind from the dawn of human history. Even so, the solution to Theodicy has not yet been found; the paradox continues. It is only Job who begins to come anywhere near finding an answer.

It is possible to discern all seven of our strands in these early 'philosophical' writings. For the Babylonians it was easy to use the pagan model plus the free use of evil spirits, a touch of dualism, but even then the unfairness of 'Why does a righteous man have to suffer?' still remains the unspoken paradox. For the Egyptians, their elaborate ideas on an afterlife in which souls are weighed and evaluated imply a certain aspect of monotheism by which eternal justice prevails in the end, regardless of how matters work out in this world. But for the Hebrews, who seem not to have had such an elaborate view of afterlife, the problem re-emerges with an extra sting, as Job, who is claimed to be perfect, falls on disaster and can make no sense of it. The reader knows that there is a 'Son of God' called Satan who has been given permission to test Job, but that is part of the irony.

Here we see the answer to the pagan model: God is supreme in heaven, which is monotheism, and yet he is not solitary. Though he is creator and active in all creation, he is still other than his creation: the answer to pantheism. For the denial of God, his wife in despair utters ‘curse God and die’, in other words, ‘go in for atheism’: but Job rejects that temptation. It is a pre-Fall situation: Job is perfect, even resisting his wife’s temptation (unlike Adam). By all human assumptions, if he has fallen on disaster, this must mean he has sinned. To read the Mosaic covenant is enough to reinforce this equation. The nearest we come to a solution is this subtle combination of monotheism with a moderated version of dualism, a scheme which came to full fruition in New Testament times. We can even discern cartoucheism in Job, for as a theological debate bordering on philosophy, it is included in the Old Testament but does not form part of the main thrust. The main message is that through God’s love, he rescues people and establishes a covenant with them, issuing promises and threats. The only relevance of this to Job is that his misfortunes cut against what he assumes in the covenant of God; all completely illogical unless you see it as a paradox of the first quality.

Job’s three ‘comforters’ continually emphasise the idea that he must have sinned. He remains firm in denying it. It is only with Elihu, the young firebrand, that any light dawns on the problem. He accuses the others of having no answer at all and indeed that is true: they simply go round in circles, like our seven strands. Although it is not stated as such, Elihu is getting away from the negative or blame aspect of the argument. He begins to see the whole thing in a positive, constructive light, something that humanity does not really understand.

Job 33:14: ‘For God speaks in one way, and in two . . . though a man does not perceive it.’

Job 33:29: ‘God does these things twice, thrice, with a man to bring his soul back from the Pit, that he may see the light of life’.

This means it is God’s method for saving people. It is here that we see a hint that ‘the Pit’, the underworld or Sheol, is not the final or permanent end of mankind. This ties in with something from the Babylonian Job (line 65): ‘Do you wish to go the way these have gone (the rich)? Rather seek the lasting reward of the gods.’[6] This sounds like a hint of rewards in the afterlife.

Job 37:13: ‘Whether for correction or for his land, or for love, he causes it to happen.' Here we have the admission that God makes misfortune happen and that he has purpose in doing it. 'For love' is quite a claim, but then we are talking about love which is not some sort of sentimental paternalism; it is a robust, caring commitment to his people, which looks at the long-term salvation, not just the satisfaction of ephemeral fancies.

It is no surprise that God answers Job out of the whirlwind, which is symbolic of humanity's confused and circulatory thoughts on the matter (31:1). In fact, arguments about Theodicy usually finish with total confusion and an array of illogicalities and circulatory movement through our seven strands. Then follows a long discourse on the wonders of nature, which to some has seemed irrelevant, but is actually very much to the point.

'Where were you when I laid the foundations of the earth?' (38:4). It goes on until Job is rendered speechless (40:4): 'Behold I am of small account ... I lay my hand on my mouth ... I will proceed no further.'

This reminds us of something in the Babylonian Job (line 292): 'My voice was not raised, my speech was kept low.'

This was for a different reason: he was just being humble in society. Job is speechless in the face of God. This may be a good example of how a monotheistic writer has reinterpreted a pagan idea.

When we see the wonders of nature and have but a feeble grasp of its ingenious workings, how can we approach the problem of Theodicy? This becomes all the more relevant today as scientific discoveries continually underline the wonders and relatedness of things in the natural world: it raises the question of how we can possibly know better than God. A quotation from Thomas Aquinas may be helpful here:[7]

> According to Augustine, God is so good that he would never allow anything evil to occur, unless he were powerful enough to be able to draw good from every instance of evil. Hence the fact that evils appear in the world is due neither to impotence or ignorance on the part of God. Rather it is due to the ordering of his wisdom and the magnitude of his goodness from which proceeds the multiplication of the various degrees of goodness in things, many of which would be lacking if he permitted no evil to occur.

Job's passage on Wisdom (28:20) brings us to a conclusion. 'Whence then is the place of Wisdom ... it is hid from the eyes of all living ... Abaddon and Death say "we have heard a rumour of it" ... God understands the way of it.'

He is saying that God knows the answer to all these things but it is concealed from all living. If you wish to make a start on it, take this as the crucial remark: 'The fear of the Lord, that is Wisdom ... and to depart from evil is understanding' (28:28).

In other words, if you begin your enquiries into Theodicy with a deep respect for God's brilliance in creation, and keep a clear conscience, you will begin to come close to seeing the deep truths of salvation.

This gives the lie to the Gnostics and the meditators with their special knowledge or mantras or techniques; the lie to the pagans with their pantheons; the lie to the denial of evil; the lie to the absence of God altogether. The final answer lies in God's hands. For those who think there is no eternal justice as stated in the Babylonian Job (line 72): 'In my youth I sought the will of my god ... but I was bearing a profitless corvee as a yoke: my god decreed, instead of wealth, destitution ... the rogue has been promoted but I have been brought low.'

But Job assures us that there is final justice, for in the last verses he is restored. This of course refers to this life, 'yet in my flesh shall I see God.' Here is also the beginnings of an awareness of hope in the next world (33:28): 'He has redeemed my soul from going down into the Pit, and my life shall see the light.'

Prometheus Bound in relation to these ideas[8]

This short drama by Aeschylus probably stems from the pre-classical era in Greek culture. It also involves itself in the question of Theodicy but because it approaches the matter in an obviously different way, it is highly unlikely that there is any interdependence with Job. It is more likely that the same difficult question is at the root of every culture on earth: it is all about 'Why does the innocent have to suffer?'

The play does not concern itself with humanity except indirectly. The actors are all gods or divinities of some lesser form. Briefly, Prometheus stole some fire from Hephaiston and gave it to mankind and helped them to develop all manner of skills and knowledge. Zeus objected to this and decided to punish Prometheus by crucifying him on a rock. When he refused to tell of the whereabouts of Io and claimed that Zeus would be dethroned, he was damned to hell.

It is possible again to discern our seven strands in this play, although not at all clearly thought-out. As with Job, we are left with no clear reason why the innocent should suffer and Prometheus's damnation remains all very unfair, at least from the human point of view, and also that of various minor divinities. The prevailing pagan assumptions are the backdrop of the play, and there is dissention between Zeus, the king of the gods and the lesser gods. Zeus himself is known to be lecherous and is seeking Io for that purpose; his wife Hera is fuming. With this kind of attitude at work in the heavens it is not difficult to see why humanity has so many problems. The Gnostic view of gods proceeding from one another is not so much stated but assumed: Prometheus is assuming, from Hesiod, that the Sky-Kings are annually overthrown and supplanted by their sons, so Zeus was to be ousted eventually by someone who may be more kindly disposed to Prometheus. There is a touch of dualism (though not very thorough-going) where Typhon opposed the gods, especially Zeus: 'Typhon will with hate, the hundred heads in fury subjugate, who dared to rise against all the hosts of God. His snake fangs hissing and a-foam with blood ... as though to strike the god's very throne.' But this is not really related to Prometheus's plight.

The denial of God is seen in the idea that Zeus can be dethroned: 'that the grief that I endure shall know of no relief nor lightening, until Zeus from heaven be cast. Can this thing be, that Zeus shall fall at last? What foe shall wrest the sceptre from his hand?'

This can hardly amount to complete atheism, since they are assuming that a replacement chief god will appear. Evil can hardly be reduced; more likely, good is understated. There is no pantheism, but regarding monotheism there is the assumption of an age of innocence in the far distant past, although Pandora's Box is assumed rather than mentioned. It is Prometheus who gives humanity a positive start, much to Zeus' disgust:

> Hear now the sorry tale of mortal man. A thing of no avail he was, until a living mind I wrought within him and new mastery of thought. I cast no blame on man: I do but crave to show what love was in the gifts I gave ... everything they did was

> without knowledge, til their eyes were oped by me to see the stars that rise ... all that of art man is, Prometheus gave.

It was out of love that he did all this and yet Zeus objected and decided to punish him. Zeus is represented as cruel and unfair, Prometheus as some sort of defiant hero, mankind as morally neutral. It is Theodicy upside down.

The two sequels to this play are lost but it is understood that Prometheus is eventually released from the abyss and reinstated. Even so, the suffering of the innocent is still beyond explanation.

One interesting feature of this play is the way Prometheus is portrayed in almost Christ-like terms: 'in this craggy high and tempest-riven gulf to crucify a god ... in bonds of brass indissoluble, nail thee against this life-deserted hill.'

This reminds us of Golgotha, the place of a skull. Prometheus comes across as a kind of saviour god, helping mankind. But the essential difference is that he is not in agreement with the 'Master's Plan' for 'which sin to all heaven he needs must pay atonement', he is not atoning for mankind's sin, but for stealing Hephaiston's fire and enlightening mankind. Even if the logic of this is markedly different, it nevertheless comes to resolution and correction with the atoning death of Jesus Christ. The whole play is characterised by doom, despair, blame, guilt and recrimination: the Christian gospel is the opposite, for out of pain and death comes resurrection, triumph and great joy.

A drama by Aristophanes, *Wealth*: a contrast to Prometheus[9]

The play *Wealth*, by Aristophanes, stands in total contrast to Prometheus. It is bawdy, lavatory humour, almost pantomimic in its approach to Theodicy. Although gods are worked into the fabric of the play, it is not really a theological approach, it is more a socio-economic argument, which makes it seem remarkably modern to some.

The main character, Chremylus, a poor farmer, states what we all would like to assume, and yet we have to admit it does not work out thus: 'it is obvious to everyone alike: that in all fairness the good people of the world should prosper and the wicked, and godless the opposite.' This is in contrast to his earlier cynical remarks, that 'temple robbers, politicians, informers, rascals' all seem to prosper. He is minded to advise his son to embark on a life of crime if he wants to get ahead in life.

But now Chremylus thinks he has found a splendid course of action which will solve the problem. Wealth is pictured as a blind and ragged old man who wanders around encountering people at random, which explains why there is no logic to who gets rich and who is destitute. The reason for his blindness is because Zeus (who resents mankind) had blinded him on purpose because he said he would only visit the just, wise and decent people. Should he ever recover his sight, he would shun the wicked. Chremylus offers to restore his sight but Wealth is fearful of Zeus's reaction. He does not realise how potentially powerful he is; a truism, as wealth does entail economic and political influence.

Now Poverty, pictured as a hideous old hag, enters. She is furious that she will be banished, saying that it is completely wrong to make the just people rich. Her reason for saying this is that becoming rich will corrupt them all with idleness. There will be no more slaves to do the menial work, so all that money will not solve any problems. It will only mean one will have to do the menial work oneself. She makes the point that poverty makes better men: the good ones are poor and the rich are arrogant and idle. (Echoes of Marxism!) 'How dare you keep denying that Poverty is the source of all your blessings?'

As the play develops, Chremylus takes Wealth along to the temple of Asclepius and a miracle takes place: Wealth can now see. But amid the rejoicings, as poor deserving people find they are suddenly rich, a complete upset is looming in the socio-economic order. The just man falls on good fortune; the informer is ruined; for the old woman with a boyfriend, the relationship has all gone wrong (she was a prostitute); Hermes reports that Zeus is furious because no one is sacrificing any more; the priest is ruined for the same reason. They are all trying to find a new role in life and the implication at the end is that they are invited to follow the procession of Wealth to his temple. This is a roundabout way of saying that everyone can be equally rich. The unspoken thought at the end is what Poverty warned: if it is poverty that gets the work done, who will do the work?

A comic play of the classical Greek era, it nevertheless hints at deeper matters. We can see it as a trivialisation of divinity: Wealth and Poverty, though seen as gods, are clearly little more than clever personifications. They talk and behave like humans and Chremylus is actually talking down to them. But the unspoken truth behind it all is that there has to be poverty for wealth to have any meaning. The reverse is true: that wealth is to no advantage unless there are poor people toiling away at the basic tasks. If everyone is equally rich, then by the same token they are equally poor. For there to be any values in life, there has to be the contrast between rich and poor.

This is as far as it goes in this comedy, but of course the implications in it can extend to theological and philosophical matters. Why is there suffering in the world? Why does the innocent have to encounter pain? The root of the problem of Theodicy; the answer may be on the same lines. If we were all equally fortunate, nothing ever went wrong, no one ever got hurt, what sort of people would we be? Poverty would probably say, 'Idle, arrogant, corrupt, domineering, dishonest, and generally greedy, failing to give thanks to God.' Are we seeing something of this in the Western world today, with the current wave of prosperity? It has blinded people to the realities of life and made them complacent and unable to respond with gratitude to God.

Superficially this play deals with the matter in a comical manner, and yet deeper and more soul-searching matters are implied even if they are not stated. One such thought, not stated at all, would be that Zeus, the chief god, deliberately blinded Wealth, which implies in a roundabout and mythological way that God is the ultimate cause of the problem of Theodicy. In this way, Aristophanes could well be in agreement with Aeschylus.

The prophet Isaiah in relation to these ideas

It is not possible to know, timewise, where Isaiah fits in relation to Job or Prometheus, but there is no reason to assume any dependence on these works. It is further evidence of the ongoing question of Theodicy in the heart of mankind in early times. The assumption here is that Isaiah is one literary production, in spite of modern ideas that there were actually three prophets at work here at differing times. Essentially it does not matter, but the unity of the book will be discussed in chapter 3.

With Isaiah we see a robust monotheism. There is never any mention of Satan, the Devil, Azazel or any other form of evil spirit. Theodicy is not the main thrust of his theology, and yet remarks relevant to Theodicy keep emerging all through the book. He has clearly not set out, like Job, to explore the matter as his main theme, and yet Theodicy is at the back of his mind all the time. It is possible that his experience of the good reign of King Uzziah, a highly prosperous time which was clearly favoured by God should end with the king developing leprosy and having to be segrated from everyone. 'The Lord had smitten him' as 2 Chronicles 26:1–23 puts it. It is no accident that the call of Isaiah (6:1) coincides with the death of Uzziah. This must have influenced his thinking. Also the fact that Hezekiah, another righteous King of Judah, came up against certain misfortunes and was only spared by the intercession of prayer, must have played a part in his thinking. The same question then arises: 'Why does the righteous have to suffer?' Isaiah does not make the mistake of trying to deal with Theodicy on a personal level; what went wrong with Uzziah? – which is what we see in the Chronicles. He keeps it on a general and theological level, so that any conclusions will be of general application rather than specific.

His ongoing theme of the unity and overwhelming power of God is important in this context: 'I am God, and there is no other' (45:22), 'I am he, I am the first and I am the last' (48:12). Essentially this is a counterblast to idolatry and false gods, but it goes further, for the logic of it is that 'I am God, and henceforth I am he: there is none who can deliver from my hand: I work and who can hinder it' (43:13). The potter and the clay is an important parable here (29:16): 'Shall the potter be regarded as the clay: that the thing made should say of its maker, "he did not make me"?'

This raises the question of how or why we go wrong at all. This emerges in 63:17: 'O Lord why dost thou make us err from thy ways and harden our heart, so that we fear thee not?' The implication here is that it is God who makes things go wrong and humanity has very little control over it, if any. This applies on a cosmic scale, for 'I clothe the heavens with blackness and make sackcloth their covering' (50:3). It comes out specifically in 45:7: 'I form light and create darkness, I make weal and create woe, I am the Lord who do all these things.' But the matter cannot rest there, for there is still guilt and a failed relationship with God, even if he is omnipotent.

Something that everyone in the ancient world would have understood (59:2): 'Your iniquities have made a separation between you and your God, and your sins have hid his face from you so that he does not hear.' This is balanced by this remark in 57:1: 'the righteous man perishes and no one lays it to heart'. People try to ignore the injustice of it but Theodicy is still there regardless. Isaiah is aware that there is a deep mystery in the workings of God (29:21): 'to do his deed ... strange is his deed: and to work his work ... alien is his work'.

There is a subtlety and depth in his workings which defy logic (45:15): 'Truly thou art a God who hidest thyself.' Verse 45:15 sums it up well: 'for my thoughts are not your thoughts, neither are your ways may ways'. Essentially we do not understand God's method and system, perhaps we never will, and yet we cannot avoid being confronted with the question of Theodicy.

Even so, Isaiah can foresee a resolution to the problem of pain somewhere in the future. One of his main themes, the reversal of values, now becomes relevant. It is expressed in powerful metaphors involving mountains and valleys, light and darkness and other striking terms; somehow it is connected with the coming of the Messiah, when all these imponderables will be straightened out. This is not something within the power of human nature (5:20): 'Woe to those who call evil good and good evil ... woe to those who are wise in their own eyes.' It is for God to resolve these matters, according to his wisdom. But the reversal of values is seen in many places in Isaiah and it amounts to the cessation of pain and suffering.

'The wolf shall dwell with the lamb ... and the lion shall eat straw like the ox ... the earth shall be full of the knowledge of God as the waters cover the sea' (11:6).

'I will put an end to the pride of the arrogant' (13:11).

'Every valley shall be lifted up ... and the rough places plain' (40:4).

'I will turn darkness before them into light ... the rough places into level ground' (42:16).

'The people that walked in darkness have seen a great light: those who dwelt in a land of deep darkness, on them has light shined' (9:2).

'To bring good tidings to the afflicted ... to bind up the broken hearts, to proclaim liberty to the captives' (61:1–2).

This is clearly to be seen in the short term as the return of the exiles from Babylon, and yet there is a deeper, more eternal quality to it, that of the whole of creation being brought to equanimity and peace in the Messianic age.

The reversal of values continues as the substratum of the Suffering Servant, for, contrary to all expectations, here is someone who has done no wrong and yet is subjected to the depths of suffering and shame. These songs, which occur from chapters 49 to 54 intermittently, are well integrated into their context and it is a mistake to try to divorce them from their surrounding literature, and indeed the entire Book of Isaiah. They delve into the problem of pain with a sensitivity and depth of understanding not seen anywhere else. It draws in the Levitical motif of the scapegoat, except that this time it is a lamb, but at least it is the most successful attempt at coping with Theodicy seen anywhere. It would be true to say that the ministry of Jesus would have had very little meaning without the backdrop of the Suffering Servant of Isaiah. There is some sort of equation between the servant and the people of Israel: their sufferings as they were defeated and exiled and the maltreatment of the servant. It is not a complete equation: the Israelites had sinned but the servant had not (27:9, 'the guilt of Jacob will be expiated').

The servant believes he had done his best but all to very little effect (49:4) but God reassures him that he will restore Israel and more than that, provide salvation to the entire world (49:6). It seems unbelievable that such a one, humiliated, rejected, despised, should allow all this to happen to him (53:7) and yet never object. Here was someone who was completely innocent (53:9) and yet had to face an horrific end, victimised by everybody. The explanation fits perfectly with Isaiah's theology. 'It was the will of the Lord to bruise him: he has put him to grief' (53:10), and now comes the reversal, 'the will of the Lord shall prosper in his hand: he shall see the fruit of the travail of his soul and be satisfied' (53:11). In a mysterious way, he has taken away the guilt, primarily of Israel but also of all mankind. 'The Lord has laid on him the iniquity of us all' (53:6), and 'because he poured out his soul to death, and was numbered with the transgressors, yet he bore the sin of many' (53:12). This is the root of the theology of vicarious suffering, a strand taken up by many Christian writers including Anselm and Calvin. It defies human logic and yet, in the wisdom of God, it works nevertheless: through suffering and loss, gain and salvation is achieved. This is an idea that Elihu was on the verge of explaining, but Isaiah has brought it out in full.

This is not to say that we have the answer to Theodicy; even so, it is the nearest we can come to coping with it in this world. The paradox of suffering being transformed into joy is not easy to comprehend; the paradox of one person shouldering everyone else's guilt and relieving them of it is also a difficult piece of logic to assimilate. It may be that the metaphor is difficult and yet the reality behind it is equally recondite. But that is the Christian understanding of suffering and it goes right to the heart of Theodicy.

An ancient and yet modern approach: Taoist philosophy

For all its antiquity, this scheme has much to offer in contemporary thought. How the Unnamable Subtle Origin turns into the yin–yang diagram is not explained: nor can it be. It is a paradox of the most basic type. The whole scheme is filled with paradoxes: the contrast between fire and wood: metal and water, and so on. How this accords with modern Physics and Chemistry is an interesting question: and yet the Taoist is not really talking on that level. It is profoundly true that the workings of Nature are essentially based on a series of paradoxes which ultimately stem from one ultimate origin.

The T'ai Chi symbol with the yin–yang is claimed to be the ultimate truth of the universe. Everything creates itself through the integration of yin and yang without the direction of any creator. Everything that exists is an expression of T'ai Chi. We see that yin and yang are slightly intertwined, with dots of opposite colours. This not the only version of the yin–yang sign. Here it is a derivative of the Unnamable Subtle Origin, which might be analogous to 'God the Father' or YHWH. From the T'ai Chi flow all the permutations of creation, water, wood, metal, fire. This superstructure as described in the *Hua Teh Ching* may not be the authentic theorisings of Lao Tzu, but later realisations; but even so it may be a fair idea of Taoist philosophy. Tao, the subtle reality of the universe, cannot be described. Even so, as an answer to Theodicy, the T'ai Chi is profound: 'as soon as the world regards something as good, evil simultaneously becomes apparent.'

An analogy from the composition of water

Water is an unusual compound in that it is a combination of two gases, hydrogen and oxygen. It is unlikely that there are any other instances of such reactions in the world of chemistry. The reaction happens spontaneously when atoms of hydrogen and oxygen encounter one another in any circumstances. H_2O is a molecule of two hydrogen atoms, positively charged, and one oxygen atom with a minus charge. It is all held together by the tension between opposite electric charges. So this tension causes two gases to form a liquid. Going on from this, the world is held together – gases, liquids and solids – by tiny electrical impulses holding each other in tension. From the gases, liquids are formed; from the liquids, solids are formed. Is it possible to extend this thought and say that from the positive and negative tensions going on in the world of the spirit, the whole created world is formed and sustained? It would mean that all the paradoxes, contradictions, balancings and tensions are there to fulfil a positive role: that of underpinning the entire physical universe.

This is not an entirely new idea. The Mayans knew that 'the continuity of all things is dependent on the yin–yang co-existence of opposites'.[10] This does not mean that they were Chinese Taoists, rather that they arrived at the same idea as the Chinese, but using different vocabulary and thought forms. They believed that humanity is dependent on death, and vice versa. This again is a profound and absolute truism. Unfortunately they worked it out in real terms by committing human sacrifice on a vast scale, on the assumption that the sun would not appear in the morning and the world would come to an end if they failed to perpetuate this system. However, it is still true that there is no life without death and there is no death without life; this points us forward to the sacrificial death of Jesus.

'The bread which I shall give for the life of the world is my flesh', John 6:51.

'The first man Adam became a living being: the last Adam (Jesus) became a life-giving spirit', 1 Corinthians 15:45.

From this we see that the death and resurrection of Jesus is not just a personal, local, limited event for those who happen to believe in him: it is a cosmic event, upon which the whole of history, life, destiny and meaning pivots. This paradox will be unpacked later.

Modern explorations

Recent explorations into outer space have shown us that there are other worlds where conditions are in total contrast to our own. Absence of atmosphere, life, graduation of heat, all essential to human life on this planet, serve to remind us how dependent we are on a vast array of contrasts. There has to be a balance between hot and cold, height and depth, dry and wet, joy and misery, to name but a few. In theological terms there is the balance between good and evil, success and failure, growth and decay. At this stage it is possible to glimpse Theodicy without some kind of moral tinge or blame mentality. In even more neutral terms, in mathematics, plus and minus, and their derivatives, multiplication and division, powers and roots. We can see what the effect is in a world with no contrasts: is it possible to conceive of a world with no balancing: everything is plus, gain, success, happiness, growth and good? It would not work. For there to be genuine gain there must be loss: good only has meaning if there is evil. Just as there is balance in Nature, so too in all other aspects of life. To have any values in life there must be an ongoing balancing act between good and evil. The yin–yang emblem is profound.

So in the theology of balance we begin to see some sort of positive reasoning in Theodicy: it is a mechanism given by God for stabilising and sustaining life. We can go further and say that each of our seven strands in theodicy contains an element of truth: no theological idea is totally wrong; the mistake comes in overemphasising one idea at the expense of others. Strict ethical monotheism is balanced by the diversity of paganism. The harshness of pure dualism is balanced by the subtle yin–yang idea. The all-inclusive passivity of pantheism is contrasted with the active spiritual world of shamanism. All these ideas are in subtle balance and this explains why religions and systems of thought persist in some shape or form despite all the shifts in world history. Even atheism can be seen as a part of the balancing mechanism for extreme levels of belief have to be mirrored by the negative possibilities of failure of faith.

This leaves us with the first and most teasing paradox: why or how did a perfect God devise a world with contrasts, differences of opinion and the tension between good and evil? Does this mean there are contrasts within God himself? Is there tension between pleasure and pain within God himself?

Strangely this is not a new idea. Heraclitus saw that tension between opposites is the eternal condition of the universe; it is in eternal flux and there is no permanence. This is a profound thought only taken up again recently, by Bergson and Whitehead. It leaves us with the paradox of permanence in God but impermanence in the creation.

Concluding remarks on the Paradox of Theodicy

The paradox of a perfect, eternal and all-powerful God having any relationship with a failed, corruptible and changing world has always been a difficult, nay impossible, question in the soul of humanity. This is no new problem and will continue unresolved until the end of all things. What has clouded the issue is the negative way in which it has been discussed, usually drawing in blame in some shape or form.

This chapter has opened up the possibility that Theodicy can be discussed in morally neutral terms and, going further, in morally positive terms. It can be seen in the balance between positive and negative principles of all kinds which allow the universe to function both physically and spiritually. Looking at it in a positive way, the fact that there is suffering and loss in life points the way to eventual gain and triumph. This does not accord too well with any canons of human logic but that is what Elihu and Isaiah were on the verge of opening up for us.

Going on further, Isaiah's theology, which is full of vibrant optimism, raises the prospect that all these matters which are a burden on the human mind will, at some stage in the future, be brought to resolution. The theology of resolution, which is an important aspect of this work, functions on different levels and in a variety of metaphors across the entire spectrum of religious experience. At its very lowest level, the failure in the Garden of Eden carries the implication that somehow all things will be restored and put to right, eventually. At another level, the activity of lawmaking implies that there is the possibility of human correction and maybe even of perfection, one day. Prophecy also, a major strand in the Bible and elsewhere, implies that the unseen powers have it in mind to resolve all the problems of this world. Mythology too, as will be seen, carries the implication that all the speculations of human nature will in some way be brought to conclusion, very often in historical terms.

So the paradox of Theodicy, far from being a problem of despair, actually carries the promise of continuity[11] in the physical world and resolution partly in this world but also in the next. Even with all this, it is not possible for us to cope with the deep mystery that Isaiah managed to discover, that out of the depths of pain comes healing: 'Who has believed what we have heard? He was bruised for our iniquities ... and with his stripes we are healed' (Isaiah 53:1–6). He is in effect saying, we cannot comprehend this, but out of total loss comes total gain, a paradox which underpins everything that Jesus Christ came to bring to completion.

Having said all this we are still left with the awkward question of Theodicy. If one takes the Taoist path, there is still the question of who or why the first clear circle, the Unnamable Subtle Origin, manages to turn into the yin–yang symbol in which half the circle is black. The same problem teases us with Western religion: how does a perfect ultimate God cause or allow a creation which is not perfect? In fact, looking at the world as it is now, it appears to be a chaotic, vicious debasement of what it ought to be. We have looked at seven possible strands of thought which might offer some sort of solution but there is none, at least not in terms of human logic (there may be in terms of divine logic), but that is concealed from us in this life. The nearest we have come to a working solution has been what the Book of Job explored: that there is a subtle balance, even a sort of 'swing-ometer', between monotheism and a moderated form of dualism. Going further there is even the suggestion that the spiritual powers of good and evil are in some sort of bargaining arrangement over the fate of mankind, even some sort of collusion. How this works in the world of the spirit is beyond us to assimilate. The basic contradiction is obvious: on the one hand there is God who is all goodness and perfection; on the other hand there is a dichotomy between good and evil at work in all of creation. This is a contradiction beyond our comprehension: it is a stunning paradox which goes right to the heart of life itself, meaning, values and destiny. We stand back from the blame mentality which confuses thoughts on Theodicy; the way forward is to see it in these terms: that the balance between good and evil is a subtle mechanism for growth, improvement and ultimate perfection.

Notes

1. *The Complete Works of Lao Tzu, Tao Teh Ching and Hua Hu Ching*, Hua-Ching Ni, p. 30.
2. Mary Boyce, *Zoroastrians*, p. 19.
3. See page 33 for the T'ai Chi or yin–yang sign.
4. C. S. Lewis, *op cit.*
5. Psalm 14:1, 'The fool says in his heart, "there is no God".'.
6. Winton Thomas, *Documents from OT Times*, pp. 99ff.
7. T. Aquinas, *On Physical and Moral Evil*, p. 162.
8. Aeschylus, *Prometheus Bound*, Loeb Library.
9. Aristophanes, *Wealth*, Loeb Library.
10. See Chapter 20 on Continuity.
11. David Drew, *The Lost Chronicles of the Mayan Kings*, p. 139.

3

The Connection Between God and Humanity

On the assumption that there are divine powers at work in another world, and yet impinging on this world, the question arises as to how any contact can be made in either direction. This is a different matter from the paradox of Theodicy: it is the paradox of communication. If one world is of the spirit and the other is physical, what method of communication can there be? The answer is that there are a variety of methods at work; they all assume that the paradox of communication can be solved but none of them is a totally conclusive, reliable or exhaustive answer. The problem remains that no one in this world really knows what God is all about. Even Jesus, who is understood to be the most accurate representative of God, does not know every detail of God's intentions. Matthew 24:36 says, 'but of that day and hour (the apocalypse) no one knows ... not the Son but the Father only'.

The methods at work can be summarised as follows for the purposes of this chapter: shamanism; sacral kingship and messianism; and prophecy and priesthood. Derivatives of these will appear in later chapters. These methods all assume some form of mediation between two worlds. None of them is a totally conclusive answer in itself: there is always the margin of questioning and doubt which is balanced by over-much credulity on the part of some.

Shamanism

At a level which is termed 'primitive' by anthropologists, there is the basic shamanism which is assumed to be a survival from the Stone Age or earlier. The word 'shaman' comes from Siberia but is applicable to many tribal groups in various remote parts of the world, such as Australia, South Africa, India and Haiti. The method there is the witch doctor, medicine man or diviner. He has many methods at his disposal which need not be elaborated here. But when the world is peopled by spirits inhabiting each and every physical thing, and there are gifted people who can make contact with these spirits and coerce them into a course of action or possibly divine what their intentions are, we have some sort of mediation. This has to be underpinned by a deep faith not only in the shaman himself but also in the people he serves. This type of mentality, though termed 'primitive', may at the same time betray a closeness to the workings of nature and God that our so-called 'advanced' societies will never understand. The witch doctor's methods, whether of curing diseases or making it rain, have a certain success rate. Should these methods not work, other reasons are found, such as another shaman working the opposite spell, or an evil spirit blocking the process. Some of the shamans are genuinely psychic; all of them are genuinely valued and feared by their people.

It is a mistake to assume that shamanism is a thing of the past or of undeveloped societies: it not only thrives in some areas but survives under different titles or in variant forms in modern Western cultures. Some of these are Christian, some sub-Christian, and some avowedly anti-Christian. There is Spiritualism, spiritual healers of varying levels of spirituality, and there are also Satanists. Many people place much faith in horoscopes and almanacs, and follow strange superstitions. Much significance is attached to heavenly movements like comets and astral conjunctions. There are jinxes and fate, strange illogical fears, Hallowe'en rituals, and observances at Stonehenge. The basic instinct in human nature is still there.

It is noticeable that shamanism, though it takes many different forms, usually influenced by climate and conditions, has a lot in common in its basic assumptions. There is *mana*, taboo, animism, myth, fetishism, ancestor worship, necromancy, magic; this is balanced by belief in one High God or Supreme Being. Not that the shaman directs his methods at the High God, for he is seen as too remote. Since shamanism is so widely scattered in remote parts of the world and still reappears in modified and secularised forms in modern 'advanced' societies, it is unlikely that there has been much borrowing or influence between groups. The conclusion could fairly be drawn that it is a basic instinctive response implanted by God: the need to try to control or at least predict the future in an uncertain world.

In this we see a balance between instinctive religious responses and the more elaborate theorisings and philosophies at work today. It is no surprise therefore that shamanism has not died out with the so-called modern scientific or logical climate. It is part of the balancing mechanism in the problem of communication.

Sacral kingship

A natural development from shamanism is the system of sacral kingship in the ancient world. Here, a mediator takes in not just one or two tribes, but an entire nation. The prime example of this is Ancient Egypt where the need for national unity produced the Pharaoh, who was King-God. This was of vital importance for the rank-and-file Egyptians, for it made sense to have not only a strong national leader with divine backing but also someone who, partaking of the correct rituals, would ensure that the Nile would flood each year, ensuring the success of the harvest. There was a form of sympathetic magic at work here, for in the rituals the King 'died' and was raised again, thus making the Nile rise again. How far the Pharaoh was ever thought of as human is debatable, as he was definitely equated with Osiris, and when he died he was assimilated into Horus in heaven. The queens too received divine status: Nefertari was equated with the goddess Hathor.[1] The inherent weakness with any form of kingship is the transfer of power from the old king to his successor, always a time of crisis in any nation. This was particularly so with sacral kingship in Egypt: as the Pharaoh grew old, there were questionings about the strength of his spirit and how this would be conveyed to the next Pharaoh without reducing the country to chaos. There were secretive and bloodthirsty methods at work to resolve these problems.

A similar situation developed in Mesopotamia, although not as extreme as in Egypt: it is unlikely that the King was seen as totally divine, but rather he was seen as a divinised human. The New Year rituals were seen as vital: to omit them was to invite failure of the harvest. Many Semitic states had a version of sacral kingship and it has been suggested that early Israel had such a procedure,[2] as is suggested by many bits of phrasing in the Psalms. While enjoying a measure of popularity at this time, this hypothesis has never gained complete acceptance.

Ancient Greece had a weaker form of kingship but even there in Mycenean thought there was a *wanax*, a human ruler but with some kind of divine aspect. There seems to be no suggestion of New Year rituals as in the East. It is with the coming of Alexander the Great that we see the apotheosis of a military genius, and it is probably a natural development to see Antiochus Epiphanes (which means 'god made manifest') promoting himself to a deity. This was clearly related to the need for stabilisation of the Seleucid kingdom. Other successors of Alexander, the Seleucids and the Ptolemies, took titles which sounded like self-deification, but it may not have been meant in quite such a literal sense.[3]

With Ancient Rome, having started with a republic, the dawn of another form of sacral kingship was clearly of importance to the unity of the empire. Julius and Augustus were regarded as 'divine' in their lifetimes and deified by the Senate after death. From Caligula onwards we see emperors claiming to be divine before death. It is probable that it was not meant in quite such a literal sense as in Egypt, although Caligula himself might have seen himself as God in a literal sense. It was an attempt, becoming increasingly clumsy, at uniting the empire in the face of strange cults coming from newly conquered lands and the incursions of barbarians.[4]

Ancient China also had a form of sacral kingship. The Chou and later emperors had a close relationship with heaven, termed *T'ien Tzu*, meaning Son of Heaven. This may not have had the same significance as in the Western world, for God in the East does not have the same active and personal dynamism as intervening in history. However annual ceremonies required the Emperor to perform sacrifices while an official recited set prayers. The harmony between heaven and earth would be disrupted without these rituals.[5]

In the Inca Empire, the Inca was regarded as a god and venerated as such. In an attempt to break this bond of loyalty, the Spaniards burnt the Inca's mummy. Even so the Incas continued to venerate the ashes of the mummy, and the other mummies of the Inca royal family were moved around in concealment to deny the Spaniards the opportunity to destroy them. A dead ruler would have a symbolic effigy provided, a *huaunge*, an idol, and this meant that in practice it was very difficult to convert the Incas to Christianity. Unfortunately, with no written records from that culture, we do not have a full understanding of that religion. It is enough to know that they had their own version of sacral kingship.[6]

With the Mayan Empire of Central America, we have more written material, much of which is still being deciphered. The rulers were termed *k'ul ahaw*, which is thought to mean 'Holy Lord' or 'Divine King'. They mediated between the gods and humans through the process of human sacrifice. On ceremonial occasions, the king would assume the guise of one of the Hero Twins and other deities. The heavenly twins were the sun and Venus: while one was visible in the sky, the other one was out of sight. Masks and elaborate costumes were used and they 'became' the gods for a time. As the maize god, he would be dressed up to appear like a stalk of maize swaying in the wind: as one of the Twins he would have a jaguar costume. The maize god was brought back to life by his sons; at death he was bound for resurrection in the sky as a star. Whether the god was some form of incarnation or the King was temporarily deified or promoted is not clear, but it is an interesting version of sacral kingship which had various features in common with the Egyptian system. Perhaps the most graphic representation of sacral kingship can be seen on the lid of Pakal's coffin at Palenque[7] (see diagram): assuming we interpret it correctly, the king is sitting in a birth position halfway between heaven and the underworld, perched on the 'World Tree': he is clearly the connection between two different worlds. This will be given more detailed treatment in Chapter 11 on Mythology.

Pakal's Tomb Palenque (simplified)

It is unfortunate that most of the Aztec codices were destroyed by the Spaniards, but we have enough information to glimpse what their system was like. In the early years, Huitzilopochtli was originally a human chief but became revered as a god, in some sort of promotion. The name actually means, 'Whose likeness you represent'. Chimalpopoca dressed up as a god and offered himself for sacrifice. Moctezuma II and his family allied themselves to the patron gods, Tezcatlipoca (the paramount), and Huitzilopochtli (the war god). The King was central to the bloodletting rituals, though the priests did most of the actual sacrificing on the step-pyramid. The reason for the Aztec Empire's abrupt collapse in the 1520s is easy to see: an ancient prophesy concerning the god Quetzalcoatl (the plumed serpent) was seen to come true at the arrival of Cortez. He made an alliance with the Nahuas and other kingdoms on the Gulf Coast; their royalty called themselves 'children of Quetzalcoatl' and Cortes, because of his beard, was thought to be the god himself. He quite cynically completed the illusion by dressing up and playing the part. Moctezuma and his court quite fatalistically took this as marking the end of their empire. This underlines a serious weakness in sacral kingship: that overcredulity can backfire and undermine one's own system.[8]

With Japan we see the Japanese Emperor traditionally regarded as the sun god, Amaterasu. Since the disaster of 1945, this system has had to be modified and yet he is still revered – perhaps not to the same extremes as before. It is interesting that widely separated parts of the world can produce their own versions of sacral kingship, the features of which are often remarkably similar. This may not be a case of shared ideas; rather it is a trait in human nature which requires one's god to be equated, or associated with, one's earthly ruler.[9]

The Christian faith, in all its variations, has never embarked on sacral kingship, since Jesus is the ultimate King. However there are aspects of it which echo sacral kingship. There was the Holy Roman Emperor, and Henry VIII proclaiming himself as the head of the English Church. Also the Papacy with its triple-crowned mitre, the 'vicar of God'. Charles I emphasised the 'divine right of kings'. No one has ever suggested that such people are anything more than human; even so, the authoritarian atmosphere that they engender has always been a matter of concern to Christians of other stances.

Tibetan sacral kingship, the Dalai Lama ('Ocean Teacher')[10]

An old tradition which has come to prominence in the modern world is the Tibetan Buddhist belief in the status of the Dalai Lama. He is a priest-king, but more than that: a Bodhisattva of the 'supreme Lord of Compassion', Avalokiteshvara, incarnated as the Dalai Lama. The present one in exile is the fourteenth and his appointment is arranged thus: when the old Dalai dies, the Panchen Lama, the regent, goes to the oracle lake, has a vision of the birthplace of the new Dalai, goes and finds a male infant, consults various auspices, and if the right baby is found he is taken to Llasa to be raised as the new head of state. The Panchen Lama is the next holiest in Tibet, and when he dies the Dalai goes through a similar procedure to appoint a new Panchen. He lives at Tashilhunpo monastery and is an incarnation of Amitabha Buddha. A problem arose in 1995, for when the new Panchen Lama was chosen, the Chinese removed the new infant and substituted one of their own choosing. It was clearly a Chinese (atheist) ruse to undermine Tibetan Buddhism. What will happen when a new Dalai Lama is needed is a matter of concern, and the present Dalai Lama has plans to modify if not rethink the methods of selection.

The present Dalai Lama is widely respected worldwide and commands a strong adherence in his own country, but as with Cortez, the system is liable to backfire on itself with a foreign power's malignant interference. Another factor in this is that the Dalai Lama is not the only Bodhisattva in Tibet, or even the Panchen, for almost everyone else in Tibet is seen in such terms. It would seem that there are thousands of Bodhisattvas, people who appear in incarnations to help poor languishing souls on earth. This raises the question of how literally the Dalai Lama is meant to be a god; or is it God in the sense of Western religions? Nevertheless it remains as a fascinating variant of sacral kingship in a modern application. The political role is clearly modified and the fertility cult aspect of it appears to be missing.

When considered against the backdrop of Buddhism in general, it could be said that the Tibetan version of it can be seen as an aberration. Siddhartha, though royalty himself, originally did not involve kingship in his teachings. One could say that the Jataka tales often refer to kings, but that is not integral to Buddhist teaching. In other Buddhist countries kingship, where it exists, is not integral to the

Buddhist system. The whole system of thought depends on acceptance of Karma and hence Bodhisattva-ism. While many will agree that the Dalai Lama is a major force for peace in the world, he can hardly be seen as Almighty God in the Judaeo-Christian understanding.

Modern secular versions of sacral kingship

With the rise of Adolf Hitler in the 1930s we see a form of sacral kingship, minus the king and minus God. Here was a man from the dosshouses of Vienna who had the gift of saying in inspiring oratory exactly what the German people wanted to hear after the humiliation of 1918. Although the fertility cult aspect was clearly lacking, the unification of the German-speaking people plus the acquisition of territory on the basis of *lebensraum* were obvious motives. The fanatical adherence by the Nazis to Hitler can be seen as a modern secularised version of messianism, albeit for a German messiah. One would imagine that with Hitler's disappearance and subsequently confirmed death, this hysteria would have died down. However, there is still a fascination for some people and he is still revered by some. This can be interpreted as his being seen as some sort of divinity, still alive in another world. How this works in relation to Christian teaching and to the existence of God would be something of a mystery. But the fascination for Hitler is still there to such an extent that the authorities dare not open his private apartments to the public for fear of them being turned into some sort of shrine. Similar impulses have been noted for Stalin and Lenin and, even more notably, Mao Tse Tung. In spite of his excesses in the Cultural Revolution, he is still revered in China. It is interesting that Kim Il Sun in North Korea, recently deceased, has been succeeded by his son. Is this the beginnings of a Communist monarchy? It is easy to see that an atheist state leaves a space for a much-respected mortal to fill the gap and receive some sort of promotion to divinity. How this works in relation to atheism is again a mystery. Since 1945, extreme dictatorships have fallen into disrepute; this does not mean there have not been any, but humanity has been able to see the flaws in such a regime and feel free to criticise. What we do see is that sacral kingship in a secularised form is not very far beneath the surface in the human mind.

Messianism: Israel's response to sacral kingship

It may be seen as a direct result of the Israelite antipathy to sacral kingship that their idea of kingship and messianism took the form that it did. It was with much reluctance that Samuel anointed their first king, Saul, purely from the motive of military leadership: there was no attempt at identifying Saul with God. With David we see the emergence of a highly effective charismatic leader who became the blueprint for all the kings down to AD 70. None of them were ever claimed to be divine; all their shortcomings and human failings were recorded. Their compromisings with paganism were blamed for the fall of both kingdoms, and the failures and cruelties of the Hasmoneans and Herods were described in bitter terms by historians. Symptomatic of the Jewish attitude towards regal claims to divinity is the account of how Agrippa I fell down dead because he failed to correct the people who hailed him as a god: 'and the angel of the Lord smote him because he did not give God the glory', Acts 12:23; also Josephus describes the same incident.

It is with Solomon at the dedication of the Temple that we see the nearest thing to sacral kingship: 'But will God indeed dwell on earth? Yet have regard to the prayer of thy servant ... and of thy people Israel ... hear thou in heaven ... and when thou hearest, forgive', 1 Kings 8:27ff.

Solomon's prayer never once suggests that he is divine in any sense, even though he has an unusually close relationship with God. He is seen as the great inaugurator of Hebrew wisdom and yet it is emphatically a gift from God, not something of his own devising.

Disillusionment with the failures of the Judean and Samarian kings led to the development of a messianic hope in the later prophets, beginning with Isaiah 9:6ff: 'For unto us a child is born: to us a son is given ... wonderful counsellor, mighty God, everlasting Father, the Prince of Peace'.

What exactly Isaiah was thinking of at that time is uncertain and the idea that the Messiah could not be anything but human became axiomatic. Even if he was to be specially gifted in virtue and leadership, he was never expected to be divine in the sense of sacral kingship. To quote the Testament of the Twelve Patriarchs, Testament of Judah 24:1-6: 'a star shall arise to you from Jacob in peace, and a *man* shall arise ... like the sun of righteousness.'

Because of this expectation there were many false claimants and pre-emptive revolts. Acts 5:33–39 mentions Judas and Theudas, two abortive messianic revolts and the culmination was the Bar Kochba debacle of AD 135. And still the messianic problem goes on today, for we have various spurious claimants, thriving on the fact that Jesus said he would come again.

With the coming of Jesus, we see a literal interpretation of 'Son of God', one of the factors which upset the Jewish establishment. The voices from heaven state it clearly: 'This is my beloved Son with whom I am well pleased', Matthew 3:17.

Jesus himself makes remarks which are tantamount to claiming divinity, at least that was how his critics interpreted them: 'he said to the paralytic, "My son, your sins are forgiven," ' Mark 2:5.

This was taken by his detractors as blasphemous: it was only blasphemy if he were an imposter. If he were truly divine, it could hardly be seen as blasphemous. But on the whole Jesus is guarded about his claims to Messiahship. In John 10:22–25 he evades a direct question: 'The Jews said to him, "How long will you keep us in suspense? If you are the Messiah, tell us plainly," and his reply is, "I told you and you do not believe." '

The Jews would probably have been delighted if he had allowed himself to start a messianic revolt. The apocalyptic literature of the age (200 BC to AD 100) clearly shows that there was fervid expectation that God would make a decisive intervention in history and bring in a new age. John 6:15 recounts how 'they were about to come and take him by force to make him a King' but Jesus avoided this.

Normally he called himself the 'Son of Man'. The title is a two-sided claim, ambiguous and enigmatic. Ezekiel was called this and it indicated that he was a prophet, human, with theophanous encounters with God, but not divine himself. This fits in well with the humility of Jesus. On the other hand, in Daniel, the Son of Man is a heavenly, glorious figure who breaks into history and brings in the Messianic Age. Jesus is alluding to this in Matthew 26:64: 'you will see the Son of Man seated at the right hand of power, coming in the clouds of heaven.' The high priest takes that as blasphemy. Jesus knows he is two things at once, human and divine, and this is on a different basis from all the other god-kings of this world. This brings us to the paradox of the Incarnation: Jesus is the ultimate mediator between God and humanity. He brings sacral kingship to a level of fulfilment far beyond anyone's imagination. His kingship was not based on power politics, violence, fertility cults. The paradox is that his power was the power of love and humility. To call him the 'King of the Jews' was a desperate insult, even if he was remotely descended from King David; the underlying paradox is that he was the king of all humanity. He was rejected for being a false claimant to messiahship but the paradox is that he was the only genuine Messiah or sacral king in the entire world.

Moving on to discuss prophecy and priesthood, we find that these also are a natural development from shamanism. Indeed many elements of shamanism can be evidenced from the Old Testament in connection with all three aspects: prophecy, priesthood and kingship. Because kingship was held in such suspicion by the Israelite people, a much greater emphasis and reliance was placed on prophets and priests, indeed in many cases the two functions were combined in one person. The difference is that while a prophet foretells and forthtells messages from the deity, a priest, usually in a ritual role, speaks to the deity on behalf of humanity. The two functions normally complement each other; occasionally they clash. At the inauguration of the new faith of Israel, Moses and Aaron, the prophet and the priest, are working in close conjunction and it is perhaps a little artificial to separate the two roles overmuch.

Prophecy

It is often the case that at the inauguration of a new faith there has to be a major prophetic figure whose influence is great enough to engender changes in people's religious thinking. This is true not least with Moses and the Sinai event. His towering influence is based on his ability to converse at length with God, something which is beyond the comprehension of most people in the modern world.

'There has not arisen a prophet since in Israel like Moses whom the Lord knew face to face, none like him for all the signs and wonders which the Lord sent him to do in the land of Egypt', Deuteronomy 34:10.

It is noticeable that although there are Shamanistic features mentioned in Exodus, we have moved on from shamanism as such. Moses is in contact not with spirits, demons or low-level divinities, but has direct contact with the Almighty. The Sinai event remains one of the seminal events in world history: the laws promulgated have been a bedrock for so many people and systems down to the present day, regardless of their stance on religion. For those who find difficulties in accepting the mediatory abilities of Moses (and others) the Book of Samuel has a telling remark with clear implications: 'and the word of the Lord was rare in those days: there was no frequent vision,' 1 Samuel 3:1.

There are times when God appears to 'go quiet' (as nowadays!) and at other times he intervenes quite heavily. Doubtless there is a reason for this and it may be bound up with the general paradox of communication. Great prophets appear at certain times when there is a need for them. There are long periods when the faithful are carried along by kings and priests. We notice that a prophet does not have to be of any special lineage or exalted background. Many of them have obscure backgrounds, Moses and Samuel are cases in point. But this is counterbalanced by the prophetic call which is an important feature of their ministry. The Biblical writers lay much stress on this aspect of prophecy. One of the most notable callings is seen in Isaiah 6:1ff: 'I saw the Lord sitting upon a throne, high and lifted up ... I heard the voice of the Lord saying, "who shall I send and who will go for us?" '

The prophet's unworthiness and ineffectualness is admitted, as with virtually every case – 'I am a man of unclean lips' – but the reply is to cleanse and reassure him for ministry. The question of human weakness has to be addressed. ' "Behold I do not know how to speak for I am only a youth" ... "I have put my words in your mouth ... I have set you this day over nations and kingdoms," ' Jeremiah 1:6.

Here we see the international aspect of prophecy: it is not a nationalistic line as with sacral kingship, neither confined to one's own religion. In fact prophecy goes beyond the bounds of religion and spokesmen for the deity are found in many diverse situations. This brings us to the major weakness in prophecy: the genuineness or falseness of the statements which are claimed to be inspired by God.

At the time of Jeremiah this matter came to a head as the Judean kingdom faced the debacle of 597 BC. Jeremiah found himself in a minority of one in the face of many spurious prophets who were offering false hope. His self-confidence was seriously affected: 'O Lord thou has deceived me and I was deceived ... I have become a laughing-stock all the day: everyone mocks me,' Jeremiah 20:7ff.

The issue of telling the truth from lies is just as acute as with false messiahs. The only way to discover the truth in both instances is to wait and see, as with the counsel of Gamaliel (Acts 5:38). Jeremiah's prediction of 70 years of exile turned out to be uncannily true, and that assured him of a leading position in Judaism ever since: 'to fulfil the word of the Lord by the mouth of Jeremiah ... to fulfil 70 years,' 1 Chronicles 36:21.

It is not possible to overemphasise the importance of prophecy throughout the whole Bible. It is an ongoing theme, how the words of the prophets come to fulfilment. One small example will suffice, but many others can be adduced.

'Do not be afraid ... of the king of Assyria ... I will put a spirit in him so that he shall hear a rumour, and return to his own land and I will cause him to fall by the sword in his own land," 2 Kings 19:16ff. And the fulfilment: 'and Sennacherib departed and went home and as he was worshipping (in his temple) his sons slew him with the sword,' 2 Kings 19:33–35ff.

This was Isaiah's oracle and was one of the items that made his reputation as a genuine prophet, the most influential of all, apart from Moses. 'I am God and there is no other, declaring the end from the beginning, and from ancient times things not yet done ... I have spoken and will bring it to pass, I have purposed and I will do it,' Isaiah 45:10.

As we see from this oracle, the implication in prophecy is that predestination is a reality, a factor very much at variance with current thinking in theology. (This will be discussed later.)

As the classic age of the Hebrew prophets drew to a close it is interesting to note the emergence of the prophet Zoroaster,[11] presumably about the time of the Exile, although no one is really sure when he appeared. It is thought, probably with some validity, that he had some influence on later Jewish thought all through the Persian period and into New Testament times. About 660 BC, it is claimed, Zoroaster received revelations, visions of angels, and his disembodied soul mounted up to meet Ahura Mazda, the god of light. This sounds like a theophanous experience not unlike what we read in Ezekiel. But it was powerful enough to create a new religion. Whatever one may think of Zoroastrianism or Parseeism, the impact of it on Judaism and Christianity cannot be ignored; Jesus himself clearly assumed this kind of dualistic mind-set and for that reason it has to be given serious consideration.

The other effect is profound on Jewish prophecy, for we now see classical prophecy fading out to be replaced by the apocalyptic mentality, a form of prognostication on a lower and more desperate level as the clouds of persecution gather, leading up to the collapse of the Jewish state in AD 70. The identities of these writers is not known to us but they claimed to be writing in the spirit of such worthies as the Twelve Patriarchs, Ezra, Moses and many others. How seriously they were taken is difficult to assess against the wishful thinking of the downtrodden Jewish people, but most of this material did not gain acceptance in the Hebrew canon in circa AD 90. Even so, its influence on Jesus and the early Christians was profound.

That the need was felt for a return of the old prophets is clear: the Jews needed authoritative guidance in the face of desperately uncertain times. The first Book of Maccabees mentions this thought several times: 1 Maccabees 4:46, 'they laid the (altar stones) in a convenient place until there should come a prophet to show what should be done with them.' Indeed the identity of John the Baptist and of Jesus is a subject for wishful speculation with the Jews: ' "are you Elijah? ... are you THE prophet?" ... he said, "no," ' John 1:20–22.

There was an expectation that one of the great prophets would return to herald the coming of the Messianic Age. The first Christians could see that Jesus was not just a great prophet, but the final and ultimate spokesman for God. The tragedy was that certain elements in the Jewish leadership failed to see this and reacted negatively to his challenging prognostications. The paradox is that the very people who should have realised his significance failed to do so and rejected him.

Running parallel to the prophets of old in Israel was the Greek tradition of oracle-making. We do not know how far back in time it went, but by the time of the Greek expansion in response to the Persian encroachment (fifth to third centuries BC) there was a system of considerable influence all over the Hellenistic world and beyond. The Oracle at Delphi was central and emissaries came from almost everywhere to consult and receive advice.[12] This is an interesting case of prophet and priest being the same person: the Pythia, a woman, would go into a trance and her words, transcribed, would be issued. The quality of the oracle could well depend on the quantity and quality of the spondulicks in the equation. It is thought that the shrine was located over a fissure in the rock, from which some form of hypnotising gas emanated. Nevertheless the oracles, if mostly gloomy, ambiguous and convoluted, had a massive influence on

Greek culture and events, and later had a heavy influence with the Romans too. In addition to this were the Sybils, of which there were many in various locations, issuing prophecies of varying quality, mostly relating to political matters. None of this material can match up to the stature, literary genius and theological insight of the Hebrew genre, and yet the Sybils were highly influential. A well-known example is of the Gordian knot: the prophecy stated that anyone who could unravel it would go on to conquer the world. When Alexander encountered it, he just hacked it apart with one blow of his sword; he went on to conquer the world.

Two incidents from Roman times give us an insight into how influential prophecy was. Tacitus[13] recounts how there was the oracle of Apollo at Clarus, visited by Tiberius. This time there was a male priest who descended into a cave and drank water from a sacred spring and then produced verses in answer to whatever the enquirer had in mind. This oracle may have been less influenced by spondulicks. This was on the west coast of Asia Minor, near Miletus. Suetonius[14] mentions an oracle at Paphos (of Venus) consulted by Titus as he worked his way up to becoming Emperor.

Aware of this, the Jews, seeking to infiltrate the Greek world, realised that they would have to produce something to out-trump the Sybils. The Sybilline oracles (of Jewish production) are a blatant attempt to produce a monotheistic Judaised version of the Sybilline material. The Christians in their turn worked the same method down to the time of Augustine. Both parties had considerable success with this approach, for the Jews heavily infiltrated the Hellenistic and Roman worlds and the Christians too found it easy to evangelise where monotheism had been introduced, ostensibly by soothsayers.[15] This is an interesting example of how one system can be hijacked by another system.

In the early seventh century AD we see the Prophet Mohammed, the instigator of Islam, make his appearance. He was hailed as the 'Last Prophet' by his adherents, and his influence has been massive. His prophetic call was a dramatic one, involving a vision of the Archangel Gabriel in a cave, and this produced the written corpus known as the Koran. We can see in this the need for Arab unification and the removal of polytheism and idolatry. Even so the Ka'aba and other features remained from pre-existing Arabic faiths. Initially, Islam was not averse to the Jews and the Christians: Mohammed did not wish to clash with anyone who was a monotheist. Unfortunately tension began to develop later. Monotheism was the core of the new faith, and in some ways Mohammed resembles Moses for his forthright message and towering influence. Prognostications about the future seem to be rather scarce, except on the general concept of an apocalypse. He seems to centre on the other aspect of prophecy, that of forthtelling about moral conduct. Detailed law-giving was to come later from the Muslim culture. There was never any suggestion of any kind of sacral kingship, but Mohammed was understood to be in a very close relationship with God.

Sura 42:51: 'It is not fitting for a man that God should speak to him except by inspiration or from behind a veil, or by sending of a messenger to reveal, with God's permission what God wills, for he is most high, Most Wise.'

The fifteenth century AD sees the appearance of Guru Nanak, the inaugural prophet of Sikhism. In common with other prophets, he has a vision of God, a theophany: 'one day after bathing in the river, Nanak disappeared in the forest and was taken in a vision to God's presence. He was offered a cup of nectar ... God said to him, "I am with thee ... abide uncontaminated by the world ... this cup of nectar ... a pledge of my regard."'[16]

In this he was cleansed and commissioned to proclaim monotheism, and to attempt to syncretise Islam and Hinduism, and as such it has had more success than other syncretistic schemes. Nanak's oracles became the basis of the Guru Granth, to be completed later by other gurus. It is an example of monotheism without a strong ethical aspect, or detailed ritual provisions, and prophetic vision without an attempt at prognosticating about the future.

> Nanak's emphasis on integrity and an inner focus on divine truth, rather than upon religion's trappings provides a basis for spiritual development ... at the heart of Sikhi are principles that can contribute strongly to inter-faith dialogue ... this has the potential to contribute from its principles of respecting spiritual paths while retaining its focus on God, the Ultimate Truth.[17]

Making comparisons between Sikhism and other faiths is liable to be misleading, but it is interesting to note that Nanak's work coincided with the Reformation in the Western world and some of his ideas are reminiscent of those of Luther and other reformers. But there the comparison must falter because the backdrop, language and mind-set involved are drastically different.

Contemporaneous with Nanak is a controversial figure called Nostradamus,[18] Michel de Notredame, a Jew converted to Catholicism and of French nationality. All his oracles are in French and are orientated to the fortunes of France, although other neighbouring countries are involved. One wonders if his detractors have actually read his oracles with a sympathetic eye. Unfortunately Nostradamus has been used as a tool for propaganda and various forgeries have confused the situation. It is enough to say that although his style is convoluted and heavily worked with symbolisms and imagery in the mentality of the ancient world, there is a hard core of material which cannot easily be dismissed. Also, to confuse matters is the fact that he rearranged all his quatrains and made alterations and anagrammatisations to avoid accusations of witchcraft. Even so those who know his methods are able to make sense of much of his writings, but some material remains obscure.

Perhaps one of the most difficult to explain away is Centuries 3:77 in which the actual date and countries involved are correctly forecast: 'The third climate under Aries in the year 1727 in October the king of Persia, captured by those of Egypt: battle, death, loss: great shame to the cross.'

This is one quatrain that he omitted to tamper with: the date, time, place and political outcome are correct, an amazing prediction 150 years in advance. There are many such oracles which are not quite so specific but are capable of interpretation in relation to salient events in European history up to the present. Nostradamus has a special interest in the French Revolution, the Napoleonic Wars, Napoleon III, the two World Wars and many other events in the twentieth century.

Another specific but partly disguised oracle comes in Centuries 3:96: 'The leader from Fossano will have his throat cut by the man who exercised the bloodhounds and greyhounds. The deed will be committed by those of the Tarpean rock, when Saturn is in Leo on 13th February.' This refers to the unstable situation after the fall of Napoleon, when the Duke de Berry, a pretender to the French throne, was murdered by a republican stable lad on 13th February 1820.

Napoleon figures large in the oracles and at one point his name in an anagram is actually cited in Centuries 8:1: 'PAU, NAY, LORON will be more of fire than blood to swim in praise, the great one to flee to the confluence, he will refuse entry to the magpies (?): Pampon and Durance will keep them confined.' This is thought to refer to the imprisonment of the Pope in 1798, and in spite of the obscurity of this oracle the first three words are an anagram of 'Napaulon Roy' (king).

Another name that appears is Hitler in Centuries 2:4. (It actually appears as 'Hister' but that may well be a disguised version of the name.) 'Beasts wild with hunger will cross the rivers, the greater part of the battlefield will be against Hitler, he will drag the leader in an iron cage, and when the child of Germany observes no law.'

This fits exactly the circumstances in May 1940 when the Germans, heavily outnumbered, invaded northern France. The beasts are the tanks and other machines (the Germans gave them animal names) and Nostradamus calls them beasts, and the iron cage is the railway coach in which the surrender was signed. Hitler and the Germans did behave lawlessly, breaking treaties and plundering conquered territories. The Second World War figures large in his oracles.

The name De Gaulle appears in Centuries 9:33 although the rest of it is obscure: 'Hercules King of Rome, and of Annemarc three times the leader of France to be surnamed De Gaule. Italy will tremble and the waters around St Mark the first to be renowned over all the kings.' No one knows what Annemarc is (unless it is a corruption of Dannemarc, a town in Alsace). Hercules is a good example of how he uses classical imagery in describing modern figures: this might be the king of Italy.

The wild beasts and the iron cage are good examples of how he describes twentieth-century things in terms of sixteenth-century vocabulary. We have mention of air travel, submarines, Polaris rockets, V weapons and the swastika. It would seem that the Twin Towers disaster of 2001 is referred to, and this is a group of oracles coming to fulfilment since Erika Cheetham's exhaustive work on the Centuries (1973).[19]

'The garden of the world near the New City in the road of the hollow mountain. It will be seized and plunged in the tank, forced to drink water poisoned with sulphur' (10:49). This is quite obscure but the reference to New York and a skyscraper (hollow mountain) is clear.

'Earthshaking fire from the centre of the earth will cause tremors at the tower of the New City. Two great rocks will war for a long time, then Arethusa will redden a new river' (1:87).

'The sky will burn at 45 degrees, fire approaches the great New City. Immediately a huge, scattered flame leaps up when they want to have proof of the Normans' (6:97).

New York is 45 degrees north and the attack did produce a massive fire and smoke. Why the Normans would be involved is not clear but that is typical of Nostradamus to slip in a remark which is quite irrelevant. See also 9:92: 'The king will want to enter the New City ... he will stay far from the enemy.' True: Bush and Bin Laden were very far separated, and Bush had to be held back from going back from Texas.

Certain features of these oracles indicated that Nostradamus's inspiration was partially visual and partly auditory. He 'sees' things in the future which would have been meaningless to anyone in the sixteenth century: also he 'hears' names which might be slightly misspelt in today's terms but would have meant nothing in his day.

For example, 3:70 is interesting: 'Great Britain, including England will be covered by very deep floods. The new league in Ausonne will make war so that they will ally against them.' In the 1550s the term 'Great Britain' would have been meaningless. After 1604 James I assumed the title of King of 'Great Britain'. There were bad floods around Bristol in 1607 and in 1605 there was a treaty called the Holy League renewed in Italy (Ausonne).

We are accustomed to thinking of prophecy as always concerning the future: however there are a number of oracles which can be termed 'retroactive' in Cheetham's terminology, that is it appears to refer to the future but is in fact extending into the past. Take for instance 9:6: 'A great number of English in Guienne will occupy it, calling it Anglaquitain. In Languedoc, Ispalme, Bordelais, which they will name after Barboxitaine.' Here we see the English occupation of large areas of France, something which has not happened since the twelfth to fifteenth centuries and is hardly likely to happen now. Is he seeing into the past?

Consider Centuries 2:72, which seems to be describing the battle of Pavia, 1525: 'The French army will be troubled in Italy, on all sides conflict and great loss. Flee the Italians, O France repelled: near the Tessin the battle at Rubicon is uncertain.' In case one was thinking that Nostradamus was just describing the past, it is not as simple as that. It was a definite victory for Italy, not an uncertain one, so some of this is slightly inaccurate. This is a feature of prophecy which will be discussed later.

An obscure oracle in Centuries 5:96 might be describing the battle of Actium, which he might have 'seen': 'The nautical oar will invite the shadows and then come to provoke the great Empire. In the Aegean sea the remains of bits of wood obstruct the Tyrhennian sea and impede it.' This can hardly be a modern naval battle with wooden wreckage floating about. The Empire mentioned is Rome and the shadows are Anthony and Cleopatra. Several oracles mention ships in classical vocabulary.

Centuries 2:21: 'The ambassador sent by the biremes is repulsed half way by an unknown man. Four triremes come reinforced with salt: he is bound with cords and chains to Negrepont (Euboea).' Is this seeing into the far distant past?

Erica Cheetham comments on the Roman flavour of the next one, Centuries 3:40: 'The great theatre will be raised up again, the dice thrown and the nets already cast. The great one who tolls the death knell will become too tired, destroyed by bows split a long time ago.'

This evokes the scene in the Coliseum at the Roman games.

Consider this oracle at 2:13: 'The body without a soul no longer at the sacrifice: at the day of death it is brought to rebirth: the divine spirit will make the soul rejoice: seeing the eternity of the word.'

Also 2:27 which is very obscure but redolent with meaning: 'The divine word will be struck by heaven and will not be able to go any further: of the resurrection the secret is closed up so that one will walk over and before.'

How much of this is evocative of the death and resurrection of Jesus Christ? Such oracles are normally written off as occult material and thus beyond penetration: but they fit with Jesus: he was called the Word of God, the Crucifixion was a sacrifice, and his death did bring about new life.

Whatever one may think of Nostradamus, it is not enough to write him off as complete nonsense: so much of his oracles makes sense if carefully analysed and interpreted. The fact that there is so much accuracy, and that he has been taken seriously by so many people, must cast an important new light on the matter of prophecy in general terms. There is now quite a problem for those who wish to deny the reality of prophecy and even more so for those who think it can all be explained away as *vaticinum ex eventu*, meaning in effect that the 'prophet' was in fact simply describing the past; in other words, a fraud.

Sadly this notion is endemic in liberalistic modern Biblical criticism; this is because they have no idea of the nature of prophetic inspiration. There are people, not many, who are genuinely psychic. If Nostradamus can be accepted as genuinely seeing into the future, why not such people as Isaiah, Jeremiah, Ezekiel, Daniel and above all, Jesus himself? Such a realisation could turn the whole of Biblical criticism upside-down. The uncomfortable thought is then that the future must be determined in some way. Erika Cheetham puts it this way:

'It is essential for thinking man to believe in free will: to believe that his future can be changed by thought and action. Prophecy denies this and declares that all futures are immutable and fixed ... I must admit the disturbing fact that although I can dismiss 95% of it as historical coincidence, there remain a few quatrains which are hard to reconcile with this.'[20]

This is something of an understatement: that Nostradamus somehow foresaw events, people, names, aeroplanes, submarines, skyscrapers to mention just a few, is beyond the comprehension of most rational people. It means that a re-evaluation of the ancient Hebrew prophets and Jesus is now not just possible but unavoidable. Also the apocalyptists of the intertestamental period, who have for a long time been regarded as spurious, may now be seen in a slightly different light. Another aspect of this is the impact and power of prophecy on people's minds. The fact is that many forgeries and the use made of it for propaganda are evidence of the massive influence Nostradamus's writings have on people's minds, and in an age when prophecy is not taken so seriously. The same goes for all genuine prophets.

Another corpus of prophecy contemporaneous with Nostradamus and also having great influence of political developments is the material found in the New World when the Spaniards arrived. It would seem that the Incas had their own prophets. About 1432 Wiracocha Inca foretold the cataclysmic destruction of Andean civilization within five generations. This was kept as a closely guarded secret in the royal family and was only made public by the last emperor as he died. They equated the Spaniards with Wiracocha and hence believed they were gods. This explains why the Inca Empire abruptly collapsed on the arrival of the Spaniards, even if some of the Incas did resist. They believed they had to submit: this exemplifies the power of prophecy, and in an area well away from the Old World.[21]

The same is largely true for the Mayans. The books of Chilam Balam, a pre-conquest scribe or prophet, known as the 'Jaguar Prophet', foresaw the coming of the Spaniards. Some of his writings were carefully hidden from the invaders and still survive, being added to until recent times. The Mayan kings wished to fix their actions precisely within the divinely ordained cycles of time, which was done through a continuous count of the *katuns* (260 years). This held its own prognosticatory complexion, since the events of one *katun* would be expected to recur in the next *katun*. This was history repeating itself: recording the past served to predict the future.[22]

The Aztecs also had a tradition of prophecy. Nezahualpilli, a neighbouring king, foretold calamities that would destroy the whole kingdom. This really upset Moctezuma and he wanted to die. He believed that Quetzalcoatl (a god) was thought to have gone off to the east and would return. When the Spaniards appeared in their ships in the Gulf of Mexico, he and his people[23] assumed it was the god returning to claim what was his own. A fatalism fell on the Aztec Empire: this shows the power of prophecy and its effect on morale. It also shows that prophecy is not just confined to the Bible or to Christian tradition. Even with its discrepancies and errors, there is a major kernel of truth about the future contained in the oracles. If it is the truth, then we cannot escape the conclusion that it is of God and not just of human devising. As with every channel of communication between two worlds, there is the danger of falsification and distortion, just as in Biblical times, and this has held true up to the present. The only way to sift truth from falsehood is to wait and see. Somewhere there is a paradox in this, chiefly in the fact that the true and eternal prophet, Jesus of Nazareth, was condemned as a false prophet by the very people who ought to have understood and appreciated him.

Isaiah, the first great literary prophet

It has been customary to divide Isaiah up into three different writers: one in the early seventh century, another in the Exile and another even after that. The assumption has been that one writer at the time of Hezekiah could not have foreseen events over 200 years later.[24] Now we see, after a consideration of Nostradamus, that it is entirely possible that one person could have produced the entire literary complex well before the events which brought it to fulfilment. The divided Isaiah theory has always had the inherent weakness that no such prophet has been clearly identified during the Exile. It is quite feasible that an amanuensis could have assembled Isaiah's works, not in any chronological order, but thematically, which would explain why the message of hope predominates after chapter 40. The following remarks will make the assumption of the unity of Isaiah, and this makes far better sense of the whole book in the light of our modified understanding of the phenomenon of prophecy.

1. The branch theology

There are many references to the 'branch', which is Isaiah's remnant theory. It assumes that the main family tree of the Kings of Judah will be cut off and yet there will be survivors who will re-establish the royal line. Isaiah 10:20 to 11:1ff: 'Then shall come forth a shoot from the stump of Jesse, and a branch shall grow out of his roots.'

This is a theme taken up by later prophets, notably Zechariah, and it gave the restorationists a certain degree of confidence in the idea of a restored monarchy. This turned out to be pre-emptive, for while a figure called Zerubbabel, a scion of the Judean royalty, became influential for a time, it all came to nothing and Judea was ruled by high priests down to the time of the Maccabean revolt. In a sense Isaiah was right but the main fulfilment of it had to wait until the coming of Jesus, the true King of the Jews and a distant descendant of King David.

2. The highway theology

Isaiah tells us that there will be a road leading the exiles back from Assyria and other places. This is a common thought in the ancient world, where the 'sacred way' was an important feature in temple worship, a processional way on which the god and his people would approach their temple. A literal understanding of this idea never materialised: the world had to wait for the messianic kingdom to level the mountains and valleys in a figurative sense. This points up the tension between literal and figurative interpretation in the prophets, a feature also seen in Nostradamus.

3. The world empires

Isaiah foresees the fall of Jerusalem to Nebuchadrezzar and the Exile to Bablyon, and the deep impression left on the Jewish people. Also the defeat of Babylon, involving the Medes and the Persians and in association with vassal states such as Lud, Put, Tubal, Javan and Tarshish. No one is completely certain of the location of some of these places but the general impression is that the northern and far-off places, the ‘coastlands’, are now involved in the future of Israel. Broadly speaking, virtually all of this came to pass.

4. The Persian Empire

Isaiah tells of the return and actually quotes the name ‘Cyrus’ twice, the Persian king who was instrumental in the restoration. The name K’ur’u(sh) was a real Persian king, the great empire builder. This name would have meant nothing in the early eighth century, but came to mean something at the end of the Exile. Obviously there was a spelling discrepancy but that was a feature common in the ancient world, with their different languages and alphabetic usages. This again can be understood in the light of Nostradamus with his proper names. The return is framed in terms of great glory and triumph, but the reality was much more modest, in fact an anticlimax in Isaianic terms. The Jews had to wait for the true Messiah to see the full glory awaiting.

5. Egypt

Isaiah tells of the diaspora, particularly of Jewish communities in Egypt. We do not know if five cities in Egypt did actually turn to the Lord (19:18) but On did become known as Heliopolis, the City of the Sun, and a Jewish temple, a replica of the Jerusalem one, was built there in Maccabean times. There must have been Jewish enclaves such as Elephantine in the land of Syene. Sadly the idea that the whole of Egypt would turn to the true God would have to wait until the Christian upsurge in the early centuries AD.

6. Rebuilding the Temple

The reconstruction under Nehemiah and Ezra is also foreseen, even some of the details (19:17). Even the provision of watchmen during the night (62:6) is referred to. However, the happy relationship with the foreigners which Isaiah mentions was not to be: the historians are honest enough to admit that Sanballat and Tobiah tried to stop the work, and foreigners were excluded from the Jewish community. The full realisation of inclusiveness would have to wait for the coming of Jesus.

7. The Messiah himself

Vast amounts of Isaiah are deeply optimistic about the coming messianic kingdom. It is amazing that so many of the details of the life and ministry of Jesus are foreshadowed in his writings. Very little of this would have made any sense in the eighth century BC, but when the early Christians read it in light of what Jesus did and suffered, it all made perfect sense. The Suffering Servant passages after chapter 40 are particularly important in this respect, but the work of the true Messiah is hinted at in so many other places too. Isaiah 29:18: ‘In that day the deaf shall hear the words of a book ... the eye of the blind shall see ... the meek shall obtain fresh joy in the Lord and the poor ... shall exult in the Holy One of Israel.’

So much of Isaiah only makes sense if seen as a genuine visionary of the eighth century BC, as opposed to a late *vaticinium ex eventu* fraud. If it had been concocted near or after the actual events, the question would arise: why did not the writer harmonise the oracles and the fulfilment more thoroughly? The truth is that Isaiah was not always completely accurate in his predictions, for instance (60:10): ‘Foreigners shall build up your walls and kings shall minister to you ... your gates shall be open continuously.’ All this is somewhat optimistic until we see the kingdom of God arriving with Jesus. Even so, there was enough of truth and fulfilment in Isaiah to make his reputation as one of the greatest prophets of all time and he is still held in great respect by people of faith the world over.

Daniel, a visionary prophet of the Exile

It has been normal to divide Daniel into two parts: chapters 1 to 6 which appear to be 'historical', and chapters 7 to 12 with visionary expectations of the End.[25] As with Isaiah, this division may be seen as artificial and unnecessary, if not misleading. Also the assumption that the work is very late, a long time after the Exile and the return, when historical events were becoming a little blurred, is also not just unnecessary but impossible and can now be seriously questioned.[26] It has always been a problem as to how Ezekiel, an exilic prophet, is seen to refer to Noah, Daniel and Job as the wise men of the past. Surely Daniel predates Ezekiel. If the book had been written late into Hellenistic times, the problem arises as to how it would ever have gained the towering reputation that it did. If it were a late forgery, simply describing events afterwards, why was he taken so seriously by so many people including Jesus? The later apocalyptists can be seen as cheap imitations of Daniel. The assumption at work in the following remarks is that Daniel is genuinely prophetic – not just the later parts, but all of it – and there is no 'historical' material in it at all. He was seeing the whole of the future from before the fall of Jerusalem. This will be a controversial view but it does make sense in the light of what we know from Nostradamus.

It has long been noted that the first line in Daniel presents problems, (1:1): 'In the third year of the reign of king Jehoiakim king of Judah, Nebuchadnezzar king of Babylon came to Jerusalem and besieged it.'

If we compare this with 2 Kings 23:36 to 24:2, it would seem that Jehoiakim had been on the throne for eight years and his last three years were under the suzerainty of Babylon. The city was taken and the first phase of the Exile began. His son, Jehoiachin, was allowed to continue as king but only for three months, whereupon his uncle Zedekiah was installed as regent. The actual defeat and exile was more complicated than seen in Daniel, and there is no mention of Jehoiakin, Zedekiah or even of Gedaliah. The mention of the 'third year' is interesting: are we seeing a prophetic impression which turned out to be true in a way but not strictly historically accurate?

Turning to the actual name 'NebuchadNezzar' we note that there are two spellings of this historical king's name. It would seem that Jeremiah and Ezekiel are more accurate in their rendering of it, 'NebuchadRezzar'. The Babylonian spelling is decisive: 'Nabu-Kudurri-usur': the R or *resh* (in Hebrew) is correct: the N or *nun* is wrong, although in the Hebrew script the letters appear rather similar. Nebuchadrezzar actually means something: 'may Nabu (a god) protect the boundary (or possibly 'the crown')'. The word 'Nebuchadnezzar' loses this meaning and in fact appears to mean nothing: would Daniel have deliberately altered it to mean nothing, from something that did have a meaning? The other possibility is that he 'heard' or 'saw' the name in a visionary context, before that king actually appeared, and recorded it with a slight inaccuracy. Such is a common feature in Nostradamus (compare Hister with Hitler). In other words, Daniel foresaw the fall of Jehoiakim and the rise of Nebuchadrezzar; it was also a fact that Jehoiakin and certain of the exiles found favour in Babylon and began to influence political affairs in their new context.

It appears to have been a common practice of Nebuchadrezzar to alter people's names to suit his expectations. So Mattaniah became Zedekiah (2 Kings 24:17). Shadrach, Meshach and Abed-Nego are all paganisations of the Hebrew names (Daniel 1:6–7): this was a policy which failed as the young men refused to compromise with Babylonian religion. Daniel became Belteshazzar, very close to Belshazzar, who is seen later. This 'king' was the son of Nabonidus, who installed him as regent in 555 BC, and in effect Belshazzar was the last Babylonian ruler before the Persian victory. He could only loosely be called the 'son' of Nebuchadrezzar; more likely he was one of his successors. But this would work if Daniel were seeing the whole scheme in general terms well before it came to pass. Darius I was actually the son of Cambyses, the Persian king who managed to conquer Egypt. As far as we know, Darius was never a Median king, although he almost certainly had Median forebears, since Cyrus had married a Median princess. Also to say that Darius was the son of Ahasuerus (Xerxes), a Mede, is again difficult: it was the other way round. Modern critical scholars have come up with all manner of ingenious rationalisations of this problem. But they are missing the point: if it were a prophecy from some time beforehand, it is easy to see how Daniel did not see things in quite the right sequence. But his general overview of history in figurative terms is remarkably good.

With this we gain the clue that while on the face of it Daniel is 'seeing' the Babylonian empire in literal terms, at the same time he is 'seeing' the later Persian and Greek situation in the long term, but in figurative terms. This is an intriguing example of double prophecy, literal and figurative, working on two levels at the same time. With hindsight, people saw the full depth and spiritual importance of his message; this explains the many imitators of Daniellic literature down to the intertestamental period, and also the Book of Maccabees, which shows how his words came to fulfilment during the Seleucid domination, and also explains why the family of Hashmon fought with such conviction and certainty of success.

In Daniel 2 we read about the second year of Nebuchadnezzar, which would be 603 BC. The King has a dream which only Daniel can explain. The great image and the King himself are now symbolic of the Babylonian Empire and its fate unfolding down to Hellenistic times, if not Roman. Modern critics have tried to equate the five parts of the image to the successive empires as we know them but it has never been seen to work convincingly. Perhaps we see in the feet of iron and clay the divided kingdom of the Ptolemies and the Seleucids. But the point is that a stone not of human origin will smash these empires and establish a kingdom not of this world. The fulfilment of this had to wait for the coming of Jesus and the Kingdom of Heaven.

The imminent collapse of the Babylonian Empire continues to be seen in chapter 4, with the great tree which is stumped and bound with iron and bronze, hinting at the dual kingdom of the Medes and Persians. History shows us that after Nebuchadrezzar died, Babylon rapidly degenerated to the point that their kings were mere ciphers, leaving it open for Persia to swallow up virtually all of the ancient orient. As a general overview as prophecy, Daniel is correct in many ways but it is folly to try to take every detail as corresponding to a known fact of history. Whether Nebuchadnezzar actually did eat grass is not known. Even so it is symbolic of the rapid humiliation of Babylon. And yet, the 'seven times' may be a hint at the time span of the Babylonian Empire (seven times equals 70 years) from the fall of Nineveh to the triumph of Cyrus. The claims that Nebuchadnezzar turned to the true God cannot be substantiated, unless we see it as figurative, in that Cyrus had a completely different attitude towards Judaism; he had a completely different religion, Zoroastrianism, which was more akin to Judaism.

The numbering of the days of his kingdom again appears in Belshazzar's feast. '*Mene*': your days are numbered; '*tekel*': weighed in the balances; '*Peres*': your kingdom is divided. All of this came true. Also there is the hint of Persia in it, '*Pharsin*'. Whether Darius was 62 is beyond us to ascertain. Scholars have tied themselves in knots over this! But it may be a hint that the Jewish exile was almost completed, that is, 70 years.

It is with chapter 7 that the most intriguing prophecies in visionary form appear. The four beasts – the lion, the bear, the leopard, and the beast with iron teeth and ten horns and a little horn with great talk – these show the successive empires down to the Hellenistic era. Much argument has ensued over which empire is which; this is because modern scholars will try to take it totally literally and miss the point. *Darius the Mede and the Four World Empires*[27] is a classic case of a liberalistic attempt at coping with Daniel as 'history'. Sadly they cannot see past the notion that Daniel is a late Maccabean forgery. There were roughly ten Seleucid kings from Alexander to Antiochus IV Epiphanes, but it depends on how they are counted: do we include the imposters? Almost everyone agrees that the 'little horn with big talk' is the one that persecuted the Jews and defiled the Temple in 167 BC. This disaster made such an impression on the Jews that it became a duty to mention in the apocalyptic material of the time. Jesus himself refers to it ('The Abomination of Desolation'). Now we see the massive influence that Daniel gained in the post-exilic world. It can hardly have been a late post-exilic production: for then why were the details not more exact, and why did not people know it to be a late fraud? His remark that that was the signal for the advent of God's Everlasting Kingdom ensured that the expectation was augmented to a massive level. Sadly the world had to wait another century and a half for it to materialise.

By this time we are seeing the symbolic and to some extent literal usage of numbers in prophecy. This may have been triggered by Jeremiah's successful prophecy of 70 years for the length of the Exile (Daniel 9:2). So for instance in 9:24, '70 weeks of years are decreed' (490 years) from Cyrus' order to rebuild the Temple down to 'an end to sin and . . . to bring in everlasting righteousness'. This is not a bad estimate to bring us to the time of Jesus and the Kingdom of God. The rest of the details in that passage are somewhat vague and difficult to attach to known historical events, but the desolation of the Temple in 167 BC for three and a half years is clearly to be seen. This may explain why the Maccabees waited three and a half years before cleansing the Temple.

In chapter 11 we see a more accurate view of the history even though some details do not quite tally. This clearly shows it to be a genuine prophecy as opposed to an account concocted after the events, in which case it would have been harmonised and made much more convincing. Four more Persian kings after Darius I is not quite true: there were five. Then we see the reaction coming from Greece and Alexander's sweeping triumph. And yet his kingdom (v. 4) is broken and divided into four: the Seleucids, the Ptolemies and two more smaller kingdoms in Asia Minor and Macedonia. From verse 5 onwards it concentrates on the Seleucids and the Ptolemies with their uneasy relations down to what seems to be the appearance of the Romans (11:30 'ships of Kittim') when Antiochus is rebuffed in Egypt and the backlash landed on the Jews. Verse 31, 'and shall appear and profane the Temple and stop the sacrificing'. The persecution of Judaism is seen and the resistance mounting: Antiochus' self-proclamation as a god (v. 36) and his eventual fall (v. 45). Now we can see the two books of the Maccabees as pointing out the fulfilment of all this: they are saying that Daniel was right; it all came to pass.

Daniel believes that after that fateful three and a half years, the End will come. He does not really see beyond to the Hasmonean kingdom, the Herods and the Roman occupation. We are left with the intriguing question of what 2390 days and 3335 days are supposed to mean. No one has convincingly explained either of these, but they are obviously symbolic of something. But from that, apocalyptists in the future have tried to use this method of prognostication, but with very little success.

In general, Daniel is a highly successful prophet of the historical events from Nebuchadrezzar down to Antiochus Epiphanes. Not all the details can be verified with hindsight, but the same applies to Nostradamus. The general overview of history is correct and most impressive. This leads us to the conclusion that Daniel was genuinely inspired by God, had foresight of the plan of history and foretold, in terms which he might not have understood himself, the coming of God's Kingdom in real terms, with Jesus the Messiah.

The fact that verbs are in both past and present tense is of very little importance: in Hebrew there is always a certain degree of vagueness in prophetic utterances and tenses cannot be taken completely literally. More interesting is the fact that the book begins in Hebrew and floats off into Aramaic at 2:4: 'O King, live for ever'. This need not be any surprise, since Aramaic became the lingua franca of the Persian Empire but originated in Chaldea. Part of Daniel's inspiration was that he could speak to the Jews and other peoples in Mesopotamia in the new language of scripture, as Hebrew gradually became obsolete.

All this may seem incomprehensible to twenty-first-century minds, but we are dealing with the ancient world in which there were people with psychic gifts and levels of inspiration which are rarely seen today. Also the dream mentality (with visions) is not taken at all seriously nowadays, but was for them of massive significance.

Ezekiel, visionary prophet of the Exile

Although roughly contemporaneous with Daniel, Ezekiel shows a remarkably different approach. He has many theophanous visions, often with ground-breaking theological truths, but his ultimate interest is in the restoration of the Temple, which is described in great detail. There is the temptation to take all his numbers and measurements as some kind of code or symbolism but this may be forcing the issue. From the point of view of prophetic fulfilment there are various elements that can be listed.

1. Chapter 4 records Ezekiel making a brick, and a portrayal of Jerusalem under siege. This refers to the second siege of 597 BC after Zedekiah had broken his agreement. The siege is said to last 390 days; this turned out to be not far off, actually 399 days according to 2 Kings 25:1ff. But the other number, 40 days (v. 6) another spell of punishment, accords well with the disfavour of King Jehoiakin in Babylon, after which, 37 years later, he was brought back into favour (2 Kings 25:29).
2. In many places Ezekiel foresees the return and the restoration of the exiles. In 37:15ff, he sees the reunification of the two Hebrew kingdoms, Israel and Judah. As far as we know this never happened: the ten tribes taken off to Assyria are assumed to be lost to history. Perhaps Ezekiel was aware that

some of the ten tribes would come back with the Judeans, but this cannot be verified.

3. What could be a very accurate prediction (in the tradition of Nostradamus) appears in 24:1ff, where we read, 'In the 9th year, in the tenth month, on the tenth day of the month', he came to realise that the siege of Jerusalem was starting. This dating only becomes clear when we read Kings 25:1: 'Zedekiah rebelled against the king of Babylon'. It is just possible that the writer of Kings was influenced by Ezekiel, yet if that were so, why did he not make use of the many other precise datings given in Ezekiel, ostensively under some kind of vision? It is interesting to note in 12:13, talking of Zedekiah, 'I will bring him to Babylon ... yet he will not see it'. Very true: Zedekiah was blinded at Riblah, before he arrived in Babylon.
4. Ezekiel foresees the involvement of Persia and other client kingdoms from the north and east, Meshech, Tubal, Cush and Put (possibly under the influence of Isaiah) but is less precise about the timings and full outcome of these developments.
5. Ezekiel believes that Babylon will defeat Egypt and send them into exile as well (29:17ff). We know that Nebuchadrezzar made punitive raids on Egypt: it was left to the Persians under Cambyses to make a complete victory and sweep up the whole of the ancient Orient into one empire. But by this time the name 'Nebuchadnezzar' was becoming symbolic for all cruel conquering tyrants.
6. Ezekiel as a messianic prophet comes out in 34:15, 34:23 and 37:22: 'I myself will be the shepherd of my sheep,' and 'I will set up over them one shepherd, my servant David.' All this had to wait for fulfilment with the coming of Jesus.

2 Esdras (Ezra): a visionary of the Persian period

Some have assigned this to very late, post-New Testament times, but this is almost certainly based on false assumptions. It is claimed to have been originally written in Aramaic; however R.H. Charles believes it has a Hebrew original.[28] The writer claims to be in the times of Artaxerxes, well into the Persian period. Which Artaxerxes is meant matters little: it is possibly the second one, some time after the coming of Nehemiah. The book is interesting for its dream-visions of the same genre as Daniel, but less vivid. Noteworthy are specific mentions of Jesus, the Christ, the Lion and also what could be taken as the Roman domination.

'For my Son Jesus shall be revealed with those that be with him, and they that remain shall rejoice within four hundred years,' 2 Esdras 7:28. Clearly we have a reference to Jesus the Son of God and his disciples. The 400 years is usually taken as meaning after his ministry, but this makes no sense: more likely it means before his ministry, which would be about right. The seventh year of Artaxerxes II was 457 BC; thus 400 years is not a bad estimate.

Verse 29 continues: 'after these years (400) shall my Son Christ die and all men that have life'. The Crucifixion is foretold and possibly also the first Christian martyrs. After this comes a period of seven days in which the dead will be raised from the 'secret places': this recalls the raising of people like Lazarus and the three days in hell before the Resurrection. If this were written after the time of Jesus by someone sympathetic to him, why not mention the Resurrection and other details?

In chapter 11 we have the vision of the all-ruling eagle and an impression of the conflicts within the Roman Empire. Trying to locate the warring factions to actual events is difficult: all this indicates that it is genuine prophecy and not *vaticinium ex eventu*. In 11:39 we have 'a roaring lion chased out of the wood ... and sent out a man's voice to the eagle' and accused him of injustice and presaged that empire's collapse. The lion is clearly equated with the Messiah (12:31); Jesus seen as a lion was taken up as a metaphor by Revelation 5:5 and the Gospel of Thomas, and so became a well-established phrase in Christian thinking. In 13:22 we have 'then shall my Son be declared whom thou sawest as a man ascending'. Are we seeing a prophecy of the Ascension? After that the Messiah appears to rebuke the nations for their wickedness; the general impression from the Gospels is that he spoke kindly to the Gentiles.

In general terms, the dreamlike quality, the occasional inaccuracy, and the surprise quotation of names all indicate that 2 Esdras is genuinely visionary. If it is maintained that it was written about AD 70, it would be like saying that Nostradamus made mention of Hitler, writing after 1940! Also one would have to explain why the book was written in Aramaic, a language that was going out of use by then; more likely it would have been originally in Greek, like the New Testament. Also the fact that the book was on the borderline for inclusion in the Hebrew canon must indicate that it had been written well before AD 90, far enough in the past to accrue a degree of authority as potential scripture which was quotable. We know that the early Christians did assume much of the apocryphal and pseudepigraphal material as scriptural.

Regardless of how one views 2 Esdras and other works in the same genre, the main issue is over the reality and influence of prophecy. It is fashionable today to discount prophecy as illusory but this cannot be the complete truth. There is enough evidence to show that a genuine prophet can successfully outline the future, though not necessarily the complete details. This again runs counter to modern thought, for people do not accept the idea that the future is planned or determined. This of course is based on sentimentality and egotistic fancies about freedom of the individual. The full debate on predestination and free will comes later in this work. We have to realise that even if the modern world tries to ignore the prophetic connection between God and humanity, the ancient world saw it as a very important channel of communication, even if some of it was obscure, spurious, convoluted and even misleading. There was enough reality in it to convince them that the other world was really speaking to them of God's plan for the future.

An important paradox in the field of prophecy is that, on the one hand, human nature is uncomfortable with the idea that events in the future can be foreseen. Evidence for this is obvious: people seem to trivialise prophecy, and try to explain it away in so-called rational terms. It challenges the idea of personal freedom; it evokes ideas of superstition and exaggerated gloom. On the other hand there is the need in human nature to control, anticipate and even take precautions against future events: forewarned is forearmed. People need some sort of assurance that the future is secure in the hands of God. Evidence for this is the eagerness with which people receive prophecy and try to locate it to known events, often overdoing it. Frauds and imitators too, an ongoing problem for genuine prophets, also point up that paradoxically the human mind cannot do without prophecy. The paradox is similar to that of sacral kingship: on the face of it, we pretend to be above such things, but the basic needs that produce these things are never very far beneath the surface, and sometimes break forth. The same will be seen to be true of priesthood.

Priesthood

The work of prophet and priest are not totally opposed. There are many examples of the same person fulfilling both roles at once. But the priest essentially represents humanity to God and speaks to God on behalf of those who find it difficult to address the Almighty.

Priesthood in the Bible begins with Melchizedek in Genesis 14:18: 'Melchizedek king of Salem brought out bread and wine: he was priest of God most High. He blessed Abraham and said, "Blessed be Abraham by God Most High ... and blessed be God Most High."'

Salem we take for Jerusalem, so he pre-empts the Temple and all the spiritual power of the Holy City. He has some sort of sacramental encounter with Abraham and issues a blessing. He has the spiritual authority to bless God too. This enigmatic figure plays a crucial role in later thinking; it is taken up again in Psalm 110:4: 'Thou art a priest for ever after the order of Melchizedek.'

There is an eternal and ongoing mediation between God and humanity, not dependent on human vagaries or varying opinions. It is different from any sort of sacral kingship or prophetic inspiration. Noticing that Melchizedek appears to have no earthly parentage, the writer of Hebrews sees Melchizedek as prefiguring Jesus, who is the ultimate, eternal priestly mediator. That Jesus was also seen as a king and a prophet does not alter the fact that his priesthood was not of this world. It is not a theory, a religion, a passing opinion, but a real, living person who is the final link between God and humanity.

'In the days of his flesh, Jesus offered up prayers ... and being made perfect he became the source of eternal salvation to all who obey him, being designated by God a high priest after the order of Melchizedek,' Hebrews 5:7. In this statement of priesthood we see mystery, spiritual strength, authority, sacramental and sacrificial role and mediation. From this standpoint we can understand every priesthood on earth of any religion, including those that try to do without priesthood.

In contrast with the above, we encounter the Aaronic system of priesthood which works on a lower level and was subordinate to Moses. In Exodus 29:4-9 we see:

> You shall bring Aaron and his sons to the tent of meeting and wash them with water ... and put the holy crown on ... and the anointing oil and pour it on his head ... and his sons ... and the

> priesthood shall be theirs by a perpetual statute. Thus you shall ordain Aaron and his sons.

This system of priesthood persisted down to the destruction of the Temple in AD 70. It ruled the country from the Exile down to the revived monarchy under the Hasmoneans, even retaining crucial political authority under the Herods and the procurators. The High Priest's ultimate role was to enter the Holy of Holies on the Day of Atonement and utter the sacred name in an undertone. This summed up mankind's attempts at speaking directly to God.

Paradoxically, it was the Aaronic line of priests that condemned Jesus to death and a certain Caiaphas who unwittingly prophesied: 'You know nothing at all: you do not understand that it is expedient for you that one man should die for the people and that the whole nation should not perish,' John 11:49. One would have thought that they would have recognised his priesthood and the two systems would have converged. But no, they could only see him as a scapegoat victim. Yet again, paradoxically, this led to the ultimate sacrifice which was not just for the benefit of Judaism but for all peoples the world over, 'To gather into one the children of God who are scattered abroad' (v. 52).

To go into every detail of the priest's role would require volumes and probably obscure the main argument, but the main matters can be briefly summarised thus:

1. To perform sacrifice (this will be examined elsewhere), although this function can be performed by others. Normally it is felt that someone dedicated for that purpose would produce more efficacious results.
2. To be in charge of a temple or other sacred terrain and all the correct rituals and formulae connected with it.
3. To adopt a lifestyle, clothing and conduct distinct from laymen. Often this means not earning a living by normal means but being subsidised by the community.
4. To issue blessings (and curses) and guidance to the populace and temporal rulers.
5. To perform *rites de passage* such as marriage, initiations, funerals, and so on.
6. To be in the forefront of divining, astrology, record-keeping of astral movements, medicine and calendar calculation.

7. To be in possession of spiritual power by training, ancestry or special appointment, and be regarded as sacrosanct, above the normal cut and thrust of daily living.

Thus it can be seen that the priest's role, though being different from the prophet's, has certain matters in common with the shaman's. He is expected to have a spiritual sensitivity that most ordinary people lack. At an instinctive level, human nature requires these features in a priest for him to be taken seriously. It is writ large in the prescriptions of Moses in Leviticus but there is an amazing degree of consistency in practice in every religion.

There are some areas where priesthood is claimed not to be a part of the system, but as with trying to leave God out of one's system, something else has to take its place:

1. Judaism. The Jewish priesthood and Sadduceeism faded out after AD 70 since there was no Temple available. The substitute has been the Rabbi, who is not a priest, but an expert in Mosaic law. That is the basis of their faith: the sacrificial system remains only as a memory, albeit an important memory.
2. Buddhism. This was a reaction (with Siddhartha) from the excessive ritualisation and sacrificing of the Hindus. Siddhartha decided it was all unnecessary and ineffective. As a substitute, in Tibet there are the lamas ('one who is superior') and there are spiritual guides and teachers. Monks receive 'ordination' but it is not priesthood even though they perform rites such as funerals.
3. Sikhism. Nanak also saw the hollowness in Hindu rituals and gave a strong feeling of equality amongst his followers. The main leadership comes from the Guru Granth, termed a 'living Guru'; also there is a Jethedar, loosely termed a chief priest, but he is only a temporal officer.
4. Christianity. It was early realised that Jesus was the ultimate priest of which there could only be one. There was never any sacrificing in the traditional sense even though Christians borrowed the Temple worship in the early years. Eventually the Eucharist came to be seen as the Christian 'sacrifice' and the officiant (principally the bishop) as the Christian 'priest'. This was always and still is a borrowed status from Jesus. At

the Reformation, many Protestant groups rejected priesthood in reaction to the sacrifice of the Mass, and the substitute was some form of minister in a position of leadership. Some groups went even further – Quakers, Salvation Army – and embarked on a far more thorough approach to equality. This inevitably led to a heavier emphasis being laid on the Bible.

5. Islam. Mohammed was never termed a priest, and priesthood has never been a feature of that faith. Leadership is exercised through Ayatollahs and imams, but the equality of each Muslim is heavily stressed. Guidance from the Koran thus becomes correspondingly more important.

With this we see that to do without priesthood generally means that something or someone else has to be found as a substitute: for leadership, or a focus of authority, is required even if there is supposed to be equality. Human nature needs some form of guidance in not just political matters but spiritual matters too. It can become a problem if someone manages to combine both guidances in the one person, as with sacral kingship, or Henry VIII as the alternative Pope, or the Brahmins who wielded more spiritual and temporal power than the gods. But to do without it can bring all manner of problems with splinter groups, contrary centres of opinion and internal strife.

It was with Martin Luther that the priesthood of all believers was reaffirmed, and this underpins virtually all of the Protestant world. The Biblical basis for it is 1 Peter 2:5: 'built into a spiritual house, to be a holy priesthood, to offer spiritual sacrifices acceptable to God through Jesus Christ'.

This is the crucial text which is a natural development from the priesthood of Jesus, which gives all Christians of any kind a firm basis in relationship to God and each other. It is St Mark who in allegorical terms shows the significance of the death of Jesus (15:37): 'Jesus uttered a loud cry and breathed his last. And the curtain of the Temple was torn in two, from top to bottom.'

This was the fine linen drape that obscured the view into the presence of God, the Holy of Holies. As the curtain is torn, we all see into the presence of God without the need for a priest or mediator. This unimpeded access to God is available to all believing souls. It is a fulfilment of Isaiah 25:7 in which the veil which is spread over all the nations will be destroyed, along with death itself. Paradoxically, there is still a veil obscuring the Gospel as St Paul explains in 2 Corinthians 4:4: 'our Gospel is veiled, it is veiled only to those who are perishing.'

Interestingly enough the Koran admits that there is a veil obscuring man's access to God (Sura 42:51). In a way, this is an admission to having an incomplete religion. Full access to God is not available, whereas in Christianity it is. The paradox is a deep one: Christ's death has cleared the way for all to come into God's presence; even so there is still a barrier set up by ourselves, our failure to accept it, and the falsehoods of this world.

Now we see an important paradox in communication with God: on the one hand there is the need for authoritative guidance in our relations with God; on the other hand we all have free access on a personal basis with the Almighty. These two statements are contradictory and irresolvable, and yet each is equally true in its own way.

Notes

1. M. Murray, *The Splendour that was Egypt*, pp. 100, 110.
2. J. Bright, *The History of Israel*, p. 35.
3. Peter Green, *Ancient Greece*, p. 171.
4. Stobart, *The Grandeur that was Rome*, pp. 161, 190, 202.
5. Scott Littleton, *The Sacred East*, pp. 100, 164.
6. Sullivan, *The Secrets of the Incas*, pp. 123ff.
7. David Drew, *The Lost Chronicles of the Mayan Kings*, p. 139.
8. Pohl and Robinson, *Aztecs and Conquistadores*, p. 114.
9. Scott Littleton, op. cit., pp.146, 165, 157.
10. Scott Littleton, op. cit., pp. 85, 91.
11. Mary Boyce, *Zoroastrians*, pp. 42–43.
12. Stobart, *The Glory that was Greece*, p. 68.
13. *Tacitus*, Penguin Classics, p. 102.
14. *Suetonius*, Penguin Classics, p. 289.
15. R.H. Charles, *Pseudepigrapha of the Old Testament*, p. 368.
16. E. Nesbitt, *Sikhism*.
17. Nesbitt, op. cit.
18. Erika Cheetham, *Nostradamus*.
19. Cheetham, op. cit.
20. Cheetham, op. cit., Introduction.
21. Sullivan, op. cit., p. 255.
22. Sullivan, op. cit.
23. David Drew, op. cit., pp. 382, 403.

24. Henshaw, *The Latter Prophets*, pp. 225, 255.
25. Henshaw, op. cit.
26. Henshaw, op. cit., p. 255, on the subject of the date of Daniel.
27. H.H. Rowley, *Darius the Mede and the Four World Empires*.
28. R.H. Charles, op. cit., p. 542, the Hebrew original.

4

Implementing the Connection

Normally any connection between God and humanity is carried out by the medium of prophet, priest or king or some combination of these three. The methods employed are various: covenant, laws, sanctions, good works, faith and sacrifice. It is not easy to separate each one of these; more often they are intertwined with one another. Some are specifically Biblical and others are widely spread amongst many religions. One can see the different emphases each one receives and this serves to underline the latent unity between faiths of all kinds.

Covenant

One of the strands in the Bible which is specifically Judaeo-Christian is the teaching on covenant.[1] The Bible is actually entitled the Old and the New Testament (Covenant). There are various covenants described and the theology of them is crucial to an understanding of Biblical faith. Since 'covenant' does not appear in other religions (with the exception of Islam), it might be concluded that that kind of thinking is peculiar to the Bible and the Koran. Even so, it is worth seeing if the thought-form appears anywhere else, perhaps under a different guise or metaphor. Is 'covenant' an instinctive impulse in human nature in relation to God or is it a purely Biblical revelation?

The word 'covenant' itself, *berith* in Hebrew, seems to be a purely Israelite word. It may be related linguistically to the Assyrian *beritu* meaning 'a fetter, an agreement', but it has none of the connotations of the Biblical usage. In translation to the Greek, *diatheke* means a 'disposition, arrangement, last will and testament', and it would probably have had none of the theological connotations of *berith* had it not been chosen as a translation of 'berith'. Actually the choice of *diatheke* is particularly apt when applied to the New

Testament, as this was actually the final arrangement given by Jesus, his 'last will and testament' at the Last Supper.[2]

It has been pointed out that the Hittite vassal treaties of the second millennium BC[3] follow a pattern closely resembling the covenant of Moses as described in the Pentateuch. There were two types of treaty: one on an equal basis, as with Egypt, two countries of equal strength; the other which involved a major power (Hittites) and a weaker nation state on the fringe of the Hittite Empire, which in effect turned the smaller kingdom into a vassal state. Many have assumed that Moses knew of these treaties and simply used that format in forging a relationship with God; it is just remotely possible that the reverse is true, that the surrounding nations derived the idea from Moses. That would be very contentious. A lot depends on how one dates things in the second millennium BC: no one can with certainty place a date on the Sinai event. Whichever way it is seen, it is clear that the Mosaic covenant fits with the political mentality of that time in history. It is also true that that type of treaty persisted down into the late Assyrian era; the form of it seems to have faded but the wordings of some of the details strongly resemble passages in Deuteronomy and other places. There has to be some relationship there, even if it is not a direct literary dependence. After the Assyrian collapse, this type of treaty went out of usage.

But the differences are more important than the similarities. The vassal treaties are purely a political tool analogous to modern-day international treaties like NATO (the North Atlantic Treaty Organization). There is nothing specifically theological about them except to say that an assortment of gods are cited as witnesses to the agreement. With Moses, however, the whole arrangement is God's plan and love for the Israelite people. At the very least we are seeing the format of ancient vassal treaties being used as an important metaphor in man's understanding of his relationship to God, and vice versa. It is worth remarking that the Hittites and other nations did not seem to have a specific word to describe such a treaty: no synonym for *berith* has so far been found. It is Moses who supplies the word and completes the thought-form. This thought-form became axiomatic in Israelite life: there are many minor covenants recorded on the level of deep friendship and even marriage. But the main and most significant covenants will now be examined.

The covenant of Noah is the first one encountered, in Genesis 9:1–

17, where the occupants of the Ark survive the Flood and Noah makes a sacrifice to God. The promise is:

'While the earth remains, seedtime and harvest, cold and heat, summer and winter, day and night shall not cease.' The covenant requires a sign, which is the rainbow, and God says: 'This is the sign of the covenant which I have established between me and all flesh that is upon the earth.'

It is noticeable that various important features apply here. This is an unconditional agreement applied by God without any consultation with Noah, just like the vassal treaties. However, unlike the vassal treaties, it makes no difference how wayward humanity might become: the seasons and the harvest will not fail. This applies to the whole of humanity, even the whole of creation regardless of whatever conduct they indulge in. Noah does not have to follow any rules, neither does anyone else. He actually says nothing, but the sacrifice, as a thank offering, sets the right context for God to be generous. What is implied here is that Almighty God has tied himself down to an unconditional commitment. We can see the paradox in that: that the omnipotent power behind all things takes the risk of underwriting the future of a failed humanity. This is a thought not found anywhere else. It speaks of the love of God in the face of the wickedness of mankind. In pagan sources it is the opposite: the Greek version of the Flood has Zeus furious that a few of humanity have survived the Flood: in Babylon, Utna-Pishtim survives the Flood but the gods are only pleased when he performs a sacrifice. There is nothing about a cosmic agreement involving a rainbow as a sign of God's goodwill.

It is difficult to assess the relationship between the covenant of Noah and the vassal treaties. We do not know when this part of Genesis was written, and whether it was actually the work of Moses or of a later hand. But the mentality behind it certainly fits with the second millennium BC. It is not out of the question that a tradition about Noah was maintained by the Patriarchs, which later worked its way into the Pentateuch. If so, the covenant of Noah might be contemporaneous with or might even pre-date the Hittite vassal treaties. That would imply a case of the pagans taking an idea from the early Hebrews.

If we compare this covenant of Noah with the mentality shown in sacral kingship, where the harvest is expected to fail unless certain quasi-magical rituals are performed by the King, clearly the pagans do not trust their gods to be generous without heavy coercion. There is a basic lack of trust there: trust is placed in the King-God and his rituals. One could take the covenant of Noah as saying to the rest of the world: 'God has promised to feed us whatever we do: all your rituals are a waste of time: just be thankful instead.'

The covenant of Noah reverberates into the New Testament where Jesus talks of God's love for mankind, regardless of their religion or lack of it.

'For God makes his sun to rise on the evil and on the good, and sends rain on the just and the unjust,' Matthew 5:45.

'For he is kind to the ungrateful and selfish: be merciful even as your Father is merciful,' Luke 6:35.

'Do not be anxious about your life, what you shall eat ... look at the birds ... they neither sow nor reap ... therefore do not be anxious saying, "what shall we eat?" for the Gentiles seek all these things ... and your heavenly Father knows that you need them all,' Matthew 6:25–33.

This is the final endorsement of the covenant of Noah and the final denial of the fertility aspect of sacral kingship. It could be that the Christian understanding of Noah's insight into God's love has resulted in the demise of this aspect of sacral kingship. Although forms of sacral kingship have been evidenced in later times, it has generally omitted the fertility cult strand and concentrated on power politics.

Assessing the Covenant of Abraham is rather more complex for there are two accounts of it in Genesis (normally explained by the claim that there are two different sources at work). In Genesis 15 we read: 'Fear not, Abram, I am your shield.'

The promises of making him a great nation and giving him a land are crucial for the future of the Hebrew people. There is then a sacrifice and a deep mystical experience which prefigures the cloud of fire and smoke at the Exodus. The second account in Genesis 17 with the same promises reveals that his name is to be graduated to Abraham. 'Abram' means 'exalted father' but 'Abraham' means 'chief of a multitude'. The insertion of one letter 'HE' alters the meaning considerably. The sign of the covenant is circumcision and another theophanous encounter with God is seen. It is difficult to assess a date for Abraham but he also may predate the Hittite Empire, or at least its heyday. If so, again, the format of this covenant could possibly have served as an idea for the Hittite politicians in their treaty-making. The essential element in it is that God, the superior power, imposes an agreement on the weaker party who does not venture to object or even try to discuss the matter. But nowhere do we see a list of rules or threats which would imply a future breakdown in the agreement. Abraham only has to trust in God: 'And behold he believed in the Lord: and he reckoned it to him as righteousness.'

In later times this crucial remark was to be seen as the key text for underpinning 'justification by faith'. It is important to see that a sound relationship with God does not have to depend on rules, rituals and procedures. He was told to 'walk before me and be blameless'. But this does not go into details about moral or ritual conduct. A lot is assumed in the early parts of Genesis on the subject of moral conduct, but nothing is formalised until we reach the Ten Commandments. It is sad that Abraham is often judged by later standards, but that is hardly fair: he was almost certainly just following the standards of his own times and knew no better.

The contrast between this and practically every other religious system in the world is obvious: here Abraham is found by God, chosen, and given an agreement. The opposite to this is found in the pagan world, where humanity tries to find a god, has limited success and then tries to manipulate the deity by various techniques. The paradox deepens as we see Almighty God tie himself down to an agreement and promises to one man, which included his family. The rest of the human race has to function on the covenant of Noah; but Abraham is in a special relationship with God. As with Noah, the agreement is unconditional; the thought that the agreement could break down is never mentioned.

It is also paradoxical that while there is an element of doubt Abraham's mind ('shall a child be born to a man who is 100 years old?'), even so we see Abraham embarking on a kind of bargaining conversation with God about the fate of Sodom. Genesis 19:22–33: 'Wilt thou indeed destroy the righteous with the wicked?' The implication here is that the believer can speak to God on a personal level and bring about an alteration in God's intentions. The same idea comes to completion in Luke 18:1–8, the parable of the Unjust Judge: 'Will not God vindicate his elect? . . . he will vindicate them speedily.' The implication here is that the true believer can bring about a modification in God's plans. This is not on the basis of some kind of moral or ritual persuasion, but on the basis of a close, trusting relationship within the covenant of Abraham.

The unconditional nature of covenant now has to face a kind of modification when we consider the covenant of Moses. This is central to the Old Testament. On the one hand the covenant of Abraham underlies the whole agreement and yet there is now a conditional element superimposed: the possibility of failure to observe the commandments rears up and the breakdown of the agreement, yet there is always the possibility of repentance and a renewed relationship. There are various phenomena which can be taken as the signs of the covenant, the Passover event, the Sinai event and various other miraculous or quasi-miraculous events. When we come to the two tables of stone, various elements begin to remind us more of the Hittite treaties: usually they were inscribed on stone monuments with rules and instructions displayed. In particular the blessings and curses to ensure observance of the treaties become increasingly similar to parts of the Pentateuch. Some would say that the Hebrew writers took ideas from the treaties; it is entirely possible that the Pentateuch was known to and copied by the later Assyrian treaty-makers.

Essentially, God has chosen the Israelites and imposed an agreement upon them. There is the personal and the national element in it (Exodus 34:27): 'The Lord said to Moses: "write these words: in accordance with these words I have made a covenant with you and with Israel." '

This runs counter to all modern ideas about freedom of choice and the assumption that one can choose a religion to suit oneself. Nevertheless, paradoxically, the people are presented with two options at the end of Deuteronomy 30:15–20. They are presented with a choice between 'life and good, death and evil ... therefore choose life'. This implies the reality of freedom of choice and of a failure of the agreement. And yet, paradoxically, the covenant is still there (Exodus 30:10): 'If you turn to the Lord your God with all your heart and all your soul.'

The other implication in this is that good conduct earns approval from God and bad conduct the opposite. This is an assumption widely evidenced in human nature the world over. It was later to be described as 'works-righteousness' by St Paul. But in this respect the Mosaic covenant is not just an Israelite assumption, it is a general back-drop in the human mind everywhere. The difference is that for Moses the same closeness to God was experienced, even closer than with Abraham: 'But you cannot see my face for man shall not see me and live. While my glory passes by ... I will cover you with my hand ... and you shall see my back but my face you shall not see,' Exodus 33:22ff.

This is an amazingly anthropomorphic passage about God. It tells of how close one can be to God, and yet he is overpowering and beyond the limits of the human mind. God is near and yet totally other. Both statements are absolutely true but are opposites, a paradox which underpins religious understanding the world over. It is only Israel that has coined a word to describe it: the relationship of 'covenant' is not described anywhere else, even though aspects of it are assumed.

The next covenant is with King David via the prophet Nathan: 'Your house and your kingdom shall be made sure for ever before me: your throne shall be established for ever,' 2 Samuel 7:16. This is all bound up with the building of the Temple, which can be taken as the sign of this covenant. But because David was engaged in so much warfare, the Temple has to be left to his successor who turns out to be Solomon; by that time the Davidic monarchy is well established and flourishing. Although the actual word 'covenant' does not appear in this context, the promises are certainly seen in that light, soon enough.

'Yes, does not my house stand so with God? For he has made with me an everlasting covenant, ordered in all things and secure.' 2 Samuel 23:5. This covenant appears to be unconditional for although the kings may go astray, God will correct them, Solomon and his successors: 'He shall build a house for my name and I will establish the throne of his kingdom for ever. I will be his father and he shall be my son ... I will chasten him ... but I will not take my steadfast love from him,' 2 Samuel 7:13.

The word for 'steadfast love', *hesed*, is pivotal here.[4] God's love, which underpins all these covenants, is not just a sentimental passing attachment: it is a deep, caring, continuing love. That there is emotion in it is clear when God commits himself to being a father to this son, the King. It is not a vapid, ephemeral fancy so often seen in the human race. The paradox of God's commitment in covenant is deeper than just a business contract or an international treaty. It shows that the Almighty God, controller of all creation, has emotions, deep caring for his people and specifically for the King.

One could ask whether the relationship between king and god as seen in the ancient sacral kingship ideas presupposes some sort of 'covenant'. The word and the idea are never stated as such in any of the pagan texts. It might be fair to say that the pagans were working towards this type of theology but never actually arrived at it; more likely their ideas were clouded by fear and distrust of their gods.

As the course of history shows us, the Judean kingdom deteriorated to the point that a complete disaster overtook them it 597 BC, which suggested that the promises had all been forgotten. Nevertheless, the optimism of the prophets, particularly Isaiah, ensured that the Davidic covenant became transformed into the messianic hope. The Jews were deeply suspicious of any attempt at monarchic revival after the Exile; although there were attempts to reformulate the Davidic monarchy, it was never the same again. The Hasmoneans and the Herods attempted to revive the issue but this never met with full acceptance by the Jewish people. The world had to wait for the coming of Jesus to see the true fulfilment of the Davidic covenant and the messianic hope. Even then the Jewish leadership failed to grasp the moment and accept him as their king.

It would be a mistake to think that the 'New Testament' was an idea solely confined to the New Testament pages. By the time of Jeremiah, it was realised that not only a modified kingship was required, but also a modified covenant, since the Mosaic covenant had clearly not carried conviction with the people. So while Ezra tried to reimpose the Mosaic disposition, others saw the need for a new approach.

'The days are coming when I will make a new covenant with the house of Israel and Judah, not like the covenant which I made with their fathers ... I will put my law in their hearts,' Jeremiah 31:31.

'I will make a covenant of peace with them,' Ezekiel 37:26.

These statements came to completion in the Gospels. The New Testament draws heavily on the pattern and imagery of the Old Testament one of Sinai with Moses. Jesus is clearly seen as the new great lawgiver, drawing all of Moses' and later legalism to a conclusion and perfection. It is crystallised into two simple commandments, which anyone can carry in his heart: 'you shall love the Lord your God with all your heart ... you shall love your neighbour as yourself. There is no other commandment greater than these,' Mark 12:29.

At the end of his earthly ministry Jesus inaugurates the New Covenant at the Last Supper, or the first Eucharist: 'This is my blood of the New Covenant which is poured out for many,' Mark 14:24.

This time the sacrifice is Jesus himself: in so doing he brings about a new relationship between God and humanity. He is clearly identified with the Passover Lamb as at the first Passover. There are promises, forgiveness, reconciliation and the prospect of a promised land not of this world but the next. Although Jesus mainly draws on the Mosaic covenant, he also draws in the others. We have already seen how Noah's covenant is referred to in the Sermon on the Mount. The closeness of Jesus to God is seen in the Gospel of John, but it is interesting how Jesus in the Garden of Gethsemane tries to persuade God to change his course of action (Mark 14:36), but withdraws the thought, knowing that the Crucifixion is inevitable.

It is easy to see how the Davidic covenant is brought to fulfilment: he was known to be a remote descendant of David, and the people hailed him and tried to persuade him to take his kingship. But the completion of this theology was that it was not any kingship of this world. So although the New Covenant works on an entirely different dimension, it draws heavily on the imagery and bedrock of all the previous ones. Looking at the pattern from Noah onwards, we see that God's relationship with humanity builds up in layers not unlike a Ziggurat or a stepped pyramid or an Aztec temple. It may be that something deep in human nature requires a 'stepped' approach to a full relationship with God. Certainly in many places of worship the world over, the worshippers approach the holy parts via a flight of steps. Often we see crosses with a stepped base. The Zoroastrian fire altars had three steps up.[5]

It is worth mentioning that the Hindus have a meditational aid, called a *yantra*, which helps to focus the mind in yoga. It goes up in four successive layers like a stepped pyramid and is crowned by a symbol called an *Om*, the most sacred symbol in Hinduism. It is the sound form of Brahman, the 'shabda-Brahman' chanted at the start and finish of ceremonies. It leads to enlightenment and immortality and is analogous to the sacred name in Judaism, YHWH. Are we seeing a stepped approach, covenant in another form of imagery? The metaphor of covenant is good: the *yantra* may be an approach to it under a different imagery.

Two basic forms of covenant are seen in the Scriptures: the Old and the New. It is not as simple as saying that all the old ones are found in the Old Testament and the new one is confined to the New Testament pages. The key to understanding the difference is the conditionality of the agreement. With Noah, Abraham, David and

Jesus, we see the pure love of God entering the world with no conditions, no threats, no suggestion that the covenant will collapse. Essentially, these covenants are 'new'. The only one left is the Mosaic covenant which although it has an unconditional starting point, becomes conditional and is basic to human nature. It is all about keeping laws and earning favour with God. This is why the debaters in Job never come near to understanding Job's misfortunes. The same assumption is seen in John 9:2–3, where the blind man is understood to be under some sort of punishment, for his own or his parents' sin. This is not just the disciples' assumption: it is basic to human nature. It goes something like this: 'I am aware of some sort of god: he has rules and expectations for me to follow. If I keep to the rules, all will go well: if I break the rules, things will go wrong. I have to do something good to obtain a blessing.'

This assumption goes on in people's minds at the instinctive level in spite of all the evidence to the contrary. The Old Testament grows out of this mind-set. It is not just a book: it is an entire pattern of thought that permeates all religious and political systems.

With the New Testament, the reverse situation applies: God comes into our world with a blessing; it is not earned or merited; we are then called to respond with good deeds – that is the crucial difference. 'If you love me, keep my commandments.'

It will now be instructive to see how much of the Old Testament thinking can be found in other religions; though the word itself does not appear in their vocabulary, the thought-form certainly does. With Islam we see the use of the word 'covenant' several times[6] but it does not go into details about it. Moreover we do not see long lists of rules, as at Sinai. Even so an entire legal system did emerge later. There is no distinction between ritual and ethical or dietary rules; all one's conduct is sacred. It is clearly stated that good deeds are essential for salvation: 'To those who believe and do deeds of righteousness hath Allah promised forgiveness and a great reward,' Sura 5:9.

In this we see the issue of faith and works emerging, but it is not fully explored or explained as in the Epistles of St Paul. Islam has been described as a revived form of Judaism. There may be a lot of truth in that, but it is not the entire truth. We can see an awareness of 'covenant' and the balance between the old and new. What appears to be absent is the closeness of God to the believing soul: God's distance from humanity, his transcendence, is constantly emphasised. It is worth remarking that Mohammed's encounter in the cave was with the Angel Gabriel; Abraham and Moses spoke directly with God himself.

'Those who believe and do deeds of righteousness will have their reward with their Lord,' Sura 2:227. Although 'covenant' is not mentioned in this context, there is some sort of 'agreement' with God at work here. It may be seen as a system of merit at work. One example of this could be that *Salat-al-isha* (the night prayer) is deemed more meritorious if done before midnight as opposed to after. After death each man is to be judged by the deeds he has committed; rewards and punishments are awarded. There is to be a resurrection at which all people will be assigned to one of three fates: hell for the companions of the left hand; heaven for the companions of the right hand; for the foremost of the foremost, actual union with God himself in a realm that is beyond all comprehension. All this is the result of one's deeds being weighed in the scales of divine justice. This could be described as a 'works righteous' system in which one buys one's way into favour with God, and this would accord well with the Mosaic covenant. Even so, Allah is known to be merciful, something which is constantly stressed. In this we see the paradox between works and faith latent in Islam but not brought out and discussed in full.

With the Hindu system, and by extension the Buddhist too, we find a fully developed promotional ladder with regard to deeds and merit. It is called the Karma Marga or Way of Works.[7] The concept of merit is endemic in this system; also the assumption that one progresses from one reincarnation to another, in an eternal series of lives, is essential. One's conduct in the present life determines one's promotion or demotion for the next life. There is the prospect of returning as an animal, or worse; good conduct might result in rebirth as a Brahmin or, even better, becoming a god or being absorbed into Brahma the Absolute. The deeds which must be performed do sound a little like the ritual prescriptions in the Pentateuch: rites, sacrifices, ceremonies all done correctly. There is not the clear ethical teaching of the Ten Commandments and their refinements. It is not moral transgression but mental error which is the root of all evil. Moral conduct, or lack of it, is not the main focus of merit.

The wheel of Karma is remorseless: there seems to be no way out of it unless one embarks on Jainism, Sikhism or Buddhism. The God of mercy is not at all well known. It is a thoroughly Old Testament pattern of thought even if portrayed in a completely different thought-form or metaphor. Even so, in fairness, there is some sort of dilemma in the Hindu mind over works and faith. It comes in the metaphor of the monkey and the cat with their babies. The 'monkey hold' means that the baby clings on to the mother's back, which betokens that salvation is the free cooperation of the believer who makes the effort. The 'cat-hold' means that the mother cat picks up the kitten in her mouth, which betokens that salvation is of God and the solution is of God's caring for the human soul. This is a powerful metaphor with a certain degree of emotion attached, but it does underline the fact that faith versus works is not just an issue confined to Christian theology. The balance between faith and works is there; also the paradox, in that there is a strong element of truth in both statements. The mistake is to ignore one aspect in favour of the other. This way the balance and paradox is lost.

When Siddhartha set to work to break out of Karma he discovered the great enlightenment in which all human pain is to be explained by human desire.[8] Finding a way to remove desire would be to reach Nirvana and break out of Karma. The method is to accept the Ten Precepts and follow the Noble Eightfold Path. Much of these sound suspiciously like the Ten Commandments. What is missing is the ritual aspect of Hinduism, and what is gained is a certain amount of ethical guidance and the need for the right sort of meditation. We can see in this a balance struck between Hindu and Buddhist methods. Following Siddhartha's method, every Buddhist believes he will achieve Nirvana, if not in this life then in the life to come. As it developed, merit became increasingly important: this can be taken as just as much an Old Testament approach as any other. One buys one's way into salvation. The difference is that there is no active personal God there to dispense the merit. Although there are gods in Buddhism, they appear to be irrelevant to the accruing of merit. It seems to work like an automatic slot machine: what one puts in one gets out in the form of blessings.

Though the metaphors and the phrasing are different, it is just another version of the Mosaic covenant intermingled with an intellectual form of Gnosticism. Where it departs from Moses is over the issue of the nearness of the personal God: 'for the commandment is not too hard for you neither is it far off ... it is not in heaven ... it is not beyond the sea ... the word is very near to you,' Deuteronomy

30:11. But with Buddhism it would be fair to say, 'the truth is not near to you: it is very far from you, above your head, and it takes all manner of mental exercises and heavy discipline to discover it.'

Again it would be unfair to say that Buddhism is an entirely 'works righteous' system. There is the same dilemma as with Hinduism. There is *jikiri*, which means works, merits, done in one's own strength. Also there is *tariki*, which means 'grace', the strength of another helping one to do the right things. This can be explained by the teaching on Amida (Amitabha), a deity in Buddhist[9] thought understood as a Bodhisattva in first-century India, though not a historical figure. Amida is understood to have immense merits that will avail for the salvation of others. One can call on the merits of Amida rather than rely on one's own actions. This is a milder version of salvation by faith alone. It is an approach to the New Testament but there is no real historical figure who undergoes an atoning death for the benefit of humanity. To find that, it is possible to find this thought-form in the Jataka tales, stories told by Siddhartha in his teachings.[10] A good example would be the 'Monkey Bridge' in which the chief of a tribe of monkeys lays down his life to save his followers from death. With this we see the basic stirrings of New Testament thought in a culture far removed from first-century Israel. Even so, the normative and basic doctrine in Buddhism is 'those who have the self for a lamp', which brings us back to merit, personal effort and buying one's way into salvation, a thoroughly Mosaic pattern of thought.

With many Oriental religions, God is not seen as a personal active force in people's lives, and this is particularly true with Taoism. Even so, human conduct is important for keeping the equilibrium of the Tao. In the early years it was the Emperor who had the task of making the correct sacrifices and procedures to ensure harmony in the natural world; later it was for each person to observe righteous behaviour. An interesting anecdote about Tsao Shen the hearth god serves as an example. On 24th December, food and wine were presented to his paper image; when burnt in the hearth he ascended up the chimney to make his annual report on the behaviour of the family. Though we have nothing like the Ten Commandments, much is assumed about good conduct for mortals and this is connected directly to another system of merits, even if under a different metaphor.

With Confucius, we have someone who would have made an

excellent Humanist with his optimistic view of human nature and ethics which do not specifically require divine backing. His law of human relationships sounds just like something out of the New Testament about mutual consideration. There are five cardinal virtues: *jen*, the motivating force in moral life; *yi*, righteousness by justice; *li*, the religious and moral ways of acting; *chih*, wisdom; and *hain*, faithfulness. His precepts were not written down by himself but were codified by later sages. His status was entirely human until later times gave him promotion to divinity. With regard to God he felt he had the backing of heaven: 'Heaven begat the power (*te*) that is in me.'[11]

He believed his message had eternal significance because it had its origin in the moral order of the world. So in spite of being vague about the nature of God, he stands like a Moses figure for the Chinese people and has influenced their mentality down to the present day. Although there are no threats or sanctions on immoral behaviour, the implication (not clearly spelt out) is that Heaven will be displeased if people cannot conform. So this appears to be another, milder version of the Mosaic covenant.

The Shinto religion has absorbed much of Confucian and of Buddhist thinking, but in addition developed the Bushido Code, 'The Imperial Knight Way'. This can be summarised under eight headings: loyalty, gratitude, courage, justice, truthfulness, politeness, reserve and honour. These all seem laudable enough, except that failure brings with it the expectation to commit suicide. This is the acceptable method of atonement. It applied principally to men but also to women, who were not expected to fight. So while there is no detailed written law code as seen elsewhere, the ethics and rituals are heavily enforced by oneself. There seems to be little mention of failure to adhere to this code and the idea of mercy and forgiveness seem to be absent.

When assessing the Mesoamerican peoples there is the difficulty that much information about the details of their religious ideas is lacking: the Incas because they had no writing, and the Mayan and the Aztecs because much of their written material was destroyed by the Spaniards. We do not know what law codes they had. The Aztec priests preached laws both ritual and moral, and Moctezuma I was known as the great lawgiver who delivered a new legal code. There was great strictness observed over various matters: for instance, for drunkenness and adultery the death penalty was applied. From the

Inca world we have the fascinating account of a family that produced twins. This was seen as problematical: did it mean the woman had committed adultery or had been raped, or was one of the twins a son of lightning? There were elaborate procedures for clearing guilt and atoning. This at least shows concern over sexual morals and family life. Beyond this it is impossible to discern whether there was anything resembling a 'covenant' of any kind.

It is with Judaism that we see the full implications of sacral legalism. First came the laws of Moses. After the return from the Exile, Ezra began the process of reinforcing, on a scale not seen before, the full observance of the Law. This was because the disaster of 597 BC was clearly the result of the failure to keep the laws of God: it was the words of Moses in Deuteronomy 28ff, seen to have come true. From then on the elaboration of laws as a fence round the Law proceeded, leading eventually to the production of the Mishnah and the Talmud. The activities of Antiochus Epiphanes and other Hellenisers gave an added spur to this process. It was then that we see the emergence of the Hasidim, the ardent lawkeepers, which resulted in the appearance of the Pharisees in New Testament times; also the Essenes who had an alternative legal system. It was Phariseeism that survived the disaster of AD 70 and the proliferation of law has gone on to this day with the rabbis. The obsession with every tiny detail of legal observance can and does run the risk of becoming counterproductive, as Jesus himself pointed out (Mark 7:8ff): 'You leave the commandment of God and hold fast the tradition of men ... thus making void the word of God through your tradition.' (It was the Corban question.)

It is easy to see with Judaism that this kind of legalism has an underlying assumption of covenant, giving it a rationale. But for many religions, the plethora of rules almost certainly does not have such an assumption underpinning it.

Sacral legalism is still with us in the Christian world since many a Church organisation has endless regulations in force, much of which, in essence, has very little to do with Christianity. In modern times sacral legalism has given way to secular legalism which is growing at a startling pace and is threatening to stifle just about every aspect of life. We are all aware of the bureaucracy dominating matters such as health and safety, transport, food, banking and finance, education, to name but a few. Strangely, the motivation for this welter of regulation is still present, even if there is no 'god' available to provide the final sanction. Possibly the 'god' is meritocracy or some sort of respectability, in spite of people's complaints on the matter. In an atheist system as seen in various communist states, we have seen meritocracy combined with heavy legalism virtually paralyse whole populations.

It is a safe generalisation to say that the Old Testament mentality has pervaded and still does pervade most of human life, whether as sacral or materialistic. The existence of copious law codes, procedures and codes of conduct, backed up by the modern mania for meritocracy, all show that the human mind functions on the level of some sort of merit system. We could phrase it thus: 'I want to be acceptable on earth and possibly in heaven too: I must keep to the rules at all costs and never be seen to be out of line. That way I shall get promotion in this life and possibly in the next (if there is one).' It is all about merit, advancement, promotion, avoidance of failure; the basic assumption at work in the Mosaic covenant.

It is St Paul in Romans who elaborates the difference between Law and Gospel. This was an issue latent in the teachings of Jesus, which had to be explained in such a way that the full paradox between Old and New Testament would become clear. Paul never used the word 'paradox' in this context, but Karl Barth did. When Paul talks about 'Law' he means the whole mind-set of the Mosaic covenant. We can extend it to include religions and political systems in every part of the world where the assumption of merit or 'works righteousness' is at work.

'For no human being will be justified in (God's) sight by works of the Law, since through the law comes knowledge of sin.' Romans 3:20. It is through the ever-increasing mass of regulations that we become aware of our failings. This does not mean that laws are a bad thing, a mistake on God's part, or even the government's. 'Shall we say that the Law is sin? By no means, yet if I had not known the law, I would not have known sin ... so the law is holy and the commandment is holy and just and good,' Romans 7:7.

There is nothing wrong with the Old Testament as given by Moses, as far as it goes. It was, as a framework of thought, implanted as an instinct in the human soul right from the start. The Mosaic teachings only tap into that assumption. The mistake is to say that it is the only arrangement possible between God and humanity: there is another one called the New Covenant. The old one cannot be dispensed with, because it is essential as a basis for the new one brought in by Jesus. This is an arrangement not seen amongst other religions of the world, although as we have seen there are indications of the dilemma, or paradox, between Law and Gospel, expressed under different metaphors. But no one has been able to anticipate the full extent and ramifications of the New Testament. Only God could have devised it: it is beyond human imagination. It follows this pattern:

1. Repent: admit to failure.
2. Christ comes into our world with love to clear guilt.
3. His love cannot be bought; it is a gift from the start.
4. A new relationship of trust is provided between God and mankind.
5. This is brought about by Christ giving himself as the final and ultimate sacrifice.

This relationship is on an entirely different dimension and logic from the old one. Akin to the arrangement with Noah, Abraham and David, it is God who initiates the situation, seals the agreement and trusts the human to adhere to the covenant. In that sense these early covenants are prophetic in relation to what Jesus brought in. It is all about God's love, not about the purchasing power of humanity. The paradox is that although Law and Gospel are opposites in thinking, neither of them is wrong: they both need each other to make sense of each other, in a sort of balancing mechanism.

'But now the righteousness of God has been manifested apart from law, although the law and the prophets bear witness to the righteousness of God through faith in Jesus Christ for all who believe,' Romans 3:21. It is important to see that 'righteousness' in this context does not mean good behaviour on the part of God or of man: what it does mean is the strength of the love of God intervening in this world to bring in salvation. It only requires the human soul to respond with trust to this new arrangement.

This does not mean that we can abolish all the laws and live as libertines. Some Christian groups tried this and failed. But early in the Christian era it was decided that the ritual and dietary rules could be dispensed with, but the moral content was to be retained and possibly intensified, while focusing on the two great commandments. It is not satisfactory to cancel one covenant in favour of another, whichever way round one sees it. The Old is the seedbed and preparation ground for the New, marking out a basic kind of safety net for all mankind. The New is the culmination and completion of the Old with the reassurance that everyone can come into God's presence cleared of failure and with a clear conscience.

Although Jesus never mentions this, there is always the possibility of losing the relationship with the New. The reaction of the disciples, especially Judas during the Passion, would be a prime example of this.

The prayer, 'take not thy Holy Spirit from us' (adapted from Psalm 51:11) is a cautionary remark for all Christians who become too complacent. But in that event, there is always the Old one waiting like a safety-net and another chance to begin again through repentance. The New Testament would have had no meaning or relevance if it had not grown out of the Old: the Old has no completion or final success without the coming of the New. They work on two different levels and at right angles to one another. There is the earthly level, basic rock-bottom human nature trying to find the correct way to behave in a world of pain and uncertainty; there is the heavenly level where Jesus reaches out and raises us up above it. So indeed the Christian finds he has one foot in this world and the other foot in the next, a difficult balancing act. This is a kind of schizoid life which Jesus himself appears to have had to endure. St Paul puts it well in Romans 7:21ff:

> So I find it to be a law that when I want to do right, evil lies close at hand. For I delight in the law of God ... but I see in my inmost self ... I see in my members another law at war with the law of my mind and making me captive to the law of sin which dwells in my members ... I of myself serve the law of God with my mind, but with my flesh I serve the law of sin.

Unfortunately he uses the word 'law' in two different senses here, but what he is trying to say is that here is a man who is working under two covenants simultaneously. Here is quite a paradox: that two relationships with God working on different dimensions, and apparently contradicting one another, can be lived at the same time by one man. It applies to us all if faith in the Messiah is allowed to transcend all earthly situations.

'Do not be conformed to this world but be transformed by the renewal of your mind, that you may prove what is the will of God, what is good and acceptable and perfect,' Romans 12:2.

For those in the Protestant world who have placed much emphasis on 'justification by faith' there are parts of the New Testament which could serve as a considerable embarrassment. The Sermon on the Mount in Matthew contains many remarks which appear to teach the exact opposite: that rewards for good conduct are quite clearly promised.

'Your alms may be in secret and your Father who sees in secret will reward you,' Matthew 6:4.

'Beware of practising your piety before men in order to be seen by them for then you will have no reward,' Matthew 6:1.

'Do not lay yourselves up treasures on earth ... but lay yourselves up treasures in heaven ... for where your treasure is, there will your heart be also,' Matthew 6:19.

'There is no man who has left home and family for the sake of the kingdom of God who will not receive manifold more in this time and in the age to come eternal life,' Luke 18:19.

Much more could be adduced and it has to be admitted that Jesus did talk about rewards for good deeds and the commitment of faith. The mistake comes when people do it purely and simply to gain praise from humanity and merit from God. Done on a trusting basis within the covenant, good deeds do carry weight with God. Even so, the opposite thought is also to be found in St Luke 19:9: 'Today salvation has come to this house ... for the Son of Man came to seek and save the lost.'

'Would not even lift up his eyes to heaven ... "God be merciful to me a sinner" ... I tell you this man went home justified,' Luke 18:13.

So here is a deep paradox indeed: on the one hand good works do bring about blessings from God; on the other hand, we are blessed by God on the basis of faith. Can we go so far as to say that both of them are the complete truth in their own way? To deny one in favour of the other unbalances the tension between them and the paradox is lost. The truth is that mysteriously God deals with us in both ways, but his dispensation of love is in his hands, not in our powers of persuasion.

It may be that 2 Esdras 9:7 comes very close to realising this paradox: 'Every one that shall be saved, shall be able to escape by works or by faith, whereby he hath believed.'

Sacrifice

This is complementary to covenant and is the other side of the implementation of the relationship between God and humanity. It is the human side of the arrangement: in the Bible it is closely interrelated with various covenants. Elsewhere some version or permutation on sacrifice is found in every religious system in the world, even secular and atheistic ones. This might suggest that the existence of God is not completely necessary in this activity, and yet it depends on what is meant by 'God'. The historical or classic understanding of sacrifice is understood on these lines: that something of value is offered to the god as some form of gift. This kind of idea may seem illogical to modern minds, but it is far from absent in modern patterns of behaviour. Even in ancient times the illogicality of it may have been glimpsed if not made explicit.

David gives his final address to the people, in 1 Chronicles 29:14: 'For all that is in the heavens and the earth are thine. For all things come from thee and of thine own do we give thee.' So the word 'give' is somewhat strange in this context, but it opens up another paradox. If God owns everything in any case, what does it mean to hand something back to him?

It may be fair to say that the idea of sacrifice is endemic in human nature and is basic to every system. It appears in three ways: a religion based on active sacrifice; a religion based on the memory of a sacrifice; a religion or secular system based on some form of transmuted version of sacrifice. The active sacrifice was prevalent in the ancient world and still goes on in some areas, for example the Hindus and the shamans. Those relying on the memory of a sacrifice would be the Jews, the Christians and the Muslims for the most part. Those working on some form of transmuted sacrifice would be the Buddhists and various political extremist groups. Since the same kind of mentality is found everywhere, it is most likely that it is deeply engrained in human nature at the instinctive level. It stands out as one of those traits implanted by God, although not using the metaphor of 'covenant' even so it implies virtually the same thing, that there is some sort of reciprocal agreement at work between two different worlds.

The full range of sacrificial offerings is much the same the world over. The more valuable the victim, the more efficacious the sacrifice. Human sacrifice has been widespread in remote prehistory, and while it declined in the Old World, the opposite happened in Mesoamerica and was only stopped by the Spaniards. Child sacrifice also was probably seen as a substitute for an adult. In the sacrifice of Isaac we can see the substitution of an animal for a child. The Canaanites committed child sacrifice on the assumption that it would relieve a dire situation: if the heir apparent were offered it would have more purchasing power with the gods. By Roman times we see the Caesars actually persecuting the Druids for their murderous behaviour, namely human sacrifice. Nowadays we see it as bloodthirsty, illogical and cruel, but the ancients almost certainly saw it in an altogether different light.

One example from the Aztecs will suffice. Vast numbers of humans were cut open and thrown down the temple steps. The Spaniards were horrified, and yet the Aztecs could not understand this. They believed that the sun would not return for its daily course and the world would come to an end if there were no daily sacrifices. On this basis warfare was a necessity in order to take enough prisoners for sacrificing. One might have thought that the prisoners would have objected and tried to escape: very much the contrary. They were very glad to be taken, and demanded it to be carried out. It was nothing to do with hate or cruelty. If you died in battle or were sacrificed as a prisoner, you went straight to heaven to assist with the sun making his daily course across the sky. After four years you would return as a humming bird and have a lovely time sipping honey. Before criticising sacrifice, one must try to see into the mentality of those who practised it.

Over the history of mankind, vast numbers of cattle, sheep and other animals were burnt on altars. In some cases the ritual involved a complete consumption by fire but also a sacramental meal in which the participants were believed to have a special closeness to the god. Other foodstuffs would be offered, some to be burnt and some to go for the upkeep of the priests. Another important substitute was the incense, which could be very expensive, but was seen as ascending up to heaven like the smoke from the altar. Vast amounts of it were produced in Arabia and shipped to virtually every part of the known world.

Looking at the motivation behind sacrifice, this can be seen mainly under four headings. Firstly, persuasion of the deity to do something or desist from a course of action, either of which would be helpful to humanity. It assumes that the deity can be bought, coerced and even blackmailed into being helpful. Many of the priests are convinced that their offering will be guaranteed to bring positive results from the other world, and if success is not seen then the sacrifice either has some fault in it or it was insufficient. Vast liturgies and complicated procedures had to accompany the act. The most prevalent issue was the success of the harvest, often in combination with some form of fertility cult, success in battle, national defence and personal wealth. This mode is 'telling God what to do', a basic motive in pagan thinking which betrays a lack of trust in God and the urge to promote oneself to divine authority. It is essentially pagan and yet there are many Christians whose minds, subconsciously, work on this level. It could be that the Muslim teaching on submission – the word 'Islam' means just that – is the final answer to human self-promotion. Sacrifice on this motive is closely connected with ideas on merit and earning power with God.

Secondly, removal or transference of guilt. The moral values of any given culture may vary considerably, but guilt over sin and mistakes made over rituals all engender guilt. It may be said that, apart from the Confessional, there is no effective way of dispelling guilt in modern Western society and this almost certainly has something to do with the prevalence of mental illnesses. The Ancients had well-established methods for clearing a troubled conscience. A glance at Leviticus 6:24 shows the general pattern of thought: 'This is the law of the sin offering.'

It is also worth considering the thought-pattern in Psalm 51 which is often assumed to be referring to David's guilt over the Bathsheba incident. Even in those remote days there is the realisation that merely performing a sacrifice is not the real answer to guilt. Psalm 51:16:

'For thou hast no delight in sacrifice: were I to give a burnt offering, thou wouldst not be pleased. The sacrifice acceptable to God is a broken spirit: a broken and contrite heart O God, thou wilt not despise.'

It would be fair to say that Moses' laws do not place an undue emphasis on this aspect of sacrifice; more emphasis can be seen in other religions on this matter. The idea is that the 'gift' clears a troubled conscience. Another aspect of this is the scapegoat motif, which relates not so much to personal guilt but to corporate or national guilt. Leviticus 16:7: 'And he shall take two goats . . . and cast lots.' One goat is sacrificed: the other has guilt loaded on to him and is sent out into the desert to AZAZEL (who is taken to be an early understanding of the Devil). The Day of Atonement, Yom Kippur, is an essential part of Judaism and is a good example of how a religious system functions on the memory of a sacrifice.

Thirdly, thanksgiving. This does not presuppose any sin or attempt at coercing the deity. It assumes a blessing has already been received and is an expression of gratitude. This is much more in accordance with New Testament thinking. Leviticus 7:11: 'This is the law of the peace offerings ... if he offers it for a thinksgiving.'

Here we see that thanksgiving is intertwined with reconciliation with God. The phrase 'peace offering' in modern parlance means something to do with restoring a failed relationship, but it may not mean quite the same thing here. The sense of loving God, having an easy relationship with him, being grateful, joyful, even trusting pervades this motif. Thanksgiving does not always involve a literal sacrifice: in the Psalms it is clearly to do with hymnody and music in general. This is a thought picked up by Calvin who saw the Christian sacrifice as the sacrifice of praise.

Fourthly, sealing an agreement. We see this several times in the Old Testament where the seriousness of a solemn promise or covenant is sealed by a sacrifice. In fact the phrase 'to cut a covenant' is seen to refer to the cutting of the animal. This was the normal thing in the ancient world; today a business contract or other agreement may be accompanied by a deposit of money or a celebratory party.

So far we have seen an important paradox in the motif of sacrifice: God is the giver of all things; mankind feels the need to give something back to God. Both of these are true but contradictory. Even in modern life where people have to some extent lost the feeling of dependence on the success of the harvest, there is still the urge to give, even if the belief in God is only vestigial. Human nature may have changed a little but not completely.

As evidence of this there are many ways in which a secular or transmuted sacrifice seems to appear in modern life. There is the insurance system in which people pay enormous sums of money on the assumption that there will be a payback somewhere in the future. Could it be that celestial insurance is actually more reliable? There are various forms of charitable giving and sometimes this may be linked to guilt: we all know the phrase 'conscience money'. There are people who give up a lucrative post or a life of ease for the purpose of some worthy cause or commitment to the ministry of some sort of religious ideal. In the last century we have seen two disastrous World Wars in which millions have perished. Looking back on it, it would seem to be a massive waste and to very little purpose. The term 'sacrifice' and 'holocaust' have been heavily used in conjunction with this loss of life. An extreme case would be the Japanese *kamikaze* pilots, but this was not the only belligerent nation to devise schemes on these lines. 'Greater love has no man ... that he lay down his life for his friends' has come to have an extra poignancy in recent times. The term 'holocaust' (which means 'whole burnt offering'), which did actually involve the 'Final Solution', is now clearly linked to the rebirth of the Jewish state in 1948. This would invoke the second and fourth motive for sacrifice. Although the Buddhists have no sacrificial system as such, even so there is the commitment to monastic life and the local community's support for the begging. We have seen totalitarian states of varying colours, in which dictatorial governments have made the state into a god and sacrificed people's individual rights and freedoms for the sake of some sort of social idea. Furthermore a full system of victimisation has been seen and this reminds us of the scapegoat.

With the Christian religion we see a distinctive pattern emerging even if there is a difference of opinion between Roman Catholic and Protestant. The root of the matter lies in Christ's own sacrifice, a situation where the incarnation of God actually allows himself to be put to death. The paradox in this will be explored later, but for now, evidence from the New Testament will help to elucidate the covenant and the sacrificial aspects of his work. In the gospels, the Crucifixion is clearly linked to the Passover sacrifice with all that that means with regard to inaugurating a covenant.

It is with Hebrews that we see the full implications of Christ's sacrifice worked out. Hebrews 4:14: 'Since we have a great high priest who has passed through the heavens ... to act on behalf of men to God ... to offer ... sacrifice for sin.' And 9:26: 'He has appeared once for all at the end of the age to put away sin by the sacrifice of himself.'

It is Hebrews that has the courage to say, in an age when blood sacrifice was the norm, 'It is impossible that the blood of bulls and goats should take away sin,' Hebrews 10:4.

What is being said here is that the death of Jesus was the culmination, the fulfilment, the completion of all the methods and motives for sacrifice the world over. There is no way that slaughtering an animal will bring about an improved relationship with God. The paradox is that God himself has provided the victim, the priest and the holy place, and brought about by himself a new relationship between humanity and himself. This might suggest that all the offerings in prehistory were a complete waste. Hebrews might have agreed, and yet the benefit was not for God but for the human mind, in the easing of consciences and building of strong relationships. Does this work nowadays for those who perform sacrifices? For those who have not understood the New Testament, this may still hold good, but for those who have come to understand the sacrifice of Christ, it is completely unnecessary and a waste. This explains why the early Church soon realised that all the Temple activities could be abandoned and their worship could centre on the Eucharist instead, the re-enactment of the Last Supper and the calling to mind of the Paschal offering. It can be seen as no accident that after the Christians began to become separate from the Jews, the Temple came to its destruction in AD 70: was this God's plan to point up the completion of the sacrificial system?

In the course of Church history, the Eucharist gradually became seen as the Christian sacrifice, which carried the implication that the Christian minister was the 'priest'. It was St Cyprian[12] who was the thinker who lit the fuse over the 'sacrifice of the Mass'. The bomb only exploded centuries later at the Reformation when it was realised by Luther and others that the Mass could not be used as a kind of bargaining chip or celestial insurance premium. The tension over merits and faith surfaced in quite a violent way. The Eucharist then became for the Protestants a memorial ceremony: they had difficulties over 'this is my body (and blood)'; the sacrificial overtones were played down or even absent. Some went further and abandoned the Lord's Supper altogether as an overdone reaction to Catholicism.

It could be seen as a fourfold paradox that Christ's death satisfies all four criteria of sacrifice at one stroke. There is the matter of buying favour with God, the celestial method: this makes no sense if everything belongs to God in the first place, and yet if God performs the sacrifice himself, it can only be seen as totally effective, in contrast to the impure and feeble efforts of mankind to buy favour. Secondly, there is the conscience-clearing aspect: here we see the one without sin take away sin and clear guilt. This is not really effective if a human priest, in spite of all his attempts at self-cleansing, performs the act. Thirdly, there is the thanksgiving peace element which is clear in the Eucharist (the word itself means 'thanksgiving') and 'Peace I leave with you' (John 14:27). Fourthly there is the element of sealing an agreement or covenant. This is clearly stated in St Mark: 'This is my blood of the New Covenant'. This was a deep, everlasting commitment on the part of God which required the most drastic act to bring it in. In this way, the mentality of sacrifice is brought to a conclusion and completion by Christ. In the one act, we see the final answer to finding a proper relationship with God, removal of guilt, the proper context for giving thanks and the acceptance of God's terms. Each one is true in its own way, but this time there is no tension between them: the paradox is a good one.

It would be tempting to say that the sacrifice of Christ is unique in world religious thought. Nevertheless the motif can be found elsewhere. The Rig Veda X:90 talks of a cosmic sacrifice performed by a cosmic man, Perusha, who produced gods from himself and they made a sacrifice of him. Though the motif is very similar, it is a mistake to say that it is the same as the sacrifice of Christ only under different wording. For one thing, the Rig Veda is not historical material: it is only poetic and mythological, which means that there is no actual historical figure called Perusha who is sacrificed. As we have seen in sacral kingship, in many cases the king-god dies what might appear to be a sacrificial death to propitiate the senior gods. Again this is not real but only play-acting in the actual fertility ceremony. The closest we come to reality is when a Mayan king,18-Rabbit, is sacrificed after a ball game in the ball court. Even then, the rationale of it, if we understand it anyhow, is not the same as with Jesus. The king, 18-Rabbit, is not the one true eternal sacrifice which finally and irrevocably alters the relationship between humanity and the one Eternal Father. The motif of dying and rising is important in pagan sources but it never comes to completion or full effect until we come to Jesus. It can be seen as God preparing the human mind for the eternal sacrifice; also it points up the deep-seated need in human nature for a final, everlasting basis of understanding between God and mankind.

On this basis we can see that there is some kind of assumption of covenant at work, something akin to the Davidic covenant combined with the covenant of Noah. The difference is that it is never developed or described in terms of covenant. There is no word or metaphor ever used which could equate to the Biblical concept of covenant. But the fact that the sacrifice, for whatever motive it is performed, does presuppose that the gods will respond accordingly, and assumes a covenant of faith underpinning the whole activity. The fact that the pagan sacrifices were done under faulty theory or wrong assumptions does not alter the fact that faith has to be at the root of it and that in itself can be described as a form of unspoken covenant.

It is also noticeable that in Islam the Koran says, in Sura 5:9: 'To those who believe and do deeds of righteousness hath Allah promised forgiveness and a great reward.' Although the word 'covenant' is mentioned in the Koran, this clause clearly presupposes some kind of underlying agreement and promise coming from God. It is not developed and explained as we see in the Bible.

It would be fair to say that the assumption of covenant coupled with the more obvious rationale of sacrifice is present in virtually every religious system in the world.

Typology

This brings us to consider another aspect of Biblical thought which might seem strange to modern minds, in fact might seem irrelevant. It is the metaphor of copies and shadows, known as typology. This is raised in Hebrews 8:5: 'They serve as a copy and shadow of the heavenly sanctuary.'

He is talking about the whole sacrificial system as seen particularly in Leviticus but more widely in other sacrificial systems. It is an indicator, a precursor, a visual aid for the true and eternal sacrifice of Christ. It is there to prepare people's minds for the event of Calvary. There is only one high priest, Jesus; all the others are a pale imitation, a cardboard cut-out, a projection on a screen. The idea of typology not only looks backwards into prehistory but also forwards into the Christian era. The Christian 'priest' is not literally 'the priest' although the temptation for some has been there to impersonate the Messiah. As a reminder, a token, an offprint of the truth, this can be the validity for talking about Christian priests. To some extent there is the tension between the literal and figurative here. Jesus gives his disciples the power to forgive sins (John 20:23): 'If you forgive the sins of any they are forgiven: if you retain the sins of any, they are retained.'

To say that to his Jewish disciples must have been a profound shock; it was startling enough when Jesus himself forgave sins when performing healings. Yet the priesthood of the Christians is only ever a borrowed status; it is completely dependent on the ultimate priesthood of Christ. It can hardly be taken as literally true. This is an interesting example of the tension between literal and figurative in the Bible, and leads us into another paradox.

Now we see another paradox in that while the world of sacrifice and priesthood that went with it came to an end with the sacrifice of Christ, even so 'priesthood' goes on and sacrifice in all manner of permutations. It appears to be a basic need in human nature. Christianity (and other religions) functions on the memory of a sacrifice, yet sacrifice is just as important as it ever was. These statements are contradictory but yet have truth in them. It forms another paradox.

The question may be asked: why does God allow such painful things as sacrifice to occur at all? It is the same question as with Theodicy: 'Why does God allow any pain at all?' The paradox of Theodicy, which is unsolvable, applies here just as much. Why does human nature have the urge to destroy things, commit cruelties, wage war, waste on a grand scale? It is essentially irrational in terms of human logic. But God almost certainly sees it in a different light. If the sacrifice of Christ brought about a completely new relationship between God and mankind, the process of sacrifice cannot be irrational in God's terms. It is almost certainly the key to life and the future of the world. We have just lived through a century in which there has been more loss of life, wastage of resources and cruelty than ever before, on a scale that beggars belief. Is it possible to say that this high-profile sacrifice has been necessary to bring in another important 'covenant' in the history of mankind, that of the United Nations Charter? It is worth thinking about!

It is interesting to sum up these remarks on covenant, sacrifice, works and faith and their interrelationship with a glance at a selection of the parables of Jesus. Although 'covenant' seldom appears in the Gospels, the assumption is often there, as is faith, works and sacrifice. The often-repeated phrase 'the first will be last and the last first' is almost certainly the key to understanding virtually all of it. With regard to sacrifice, the Widow's Mite shows us that it is not the total amount in human terms that matters to God: it is the humility in the giving that influences God. The mite was far more important to her than the vast sums given by the rich. The Prodigal Son makes a big assumption about covenant as an unbroken love binding father and sons regardless of their worthiness. The father loves them both; the paradox is that the wayward but repentant son receives more of a welcome than the faithful son. But the unwritten covenant between father and son is a reminder to us all today in respect of family relationships.

It is the Labourers in the Vineyard (Matthew 20:1–16) that is the most relevant to these issues. As with many of the parables there are aspects of it that defy human rationality, and that is because divine logic is woven into the story. The gist of the story is that the vineyard owner takes on labourers at three different times in a day, the first being at nine o'clock, being promised a denarius. He is cagey about how much the others will receive but they are assuming it will be something less. At the end of the day they all receive the same, much to the annoyance of the early birds. But the reply is, 'do you begrudge my generosity?' and 'am I not allowed to do what I choose with what belongs to me?' By human canons of common sense, this is very difficult. For those whose minds work purely on the basis of merit, the more effort expended will result in greater rewards. He is saying that although there are rewards, it is not quite as simple as calculating a payslip with God. God is saying, 'my kindness is not conditioned by your efforts. You cannot coerce me by trying harder. I will be open-handed with whom I wish, not whom you wish.' There is an agreement and a bond of promise between God and all his adherents, but it is no use trying to calculate it in human terms. The rewards will be there but not necessarily quite what we expected, perhaps in this life, perhaps in the next.

But over and above it all, and underpinning the whole arrangement is the faith that is required in the believing soul. There is also the implication that those who think they are so virtuous should always remember that God judges not by appearances but the inner heart of man. The one that might appear to be a complete failure, a spiritual wreck, a no-hoper for the kingdom, might turn out to be occupying a seat at the top table at the Messianic banquet. The paradox is that faith and repentance are just as much required as good works and faithful service. God's love for us is based not on our efforts and expectations, but on his wisdom in knowing what is the right thing for each and every one of us. In this way this brings us back to Theodicy.

Notes

1. Walter Eichrodt, *Theology of the Old Testament*, is a thorough treatment of the rationale of covenant.
2. The logic of covenant is worked out in Hebrews 9:15ff.
3. John Bright, *The History of Israel*, p. 134.
4. HESED, steadfast love, commitment, translated into AGAPE in the New Testament.
5. Mary Boyce, *Zoroastrianism.*
6. The Koran makes mention of 'covenant' but does not go into details or specify which one. The Koran mainly focuses on Noah, Abraham and Moses.
7. Littleton, *The Sacred East*, p. 31.
8. Bouquet, *Religions.*
9. Bouquet, op. cit.
10. Noor Inyat, *The Jataka Tales.*
11. D.C. Lau, *The Analects of Confucius*, 1979, 7:21.
12. Bettenson, *Documents of the Christian Church*, p. 108.

5

Free Will and Predestination

This is another issue like Theodicy which has teased the mind of man since the dawn of time. It is not necessarily a theological matter: philosophers of all opinions, theist and atheist, have pondered this question and it is still an open matter to this day. Unfortunately the dilemma has been confused by the modern tendency to smother everything with sentimentality, with the result that predestination is out of favour and free will, which coincides with ideas about democracy and freedom of choice, is now paramount. These are worthy matters in their own right but do not answer the basic question. As with theodicy, there is a deep paradox at work here and this time the Bible does not have an entire Book of Wisdom dedicated to exploring the matter. Instead we have the Book of Ecclesiastes in which these issues are explored with passing remarks but there is no attempt to arrive at any conclusion. Indeed, would it be possible to come to a conclusion on the matter? After all, the great philosophers from Ancient Greece to the present day have not achieved a convincing solution to this paradox.[1]

There is enough said in Ecclesiastes and the Bible generally to leave us confused. The Bible was never meant to be a philosophical debate and yet it furnishes us with enough in the way of theological thought and indirect remarks to fuel the dilemma even in today's world. With the wisdom literature of the Bible we see the nearest that the Hebrew tradition comes to philosophy, and yet it is so bound up with the power of the One God that they could never have produced anything like what the Ancient Greeks achieved; the balance between them results in another paradox.

There are numerous instances in the Bible where free will is clearly assumed: the ability to choose between right and wrong actions takes centre stage. The Garden of Eden, Deuteronomy 30:19: 'I have set before you life and death ... therefore choose life,' and at the Temptations of Jesus, there is the implication that he could have made the wrong choice. It is fruitless to speculate on what the outcome of that would have been, but it is senseless to say that he had to have resisted temptation. Wickedness or virtue have no meaning if humanity is not given genuine freedom of choice.

To balance this there are remarks in the Bible that would indicate the opposite view. Job 42:1: 'I know that thou canst do all things and that no purpose of thine can be thwarted.' Many of the prophets describe how they were called to perform a mission and not really given any option. This comes out in Jonah where the prophet tries to avoid his commission but is thrown back into it again later. The whole idea of prophecy and fulfilment (as explored earlier in chapter 3) presupposes that God has a plan for history, and the implication is that all people are included in the plan in spite of their attempts to avoid it. The word 'predestination' never occurs in the Old Testament – it does in the New – neither does any phrasing about free will. And yet the basics of both views are latent. The paradox is never explicit, never explored properly, but the balance between the two ideas is certainly beginning to appear.

The Book of Ecclesiastes on the subject of free will and predestination

It has long been noted that the book appears self-contradictory.[2] It is easy to write off such matters as a corrupt text or a collection from a variety of people. To read the book through reveals a consistency of style and tone, and it seems reasonable to assume the integrity of the book. The date of this work is uncertain but its claim to be the product of the son of David (Solomon) does not seem unreasonable. Certainly its theology of afterlife sounds early.

The writer is wrestling with the deep questions of life, theodicy being one of them, although he does not make it a major theme as in Job. He claims to have thought deeply but is unable to come to any conclusion (7:27). This is a feeling that many of us have, that the deep things of God are well beyond us to explain (8:17): 'Then I saw all the work of God, that man cannot find out the work that is done ... however much a man may toil in seeking, he will not find it out: even though a wise man claims to know, he cannot find it out.'

The main theme is the futility and nonsense of human life, and the advice to enjoy oneself while the opportunity is there. Nevertheless he is beginning to stumble on to the deep contradictions and paradoxes of life. There is no attempt to produce a system of thought: he just has a consommé of ideas, many of which at times seem unrelated and haphazard.

With regard to determinism we can adduce various remarks.

'Consider the work of God: who can make straight what he has made crooked' (7:13).

'How the righteous and the wise and their deeds are in the hand of God' (9:1).

'Go eat your bread with enjoyment ... for God has already approved what you do' (9:7).

'I know that whatever God does, endures for ever. Nothing can be added to it nor ... taken from it. God has made it so in order that man should fear before him' (3:14).

'Whatever has come to pass already has been named' (6:10).

'In the day of prosperity be joyful: and in the day of adversity consider. God has made the one as well as the other so that a man may not find out anything that will be after him' (6:10).

But the contrary feeling comes over with the following remarks:

'God has made man upright but they have sought out many devices' (7:29).

'But time and chance happen to them all' (9:11).

'For to the man who pleases him, God gives wisdom and knowledge and joy ... only to give to one who pleases God' (2:26).

'The king does all that he pleases' (8:2).

'A wise man's heart inclines him to the right but a fool's heart to the left' (10:2).

'Fear God and keep his commandments for this is the whole duty of man ... for God will bring every deed into judgement' (12:13).

The famous passage of 3:1–9 is of great relevance to this dilemma: 'For everything there is a season, and a time for every matter under heaven.' On the one hand there is a feeling of inevitability, that events will occur whatever we do and there is not much latitude for choice ('a time to be born and a time to die'). And yet there is also the feeling of choice, sometimes with a moral implication in it ('a time to kill and a time to heal'). There are 14 clauses, arranged in 7 pairs, the number of eternity. It is trying to describe the full range of possibilities in life; and the tension between predestination and free will is latent and is a substratum beneath the whole idea. The passage carries its own conviction which explains why it has become so famous and impossible to deny. In a way, Ecclesiastes starts the dilemma of free will and predestination in the early years of Israel's history, a contradiction which is still with us to this day. The only satisfactory way of seeing it is as a profound paradox.

Apocalyptic material

When considering the apocalyptic literature both within and outside the Bible, we find again an uncertain situation with a latent contradiction. It is a major feature of these writings that world history is divided up into ages, and it is not possible to avoid the conclusion that history is planned from start to finish. 'Determinism became a leading characteristic of Jewish apocalyptic: and its conception of history ... was often mechanical rather than organic'.[3] We begin to see the influence of astrology, calendar calculation and zodiac work coming in increasingly. This is no surprise since the Greeks and the Persians were thoroughly immersed in such areas of thought, so too the Mesoamericans. It may well be another innate requirement in human nature: the need to see some kind of framework in history and an awareness of the beginning and the end.

As far as free will is concerned, this is mentioned quite freely as if there is no contradiction with determinism. An instance of this is in 2 Enoch 52:2, that each man's work has been written out before creation; but elsewhere it is stated that God bestowed on man the gift of free will so that he might distinguish the knowledge of good from evil (30:15). It seems not to have occurred to these writers that a contradiction is latent here, for the clash is never discussed: their main focus is to warn mankind of the impending judgement day and the coming of the Messiah.

It is no surprise that the New Testament and the thought-processes of Jesus himself strongly assume all this material, even if much of it had not and never would be accepted as canonical. It was the spirit of the age. We only need to look at the genealogy of Jesus in Matthew to see that it is divided up into equal periods of 14 generations, a scheme betraying the apocalyptic mentality. When Jesus begins to preach, 'Repent for the Kingdom of Heaven is at hand,' he was simply saying that the final epoch was dawning. The Gospels, especially John, are pervaded with a sense of inevitability about the course of history and the ministry of Jesus, how it all leads in one direction, to Calvary. 'Jesus began to show his disciples that he must go up to Jerusalem and ... be killed and on the third day, raised,' Matthew 16:21.

The way of the cross is heavily underlined in every gospel, but at the same time, the freedom to make the choice is still there, for himself and his followers: 'If any man would come after me, let him deny himself, take up his cross and follow me ... whoever would save his life will lose it: whoever loses his life for my sake will save it,' Matthew 16:24.

Here we have free will and determinism worked in together but the contradiction is not brought to the surface, still less is it discussed. This leads on to the betrayal: Jesus knew in advance about Judas's scheming, knew it was a part of the plan, and yet Judas was free to decide on that course of action and was going to feel the full weight of guilt brought on by treachery. There is a deep paradox here which will be developed later in this chapter. 'For the Son of Man goes as it has been determined: but woe to the man by whom he is betrayed,' Luke 22:22.

It is in St John that we have the strongest feeling of the timing of the last events in the life of Jesus: 'No one laid hands on him for his hour had not yet come,' (7:30 and 8:30). And 'Father save me from this hour ... no, for this purpose have I come to this hour,' (12:30).

Pontius Pilate thinks he has the power to release or condemn Jesus, but the ultimate truth is that 'you have no power over me unless it had been given you from above'. In the Acts it is now clearly stated, 'This Jesus, delivered up according to the definite plan and foreknowledge of God, you crucified ... but God raised him up,' Acts 2:23.

It follows that if the life of Jesus was determined, then so too the election and activities of his followers. St Paul brings it out in Romans and Ephesians.

'For those whom he foreknew he also predestined to be conformed to the image of his Son ... that he might be the firstborn among many brethren. And those whom he predestined he also called,' Romans 8:29.

'He destined us in love to be his sons ... as a plan for the fullness of time,' Ephesians 1:3–10.

But paradoxically, for those who have come to faith in Christ there is a sense in which they have been set free. It is the freedom of the Spirit: 'The law of the Spirit of life in Christ Jesus has set me free from the law of sin and death,' (Romans 8:11). In one sense we are predestined but in another sense we have free will; a paradox which is now beginning to become more obvious. At this stage he is not really talking about absolute determinism for all people, or free will. But the logic of it being allowed to play out, means that all people are under this subtle paradox.

Through the years of the early Church the main focus of attention was not on this issue, but by the time of Augustine it surfaced over the Pelagian controversy. Pelagius asserted free will and Augustine reasserted the Pauline doctrine on predestination. Neither of them thought to apply the idea of paradox to the dilemma. It is claimed that with Boethius[4] the issue actually attracted the word 'paradox', but if he did he does not allow the full rationale of paradox to elucidate the matter. He makes it into a rather unsatisfactory compromise but that is not the way to cope with a true paradox. It is not a mean between two extremes; it is two true statements which are contradictory and both are absolutely true.

The same could be said of the newly emerging religion of Islam. According to the Koran, nothing can happen without it having a place in the cosmic scheme of things being ordered and structured in accordance with a 'predetermined measure'. There is a plan for everyone as part of God's timeless, eternal knowledge. This applies to the whole of the created world. There is nothing that is random, accidental or the result of chance: everything is measured, planned, determined and decreed by God. It sounds like a world which is like a machine where there is no room for human freedom. If God knows all our actions in advance, how can we be said to be free? So moral choices mean nothing and punishment is senseless.

Predestination at this level of extreme determinism nearly became the sixth article of faith, but opinion within Islam polarised at an early stage. One group took the idea of JABR[5] (total predestination), and another group, free will. There were those who like Boethius wanted a mean between two extremes: the Shi'ites, the Asharites and the Maturidites. This a good example of how a dilemma like this can surface in a new religion and yet there is no totally satisfactory solution to it. The saying was, 'It is neither compulsion nor free will but something between the two.' The argument went as follows: as far as the past is concerned, we should see ourselves as 'predestined', but as far as the future is concerned, the road is well and truly open.

Even to say we are predestined does not mean we are compelled: only the truly free can be compelled to do anything. The fact that God knows in advance what we shall do does not mean we are forced to make such and such choices. Nobody at this time thought to say that they were dealing with a most profound paradox. The word simply does not come into the discussion. Instead they go round in circles trying to reduce it to compromises and tying themselves in knots. If somebody had had the courage to say that both statements are entirely true:

> God plans, guides and brings everyone's life to a given conclusion and result.
> God gives us the freedom to make good and bad choices and we are meant to feel responsible for the outcome of our lives.

then the paradox would have been patently obvious: both statements are contradictory and yet both are entirely true. Both are based on the spiritual experience and accumulated wisdom of the ages. It is not enough to try to find an average or compromise position in between; it is part of God's creative genius that he can work on us with both truths concurrently. But how he does it is beyond our comprehension, just as with Theodicy and other paradoxes.

It is no surprise then that the Christian scholastic theologians of the late Mediaeval period all went in for free will. It can be seen as a reaction against the 'Kismet' of Islam. As Guru Nanak[6] appeared at the end of the Mediaeval period we find that predestination works its way into Sikhism, as one of the elements taken from Islam in an attempt to find a compromise with Hinduism.

It is also interesting that the same dilemma again surfaces at the Reformation as a battle of ideas ensued between Luther and Erasmus. Whether this was some sort of reaction from Islamic influence is hard to say. It is more likely that Luther was reacting against the moribund ramblings of the schoolmen when he reverted to Augustine and St Paul on the subject of predestination. Looking at their arguments, which seem strange by today's standards, we see the same circular and inconsistent reasonings which lead nowhere. Moreover they appear to be thinking on different levels: Luther is thinking in terms of election in which certain people are chosen by God to be his disciples. This does not necessarily involve complete determinism, as in some elements of Islam. But Erasmus is assuming complete determinism, and so finds it unacceptable. It is obvious that they would never come to agreement, still less discover the paradox in it. Strangely there was enough in Erasmus's use of scripture to arrive at the paradox, but he does not seem to see it.

'I conceive of "free will" in this context as a power of the human will by which a man may apply himself to those things that lead to eternal salvation or to turn away from the same.'[7] *The Diatribe* allows that 'God works all in all, and that without him nothing is effected or effective, for he is omnipotent and effective action belongs to his omnipotence.'

But Luther was not arguing on the same level. In his book[8] we see a strong return to Pauline theology. He is not talking about free will as the ability to follow one course of action or another: he means that whatever fallen humanity does, it has no purchasing power with God. Man's will is tied down by sin and the corruption of human nature. Only God's loving power can give release and a new life of freedom for those who are in Christ. Because of sin, all our actions are vitiated and we are unable to make entirely free choices. And yet in the Spirit there is freedom and release. Strangely, Luther does not draw Romans 8:29 or Ephesians 1:3–10 into the argument or even comment on them. Nevertheless he would hardly have denied them: he firmly believed in 'election' but does not go on to force the logic of it to include non-selection of others. So God's choice of people to be saved is a positive one, not negative.

It is with Calvin that we see the logic of it played out in full. Is this a case of human logic interacting wrongly with divine logic?

'By predestination we mean, the eternal decree of God, by which he determined with himself whatever he wished to happen with regard to every man. All are not created on equal terms but some are preordained to eternal life and others to eternal damnation.'[9]

This is taking the matter to its logical consequence, a position not explicitly stated in the Scriptures. Naturally there was a hardening of attitudes over this as the 'unfairness' of it occurred to many people. It would have made sense to say that having had the choice (Deuteronomy) and failed to take the correct course, people then had to face damnation; but that is not what Calvin is saying. Calvin's predestinatory ideas have always been a liability, not just in the Protestant world but for Christianity generally.

It was with Arminius that a more reasonable position was offered on these lines: that God has elected all men to salvation through the

Atonement of Christ, but not all men reach the pitch of faith which makes forgiveness available to them, hence they perish through their own lack. The position, though condemned in 1619, nevertheless worked its way into many a Reformed Church and is still with us to this day. This, combined with the Protestant belief in Providence, would give a fair idea of predestination combined with free will in the Protestant orbit. It is determinism that does not go as far as 'Kismet' but does allow for God's guiding hand in people's lives.[10]

Luther and Erasmus were using the methods and assumptions of their day and age: their arguments are drawn from Scripture and a little from later theologians. As we approach the twentieth century, this dilemma does not dwindle away: rather, it intensifies on a different level. The fact that modern liberalism has managed to lubricate everything with a generous helping of sentimentality has not really removed the deep urge in human nature to ponder the truths of free will and predestination. On the one hand, we have the upsurge for freedom, political, religious and personal, given a final stimulus by the excesses of the Third Reich. The whole basis of the United Nations was to ensure freedom for all people across the world, and in itself it is a worthy concept. On the other hand, the scientific world has uncovered all manner of factors that argue for determinism of various kinds. Genes, chromosomes, environment, heredity, conditioning, socialisation, indoctrination: all these suggest that human nature is far from free, and possibly every detail of our lives is conditioned in some way. The dilemma now continues without the active force of God in the equation and the wisdom of that is already being questioned. If we are determined, are we really determined by nothing? Does that hold any logic? If we are free to assert our personal choices, for what purpose, if there is no ultimate reference point as guidance?

It is clear that despite all the modern scientific and philosophical claims on the subject, the full range of opinion is still there in people's minds, and always will be. Since the dilemma is never going to be resolved it will be even harder to resolve it if God is left out of the equation. No one today seems to be saying that this contradiction is a paradox, and the only way of coping with it is to say that both propositions are entirely true, and the only way it can work is to allow God to work it out in his own mysterious and wonderful way. Obviously this is a circular argument; but then everything is in the spheres of science, religion and philosophy too. To those who find difficulties in seeing God in the equation, then the non-answer will always be some sort of muddle between one set of modernistic ideas and another. For those who do understand God as a power active in personal life and world history, the matter is far simpler: that he gives us a plan and a destiny for life and yet gives us freedom to have a clear or a muddied conscience. How he works this is beyond us to explain. It is an offspin from Theodicy and is equally inexplicable, and yet a paradox which haunts every human soul of whatever faith they may espouse.

An example of how this dilemma has resurfaced in recent times can be seen in the thoughts of Laplace on the subject of free will and determinism. It is possible that he comes the closest to seeing the matter as a profound paradox. He imagined a 'super intelligent demon' that controls everything including human behaviour. How much simpler it would have been to assume that it is God who conditions the whole matter via a most profound paradox. But Laplace does not seem to go that far. It seems that virtually every philosopher, trained or amateur, slides into some sort of muddled compromise which only augments itself if God is omitted from the equation.[11]

The example of Judas Iscariot's betrayal

The nearest that the Bible comes to dealing with the contradiction between free will and predestination is over the matter of Judas's betrayal. All four gospel writers include the matter, but in a slightly different light. This may indicate that none of them really understood what had happened. It is even possible that Jesus himself was not completely clear in his mind about the situation. It is also interesting that in the classic battle of words between Luther and Erasmus, neither of them really arrive at the paradox. Much speculation has taken place over the years of Church history as to Judas's motives and aims in what he did. No one has a conclusive answer, any more than the first disciples did. The following remarks are offered as possible ways of seeing the problem, but there is no claim here to solving the mystery at all.

The first possibility is that Judas did it for greed. In Matthew, Judas sounds grasping as he demands, 'What will you give me if I deliver him to you?' Thirty pieces of silver are quoted; other gospels do not mention the amount. It would seem a trifling amount to hand over someone as influential as a potential Messiah for a trial: one might have expected a vastly greater sum. It is suggested that he was stealing from the common purse, being the treasurer. But this may not have been the foremost thing in his mind. In Luke he is offered money and then agrees. It may be that for Judas the money was some sort of earnest of intent from the priests.

The second possibility is that Judas just had a complete change of feelings about Jesus. Matthew records how a woman anointed Jesus with an expensive unguent, and this occasioned disgust at the waste involved. For Judas this might have been the last straw: that it was against all rationality. Coinciding with this is Luke's remark that 'Satan entered into Judas,' and John, 'the Devil had already put it into the heart of Judas' and 'after the morsel, Satan entered into him'. In modern secular terms this might equate to 'Judas just turned nasty and lost all regard for Jesus'. It is noticeable that Judas is not always present with the other disciples at various times, and may have been trying to disentangle himself from the close circle of the nascent Church.

A third possibility is that Judas had reasoned it out that he was doing something helpful for the cause of the 'potential Messiah'. It may be that he had the impression that Jesus was in approval of his scheme. It would be a confrontation with the authorities and would bring things to a head. He had heard such remarks from Jesus about 'his hour coming' and the inevitability of a big crisis at the coming Passover. John 13:27: 'Jesus said to him "What you are going to do, do quickly."' This to Judas must have sounded like an endorsement of his plan, and that Jesus knew it was Judas who was doing it, and that Jesus had prescience of the idea in detail. It may be that the Kiss indicated that Judas still had quite an affection for Jesus, even hopeful respect. Jesus takes no steps to prevent the betrayal and does not clarify the matter to the disciples so that they are kept in ignorance as to what is really happening. Judas must have felt just a little special and clever, even self-congratulatory.

A fourth possibility is that Judas thought that God or Jesus ought to be put to the test so that a conclusive result would settle the matter. He had reasoned it out that when Jesus was put on trial, he would display his Messiahship, convince them all and gain total victory over all the carping criticism of the various factions in

Judaism. John has Jesus handing Judas a morsel of bread as a kind of 'ticket' to get started. It is slightly differently recorded in Matthew and loses some of its force. But John, intent on relating it to so much of the prophets, is probably trying to evoke an idea from Psalm 78:19 which may shed some light on the strange gesture: 'They tested God in their hearts by demanding the food they craved. They spoke against God saying, "Can God spread a table in the wilderness? Can he also give bread or provide meat for his people?"'

What is Jesus saying with this mysterious act of passing a morsel to Judas? Perhaps he is saying in a roundabout way, 'Go on, you want to test me, here is a token that it will work just as it did in the wilderness.' The passage is in the context of the Israelites not having faith in God to feed them. The answer is that they should have had faith; and now Judas can have faith in what he is planning. It probably never occurred to Judas that Jesus would allow the trial to go against him, still less that he would allow himself to be condemned to death. Even then, even if it had come to a crucifixion, Judas must have been confident that Jesus would never have allowed himself to be killed. There were those who thought that if Jesus were provoked to the extreme he would break free and demonstrate dramatically and conclusively his Messiahship: 'If you are the Son of God, come down from the cross ... let him come down from the cross and we will believe in him,' Matthew 27:40.

This was the ultimate temptation in the final moments of agony; but to give in would wreck the eternal plan. It was when Judas's plan went badly 'wrong' that he was smitten with guilt, threw down the money and went and hanged himself in despair. This is a critical case of human logic not being the same as divine logic: all our earthly canons of logic, about self-preservation, proof, the easy way out, not appearing to be a failure, come crashing down to dust as the Messiah gives himself completely. Judas realises he has done something 'wrong' and yet it is actually 'right', and we are left speculating on his eternal fate.

To allude to Erasmus again, *The Diatribe* says, 'In respect of the infallible foreknowledge of God, Judas was necessarily bound to become a traitor: nonetheless, Judas was able to change his will.' Luther tries to make out that Judas could not have changed his will (therefore he had no freedom of will) and yet the way it is recorded in the Gospels, he could have changed his mind or resisted temptation. To allow free will here would be to deny God's infallibility. Luther then ties himself in knots of circular argumentation and neither of them come to the point or see the paradox.[12]

The basic truth is that Judas, regardless of his motives, thought he was planning a clever device to force a clarification of the strained situation where a 'messiah' was on the brink of being universally accepted or rejected: God's plan, which had the same ingredients was to bring about a crisis in which the final and eternal sacrifice would be brought about. In this case we see that 'evil' is not necessarily quite what it might appear to be. It is no surprise that the Christians entitled that fateful Friday as 'Good Friday'.

This difficult account does however shed light on two major issues: free will and theodicy. On the one hand, Judas was destined to be the means by which Jesus came to the Crucifixion, and yet it was his own will and intention (regardless of motives) to betray Jesus. These statements are in complete contradiction, beyond resolution, which makes them a paradox. The account of Judas's betrayal is indicative of the whole issue of free will and predestination. With regard to theodicy, we see that good and evil are very closely interwoven, and there is a subtle balancing going on between them.

'Simon, Simon, behold, Satan demanded to have you that he might sift you like wheat, but I have prayed for you that your faith might not fail,' Luke 22:31. This telling remark from Jesus indicates that at a certain spiritual level, God and the Devil are in some sort of discussion or even collusion about the fate of mankind. This reminds us of Job. 'Good' and 'evil' are not always complete opposites: in some ways they complement each other.

So with Judas, he did a filthy treacherous act which he may have thought was for the long-term good, only to find that the stratagem had come unstitched. And yet the stratagem was perfect for God's purposes. This explains why Jesus made no attempt to thwart it. So evil is transferred into good by God's own Wisdom, but not by human wisdom. The one needs the other: if there had been no betrayal, then no Crucifixion, and no Resurrection. Evil needs good and good needs evil for anything to work in this world, just as plus and minus need each other. Essentially God is good, but evil has to play its part in the great workings of things.

Notes

1. Philosophers in the main are uncertain about free will and predestination. Virtually all of them are confused and none of them seems to see that both propositions are true in their own way.
2. Henshaw, *The Writings*, pp. 226–7.
3. D.S. Russell, *The Method and Message of Jewish Apocalyptic*, pp. 230ff. This also includes references to F. Porter, *The Messages of the Apocalyptic Writers*, 1905, pp. 66ff.
4. Boethius, AD 480–524, *De Consolatione Philosophiae*, a Christian philosopher who had immense influence in the later Middle Ages.
5. Maqsood, *Islam*, p. 157, and p. 80 on the subject of JABR.
6. Eleanor Nesbitt, *Sikhism*.
7. Erasmus, *The Diatribe*, 1524.
8. Luther, *The Bondage of the Will*, Packer and Johnston, 1957.
9. Calvin, *Wendel*, 1965, pp. 263ff.
10. Arminius, *Theological Works*, 1629.
11. 'Laplace's demon', p. 76, in Barry Loewe, *30-Second Philosophies*.
12. Luther, *The Bondage of the Will* and Erasmus, *The Diatribe*.

6

Sacred Language, Literature and Authority

It would be fair to say that all religions, and secularised versions of them, have some form of authoritative corpus of recorded material. With this usually goes the authority of antiquity, for any kind of reference material has to have stood the test of time and been sanctified by age and prolonged usage. That is not to say that everything is in writing. We know that oral material, often built up as a corpus over many centuries, lies behind much of the sacred literature of religions. The need is usually felt to enshrine these matters in some form of book and in a language which is worthy of the antiquity or holiness that it serves. The exception to this would be with the Incas, whose sacred traditions never were committed to writing since they had no script: this material was retained by professional historians who retained all the material orally, and in a language which was only used in royal circles. The assumption is that God is ancient, so language about him must be antique or verging on obsolete. One exception to this would be *Mein Kampf* by Hitler which had virtually no oral period and gained very rapid acceptance by the German people. The test of time was to prove it totally wrong. Another exception would be the New Testament, which is written in Koine Greek, the patois of the eastern Roman Empire: parts of it had no oral period at all (Epistles) and the Gospels may have had a very short oral period, probably shorter than most scholars imagine. Another example is the Koran, which was given in written form very soon after the encounters with the angel in the cave. For the most part, sacred literature has to grow and develop and be edited, and even translated, over a long period of time, thus gradually assuming scriptural authority.

Holy writ is normally an offspin of mediation, as seen in Chapter 2. Normally it is the product of prophet, priest or king. So far I have used such writings in a literal sense without allowing the assumptions of modern critical analysis to confuse matters. It is far easier and more effective to allow a corpus of material to speak for itself rather than subjecting it to a form of criticism which presupposes modern preconceptions. It is important to allow the ancients to speak for themselves rather than to impose on them the faulty assumptions of modern liberalism. A classic example of this would be the *vaticinium ex eventu* mentality of today which may now be seen as totally erroneous and misleading.

However there comes a point where a completely literal assumption is not always reasonable or possible, and it is now the right moment to consider the nature of holy writ across the world and see how it is used and misused. It is a dangerous assumption to say that all sacred writings are of equal value: they are manifestly not, and yet they all shed some light on the mind of humanity in relation to the divine. Always there are paradoxes inherent in them, some more than others, which make us aware that God cannot be described purely and simply in ordinary thought-forms. There is the tension between literalism and figurativism; mythology and historical account; legal and liturgical material; poetry and prose – to name but a few contrasts. A table showing which religion relies on what holy writ will be helpful.

The holy writings of each religion or secular faith

Religion	**Holy writ**	**Language**
Jewish	Torah, Old Testament	Hebrew (Aramaic)
Christian	Old and New Testaments	Greek
Islam	Koran (and Bible)	Arabic
Hindu	Upanishads, Bhagavad Gita, Rig Veda and others	Sanskrit
Buddhism	Pitakas, Pali Canon, Sutras, Dharmapada	Pali
Shinto	Kojiki, Nihongi, Manyoshu	Japanese
Taoism	Tao Teh Ching, Hua hu Ching	Chinese
Confucianism	Analects	Chinese
Sikhism	Guru Granth	Gurmukhi script
Parsee	Videvdat, Avesta	Pahlevi
Zoroastrianism	Gathas	Aramaic
Baha'i	Kitab-i-Aqdas and others	Arabic

Maya and Aztec	Ancient codices and inscriptions	
Christian Science	Science and Health by Mary Baker Eddy	English
Mormons	Book of Mormon	English
Communist	Das Kapital by Karl Marx	German
	Little Red Book by Chairman Mao	Chinese
Nazi (Fascist)	Mein Kampf by Adolf Hitler	German

Sacred language

It will be seen from this list that many sacred writings are enshrined in a language which is often antique, verging on obsolete and shrouded in antiquity. Perhaps this is most strongly seen with the Guru Granth which is such an obscure text that it is virtually untranslatable. The obscure language mentality is also seen with Pali, the Arabic of the Koran, and the Old Testament Hebrew.

The feeling that God is too holy to be committed to a page of commonplace writing is understandable. The best example can be evidenced from the use of the divine tetragrammaton YHWH,[1] which is not supposed to be spoken out loud but rendered as 'The Lord'. The word remained as untransliterated from the ancient pre-exilic script of Hebrew when the later script came in under the influence of Aramaic. This feature is seen in the Dead Sea Scrolls. Another trait on the same lines is the reluctance to use the names of pagan gods in the text, without some form of alteration: so for instance in 2 Samuel 4, both Ishbosheth and Mephibosheth are word alterations of Ishbaal and Mephibaal, Baal being the Canaanite god but *bosheth* meaning 'shame'. Similar things happen with Nebuchadrezzar and Nebuchadnezzer and Nebuchodnozor.[2] Similar vowel and consonant transplantations are common in the Old Testament.

Conversely and paradoxically the Jews could see the importance of rendering their scriptures in languages more readily understood by non-Hebrew readers and potential converts. So the Septuagint appears and other renderings in a variety of Near Eastern languages, before New Testament times.[3] The early Christians could see the importance of rendering the message of Jesus in a medium readily understood by the majority of people in the eastern Roman Empire, Koine Greek, even if traces of Aramaisms show through in the early teachings. A similar urge was seen with Siddhartha who wanted his words to appear in Pali, as distinct from Sanskrit, which was the old and legalistic tongue of India. Paradoxically, Pali has become the obscure and hallowed-by-usage language of Buddhism.

Retaining the original language of basic texts has its advantages. It is very true that something is lost when a translation into a later tongue is made. This becomes even more apparent when a modern paraphrase like the New English Bible is made. Much of the pejorative loading of certain words is lost. A prime example of that would be HESED[4] meaning 'love' (as already discussed). The same is true of many other Biblical words which are leeched of their full implications in translation. We can sympathise with the Muslims in keeping Arabic in their worship; the Jews in keeping Hebrew. The same mentality appears in the retention of the Authorised Version and the 1662 Prayer Book. It is all part of the tendency to associate God with antiquity and attempts at breaking this down usually run into some sort of difficulty.[5] The paradox then emerges: on the one hand is the need to present one's religion in contemporary terms and make it relevant to modern conditions: on the other hand to enshroud it in antiquity thus giving it an aura of authority and holiness.

Mythology and eschatology

These can be considered together as they are of much the same genre of literature. There is usually an admixture of poetry and prose and sometimes a medium somewhere in between. It is also worth commenting that mythology and eschatology are not confined solely to sacred writings. Philosophers, poets and visionaries in many cultures have offered thoughts on the matter and only a small amount has been accepted as holy writ. The reason for discussing these two matters together is a valid one: they stand like bookends at the beginning and end of human history, and examine the beginning and the end very often in the same language and metaphors. It would seem that the human mind needs to ponder the beginning and the end.

At this point it is worth remarking that the word 'myth' needs to be defined carefully. In its common usage today, it is assumed to mean a 'lie' or, more tactfully, a 'misapprehension'. The true use of this word in this context is some kind of speculation about the beginning of all things. Mostly these ideas are handed down in use from the remote past and are not taken too seriously. The best-known are the two accounts of creation in Genesis 1–2, but there are many more on record from just about every corner of the world. They will be given a full treatment in Chapter 11. It is important however not to dismiss them all as trivial, idle and of no value: on the contrary, they tell us much about human nature and its attempts at understanding the divine. It is interesting to see how the myth-makers have projected human matters, relationships, problems and moral issues into the skies. It would be a mistake to assume that myth-making is an entirely ancient pursuit: we have our own modern myths usually justified by some kind of alleged 'scientific fact'. The most influential myth at this time is a thing called 'evolution', a word which is thrown around without much thought as to its implications, but is supposed to be some sort of blanket explanation for just about everything. Also we have notions of a 'Big Bang', which is an unprovable idea, intermingled with the modern obsession for something analogous to human life just waiting to be discovered on a far-away planet. All this kind of thing is sheer speculation, often adapting ideas taken from ancient mythology. The habit of myth-making is still with us, even if under different vocabulary and metaphors. The question arises as to how we must interpret these ideas and the degree of credulity we must allow for them. After all, who knows really how the world began and how it will end?

One problem in all this is that people then and now have a tendency to take mythology far too literally. It is a good question as to whether the ancients ever intended these ideas to be taken purely at face value. It is not unknown for more than one myth to be prevalent in one civilisation: Ancient Greece is a case in point, where there were at least four differing accounts of creation in circulation. The Bible too has two accounts side by side in Genesis. The differing cultures of the ancient world must have been aware of the divergent ideas in circulation but there seems not to have been a serious disagreement over it. The Mesoamericans admittedly had their own mythologies; even then there were many features in common in their thinking with the Old World. But we have seen in modern times a disturbing tendency to take a selected myth far too literally and turn it into some kind of political or social policy. Japanese mythology was turned into the *kamikaze* weapon of 1945. The Nazis reverted to ancient Norse ideas, and combined with evolution this has been used to justify the idea that the weak must go to the wall.[6] Also we have some sort of deadlock between creationists and evolutionists, and various somewhat clumsy attempts at forming a compromise between the two. This has confused the issue between science and religion for many people: there is the false assumption that the two things are opposed and that one cannot be a Christian and a scientist at the same time. The matter does not have to be a problem when it is realised that mythology and science are two different areas of human mentality, working on two different levels, and there is no need for a clash, still less for bruised consciences on the matter.

Each and every mythology has its part to play in the cultural and linguistic identity of each and every nation. As to where the truth lies, it is impossible for us to decide, and yet people need to have some idea to cling on to; it may be a way of stabilising one's own spiritual equilibrium.

By the same token, eschatology is a feature widely found in many religions, admittedly not so emphasised in Chinese thought, though it is not completely absent. The idea of destiny in history, the Last Judgement, the return of the Messiah, the Antichrist, the final defeat of evil and a new era of bliss, are all ingredients. We see the same literary techniques at work, to excite, terrify and inspire the human soul, usually done with exaggeration and inflammatory language. Again there are all manner of different ideas at work, the disagreements of which are hardly of any importance. Again this must indicate that a literal acceptance of these matters was never really contemplated. Jesus himself must have been familiar with much of the apocryphal writings which hardly became canonical in his times; he uses this genre but does not allow it to become the main thrust of his teachings. It is John Milton who takes the whole thing far too literally and produces an entire work, *Paradise Lost*, which is over-exaggerated with gratuitous ideas thrown in, making wonderful literature but pure imagination.[7]

Looking at the whole gamut of mythology and eschatology there is a balance to be seen. This is best seen in the total shape of the Bible: mythology at the start and Apocalypse at the end; in between we see human history going downhill in a steady debasement clouded with despair up to Malachi. Even with the Apocrypha this makes little difference. Then at the bottom of the trough the Messiah appears and hope and a fresh start raises us up to new heights and fulfilment. With this we see a pattern like a chiasmus.[8] How Jesus saw himself in relation to this will be examined later on. Just as the Messiah's ministry is worked out against a backdrop of humility, secrecy, hostility and understatement, so the opposite happens in Revelation: the work of salvation is worked out against a backdrop of massive drama, cosmic consequences and ultimate fulfilment.

An examination of the creation myths in Genesis 1–2

The influence of the first parts of Genesis on world culture cannot be underestimated: most people take one day a week off, even if they are outright non-believers. The seven-day week has become a normal assumption for most people: for the Jews their holy day is Saturday, for the Christians it is Sunday, and many other religions take another day as their holy day.

Who wrote this passage and at what age is not clear for us to assess, but he seems to have taken ideas from the Babylonian myths mainly, and perhaps a few from Egypt. For centuries it has been assumed that Moses produced it along with the rest of the Pentateuch. Recent criticism has cast doubt on this but no one has realistically offered an alternative suggestion for an author. It must have required someone with massive spiritual authority for such a passage to have gained acceptance. Names such as Samuel, Isaiah and Jeremiah spring to mind. And yet, when talking about great spiritual influence on the Hebrew people, the first name that comes to mind is that of Moses. The monotheism that the passages presuppose clearly relates to the Ten Commandments. The Genesis myth, however it was composed or inspired, is clearly at variance with almost every other system at work in the ancient world, and would have seemed incomprehensible to other cultures. The exceptions to this would have been the Atenist 'heresy' in Egypt and Zoroastrianism which both arrived at a kind of monotheism; then again they may have derived the idea from Moses.

The main features of the first account, Genesis 1:1 to 2:4, are as follows:

1. In the beginning there is One God, even if plural forms in the Hebrew are used: '*elohim*' and 'let *us* make man' and the Spirit of God is mentioned as if something separate.

2. God has a plan which is logical and creation follows a pattern from basic things to more complex things in a time-series. On the seventh day he 'rested'. This is where the style is something between prose and poetry, using an ostinato, 'the evening and the morning were the ... day'.
3. 'Let there be light': the creation of day and night is not the same as the appointment of the sun, the moon and the stars (v. 16).
4. Mankind is the apex of God's creation, 'created man in his own image ... male and female he created them'. They are in charge of the whole of creation, and can eat, utilise and modify anything.
5. God has created everything, not just some things, the implication being that all things are there for a purpose and nothing is accidental, incidental or aberrational.
6. The passage assumes what most ancient people took to be obvious: that while there is water below there is also water above in the sky, and that land appeared later.
7. The passage does not indulge in exaggerated, overemotional, overdramatised thought. It is all rather restrained in contrast to other mythologies elsewhere.
8. The passage concentrates on the Godward side of the theme, mankind only being mentioned towards the end after the main structures of the cosmos are established.

Another creation account in Genesis 2:4 to 3:24 is markedly different and forms a contrast with the previous one. Modern scholarship has explained this passage as coming from a different source:

1. It concentrates on the manward side of Creation, including many social, economic and biological matters of importance.
2. Creation appears to take place in one day (v.4b). Things appear in a different order without any kind of time-scheme. A man appears without a woman, and she appears to be a kind of afterthought.
3. The account of the Garden of Eden, the Tree of Life, the Temptation, the Fall, all form a powerful account which has influenced theology and many other disciplines of thought down to the present day.

4. Matters such as shame over nakedness, guilt over sexual relations, different languages, crime, fear, all are touched on.
5. Humanity's relationship to animals is also dealt with in more detail, including man's understanding of snakes.
6. God is very close to humanity, on conversational terms, even when things have been vitiated by disobedience. This is in contrast with virtually every other creation myth. God is described in anthropomorphic terms, but not outright crudities as in Greece or Japan.
7. The literary style is mostly prose but with sections of poetry (3:14–19). It is not overexaggerated or dramatic. Flamboyant language almost surfaces at verse 24: 'He placed the cherubim and a flaming sword ... to guard the way of the tree of life.'
8. The account progresses naturally into other early accounts such as the Tower of Babel and the Flood, a process seen in other mythologies, making it difficult to know where myth ends and historical realities begin.
9. The psychology of the passage is penetrating and the social ramifications of the account are far-reaching, irrespective of one's views in the modern world. This is where one's level of literal interpretation needs to be examined.

It is a good question as to whether either of these accounts were ever intended to be taken totally at face value. A slavishly literal interpretation will produce all manner of problems. One such issue concerns snakes: are they really inherently evil? Later generations were to equate the serpent with the Devil, but this is never stated in the passage. We are clearly in the realms of metaphor and personification, which as literary devices are excellent, but as biological and moral indicators are completely misleading. The stories must be taken as symbolic. No one ever thinks of taking the Jataka stories[9] (early Buddhist) literally, so why take these early stories from Genesis as anything other than symbolic?

The two passages are dealing with matters on two different levels: firstly, the process of creation, the Godward aspect done in stages, which the evolutionists would probably agree with in general terms; and secondly, the manward aspect in which a human soul and human consciousness is created. This is a severe problem for the evolutionists as creation is not just purely and simply about biological progression. There is the balance to be seen between the two passages; the contradiction lies in the approach taken, but is not a serious one. The paradox comes in that the One Eternal God, who created the universe, has time and occasion to talk on a personal basis with a man and his wife. God is eternal and above us all; God is on our level and known to every human soul regardless of one's worthiness or one's response. The two statements are fundamentally true but form a fine paradox.

Psalm 104 as a creation account

It would be a mistake to assume that there are no more creation accounts in the Hebrew scriptures: Psalm 104, not so well known or associated with Genesis 1–2, is another account in markedly different style. It ties in well with the first account, less so with the second. As to its authorship, it would be a fair assumption that David wrote it, or at least someone following in his tradition. The passage is one of the most amazing poetic renditions in the Old Testament: the flow of metaphor and parallelism is of the highest quality. It would be difficult if not absurd to attempt a literal interpretation of the passage. And yet it says so much about the power and wonder of God in creation. Some of the features of the passage are now examined:

1. 'Light' appears at the beginning, as independent of the heavenly bodies like the sun and moon.
2. God is described in a subtle blend of anthropomorphic terms with spiritual, but there is no clash or mental struggle over this.
3. It assumes the waters below and above the dry land are given a demarcation later.
4. Living creatures appear not completely in schematic order. There is no detailed account of the appearance of mankind.
5. All creatures are there for a purpose: 'In wisdom hast thou made them all.'
6. The dependence of all creatures on God to sustain them is heavily emphasised. There is no suggestion that God would have a day of rest. Verse 27: 'These all look to thee to give them their food in due season.'
7. The Spirit is mentioned as separate from God. Verse 30: 'When thou sendest forth thy Spirit they are created.'

8. The sun and moon have their appointed times and are under God's control; this is in contrast to the pagan idea that they are actually gods who must be propitiated.
9. There may be an indirect reference to the Flood incident in verse 35: 'Let the wicked be no more.' But there is nothing about the Garden of Eden event.
10. The major impression is that of highly emotional language and literary expression of the highest order as the psalmist goes into raptures about the greatness of God: 'I will sing to the Lord as long as I live'.

All this is evidence that creation mythology is not a simple matter of recording scientific facts, biological or any other. It is the human soul exploring the meaning of the world in which he lives and acknowledging that it is the product of powers greater than anything we can understand. For the pagans, much of this is overcast with fear and distrust of the gods; for the Hebrews it was sheer rapture and joy at God's loving care in creation and his determination to bless all living things.

Subtle adaptation of the creation myth in 2 Esdras 6:38ff

Although Genesis 1 is seldom referred to in later parts of the Old Testament, in 2 Esdras (Apocrypha) we see a full reference to it in detail but with slight alterations. The book purports to be the work of Ezra and belongs to the exilic period, by which time Genesis 1 would have been a well-established scriptural text. The book was originally in Hebrew but must have been one of the last such productions before Aramaic became the norm. That Ezra could hardly be a literalist or fundamentalist is seen in the way he rephrases and alters some of the details of the scheme. He is in agreement with virtually everything in Genesis 1; a few slight alterations are listed below:

1. Verse 39 'The sound of man's voice was not yet formed.' The whole of creation is performed for the future benefit of mankind.

2. The heavenly light as distinct from the sun and moon was given ‘that thy work might appear’, that is, so that mankind could be enlightened. (Compare this with *Prometheus Bound.*)
3. Verse 42, the waters below are confined to a seventh of the world’s area: six-sevenths of it dried out to become land.
4. Verse 39, Enoch and Leviathan are created; Behemoth is a variant reading on Enoch. Is this a claim that one of Israel’s visionaries predated Adam?
5. Ezra notes that the Jews and Gentiles both stem from Adam but reckons the Gentiles as ‘spittle’ (v. 56).
6. Now we see the motive for quoting this passage: that ‘thou madest the world for our sakes’ (the Jews). The heathen, who are reckoned as nothing, ‘have begun to be lords over us’. ‘If the world were made for our sakes, why do we not possess an inheritance with the world?’

A subtle adaptation of the creation myth: God’s motive in creation was to provide a world first and foremost for the Jews; coincidentally for the rest of humanity. The language is slightly more emotional than Genesis but not excessively so. The power of God in creation is built up, ‘for as soon as thy word went forth the work was made’. The general context in 2 Esdras is of the difficulty of reaching the future world of felicity because of the corruption of the present world. It is a deformity of the original intention in creation. No mention is made of the Fall. The devotion of the Jews to God is stressed and the unfairness of it all is hinted at. By 7:17–18, Theodicy again is touched on and the response is, ‘There is no judge above God’ (v. 19). Thus this is a creation myth brought into relevance in the contemporary crises of the Jewish nation.

Hyperbole in eschatological writing

It has already been mentioned that exaggeration is a feature of apocalyptic material. It is possible that many find this genre difficult to cope with because it has not been realised that this is a feature of its style. Exaggeration is not confined to apocalypses but is a well-established literary feature in sacred literature. One would also expect understatement to be used: it is, but in nothing like the same lavish quantity as hyperbole.

Consider this passage from Jonah 3:3b: 'Now Nineveh was an exceedingly great city: three days' journey in breadth.' The archaeologists will affirm that Nineveh was not of such dimensions and we can see here a blatant exaggeration. It ties in with Jonah's ordeal in the belly of the fish for three days. At the very least the writer is giving us a signal not to take this work at face value, but as symbolic. In later times the Christians would see this as a prophecy of the three days of Jesus in the tomb.

Consider this passage from Psalm 29:9ff: 'The voice of the Lord breaks the cedars ... the voice of the Lord flashes forth flames of fire ... the voice of the Lord makes the oaks to whirl.' Some of the most powerful poetry in the Scriptures uses grand overstatement to convey a message with force. Here the message (v. 4) is, 'The voice of the Lord is powerful ... full of majesty.'

It is with the Book of Daniel that we see the full and free usage of exaggeration. The visionary work belonging to the exilic period exudes a dream-like quality but has had a massive influence on later generations, not least on Jesus himself. No one has really come to terms with the hyperbolic mentality which makes the work so vivid. Daniel has had many imitators but none of them in the intertestamental period come anywhere near the depth and quality he has. To take a few examples from Daniel:

1. The great image of mixed materials is struck down by a stone which fills the whole earth (2:35).
2. The fiery furnace is heated to seven times more than normal (3:19).
3. The informers against Daniel are torn apart by the lions before they even reach the ground (6:24).
4. The three men coming out of the furnace had no smell of fire about them, not a hair singed (3:27).
5. The tree of great height reached to heaven and was visible to the end of the earth (4:11).
6. The Ancient of Days has a throne of fiery flames and its wheels are burning fire (7:9).

Many other examples could be found; as a literary method it works up the emotion, expectation and fear. It works well with the climactic way in which other things are described repetitiously: the magicians, the enchanters, the sorcerers, the Chaldeans (2:2). The sound of the horn, pipe, lyre, trigon, harp, bagpipe, and every kind of music (3:7); as a sort of ostinato which builds up the emotion. The whole book raises us to an expectation of the final confrontation with tyrannical evil and the end of all things.

In the New Testament apocalypse by St John we see the same literary techniques at work and often direct and indirect references to Daniel. 'The idols of gold and silver and bronze, stone and wood' (9:20), and 'one like a Son of man with a golden girdle' (1:13ff).

The whole of world history is brought to a measured but highly dramatic fulfilment with evil finally defeated and a vision of heaven writ large in the most exaggerated terms. 'I saw a new heaven and a new earth ... I saw the holy city, new Jerusalem ... he will wipe away every tear ... death shall be no more nor crying nor pain'. In other words, the Fall in the Garden of Eden is reversed and all is bliss again, except that it is on a cosmic canvas in the most exalted vocabulary.

As a piece of visionary literature, the Revelation stands out as almost certainly the pinnacle of emotional expression. It is the work of the humble Messiah magnified and projected in lurid terms against the backdrop of the skies and the underworld. For those who wish to underestimate the force and the truth of this book, St John has a warning: 'I warn you ... if anyone adds to it ... and if anyone takes away from the words of this prophecy,' there will be problems in store for them (Revelation 22:18).

When considering the words of Jesus we see that exaggeration is a major feature of his preaching; his rhetorical method is powerful oratory. These are best seen in the Sermon on the Mount, but this is by no means the only place.

'Why do you see the speck that is in your brother's eye but do not notice the log that is in your eye?' Matthew 7:3ff.

'If your right eye causes you to sin, pluck it out ... if your right hand causes you to sin, cut it off,' Matthew 5:29.

Did Jesus really expect anyone to take this literally? All manner of follies have been committed by people who took these dicta totally at face value. He is talking figuratively.

Jesus is also one of the apocalyptists, but the extent of it is limited; it is not the main thrust of his teachings. St John's Gospel avoids it altogether, which might amount to understatement; Matthew devotes an entire chapter to it and manages to hyperbolise it. St Mark is more concerned about false messiahs (13:22); and St Luke tells us of hope in spite of fear, and again it is understated.

A basic teaching underlying all the Gospel eschatology is that we should always be ready for his coming, not that one can speculate on its timing, but be aware that the moment of truth could arrive literally at any time. Many of the parables, especially in Matthew, have as their theme the moment of crisis when God intervenes in history and the Messiah unexpectedly appears. The Labourers in the Vineyard, the Ten Virgins, the Marriage Feast, all speak of that moment of truth when judgement comes and a new world appears. His method, in the parables, is in a more restrained and normal language, unlike the full flourish of eschatological expression. How literally they are meant is a matter for personal faith, but there is no doubt that for all human souls there comes a time of decision, whether it is on a personal level, or national or even international.

That there is a need for eschatology in the human soul is obvious. Recent attempts within the Christian orbit to undervalue and minimise this aspect of faith have never been really convincing. The recent trend in liberal theology which has sought to ignore this aspect of the teaching of Jesus has simply given added incentive to splinter groups with a doomsday mentality. It could be seen as a reaction to the extremes of Calvinism: 'I cannot accept that some people will be eternally damned, therefore I will mentally ignore this aspect of the Gospels' teaching. Far safer (for myself) to say that Jesus never said such things and then I do not have to worry about eternal damnation.' Of course this mentality, which is at the root of much Gospel criticism in recent times, is completely circular in its logic, and verging on dishonest. One underlying assumption in this work is that we must take these ancient texts as integral, carefully thought-out, and as near to the honest truth as is reasonable to expect. Only then do we see the full gist of what these writers were attempting to convey to us. We need to appreciate that the ministry of Jesus brings to completion every aspect of spiritual needs in the human soul, mythology and eschatology being two important drives in our make-up.

Historical Account and Interpretation

The historical material in the Bible begins about Genesis 12 and continues in a more or less connected narrative right through to the Persian period with King Artaxerxes (Ahasuerus). Much of the post-exilic period is guesswork until we come to the appearance of Alexander the Great and the Maccabean revolt. The New Testament also has historical material: it is the fashion to undervalue the Gospels as history, and yet carefully interpreted they give a fascinatingly detailed impression of events in the early first century AD. It is not good enough to assume it is unreliable information: their main concern was to explore the significance of this Messiah Jesus rather than to give just a bald account of events. Looking at other sacred writings, there is nothing to compare with the Biblical historical material, especially the Gospels. The reason for this is that only in the Hebrew mentality (governed by 'covenant') do we see God as personally active and guiding in the affairs of mankind. Other religions see God as too remote or detached from human history, or they 'borrow' from the Bible for the basis of their own faith.

To omit any mention of other historical writers contemporaneous with the Bible would be a mistake. We have Herodotus, the Greek historian who has been dubbed the father of historical writing; however he was most likely preceded by the early Hebrew writers. He belongs to the late post-exilic period and his main slant is to explain the antagonism between the Greeks and the Persians. He throws much light on the events surrounding Alexander's triumphs; interestingly enough he records that King Artaxerxes had a queen called Amestris.[10] The Jews called her Esther; the vocalic and consonantal connection between the two names is fairly clear: are these one and the same person? But to equate Herodotus with Biblical history is quite misleading: he has no idea of God active in history, in fact it is a purely secular account. Maybe he was an atheist?

Another writer of Greek antiquity is Homer. This too bears no comparison with the Bible. In the Trojan Wars we see endless conflict which is heavily interfered with by numerous gods, but there is no sense of God's love and covenanted commitment to caring for humanity. The margin between mythology and history is not at all clearly defined; even so, recent thought has been to take Homer seriously and excavate what is assumed to be ancient Troy (Ilium).

Filling many of the gaps in our knowledge of Israel's history is Josephus, a late first-century historian of the Sadducean party who sided with the Romans. His bias is clear: that the mainstream reasonable Jews never wanted a revolt, still less to bring about the disaster of AD 70. It was the idiocy of the fanatics that precipitated the debacle. Sadly he was not alive to record the debacle of AD 135 when Bar Kochba made another attempt at Jewish messianism, and that revolt is nowhere near as well recorded. It is interesting that Josephus refers to John the Baptist in sympathetic terms, and describes Jesus as 'a good man' and 'Christ'. As part of the trend of denial, people have tried to minimise or erase such references; that may have been the Jews who could not bring themselves to admit that Jesus was the true Messiah.[11]

It is an unavoidable truth that every historical writer has his axe to grind. The difficulty often lies in discerning how much and what bias is taking place. Another problem is how long after the events they were recorded, on the assumption that the longer it takes, the more inaccuracies will creep in. The authorship of such works is often argued over, as if this will substantiate the authority of a given work. To read these pages in the Bible one is often struck by the honesty and integrity displayed by the authors. The kings are portrayed 'warts and all'; this is in contrast with the annals of surrounding empires where their kings are always fantastic, defeats are never mentioned and stalemates somehow grow into glorious victories. Honesty somehow takes a back seat! The Biblical writers (especially the Gospel writers) are content to give differing accounts of the same event without trying to comb out the discrepancies. If there is an element of exaggeration or distortion which is often difficult to assess, it has to be forgiven. It is only human nature.

In our own times the issue of historical accuracy is just as real with regard to our own annalists. We only have to consider the incident of the 'Dambusters' in 1943 to realise that within only a few years and with many living witnesses, all manner of minor differences in detail had crept into the story. By 1952 with the publication of Paul Brickhill's book[12] and the film based on it, various distortions were being allowed to give a mistaken impression. The Germans had their own version of it which was in many respects different, and it is only recently with the release of classified material that certain wrong impressions have been clarified. Even worse still is the Holocaust denial mentality emanating from various neo-fascist groups; and this, with living witnesses as survivors from Auschwitz and other camps, beggars belief. Distortion in historical account is nothing new. A certain degree of skill and insight is always required in the interpretation of any account.

With the Gospel writers there was a heavy onus to be careful and substantiate their claims. St Luke actually admits the need to produce a carefully researched account (Luke 1:1–5): 'by those who from the beginning were eyewitnesses ... to write an orderly account ... that you may know the truth.'

It is normally assumed nowadays that Mark was the first Gospel to be written[13] and that Matthew and Luke copied him, also using an unknown source termed Q (Quelle) which was unknown to Mark; this was followed by John much later on. Much of this rests on the gratuitous assumption that Jesus could not have uttered those long discourses which are so personal and intimate. Few people have the courage to say that John was written first by a disciple who was very close to Jesus and before his recollections began to fade. The whole idea that the Gospels were written a long time after the ministry of Jesus is plainly nonsense: there was every motive for recording as soon as possible the extraordinary events that were being denied by the Jewish authorities. The Resurrection is a case in point. In Matthew we already see the attempts by the authorities to smother the Resurrection, and this type of denial continued and still crops up in the present day. The first Christians had a very strong need to substantiate these amazing events by every means possible.

Another aspect of this is acceptance by the Christian community. It takes a long time for a potential scriptural work to gain acceptance and authority. This would indicate an early date for all the Gospels.[14] By the time of Irenaeus they were all being quoted as scriptural, and even before that with Ignatius and Justin Martyr. Also by the turn of the century the early Christians were discerning which literature was reliable and which was on the road to rejection. We must remember that living witnesses would have been extant up to the time of Josephus and would have been able to correct anything unreliable in the emerging Gospels. It is interesting that the Gospels have been submitted to so much undue scepticism, especially in recent times. We ought to beware of too much destructive criticism: it can spring back in one's face. A good example of this is found in St John, where he mentions the 'pavement' in the Roman fortress, the '*lithostroton*'. This was thought to be a fantasy on the part of St John, since no one could actually find it in Jerusalem. Now, we can visit it, 40 feet below street level. The same goes for the Pool of Bethesda, which could not be found; however, it was there, complete with five porticoes, deep down below ground level in Jerusalem. If we learn anything from this it should be that St John is nearer to the actual events than we realise, and not to regard claims made by him as impossible or pure fantasy.

These remarks can apply equally well to much of the Old Testament historical material. There has been a tendency motivated by modern liberalism to relegate much of this literature to the late post-exilic period. The trend now is to assume that the events recorded are much nearer to the times they are describing. Assuming that it is a long drawn-out process for such material to became accepted, books only become authoritative after their spiritual and antique value has been experienced. We can see the tendency in the post-exilic period for much spurious literature to be produced, and the drive to give it some sort of plastic authority. Usually it was claimed as the work of such people as Enoch, or one of the Patriarchs. Fortunately the Jews seem not to have been deceived by this and saw the need for canon-closure. So by AD 90, at the council of Jamnia, borderline material was finally rejected, that is, the Apocrypha, and the Old Testament received its final form. At the same time it would be prudent to re-evaluate the material that was accepted, on the assumption that it is more reliable and authentic than has often been assumed. The Christians too, in the fourth century, went through the same process, rejecting certain items of literature which were seen as borderline in quality or reliability. One of the criteria used was as to whether a given work was known to be Apostolic.[15]

The legal material

In contrast to the mythological material, the legal material in the Old Testament was and still is regarded as of the highest authority. It is mostly enshrined in the historical narrative of the Exodus and occupies vast areas of the Pentateuch. It purports to be the direct instructions from God to Moses and concerns moral, liturgical and ritual matters for the conduct of the newly formed nation of Israel.

It is not until we arrive at the New Testament that Jesus in the Gospels resumes the lawmaking, largely in the two great sermons and to a lesser extent elsewhere. He clearly refers to the Mosaic tradition and builds it up with a degree of exaggeration to a level which is staggeringly impossible: ‘You must be perfect, as your Heavenly Father is perfect,’ Matthew 5:48.

The liturgical and ritual matters are of far less interest to him, which goes a long way to explaining why the early Christians soon abandoned these matters to concentrate on the moral areas.

It would be misleading to claim that this genre of literature is not to be found in other sacred writings. Similar ideas and instructions are to be found, but to nowhere near the same extent, or the same level, or the same motivation, or indeed the same authority relying on divine backing. Compare these two quotations.

Matthew 7:13: 'Enter by the narrow gate, for the gate is wide and the way is easy that leads to destruction . . . for the gate is narrow and the way is hard that leads to life and those who find it are few.'

And with the Katha Upanishad part 3: 'strive for the highest and be in the light! Sages say that the path is narrow and difficult to tread, narrow as the edge of a razor.'[16]

The tone from Moses and Jesus is far more overwhelming. A different tone is seen in Confucius' teaching. It is all about Li, the highest propriety or the golden mean.[17] 'Kindness in the father, filial piety in the son. Gentility in the eldest brother, humility and respect in the younger: righteous behaviour in the husband, obedience in the wife, humane consideration in elders: deference in juniors. Benevolence in rulers, loyalty in ministers and subjects.'

This reminds us of Colossians 3:18 where family relationships are given guidance by St Paul. The difference is in the motivation. He is talking to the redeemed, 'God's chosen ones'; Confucius is talking generally about cosmic harmony between humanity and earth and heaven, including equilibrium in Nature.

The Taittiriya Upanishad 1.5, the words of divine law: 'What is needful? Righteousness, and sacred teaching and learning, Truth, Meditation, Self-control, Peace, Ritual and Humanity.'
Again this reminds us of the moral sections in many of the Pauline epistles, Galatians 5:22: 'But the fruit of the Spirit is love, joy, peace, patience, kindness, goodness, faithfulness, gentleness, self-control.'

The 'thou shalt not' mentality of the Pentateuch is not in evidence here; the tone is far more positive and encouraging. For St Paul it is all a result of living with the Spirit of the Lord. With the Upanishads, there is the impression of it being divine law, but there is nothing like the Mosaic legal system. Righteousness is often referred to but there seems to be no attempt to go into details as to what this consists of. Do we have to desist from murder, theft and adultery?

Wisdom Literature

This is found largely in Proverbs, Job, Ecclesiastes but also scattered pieces in other books. The Wisdom of Solomon and Ecclesiasticus are found in the Apocrypha. It is almost all in the medium of poetry. In the Hebrew frame of mind, it all stems from Solomon and runs along parallel with other genres as comment and advice rather than commandments. One might comment that, on the face of it, it has nothing to do with 'covenant' for such matters are never referred to. Nevertheless, we have to recall that if Solomon was the heir to the Davidic covenant, then all his skills are a by-product of that relationship. That is not to say that Solomon wrote all the wisdom literature: he stands as the chief inspiration behind it and his imitators in later times. The genre is valuable for its attempt to tackle some of the deepest questions in life, Theodicy (Job), and predestination and free will (Ecclesiastes).

An important feature of wisdom literature is the way that Wisdom is not just an abstract idea, but is given an exalted personification as a subordinate presence in the skies. In this way, it connects with mythology, although there is no mention of this in the Genesis creation accounts. In this we are seeing the Hebrews reaching back into the pre-history of the universe.

'The Lord created me at the beginning of his work, the first of his acts of old,' Proverbs 8:22.

'He created me from the beginning before the world and I shall never fail' and 'I came out of the mouth of the Most High and covered the earth as a cloud ... my throne is a cloudy pillar,' Ecclesiasticus 24:9 and 3.

Wisdom of Solomon 7:25 investigates how the king grew to greatness with the aid of Wisdom, pictured as a female. 'For she is the breath of the power of God ... for she is the brightness of the everlasting light.'

How literally we can take this is difficult to say: it has to be a sustained personification. It is easy to see, in spite of Wisdom being seen as feminine, how the early Christians quickly took it to signify the pre-existent Christ, through whom all things were made (St John). This goes a long way to explain why there is no wisdom literature in the New Testament: the nearest thing would be various aspects of the Epistles. Jesus himself was seen as the ultimate and final wisdom, bringing the whole system of thought to completion.

While the Greeks were coming to grips with philosophy, the Hebrews were considering the deepest matters of life in the wisdom literature.

To say that wisdom is found in other sacred writings would be much safer than regarding other genres. Many analogous ideas are to be seen elsewhere. The Upanishads, Katha 3, says:

> He who has not right understanding and whose mind is never steady is not the ruler of his life, like a bad driver with wild horses. But he who has right understanding and whose mind is ever steady is the ruler of his life ... like a good driver with well trained horses ... He who has not right understanding is careless and never pure, reaches not the end of the journey but wanders on from death to death. But he who has understanding, is careful and ever pure, reaches the end of his journey from which he never returns.

This can be matched from Proverbs 4:25: 'let your eyes look forward ... take heed to the path of your feet ... do not swerve to the right or left ... be attentive to my wisdom, incline your ear to my understanding.'

That there is a carefully thought-out rationale of wisdom in Hindu philosophy is sensed in Mundaka Upanishad part 1, chapter 1: 'Sages say there are two kinds of Wisdom, the higher and the lower ... the lower wisdom is in the sacred Vedas and the six kinds of knowledge ... but the higher wisdom is that which leads to the Eternal ... whom the sages see as the source of all creation.'[18]

But in Hebrew thought it is simpler, more direct and God-oriented. Ecclesiasticus 1:14:

> To fear the Lord is the beginning of Wisdom and it was created with the faithful in the womb... the fear of the Lord is a crown of Wisdom, making peace and perfect health ... both which are the gifts of God: and it enlargeth their rejoicing that love him. Wisdom raineth down skill and knowledge of understanding.

In the Buddhist scriptures there is a 'Hymn to perfect Wisdom': 'Homage to thee, Perfect Wisdom, boundless and transcending thought. All thy limbs are without blemish, faultless those who thee discern.'[19]

It would seem that 'wisdom' approximates to *gnosis*. This became a major feature of Gnosticism, which was prevalent in the Hellenistic and Roman world. In many ways Hindu and Buddhist thought contains Gnostic patterns, and they may be seen as an Eastern version of Gnosticism. Vice versa, Gnosticism may have been derived from the East. In general though, wisdom as a feature of religious thought, as an aspect of mythology, crosses many boundaries and is not purely confined to Judaism.

The canonical prophets

This corpus stretches from Isaiah through to Malachi and is not in strict chronological order. Several of them cannot be dated at all: Amos and Hosea stand out as the first oracles to appear in writing, and concern the imminent collapse of the Northern Kingdom. Most of this material is in poetry and some is literary expression of the highest order. As a genre they stand out as unique in world religious expression. Even with Mohammed being a literary prophet, the Koran is of a completely different tone and purpose. The reason for this is the messianic hope which gathered momentum from the eighth century onwards. This was a spin-off from the covenant of David. When it was realised that the promises were not being fulfilled and the people were increasingly inclined to ignore the covenants, then it was clear that something drastic would have to happen if God's people were to continue to survive. An ideal king, or a new covenant, a remnant, a scion of the house of David: all this suggested that a new order would have to be inaugurated by God. For those who can see Jesus of Nazareth as the true completion and fulfilment of all this material, it remains as an amazing thing that so much of it prefigures his life and ministry. For those who cannot see it, vast amounts of the prophetic material remain a puzzle, unfulfilled and galling. The paradox is that the very people who ought to have realised the significance of Jesus, failed to do so; the Gentile world, however, saw him for what he really was.

The great age of prophecy petered out after the return from Exile. By this time, much of it was in imitation of Isaiah and did not offer much original thought. But it left the Jews with an expectation that since prophecy had not been brought to completion, then somehow another great prophet would emerge, or alternatively one of the great ones from the past would somehow come back to life. Elijah was a favourite for this task and indeed John the Baptist and Jesus were believed by some to be just such. Elijah was expected to come and rescue Jesus from the cross. But the great age of the canonical prophets was over: the age of the apocalyptists had arrived, but their literary quality and prognosticatory abilities were nowhere near the standard of their predecessors. This goes a long way to explain why such books as the Jubilees, the Testaments of the Twelve Patriarchs and many others were not accepted for the Hebrew canon.

It is important to recognise that the prophets must be seen against the preconceptions of their day. The assumptions of the modern world, which include the idea that these people could not possibly have foretold future events, must be kept out of any serious attempt to understand them. The failure of modern man to cope with predestination largely explains why experts are in denial over prophecy. As we have seen with Nostradamus, a whole new look at prophecy is needed. Prophecy in the ancient world was held in very high esteem: prophets were held to be genuinely psychic and capable of miracles. It was a bit like printing money: there were genuine ones and forgeries. The world found it hard to cope with false prophecy and yet this did not detract from the power and influence of the genuine prophets. By and large this influence had to be accrued later when the pronouncements of oracles were seen to come true, but Isaiah stands out as one who in his own lifetime was accepted as reliable.

Songs and Psalms

As a variant on poetry, songs and psalms are found mostly in the Book of Psalms. It is a well-accepted tradition that David was the chief inspiration behind Hebrew psalmody, although other composers almost certainly had a hand in the composition of the psalter. That this genre began with David is almost certainly untrue. There are substantial songs to be found in the Pentateuch and these are understood to be of the earliest written material in the Bible. The Blessing of Jacob (Genesis 49), the Song of Moses (Exodus 15), another Song of Moses (Deuteronomy 33), and the Song of Hannah (1 Samuel 2) are noteworthy and theologically important. Sung material in a liturgical setting is a widespread feature of religion and serves to heighten the emotion and give expanded expression to other genres. Psalm 104 is a prime example of a poetic rendering of the creation myth: 'Thou coverest thyself with light as with a garment.'

Similar ideas can be found in the Rig Veda, 129th hymn in the tenth book: 'Darkness was hidden in a deeper darkness, the All was as a sea without dimension: the Void still held unformed what was potential until the power of Warmth produced the sole ON.'[20]

All manner of literary techniques are employed. One notable feature is the use of repetitions. Chandogya Upanishad 3.15.3: 'I go to the imperishable treasure: by his grace, by his grace, by his grace.'[21] And Psalm 118:1-4: 'Let Israel say: his HESED endures for ever. Let the house of Aaron say: his HESED endures for ever.'

The use of a chorus or ostinato is important in music, in an age when there were presumably no hymnbooks. Psalmody has been a major underpinning factor in Christian worship to this day. The psalms give vent to all manner of emotions ranging from pure hate to the heights of bliss. This works like a safety valve by which the believer, in concert with others, can allow all pressures to be released, rather like a communal confessional. The paradox is that the believer can offload all manner of emotions, human and even subhuman, in the presence of a pure and all-knowing God.

A classic contradiction in the Gospels

For those who wish to take the Bible as the literal truth, there is a problem lurking at the end of the Gospels.[22] The Synoptics and Paul have Jesus eating a Passover meal on what appears to be the evening of the Thursday (although the 'fifth' day is not actually stated). This would be in Jewish reckoning the beginning of the Friday, that is, after 6 p.m. on the Thursday. This means that the Day of the Passover was actually on the Friday. St John has the Friday as the Day of Preparation, which meant that the Passover began at 6 p.m. on the Friday, thus making the Sabbath (Saturday) coincide with the Day of the Passover. This explains why the last meal together was not seen as a Passover meal because Jesus was being buried at 6 pm. on the Friday.

The evidence from the Gospels is varied but the critical quotations are as follows. Mark 14:12: 'On the first day of Unleavened bread when they sacrificed the Passover lamb.' It appears to be the

Thursday afternoon, with what is clearly a Passover meal taking place after 6 p.m. as Friday begins. The other Synoptics support this, it being assumed that they were copying Mark.

St John however says (19:31): 'On the first Day of Unleavened Bread, since it was the Day of Preparation when they sacrificed the Passover lamb,' and also, the priests 'did not enter the Praetorium so that they might not be defiled but might eat the Passover.' This is the Friday and the Passover is still in the future at 6 p.m. that day and on into the Saturday (Sabbath).

The contradiction is not helped by St Luke who may have copied St John in 23:54: 'It was the Day of Preparation and the Sabbath was beginning'. This contradicts his earlier remark in 22:7 where the Passover lamb had to be sacrificed, clearly on the Thursday afternoon.

This problem has teased the minds of experts down to the present day and there has been no conclusive answer to it. For an up-to-date discussion of it, see C.K. Barrett's Commentary on St John.[23] It is always possible that since we do not know every detail of how the Passover festival was carried out at that time, some new facts may come to light, and this contradiction may be resolved. As it stands, the contradiction cannot be solved on the historical level. But on the theological level we may be looking at another paradox, something which seems not to have occurred to anyone so far. The nub of the matter is which day was the Day of the Passover: the Friday or the Saturday? Does it actually matter? The writers of both versions deeply espouse the views they take and it is not just a trivial mistake on the part of one writer. Each writer is trying to convey an important interpretation about these events. Taking Hepburn's approach, 'paradoxes unfold themselves fully only if the concept of God is submitted to logical analysis. But at whatever level they appear, the pervasiveness of paradox cannot be denied.'[24] How true! The contradiction between John and the Synoptics only emerges from rational analysis. But this is not something to destroy faith: the question is, what positive matters which give a deepening of faith will emerge from this research?

What is St Mark trying to say? The original rescue of Israel from Egypt took place on the night of the Passover with that special meal, and that was the opening phase for the covenant of Moses at Sinai. Jesus himself is the sacrificial victim who seals the New Covenant with his body and blood. The giving of his own life brings new life and hope to a world overloaded with sin and death. The link between the Passover meal and the Last Supper is crucial: God gives of his very self to heal a broken world. Also the allusion to the messianic banquet as seen in many of the parables comes as an enigma. Jesus appears to desist from eating and drinking for the reason that he is expecting to partake when the Kingdom of God comes in, after he has suffered. Was this a way of saying that he had to die first in order that the new relationship with God could come into force? Does he expect his disciples to die as well, since he expects to be eating 'with them', according to Matthew? Or does he mean he will be raised from the dead in order to eat with them again?

During the trials, Jesus hardly says anything in his defence and actually gives them the evidence they want (14:61). But this is just one case of how he was consistently misunderstood by his enemies, and how cruel it was when he said, 'My God why have you forsaken me?' which they take to be an appeal to Elijah who is imagined to be on hand to rescue him. In truth, this was the final desolation and rejection. But through it, the veil of the Temple is rent, signifying the end of the Old Covenant. It is the Centurion who concludes that Jesus is actually the Son of God, thus completing the paradox that his enemies, who should have realised his true identity, scorned him as a fraud. The hidden Messiah, which is heavily stressed in Mark, is now revealed as the true one, and the realities about God are now plain for all to see. This is the true and ultimate Passover for all people.

What is St John saying? As Jesus is dying at the same time as the lambs are being slaughtered, he is the true Lamb of God that takes away the sin of the world. 'Not a bone of him shall be broken,' in spite of all the rough treatment he has received. The blood and the water from the spear wound (which does not appear in the other Gospels) is suggestive of so much in the first Passover and the Christian Eucharist, and also the medium of cleansing. Strangely, the Last Supper is only indirectly mentioned. But the message is the same. Jesus is the final, ultimate sacrificial victim: God giving of his very self to save the world.

St John goes further: he emphasises the Kingship of Jesus more heavily than the other writers. The sign, 'The King of the Jews', goes up in three languages which implies he is more than just a national king. Pilate refuses to alter it. Jesus has a long conversation with Pilate, who does not know what 'truth' is; and yet paradoxically he does have the truth inscribed on the sign, and he is staring at Jesus, 'the way, the truth and the life'. Another paradox. There is no crown of thorns this time, but 'here is your King' (19:14) underscores the majesty of Jesus: he is reigning from the cross.

The desolation and degradation is understated. It is more a matter of fulfilment and completion, if not triumph. 'It is finished' (*tetelestai*)[25] means that he has brought all the prophecies, the laws, the deepest needs in human spirituality, to completion. Nothing dramatic happens such as the veil being torn, nor indeed darkness or earthquakes. That aspect of it is noticeably understated, but sympathy for him begins to appear. 'They shall look on him whom they pierced,' quoted from Zechariah 12:10 in which a 'spirit of compassion and mourning, and weeping as for a first-born child' reminds us of the first Passover in which the first-born of Egypt had to die; this time the first-born of all creation is the one who has to die to bring about the salvation of the world. John never mentions 'covenant' and yet the metaphor is implicit in the whole account. The sacrificial element is heavily emphasised but in a different way to St Mark.

Instead of the veil being torn, Jesus' tunic is not torn; is St John talking about the unity of Christian people? The timing of his death is important: he dies just in time to be entombed (in a new tomb) as the darkness falls and the Sabbath begins. He is entering into his 'rest' on the seventh day, just as God did in creation, and that happens to coincide with the Passover.

The contradiction between St John and the Synoptics is not a reason for loss of faith and confused belief. They put together two vital elements in a wonderful paradox. It is no use trying to discount one in favour of the other. This reminds us of the mathematical paradox in Chapter 1: both lines of working are absolutely true, the result is the same, but the workings are different. St Mark uses the metaphor of the New Covenant at the Passover meal; St John uses the sacrificial motif and the imminence of the Sabbath. To gain the full picture, both systems of metaphor are needed. From this we see that paradox is not an inconvenience or a worry to those whose logical processes impede their faith. The opposite is true: paradoxes are there to bring out the fuller and deeper truths of religious experience. They are there to enrich faith, give greater depth, give differing understandings of bare facts.

Again quoting Hepburn: 'We have not attempted to reconcile the paradoxes . . . we have taken a different approach, namely to enquire whether there are ways open to us whereby we may accept the paradoxes if we have to do so, but without abandoning belief.'[26] With this he entirely misses the point. Paradox is not there to confuse or destroy faith: it is there to deepen, show differing levels of belief, increase depth and mystery in faith. It is not a negative problem: it is a positive catalyst for the growth of spirituality.

When we review the sacred literature, largely in the Bible but not entirely, we see that the need in the human soul for something in writing, some reference material stemming from some authoritative figure in antiquity, is fulfilled is various ways. There is the hyperbolic language in mythology, the appeal to real actions in historical account, the appeal to poetry and song. But principally, there is the assertion that God is not a passive principle far away in the skies, but an active personal force impinging on the human soul from day to day. This is the deepest claim in holy writ and evokes the deepest paradox, that of how an eternal spirit can speak in the language of humanity to every living soul. This brings us to the next question: that of Incarnation, by which God came into this world and spoke to humanity in their own words and thought-forms.

A paradigm from a 3D viewer

A boy was rummaging in the attic and found a collection of photographic prints, on cards and in pairs. He noticed that the pairs appeared to be slightly different although the main features of the picture were the same. He pointed it out to his father and asked, 'Does that mean that one picture is wrong and the other correct?' In answer, his father produced a gadget which when the photographs were placed on the right spot, the two pictures merged and became a 3D image. The whole picture sprang to life in each case. His father explained that just as we have two eyes which can see the same view but from two slightly different angles, thus bringing the view to a reality which would not be so if we had just one eye, so there is a camera that can take two shots at once and can produce a three-dimensional view. It all comes out a lot more real in 3D.

The same is true with the differences between St John and the Synoptics: they present a slightly different view of the Passion, some of which amounts to paradoxes. It is useless to say that one view is wrong; when put together, the differing views blend in together to produce a result which comes to life in a way that a flat picture cannot.

Tatian, in the second century, tried to harmonise the gospel accounts and produce one flat picture of the whole thing.[27] This did not work: it did not last. Just producing one flat picture from four flat pictures does not produce anything instructive. The paradoxes in the Gospels, and generally in sacred writing, are not there to confuse and destroy belief: they are there to engender depth, deeper meaning and mystery. After all, the interaction between God and humanity is a mystery which cannot be rendered down to a flat picture: it can only achieve its full implications through metaphor, hyperbole and sometimes understatement. Such is the mystery of the Incarnation.

In conclusion about language and literature

We have seen an era over the last 150 years in which the Bible has been submitted to ferocious and destructive criticism. This may be seen as a reaction to the undue uncritical acceptance of it at purely face value. Clearly a balance between the two has to be struck. It is strange that other ancient texts such as Josephus, Herodotus and especially the Koran have not been subjected to such levels of scepticism. The irony is that believing people still continue to take the Bible as their mainstay of faith in spite of all the doubt thrown in their way.

Underneath it all is the assumption that these ancient people were stupid, or at least not as intelligent as we are today. One wonders if the reverse is not true! We have only to look at some of their achievements in the fields of mathematics, technology and theology to realise that they were probably, in proportion, more intelligent than us. The legacy of many of their findings is still with us to this day, not least in the field of religious thought.

Just one example may give cause for thought. There is a passage in Jeremiah 10:1–22 which on the face of it may appear somewhat commonplace, if not confused. There is a portion of Aramaic inserted in verse 11 which has been assumed by experts to be a later insertion, or an indication that Jeremiah could not have written it.

Looking at it more carefully, verses 1–5 have the theme 'do not be afraid' with the impotence of the idols sandwiched in between. It forms a pattern ABA, like a mini-chiasmus. The same thing happens in verses 6–10, the incomparable nature of God with the stupidity of idolatry in between, CBC, another little chiasmus. Then comes verse 11 in Aramaic which is also a mini-chiasmus. Verses 12–16 also follow the same pattern, the greatness of God in creation, with the stupidity of idolatry in between: CBC again. Verses 17–22 now tell of the approaching Exile, with the stupidity of the shepherds (who went in for false religion) sandwiched in between: DBD is another chiasmus. The small chiasmi form a large chiasmus from verses 1–22, with verse 11, the Aramaic verse, as the central or pivoting point. What could be the purpose of this? That Jeremiah intentionally put in the Aramaic as a pointer to the identity of the attacking nation, Babylon, coming from the north and famous for its lavish idolatry. Because of this stupidity, the original Tabernacle of the Lord in the wilderness is lost, and false religion from foreign influences has taken over in such a destructive way. The whole passage is carefully structured with subtleties for those who look carefully. The underlying hint is that those who are not stupid will see the truth of God's creative wonder and know the folly of idolatry.

Many such instances could be found in the Biblical literature which tells us that these writers were not fools: they wrote these things with care and skill, and at our peril do we dismiss them as ignorant or trivial.

Notes

1. YHWH rendered as 'Jehovah': it is a hybrid between the consonants of YHWH and the vowels from Adonai (the Lord).
2. Nebuchadrezzar is the correct spelling, 'Nabu-kudurri-usur' meaning 'Nabu protect the boundary (or crown)'. Daniel slightly alters the spelling, Nebuchadnezzar, and now the meaning is lost or distorted. With Nebuchodnozor (Judith 14:18) we see the vowel transplantation from *bosheth* (shame).
3. For instance Syriac and Etheopic, but the Septuagint was the most important attempt to render the Hebrew scriptures intelligible to the Hellenistic world.
4. HESED has a very wide range of meaning: basically, kindness, mercy, faithfulness, being helpful to the poor, God's consistent love within the covenant.
5. This raises the issue of continuity: see Chapter 20.
6. Hitler, in *Mein Kampf*, asserted that evolution meant that the weak must go to the wall.

7. John Milton, *Paradise Lost.*
8. Chiasmus is a literary form often used in Hebrew literature: A,B,C,D,C,B,A for instance.
9. Noor Inyat, *The Jataka Tales* (various editions).
10. Herodotus, in the *Histories*, records that Xerxes had a queen called Amestris, pp. 479 and 620ff. The Book of Esther records Artaxerxes as having a queen called 'Esther'. The two names are clearly related consonantally. The name Esther in Persian (*stara*) means a star. The prefix 'm' would mean associated with, related to, connected with. Are we looking at the same name but with a prefix, indicating that Amestris was derived from 'the people of a star', namely the Jews? The fact that she presents the king with a coat of many colours is very interesting: a lady with a Jewish background would have seen that as a major compliment for a king, and an object of envy.
11. S. Mason, *Josephus and the New Testament*, 2003.
12. Paul Brickhill, *The Dambusters*, 1952
13. The primacy of Mark is a modern assumption (and a fair one). Much of Mark is in the present tense which makes it all very vivid. Could Mark have been an eye-witness, perhaps Peter's workman?
14. C.E. Hill, *Who Chose the Gospels?* The trend now is to take the four canonical Gospels as more basic and earlier, and the so-called apocryphal gospels as later.
15. The Council of Laodicea, AD 346, by which time the NT canon was virtually stabilised.
16. *Upanishads*, Penguin Classics, 1961, p. 61.
17. Analects of Confucius.
18. Upanishads, p. 75.
19. Buddhist Scriptures, Penguin, 1959, pp. 168ff. It is interesting that Wisdom is personified as a mother.
20. Rig Veda, Sookta-wise translation, Pandey, Diamond books, pp. 160ff.
21. Upanishads, p. 75.
22. C.K. Barrett, *The Gospel According to St John*, pp. 48–54, for a full and up-to-date treatment of this problem. He does not have a clear answer, but there is the possibility of an alternative timing for the Last Supper. See also Chapter 14 on Calenders.
23. Barrett, op. cit.
24. Hepburn, *Christianity and Paradox.*
25. *Tetelestai*, 'it is finished'. This is a perfect passive in Greek. *Telos* implies not just the 'end' but completion, finality, accomplishment, final achievement. It is better rendered as 'it has been finally accomplished' but even this does not bring out the full implications. Jesus is saying, 'All I came to do, I have managed to finish off.'
26. Hepburn, op. cit., p. 186.
27. Tatian, Diatessaron, c.180 AD. He was not the only one to produce a Gospel conflation. None of these were a success. See Hill, *Who chose the Gospels?* p.104.

7

Incarnation and Apotheosis

For the purposes of this chapter, Incarnation means God becoming a human for a time. Looking at the other channels of mediation seen so far, this is the ultimate mode in which the highest authority in the world of the spirit comes into this world and discloses himself in a way which has not been seen before, and presumably will not be seen again. That the idea was not totally new to the world when Jesus came, would be true to some extent, but nowhere in the Jewish tradition does this mode appear. The Messiah is always assumed to be fully human; the Son of Man, as seen in Daniel, remains as heavenly. There is no attempt at combining the two, and when Jesus did just that, the Jewish authorities found that unacceptable.

It would be misleading to say that 'incarnation' in Eastern religions predates the Christian one. To take each possibility in turn, Mahavira, the first Jainist, was believed to be the last in a long line of saviour beings, coming down from heaven and having a supernatural birth. He had an advantageous start in life, being royalty, and embarked on asceticism. His humanity would be easy to accept; his divinity less so, since he is not claimed anywhere to be the Ultimate God (Brahman) in human flesh. The same could be said of Siddhartha, whose life is remarkably similar to Mahavira's. Buddha was seen as a reincarnation of some spiritual being but not of the remote principle of the universe which is far too distant, and in fact Buddhism, strictly speaking, does not have to involve the Eternal God in its system. There are gods on a lower level in the Wheel of Becoming but Buddha is not an incarnation of one of them. Looking at Hinduism we notice that there are gods who 'come to earth' as an avatar, as recorded in Vedic mythology: principally Vishnu, but this can include Krishna. This involves a god appearing at various times and in various forms, possibly as an animal.

Bouquet[1] comments that an avatar (or descent) is not a real incarnation, but rather an accommodation to human weakness and limitations. The god engages in a sort of 'will-o'-the-wisp' appearance, a beneficent illusion. The matter is left suitably vague and is never explored or explained properly. The assumption would be that the god would remain purely a god and not become a real human. In Zoroastrianism, the prophet has a remarkable birth and life full of miracles, but nowhere is it claimed that he is the incarnation of Ahura Mazda. Zoroaster was definitely human but only 'god-like'. According to Bouquet there is a Japanese sect called Konkokyo which has a founder called Bunjiro. He is alleged to have had a dual consciousness which might be analogous to that of Jesus, with divine and human nature. This seems to be a prophetic monotheism not derived from the Bible. It would be easy to describe Bunjiro as human but it is unlikely that anyone has concluded that he is also the Eternal God.

There is much in this to establish a kind of corporate union between God and man, but none of this is actually the same as what is claimed for Jesus of Nazareth. It could be said that God was preparing the human mind for the ultimate incarnation, and in this way Jesus can be seen as the completion of this idea. It can also be said that the human mind has a need for some kind of final connection between divinity and humanity. Even so, Eastern theories about incarnation come a long way short of what is shown to us in the New Testament and the early Church fathers. The ultimate connection between God and mankind is not a theory, a list of rules, a myth, a complicated philosophy, but a living person who relates in real terms to God and mankind and ties the two together.

There seem to be two ways of approaching the matter. One is to try to assess what Jesus thought about himself, his own estimate of his real identity; and the other is to attempt to assess what his close associates thought of him. A third way, that of reviewing the opinions of the early Church fathers, may be helpful but will always be dependent on the first and second approach. It is worth remarking that the word 'incarnation' is never used in the New Testament, probably because the word had not been coined, nor even a synonym of it. Even so, there are various phrases which would lead in the course of time to such terminology. Hebrews 5:7, 'In the days of his flesh', is just one of the various remarks which introduce the notion of incarnation. A complicating factor in this assessment is the inability of many experts to give St John credit for his alleged record of Jesus' own remarks to his disciples. There is a lot of circular argument involved here: it is assumed by some that John was written much later than the other Gospels and that because it is late, it is less authentic or reliable; in other words, some sort of invention. It seldom occurs to them that St John might be the nearest thing we have to the real Jesus and could be more reliable than the others. Even then, it is a gratuitous assumption to say that if a record is 'late' it is therefore more unreliable than the other Gospels. The approach taken here is thus: to allow each Gospel to speak for itself, leaving out the 'scissor and paste' mentality of recent years, and allowing each writer to tell us what he believes. That way we shall learn a lot more. The actual authorship of the Gospels is not strictly relevant here: whoever wrote them, they were clearly inspired and attempting to be honest. It would be fair to say that the first disciples were so astonished, confused and often terrified that they were unable to rationalise their experiences of Jesus, let alone arrive at an estimate of his identity. It would be also fair to say that only on reflection, later on, did they begin to formulate any firm doctrine about the significance of the ministry of Jesus.

To begin with St Mark, the theme of the 'messianic secret', we are struck by the fact that Jesus does not go round making vast claims in public proclamations. Much the opposite, he tries to understate himself, a deliberate policy for three reasons: he wanted the disciples and the wider public to come to their own conclusions without trying to tell them what to think; also he did not want to be equated with the fanatic insurrectionist element which was causing so much trouble at that time; and he thought of himself as the 'Servant' not as the master, humility not hubris. This explains why in Mark 8:29–30, when Peter concludes that Jesus is the Messiah, he is told to keep it quiet. It is also clear from St Mark that Jesus knows he has power over the spirit world and the elements. He makes remarks which imply he is God: 'my son, your sins are forgiven.' This was a profound shock to everyone, especially the legal purists. He implies that he is the 'bridegroom' (Mark 2:19): that could only mean that God was about to come and claim his bride, the people of Israel. The whole Gospel is structured around the theme 'Son of God': at the Baptism, the Transfiguration and twice at the Crucifixion he is proclaimed as such; he could hardly have had a divergent opinion from the voice from heaven. In calling himself the 'Servant' (Mark 10:45) this relates him to the songs in Isaiah and hints at the sufferings to be faced. Mostly it is the title 'Son of Man' that he uses, with all that that implied. Even here, before any serious theory of the Incarnation is apparent, the paradox of his being purely human and yet with an unmistakably divine aspect has arrived. How could he be the suffering servant and yet be the Son of Man sitting at the right hand of Power? Mark does not try to explain it, but the paradox is already emerging.

St Matthew clearly builds on this. The Temptations are obviously intended for someone who is more than just human. Yet the people of Nazareth cannot cope with him, since they know him as the 'lad from down the road'. The Son of Man now appears as the eternal judge and wears a red gown at the encounter with Pilate (Roman judges wore red gowns), and yet Matthew emphasises the servant motif from Isaiah (12:18). The paradox continues to build up. St Luke would hardly have disagreed with any of this. We now begin to see the use of the term 'the Lord' (Luke 22:61) in relation to Jesus, with all the implications it carried about Adonai in the Old Testament, YHWH. It is Luke who talks of the miraculous conception of Jesus and yet relates his origins back through Abraham to Adam. He is fully human and yet divine. When we add in the Star of Bethlehem, the cosmic importance of Jesus begins to unfold. The paradox is there just waiting for later generations to ponder over. It would be St Luke who would laugh at the speculations, theories, and doubts leading up to the present day. Luke 22:67 says: '"If you are the Christ, tell us." But he said to them, "If I tell you, you will not believe."' Very apt: no matter what evidence we may be given, there is always someone who manages to disregard it; how true of today!

The evasive and taciturn approach seen in the Synoptics is reversed in St John. For many people this is seen as later followers exaggerating Jesus' claims. What they fail to see is that a paradox emerges between understatement and exaggeration. It is quite feasible that Jesus was cagey about his estimate of himself in public but prepared to explain things in more detail to his closest confidantes. Why there should be any problem over John 14:11 – 'Believe me that I am in the Father and the Father in me' – is a mystery but he is emphasising it in the face of all those, like Philip, who have problems with it. The important 'I am' passages in St John also indicate what Jesus thought about himself: that he was the fulfilment of the incomplete statement in Exodus, 'I am that I am.' He prays to the Father and acknowledges God's love for him before the foundation of the world (17:24). This all sounds contradictory but is in fact the paradox of the Incarnation on the lips of Jesus.

Some have supposed that one can see into the mind of Jesus and assess his thoughts on incarnation as something distinct from the disciples' estimate. This is impossible for two reasons. Firstly, we cannot seriously imagine that we can see into the mind of Jesus any more than we can penetrate the mind of God. Secondly, all that we know about the mind of Jesus is reported in the words and thought-forms of his disciples, and in turn they were only describing him against the backdrop of their day and age. It was a time of crisis when God was expected to intervene dramatically: demons, angels, prophets, pagan emperors and even astral conjunctions: all these had people on a cliff-hanger of expectation. The disciples were right that Jesus was the key to the situation in one sense, but they drastically misunderstood him in many other ways. Who knows what really went through Jesus' mind? It is idle to speculate, and yet so many incarnation 'theories' have tried to do this.

Moving on to the opinions of his earliest followers, there is the Prologue of St John which can hardly be the actual words of Jesus but is a realisation of many of the sayings to be found in the Gospel, 1:18:

> In the beginning was the Word (logos) and the Word was with God and the Word was God ... all things were made through him ... and the Word became flesh and dwelt among us, full of grace and truth: we have beheld his glory, glory as of the only Son of the Father ... no one has ever seen God: the only Son who is in the bosom of the Father, he has made him known.

So in quasi-philosophical, quasi-poetic terms John makes an unequivocal identification between God and Jesus. '*Logos*' was a sort of catch-word in the Graeco-Roman world and had a wide range of meaning. Here Jesus is clearly identified with the personified Wisdom seen the wisdom literature. In case one would assume from this that his divinity is clear but his humanity is in question, we must recall that at the end he is crucified and he really is wounded and dies. John emphasises this. The reason for this was that those of a Gnostic turn of mind could happily say that Jesus was divine but not really human: the flesh was degraded and he could never really have had a human body, still less be put to death. It was all a fantasy. This is a heresy which still keeps reappearing to this day.

Another important text is Hebrews 1:1–4, using different metaphors:

> In many and various ways God spoke to our fathers by the prophets: but in these last days he has spoken to us by a Son, who he appointed the heir of all things, through whom he also created the world. He reflects the glory of God and bears the very stamp of his nature . . . having become as much superior to angels as the name he has obtained is more excellent than theirs.

If we learn anything from this passage it would be that different metaphors can be used in discussing the Incarnation, not just one. It is important not to allow just one metaphor to monopolise our thinking.

There is the faintest suggestion of him 'earning' his exalted status. Hebrews may have sensed the dilemma over this, as in 5:5–9 he offers both sides of the argument. '"Thou art my Son, today have I begotten thee" . . . in the days of his flesh, Jesus offered up prayers . . . although he was a Son, he learned obedience through what he suffered, and being made perfect he became the source of eternal salvation.'

Again there is the suggestion of adoptionism and yet it is juxtaposed with his eternal begetting. Another paradox is unfolding here. This is even more obvious in the 'Hymn of Philippians' (2:6–11), which may be St Paul's understanding of the matter:

> in Jesus Christ, who though he was in the form of God, did not count equality with God a thing to be grasped, but emptied himself, taking the form of a servant, being born in the likeness of men. And being found in human form he humbled himself and became obedient unto death, even the death on a cross. Therefore God has highly exalted him and bestowed on him the name which is above every name, that at the name of Jesus every knee should bow . . . and every tongue confess that Jesus Christ is Lord to the glory of God the Father.

Paul is not trying to address the logic of incarnation here: his main concern is humility between Christian people. If we take every word of this at face value, there is enough here to fuel adoptionism and various other heresies. The main point at issue is that the humble carpenter is now the supreme controlling authority in the universe, no matter how tortuous the logic of it may be.

So far we have seen that the claim that Jesus is truly God and yet truly human is well authenticated from a wide range of New Testament references. That this is a paradox of the first quality cannot be denied. Many people, including the Jews and the Muslims, cannot cope with it, and yet if God is to be fully represented to humanity, and humanity represented to God, it requires something of this level of contradiction. It is beyond our ability to rationalise or explain. Moving on from this is the question of pre-existence: what or where was Jesus before he was born, and if he died on the cross, does that mean that God died as well? Here lies another paradox: that in one sense he 'began' as a baby in Bethlehem and followed the normal routines of any human being, including having to die; and yet in another sense he was with the Eternal Father from the beginning of all things, and carries on to this day shaping the course of history. Again the two statements are contradictions beyond resolution; they form a secondary paradox within the main paradox of the Incarnation. And this one is clearly related to the paradox of Theodicy, for why did he have to suffer if he never did anything wrong in his earthly life?

As the New Testament age began to fade, the early Church fathers began to unravel the mind-boggling implications of the Incarnation. This was in the face of various cranky heresies which can clearly be seen as a crude attempt to harmonise nascent Christianity with the current philosophies and metaphysics of the day. It was Irenaeus who came out with what now seems to be pure common sense, in 2 Adversus Haereses 28:7:[2]

> If anyone asks how the Son was 'produced' from the Father, we reply that no one understands that 'production' or 'generation' or 'calling' or 'revelation' or whatever term one applies to his begetting which in truth is indescribable ... it is not our duty ... to make guesses about infinite things which concern God. The knowledge of such matters is to be left to God.

If it had been left at that, there may never have been any need for heresies, splinter groups, and possibly not even Islam. Unfortunately those who wished to argue it through in every detail forced the Church fathers to hammer out a full doctrine culminating in the Creeds and the Chalcedonian Definition. To quote Irenaeus again, 19:6: 'For it was incumbent on the Mediator between God and man, by his relationship with both, to bring both to friendship and concord, and present man to God, while he revealed God to man.' This is the core purpose of the Incarnation and to probe into it and attempt to rationalise it soon destroys the paradox.[3]

To relate in detail all the various heresies of the early years would be tedious and unnecessary. They can be listed roughly as follows: those who claimed Jesus was not fully human, Basileides, Valentinus, Marcion, Montanus, Apollinarius and the Patripassionist branch of Monarchianism. Those who claimed he was not fully divine: Ebionites, Celsus, Arius, Nestorius and the Adoptionist branch of Monarchianism. Some of these were truly fantastic, others only slightly at variance with what was to become the orthodox position. It would be fair to say that they all, including the orthodox, tried to cope with it in terms of the jargon of the current philosophical notions of the time. While it is fair to try to find a helpful metaphor, it is a delusion to allow one particular metaphor to become over-emphasised and rule out all others. All the time there were those who were not thinking in terms of figurative language but analysing the Incarnation in some sort of clinical, factual manner. This explains why much intolerance and strife was engendered by these differences of opinion. It is important to beware of a religion or theological system which has a collection of easy answers, clever rationalisations and convincing arguments, leaving us with no mystery, no challenge to faith, and no space for divine logic which is other than the thought-forms of this world. The reality that the relationship is beyond human explanation did occur to some, but not to others. Even more so, the idea that it was a paradox of the first quality seems to have escaped them. The word or a synonym for it was available at that time, but it was strangely lacking from these heated altercations.

It would be unnecessary to quote all of the Chalcedonian Definition but the key clauses should be recalled:

> complete in Godhead and complete in Manhood, truly God and truly man ... of one substance with the Father ... and one substance (homoousios) with us ... recognised in two natures, without confusion, without change, without division, without

> separation... each nature coming together to form one person and subsistence (hypostasis)

So, by AD 451, all the known deviations from the middle course were ruled out, and complete equality between divine and human nature in Jesus was affirmed and dogmatically enforced. This was to be the position until comparatively recent times. No one, except the Jews and the Muslims, seriously ventured to tamper with this statement.

It is only within recent times that the whole matter of the Incarnation has again surfaced. It is part of the general questioning of everything. Mercifully there do not seem to be the hysterical accusations of heresy that would have ensued in past ages. People seem able to discuss the matter in a calmer and more constructive fashion. It is interesting that the same old deviations from Chalcedon have surfaced again, using the thought-forms and jargon of contemporary disciplines. Sociology, psychology and even Venn diagrams have managed to creep in. Some of the 'explanations' for the Incarnation are couched in all manner of elevated language and intricate thinking, but they all fail. No one appears to have realised the paradox of the Incarnation which means it is an insoluble problem for the human mind. Even Hick, who actually uses the word 'paradox', does not set to work to elaborate on it. To quote him in selective parts: '(Chalcedon) ... merely asserted that Jesus was "truly God and truly man" without attempting to say how such a paradox is possible.'[4]

But it is in the nature of a paradox to be beyond explanation! The orthodox fathers were right not to try to 'spell out an intelligible way' of explaining it. Hick seems to think that Chalcedon 'sets before us a mystery rather than a clear and distinct idea ... it was not a divine mystery but one created by the (Council).' This is where he is totally mistaken. The mystery of the identity of Jesus Christ was not a Chalcedonian invention. It was a reality patent to the first followers of Jesus during his ministry, starting with Mary who 'pondered these things in her heart', and continuing right through to the trials and execution. Who or what was this amazing person who defied all attempts at an explanation? We can sense the mood of confusion, fear, brain-wracking doubt, and flights of emotional commitment. It was easy for his detractors to label him as a fraud or an imposter; this still goes on today with those who try to deny his historical existence. But the reality is that he cannot be airbrushed out of history and the phenomena that are claimed for him cannot lightly be dismissed. No: the mystery of the Incarnation began with the life of Jesus himself and has continued to be beyond explanation ever since. The best way to approach it is not through some clever rationalisation or theory, but to use Jesus' own favourite method, that of parables and allegories. The strength in them is that they are far more real, personal, vivid, undogmatic. A series of parables, each highlighting one or two aspects of the matter, avoids some sort of dogmatic position and brings the whole issue up in 3D. It is a paradox that can be coped with as long as it remains open and capable of discussion. To allow one idea to become pre-eminent unbalances the matter and very quickly the paradox is lost.

That figurative language was understood to have been used by Jesus is clear from John 16:29, 'now you are speaking plainly and not in any figure', and the frustration at not being favoured with plain language is sensed in this passage. However there is the promise that at some stage Jesus will tell them everything *en clair*, something that successive ages have attempted to achieve but never managed to move beyond the figurative level.

Another important issue connected with the Incarnation is the 'problem of particularity'. This means that with Jesus coming at a particular time in history and to a geographical location, how can this be fair on those who lived in the centuries before he came, or indeed those living in far-away countries who never had a chance to know about his coming? Does this mean that they miss out on salvation? What about the other major religious leaders in history: are they another incarnation of the same God? To quote Hick, 'the idea of divine incarnations seems dangerous to many Christians ... the hypothesis of a number of incarnations ... is logically and theologically permissible'![5] This may seem totally shocking, and yet in our modern world where there is now an awareness of outer space and other planets which in theory could be expected to support life, would, should or ought God to have visited these places at other times and in other ways apart from the ministry of Jesus? To answer these points is not easy and there is no final answer to it.

As to whether there is life on other planets, this quest amounts to an obsession with certain elements of humanity at the moment. We have only to think of such a programme as *Star Trek* to realise that people like to project humanity into outer space to conjure up all manner of frightening consequences. This of course is all speculation and modern mythology. There is, as yet, no evidence for any life forms on any planet, and to assume that if there were they would be something analogous to humanity is, so far, pure fantasy. If such a discovery were ever to be made, it would then be a major undertaking and expense to reach such a planet and ascertain what the situation actually was.

The possibility that other world religious leaders have been some sort of 'incarnation' of God or Jesus is a rather more definite and less speculative proposition. However, when one comes to inspect these people, the first question is, 'What did they claim for themselves?' and secondly, 'What did their followers claim for them?' The answer is that their claims come nowhere near what Jesus understood himself to be, or additionally what his followers came to believe about him. A possible candidate might conceivably be Siddhartha, and yet he never claimed to be the Ultimate Principle, still less a God that probably did not exist!

To cope with the problem of particularity, it can be seen that the matter had occurred to the New Testament writers and they have various ways of dealing with it, again in metaphors and mythology, and yet surprisingly unanimous. It is Hebrews which points out the uniqueness of Christ's ministry, 9:28: '[Jesus] ... has appeared once for all at the end of the age to put away sin by the sacrifice of himself ... Christ having been offered once to bear the sins of many.'

There was no need for him to have done it repeatedly: once was enough. Interestingly, the Zoroastrians believed that there was a series of world saviours who would appear every thousand years.[6] The precise number of them was never actually agreed, but this had features in common with Gnosticism. We can see in this the urge to have the saviour covering more than just one historical milieu. Now we see an extra relevance in what Hebrews is saying here: Jesus only had to come once. Even so, though it was tied down to a particular time and place, it had cosmic consequences. It brought in a new relationship between the Creator and the creation. How this worked is again beyond us to explain, any more than the Incarnation itself, and yet here we see another paradox emerging, subsidiary to the main one.

It is easy to say that the Messiah is known to and active among people in the AD period, in the form of the Holy Spirit. It is helpful to see the Roman Empire as a communications network ideal for the spread of the new faith to all parts of the known world. But there must have been millions who lived and died before Christ's coming. This is where the concept of the pre-existent Christ becomes important. If he was in 'the bosom of the Father' from all eternity and active in human history from the start, then he was, as a Holy Spirit, present in people's lives in the BC era as well as the AD period.[7]

But St Matthew goes further than this in 27:52: 'The tombs were opened and many bodies of the saints who had fallen asleep were raised.' In other words, many did come back from prehistory to find out about the Messiah. This ties in with the belief which was rife in apocalyptic literature concerning resurrection, to which all would be summoned to judgement, something that the Pharisees would have agreed with.

Also in 1 Peter 3:19 it says: 'in which he went and preached to the spirits who formerly did not obey.' He is talking about the three days in hell, which means that those who were thought to have been damned did encounter the Messiah and were offered release. In the same passage, Peter explains that Christ died for the righteous and the unrighteous ('the world' as St John would have said), which would mean the whole of humanity, past, present and future. The new relationship between God and mankind is not limited by time and place: it is a universal sea-change, applicable to all creatures of every kind.

St John phrases it another way in 5:28: 'Do not marvel at this: for the hour is coming when all who are in the tombs will hear his voice and come forth, those who have done good to the resurrection of life and those who have done evil to the resurrection of judgement.'

This is hammered home by the miracle of the raising of Lazarus and the eternally significant remark, '"I am the resurrection and the life ... he who believes in me shall never die."' The implication in this is that death is no barrier to knowing the Messiah. His ministry and the new relationship with God crosses all barriers and frontiers.

From this it can be seen that the New Testament writers were aware of the problem of particularity and did have answers ready. It may be said that these answers sound as if they are verging on the mythological; that would not apply to St John. However it is a good example of how history and mythology converge in the ministry of Jesus. It is a big mistake to try to separate history and mythology overmuch. They act together like the chicken and the egg: they influence one another in a reciprocal manner. It is important for mankind to have an impression of how all things began in some sort of myth; it is also important for us to know that God came into history in 'real' terms and performed actual deeds for all to see, rather than some theory or general principle. It is also important that we have a myth relating to the future, and that is what we are busily engaged in at the moment. Mythology will receive a closer treatment in Chapter 11.

The importance of mythology in relation to the ministry of Jesus cannot be underestimated. It is idle to relegate mythology to the realms of superstition and illogical fears. These matters are a vital part of human nature, implanted by God. If Jesus were fully human, as is claimed, he would be making the same mythological and cosmological assumptions as anyone else of his times. He was a child of his age, just as we are of ours. What was he assuming? It was a world influenced by demons, angels, the Devil (under various names), prophecies from the past and eschatological prognostications at the present. If asked about 'Theodicy' Jesus might well have said that Satan was the cause of all pain and loss. To us now this might all sound rather quaint; our ideas now will seem ludicrous in 20 centuries' time!

But the whole matter can be seen another way round: that God had allowed Zoroastrian ideas about the conflict between good and evil to work their way into Judaism and then into Christianity for a purpose. That purpose was concerning the final battle between good and evil which would come to a crisis at the Crucifixion: not just a local battle, but a cosmic conflict. Mankind would see it as such and not just as an unfortunate miscarriage of justice which was irrelevant to this world or the next. Other ideas on Theodicy would not have worked with these events at all. The multi-deity and its modifications; the denial of evil or of God; the purely strict monotheism; none of these would have had any meaning in relation to an event like the Crucifixion. But because of the dualistic assumptions of the day, the Passion is full of meaning and the new relationship between God and mankind is seen to be redolent with power in both worlds. It was no accident that dualism had become the prevailing theological mind-set of the day. Does that have to mean it must be so in today's world? Do we now have to believe in Satan? That is at the least debatable. It may be that strict monotheism is now the prevailing assumption, in view of how scientific investigations have brought into sharper focus the unity, complexity and subtle balancing in the natural world. This is where the Muslims and Jews will score.

Incarnational paradox in summary

The application of the term 'paradox' is not a new idea by any means, but previous writers have not teased out the full ramifications of such a claim. It might be summarised as follows:

1. The main paradox: that Jesus was wholly God and wholly man in one person, the Chalcedonian position. Forming a balancing situation around this are various heresies which emphasised either the humanity at the expense of the divinity, or vice versa. The same situation still applies to this day.
2. In one sense Jesus the man began as a baby and ended by dying, having gone through the same human processes as anyone else. (Some have suggested that he might have been married.) In another sense he was eternal with God the Father, and continued to be right through his earthly ministry, and after. A secondary paradox.
3. The problem of particularity is not a problem, for although his earthly ministry was restricted to a certain time and place, the ramifications of it were cosmic. It brought in a new relationship between God and his creation, and that applied to both worlds at once. All these three are impossible according to canons of human rationality. God's system of rationality is other, and if we did understand it, it would all become clear and logical.

Subsidiary to these three are many and various features of Christ's ministry which appear to make no sense in terms of human logic. The Temptations stand out as very strange: how could the Messiah be tempted to do wrong, and what would have happened if he had fallen for the temptation? At the Baptism, why did Jesus think he had to be initiated into his own religion? If he were sinless, why would he need to be cleansed from sin? If he were God, how or why does he pray to God like a little child? One moment he is displaying humility and the next minute he is exerting power over the demonic powers of the other world, a balancing act which can only be seen as a paradox. Many more examples could be found in the Gospels. And the final paradox in all this is that while on the one hand his ministry brings in a new relationship which saves the whole world at one stroke, nevertheless few people have heard of him and the Gospel has to be preached all over the world to all creatures.

All these lesser paradoxes are dependent on the first three. The whole matter of the Incarnation is a much more complex situation than just debating whether Jesus is God or man. It is interrelated with Theodicy, and salvation by faith or works, and free will and predestination, and even the relationship between mythology and historicity.

Even within the New Testament there is the mysterious side of the whole thing. Looking at Luke 4:30: 'But passing through the midst of them he went away.' This was walking off from a mob intent on murdering him. Mark 6:45 has Jesus walking on the sea and making as if to pass by the disciples. In John 18:6 those sent to arrest him collapse to the ground when he says 'I am He,' but then shortly afterwards they arrest him and he is in their power. All four Gospels relate that Judas has to be enlisted to identify Jesus, to be certain of arresting the right man. This is strange since many people had seen Jesus in the city and the Temple and presumably there should have been no problem in apprehending the right man. Does this mean that his appearance was known to change somehow? In three Resurrection appearances, people who knew him well do not realise at first who it was.

We have instances of the risen Christ appearing to people in the post-Incarnation times. St Paul's conversion on the Damascus Road is a dramatic case in point, but there have been many others over the years. The strange case of Linda Martel, excellently documented by Charles Graves, is a modern example of a little child who had experiences of Jesus and was able to do miraculous healings.[8]

Even more mysterious is the situation in the Inca Empire as the Spaniards came to understand that their god Viracocha had appeared to them in ancient times. He was a tall man with a white robe reaching down to his feet, the robe had a belt, his hair was short and there was a crown on his head like that of a priest. He carried a book like a breviary. He was a white man, tall, who aroused great respect and veneration. He came to the sea and spread his cloak and walked on the water, never to be seen again. The name Viracocha means 'foam of the sea'. It is difficult to evaluate this account, but seen through the eyes of Spaniards who were hostile to Inca religion, it is amazing. One recalls the walking on the sea in St Mark and other aspects that remind us of Jesus either incarnate or as post-Resurrection. We do not know when this encounter occurred.[9] It may be highly relevant to the problem of particularity.

What we can learn from these remarks is that the matter of Christ's appearances or disappearances in this world is a whole lot more mysterious, deep and beyond the canons of human comprehension that we can ever understand. Clever theories and easy explanations simply confuse the issue. The way to cope with it is through metaphor and parable. That is the method that Jesus himself gave us, and at our peril do we try to employ a different method.

Parables concerning the Incarnation

1. There was a pond with still water. Someone threw a stone into the middle of it. There was an enormous splash and then the ripples began to spread out across the water. They eventually worked their way into the reedbeds and then bounced back again causing turbulence everywhere.

So too with the coming of Jesus: it made a big sensation in Israel at a particular time, but the implications of it affected the entire world, or cosmos, to and fro, affecting everyone, one way or another. Hick might well agree with this image, but on the basis of his modern liberalistic assumptions. Page 132: 'the voluntary acceptance of death by a holy person has a moral power that reverberates beyond any words that we can frame to express it ... enriching and enhancing the human community.' But the reverberations went much further than just humanity: they reached out to and permeated the whole of creation, producing a new relationship between the Creator and the creation. It was a change not just local or even worldwide: it was a cosmic change affecting the entire universe.

2. A boy placed a stick into water. He noticed that the stick was 'bent' and also that the colour was slightly different. He told his teacher, who replied that it was a well-known optical illusion which can be explained by the theory known as refraction. The stick is straight and never actually bends. On the other hand, when placed in water, the bit that is immersed appears to bend but is still straight;

the bit above water does not bend. There are two facts here which are contradictory: the stick is straight, the stick is bent; also the colour changes slightly. It is still the same stick but seen in altered circumstances.

So too with the Incarnation. The Messiah is the same before and after, and even during his immersion in human affairs. And yet during his lifetime, as seen by the human race, he appeared not totally different, but different in many important respects. We can explain the altered appearance of the stick, so it is not really a paradox; we cannot explain the altered appearance of the Messiah, knowing that he is eternal and yet human at the same time: that is the paradox.

3. A girl was making bread with her mother. When the lump of dough was ready, she produced a pinch of yeast to leaven the bread. Just a tiny pinch in one place was enough. 'Why don't we put in some more yeast in different places?' asked the girl. 'There's no need,' said the mother, 'just give it time and the yeast will spread right through and the whole lump will rise up. Then we bake it in the oven.'

So too with the Messiah: he only had to come once in one specially prepared place, to have his effect on the whole of humanity. If he had not come, the dough would not have risen and humanity would still be left with the 'old' arrangement between God and mankind, a flat, two-dimensional relationship like a *matzo* (unleavened bread). This is all right as far as it goes, but is not the full and final loaf when the bread rises up and gains its full flavour. St Paul might have liked this image.

4. A boy asked his father, 'What does Uncle Fred look like?' His father replied, 'A bit like me because I'm his brother.' But the lad was not satisfied: 'Haven't you got a photo of him to show me?' In answer to this his father produced a photographic negative and said, 'This is the only thing I've got. Uncle Fred was very shy and every time someone produced a camera he hid his face: but we managed to catch him unawares one day.' The boy looked at the negative and said, 'Well I can't make this out at all. It's just a blurry mess.' In reply, his father took the negative and made a print from it. It was a good impression though it did not show Uncle Fred totally in every detail, but it was enough to give a fair likeness so that he could be identified.

Jeremiah would have agreed with this, for 'Surely thou art a God that hidest thyself!' Nevertheless, there was one occasion when a fair impression of God was given to humanity: the 'offprint' of Jesus. If we try to discern God in the Old Testament it is like trying to figure out a photographic negative; but when the Messiah came, the only positive print we have of him, it was not every intricate detail of God, but as much as humanity can actually cope with. He is our one permitted icon. It is not idolatry, because he provided the picture, not us. It was he who completed all those definitions which began with 'I am.'

Strangely, this metaphor, which would have meant nothing in the ancient world, has come into its own with the discovery that the Turin Shroud is not just a photographic negative, but a 3D negative.[10] The artefact remains a mystery in spite of all the scientific attempts to explain it away. What is instructive is the reaction to it from all manner of people: for some it is the authentic burial shroud of Jesus and elicits absolute wonder and acceptance; for others it stimulates incredulity and disbelief, as if people are in denial of it. How strange! The same reactions were seen towards the earthly Jesus: those of acceptance and those of refusal to understand.

5. A teacher had a very difficult class to cope with. They simply refused to take anything he said seriously, let alone learn anything. At the same time, the local drug dealers had developed a particularly nasty version of a drug which initially gave great pleasure and excitement, but in the medium to long term was deeply damaging to health and personal relationships. The headmaster asked the teacher to give lessons on the matter to warn the children to steer clear of these substances. The teacher assumed that since it was such an important matter, the pupils would at least listen and give the matter serious thought. But they did not: they sneered, brought up objections and made out that the teacher was wrongly informed. The lesson turned into a riot. In desperation, the teacher tried to reassure the few pupils who did take the matter seriously that he would try again. They suggested that he obtained a police video to make it all seem much more real. So he did. Many more of the pupils began to take the issue much more seriously because it all seemed so much more real. There were others who thought it was a joke but beneath it all they began to think seriously about it. And there were a few (whose parents were actually the pushers) who reacted angrily and tried to smash the video machine.

So too, when God comes into our world for real, some can see the truth of it: others react badly and try to silence him.

6. There was an oil-painting in an art gallery, of outstanding skill and beauty, painted by an Old Master and of great value. It stood out from all the other pictures in its quality and depth. Some of the other pictures were a cheap imitation of it, but were obviously copies. To look at it closely (as with all oil paintings) reveals just a mass of squiggles and smears which do not form into any sort of coherent picture. It is necessary to stand back a little and then the picture begins to take shape. The smears and squiggles begin to relate to one another and form a clearer impression: the whole picture merges into one, and all manner of light and shade, depth and interpretation are seen, complete with the ornate framework. The framework is important too as it must be appropriate in style and skill to the picture. One is impressed by the thought that the artist must have been highly skilled to paint with a short brush something that can only make sense when seen from a distance.

So too with the Incarnation: the impression on the first disciples in their 'close-up' of Jesus was not at all clear. They were confused, fearful and groping around for words to cope with it; sometimes they formed the wrong impression. A little later, in the Apostolic age, the picture is beginning to take a coherent shape; and then from the distance of the early Church fathers the whole picture with all its richness becomes more obvious and easier to appreciate. Not that we can explain it, for the skill of the artist is still beyond easy rationality. But the Old Testament framework now appears to be highly appropriate to what they could all see: that Jesus was the fulfilment of all that went before. Also, other pictures which are claimed to be of a certain merit do not come anywhere near the quality of this picture, and the ones that are merely cheap reproductions can clearly be seen as such.

7. There was a composer who wrote a beautiful orchestral symphony. There was great skill involved in the fashioning of the chords with passing notes and counterpoint, all making a deep and rich texture. It took top-rate performers to do justice to this piece; mediocre musicians simply could not cope with its exacting standards. When performed well, the symphony had a riveting effect on the audience. There were some who said: 'Let's simplify it so that lesser musicians can attempt it: let's make a piano realisation of it.' But the result was nothing like the original. The oversimplification that had promised to make it available to a wider base of skill had fatally robbed it of depth and enervation.

So too with the Incarnation. It is a wonderful work full of depth and mystery. All the attempts at explaining it away in easy terms (the heresies) have failed to do justice to it. People are left dissatisfied, and eager to sample the full truth and glory of the composer's original production. So a heresy or a botched version of the Incarnation may give ephemeral satisfaction for some, but the full truth of it is still there in the background, demanding a deeper commitment. It is essentially not us who are writing the tune: it is God, and tampering with the harmonies only destroys the paradoxes.

8. There was a factory owner who had a son who was destined to inherit the firm when he was old enough. The father did not want the boy to go in there behaving like Lord Muck and taking advantage of his potential status as owner one day. He decided that it would be far healthier if the boy started on the shop floor and learnt first hand of the conditions that the workers had to face. There had been much unrest, with wage claims and a 'them-and-us' attitude, largely fostered by a small group of troublemakers. The lad had to start as tea boy and then take a turn in each department, being under the orders of each departmental manager.

There was very little secrecy about it: it was soon realised that the boy was the boss's son and that he was working for a wage the same as everyone else, also under the same discipline. Most of the workforce appreciated the idea of the lad working along with them and could see the purpose of it; a few of the troublemakers never really reconciled themselves to it and played up, trying to victimise him. Eventually the boss decided that the time had come for his son's promotion and he graduated to the board of directors. But the experience he had gained and his sympathy for the workforce meant that industrial disputes were more easily dealt with and pay rises were usually more generous than before. It made for a happier firm, although there were still a few that were envious and did not wish to cooperate.

So it is with the Incarnation. The Son, Jesus, comes into our world and works along with us as a normal apprentice, working his way up and discovering what the human condition is really like. Some could see the purpose of it and were very glad; others objected to him and tried to dispatch him. It was a painful business being victimised in one's own firm. All the time he was one of the workers, this did not alter the fact that he was heir to the entire enterprise. But being eventually promoted to the highest authority in the works, he had first-hand understanding of the human condition and could advise his father, and other board members, and moderate their attitude. In this sense, there is a degree of truth in the Adoptionist approach but it is a mistake to allow it to become the only aspect of things. It can relapse into works righteousness and an obsession with merits for all believers. But that is an important paradox: that on the one hand he was the eternal Logos with the Creator, and yet concurrently he allowed himself to take on the human condition and bring about a new relationship between the chief and the workers.

An awareness of the paradox of incarnation in the sub-Apostolic age

The Acts of St Peter[11] is a fascinating piece of literature to read. It is thought that it appeared in the late second century, but even so it may contain various traditions about St Peter as the first Bishop of Rome and his martyrdom. How seriously we may take his 'miracle contest' with Simon Magus is a matter for debate, but it may be an echo of a genuine struggle between the early Roman Christians and the pagan objectors. What is significant is the clear awareness of paradox with regard to the Incarnation, a factor that the pagans could not cope with but the believers accepted. The only word missing is actually 'paradox', or even 'oxymoron'. Acts of St Peter 22:

> for he is in the Father and the Father in him: in him also is the fullness of majesty, who has shown us all his benefits. He ate and drank on our account though he was neither hungry nor thirsty ... this great and small one, this beautiful and ugly one, this young man and old man, appearing in time, yet utterly invisible in eternity, whom a human hand has not grasped, yet is held by his servants: whom flesh has not seen and now sees: who has not been heard, but is known now as the word that is heard: never chastised, but now chastised: who was before the world and is now perceived in time beginning greater than all dominion yet delivered to the princes: glorious but lowly among us: ugly yet foreseeing.

At the end of chapter 23 Simon Magus asks the Romans, 'Is a God born? Is he crucified? Whoever has a master is no God,' and the

Roman populace agrees with him. Here we see the basic problem of the difference between divine and human logic: if Jesus were divine in some sense, how could he allow himself to be put to death as a criminal? Peter attempts to deal with this in a more theological manner by referring to the prophets. One wonders how much of the Hebrew prophets were known to the Roman public; alternatively, it may be indirect evidence that the Hebrew prophets were widely known in the Gentile world at that time. A few selected verses from chapter 24 will suffice.

'A child shall be born of the Holy Spirit: his mother knows not a man and no one claims that he is his father.'

'She has given birth and has not given birth.'

'He came not out of the womb of a woman but descended from a heavenly place.'

We notice that there is a certain Gnostic influence here. However, Peter goes on to say, 'if you knew the prophetical writings I would explain everything to you. It was necessary that through them it should be a mystery and the kingdom of God be completed.' The realisation of the Incarnation being a mystery is being admitted here. The paradoxical situation of Jesus being born and yet being eternal is heavily emphasised. Peter rightly does not attempt to explain it away: he uses the authority of the ancient prophets to substantiate it. 'Who shall declare his generation?' (from Isaiah) is very aptly quoted.

Notes

1. Bouquet, *Comparative Religion.*
2. Irenaeus, in Bettenson, *Documents of the Early Christian Church.*
3. 'Paradox' was coined in Greek philosophy well before the Christian era. See Chapter 1.
4. Hick, *The Metaphor of God Incarnate*, SCM 1993, chapter 9.
5. Hick, op. cit.
6. Mary Boyce, *Zoroastrians*, 1979, pp. 74ff.
7. Hanson, *Jesus Christ in the Old Testament.*
8. Charles Graves, *The Legend of Linda Martel.*
9. John Hemming, *The Conquest of the Incas*, p. 88.
10. Ian Wilson, *The Turin Shroud.*
11. Bart Ehrman, *Lost Scriptures, The Acts of Peter*, pp. 135ff.

8

The Trinity

The doctrine of God being Three and yet One springs naturally from the paradoxes associated with the Incarnation. If Jesus' time on earth ended with him being assumed into heaven, and if he imparted his Spirit to his followers after his departure, then that leaves us with God in three distinct methods or modes of operation. It has been pointed out that the idea of 'trinity' is also to be found in other religions, but none of them come anywhere near the arrangement seen in the Christian teaching.

In the Hindu tradition, there is a form of trinity: Brahma, Vishnu and Shiva. Brahma is the ground of all existence, the sacred and most high God who embraces all phenomena and yet is beyond definition: a non-being as well as a being (notice the paradox). Vishnu is the preserver, always benevolent; he comes in avatars to defeat evil and champion good. Shiva is the destroyer and yet paradoxically he brings enlightenment; he is ascetic and yet is erotic (another paradox). It is a threefold manifestation, a 'Trimurti' in which three gods represent three basic functions in the life of the world.[1] We notice that all three of these functions could be subsumed in the work of God the Father, the Creator. Also it is to be noticed that each one contains paradoxes. It must be remembered that this arrangement is three separate gods and, further, there are literally hundreds of other gods in Hindu thought. There is nothing about One God who came as one Incarnation as a historical event, still less imparting his Holy Spirit to his adherents. The Christians never allowed the Trinity to degenerate into polytheism, in spite of attempts to make it seem like that.

The Buddhists also have something on similar lines, the 'Trikaya' or Triple Body, a more abstract, philosophical approach.[2] The Body of Essence and Being, the Body of Spiritual Bliss, the Body of Earthly forms – these are elaborated below:

1. The Dharmakaya: the eternal principle of truth, transcending time and space. This says nothing about creation or a personal Creator God, the Father of all. It is the eternal reality, the Absolute Suchness, the Void, undifferentiated and impersonal.
2. The Sambhogakaya: the heavenly manifestation of no. 1: differentiated and personal. These are bliss bodies, images of Buddhas that are not historical but archetypal. Each one represents a different aspect of enlightenment. It is not one person but hundreds of different aspects, not living people but theoretical ideas and principles.
3. The Nirmanakaya: form body, earthly manifestations of no. 2. The historical Buddha, Siddhartha, is a particular expression in one place and time of the eternal truths of the Dharma.

This is a very different sort of Trinity from the Christian one. None of these are actually gods, but abstract ideas which have nothing to do with Father, Son and Holy Spirit. There are gods in Buddhism but they have nothing to do with this kind of trinity. To find them we must study the Wheel of Becoming (see diagram), which is divided into six samsaric realms:

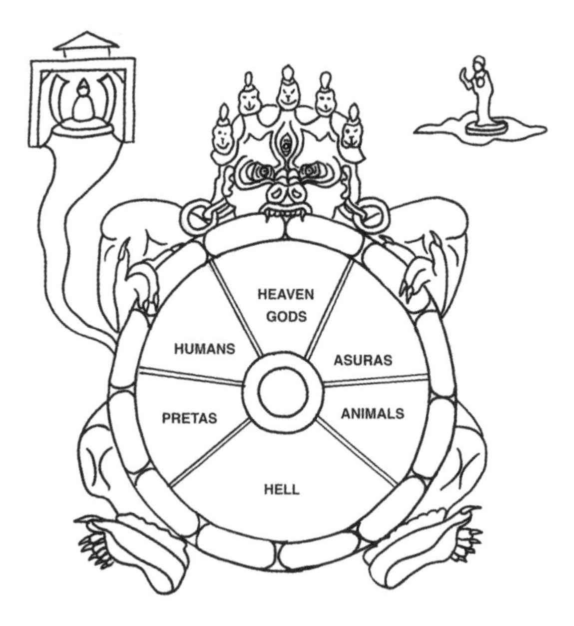

The Wheel of Becoming (simplified)

1. At the top, the devas or gods in heaven: at ease and with great luxury and pleasure.
2. Going right and downwards: the asuras, jealous gods who desire to reach to no. 1.
3. The animal realm: ignorance and greed, seeking food by eating each other.
4. The bottom realm: hell, a state of torment where they burn and freeze and die.
5. Coming up on the left: the hungry ghosts, pretas, constantly hungry and thirsty, with swollen bellies.
6. The humans who carry on normal life with its hardships, and see the possibility of escape upwards to no. 1.

It is also to be noted that there are various versions of this analysis, with different regions. All pass through these stages through rebirth and it is possible to go round in clockwise motion eternally; however Buddha is there at each stage, offering an escape from this inexorable wheel. It means that humans can become gods; gods can be demoted to devils and hell. They are trapped in the same cycle as everyone else. There is no sense of a Creator God who is supreme and controlling the whole picture. Where does the Buddha fit into this scheme? He is a Boddhisattva who compassionately came down to earth to be the historical Siddhartha. Having discovered a way to achieve Nirvana he returned to the Dharmakaya (Nirvana). But this is not a one-off situation: hundreds of Boddhisattvas are thought to have been active in human history and are some kind of emanation of numbers 1 and 2. Buddhism has been described as a form of Gnosticism and this is probably fair: essentially it assumes that human nature is beyond redemption and that the heavenly principles must be insulated somehow from the corruption. The idea of a trinity is only very superficially there, in contrast to the Christian Trinity.

The Taoists also have a form of 'trinity', the Three Purities: the Jade Emperor, Lao Tzu, the founder of Taoism (the Emperor of mysterious origin), and Ling Pao, the marshal of the supernatural beings. This bears no relation to any Ultimate God or of him coming in human form. These three are divine but the relationship between them is imprecise and there are still many other gods in the scheme. It is only a very superficial similarity to the Christian Trinity. The only worthwhile aspect of it is that the relationship between the three is not investigated in great detail in some sort of philosophical analysis.

What all this indicates is that the human mind seems to require a configuration of three, whether as a triangle or as a series in a kind emanation. The fascination is still there. Many aspects of liturgy contain a threefold method or repetition. It is a very real possibility that God has prepared the human mind in that way: that three holds a fascination that other numbers do not (except for seven). But the full completion of it comes with the Trinity given to us by God in the Bible.[3]

The Trinity and the Bible

Nowhere in the Bible is there a clearly formulated doctrine of the Trinity, in fact the word itself does not appear in Christian literature until Theophilus of Antioch (AD 180) used the word *trias*. Nevertheless the rudiments of this concept are to be found in many parts of the Scriptures but without any attempt at formalisation. As with the Incarnation, this was to come during the early Church leading up to the Catholic creeds and the Chalcedonian Definition. It was inevitable that some kind of threefold arrangement would appear, since much mention had been made of God as Creator, the coming of the Messiah Jesus as his Son, and frequent mention of the Spirit of God in both Testaments. The relationship between them had to be discussed even if it became increasingly clear that it was just as deep a paradox as all the others. Strangely, no one thought to call it a paradox at the time. If any of the New Testament writers had been asked to comment on it, the answer might have been somewhat vague (2 Corinthians 13:14): 'The grace of our Lord Jesus Christ and the love of God and the fellowship of the Holy Spirit be with you all.'

This says nothing about how they are related, and if asked St Paul might have offered what we would see as a somewhat confused answer: 'Now the Lord is the Spirit' (2 Corinthians 3:17), and when he says 'The Lord' he almost certainly means Jesus. He had not begun to think it through, and indeed why should any of them in the primitive Church? It was only the cranky and hairsplitting ideas of the heretics that forced the Church fathers to particularise and formalise.

The most helpful account from the New Testament comes in John 14:16: 'I (Jesus) will pray the Father and he will give you another Counsellor ... the Spirit of Truth.' There is no attempt to delve into the intricacies of the inner workings of God, and yet later generations were to attempt this impossible task. St John here is encouraging faith and confidence in the disciples rather than to embark on a doctrinal wrangle.

We see the beginnings of the issue of equality emerging when Clement of Rome says: 'As God lives, and the Lord Jesus Christ lives, and the Holy Spirit, the faith and hope of the elect,' Epistle to the Corinthians 57:2, but not fully thought out.[4]

With Irenaeus we see the thinking is still functional rather than theoretical:

'The Father decides and commands, the Son carries out the Father's plan, the Spirit supports and hastens the process,' AH 4:38:3.

'Through the Spirit man ascends to the Son: through the Son to the Father,' AH 5:36:3.[5]

'The Spirit supplies knowledge of the truth and has made known the ways of the Father and the Son towards man,' AH 4:38:3.

By the time of Tertullian we see the issue of 'three gods' surfacing. But the Christians always resisted this attempt at rationalising their faith with the pagan polytheism of the Roman world.

'We have always believed in one only God yet subject to the "dispensation" that the one only God has also a Son, his own word ... it is impossible to believe in the unity of God without identifying the Father, the Son and the Holy Spirit ... through unity of substance,' (Adversus Praxeam 2).[6]

Here we see with the word 'dispensation' and the use of 'economy' that figurative language derived from the Roman world is being used to help explain the Trinity. Also we see the emergence of paradox here in the way he contradicts himself, even though the actual word does not appear: 'people are dismayed by the idea of "economy" ... they do not understand that while believing in the unity of God they must believe it together with his "economy" ... but the truth is that the unity in deriving the trinity from itself is not destroyed thereby but dispensed,' Ad. Prax. 3.

At this point theorisings in the light of current philosophical assumptions begin to creep in. The dilemma between having three gods and one God was always an undercurrent in the disagreements:

by and large, the Patripassionists, the Modalists, the Sabellians and the Monarchians emphasised the unity of God at the expense of the Trinity: Valentinus, Basileides, Marcion and the Manichees speculated on two or more gods, sometimes trying to drive a wedge between 'the God of the Old Testament' and 'the God of the New Testament' (Marcion).

That there must have been an awareness of the shortcomings of metaphor is glimpsed in the words of Origen. We can picture such a phrase as 'only begotten Son' being taken by the populace to imply something like what Zeus did with the ladies. Although Origen does not actually say so in so many words, he is pointing out that such language is not meant literally:[7]

> the way in which God the Father begets and sustains his only-begotten Son is not equivalent to the begetting of man by man or animal by animal: there must needs be a great difference ... human thought cannot apprehend how the unbegotten God becomes the Father of the only-begotten Son. For it is an eternal and ceaseless generation (De Prin. 1:2:1).

Origen, in company with many of the fathers, likes to adduce an array of metaphors: 'He is the radiance of the eternal light: the unblemished mirror of the activity of God, the image of his goodness.'[8]

But some of his thoughts would in later times be seriously questionable: 'The Son is inferior to the Father ... he is subordinate to the Father. The Holy Spirit is still lower in degree ... the power of the Father is superior to the Son and the Holy Spirit, the Son's power is greater than the Holy Spirit,' and yet in the same breath he says, 'there must be no question of lesser or greater in the Trinity, since the source of the one godhead holds sway over all things by his Word and Reason and sanctifies by the Spirit of his mouth.'

With this we see the paradoxical nature of Trinitarian thinking beginning to emerge. But the controversies continued until the age of Athanasius. He could sense the futility of attempting to analyse the inner workings of God:

> Much more mad is the presumption in making such inquiries about God: for the truth about the godhead is not given by a display of arguments ... but by faith and reason exercised with

> reverent caution ... yet such perplexity may be remedied, firstly and chiefly by faith, but in the second place by such analogies as those of image and brightness'

With this we see the perceptiveness of Athanasius, that he realises that the Trinity can only be discussed with the aid of metaphors (or parables). He also is valuable for asserting in the face of the Arian controversy, the unity of God and the equality of the three in one. He was instrumental in framing the Nicene Creed, which was amplified as the Creed of Constantinople. These have stabilised the situation up to relatively modern times.

It is worth remarking that the Creeds that were accepted were bare minimum statements. When we compare them with some of the other elaborate and speculative statements of the time, it is clear that the orthodox party wanted to particularise as little as possible about the nature of God and his workings before the creation of the universe. The mistake made by many of the heretics was to imagine that they could speculate about the activities of God in 'producing' a Son and the Holy Spirit, matters which are beyond the human mind to comprehend. Arius made the mistake of taking the word 'beget' far too literally and then saying that since God the Father was *agennetos*, unoriginated or self-existent, then the Son of God could not be fully or totally God.[9] He was a creature and so was the Holy Spirit. The word *homoiousios* is important here: it meant 'of like substance' but not completely the same. So he thought up the scheme whereby there was God, then Jesus as a demi-god and the Holy Spirit one step lower. It was a misuse of Origen and a return to a simplified form of Gnosticism.

In the Creeds we see the words, 'of one substance' (with the Father). *Homoousios* means 'of one substance' but notice the very slight difference in spelling and meaning.[10] In today's world such hair-splitting and quibbling would almost certainly be treated with derision and yet at the time it was of vital importance. Today we are more inclined to be less dogmatic about the workings of God in the far distant past: more absorbed with the 'Big Bang' theory and other such speculations. Arius managed to render the Trinity down to something rational, explicable and semi-pagan. If at the time the disputants had realised that they were dealing with a most profound three-way paradox, it might have been a very different matter. Fortunately the orthodox camp managed to retain the unity of God with the Trinity as eternal, co-equal and fully divine. Only by that arrangement, which is beyond explanation, can the true paradox be seen.

The important influence of Athanasius cannot be underestimated. As an indicator of this, the later so-called Athanasian Creed carries his name but is now thought to be the work of Ambrose. The phrases such as 'the Father incomprehensible, the Son incomprehensible, the Holy Ghost incomprehensible' are the nearest we come, in ancient times, to an admission that the whole matter is a paradox well beyond the comprehension of the human mind. Even though there were subsequent doctrinal disputes on this matter, the situation soon stabilised itself around the official creeds up until modern times.

The central position of the Trinity for Christian theology and practice cannot be underestimated. Once the mystery of the Incarnation is accepted, the question then arises: how can God be properly represented to mankind unless Jesus is truly and fully God? Also, how can mankind be properly represented to God unless Jesus really is human? If any of this is denied then there is no final and ultimate mediation between God and humanity. This would apply whether Jesus is seen as prophet, priest or king, but particularly as priest. So the first paradox in the Trinity is the Incarnation. Then the question arises: how is the mediation to be continued after the earthly ministry of Jesus? The answer is that the Holy Spirit, working in the hearts of the faithful and the Church and in the world generally, keeps the presence of Jesus going on into the future. Here then is another three-way paradox, that the Holy Spirit is in action in three areas at once: the faithful believing soul, the community of believers and then the world at large.

The question then arises: what about the time before Jesus' earthly ministry? It is well attested that the Holy Spirit was active in this way in the BC period, in creation, in the hearts of the great leaders and prophets, and also paradoxically in the actions of some of Israel's enemies. So now we have another three-way paradox: that the Holy Spirit was active from the beginning, then during the ministry of Jesus, and then in the AD period. Add to this that the Holy Spirit came upon Jesus at the Baptism and was active all through the ministry of Jesus, and then is imparted to the disciples at the end of the ministry, at Pentecost. All this sounds contradictory, and it is, in strictly logical terms. But we are dealing with profound paradoxes and on that basis these are beyond human explanation.

Another aspect of it is that the Trinity is the final answer to polytheism. On the one hand God is emphasised as One; on the other hand he is not just singular but in a mysterious way plural. In this way polytheism comes to completion and obsolescence. One of the major problems with the early heresies was the tendency to slide into 'three gods', in other words, back into polytheism. But the Trinity is the corrective and the fulfilment of all that. In addition to this, it is the final answer to idolatry. The attempt to portray God or gods in some form of artwork or even imagination is not just a pagan characteristic: many a Jew, Muslim or Christian have some kind of mental picture or even an artistic portrayal of God. But the three-way paradox of the Trinity removes the need for this: firstly, God is beyond human imagining; secondly, he provided an icon of himself in Jesus; thirdly, the Spirit comes into our lives giving a closeness to God that obviates any picture of human invention.

It has only been in modern times that serious rethinking of the doctrine of the Trinity has appeared. The same factors as before, concerning the equality or non-equality of the three in one, have emerged, but the difference is that at last the word 'paradox' has begun to appear, although strangely it has not been discussed with any thoroughness. There is an awareness that such phrases as 'only begotten Son' and 'of one substance' and 'three Persons in one God', though helpful in their day and age are now obsolete metaphors. The word *persona* (Latin) does carry different connotations from the word 'person' in English today. The word 'substance' now means very little: it fitted well with Neo-Platonist ideas on philosophy but our philosophy today works in different ways and uses different language. All the same, to eliminate such ancient formulae is not entirely wise: they remain as important ingredients in the Nicene Creed, a document that holds Christianity together in spite of all its variations.

So with Barth we see his idea of three 'modes of being' rather than 'persons'. This sounds like a return to the modalist idea that Sabellius put forward, but is probably not such. We need to avoid confusing the imagery of the Roman Empire with the metaphors of today. Another idea, thinking of three distinct personal beings (Webb), recalls the Cappadocian fathers, Basil and the two Gregories. Again we see the same hairsplitting mentality which leads nowhere in the end. To quote Baillie:

> it spoke of personality IN God rather than the personality OF God: it conceived of God as consisting of a unity of three personalities, not as one personality ... he would speak of personality in God, or of God as the unity of three Persons, than of God as a Person.[11]

Does this actually mean anything? Is it possible to conceive of God at all by human rationality or imagination? Even so, the possibility of modern metaphors is always a reality. One such strand could be called the 'social life of the Blessed Trinity', which would involve picturing God as not just personal but social within himself. It is easy to guess the influence of modern social sciences on this imagery, but it is a healthy sign that new metaphors are being sought.

To summarise the position now: the unity of God and of his Creation is being realised more than ever; also the diversity that goes on within God himself, a diversity which means that different and sometimes contradictory things happen in the Creation. Also that God is subject to hurt and pain himself, something that earlier centuries have found very difficult to stomach, and indeed is still a paradox for us now. The way forward is to minimise the speculation, in philosophical terms, about the inner workings of God (which we cannot begin to understand), and concentrate on metaphor, imagery, parable and allegory. After all, this is the method that Jesus relied on almost exclusively. Nearly all of his figurative language was dependent on the agricultural life of Palestine under the Roman Empire; we now live in a 'post-industrial' age dominated by electronic gadgets and instant communications. The challenge is to devise new metaphors which reflect this thinking, but not allow just one metaphor to occupy centre stage.

An assemblage of metaphors, old and new

1. Take the shamrock (or clover) leaf. It is three leaves, of the same colour, weight and shape, absolutely equal. They are also connected together by the one stalk. This speaks of the co-equal connectedness of God in Trinity. The shortcoming of it is that all three leaves are the same, and yet the persons of the Trinity act in different ways, or

are experienced by the believer as taking different roles. This image is credited to St Patrick but is still in use to this day.

2. 'When a ray is projected from the sun it is a portion of the whole sun.' This is a useful analogy. The sun radiates light and heat to the earth and has a vitally important effect on all of us. So, the Father sends out his Son to us and the Spirit enlightens and encourages us. It is all one process, God loving and caring for us through the medium of the Trinity. A possible problem with this is the temptation to equate God with the sun, a common pagan assumption. Also, one might think there is no real difference between the workings of the three. Tertullian can be credited with this idea.

3. A similar idea is taken from the sphere of geography. A river can be seen as having three phases: youth, when it appears as a spring high up in the mountains; maturity, when it flows through a well-eroded valley; old age, when it goes into an estuary or delta. The speed of its flow, the effect on the surrounding areas, the rate of erosion or deposition are all differing aspects of its behaviour. And yet, it is all one substance, namely water. In its favour, is the evocation of the water of Baptism, the Red Sea and the River Jordan. It speaks of the unity of God but is not quite so adventurous on the varied activities of the Trinity. Athanasius originated this idea.

4. In the sphere of chemistry, there are many situations where two substances put together do not react unless a catalyst is added. A case in point would be when hydrogen peroxide has water added in order to produce oxygen. At first very little of the gas is produced; when a few grains of manganese dioxide are added, the reaction works freely. Notice that all three substances have abundant oxygen in them, locked up until a catalyst facilitates the reaction. The result is a life-giving gas. God gives life to the world by the combination of three substances which consist of the same material but are different in appearance and activity. To take the analogy further, a slight adulteration from a trace of another element in the experiment might alter or confuse the reaction. So too with the realities of failure in faith and of blocking the work of the Spirit in the Church. This might be helpful on the subject of Theodicy.

The strength of this analogy is that God is present in full in all three participants in the experiment. All three substances on their own appear to behave differently and yet together they react to produce something vital. In the reaction they are dependent upon and interacting with one another. It is not as if the persons of the

Trinity could act independently of one another. The shortcoming here is that each substance can be used for other experiments and usages not connected with the production of oxygen. It is never wise to force the analogy too far. The idea of the Spirit being a facilitator, which is much the same as a catalyst, is found in the fathers, starting with Irenaeus, although he did not expand on this.[12]

5. In politics, many countries have a monarchy. The king might invest his son, the heir apparent, with the authority to implement his policies, and may also find he has confidence in a close relative or associate to be a kind of prime minister who will frame laws and advise on courses of action. Seldom does a monarch proceed on totally autocratic lines: even with extreme dictatorships there is some form of consultation and implementation through intermediaries. There is a certain strength in this image in that there is unity of purpose in the work of God the King. The problem is that in the modern world most monarchies are constitutionally organised, which means that the people through elections have a very large say in policies. Also the republicans will hardly like this figure. The connecting thought is the authority coming from the top: the weakness is that many modern governments of all types function on so-called consultation, which in fact means endless wrangles in the halls of power. This would doubtless please the polytheists. This monarchist idea goes back to Tertullian and was the impetus for a certain brand of heresy when the metaphor was forced too far. Nevertheless, in the world of the Roman emperors who paid lip service to democracy but in fact behaved like modern-day dictators, this image would have had a lot of influence.

6. A modern idea taken from Tertullian. A welder (using gas or arc-welding) proceeds in his work with a torch against bits of metal. The light and heat given off are far too brilliant for the naked eye to cope with. He must have a piece of darkened glass set in a hood arrangement to see the job safely and clearly. The Father is the brilliant light; the Son is the window; the Spirit is the image received by the eyes and the brain. It is not difficult to know God as too brilliant for us to stare at: after all Moses had this problem when he encountered God face to face. The idea of the Son being a window maybe difficult for some, but he did actually call himself 'the door' or the 'door of the sheepfold'. Is a door all that different from a window? The Spirit working on our hearts and minds is what most believers know to be true from personal experience in the life of

faith. The analogy breaks down when Jesus is seen as a darkened glass, the opposite of God's pure light. And yet this raises up another paradox, for while Jesus removed the veil that impedes our access to the heart of God, on the other hand he is the filter which prevents the power of God overwhelming us, with our feeble human minds. There is no need to push this analogy any further, such as to say that it is the welder who actually causes the reaction: we do not cause God to be brilliant; he causes us to exist. Every metaphor has its strengths and weaknesses. This is why it is important not to let any one figure dominate the picture.

7. Another idea from chemistry: there is an element called carbon which is very plentiful in this world but also essential. It occurs in three forms: firstly as a fine black powder, secondly as graphite, thirdly as diamond. What is the difference between them? The black powder occurs in many situations from soot in one's chimney to calcium carbonate, and combines with all manner of other elements to produce different substances. It is even useful in carbon dating because (it is assumed) that its radiation decays at a steady rate over time. Graphite is a form of pure carbon with strength in one dimension but not in the other; it is used in pencils, though not in its pure form. Diamonds, again pure carbon, have strength in two dimensions and are one of the hardest known substances. They are very important for industrial use, in cutting softer materials, and also high-quality ones can be cut to make top-range jewellery. They are very different in appearances but are essentially the same ingredient. All three have their very different uses. All three are essential in their own way. As an image of the Trinity, it is not necessary to push the metaphor too far. They do not 'proceed' from each other; they appear independently according to different circumstances. Even so, there is certain level of suggestion for each one. That black powder is an essential ingredient in the created world; so many things are dependent on it; it has its own 'cycle' like water and nitrogen. It goes on for ever round in circles. Is this the Father? The graphite is a grey, flaky substance used in the early pencils but also has implications for electrical conductivity. Is this the Son? The diamond is noted for its brilliance and fascination as virtually indestructible. Is this the Spirit? All this can be left to one's imagination but not to dogmatism.

8. An image taken from anointing, a sacrament of the Old Testament, in which prophet, priest or king was inaugurated in a special

ceremony. Much importance was laid on the anointing and it implied that God's spirit would rest upon that person and give inspiration and protection. Suppose we see the Father as the one who performs the ceremony, the anointer; the Son as the anointed, hence the term 'Christ'; and the Holy Spirit as the medium, namely the holy oil? This will appeal to those of a sacramental turn of mind. This is a very ancient image outlined by Irenaeus, but with all manner of possibilities.[13]

9. The kaleidoscope. This is a fascinating gadget based on certain light effects which can be explained from the world of physics. There is a tube with three longitudinal mirrors aligned to form a triangle. Circular pieces of glass at each end hold the structure together and trap a collection of translucent beads at one end. Squinting down the tube, a magnificent effect is seen as the beads tumble about and produce different patterns. It is the action and interaction of the three mirrors which cause the effect. If we see the Trinity as three equal factors relating and interrelating with each other, the beads are the human race as much as the believing community. It is a fact that the patterns are never the same; so too with people, even twins. They are always slightly different in some way. Could this explain why humans are all different in ideas, feelings, reactions, appearance, fingerprints, DNA? Also that there are different religions and groupings within them? This could extend to political leanings of all kinds. If God were absolutely Unitary, could we expect everybody to be exactly the same, like clones?!

Notes

1. Littleton, *The Sacred East*, p. 38.
2. Littleton, *The Sacred East*, p. 84.
3. Christians have pointed out Abraham's encounter with the three strangers, Genesis 18:1ff. One of the most famous icons is the *Old Testament Trinity* by Alexander Rublev, which turns the encounter into an angelic, primordial Eucharistic experience. See Karen Armstrong, *The Case for God*, p. 118.
4. Clement of Rome, 'Epistle to the Corinthians', in *Apostolic Fathers*.
5. Bettenson, *The Early Christian Fathers*, p. 120. AH = Adversus Haereses.
6. Bettenson, p. 184.
7. Bettenson, p. 319. De Prin = De Principiis.
8. Bettenson, p. 410ff.
9. Stevenson, *A New Eusebius*, p. 351.

10 *Homoousios* means 'of the same substance' (as in the Creed). *Homoiousios* means 'of similar substance'.
11. Baillie, *God was in Christ*.
12. Clement of Rome, op. cit.
13. Bettenson, op. cit., p. 120.

9

The Atonement

In contrast to the Trinity and the Incarnation, the Atonement has not been subjected to such rigorous discussion and to this day no firm conclusion has been reached. There is no creedal definitive statement on the matter: just an assemblage of metaphor, imagery and allegory. There have been many attempts at explaining it away in ephemeral philosophical terms but no general agreement has been reached. For this reason the matter is much fresher in Christian thinking and we are not hampered by the thought of heresy-hunting. Even so we see the same lines of argument as with the Trinity and Incarnation, on the assumption that the mind of God can be analysed and predicted. The modern trend is to subject the matter to liberal doses of sentimentality, and the selective use of Scripture is just as prevalent as ever.

Taking Atonement to mean restoring a broken relationship between God and humanity, we can see that it is basic to religious awareness the world over. Wherever there is a feeling of guilt, remorse, angst, or even a feeling that all is not in harmony between the world of the spirit and the world of mankind, there is some kind of procedure for coping with the problem. As we have seen, an important method widely used is that of sacrifice, either in its literal form, or in some kind of transferred procedure. The word 'atonement' does not have to be there, but the same processes of thought are undeniably present everywhere.

The word itself stems from Judaism, Yom Kippur,[1] which is now the most holy day in the Jewish calendar as stipulated in Leviticus 16:30. This, coupled with guilt offerings, would have been understood by virtually every culture in the ancient world. When Hebrews elaborated on this and showed that Jesus was the eternal sacrifice in 9:12, this would have struck a chord with virtually every race and culture in the Roman world and beyond. This may also help to explain why the Church fathers tended not to delve into this matter, but concentrated on the Trinity and Incarnation which were not so clearly understood.

But the question has always been: how did the life and death of Jesus bring about the new relationship of trust, peace, removal of guilt and transformation of death? Is it possible to describe the process? In the Bible there are many remarks which can be used to fuel any theory, but there is no definitive idea covering the whole matter. The interesting feature of all attempts to make the Bible tell us the answer is the selective way in which evidence is used. Theologians almost always start with various presuppositions and then try to bend the scriptural evidence to support their views. There seems to be no one who can use all the evidence in a balanced fashion and be honest enough to conclude that there is no final, rational solution, as far as human reasoning is concerned. In general terms, there are three main strands for coping with the Atonement – the ransom theory, the sacrificial theory and the moral theory – but there are many permutations on these. The first and third would be more specifically Christian and the second more general for all people. All three have some degree of relationship with the notion of 'covenant' as discussed above.

The ransom theory

Nowhere is this strand of thought worked out as a logical system in the way that the sacrificial system was. It is the general assumption that was prevalent among the early Church fathers down to the end of the Roman Empire. In recent times it has seen a rejuvenation largely by the influence of Gustav Aulen.[2] It has almost always been conveyed in highly metaphoric, and luridly mythological terms and this is why many later writers have either rejected it or tried to reinterpret it in such a way as to alter its thrust drastically.

The essentials of this strand of thought are as follows: Jesus made a remark, in Mark 10:45: 'For the Son of Man came … to give his life as a ransom for many.' This metaphor would have been clearly understood by anyone in the Roman world: the idea of a slave being bought out by a rich man and set free was a common procedure. To whom would the ransom be paid: who was the slavemaster? The answer is, it was paid to the Devil who had kept mankind captive since the calamity in the Garden of Eden. God would 'buy out' an enthralled humanity. This, for the Jews, would evoke the same situation as at the Exodus, when God rescued Israel from captivity in Egypt. This brought in the Old Covenant; the rescue performed by Jesus would bring in the New Covenant. For this reason, this strand of thought is closely aligned with the metaphor of covenant, simply a continuation of that process of thought. Such phrases as 'you were bought with a price,' 1 Corinthians 6:20; 'one man's act of righteousness leads to acquittal and life for all men,' Romans 5:18; 'in him we have redemption through his blood,' Ephesians 1:7, all point to the same process of thought. Essentially it implies that God, as the Messiah, comes into our world to effect a rescue mission, since mankind is under the menace of sin, death, guilt, all the work of the powers of evil. In the ministry of Jesus, evil is overcome and a fresh start, the New Covenant, is ready for all who can accept it.

Some might say that this theory is dependent on a literal acceptance of the Fall; this is not necessarily so. More essential is the acceptance of the reality of evil, as personified by the Devil, or Satan. Many have tried to relegate this kind of thinking to the lumber-room of theological history, but this cannot work. Consider this quotation from Luke 10:18: 'And Jesus said to them, "I saw Satan fall like lightning from heaven ... I have given you authority to tread upon serpents and scorpions and over all the power of the enemy."'

Several factors emerge from this remark: Jesus clearly sees his ministry as a battle against the powers of evil; he sees it as a reversal of the Garden of Eden situation; he sees this work as in train during his earthly ministry and not just at the crucial moment at the end, his death; also he knows he is winning and it will result in victory. It is not enough to say that belief in the Devil is an outmoded, superstitious mythological notion. This is the belief that Jesus held, and it is more than just a suspicion; he had, we understand, a situation of dire temptation with the Devil in the wilderness. He had first-hand knowledge of the world of the spirit and that included evil spirits. St Mark goes to some lengths to point this out. It may well be that it was Zoroastrianism that introduced this idea of dualism into Judaism and then into Christianity, but that does not have to mean that it is a mistake: more likely it was God's design to implant that idea. In any case dualism, as a candidate for coping with Theodicy, has been an important aspect of Christian thinking through the ages, and still is, in spite of the modern tendency to attempt to airbrush it out of theology. The fact remains that dualism was an important factor in the mind-set of Jesus, not just some sort of pretence, and as such ought to be given more respect than some have in recent times.

What exactly Jesus meant when he said he would be ransom for 'many' is not clear. Some have taken it to mean that some people will be saved and others not. It may be that he had in mind something from Isaiah where the suffering servant says, 'by his knowledge ... my servant will make many to be accounted righteous,' and 'yet he bore the sin of many,' Isaiah 53:12. This is balanced and filled out by St Paul in 1 Timothy 2:6: 'Jesus who gave himself as a ransom for all.' The whole of mankind is included in the rescue, not just a few selected favourites.

The ransom approach keeps on appearing in the patristic period. Irenaeus (Adversus Haereses v. 1.1–3)[3] says: 'He who was powerful Word and also truly man redeemed us by his own blood by a rational transaction and gave himself as a ransom,' and also, 'the Lord redeemed us by his blood and gave his life for our life, his flesh for our flesh and poured out the Spirit of the Father to unite us and reconcile God and man,' and 'on our behalf he propitiated the Father ... and cancelled our disobedience by his obedience.'

With this we see the beginnings of a paradox, not spelt out, but latent: in one breath he talks of a ransom which works out as some sort of transaction with the Devil, and yet in the next breath he talks about propitiation, which implies a sacrifice to clear guilt with God. We see traces of the 'recapitulation' idea, derived from St Paul, but now worked out more fully. It implies that the whole life of Christ, not just his death, is significant in rescuing fallen mankind. This is a great strength in his thinking also: the Holy Spirit is included in the scheme, a factor not very often seen in later thinking.

With Tertullian[4] we see the gradual enlargement of this imagery, the transactional metaphor beginning to take centre stage. De Fuga in Persecutione:

> What kind of man is he ... who depreciates and soils the merchandise which he acquired at so great a price ... his most precious blood? The Lord ransomed him from the angelic powers who rule the world, from the spirits of iniquity, from the darkness of this world, from eternal judgement, from everlasting death.

Here the image has slipped a little, for it is God who is ransoming Jesus from the Devil. Even so, the train of thought is the same.

With Origen the imagery goes further. Commentary on Matthew 16:8:

> To whom was the ransom paid? Not to God: can it be to the evil one? For he had power over us until the ransom was given to him on our behalf, namely the life of Jesus: and he was deceived into thinking that he could keep his soul in his power ... had no power over him who became 'free among the dead' and stronger than the authority of death.

Also, 'Jesus was offered as a sacrifice not only for things on earth but for things in heaven ... he offered up in sacrifice the vital power of his body, as a kind of spiritual sacrifice.'[5]

Here we see the element of deceit creeping in, that the Devil did not realise what he was attacking and so was defeated. This idea occurs frequently in the fathers, and the imagery comes to its most lurid and off-putting when Gregory of Nyssa likens Jesus to the bait on a fisherman's hook: the Devil swallows it, not realising that he will be caught and landed. The divine nature was hidden in the human nature and the Devil thought it was easy prey. The imagery in Gregory the Great goes even further and becomes grotesque. This explains why later generations found this theory unacceptable and rejected it: they failed to see the spiritual realities behind it. The strength in this theory can be seen in various ways.

There is a unity of purpose between God and the Messiah, a straight line coming from God, through the humanity of Jesus to tackle the problem of evil. Evil is a reality, not just a theory or a facade. Also, God does not proceed by means of force to accomplish his victory: he includes himself in the process of victory, not just using agents. The greatest force was shown through love and humility, not tyrannical methods. Another truism is that evil generally overreaches itself or exceeds its remit. This implies that the Devil is not just the enemy of God but also in a way his agent. Here comes another paradox, but one that is well supported by Job. This copes with the strange notion that the Devil could acquire 'rights' over mankind. From there the metaphor of ransom is quite appropriate. Looking beneath all the imagery and mythology, the basic train of thought is as follows: God comes in mercy and forgiveness, in the form of his Messiah, to contend with this problem and bring release to all mankind. How this is actually performed, the mechanics of it, is a long way beyond human comprehension, and yet we still try to analyse it.

This theory relates well to the paradox of Theodicy, also to the Incarnation and also the total life and ministry of Jesus. The resurrection too is implicated, although it is seldom mentioned specifically. The conquest of death clearly refers to Jesus rising from the dead.

In recent times the ransom theory has found renewed interest. The difficult imagery associated with it is still a problem for those who wish to take it literally. Another problem lies in the failure to understand the reality of evil, and in fact to try to airbrush sin and guilt out of the scheme. Death too cannot be faced realistically. This is rather strange since we have just lived through a century in which there has been an unprecedented outpouring of evil, wickedness in high places and death on a grand scale. And yet connecting this with the ransom theory of Atonement is far from people's minds. But for those who do understand it, divine intervention is clearly the only way of escape from these horrors.

Another related issue which surfaced in the patristic period centred on whether 'redemption' was for all or only for some, namely the ones who had committed themselves to the new faith. 'A ransom for many,' as seen in Mark 10:45, might suggest that God was only going to save certain selected persons. An awareness of this might be seen in 1 Timothy 2:20:

'In a great house there are not only vessels of gold and silver but also of wood and earthenware, some for noble use and some for ignoble.'

St Paul was talking about youthful passions and pointless wrangles. But Origen, cleverly (Hom. In Ieremiam 20:3), uses this as a basis for discriminating between the genuinely saved, the frauds, and the ones not yet included in the Church: 'While the rest, that is ordinary men, who are outside the treasury ... will yet be able to be vessels in the great house.' We may sense that Origen is somewhat undecided about this question of salvation for all, or some. He includes the remark, 'according to the mysterious dispensation of God', which might indicate that he is aware of a dilemma here, but does not take it further to develop a paradox.[6]

Augustine thought that the Atonement only availed for the elect.

Others, Gregory the Great and Gregory of Nyssa, believed in universal redemption, including not just all of mankind but the Devil and all his angels too.[7] Both these views can be supported by clever quotation of Scripture. It seems that the Biblical writers never addressed themselves to this potential contradiction. This is a difference of opinion that has worked its way through Church history and is still with us to this day, somehow intermingled with denominationalism. We may be looking at another paradox: that in one sense the entire Creation is saved; on the other hand only those who respond in faith to the rescue mission of the Messiah are saved. Or are we looking at a temporary rescue effected by Jesus for those who respond to him, with the full universal rescue still in the future at his Second Coming? It could be seen both ways.

The satisfaction theory

By the eleventh century a new initiative in Atonement thinking arrived with Anselm. He stands as a focal point in the development of this area and has influenced thought ever since, even with modern liberalistic departures. He claimed to subject the whole matter to reason and logical processes, but even so makes as many assumptions as anyone else. The chief change in thinking was the altered legalistic assumptions of the day: gone was the Roman system and arrived was the Mediaeval scenario of allegiance. Anselm rejects totally the idea of a ransom being paid to the Devil: the true receiver of the Ransom was none other than God.[8] This was because God was outraged by man's sin, and satisfaction was the only solution to bring about reconciliation. The sacrifice of Christ was the crucial thing that brought about a new relationship between man and God.

An important strength in this theory lies in its universal application. Not only does it employ imagery from the sacrificial system in the Old Testament and also through the realisation of it in Hebrews, but it also appeals to the sacrificial mentality seen in virtually every other religion in the world. It is possible to say that the sacrifice of Christ brings all sacrificial activity and thinking to a climax of completion, and in some respects to obsolescence. As a metaphor, this is very useful as far as it goes: of course there were many who forced the metaphor into all manner of permutations, with the result that the original value of it is soon lost.

Some of the assumptions in this theory may be somewhat questionable. The idea of merit had been current since Tertullian, but the idea of 'superabundant merit' was a different matter. We have seen this idea in Buddhism with the merits of Amida, but the Western world was yet to find its feet with this idea. It developed into the idea that merit could be transferred from one person to another and also, by dint of logic, guilt could be transferred. So by a clever transaction, the guilt of mankind could be loaded on to Jesus and the merits of Jesus could be made available for us all. Sin was seen as a debt owed by everyone to God, but since no one could manage to pay off the debt, it needed God himself to come in the form of his Son to pay off the debt. The sufferings on the cross cancelled out all human guilt. This metaphor too was taken far too literally when people began to assess the exact amount of suffering and balance it with the total debt involved, just like creative bookkeeping!

The idea of transferring guilt was by no means a new one. Strangely, the scapegoat motif from Leviticus is seldom if ever mentioned, but of course it is the same assumption: that guilt is a commodity which can be relocated. Origen (Comm. on John 28:19)[9] points out that certain barbaric tribes in Greece would, in the case of disaster, find release through one man's offer of himself for sacrifice, the assumption being that communal guilt would be loaded on to the victim. This motif is seen in Isaiah with the Suffering Servant, 53:4–6: 'Surely he has borne out griefs ... bruised for our iniquities ... and with his stripes we are healed ... the Lord has laid on him the iniquity of us all.'

The liberalistic mentality of later generations found this notion morally repugnant and totally unfair, as indeed it would seem to be. What they fail to realise is that 'scapegoatism' or victimisation is an all too common a factor in human activity. It stems from a nasty instinct which demands that someone has to be ostracised, usually a soft target, in order to put things right, somehow. Mankind has just lived through a century which included the Holocaust, involving the extreme victimisation of whole classes of people who were imagined to be 'inferior' and having a deleterious effect on society. Even with an awareness of such prejudices, and legislation to counter it, victimisation still goes on regardless, albeit in different permutations. The ancients were right in a way: we are fools to ignore this nasty streak in human nature. But in relation to the Atonement, it can be seen in this light: that God allowed all the evil in human nature to play itself out by inflicting it on Jesus, who appeared to be a 'soft target' or 'whipping boy'. In that sense there is a deep spiritual reality in the scapegoat motif.

Other difficulties with Anselm's view centre on the transactional mentality involved. It is all very mechanical, pecuniary and legalistic, verging on a commercial trade-off. It involves a conception of a God who stands on his dignity; his holiness is too great to allow of a debt being cancelled. He sounds like a mediaeval lord who requires the full dividend from his underlings. This is at variance with the scriptural view in which God proclaims himself as ready to forgive and accept the genuinely repentant sinner. It has been pointed out that sin and guilt are a far deeper matter than just a commodity that can be relocated or paid off in some sort of transaction. But of course if we take Anselm's metaphors literally, it is easy to object and reject. Another problem is that the sacrificial motif has very little to do with the ministry of Christ before the Crucifixion; also the Resurrection and the Holy Spirit hardly ever seem to enter the picture.

If we look at how Hebrews treats the matter, the picture is somewhat different (9:26): 'He (Jesus) appeared at the end of the age to put away sin by the sacrifice of himself.' Hebrews goes on to give a fuller picture, for Jesus is not just the victim but also the final High Priest and also the altar upon which it is performed (9:11ff). The metaphor here is somewhat mixed and yet all-encompassing. He takes it on to work in the New Covenant (v. 15) and answers the question of why Jesus had to die: it was to ratify the New Testament. If he had not died, his 'Will' could not have come into force. 'Without the shedding of blood there is no forgiveness of sins.' Moreover, the earlier incidents of Jesus' ministry play a part in this scheme. The temptation to sin is referred to (4:15), and in 5:7 we see mention of Jesus praying and his obedience. This means that the whole of his ministry is involved, not just the sacrificial death. Unfortunately this aspect of it is normally ignored or played down by the satisfaction theorists. The reality of the Devil is implied in Hebrews, but for Anselm this aspect is virtually ignored: the transaction is between God and Christ. If this appears to drive a wedge between Father and Son, that could be a fair criticism. The straight line of the ransom theory is gone: instead, there is a reflected line. The Father sends the Son into the world and the Son responds as the line goes back to the Father. This line does not seem to involve the disciples, the Holy Spirit or anyone else. It is all performed over our heads and does not really get to grips with evil. But Hebrews does relate it to us (4:15): 'Let us then with confidence draw near to the throne of grace that we may receive mercy and find grace to help in time of need.'

The sacrificial aspect and motif of the Atonement is valuable and has great depth, and the way the Biblical writers handle it is admirable. But so easily the imagery can be overworked, distorted and spoiled. Already we see a paradox emerging over to whom the ransom should be paid: the Devil or to God? The answer is that both are true in their own way. It is a big mistake to relegate one of them to the dustbin. Another paradox already seen is that God performs a sacrifice to himself: what meaning can this have? It brings us back to the Trinity and Incarnation, and the reciprocal relationship between Father and Son. If we could be content with St John the Baptist's remark in John 1:29, 'Behold the Lamb of God who takes away the sin of the world', this would answer all the questions. The work of Christ is of cosmic significance; he brings in a new relationship of trust and freedom from guilt for all people; it is the final rescue mission by God, mirrored in the first Exodus. The whole Atonement is summed up in this. And yet people are not satisfied with that.

The penal theory

With the Reformation we see various stirrings on the subject of the Atonement. With Luther, we see the brief re-emergence of the ransom theory, but unfortunately his associates and successors did not really take on board what he was saying and slid back into the Anselmic mentality of satisfaction and sacrifice. So with Calvin we see the penal theory spelt out but it was only the satisfaction theory re-expressed in altered imagery and metaphor. The line from God to mankind in Jesus is reflected back and the Devil is not really involved. This is strange since Calvin had a strong impression of the powers of evil, but does not work them into his theory of Atonement. Like Anselm, his theory is all logical and convincing, assuming we accept his basic assumptions. But what we must remember is that the neater and more rational the theory, the more likely it is to be a product of human logic, not of divine theorising. We should learn our lesson from the Trinitarian theorisers, such as Arius, who made a very convincing argument of it but was deemed heretical. Fortunately there are no heretics in the sphere of Atonement.

With Calvin we have the free use of 'wrath', 'merit' and 'appeasement', all of which caused problems for succeeding generations of Christians. Institutes 2:15:6:

> Because the curse from the time of Adam has justly closed the entrance to heaven, and that God, inasmuch as he is judge, is against us, it was necessary that the sacrifice, in order to open the way to grace and to appease the wrath of God, should intervene with satisfaction: and therefore Jesus Christ, to acquit himself of his office, had to go before with sacrifice. But this sacrifice consists in his passion and his death ... instead and in place of sinful humanity ... by taking on himself the punishment prepared for every sinner by the just judgement of God ... he abolished by his blood the iniquities which had caused enmity between God and man ... by that payment God was satisfied.[10]

Many people have found such phraseology difficult, but it was only a slightly more severely worded version of Anselm; not that Calvin would ever have wished to admit it! Again we see that the focus of the Atonement is on the death of Jesus; other issues seem not to be of much relevance here: the Resurrection, the Holy Spirit, the whole earthly ministry of Jesus. It is only fair to say that Calvin does make the obedience of Jesus in his life connect with the Passion, but there is scant mention of all his teachings, miracles and parables. Even less is there mention of how Jesus loved and forgave people when they asked for help.

To be fair to Calvin, his metaphors, bound up with mythology, may have found a ready market at that time in history. We can see a significant use of more moderate metaphor in such phrasing as in Institutes 2:16:2: 'Now such ways of speaking are accommodated to our minds in order to make us better able to understand how wretched the condition is without Christ.'

Wendel points out that this is a pedagogic adaptation to human capacities: is this an admission that Calvin's imagery was overdone, overstated and plain frightening? But there is even more to it than that. Calvin runs the risk of contradicting the New Testament. The Messiah comes in love and forgiveness at the start, as stated in 2

Corinthians 5:19: 'God was in Christ reconciling the world to himself, not counting their trespasses against them.' There is no legal wrangle about paying off debts with God.

More difficult still is Calvin's belief in predestination to election (and the opposite) to be tied in with the Atonement.[10] If it were true that certain persons were destined for heaven and others for hell, what would be the point of Jesus paying off all those debts to God? Now we can see that imagery is taking over to the point where it is being taken literally and starting to damage people's trust in God. Calvin managed (like Duns Scotus) to argue that redemption is included in predestination and founded upon it.[11]

'Wrath of God' has always been a problem for later thinkers. Later Protestant theorists tried to tone down or explain away such phraseology. Strangely it never occurred to them to see it as heavy metaphor with mythological overtones. What is really being said here is that mankind having not followed God's instructions, found itself in some sort of distancing or estrangement with God. This produced problems of conscience and guilt. The only way to resolve this was for God to come to us, in real terms and remove the problem himself: something that mankind could not achieve. If that is what Calvin is trying to say, regardless of the lurid language, then he is right. Sadly people have been disturbed by his mode of expression, taking it far too literally.

It is ironic that while Anselm and Calvin are basically in agreement over the logic of Atonement, the way it worked out produced diametrically opposite approaches to liturgy. So while the Roman Catholics made the 'sacrifice of the Mass' dominate their worship, with all its implications of purchasing power with God, the Protestants played down the Eucharist and went in for churches which resembled courtrooms, in which heavenly legalities were assumed to be resolved. Divided by metaphor rather than truth!

It is clear that Calvin's phraseology gave much impetus to the later Protestant liberalistic ideas of the 'Enlightenment'. They set to work to demolish his theory but never really succeeded in removing it from people's minds. Calvin resonates with something in human nature, even if it is in a negative fashion. There was a resurgence of Calvinistic thought in the late nineteenth and early twentieth centuries with such figures as Dale, Denney, Mozley, Edwards and others, in an attempt to ameliorate Calvin. The truth is that they cannot get away from it: none of them seem to realise that they are objecting to the imagery rather than the truth behind it. Sadly the liberals have no substantial imagery or attractive metaphors to employ as a substitute. They try to use literal language and the result is that it descends into hair-splitting and endless wrangles not unlike the efforts of the schoolmen.[12]

The moral theory

Recent times have seen the emergence of the moral theory. Other titles have been applied, such as the subjective theory, the exemplarist theory and the moral influence theory. But what this means is that there is no one established logical pattern with this one, just an assemblage of ideas that work basically on the same lines. The line here is not of one coming from God through Jesus to the Devil. The Devil is definitely discounted as some sort of superstitious nonsense. Neither is the line from God to Jesus and reflected back, for the reality of God is often a little uncertain or obscured from the plan. If there is a line, it is a reciprocal line between Jesus and mankind, the two things interacting in some kind of love-trust relationship. It would be a mistake to assume that this is an entirely new idea: traces of it can be found in the patristic period, and Peter Abelard was the first clear exponent of it, although he was shouted down by his contemporaries. It is with Schleirmacher with the liberalistic view of Christian matters that the inception of this train of thought begins to re-emerge.[13] Other names associated with it would be Ritschl, Rashdall, Bushnell and Franks. It would be quiet unfair to label the moral theorists as agnostics or atheists: very far from it.[14] But their thinking is very much inclined to the modern Humanist cast of mind and the reality of God intervening in real terms in this world is for them somewhat of a strain on the imagination.

To quote Abelard, who is the inspiration behind this line of thought, 'I think that the purpose and cause of the Incarnation was that God might illumine the world by his wisdom and excite in us a love for himself: Every man is made better, that is, becomes more loving to the Lord, after the Passion of Christ than before, because a benefit merely hoped for ... our redemption then, is that supreme love shows to us in the passion which, not only frees us from the slavery of sin, but acquires for us the true liberty of the sons of God.'[15]

From this we see that the lurid imagery of other theories is discounted and a much more positive and optimistic feeling about salvation is felt. The moralists concentrate on the earthly ministry of Jesus. This is a strength: we can see that all his teachings which introduced a higher ethic, his parables, his works of caring and obedience, are a wonderful example to us all. Even the passion is worked in, although for many the Crucifixion is a problem which has to be toned down. The Atonement means a change in mankind: they are more inclined to repent, seek help, trust in God. Jesus acts like a sort of magnet, bringing out the latent goodness in people. When people repent like this, God's forgiveness flows freely. The alteration is in man's attitude; not with God, who remains the same.

This train of thought may sound attractive to modern ears; that is because we have grown accustomed to hearing it within recent times. But there are problems with it. Firstly, it renders God as virtually inactive in the work of salvation. Jesus is active but the Father is not; is this another wedge driven between Father and Son? Secondly, the idea of human sin is superficial. The sense of deep corruption in human nature is played down, and the idea that evil is not just a personal failure but a cosmic disaster. The Devil is non-existent here and yet in the Gospels Satan is a major factor. Thirdly, the Gospels point out that while some people were attracted by Jesus' goodness, others were actually repelled by him. So salvation is only a limited thing, not general or cosmic. Fourthly, one is left wondering why Jesus had to die, why he could not rather have faded out gently like the Buddha and other great spiritual leaders. Why was his death so horrific? This has always been a problem for the humanistic liberals. Going further, the Resurrection seems to hold very little place in the scheme: it is virtually irrelevant. As a subjective theory, verging on mysticism, it is understandable and reasonably consistent, but Christianity is concerned with a balance between subjective and objective. It is rooted in history, unlike some religions which thrive almost entirely on meditation and inner life. Finally, having eliminated all the imagery of the past, they are unable or unwilling to provide any new metaphors. This makes it all very banal: there is no poetry in it. What we need are new parables, reflecting modern conditions and thought-forms. It is not a matter of devising a new rationale of the Atonement, it is more a matter of finding an array of new metaphors to complement the old ones and produce a balanced picture, even if they are contradictory. From this, the deep paradoxes of the Atonement will begin to emerge more clearly.

In recent times the moral theory has worn thin against the political developments of two World Wars and the realisation that human nature is not quite as innocent as the Humanists would have us believe. The theories have made a resurgence; the ransom theory, redrafted and reinvigorated by Gustav Aulen, and Donald Baillie, the sacrificial theory. There are no new theories in theology, just circulating ideas. It is with Baillie that there has at last seen an awareness of paradox. But he is also aware that the imagery of the past is figurative and yet cannot just be jettisoned. To quote Baillie: 'It is good to let one figure of speech correct and supplement another and to remind ourselves that all of these are but attempts to exhibit the love of God in dealing with the sin of the world and overcoming it as only love can do.'[16]

When it comes to deciding on the truth of these three theories of Atonement, it is only fair to say that it is not good enough to say that one is correct and the others wrong. All three of them bear some relationship or reflect in some way genuine spiritual awareness and experience. This is where we can say that all three of them are correct in their own way, even taking into account their defects and slight differences of opinion. Are we looking at another major paradox, this time a three-way one, like the Trinity? All three of them balance each other and the contradictions between them cannot be resolved unless we see it as a paradox. Within this major paradox lie various subsidiary ones, some of which have already been seen.

With the Ransom Theory, regardless of the idea of paying a ransom to the Devil, which is of course a piece of imagery, the underlying truth is that this humble carpenter could have the mastery over evil spirits and, yet again, did not attempt to overrule the evil that was in those who tried to silence him. Does this tell us that in God's wisdom, humility and love are the strongest elements in life, as opposed to hate and tyranny? With the satisfaction theory, one wonders at the logic of God performing a sacrifice to himself. But the underlying truth is that the love of God involves humility, obedience and giving, rather than bullying and frightening people. It raises the thought that God, the ruler of the universe, allows himself to be hurt and to modify his policy. With the moral theory, it seems inexplicable that when the ultimate goodness and love is displayed to people, some of them reject it. Does this mean that evil is firmly ensconced in certain people: certain people are earmarked for destruction and will never be saved? Whichever it is, those ideas lead us back to the other two theories. Paradoxically, all three theories need each other to bring them all to completion.

The theology of completion is an important ingredient in all three and is almost always ignored by theorists. With the ransom theory, the completion consists of various elements: the recapitulation of the Fall in the work of the Messiah (as elaborated by Irenaeus); the defeat of the Devil, bringing dualism to a finale; and the defeat of Death as seen in the Resurrection. Jesus is seen to fulfil all things: he actually says on the cross, 'It is finished.'[17] With the satisfaction theory, the sacrificial system, not just of the Jews but of everyone, is brought to a conclusion and obsolescence, and that includes all the ritual prescriptions of the Old Testament. Hebrews explains this at length but the writer is not the only one to think like this. St John, who speaks about 'the Lamb of God', shows that the sacrifice of Christ brings the Exodus and the Old Covenant to a conclusion. With the moral theory, we see the perfect Son of God bringing the laws, ethics and basic precepts of Moses to a conclusion and providing a final example of love, caring and obedience, beyond which it is not possible to go. 'Greater love has no man that he lay down his life for his friends,' John 15:13. So the whole work of Atonement came to a climax of completion with Christ's death, but also his resurrection. If he had died and remained in death, his work would have died with him, but as it was, he rose again in triumph, something that most theorists omit to consider, which means that his atoning work goes on not just in this world but eternally. This leads us to the Ascension, but he did not leave his earthly body behind since he ascended as one person, complete in two natures, and is with God for ever.

Now we see another paradox emerging, that while the Atonement takes place in the earthly life of Jesus, and is completed, in another sense it goes on eternally in the heart of God. Baillie is one of the few theorists who remarks on this, but it is not just a spurious theory, it is endemic in Hebrews 8:1: 'Now the point in what we are saying is this: we have such a high priest, one who is seated at the right hand of the throne of the Majesty in heaven.'

The implication in this is that Jesus perpetually intercedes for us in his capacity as the only one true high priest, and endured what we have to cope with, all the rigours of a genuine human life pattern, he is the only one who can really understand our problems, and so can represent them to the Father. So Atonement, paradoxically, is a continuing process, not just a completed jigsaw. This applies also to the sacrificial aspect of it, but of course the ransom aspect is also ongoing. Evil was defeated in the work of Jesus, yet still there is evil at work in the world: people still die and get involved in wickedness. The difference is that Christ's triumph has put a clear limit on what evil can do. There is no need for anyone to become enmeshed in evil, if the Holy Spirit helps us to know what wickedness is and avoid it. Death, although still a reality, is seen by every Christian as merely a transition from this world to the next, from life on a limited scale to life on a 'raised' dimension, which is yet to be revealed to us each and every one. It also applies to the moral aspect of things. For if we know that Jesus is the ultimate in love, virtue and obedience, then with the help of the Holy Spirit we can orientate ourselves to this wonderful standard. This does not mean that we become perfect, but it does mean that with a conscience cleared of guilt we can make the effort and be assured of forgiveness in the event of failure. Somehow, paradoxically, he is able to justify our actions even if they do appear to us to be wrong somehow. The case of Judas Iscariot comes to mind. In this way, the Resurrection, the Ascension and the Holy Spirit, usually ignored by Atonement theorists, become of the highest relevance and complete the picture. It also implies that the total completion will come one day at his Second Coming when all things are brought to a conclusion, and God comes into his final Sabbath, bringing us all with him.

Baillie says, 'The work of Atonement is his own work, incarnate in the Passion of Jesus Christ because it is "eternal in the heavens" in the very life of God, the love of God bearing the sin of the world.'[18] The marks of his wounds were not removed simply because he was raised from the dead: the wounds were left as an everlasting reminder to all. Relevant to this is a phenomenon known as stigmatisation, in which certain persons have experienced, either outwardly or inwardly, the wounds of Christ. Francis of Assisi, Catherine of Siena and Father Pio are the most notable cases, but 330 people are thought to have had this infliction. In a way, it is a reminder of the ongoing Atonement. The wounds are beyond medical explanation. The Turin Shroud also is (so far) beyond scientific explanation. That too is a mysterious reminder of the ongoing Atonement. Whether it is genuinely the burial shroud of Jesus or not is of no account as it still serves as a fascinating reminder of the Passion of Jesus.[19]

Atonement is thus a completed process; also a continuing process, eternally in the heart of God – a stunning paradox.

A collection of allegories

The inherent weakness with all exponents of the Atonement is that when they find a useful metaphor, they overwork it and stretch it to imply other matters which can be actually contradictory or misleading. Another problem is that such matters as the Holy Spirit, the Resurrection, the Ascension and even the Second Coming hardly ever seem to relate to the Atonement. The resort to rationality, often with legalistic impedimenta, needs to be kept in proportion, for God's rationality and eternal justice work on a different dimension. The matter is beyond us to explain and yet the urge is there to attempt it. The faithful through the centuries have found through Christian practice that a new relationship of trust and love has been engendered by the intervention of God's Messiah in historical circumstances. How this actually worked is still being debated: the sound approach to it is to find new metaphors, parables and allegories which are relevant to today's world.

1. A blacksmith found a piece of steel; it was roughly what he wanted but it was all bent and misshapen. He could not use it as it was; it needed to be straightened out. He warmed it up in the fire and then hammered it in all its contortions, using great skill, until it was really straight and even. Then to stop it bending again, he quenched it in the water trough. Humanity was wayward and bent; God took a hammer and a furnace, Jesus and the Holy Spirit, and worked on it until it was straightened up. Using the hammer made his arm ache; it took pain, toil and sweat from God to do the work. To stop it being too soft, he quenched it: the Resurrection clinched the whole process. The new relationship is there for ever even if people try to distort it again.

The temptation is to push the metaphor too far: do we really need to theorise on how the steel got bent in the first place? To concentrate on the main point, that God straightened out wayward humanity, is the main thrust of the picture.

2. An allegory from alcoholism. A man slid into alcohol abuse, drinking increasingly heavily. His job went, his marriage was on the brink of collapse, his savings were gone, he was starting to steal to fuel the habit. It was a self-augmenting problem and yet he was convinced that the drink was doing him good. All attempts at talking him out of it failed: he knew better. Until one day he overheard a chance remark which made him think; it dawned on him that

everyone knew about it and people were sneering about him behind his back. It is not an easy matter to stop; it needs someone from Alcoholics Anonymous, someone completely new and who has been through the problem and understands exactly what it is like. It was a long hard struggle but now he is off the drink and is enjoying a new relationship with his wife and friends. He has to straighten things up with everyone he has deceived. Very often this new life involves an awareness of God.

Sin and temptation usually is some sort of slippery slope and not within our own power to arrest or reverse. It takes the active intervention from someone free of it and yet knowing what it actually consists of (Jesus). The chance remark or incident can be seen as God organising a situation where one is confronted with one's failings and the need to repent. There is no need to push the analogy any further: divine intervention is the essence of this situation.

3. The lifeboat situation. A lone yachtsman, for a dare, undertook to sail his boat singlehanded through a dangerous strait. A storm blew up and his vessel was soon on the rocks. He could have managed except that he was injured and lost control of the boat. It was too near to the cliffs for the helicopter to risk hovering and drop a line. The lifeboat was called. At great risk they could only come within a few yards of the yacht. The skipper called for a volunteer and when a rocket was shot across, a line was secured for Fred Bloggs to go over and bring the injured yachtsman back. Halfway back, the line worked loose and both of them fell into the sea; it was a crucial moment. But the skipper had every man hauling on the line and they were pulled to safety in the nick of time. Back at the village there was great rejoicing and Fred Bloggs was the hero of the day and received the George Medal.

The strength in this scheme is that the Holy Spirit (the rocket) and the Resurrection both have a part to play. It is a picture of great joy and relief as a dangerous situation is turned into a great triumph. Also the legal overtones, usually bearing down on the Atonement, are absent. No one need feel any guilt except the yachtsman (humanity) who was a fool to himself.

4. There was a party to which all manner of people were invited, mostly complete strangers to one another. In typical British fashion they stood there sipping sherry and eyeing each other with deepest suspicion and wondering why they could not find someone they recognised to talk to. The party was clearly going to be a frost. The

host was beginning to despair: how are we going to make the party go with a swing? The solution came when a young man got up and began to make a speech; everyone inwardly groaned. But he reeled off half a dozen of his funniest jokes, then smirks grew into grins, grins grew into giggles, giggles into guffaws. Everybody was laughing and exchanging pleasantries. The ice was broken. Everybody was happy, trust was engendered, new friendships forged, new business deals began to emerge; it was all a great success after all.

This image speaks of a failed relationship between God and humanity, and between men themselves. It requires someone to break the ice, to engender a relaxed atmosphere where trust and joy can emerge. Jesus was the one who made the decisive move to facilitate a new and improved atmosphere in the party of life. To push the analogy too far would mean trivialising the life of Christ, and yet he was there to introduce joy and love to the world.

5. A *Gardener's World* special. A keen gardener was given a job to tame a garden: it had originally been planted with some really expensive flowers and fruit trees, but because it had been neglected it was way out of control and just a wilderness. At first he considered spraying the lot with weedkiller, but that would have meant anything worthwhile would perish too. He tried pulling weeds out by hand but this only disturbed the flowers. In the end he decided on a drastic plan: he would derive seeds and cuttings from the worthwhile material and then tear out the whole lot and start afresh. He was a bit old and stiff in the back to do the heavy work himself; he called in a young lad who stripped the garden out completely, leaving just bare earth. Then the old gardener began to replant, using his seeds and cuttings. Now the garden is a beautiful sight: weeds do still keep coming through but nothing too drastic that cannot be kept under control, and people of all kinds come to visit and admire it.

It took a big decision, after a lot of preparation, to make a completely fresh start. This is the essence of the New Testament and the arrival of the Kingdom of Heaven. We all need a fresh start through repentance and baptism. It takes a vigorous young man to shoulder the actual toil, sweat and aching limbs, but all the time the old man is waiting to replant with the original flowers and trees. Very little in the New Testament is actually a completely new idea: it is simply placed in a new setting and given a transformed meaning. It is not just a patch-up, it is a root and branch reforming. Then comes the joy of the Resurrection when the flowers come out again and it is a beautiful sight.

6. Family tensions. A kind uncle decided to give young Fred his nephew a superb toy fire engine for his birthday. Fred was completely captivated by his new toy, did not bother to thank his uncle, and even supposed it had come through the post as some sort of freebie. He played with it, did not bother to read the instructions, manhandled it, thrashed it around, and when it did not work properly, hurled it across the room and cracked a window. Fred did not know what to do: would they be furious with him? His aunt came in and said, 'Why don't you come with me to your uncle and sort this out?' 'But he will take the fire engine off me,' sobbed Fred. But the kind uncle, when approached diplomatically, showed Fred how it could be mended and how to operate it with a certain amount of care. Fred came to the point where he was so trusting of his uncle that he hugged him with joy and thanked him from the bottom of his heart.

Life is like the fire engine: easily abused and smashed, and yet with proper guidance can be a wonderful thing to operate. It is a gift which involves gratitude. Also it needs the help of a go-between, someone who is related to God and mankind, to bring about healing to a failed relationship. Both the uncle and the nephew were upset, but with the right touch from the aunt, a new and deeper relationship emerged.

7. The dangerous dog. The master of the house had a mastiff who was an excellent guard dog but quite unpredictable. He was deceptively calm and friendly as long as the master was with him; the minute his back was turned, the dog was looking for trouble and would attack anyone. It was a problem delivering a message through the letter-box as Fido would object to that also. People tried to throw him off the scent but nothing was really effective. The master was concerned at all the people with injuries who were terrified to come to the door. He did not want to have Fido put down because he had his uses. In the end he decided to call in the vet and have the dog chained up and muzzled. The vet had some idea of how to deal with fierce animals, and after an almighty struggle, Fido was brought under control. The vet was badly bitten. Fido had a long chain so that he could roam about but people could, if they were careful, keep out of his way. A sign was put up advising people not to provoke the dog or try to remove his muzzle. Most sensible people heed this

advice but there is always some idiot who will come too close to the dog, or try, with the best of intentions, to remove his muzzle.

So evil has been brought under control, not finally destroyed as yet. It took the right person with enough courage, and who knew the task, to chain and muzzle the dog. The master is much easier to contact either by letter or just by tapping on the door. He (God) is always glad to have callers as long as they heed his advice not to provoke the dog and try to remove his muzzle. But there are always those who wish to undo the work of the Messiah.

8. The venomous snake. In the master's garden lived a frightful venomous snake. Normally he would keep out of sight but when he got hungry he would come out and find something to bite. Woe betide anyone lingering about at the wrong time of day. The master wondered what to do: the snake did a useful job in keeping the vermin down and he did not want to have him killed. He took advice. In the end a snake charmer came and mesmerised the snake, caught him by the neck and overpowered him. The vet came and removed his poison gland and rendered him harmless. Now, even if you are bitten, you do not have to die, although you might die of fright. That would be because you ignored the sign that said, 'The snake is harmless: do not fear him.' There is always someone who refuses to heed sound advice. They tap on the door and say, 'I'm dying, Mister, that snake of yours has just bitten me.' But the answer is, 'You only think you are dying. The snake is harmless: I had someone deal with him. Do not go into a panic.'

So too with the Atonement: Jesus at great risk got evil under control. Now Satan is only harmful to those who allow themselves to be tangled up with him. Death is not death any more: it is only a transition from this life to the next. God assures us that if we heed his words, there is no need to go into a panic; we just need to trust him and accept his help.

9. The magnetic mine. Early in the Second World War there were several ships sunk by some strange method: it was not a torpedo, but an explosion from under the ship which was powerful enough to cripple the ship and sink it. No one knew what it was. Then one day, a strange object was spotted in shallow water off the Kent coast. Ouvery of the Royal Navy approached the object, and at great risk to himself and his assistant, managed to dismantle it and render it safe. As suspected, it was a magnetic mine which would be triggered by a large metal object such as a ship passing close by.

Countermeasures were now sought. Ouvery got a medal for his daring and successful coup. But it was a scientist who devised a method of demagnetising the ship, called 'degaussing'. A girdle of electrically charged material was hoisted up and down the ships' hulls, all the way round, and this reduced the magnetic signature of the ship. Later it was realised that this cumbersome and labour-intensive method was not needed. A copper wire was installed round the inside of the ship's hull and an electric charge was passed through it, continuously. This was more effective, except that if one switched it off, one was liable to blow oneself up (as did actually happen). The final answer to the menace of the magnetic mine was to assemble the minesweepers and comb the seas for them and explode them.

The destructiveness of evil is always with us but it can be thwarted if we take note of what the experts tell us. Firstly, a brave man managed to unlock its secrets; we need to come to terms with evil, be realistic about it. The inevitability of temptation and the progressive ruination of our lives by evil has to be faced, but Jesus the Son of God came to elucidate this to us and put his own life on the line to take the fuse out of evil and give us a solution. The degaussing process is now available to us all if we would use it. Failing to use it is asking for trouble if we happen to encounter the lurking evil. The Holy Spirit is our safeguard but only if we allow him to do his work in our own personal lives. The final answer of course is to explode all the mines. But that is in the future, when, as the Messiah promised, he would come in glory to bring all things to a conclusion and finally defeat evil. The lesson is that although evil is still present in the world, we do not have to succumb to it. We can, with the help of the Holy Spirit, overcome it and triumph, but only because the Son of God himself laid down his life to defeat the menace in the first place.

10. Radio waves. A most helpful modern discovery has been that of radio waves. These can be of various qualities and frequencies. Back in the early twentieth century it was discovered that messages could be sent from one person to another at some distance. Also a transmitter like that at Alexandra Palace could send messages to radio sets all over the country and further afield. To send messages to somewhere like Australia which is not a direct line of transmission on the other side of the world is also possible, but it involves sending waves up to bounce off the ionosphere, down to ground level, and so on until the waves reach Australia. At the same time, paradoxically, the waves go off into space and do not bounce back, unless they

encounter some form of satellite (natural or artificial). The space explorers found that when they went behind the Moon, radio contact was lost: the waves will not go through a solid mass like a planet.

How does this relate to the Atonement? At the level of the moral theory, there is the direct fairly local contact between the historical Jesus and the human race. Not that everyone bothers to switch on their spiritual radio sets, and yet the transmission of God's love is always on the air. For the ransom theory, the radio waves go from the transmitter out into the entire universe as well as locally. There is a direct link of communication between the Eternal Father and humanity. Paradoxically, for the satisfaction theory, the line of contact is refracted off the ionosphere, which means that all parts of the world can receive the message: there is a reciprocal line between Father and Son perpetually. In a strange sort of way God is listening to his own programme all the time and knows what is going on at ground level with every living soul. There are certain areas where the radio waves will not reach: behind the Moon, deep inside a mountain, the bottom of the ocean. There is always someone who refuses to listen to the programme, or who finds that interference makes it very difficult to make out what is being said. But that accounts for atheism, agnosticism and all other attempts at ignoring what God is saying.

Can we take the metaphor a little further? The radio operator has to adjust the frequencies to contact people at various locations. Jesus is the one who communicates with us at varying levels. He is able to speak to every living soul; but that depends very much on whether one's radio set is switched on.

To push the analogy too far will spoil it. What is being said here is that God's outreach of love is on varying levels: the personal, the local, the intercontinental, the interplanetary and even the universal. The intervention of God by his Messiah was not just a local thing but was of cosmic significance, by which God, the unseen world of the spirit and the whole created world, were brought into a new relationship of trust and justification.

Notes

1. Yom Kippur, the Day of Atonement. *Kippur* means to 'cover over', 'pacify', 'make propitiation', 'a price for ransom'.

2. Aulen, *Christus Victor*.
3. Irenaeus, Bettenson, *Early Christian Fathers*, p. 109.
4. Tertullian, Bettenson, *Early Christian Fathers*, p. 177.
5. Origen, op. cit., p. 308.
6. Origen, op. cit.
7. Augustine, *Basil and the Gregories*.
8. Anselm, *Cur Deus Homo?*
9. Origen, op. cit., p. 310.
10. Wendel, *Calvin*, p. 226.
11. Wendel, op. cit., pp. 231ff.
12. Wendel, op. cit., p. 211.
13. T.H. Hughes, *The Atonement*, pp. 66ff.
14. Grensted, *The Atonement*, pp. 104ff.
15. Hughes, op. cit., pp. 200ff.
16. Baillie, *God was in Christ*, p. 200.
17. *Tetelestai* is a perfect passive full of meaning. The root 'telos' implies completion, an end achieved, fulfilment.
18. Baillie, op. cit., p. 194.
19. Wilson, *The Turin Shroud*.

10

Parable, Allegory, Literalism and Imagery

So far, I have referred to parable and allegory in a general way without much thought as to any analysis of them. It was the main way in which Jesus conveyed eternal truths to his hearers. Actual allegories are rather few: his main method is the use of parable, sometimes very short and at other times quite prolonged. But they are always challenging, disconcerting, and often contain difficult paradoxes. This sometimes renders them difficult to interpret and yet there is some sort of appeal to the human soul with a question that will not go away. Picture language of this type is not confined to the Judaeo-Christian tradition but it is an important aspect of understanding the workings of God without resorting to idolatry. The importance of avoiding idolatry is emphasised heavily in the Bible and it can clearly be seen as a reaction against the absurdity of god-manufacture in the ancient world. But idolatry goes deeper than that: it is a condition of the soul, in which one creates a god in one's own image. This becomes a corrupting influence: expecting God to conform to our expectations. It is even more relevant in today's world where other idolatries such as drugs, alcohol and obsessions of all kinds come to dominate people's lives to the exclusion of all else.

An interesting example of how an allegory can be embellished and brought to fulfilment by a great prophet comes with the Vineyard from Isaiah 5:1–7: 'Let me sing for my beloved a love song concerning his vineyard.' It all started well with the planter doing all he could to ensure a full crop of grapes. But the results were disappointing. So he decided to destroy it. Then we see the allegorical interpretation of it: the two kingdoms of Judah and Israel are the vineyard and they both failed to respond to God's requirements.

'And he looked for justice, and behold, bloodshed: for righteousness, and behold, a cry!' The message is very much in the mood of the eighth-century prophets and warns of the destruction of both kingdoms. It does not have any messianic overtones at this stage.

There are three expanded versions of this image in the Gospels, very largely the same except for a few details in the wording. The image of the vineyard is described in terms clearly evoking Isaiah but then it develops, in that God sends in his agents to collect the profits and each is maltreated. Eventually the beloved Son appears on the assumption that the husbandmen will respect him; but no, he is murdered on the strange assumption that the ownership will pass to the workers. But seen from the point of view of the fulfilment of the allegory, the Jewish leadership believed that they were the sons of God and the land of Israel was indeed their inheritance. But the expectation is that the owner will reappear and wreak vengeance and appoint new workmen.

The allegory is clearly directed at the Jewish authorities, as in the original, and they clearly know it is directed at them. St Luke has them saying, 'God forbid' (since that was the thing they most feared) and St Matthew has them saying 'he will destroy those miserable men', but then it backfires on them when they realise that they are the 'miserable men'.

There is no need to take every phrase in this story as exactly matching some aspect of the work of God in history, but the main gist of it is seen to have worked out perfectly as the scheme of salvation did materialise. It also raises the question of whose kingdom is it anyway: God's or man's? Jesus was able to show that through the rejection of the prophets and of the Messiah, the old regime will be destroyed and the ministry of God's servants will be extended to others and thrown open to all comers. Jesus' oft-repeated remark, 'the first will be last and the last first', a paradox underpinning many of his parables, is now specifically applied to himself: 'the stone which the builders rejected has become the head of the corner.' Moreover, the way this is quoted from Psalm 118:21–26 puts it in a specific context: that of the triumphal entry into Jerusalem, with the implication that he, Jesus, is the blessed one who enters in the name of the Lord. All three Gospels have this parable in the context of the triumphal entry. They all agree that from then the plot to eliminate him took a more decisive turn: it was not just because the authorities feared that the Romans would come and remove them, it was also because Jesus was indirectly claiming here to be the Messiah, the beloved Son, and they could not cope with that. St John provides the completion of this thought in 11:51: 'that Jesus should die for the nation, and not for the nation only, but to gather into one the children of God who are scattered abroad.'

God is capable of providing new people who are not a physical continuation of the Jewish race: he can raise up children for Abraham (Matthew 3:9). Just to imagine that one is a title-holder of God's kingdom because one was chosen in the past does not ensure that it is a permanent claim; there is a serious need for repentance while there is still time.

Taking the main gist and message of the allegory is what Jesus and the Gospel writers intended. There have been those who elaborated on it, saying that the 'tower' is the Temple, the 'hedge' would be the fence around the Law. This kind of approach, while intriguing, can so easily destroy the main thrust of the picture. Stretching the interpretation too far can become destructive and even derisory. It was a tendency seen in the patristic era, and St Augustine's treatment of the Good Samaritan is a prime example of it:

> A certain man went down from Jerusalem to Jericho: Adam himself is meant: Jerusalem is the heavenly city of peace: Jericho means the moon, ... our mortality ... thieves are the devil and his angels who stripped him ... of his mortality, beat him, persuading him to sin and left him half-dead ... in one sense he lives because he still knows God: in another sense he is dead because he is oppressed by sin.[1]

It continues in the same vein and later thinkers even elaborated on this overdone if not fanciful approach. It is unlikely that Jesus ever intended it to be taken in this way. The original intention is clearly stated: to point out the question, 'Who is my neighbour?' It is easy to forget the shock that this parable would have produced in the Jews of that time: a Jewish traveller attacked on a lonely road, one might have expected his co-religionists to have helped, but it was the hated Samaritan who gave an excess of assistance. This must have infuriated them as indeed many of the other teachings did. He was not just telling idle tales, he was stirring people up, forcing them to ask questions about themselves, pointing them to the realities of God's Kingdom.

Usually the point is not a complicated one. The parables usually try to make one point; sometimes two or more points are worked in, but the details are incidental. Most of the illustrations are parabolic, in that most of the details are not intended to carry some heavy interpretation. Occasionally he gives us an allegory, such as the Workmen in the Vineyard and the Sower, but even then, the interpretation does not need to be overdone. There are several ongoing themes in the parables and they cohere quite well as an array of pictures of the various aspects of God's intervention in this world, namely the Kingdom of God. They can be grouped together into various categories. It has been popular to discount some of them as 'secondary' (whatever that might mean) but it will be seen that they all cohere well into one consistent theme across the Synoptic Gospels, and connect well with St John, who works on a different dimension. Also various paradoxes can be discerned.

Ongoing themes in the parables

The Kingdom of God has arrived

1. The Gospels present us with a double-sided view of the coming of the Kingdom: in one sense it has actually arrived with the proclamation of John the Baptist; in another it is still imminent. This can be substantiated with various quotations: 'The Law and the Prophets were until John: from that time on the Kingdom of God is proclaimed and everyone forces his way into it,' Luke 16:16.

John the Baptist is the final prophet who draws a line in the sand of history: 'Repent for the Kingdom of Heaven is at hand'. From now on, it is the realm of the Gospel and the new dispensation. However it is not the spectacular situation that many would have expected: 'the Kingdom of God is not coming with signs to be observed: nor will they say, "Lo it is here" or "there", for behold the Kingdom of God is in the midst of you,' Luke 17:20.

In one sense it is working quietly if not secretly even though some people are aware of its arrival. St Mark brings this out with his theme of the hidden Messiah and the secrecy of the Kingdom; not that this is absent from the other Gospels, but it is not so heavily emphasised. Evil was being defeated now as an ongoing battle during his ministry, starting with the Temptations, and every time Satan is seen to be interfering with the process, and up to the Crucifixion. Jesus is almost certainly talking about himself when he says that the Kingdom is in the midst of you. He himself was actually doing God's work in bringing evil under control. But it was not an over-dramatised conflict at that time; that was to come later. Parables which work on this theme are as follows:

Mark 4:26–29, the Sower who waits and 'does not know'.
Mark 4:30, the Mustard Seed, virtually the same message.
Mark 4:21, the Lamp under the Bushel.
Luke 13:20, the Lump of leaven working away in the dough.
Matthew 13:44, the Treasure hidden in the field.
Luke 15:8, the Lost Coin.
Matthew 25:18, the Hidden Talent.

All these contain the expectation that whatever is hidden or secret will one day be revealed, usually to great rejoicing and fulfilment. 'Nothing is covered up that shall not be revealed, or hidden that will not be known. Whatever you said in the dark shall be heard in the light, and what you have whispered in private rooms shall be proclaimed upon the housetops,' Luke 12:2.

The Kingdom is yet to come

2. This leads on to the next paradoxical element, that the Kingdom is yet to come; the Kingdom of God is still imminent. Jesus understood himself to be the Son of Man, the heavenly being who would establish God's rule on earth, and yet that is still something for the future. 'Thy Kingdom come' speaks of a dramatic divine intervention in history, an apocalypse and the final defeat of evil. But in the meantime there is an interim period of waiting: who knows how long it will be? But it seems in the first instance to refer to the earthly ministry of Jesus. There are many parables that include this motif in one way or another. They begin with the master being known to his minions and leaving them with a task: he goes away with the implication that he will suddenly return to bring things to a conclusion. The interim period is important for preparation and expectation but not overexcitement. Seldom is this idea mentioned by theologians. It is Baillie[2] who remarks on the interim period, but sees it as the time that must elapse before the Second Coming and the end of history. No one sees this as a paradox: that in one sense the interim period is actually the earthly ministry of Jesus, but on the

other hand it is the period leading up to the Second Coming. Whichever way it is, there are many parables that demonstrate this motif:

Matthew 24:25, the Faithful Servant.
Matthew 25:1, the Ten Virgins with their Lamps.
Matthew 25:14, the Talents.
Mark 13:24, the Man going on a Journey.

It is never too late to accept the Kingdom

3. During this interim period, there is ample opportunity to accept God's invitation to repent and make a decision in favour of the Kingdom. Even if those who have made an early decision might murmur about what appears to be the unfairness of it, Jesus still accepts people up to the last minute. This is most clearly seen in the Labourers in the Vineyard (Matthew 20:1–6). The workmen come to join in the harvest at various times in the day and this is of no importance: they are all valued as responding to God's call. Often there is the backtaste of earlier workers expecting to have a preferential deal; possibly the Jewish authorities assuming they would have a superior deal; the elder brother complex. There are various parables which include this thought, also that the interim period will come to an end, which implies that there comes a point when it will be too late: God will not extend the offer for ever. In this we see another paradox: on the one hand God is ready to forgive and accept; on the other hand there is a sense in which one can delay repentance too long and then comes judgement. This has the effect of augmenting the urgency of accepting the Kingdom. Often there is the implication that God initiates the response: it is not just one's own bright idea to join the work. Other parables containing the same thought incidentally or as a main theme are as follows:

Luke 15:11, the Prodigal Son.
Matthew 25:1, the Ten Maidens: five left it too late.
Luke 13:6ff, the Fig Tree, given a reprieve.
Luke 11:5, the Friend at Midnight. Here the paradox is exposed: in one sense the friend arrives too late at night, but his friend gives in and helps him out. The general impression is that

God may at first seem intractable, but he is open to persuasion and sympathy.
Luke 13:23, the Householder who closes up: there comes a point when it is too late and the door is closed; even so the prophets and the Gentiles will be able to enter.
Luke 15:3ff, the Lost Sheep: there seems to be no time limit on this one, but the sheep does not come back on his own initiative; the shepherd goes out to find him.
Luke 20:9ff, the Tenants in the Vineyard: they had various opportunities to play straight with the owner but they left it too late and the whole situation caught up with them.
Matthew 20:1–16, the Labourers in the Vineyard.
Luke 6:1–7, the Unjust Steward.
Matthew 13:6, the Fruitless Fig Tree: it even hints at the three-year ministry of Jesus.
Luke 12:16ff, the Rich Fool.

It can be seen that sometimes the interim period followed by the divine intervention is not the main thrust of the parables. Even if the interim period is the second or third element in the picture, it still indicates that this was a major assumption in the mind of Jesus. During the interim period, good and evil appear to coexist, intermingled and intertwined in such a way as to make it unrealistic to try to root out evil piecemeal. But the final act of God's intervention brings about the rooting out of evil and preservation of the good. Parables on this line are as follows, mainly Matthew:

Matthew 13:24ff, the Wheat and the Tares.
Matthew 13:47ff, the Dragnet and the Fish.
Matthew 25:31ff, the Sheep and the Goats.

It can be noticed that the good and evil are not easy to discriminate by appearances: the wheat and the tares look much alike until harvest time; the sheep and the goats in Israel also strongly resemble each other. Only God knows the true difference.

The moment of separation and judgement

4. This concept, whether related to the inception of Jesus' ministry or the conclusion, speaks of the final rooting out of evil and a new age of innocence, back to the Garden of Eden. The motif of segregating the elect from the non-elect appears in many guises in the Gospels. Some of the parables talk of hellfire and damnation, especially in Matthew, the sort of thing that Calvin would enjoy quoting. But do we have to take this completely literally? It has to be balanced against the opposite thought coming in the section below. The main point in all these parables is that God intervenes and there is judgement. In an important sense the coming of Jesus brings about a division in mankind and this is seen in the way people react to him, either adoration or pure hate. It is a sad fact. This is why he said, 'Think not that I have come to bring peace on earth, but a sword . . . for I have come to set a man against his father,' (Matthew 10:34). Paradoxically the Prince of Peace brings in a sword. Parables on this line are as follows:

Matthew 24:40, Two Men in the field: two women grinding.
Luke 16:19ff, Dives and Lazarus.
Matthew 25:31ff, the Sheep and the Goats.
Matthew 25:14ff, the Talents.
Luke 19:11ff, the Pounds.

We notice in the Pounds a slightly different version of the Talents, not so heavily based on hellfire. Even so the motif of a separation at the judgement is important, but the Lord's enemies and backsliders are in trouble because of their own shortcomings and attitude. They asked for condemnation and the 'reward' they received. Sometimes the judgement is not the main point of the parable, and yet it is clear that Jesus had in mind a major judgement session. His feelings about judgement seem to be somewhat negative – 'Judge not that ye be not judged' (Matthew 7:1) – and he himself tried to avoid judging people, or condemning them. He is far more inclined to offer forgiveness, as seen in Matthew 18:21–35 which includes the parable of the Wicked Servant, the one who was forgiven but failed to forgive others.

Inclusion, acceptance and forgiveness

5. In contrast to the section above, Jesus draws all men to himself and redeems the whole world, not just some of it (John 12:22). This results in an important paradox, since in one sense people are all judged and separated and yet in another sense they are all included in salvation. There is no way that this can be explained away, but it is a good example of the theology of balance, the juxtaposition of being saved and lost. Jesus appeals to all people, influencing them even if they do not realise it. God is always looking out to receive anyone who has gone astray and comes back asking for acceptance. The opportunity for the Gentiles to be included in the Kingdom is clearly there. It seems that Jesus does not wish to reject anyone. This aspect of his teaching will be in favour nowadays, since we have integration, anti-racialism, democracy, and the blurring of extremes in all spheres of life, especially religion. Damnation is not a comfortable thought, and yet it still happens when people are rejected and discriminated against. Parables concerning inclusion, mainly from Luke, are as follows:

Luke 12:57, the Defendant.
Luke 14:16ff, the Great Banquet.
Luke 13:20ff, the Leaven in the Dough.
Luke 15:3ff, the Lost Sheep.
Luke 15:8ff, the Lost Coin.
Luke 15:11ff, the Prodigal Son.
Matthew 22:1–14, the Great Wedding Feast.

The dilemma between separation and inclusion is a problem which has haunted theologians up to the present day, and is one aspect of the clash which produces petty denominationalism in the Christian world. If we try to eliminate one strand in relation to the other, it emasculates both and the cutting edge of the Gospel is lost. There is mercy; there is also rejection. If this had been understood as a paradox, the answer to which lies in God's hands, not ours, it could have been major factor in Christian understanding and unity.

The secrecy of the growing Kingdom

6. This is most heavily emphasised in St Mark and fits in well with the concept of the interim period. This theme is important if only for the fact that Mark saw Jesus as reluctant to allow too much fame and excitement to precipitate an abortive messianic upsurge. At the raising of Jairus's daughter, Mark 7:43, 'he strictly charged them that no one should know this.' It was all a part of his humility and intention to serve and give his life. Jesus never boasts about his miraculous powers. Many of the miracles remain a mystery to virtually everybody. He is not prepared to be forced into becoming a king. At times he disappears off into lonely places to escape the crowd.

The fact that he spoke in parables itself shows that he was offering truths about the Kingdom in such a way that those who were predisposed to understand would receive his message. It is the inner circle of his followers who are given the interpretation and even then they do not really take in what he is saying: 'With many such parables he spoke the word to them as they were able to hear it. He didn't speak to them without a parable, but privately to his disciples he explained everything,' Mark 4:33.

Matthew also takes up the secrecy element, (12:15–21, quoting the Suffering Servant: 'Behold my servant ... I will pour out my spirit on him ... He will not wrangle or cry aloud, nor will any one hear his voice in the streets: he will not break a bruised reed or quench a smouldering wick, till he brings justice to victory.'

This ties in with Matthew 12:38. The Pharisees try to talk him into doing a miracle but he refuses and offers them the sign of the prophet Jonah. He was clearly talking about his death and Resurrection, including the three days in hell. Again this was a modest way of predicting the climax of his earthly ministry. But another aspect of it was that the call to repentance, which the men of Nineveh heeded, is being ignored now. These are the Pharisees who love to indulge in ostentatious religiosity and think they have the right relationship with God. But there is something vitally wrong with them: they cannot admit to their failings. 'He who has ears to hear' is directed at them and anyone else who fails to see the need for repentance. But the implication is that they could have accepted Jesus' message (as some did) and once again become the salt of the earth.

At this point the parable of the Salt is relevant (Mark 9:50). It is a puzzle as to how the salt can loose its saltiness: it can only be done if it is adulterated or diluted. But its saltiness can be recovered through crystallisation. Is Jesus saying that the Jewish faith was and still should be the 'salt of the earth' and could recover that tanginess if the Jews decided to repent and stop bickering amongst themselves? With that we see one of the most cryptic remarks he ever made.

The fame of the Kingdom

7. Juxtaposed with the secrecy is the awareness of the Kingdom. Paradoxically, in one sense the growing Kingdom is hidden and in another sense it has vast publicity. Jesus seems to attract vast crowds, a sort of magnetism only recently seen at the Billy Graham rallies in the last century. In a sense, Jesus is clearly identified at the Baptism, the Transfiguration and the events of Holy Week, and in various less crucial places. Even though the parables keep a certain degree of mystery and secrecy there are some that understand or at least find him irresistible. Parables which relate to this include Matthew 5:15, the Light on the Lampstand (see also Luke 11:33):

> You are the light of the world: a city set on a hill cannot be hid. Nor do men light a lamp and put it under a bushel, but on a stand and it gives light to all the house. Let your light so shine before men that they may see your good works and give glory to your Father who is in heaven.

Here we have the opposite to the light placed under a bushel. It is a good paradox: in one sense the Kingdom is hidden, but in another sense it is being acclaimed and all can see it. Jesus is critical of ostentatious hypocritical religion and yet wishes the true and solid values of love for God and mankind to be made plain to all. In the context of false messiahs, Matthew 24:27 says that the coming of the Son of Man will be as obvious and dramatic as the lightning. Think of a carcass: it is obvous where it is because of the scavengers circling overhead. The thought continues with the motif of the fig tree coming into blossom (Matthew 24:31), an unmistakable sign: 'You know that he is at the very gates.' Is this a cryptic reference to the triumphal entry?

He reaches out for the ultimate in highlighting of his ministry:

'Heaven and earth will pass away, but my words will not pass away.' How true! His words have echoed down the centuries and are still poignant, relevant, and challenging today. The only problem is that some of his cryptic remarks still confuse people and yet they still contain a power which appeals to something spiritual deep in the heart of mankind.

Another side to it is that the paradox takes another twist (Luke 10:21): 'I thank thee Father that thou hast hidden these things from the wise ... and revealed them to babes' (the disciples). In a sense they do understand what is happening with the coming of the Messiah; and yet they still do not understand the full significance of it even after he has explained it to them. This still applied after the Resurrection. It still applies to many to this day!

A new relationship of joy and salvation

8. Although Jesus seldom uses the term 'New Testament' as opposed to the Old, it is implied in many parables where a new start, a fresh approach is accompanied with celebration and a ceremony hinting at a messianic banquet. It is clear that some kind of amendment or repair of the old system is of no use: we all need to start afresh. Mark 2:15–21 shows the skins and the patched garment, a pair which show the futility of simply trying to adjust the old regime. These two parables are in the general context (2:15–22) of a meal at which he hints at himself being the bridegroom. This metaphor is often used to describe himself in relation to Israel whom he has come to claim as his own. Jesus breaks through the strict exactitudes of Jewish legalism and engenders an atmosphere of rejoicing. Parables on this line are:

Matthew 15:1, the Ten Maidens with Lamps.
Luke 25:1, the Master coming home from the Wedding Feast.
Matthew 22:1, the Marriage Feast.

A wedding feast is planned but the guests make all manner of excuses. In the end all manner of people are invited. With this we see the failure of the Jewish authorities to respond to God's call: now it is open for the Gentiles to take their place. Sadly one guest failed to come in his best suit and was ejected. In this we see the motif of inclusion and rejoicing at the new relationship; also there is separation. The important message at the end is 'for many are called but few are chosen', which in itself is a paradox, but one which Jesus often uses to conclude his parables.

The same thought but slightly differently worded, 'the first will be last and the last first', shows the reversal of the old order. It applies especially to those who thought that they had the ideal relationship with God, all legal and correct in every detail. But Jesus points out that the rotters, the scum, the rejects and the swindlers will be at the forefront in this new Kingdom. The parable of the Pharisee and the Publican (Luke 18:9ff), the self-congratulatory attitude of the super-righteous compared with the despair of the man who has sunk to the bottom, sums up the difference. All need to repent, even if they think they are so virtuous. Mark 2:17 sums it up: 'Those who are well have no need of a doctor, but those who are sick,' and in this there is a certain touch of sarcasm. Luke 13:29 has a slightly ameliorated version, showing that Jesus could be quite categorical and given to exaggeration at times, but not always. 'Some who are first will be last: and some who are last will be first.' The paradox is the same as above; it also involves the issue of works versus faith as discussed in an earlier chapter.

The issue of wealth versus poverty

9. This motif appears often in the Gospels but this does not mean that Jesus has to be a fully qualified socialist. St Luke actually might have been, since he makes the cause of the underprivileged a major theme in his Gospel. Luke 1:51ff sets the tone for the whole ministry: 'He has scattered the proud in the imagination of their hearts: he has put down the mighty from their thrones and exalted those of low degree: he has filled the hungry with good things and the rich he has sent empty away.'

With this we see the double-sided aspect of wealth and poverty, for wealth is not just a material condition, it also involves a spiritual side; so too with poverty. If we compare two remarks from the two great sermons, Matthew 5:3 has, 'Blessed are the poor in spirit for theirs is the Kingdom of Heaven,' but Luke 6:20 has, 'Blessed are you poor, for yours is the Kingdom of God.' There is no need to say that one is inaccurate; both are true in their own way, they both reflect the double-sided nature of wealth and poverty. There is no reason why Jesus could not have said both sayings as complementary to one another. So often in the parables there is a reversal of the situation, something seen in Isaiah, and this ties in with the reversal of Old and New Testamental configuration. The parable of Dives and Lazarus (Luke 16:19) is a prime example of this, even though the main thrust is that people will not take his words on board even if someone came back from the dead to warn them: they are so obstinate. Luke 21:1ff speaks of the Widow's Mite being worth more than all the heavy spondulicks of the rich. Another widow (Luke 18:1ff) appears in the Unjust Judge, and she managed to receive a favourable decision because she kept on trying. Poverty is not the main theme in this parable, but the impression of sympathy for the poor is present. It also hints at poverty not just being a material issue: it is concerned with faithfulness in prayer and expectation of God's merciful intervention.

Jesus has a lot to say about 'treasure'; it is not always an accumulation of money. Luke 6:45 speaks of good and bad treasure: 'The good man out of the good treasure of his heart produces good, and the evil man out of his evil treasure produces evil. For out of the abundance of his heart his mouth speaks.'

On the one hand, Jesus advises people to give their money away (Luke 12:33) so that there will be treasures awaiting them in heaven. He goes further and says that there will be rewards waiting not just in the next life but in this life also (Luke 18:30): 'There is no man who has left house . . . for the sake of the Kingdom . . . who will not receive manifold more in this time, and in the age to come eternal life.'

The parable of the Talents has to be juxtaposed with this. Matthew 25:14ff is not a charter for capitalistic greed; it refers to deeper matters. The servants who gained money are given more, and the one who wasted money has it taken off him. There is a sense in which the rich get richer and the poor get poorer. It is another aspect of the parable of the Sower, Matthew 13:12: 'For to him who has will more be given . . . but from him who has not, even what he has will be taken away.' This sounds illogical until we realise that it is not just talking about material wealth: it is one's attitude towards the call of God and the effort put in for the Kingdom. In this we see another paradox: on the one hand we need to be rich towards God and receive his treasures; on the other hand we need to show humility and real repentance – we are all beggars in God's sight.

10. Making the crucial decision and adhering to it. There is one parable, the Unjust Steward in Luke 16:1–7, which stands out as probably the most difficult of Jesus' parables. At the very least, it is not necessary to take it as an encouragement to dishonesty; this in itself should warn us not to take the story purely at face value. That is true for many of his other parables. This parable is making more than one point, in fact most of our themes are worked in one way or another. The very inconsistencies in the story suggest that the underlying meaning is not meant to be easy to discover. Verses 10–14 have been seen as varying attempts at drawing out the meaning in later times, not always succeeding. It is more profitable to say that Jesus himself added these words, and that they illustrate the discrepancy between human and divine logic. Being such a difficult one, it testifies to the honesty of St Luke in including it in his Gospel (unlike the others!). With various themes already outlined in the earlier part of this chapter, it is easier to discern some of the possibilities contained in the story.

Questions raised are: why did the rich man not dismiss the steward on the spot, rather than letting him continue at the risk of committing more fraud? Was he being given a chance to repent? Again we see the 'interim period': he was being given a chance to make a crucial decision. The rich man appears at the start and at the end but the moment of truth has to come sometime.

Another question: how did the steward think he would succeed in his clever dealings when the rich man would certainly discover what had been happening? To our amazement, the steward is congratulated for his prudence! Is that logical? Not by human canons of rationality. Here is a case where human and divine logic are at complete variance. The discrepancy between the two versions of logic actually surface in the next verse, 'for the sons of this world are wiser in their own generation than the sons of light' (see Luke 16:15). As St Paul points out, the believer does appear foolish by comparison with the wisdom of this world.

At least the steward had the courage and clear-sightedness to make a decision and adhere to it. This may be the basic message of the parable: make your mind up. Here we have the moment of truth when men are segregated. The difference here is that he segregated himself, albeit for the old regime, but at least he would have the old regime to work with. Making up one's mind and staying with it again surfaces in verse 13: 'no servant can serve two masters ... you cannot serve God and mammon.' Here the old system of works righteousness is associated with greed and ostentatious religion. This ties in with Luke 16:14 where the Pharisees are seen as 'lovers of money' and their outward show of religiosity was well known. But this was the Old Testament taken to its logical conclusion: by works and empty legalism. It is interesting how this is associated with financial greed. Beneath it all are God's values which are totally opposite to those of humanity, 'for what is exalted among men is an abomination in the sight of God'. One has to make a decision for one or the other: there is no sort of happy average between the Kingdom of God and the kingdom of this world. That explains why Jesus told the rich young man to give up everything, make a clean break (Matthew 19:22).

But to opt for the old system, like the steward, there is something positive waiting. We are assured that there is a reward for that sort of religion (Matthew 6:16): 'truly I say to you they have their reward.' But the eternal habitations awaiting them will be somewhat different from what is the true heavenly treasure for those who genuinely love God.

The next difficult piece is in verses 10–12: this can be seen as an example of Hebrew parallelism which is a feature of Hebrew poetry and may indicate it is original to Jesus, just as parts of the Sermon on the Mount are so regarded.

'He who is faithful in a very little is faithful also in much.' Very true.

'He who is dishonest in a very little is dishonest also in much.' That follows.

'If you have not been faithful in the unrighteous mammon, who will entrust you with the true riches?' (What does it mean by 'true riches'?)

'If you have not been faithful in that which is another's, who will give you that which is your own?' This sounds rather strange: 'that which is your own' ought to be yours in any case.

The last two lines need to be read together, and explain each other. The true riches are the heavenly wealth, which would be 'your own' if you had taken that option. But the steward had opted for earthly gain and greed which all too often does involve sharp practice. The contrast between seeking heavenly treasure and earthly spondulicks is sharply drawn here, and the implication is to make one's mind up, as seen in verse 13. Matthew would say that the true treasure is what one lays up in heaven where one's heart is truly fixed (6:20). Interestingly enough that comes in the context of dishonesty where thieves are likely to steal one's earthly treasure, and also just before the hypocrisy of ostentatious religion is discussed, and that God in secret will provide a reward. Here the secrecy aspect reappears. But the main message is for one to make a decision between God and mammon and stay with it: there is no compromise.

This parable stands out as one of the most profound and multi-faceted ones that Jesus offered. On the face of it, it seems illogical, and that explains why the Pharisees in verse 14 sneered at him, assuming him to be deranged. But the parable involves virtually all ingredients of his parabolic message, as seen earlier. It is not easy to expound because it has a depth and eternal feel to it which is in contrast to all earthly values and common sense. It brings out the paradox of God's logic being other than human; also that the two covenants work on two levels, and yet there are rewards awaiting those who follow either system, but not something in between in a sort of compromise. The paradox of the interim period is also there.

Parables allied to this one come in Luke 14:28, Building a Tower and a King going off to War. In each case it is shown that the cost involved, the commitment and the advisability of backing off are important. The new Kingdom requires a complete commitment and firm decision, not some sort of half-measure. Then comes the toughest remark of all: 'whoever does not renounce all that he has, cannot be my disciple.' Categorical, exaggerated, soul-searching. Too many people have tried to take this totally at face value with disastrous results. There is a sense in which the true disciple lives in two worlds at once: he has to cope with all the normal things in life, and yet he has the distinct feeling that he owns nothing and that God will provide. It is a difficult balancing act, leading to another paradox: we are citizens of two worlds at once and yet we have to make up our minds which world we really belong to. Moreover if we take the parables totally at face value and literally, we engender all manner of problems.

Another parable allied to this is Luke 11:22, the Strong Man in his Palace. This time it is not God who is the principal actor but the Devil. He is defeated by a stronger man invading, who appropriates all his assets. This is not meant as an encouragement to midnight marauding; it tells of Christ overcoming evil and people having to make their minds up which side they are on. A telling remark is, 'he who is not with me is against me': either one belongs to the Kingdom of God or one does not. Paradoxically, 'He who is not against us is with us', but that appears in a different context.

Another parable, Matthew 21:18ff, the Two Sons and the Vineyard, raises the question of making a decision and implementing it. This time it is directed at the chief priests and elders, as opposed to the Pharisees. Again it reminds us of the first becoming the last and vice versa. Sinners will be accepted in the Kingdom sooner than the super-righteous. And this is another paradox when we consider the Unjust Steward.

Summary

To summarise this treatment of the parables, usually the main message or theme of each parable is given at the end or possibly the beginning. Some of them are multifaceted and others relatively simple. There are several ongoing recurring themes which appear often, not always as the main thought, but when the full array of parables is considered it becomes increasingly clear what Jesus was trying to say. They are full of paradoxes; to the casual reader they come up as contradictions. There is plenty there for the doubter to conclude that Jesus was deranged, as indeed his detractors did at the time. But still there is a quality of fascination, depth and eternal significance about them, not seen in lesser story-telling. The difference will be seen as we consider the Apocryphal Gospels and the Jataka tales.

The use and misuse of parable in sub-New Testament times

An early but recently discovered corpus of literature is the so-called Gospel of Thomas. It contains 114 sayings, some of which have either been lost from the tradition of the Apostolic Church, or invented by 'Thomas'. To call it a 'gospel' is a misnomer since it has no Passion narrative. This alerts us to the possibility that this is a Gnostic work, and indeed many of the sayings appear to have some kind of Gnostic influence.

Known and unknown sayings of Jesus are often interwoven (89:12–23):[3] 'Jesus said: it is impossible for a man to mount two horses and stretch two bows.' This continues with the wineskins and the patched garment: 'no one drinks old wine and then desires new wine ... an old patch is not put on a new garment.' Even if the wording is slightly altered we still have the importance of making a decision and staying with it; so too the difference between the Old and New Testaments.

Thomas gives another version of the Dragnet, cleverly altered to suit a Gnostic frame of thought (81:28ff): 'Man is like a wise fisherman who cast his net ... it was full of little fishes. Among them was found a good large fish. All the little fish were cast back into the sea.' Gone is the notion of 'fish of all kinds, good and bad', which would not suit the Gnostic view, which is that only Gnostics are selected by Jesus, or that Gnostics select Christ. Gone is the catholicity of acceptance of many different kinds of people: the motif of judgement is weakened if the vast majority of people are rejected just because they have not got that special insight.

A deeply obscure parable, probably pleasing to the Gnostics (81:23ff): 'Blessed is the lion which man will eat, that the lion will become a man. And cursed is the man whom the lion will eat, that the lion will become a man.'

As there is no parallel to this in the canonical gospels, and no tradition of interpretation to go with it, we can only guess at its meaning. The lion may be symbolic of many things but Jesus as the 'lion of Judah' comes to mind: he is also termed 'the lion' in Revelation. He is the bread of life which men do eat. Jesus did become a man in the Incarnation, but if a man gets it wrong with Jesus, there is rejection. The Gnostics did not value the flesh, which helps to explain why there is no mention of the Last Supper and eating 'his flesh'. It is possible that 'Thomas' has preserved this saying which he thought would favour a Gnostic interpretation, but actually was never meant in that way at all. How this relates to the criteria already seen is a good question.

More familiar is 87:10–18, with one slightly unfamiliar element: 'What you hear in your ear preach to another upon your roofs. For no one lights a lamp and puts it under a bushel.' It is a combination of elements from Matthew, Mark and Luke, and the fame of the Kingdom is clearly shown here. That the Kingdom of God has come is seen in Thomas, but the interim period somehow does not receive a mention.

87:27ff gives a teaching not known in the Gospels: 'The disciples said, 'On what day will you appear to us?' Jesus said: 'When you undress yourselves and are not ashamed. Take off your clothing ... like little children.' This seems contrary to Jewish feelings about modesty: it is rather a Gnostic idea that the body needs to be stripped away, leaving just the soul. The body is a garment of shame. Thomas would say the Kingdom has arrived but has not been recognised. This is slightly different from what we see in the Gospels. Another approach to this is that nakedness reminds us of Adam and Eve: Jesus could be saying in effect, 'when you return to pure innocence like little children who play around naked, then the Kingdom will return, as in the Garden of Eden.'

Another very obscure parable at 91:9ff is not known from anywhere else: 'A Samaritan bringing a lamb as he entered Judea. In order to kill and eat it ... as long as it lives he will not eat it but only if he kills it and it becomes a corpse.' This has overtones of the 'Lamb of God' and the Eucharist, and the inauguration of the New Testament which can only happen if Jesus dies (Hebrews). If so, this speaks of the end of the interim period and the final moment of truth. Thomas however seems as much confused by this parable as everyone else.

Not quite so obscure is this parable (97:7–15): 'the Kingdom ... is like a woman who carries a vessel full of meal and goes a long way. The handle of the vessel broke and the meal flowed out behind her on the way ... she did not notice it.' Grant and Freedman cannot decipher this motif; even so we can see the idea of the Kingdom growing in secrecy, with certain people realising what is happening, and then at the end she realises it herself. There is a certain allusion to the interim period here.

Concerning making a decision and assessing one's capability of coping with it, is 97:15, the Murderer: 'The Kingdom ... is like a man who wanted to kill another great man. He drew his sword in his house and ran it through the wall in order to know whether his hand was strong enough: then he killed the strong man.' There is the element of commitment in this: also the need to assess one's capability of coping with the commitment.

The Parable of the Lost Sheep has a subtle alteration made (92:22ff). The lost sheep is the 'largest' one, like the big fish. He says to the one he recovers, 'I love you more than the ninety-nine.' The largest one is the Gnostic who is prized for his inner knowledge, thus missing the point about inclusion.

A saying which recurs in Thomas and other writings (94:22–28): 'Jesus said, 'I am the light which is over everything. I am the All: the All has gone forth and to me the All has returned. Split the wood: I am there. Lift the stone, and you will find me there.' Here we see a contrast between the obvious Messiah and the secret Messiah. This has clear Gnostic thought, possibly related to Buddhism (the All); also there is a touch of pantheism, if God can be found concealed in natural things like stone and wood. The secrecy-publicity strand is present here, but not in the same way as in the Gospels.

Another parable which did relate to secrecy and the importance of making a commitment to it, the Treasure in the Field, receives rather a strange treatment (98:31ff): 'The Kingdom is like a man who has in his field a treasure which is hidden, of which he knows nothing ... and sold it ... A buyer came, ploughed it and found the treasure ... he began to lend money at interest,' with a view to buying the field.

The story is more verbose, rambling, and the point is not clear. In Matthew 13:44 we do see the point: the secrecy of the Kingdom and the need to know its value and go all out to get it. It is thought that this idea was a current popular tale since it occurs in Aesop, the Talmud and the Jataka tales. Jesus often took an idea and adapted it to his own purposes. In Thomas however we often see slight modifications or misunderstandings of Jesus, which can be explained as the Gnostic mentality at work in the background. The main themes in the genuine parables of Jesus are not completely lost but are blunted and obscured by someone who appears not to have understood them properly or perhaps heard a garbled version of them.

The Epistle of the Apostles

Not all such literature bends the message of Jesus to favour a heresy: the Epistle of the Apostles (AD 160?) verse 43, uses the Parable of the Ten Virgins quite faithfully, but at length expounds it as an allegory: 'The five wise are Faith, Love, Grace, Peace and Hope. And the five foolish are Knowledge, Understanding, Obedience, Patience and Compassion.'[4] And it seems strange that they would be excluded. The message here is more hard and fast: those excluded will stay out to be devoured by wolves. 'By five shall men enter the Kingdom: by five shall men remain without.' There is the tendency to allegorise every detail; also to take it more at face value, an intention that Jesus may not even have thought about.

The Book of John the Evangelist (very late) has John asking Jesus all manner of questions: the second one could be an attempt at coping with Theodicy by using the parable of the Unjust Steward. The fall of Satan is described in speculative terms, in such a way as to lift the 'successful swindle' into cosmic terms: 'Satan said to the angel, "How much owest thou thy Lord": "A hundred measures of wheat" ... "take pen and ink and write sixty."'

Having seduced various angels, a voice came, 'What doest thou, O denier of the Father?' and the angels are stripped of their clothing and crowns and lose their stewardship of the heavens. Here we see a subtle alteration in the story which amounts to lifting guilt away from humanity and making sin a cosmic problem.[5] The multifaceted nature of the original parable is lost, probably never understood in the first place.

The Acts of John contain an interesting usage of the parable of Dives and Lazarus (Luke 16:19ff). The Lukan text is quite faithfully followed without an attempt at a fanciful interpretation: instead, a basic face-value interpretation frames the whole image: 'Be rich for the time that ye may be beggars for ever.' God has made 'a conflict for souls, that they may believe that they have eternal riches, who ... have refused temporal wealth.'[6]

The hint here is that being poor on purpose will engender wealth in heaven, and the opposite. This is not quite what Jesus said. The motif of separation and making a decision in good time is not lost, however, thus according well with the original intention of Jesus; also the issue of wealth versus poverty. The tail piece of the parable in John is about making people believe. A dead young man is brought in and is brought back to life 'and confirmed all his words'. This is more like the opposite to the intention of Jesus who said that no sign would be given to convince those who lacked faith. 'A conflict for souls' is interesting: are we seeing a rudimentary awareness of paradox, even though the word itself is not yet being used?

The Gospel of St John in relation to the parables

It has often been noted that St John does not use parables: his preferred method is to use certain selected miracles which serve the same purpose, as signs or indications of the Kingdom and the glory of the Messiah.

In John 2:1–11, the Marriage at Cana, the water is changed into wine. This is redolent of so many aspects of the new faith, the Eucharist and also many parables. The bridegroom enquires why the best wine has been kept to the end; the inference is that the New Testament (unexpectedly) comes in after the Old and is of a completely different quality. Also the wedding feast mirrors the coming of the new relationship with joy. The new wine emerges from the existing Jewish rites of purification (works righteousness) but no one knows how it comes about. The servants do know: they are the 'babes' in the parables, but they know the deeper truth. We even have a hint at the interim period: 'my hour has not yet come'. This is not to say that the account is purely made up to support the parables, but the miracle underscores the miracle of the transformation of the Old to the New, which so many find beyond their comprehension.

John 6:1–15, the Feeding of the Five Thousand, is clearly linked to the Passover, the occasion when the old covenant was inaugurated: now a new one is coming in as Jesus gives thanks, in an embryonic eucharist. Although no mention of the new covenant is made, the implication is there, that Jesus gives the true life from heaven: this is developed later with 'I am the bread of life'. The manna in the wilderness is mentioned. The contrast between the public and the secret life of messiahship is seen when the people realise he is a prophet and decide to make him a king; with that he disappears to the hills by himself. Also there is the open-ended acceptance of all people: a vast crowd is fed with plenty left over for more. The new dispensation is generous, non-discriminatory and catholic. The development of this goes on into chapter 7 where again a Jewish feast, that of Tabernacles, is the background. No miracle is cited but the secrecy versus the publicity issue is discussed in full. His brothers want him to work openly; he wants to keep things in reserve, and yet, paradoxically, he appears in the Temple and speaks openly. Also there is another hint at the interim period, 'for my time has not yet fully come' (v. 8).

In John 9:1–12, the healing of the blind man, at the start the contrast between the old regime of guilt and punishment emerges with 'who sinned, this man or his parents?' This takes us back to Job and brings in Theodicy too. But Jesus (like Elihu) lifts the whole thing on to an entirely new level: 'that the works of God might be manifest in him.' It is now a positive matter, unlike most people's thoughts on Theodicy, which are of a negative tone. It is an opportunity for the light of the world to shine forth. This reminds us of those parables where in one sense the light is under a bushel and yet paradoxically it is stuck on a lampstand. An oblique reference to the interim period emerges: 'we must work the works of God while it is day ... as long as I am in the world.' The Pharisees cannot understand what has happened, and take offence at it being done on a Sabbath, like many of John's miracles. Are we seeing an interpretation of the Sabbath as the interim period 'while the master is away' as the Synoptics would have put it? And yet, paradoxically, the Master has appeared to find the 'tenants' not prepared to cooperate at all and rejecting and resisting everything he tries to show them. It would be unfair to say that all of them should be condemned: there was a division amongst the Jews (v. 16). Here the separation referred to in the Synoptics is not so much a dramatic Judgement Day situation as with the sheep and the goats. Rather they divide themselves, but the rift between them is every bit as real.

In John 11:17–44, the raising of Lazarus, there is less of the secrecy and more of the light and glory of God emphasised in the miracle: 'Did I not tell you that if you would believe you would see the glory of God?' (v. 40). The background of this is the Jews weeping and finding fault with Jesus. There is no festival mentioned in relation to this miracle, and yet in a way, because it evokes sorrow and fault-finding, it does evoke the Day of Atonement and the general mood of guilt and negative feeling associated with the Old Testament in its 'works righteous' mode. The Jews simply do not understand the new life of freedom, Resurrection and forgiveness that is coming into the world. Many who saw the miracle did believe; here we see the separation again. The interim period also appears: 'are there not twelve hours in the day?' Crucially it was the raising of Lazarus that precipitated the rulers into a final desperate plot to eliminate Jesus. This is where the 'tenants' decide to kill the beloved Son, but they do not realise that in so doing it will stimulate the owner into the drastic remedy of removing them and inviting in all manner of other people.

It is Caiaphas who correctly and inadvertently prophesied that one man would have to die for the people, 'that the whole nation should not perish ... and not for the nation only, but to gather into one the children of God who are scattered abroad.' Also John works up the imminence of God's intervention as the approaching crisis develops: the Jewish authorities become increasingly frantic while Jesus waits for the right moment and the right situation to allow himself to be taken. The old wineskins and the patched garment turn out to be deep truism: Judaism cannot just be adapted with a judicious piece of alteration; a new and radical start is needed.

In John 4:46 to 5:18 are two healings, the official's son and the paralytic by the pool of Bethesda. The two miracles juxtaposed here are both associated with unspecified Jewish festivals. The 'seventh hour' is matched with the seventh day. The messianic feast, often seen in the parables, now receives a new dimension for the feasts of the Jews become the feasts of new health and life. The contrast between the important man with servants and the lone beggar by the pool does not escape us: this is a rare occasion in which the issue of wealth versus poverty occurs in John; it is widely seen in the Synoptics. The new regime is for all, not just the 'rich' or the 'poor', whichever understanding of this is taken. The legalists become entangled over arguments over the Sabbath; but we have the hint that the Sabbath is actually the interim period in which God is active in this world.

Virtually every aspect of the message of the parables can be found in St John, often quite heavily emphasised. It is principally found in the miracles, but not exclusively, for many of the long discourses include these matters. This does not have to imply that St John's Gospel has to have been written after the Synoptics: it simply works on a different level. It would be easy to say that John is concerned with the private and inner side of Christ's ministry; the Synoptics with the obvious and public side. This is a hopeless over-simplification: they both know of the private and public side of the ministry, but describe it in different terms.

It is unfortunate for us now, with our experience of the Holocaust fresh in our minds, that John is quite free with his criticism of the 'Jews'. It may be that he did not mean it literally in the sense of every member of the Jewish nation. After all, Jesus himself and the primitive Church were nearly all Jewish. Taking a liberty, it might be helpful to rephrase 'the Jews' as the 'strict legalists of the Old

Testament'. Those who have the works righteous strict legalism as their religion are not confined to Judaism: they are to be found in virtually every religious and political system in the world, even in some versions of Christianity. But St John, if asked, would not have wanted to issue blanket condemnation: he would rather be positive and say that those who did understand the message of the New Testament were to be gathered into God's presence in love and acceptance. 'But to all who received him, who believed in his name, he gave power to become the children of God,' (1:12).

The use of parable in the Shepherd of Hermas

This fascinating work is believed to be a second-century book written by Hermas the brother of Pius, bishop of Rome. For many it was regarded as scriptural, only being rejected from canonical status in the fourth century; it was a strong contender for acceptance. It is relevant here because it includes various parables of differing quality, not claimed to stem from Jesus but from an angel, the 'shepherd' who spoke to Hermas. There are ten parables, or similitudes, some of which might not qualify as parables at all. A selection will suffice for comparison with the canonical Gospels.[7]

The Vine and the Elm Tree, Hermas 51:1–10.

The relationship between the elm and the vine appears to be a new idea. The elm tree does not bear fruit itself, but the vine climbing up the elm does bear fruit. Without support from the elm, the grapes would lie on the ground and rot. So there is a constructive and positive relationship between the two trees. The angel then turns it into an allegory, concerning the slaves of God, the rich and the poor. Here we see a positive cooperation between the rich and the poor: gone is the chasm between them as with Dives and Lazarus. However, the realisation that wealth and poverty are not purely and simply material matters, they are also a spiritual condition, is important:

> The rich person has money but is poor towards the Lord ... so when the rich man depends upon the poor man and supplies

> him with what he needs ... helping the poor man he will find his recompense before God. The poor man is rich in his petition ... and so both accomplish their work (Hermas 51:5).

In this we see a more positive and constructive approach to the issue of wealth and poverty. Rather than just issuing a blank condemnation of wealth, Hermas is saying that both states have their part to play and can interrelate constructively. There is also a sense of fulfilment or completion in verse 8: 'The poor who pray to the Lord on behalf of the rich bring their own wealth to completion: and the rich who supply the poor with what they need bring their own souls to completion.'

The Trees in Winter: also in spring, Hermas 52 and 53

Many trees appeared withered: the living and the dead could not be distinguished (53:3): 'just as the trees that shed their leaves in winter all look alike, with the withered indistinguishable from the living, so too in this age it is not clear who the upright are and who the sinners, but they all appear alike.'

This is the perennial question for Christians: how do we tell the difference between the genuine believer and the imposter? This recalls the New Testament parables such as the Wheat and the Tares, and the Sheep and the Goats (recalling that sheep and goats in Israel look very much alike). The answer is that we have to wait for the spring, the new age, to see the difference as the living trees come into bud but the dead trees do not. Hermas 53:3: 'just as the fruits of each individual tree appear in the summer ... so too the fruits of the upright will appear ... in that age they will be blossoming.'

Firstly, this contains the expectation of a new age, an apocalypse, although the interim age is now of much less relevance. The early Church did stand in great expectation of the return of Jesus, and the righting of all wrongs. Also the parable in a way expands on Jesus' dictum, 'by their fruits you shall know them'. In other words, the genuine Christians will be doing something worthwhile as opposed to just talking about it. There is also the element (unstated) of the secrecy of the Kingdom: in the 'winter' the people of God are not easily distinguished, but when the 'spring' comes, the Kingdom becomes much more obvious.

The parable about Fasting, Hermas 55:1 to 58:5

This parable, much closer to an allegory, is more obviously related to New Testament thinking. A master plants a vineyard and leaves a chosen slave in charge to build a fence, with the promise of him gaining his freedom on the master's return. The slave did the work and much more besides, clearing weeds and digging it over. On his return, the master was delighted, and called his beloved son and heir and upgraded the slave to the status of joint heir; the son approved of this. Later the master gave a dinner and sent the slave some food. He gave some away to his fellow slaves; now he was in even greater favour. In case one should wonder how this relates to fasting, the angel explains: fasting is not simply about denial of food. It is about putting in the effort to help people and be of service. See verse 8: 'If you complete your fast like this ... your sacrifice will be acceptable before God ... and will be recorded.'

In 58:1–5 the full allegory is played out. The fence posts are the angels who surround God's people; the weeds are the lawless deeds of the slaves of God; the food sent from the dinner are the commandments; the field is this world. In case one might think that the good slave is the Gentiles who gained favour and the son and heir is the Jewish people: not so. They are not really mentioned in Hermas. The Son is the Holy Spirit and the slave is the Son of God, Jesus. In this we see a clever rearrangement of the vineyard metaphor, even if there is a hint of adoptionism with regard to Jesus. The interim period is there, though not seen as the earthly ministry of Jesus. The idea of Jesus being a slave clearly grates on Hermas (v. 5) but the angel cleverly works his way round this (59:7):

> Thus he took his Son and the angels ... served blamelessly as the Spirit's slave ... and not appear to have lost the reward for serving as a slave. For all flesh in which the Holy Spirit has dwelled: and which has been found undefiled and spotless ... will receive a reward.

This is evidence that Hermas was not influenced by Gnosticism since the flesh is capable of being pure and redeemable (60:1): 'Guard this flesh and ... to keep it clean and undefiled ... your flesh may be made upright.'

But the main lesson from the parable remains that the Son of God was appointed to tend the people of God; he not only did the basic work but did much more besides and showed compassion on his fellow workers. The Master (God) was delighted with his work and attitude and gave him the ultimate promotion, that of being accepted as 'family'. It would be unfair to see Hermas as a full-blown adoptionist, but of course it could be taken that way. In this we see a parable using New Testament metaphors but using a slightly modified interpretation.

The Shepherd of Hermas stands as a remarkably sane, almost demythologised apocalyptic work of the sub-Apostolic age. It reminds one of the style of Ezekiel or Jeremiah, or even of the style of the wisdom literature of the Old Testament. It can be termed as 'proto-orthodox' and was only rejected for the New Testament canon because it was clearly not written by one of the original apostles.

The Jataka tales

These fascinating stories[8] stem from the pre-history of Buddhism and are closely associated with the ministry of Siddhartha himself. This kind of story is not exactly a parable or an allegory, but more akin to a 'Just-So' story. Their influence has been widespread, having worked their way into literature such as Aesop, Boccaccio, Chaucer and La Fontaine. Sometimes it is in a modified form: occasionally more obviously as having been borrowed. The case of the Pearl of Great Price is a case in point: this may indicate that Jesus had heard some of these stories.

On one level they make lovely children's bedtime reading; on another level they are tied up with the Birth Stories of the Buddha. Buddhists see them as relating to Siddhartha in his previous existences: the main character is usually the Buddha, though not necessarily always. Strangely there is no mention of Karma or reincarnation. Many of the stories appear to have no clear theological content, just a simple moral, usually implied and occasionally stated clearly. As a corpus of literature they are roughly analogous to the parables of Jesus. Even so, the mentality and assumptions are markedly different. Their authorship is lost in the mists of time; even so Siddhartha made extensive use of them in his preaching.

To take one element in the stories, the motif of self-sacrifice by some leader, is quite significant. A good example would be Banyan, King of the Deer (p. 13). The king of the deer is prepared to offer his life in place of a mother deer with a baby. In the Monkey Bridge, the chief of the monkeys makes himself into a bridge to allow his people to escape from death over a river. He dies in the process but not without his message of love being brought home to the king who wanted to kill all the monkeys. The Forest Fire and the Little Quail is another case of death-defying courage to save all the animals of the forest (p. 56). In the Swan Kingdom (p. 29) the King of the Swans is trapped but his second in command refuses to desert him even though the rest of the swans depart in panic. Because of this selfless act, the King of Benares is so impressed that both swans are spared and are allowed to go free. In so many cases, there is the leader laying down his life for the sake of his subjects, a noble thought found in the New Testament. The essential difference is that the brave soul who offers his life is usually spared and restored; there is no thought of total sacrifice of his life followed by a resurrection or even life in another existence. It seems that the Buddhists are groping towards the motif of a sacrificial death but stop short of completion and triumph. This theme is brought to completion in the life of Jesus.

Another aspect which pervades the Jataka stories is the ongoing theme of kingship, or some form of leadership which amounts to the same thing. Kingship is not just found in the human orbit but in various realms of the animal kingdom, and the lion as the king of beasts is the same as in Western thought. The implication for the Buddhists is that Siddhartha is equated with the leading character, and yet there is sometimes more than one king in the story. It is of interest that Jesus was described as the Lion of Judah. Never is there any suggestion that the king is the eternal Father, God. In fact, gods are strangely absent from these tales. This may explain why, in Buddhism, monarchy is not a particularly strong element; the exception being Tibetan Buddhism. It remains as an interesting sidelight on the whole matter of sacral kingship and how it works out in relation to the ministry of Jesus. The motif of a king loving and caring for his people is heavily emphasised and comes to ultimate fulfilment in Jesus. The Banyan Tale: ‘Love had entered into the heart of the king, and he reigned with love over his people and all the living creatures in his realm were happy ever after,’ (p. 12).

An important assumption which pervades almost every story is the unity of creation. Humans and animals speak to one another, as also different species, and in addition elements such as fire. One important message from this is kindness to animals and consideration for the natural world. This can be seen against the assumption (never actually stated) that an animal might reappear as a human and vice versa, according to Karma. Strangely, merits are only faintly alluded to, and even then not in the context of Karma. But there is a warm, inclusive feeling about the unity of creation, verging on the sentimental. Such traits do occur in the Bible but nowhere near as heavily emphasised.

A noteworthy story is the Sandy Road (p. 23) where a merchant caravan is crossing a desert and begins to run out of supplies. Superficially this story is reminiscent of the Meribah incident in Exodus, where Moses produces water from the rock. This time a little boy strikes the rock and saves the day. This may be a case of the Buddhist tradition adapting something from the Hebrew tradition. But there the similarity ends: the message from Exodus is quite explicit in that God provides a last-minute rescue for his people in spite of them being totally unworthy, and they go on to complain. The Sandy Road has the men set up a flag to tell other people of the water and then go on to sell their goods and make a profit and go home feeling pleased with themselves. This is quite a different thrust.

The Merchant of Seri has been noted as reminiscent of the Pearl of Great Price or the Treasure in the Field. In both cases, a merchant becomes aware of something of great value that others do not realise: he goes all out to obtain it, without admitting to its true value. That is where the similarity ends: if Jesus had known this story from Buddhist tradition, he adapts it to a completely different message. While there are two merchants of Seri, one greedy and the other honest, the moral comes out that one should not be greedy but pay a realistic price. With Jesus, however, he is talking about the secrecy of the Kingdom of God and the need to make a full commitment. The greed element is only a minor issue, if there at all.

The end of the world is also a thought, though not a major theme in the Jatakas. It appears in two versions of the same account, basically the same plot, that a hare (or a rabbit) wondered what would happen if the world came to an end. In a panic he had all the other animals in a turmoil until they came to the lion, who had the sense to keep calm and find out exactly what was happening. It turned out to be a lot of frenzy and imagination. The story is told with a certain touch of comic sarcasm; it may indicate that in

Buddhism the world is understood to have an ending somewhere, but there is no point in worrying about it. The Buddha is courageous and a steadying influence. What is missing, as seen in the Gospels, is a sense of a coming crisis, a decisive moment in human history, the active intervention of God who brings reconciliation to this world. It is just possible that the Buddhists are offering a mildly sarcastic answer to the Apocalyptists of the post-exilic age (since Buddhism emerged at about this time). Thence Jesus provides the fulfilment and completion of this idea: that of events in human history. Not that the normal human processes will cease, but that God is present in a new relationship with mankind in a way that was not possible before. None of this is seen in the Jatakas.

And finally, the happy ending, 'they all lived happily ever after', a wish rather than a reality, concludes virtually every story. This is actually a facile understanding of life and is rarely experienced by anyone in any religion or philosophy. None of the parables of Jesus end like that: they all end with some kind of warning, question mark or challenge. For those who think that life is wonderful and there is no need to bother, the threat is that it can all end very abruptly; for those who toil, sweat and are in despair, there is relief and promise. The first will be last and the last first. It is a complete reversal of human expectation. None of this emerges in the Jataka stories, so while they are evocative and entertaining there is a heavy feeling of unreality about them.

Other examples of how Jesus adapts parabolic material

2 Samuel 12ff recounts how Nathan the prophet challenged King David over the Bathsheba incident. There was a rich man and a poor man: the one with plenty of sheep, the other with one little pet lamb. The rich man stole the pet lamb and served it up for lunch. David was furious at this and decreed a death sentence on the rich man. But then it dawned on him that *he* was the rich man, who had disposed of Uriah and stolen his wife, Bathsheba. Although this plot never appears in the Gospels, the self-accusatory mode does, when the Pharisees realise that they are the 'wicked husbandmen'. Also the sentimental tone in places, evoking emotions over the pet lamb and the division between rich and poor, is a mode seen often in the Gospels. The Lost Sheep, the Prodigal Son, and Dives and Lazarus

show that Jesus has not invented this line of thought. In the self-accusatory method 'God forbid' (Luke) we see a solid reason for using parable as a medium for teaching: 'if the cap fits, wear it'! It was suggestive without being too dogmatic; it was open to allegorisation without forcing a set interpretation.

From the Apocrypha, 2 Esdras 8:41, we see the passing use of a parable which at first sight resembles the Sower:

> For as the husbandman soweth much seed upon the ground and planteth many trees, and yet the thing that is sown good in his season cometh not up, neither doth all that is planted take root: even so it is of them that are sown in the world they shall not all be saved.

It is quite likely that Jesus knew this book and used this motif. If so he has considerably adapted it to alter the thrust. Esdras only thinks of two results: one seed that grows and the other that fails to grow. This reminds us of separation in the Gospels: the sheep and the goats, the dragnet. 'They shall not all be saved'; he does not take the positive line that some will be saved. It is not clear why 'many trees' are mentioned, unless it hints at the tree of life as in verse 52.

But with Jesus the whole tone is far more positive, for while much of the seed fails to produce anything, much of it does, thirty-, sixty- and a hundredfold. He hints more at the reasons for failure, but the implication is that the separation is one's own fault, if salvation is not achieved. Jesus has developed the sower motif to bring out two elements, more optimistic than in Esdras.

In Ezekiel the motif of Sheep and Shepherd (34:1–19) gives a lengthy and self-explanatory parable. It is much more of an allegory and yet clearly Jesus used this idea for the Good Shepherd and other teachings so related. Ezekiel is talking about the failed shepherds who do not tend the flock properly, the faulty rulers of Israel. The scattering of the sheep appears in Mark 14:27 and Matthew 10:6, 'go rather to the lost sheep of the house of Israel,' (Ezekiel 34:6). By verse 11, God begins to say that he will perform the task of shepherd, but not for one, rather the elements of his flock that have gone missing, which is talking about the return of the exiles. 'I myself will be the shepherd of my sheep ... I will seek the lost,' (v. 16). Here the Lukan version begins to surface. Ezekiel goes on to judgement: sheep and he-goats appear, then the fat sheep and the lean. This element is seen in other parables of Jesus. We see two versions of this: Luke 15:3ff is in the context of the Pharisees (the bad shepherds) complaining about Jesus associating with sinners. The true shepherd leaves 99 sheep in the wilderness and goes off to find the one that has gone astray. There is great rejoicing over one sinner that repents. This is followed by the ten silver coins and the Prodigal Son. Matthew has the Lost Sheep in a different context: that of the 'little child' who must not be allowed to be despised or perish. The child might not be a sinner; more likely a 'babe', whose childlike faith is essential for entering the Kingdom. Jesus puts a far more joyful and positive tone to this motif: there is no mention of rejection or judgement here. It is another example of how Jesus transforms a parabolic motif and gives it simplification and a more positive message.

We have seen how Jesus used pre-existing parabolic material from earlier sources and also how later imitators have adapted his parables for their own purposes. It is important to see that in Jesus' teachings we have balance, paradox and completion at work, matters which are usually absent or misunderstood with other writers. There is separation and inclusion; secrecy and fame; the coming of the Kingdom at the beginning and the end, with the interim period; there is the urgent need to repent, juxtaposed with the coming joy and celebration. So many paradoxes pervade these matters, all adding to the mystery of the Kingdom and God's personal intervention in human history.

Notes

1. Augustine, in C.H. Dodd, *The Parables of the Kingdom*, p.13.
2. Baillie, *God was in Christ*, p. 75.
3. Grant and Freedman, *The Gospel of Thomas*.
4. James, *The Apocryphal New Testament*, p. 485.
5. James, op, cit., p. 187.
6. James, op. cit., p. 228.
7. B.D. Ehrman, *Lost Scriptures*.
8. Noor Inyat, *The Jataka Tales*.

11

Personal Destiny, World View and Mythology

The word 'myth' in contemporary English now means 'lie' or at best 'misapprehension', but mythology here means some form of speculation: on the subject of mankind's origins, our world view, and ultimate destiny. To quote Burridge: 'To modern minds "myth" means something untrue, a fairy story. In the ancient world myth was the medium whereby profound truth, more truly true than facts could ever be, was communicated.'[1] We can go further and say that myth is still with us and shows no sign of fading away; on the contrary, new myths constantly keep emerging. Always there is the tendency to take mythical material as literally true and this very often confuses the issue when religious or theological matters are being discussed. Every known culture across the broad spectrum of humanity has had and still does have some form of mythology, and that includes the extremist political cultures of the last century. It cannot be held up as evidence of anything except to say that it tells us something about the human mind: that there is a need to understand our origins and our destiny. Although each culture has produced its own mythology, there are certain elements that remain constant regardless of the variations.

Seldom does a culture have a completely consistent and logical scheme: there are differing ideas at work even in the same area or race. This would tend to support the view that mythologies cannot and were never intended to be taken literally. A figurative and interpretative approach is always more instructive. Those who have taken a completely literal approach to mythology have given themselves all manner of problems and yet the urge is there. For all our modern scientific notions, many of which are literally true, mythology is far from dead, and much of it lies close to the surface, requiring only a change in circumstances to bring it back to the forefront of thought.

When considering the Bible, we see that mythology and historical account are both used freely, not just at the beginning but in various places right through to the end. Indeed, there is a subtle blending of the two, making it impossible, if not unwise to attempt to separate the two modes. A modern trend originating with Bultmann and others has been to demythologise the Gospels. These matters will be discussed later. This is an issue which hardly surfaces with other sacred writings from other religions. They do not have to contend with the paradox of the Eternal God breaking into human history in real terms. This explains why history and myth are closely intertwined and inseparable in the Scriptures, especially in the Gospels but also in the rest of the Bible. This is where balance, and paradox, and also completion are important factors. It is not a matter of some sort of happy average between myth and history: the Bible has a balance, a sense of completion, and a tacit understanding of paradox: that of the Eternal coming into the affairs of mankind, the Incarnation being its final expression. We need both myth and history: the deep truths of myth are juxtaposed with the facts of human history; there is a balance struck between the two; they both need each other; the one interprets the other; the other justifies the one. History brings mythology to a fulfilment and completion. None of it makes any sense unless it is understood as God interacting with his creation.

Personal destiny and identity

This can be seen as a subset of mythology and yet it is a useful starting point because much of it is in common the world over. There appear to be substantially three main assumptions in the world: the Chinese, the Indian, and the Western mind-sets. The Mesoamerican idea may have formed a fourth one but since so much of the evidence was destroyed by the Spaniards, we do not know in detail what the Aztecs believed; it may have been something akin to Karma. All three make the assumption that there is some form of personal survival after one's earthly life, and that one's lifestyle in this life has a distinct bearing on one's condition in the next life. To put it in very crude terms: if you are good, you go up; and if you are bad, you go down. The thought forms and imagery may vary to a large extent but the main gist of it is the same the world over. How this comes about, historically, is not clear. It is uncertain how much borrowing or exchange of ideas went on in remote prehistory between isolated parts of the world, such as China and the West, even more so Mesoamerica. It is possible that we are looking at an important instinct in the mind of mankind, just as fundamental as Theodicy, sacrifice, prophecy and other factors. If this issue is denied then one would have to render an explanation for why such assumptions are so widespread and fundamental to religions of all kinds. And this is in the face of the secularist-atheist ideas which try to deny it but do not have much success.

It is prudent to make as few assumptions as possible about how our existence in the next world will be played out. Just as we have problems when trying to use human thought forms for describing God, so too we try to describe the next world using vocabulary developed in this world. The truth is that we have no idea what it will be like. The one person who did have knowledge of both worlds at once was remarkably taciturn on the subject, and pointed out that we cannot conceive of it in terms of this world. One factor which did emerge was that there is some sort of 'insulation' between this world and the next, which keeps humanity back from death. In spite of our obsession with it, we are all in denial of it. Human nature grasps on to this life: suicide takes a massive effort of will to overcome the instinct of self-preservation. Elixirs have been sought from remote antiquity and still are. There are all manner of ways that we try to sidestep death. Strangely there is the urge to interfere with the departed, and much of this may be pure self-delusion.

The Chinese mind-set (mainly Taoism, but not confined to it)

The basic assumption here is the harmony between heaven and earth. The Jade Emperor is the essential element in this system. There are various heavens, earth, and various hells.[2] There is a strong assumption that the family holds together across the divide of life and death. Ancestor worship is a major feature. The living do have some influence over the fate of the dead souls. The living will do all manner of things to lift their dead forebears out of hell. This reminds us of Dives and Lazarus. There is a lot of vagueness about the location of heaven and hell, in fact there is suitable vagueness about almost everything. History itself is a vague concept with little sense of direction or end destination. There is the assumption of a Golden Age in the remote past and an idea that the Jade Emperor made humans out of clay, but the future and human destiny in general is not really at all clear.

It is important to see this mind-set as closely interwoven with the view of family continuity between this world and the next. Of course this element is not confined to Taoism or even Chinese culture in general. It is a trait found in many cultures with varying degrees of emphasis. There is the family album, the immaculately kept grave, the observance of All Soul's tide. People have an acute awareness of the departed being 'alive', never lost or ignored. This is in spite of Jesus saying 'let the dead bury their dead'. Active survival beyond the grave is deeply rooted in human consciousness.

The Indian mind-set, Hindu and Buddhist

Axiomatic to this mind-set is the doctrine of Karma: reincarnation. The human soul is seen as indestructible and continues reappearing in different life-forms infinitely. Life is an eternal round of existence from one life to another. What determines one's status in the next life is one's conduct in the previous life. Life is seen as a gigantic system of shelves starting at the bottom and going up to the top. Brahma, the ultimate God, is way above the top and is not really involved in what happens.[3] There is some involvement of him as a creator, but this function is mainly performed by lower gods. Those who reach to the top may eventually be absorbed into Brahma and cease to exist as such. Lower down we see the realms of the gods, various heavens, then human life which involves the caste system, below that the animal world, and below that various hells. All this is activated by merit; it is not personal and no god is activating the system; it is purely mechanical. Reincarnation is essential to this system; there is no way that it can be proved or disproved, although Hindus have been known to attempt to evidence it with memories of a previous life. There is no denying that Karma exerts a fascination for people of other beliefs, although it may seem faintly comical at times.

Behind it all we see that there is a sense of eternal and everlasting justice: you reap what you sow. The Ultimate God, Brahma, is far too remote and impersonal to be involved. Even so, Hinduism does contain a notion of a god rescuing people from their sins. Rig Veda

p. 74:[4] 'May Agni, bright as the sun, remove all the sins troubling our yagya performers.'

There is frequent reference to Agni removing sins, but whether this is moral failure or ritual inaccuracy is not quite clear. Quite how this works in relation to Karma is also not clear: the Rig Veda never mentions Karma. We may be looking at a paradox not unlike the works faith–dilemma as in Christianity. It is a little clearer in other parts of the Rig Veda, p. 80: 'I want to know about those who by dint of their performance of the Yagya have ascended to heavens. They are believed to have attained this exalted position by exercising better control of mind and performing good and noble deeds.'

One strength in this is the positive relationship between all forms of life, especially human and animal. There is a kind of unity and continuity between various species and the castes of mankind. To Western ears it might seem comical if not repugnant to think of one's dead relative coming back as a cobra, a slug or a mosquito. The positive side of it is that even a slug could work his way up to become a god. The basic assumption is that animals do have a soul and need to be treated with respect as a potential human or a god. Another permutation on this is that there have been gods who have appeared as an avatar, as in human or animal form. Rama and Krishna are mostly associated with this and here we see the Hindu approach to god active in the world of humanity. Brahma does not: the lower gods do intervene but in deep disguise. Quite how this works in relation to Karma is not really clear.

That this system of thought is not a particularly optimistic one became patent in early times. An endless cycle of lives with the constant concern that one might be demoted tended to drive people to despair. Various schemes were hatched to try to provide an escape mechanism: Jainism, Sikhism and Buddhism. Each of these offered a 'short-cut' to Nirvana. It is tempting to equate Nirvana with heaven in the Christian sense, but that assumption is possibly somewhat facile. Although Nirvana is roughly analogous to heaven, we must remember that in Buddhist thinking, heaven is something else. It is one of the Samsaric realms in the Wheel of Becoming, the place where the gods live.[5] They too, with the help of the Buddha, need to break out of Karma and find Nirvana, which is a different level of existence, of 'non-being'.

The Buddhist system is heavily reliant on Hindu thought: the assumption of Karma is basic to it. Without a belief in reincarnation,

Buddhism has no meaning. The main difference lies in the assumption that instead of a stack of shelves, all of life proceeds in circular motion as seen in the Wheel of Becoming. Everybody, including humans, animals, gods, devils, ghosts, all forms of life, go round eternally unless with the help of Buddha they make their escape to Nirvana. The symbolism in the Samsaric realms is profound and thought-provoking and yet it is also deeply pessimistic. There is no active almighty God eager to rescue one from this roundabout: Brahma (if he is there at all: a Buddhist might just as well be an atheist), does not intervene at all. Rather, the whole scheme is presided over by Yama, the god of the dead, a frightening skull image ensconced over the top of the Wheel. Yama holds the Wheel up to us like a mirror, to show us what we really are. As with Hindu thought, there is a generous application of despair.[6]

A permutation of this is the Chinese idea, Yen Wang, in which the wheel of transmigration is supervised by the tenth Yama king. He takes care that the soul is suitably placed in a body for the next life. This is unlikely to be original Taoist thought: rather Buddhist influence in later times.[7]

The notions of heaven, hell and personal existence in this and the next life are clearly present. The weakness in it, as with the Chinese view, is that there is very little sense of an active merciful and controlling God supervising the universe. Everything is essentially circular with little sense of personal or national or even international progress in a straight line towards some sort of goal or fulfilment.[8]

The Western mind-set: Christian, Jewish and Muslim

The assumptions in this are markedly different. There is no reincarnation: each soul lives once and has to face God at the end of his life. Biblical support for this is seen in Hebrews 9:27: 'Just as it is appointed for men to die once, and after that comes judgement.'[9]

This is stated not so much as a dogma but as a general assumption, which supports the teaching that Christ only needed to live and die once. There is heaven and hell, and one's destiny is connected with one's conduct in the present life. God is a personal God who is not remote but active in the lives of individuals, nations, and world history. There is a beginning and an end, with God in control of the whole pattern.

In the early years of Judaism, 'Sheol' was the term for the underworld: this was a shadowy purposeless existence until the Zoroastrians worked in the notions of fires and torments.[10] The term '(David) ... slept with his fathers', common in the Book of Kings, suggests that the souls of the dead are awaiting an awakening, but this is not explained. It was not all pessimistic, as seen in Psalm 16:9–10: 'Therefore my heart is glad ... for thou dost not give me up to Sheol or let thy godly one see the Pit.'

Satan is not related to hell until later: initially he was very much a this-worldly figure, even if an agent of God. It was understood that certain selected persons such as Moses and Elijah could progress to heaven at their death: the term for this was 'assumption'.

By the time of Jesus, the literature of the day gave a lurid account of heaven and hell with the strong advice that one's conduct would decide one's fate. For those who were in Christ, there would be no condemnation. This left something of a dilemma for Christians up to recent times: an awareness of damnation, and yet an assurance of salvation for all. This paradox has been discussed earlier. There was even the speculation that at the Apocalypse, even the Devil would be redeemed and the whole of creation put to rights by God's overwhelming intervention (Basil).[11] The strength in this mind-set is that of personal responsibility before God for each human soul. Eternal justice is juxtaposed with eternal love and mercy; coping with this contradiction can only be seen in terms of a profound paradox. But the general tenor of the system is hope: that the whole of creation has been and will be rescued from its own self-destruction, by a personal God who is active in human affairs from day to day.

One weakness in this system is that the animal kingdom appears to have very little relevance to the scheme. Although it is clearly shown in the Bible that God cares for all his creatures, even a 'sparrow falling to the ground', there is no mention of animals having an immortal soul. Some would say this is a gap in the Western mind-set. When considering such things as ghosts, fallen angels, devils, and other entities that are difficult to define, the West does not have any clear way of working them into any sort of system analogous to the Buddhist Wheel of Becoming.

In recent times the Western view has undergone certain modifications. There have been those such as Milton[12] who have gone into detail and produced all manner of speculatory and frightening accounts of hell: this has not helped the Christian image at all. Now that we are in an age of sentimentality and alleged fairness, hell and damnation are labelled by many as sub-Christian. It all depends on what one means by Christian. The Zoroastrian influence is now soft-pedalled and demythologised. Hell is now seen as 'separation from God' and damnation, if it exists at all, is deemed to be only temporary. Even evil is supposed not to exist, in spite of all the wickedness that occurred in the twentieth century. The Christians have largely shifted their ground with a bit of clever modification; the Muslims have not. The irony of it is that while hellfire is denied in all its horror, we have managed to drag hell up on to the earth-plane with two disastrous World Wars and the threat of nuclear destruction. Hell has moved into this world.

Heaven, however, does not seem to be out of favour and there is a common assumption that it is one's ultimate destination even if one's conduct has not been of the highest quality. The concept of limbo and purgatory, though still in use in common parlance, have faded largely under the influence of Protestantism. Even so, the question of allowing an unbaptised infant to die still worries people: is this latent superstition or a symptom of a deeper need in human nature? These backdrop assumptions about heaven, hell, angels and devils are still current in human thinking and seem unaffected by modern trends in secularisation, atheism and scientific 'progress'.

As with hell, there have been attempts to create heaven on earth. With the post-war rise in prosperity and the assumption that nothing can come along to stop its inevitable progression, there are many who think that utopia has arrived. It is only now that with fears of global warming, the end of this era of ease might be in sight.

General conclusions on personal destiny

Perhaps the greatest value in the Western mind-set is the centrality of history as a reality and a progression under a guiding hand. This conception is largely absent from the other two mind-sets. The result is a vague, purposeless, drifting mentality which relapses into the idea that life is not real but a series of illusions or even self-delusions. But to read the Bible one is struck by the reality of events and personalities in a progression, even if it is the subject of interpretation. The chief interpreter is God; in some ways the great prophets contribute to it but never invent it for themselves. The interaction between a living God and real events and people is paramount, and in contrast to the Eastern views.

This process began with the authors of the early historical material. It is difficult to escape the conclusion that Moses, Samuel, Isaiah and Jeremiah had an important part to play in this process even if they did not actually write the material themselves. Moving into the Hellenistic world, Herodotus, the so-called 'Father of History',[13] and Josephus[14] were highly influential, along with a collection of Roman historians.[15] We come down to our own times with Winston Churchill.[16] A spin-off of this is the sciences of archaeology, palaeontology, anthropology and other related disciplines. People in the West are fascinated by the processes of history, they are obsessive about museums and preservationism. It is also interesting to see which aspects of history are seen to be inconvenient and are 'air-brushed' out, possibly to ease various consciences. The existence of Holocaust deniers is a prime example of this. We have to contend with the fact that any historian writes with his own presuppositions and bias in mind. This is unavoidable. We see it in Herodotus and Josephus, Winston Churchill too. It would seem that there is always selectivity of facts. Even so, the concept of history is a product of a personal God controlling history, and each individual.

The truth is that no one really knows what happens when we die. What we can learn from these remarks is that it is unsafe to be over-dogmatic and obsessional about these matters. A case in point would be the late mediaeval obsession with hell and methods for avoiding it. This resulted in chantry chapels, indulgences and paper-pardonings which obscured the true message of love and mercy in the Gospels. In other words, it cancelled out its own faith. There is something to be said for the Chinese view: that such matters as heaven and hell, though they are a reality, can be left suitably vague, imprecise and unworrying.

That there is some kind of 'insulation' between this world and the next could be a helpful way of seeing the problem. 'Insulation' is a modern word born of the advent of electricity, nuclear fission and temperature retention. It forms a barrier between two factors which would cause a problem if allowed to come into contact. So too with the physical and the spiritual worlds. We can see that some kind of barrier exists between them, and any attempt to break through them pre-emptively is fraught with problems. So called 'primitive' beliefs usually include some form of necromancy, the preserve of the shaman or the medium. At the very least this is evidence of the need to be reassured of the survival or the fate of the dead. It shows that people find it hard to 'let people go' when they die. But is this a genuine contact with the other world or some sort of mental construct or wishful thinking? In some cases it has been pure theatre and exploitation of the bereaved.

The Biblical thought on this matter is to forbid attempts to raise the spirits or force some sort of irregular contact with the other world. Deuteronomy 18:11 is categorical in saying that it is an abomination. The story of Saul (1 Samuel 28:8ff) is interesting, for it does not deny the genuineness of necromancy; what it does is to show how it can backfire on one, especially as Saul's interest was completely hypocritical. He was deeply shaken, a condition often seen in those who experiment with spiritualism today. Spiritualism can be seen as a reaction to the materialism of the modern world; also to the failure of mainstream churches to give clear guidance on the matter. We can also say that the genuine core of it very easily becomes entangled with vagaries and self-delusion.

Looking at it the other way, there are many examples on record, in the Scriptures and elsewhere, where the other world makes contact with this world. This is not forbidden; it is not mankind interfering with the unseen powers. So, for instance, dreams, angels, theophanies and ghosts are examples of God making direct contact with us; this is usually a warning or a piece of encouragement, never something trivial or ephemeral. It is possible to see Jesus as the ultimate intermediary between the two worlds. But he never uses the techniques belonging to necromancy, never tries to 'raise the departed spirits'. On the contrary, the 'dead' come to raise him, as seen at the Transfiguration. In this way, we allow the next world to break into ours, at their pleasure, not ours. The insulation is a one-way process. Jesus was generally taciturn about his knowledge of the next world. In this way, the insulation between two worlds is maintained and yet allows contact on God's terms, not ours.

The modern world has now invented a particularly clever type of insulation: a plastic sheet has pores which allow moisture to pass through from one side to the other but will not allow the moisture to pass back again. It is used for insulating bridges, damp walls in houses, or as a membrane under a tiled roof. This seems to be a useful paradigm for celestial intrusion, in that the world of the spirit can pass through in tiny amounts to this world, but we cannot, or should not, pass through to them. The exception comes at the moment of death. Some might say that the 'out-of-body experience' could be another way through. This is a contentious matter about which few generalisations can be made.[17] Those who have returned from such a 'temporary death' have not gone into details about what heaven consists of or any other important matters. The evaluation of this is still to be tested.

The question then arises: how does Nirvana relate to these matters? The way it is described and the techniques needed to achieve it would suggest that it has nothing to do with the world of the spirit either in the Christian or the Buddhist understanding. It is a technique of mental discipline which induces a certain state of mind, which might be analogous to self-hypnosis or some kind of mental anaesthetic. It has nothing to do with gods, angels or devils; it does not relate to or rely on the ultimate God, if he 'exists' at all. Nirvana may be seen as below the level of insulation between this world and the next. Nirvana can be achieved in this world; what happens after death is as uncertain for the Buddhists as it is for everyone else. It is only an assumption that breaking out of Karma results in a permanent Nirvana after death.

The fact remains that no one really knows what the next world really consists of, in spite of all the speculation, overwrought imagination and dogmatisms that have emerged in theology through the ages. Even so, the assumption that there is some form of personal survival after death is just as prevalent as it ever was and this cuts across all manner of religions, philosophies, and theories of all kinds. Like the Old Testament mentality of works righteousness which accompanies the assumptions about heaven, earth and hell, it is deeply embedded in the human mind at the instinctive level.

World mythologies and their resolution

Mythology has been touched on earlier, mainly in the matter of sacral kingship, but there is a whole world of mythology pertaining to every known human culture. It is not good enough to write it off as superstitious nonsense. It is interesting that Rudolph Bultmann,[18] who tries to demythologise everything in the New Testament, never seems to make any reference to other mythologies in other faiths, still less to draw any comparisons or general conclusions. The fact is that there are many aspects which are the same from one mythology to another, even if they are expressed in different thought-forms or metaphors. This has to mean something: it cannot be held up as proof of anything, such as the existence of God, but it is a strong indication that the human soul functions in the same way regardless of race, climate or social conditions. It is also worth saying that seldom does any race or culture have a totally consistent and logical scheme: there are contradictions and variant explanations at work even in the same area. This could be taken to indicate that mythologies were never intended to be taken purely at face value. A figurative and interpretative approach is always more instructive. In this sense, Bultmann has thrown some light on the matter. We can recall that in Genesis there are two creation myths (already discussed); to take them totally at face value is to involve oneself in all manner of difficulties. The same is true in Ancient Greece where there were at least four mythologies (to be discussed later). To take them literally can so easily engender all manner of problems. Conversely, to try to cancel them out and ignore them can also produce other problems. The modern process of demythologisation, which is nothing new, ignores the fact that we all need some sort of myth to give ourselves a rationale in life. It is no surprise that in trying to abolish ancient myths, contemporary mankind has begun to fabricate new myths, often more fantastic and mind-boggling than the ancient ones.

I begin by drawing out the major features of world mythologies and how they may be brought to resolution. The New Testament particularly, and the Bible in general, has a subtle way of bringing so many features of mythology to completion. This does not have to mean that the Biblical writers knew all the details of every mythology around the world, but they did understand the human mind and how these fundamental questions could be answered in the intervention of the Living God in this world. Minor features, some not found in every culture, can be mentioned but there is a limit to the detail that can be delved into in a work of this scope.

Chaos and darkness

'Chaos' is a Greek word, but the same concept occurs, using synonyms, in every culture. We begin with utter darkness and nothingness, usually depicted as darkness, before any kind of life begins, including gods. That is a very difficult concept for anyone to cope with, whether on the crude levels of some systems or the high-flown systems of Greece and China. Interestingly we have the same problem now with explorations into deep space: it is very difficult to assimilate distances described in terms of hundreds of light years and massive areas of vacuum. Nothingness is impossible for us to imagine, who live in a world which entirely consists of 'somethings'. The astrophysicists now are beginning to admit that they are just beginning to grapple with what lies out there in space, and are constantly altering their view of things. Even so, we all assume there was a time when there was absolutely nothing. Even the Hindus, who think everything is eternal, allow that 'Initially nothing was existent' (Rig Veda, p. 175).

The beginning of all things

At some remote point, created things began to appear. Hardly any culture imagines that this happened all by itself: something must have caused it to happen. 'Nothing comes of nothing' is a truism not just for Shakespeare but for all of us. So we arrive at a supreme deity, an ultimate principle who is the original creator at the start of all things: 'It is due to Supreme God's grace that everything appeared ... when he desired to have the creation, everything appeared by his will,' (Rig Veda, p. 175).

It will be noticed that this is already following the thought-processes of 'proofs for the existence of God' (to be examined later). How nothing becomes something is a brain-teaser for everyone, regardless of their level of intelligence or religious faith. This is because it is the first major paradox. Virtually every mythology has a basic, supreme, if distant God.

God or gods

Virtually every mythology makes the assumption that the supreme God has an entire team of underlings at work in the created world. Sometimes they appear spontaneously: otherwise they emanate from the God via some kind of channel. There is clearly a dilemma as to how far to go with anthropomorphism and since no one really knows how a god is produced, there is a rich variety of drama and metaphor at work: the crudest and most subtle both coming from Greece. The only exception to this is the monotheism of Hebrew thought. Even there we are confronted with the suggestion of plurality in the Godhead. The word *elohim* is a plural form, and God says to himself, 'Let us make man in our own image.' This does not compromise monotheism: it indicates that the workings of God are not totally monochrome. Many systems have some form of triadic configuration in the senior echelons of divinity. It is also to be noted that many of the gods are multifaceted: sometimes their roles are self-contradictory. Often they oppose each other. This tells us at the very least that the gods' intentions are uncertain. On this basis it is not difficult to cope with Theodicy: it brings the problem almost to the level of non-paradox. Even so, the question is bound to arise, 'How can the lesser gods be in disagreement with each other, and with the Supreme God?' This is where the paradox re-emerges.

Eternal conflict

Because the various gods have different attitudes and roles, there is an ongoing conflict involving battles, bloodshed, and vendettas. In one sense it can be seen as human aggression and blood-lust projected into the skies, and yet, it also shows that humanity senses that there is turmoil in the universe. Perhaps the most lurid one is the Teutonic one; the least violent could be the Chinese one. At a lower level than the gods is the 'yin–yang' configuration, which, in a cartouche, indicates the tensions which cannot be resolved in nature. In this we see an awareness that life is not the harmonious experience that it ought to be. It is a time of uncertainty and yet it carries the implication that somewhere in the future it will all be resolved. The battles in the skies will one day come to an armistice.

Dualism

This is a simplified version of the conflict idea. It is the opposition of two gods, one good and one bad, which explains the cosmic battle going on behind the scenes of life. Sometimes this appears in a cartouche and is somehow included in the vast array of divine activity; otherwise it can be the main feature of the myth. One example is the Slavonic Black and White gods and also the good and bad genii of the Assyrio-Babylonian myth. Of course the Persian Zoroastrian system is the best known. Dualism appears late in the Biblical material, post-exilic and New Testament times. It is not enough to attempt to ignore this motif as superstitious nonsense. It was the basic thought-form of Jesus himself. Bultmann would like to eliminate such thinking with his demythologising method. But this is not being realistic: the idea still goes on in people's minds regardless of modern trends and clever philosophies.

Heaven, Earth and Hell

There is no culture on earth that does not assume some sort of three-tier structure. This has been partly discussed before. To give a little more detail, the world of the gods (above) may extend to as much as nine levels (Aztec). Heaven is known under different names such as Paradise or the Elysian Fields. With regard to Hell, there might be up to 18 of them (Taoist). In Finland there are no hells, and yet the evil spirits mysteriously emerge from the forests. In Buddhism, heaven, earth and hell are included in the Wheel of Becoming, which is a cartouche. This mythological world has largely been abandoned with modern geographical knowledge of the solar system. But the three-tier system is nothing to do with the realities of space exploration; the idea still goes on in people's minds and parlance, regardless. Some cultures view the creation as of an immense egg hatching out and giving birth to the whole of life; even so, the three-tier system is included within it. The egg metaphor is not generally known throughout the world, more likely is the 'arch' idea, seeing the sky as a vault which has to be held up over the ground, usually by a gigantic god (Atlas). Heaven and hell are still with us despite the efforts of Bultmann; some people take it as near to literality as is possible; most people manage to interpret it into some sort of relevance.

The connection between the tiers

Assuming a three-tier universe, the question arises as to what connection there can be between the layers. There is no general agreement on the method except to say that there has to be some form of gadget. A very common idea is the 'bridge' from earth to heaven, seen in real terms as the rainbow. Teutonic and Japanese thought have this idea. For the Romans, bridges were of much religious significance. The term *pontifex* means a bridge-builder, and he was in charge of the calendar (a matter to be discussed later), and the Emperor was the Pontifex Maximus. This motif worked its way into the Papacy, whence the Pope is still termed the Pontiff. Where the bridge is absent there are other metaphors at work: the ladder (Egypt), the spider's web (Sioux Indians), a flight of steps (Hindu). We recall Jacob's ladder. 'Learning about the stair-case going from the earth to the sky, Agni moves on them amidst the earth and the sky,' (Rig Veda, p. 90).

By the same token there is a connection from earth to the underworld. This is usually some form of perilous pathway, a boat trip on a subterranean lake, or a cave. On arrival at this kingdom there is often some kind of admission procedure to persuade someone to open the gates. We note that on the Turin Shroud, there seem to be two tiny coins placed on the eyes of the face; the question arises, 'Who pays the ferryman?'!

Another important aspect of the connection motif is the tree. Practically every myth has at least one tree, if not more. The significance of this is profound. We note that the tree is rooted in the ground, reaching down into the underworld. Its bole is plain enough in the world of mortals. Its branches reach up to the heavens. In Oceania, trees appear squat because originally they held up the sky, until a giant came along and relieved them of the burden. The tree is a symbol of the connection between heaven, earth and hell. It does not matter what kind of tree it is: a tamarisk in Egypt, or an oak in Germany, or a fig tree in other areas. We can recall the fig tree and the mustard tree in the Gospels. It is through some kind of sacred tree that knowledge or understanding of eternal matters is given to mankind. In India we have a god nestling in the branches as he observes the shepherdesses bathing. Highly significant is the Mayan idea of the World Tree,[19] which was cruciform: it supports the world and sprouts corn foliage which feeds mankind. If we interpret it aright, the lid of Pakal's sarcophagus at Palenque has a snake in its branches. Pakal falls on his back into the underworld on a bowl that holds blood-letting instruments. The tree connects all levels of the cosmos; he enters the earth as a kernel of regeneration; he spawns the tree of life; his death is a sacrifice which brings renewal of life; he will be resurrected and ascend the tree to be an ancestral deity in the sky. He is in the normal position for childbirth; he is giving birth to the tree; he signals his own rebirth. For the Judeao-Christian system, the tree is of very great significance: we start in the Garden of Eden with one, then Jesus is crucified on one; the Revelation includes one in the last chapter. The symbolism of it is profound; one wonders if Bultmann has ever seen it this way. Siddhartha sat under a Bodhi tree for his enlightenment; now we see myth and historical reality interwoven; it is folly to try to disentangle them.

Life and death

Related to the three tiers is the whole question of life and death, not just for humans but for gods too. The unspoken question is, 'Is this the end?' when thinking about death. Every system has some form of spiritual survival beyond the grave, and life being restored in some form of resurrection. This has been examined in detail earlier. One of the most noticeable themes is the death of a god and his restoration to life. This is usually accomplished by another more powerful god who is struck by the unfairness of it, and is moved to battle with the powers of the underworld. This is often related to the passing of the seasons but not always. This is where sacral kingship acts as a kind of transition from myth to historical reality. In many cases the myth contains a champion of the gods, an action man or great hero who is always victorious in battle (Thor, Marduk, Bel). Often the hero is slain in battle but raised again to fresh exploits. What this tells us is that resurrection is there as a basic need or wish-fulfilment in human nature, and can be seen as a preparatory mind-set for the ministry and resurrection of Jesus.

Related to life and death is the motif of the serpent, which appears in many ways in virtually every myth the world over. Where there is no snake, an octopus is a substitute; often there is a multitude of snakes. What does this imply? Snakes have always struck fear into humans and yet fascination. They are mysterious and lead an uncanny life which seems indestructible. They also symbolise fecundity. Here is a creature that goes on surviving, regardless of how many heads are chopped off: it is an indestructible form of life. It is related to death but also to survival of death. We recall how Moses made a bronze serpent, Nehushtan, and brought people back to life; a theme taken up again in St John's Gospel. The serpent is a multifaceted symbol, paradoxical, and another good example of myth being closely interwoven with historicity. This symbol resonates with people's minds the world over, even if there are no snakes in their area.

Another motif very commonly encountered but not in quite every myth is the appeal to gold, jewels, crystal, translucent stones and mirrors. Again we see the appeal to life and the survival of life. Gold is incorruptible (so too silver) and its lustre holds a fascination. It was widely used in alchemy and much effort went into fabricating it, the motive being to extend human life. Mercury too was thought to extend one's life-span. Jewels, with their lustrous qualities, suggested indestructible life. So too with semi-precious stones with a translucent quality such as jade, onyx, and alabaster. A ring too, especially if it is of gold, symbolises eternity. All these tell of the preciousness of life: it ought to last for ever. All these matters speak deeply to the human soul and are there as a preparation for the work of Jesus.

Moving up and down: incarnation

The connection between the three tiers has been mentioned before. The gods come down into this world, often in disguise. Vishnu with his multiple avatars is most noteworthy but there are others, such as Odin and Asshur. Some humans can gain promotion and be assumed into the skies, or even become a god on earth. Also the two-way traffic between earth and hell is a reality for humans and even for gods. In the Buddhist Wheel of Becoming the whole scheme of mobility is set in a cartouche: people circulate between heaven and hell and all stages in between. What this indicates is that though there is an unseen barrier between these stages, there is movement between them, and one's god might be very close to one. Incarnation in its various permutations is a deeply held need in human nature, and is there as a receptor for the Incarnation of Jesus.

Eternal justice

The unspoken assumption behind every mythical system is ethical values and everlasting justice. When the gods misbehave themselves there is the presupposition that there will be a reckoning to be faced. This is morality at its crudest; yet the basic values surrounding the sanctity of life, of property and of the person are common to gods and humans alike. The connection between good conduct and eternal justice is assumed everywhere. By the time we come to Hammurabi (1750 BC) we see myth sliding into historical reality. Before this, laws were simply assumed to be given by divinity, and failure to conform would lead to retribution. This is the Old Testament mentality: it is the main form of preparation for the coming of Jesus.

Related to this, mythically, is the appearance of the sword. It occurs in virtually every myth, and where it is absent a spear or even an arrow is a substitute. This speaks of eternal justice, retribution, the righting of all wrongs, and of truth. There is in our minds the need for fair play, just desserts; to see some injustice not resolved somehow leaves an imbalance in people's minds. That is why Theodicy is a problem for us all.

Relevant to this is the motif of purification, a need seen everywhere. If one has failed to live up to the standards expected by eternal justice or some sense of unworthiness, then cleansing is needed. Water is the main agent for this; fire is another. Both modes appear in the Bible. Interestingly, many myths from widely scattered areas of the world contain some kind of flood motif. The accounts sound remarkably similar to those of Noah and Utnapishtim. This may be some kind of folk-recollection of a real flood disaster in remote prehistory. As far as Noah is concerned there is archaeological evidence for severe flooding in Mesopotamia, and this is another case where myth and historical reality merge together. The underlying thought is the same: that mankind was not worth saving; the earth was cleansed by water. In some myths the gods are disgusted that a few humans survived. Nevertheless a new humanity and a fresh start is given. In Noah's case it was a foretaste of the New Testament. The flood motif has a fascination for us all. The present-day mania for tracing the Ark on Mount Ararat is just a symptom of the hold it exerts on people's minds, and the spiritual reality of the need for purification, not just of the individual but of the whole of creation.

Unusual cases

There are many other features of mythology which could be mentioned, but are not as widespread as the foregoing. It is now worth recounting one system which is unique and yet holds many features in common with other systems. The Chinese (Taoist) conception is like this. There is the Jade Emperor who lives in a heavenly palace, the Jade Heaven. It is an exact replica of the palace in Peking. He is the Father-Heaven who made all humans out of clay. He is the greatest of the gods, but only second in a triad. The first is the heavenly master of the first origin, the heavenly master of the dawn jade of the golden door. The Jade Emperor has an 'action man', the great emperor of the eastern peak who actually deals with day-to-day matters with humanity. There is a mass of subsidiary gods who perform a wealth of bureaucratic, commercial and professional roles. The whole thing is a bureaucratic projection into the skies. God is the ultimate 'jack-in-the-office': a complete system in the sky as it is in central government in Peking. This turns out to be another variant on sacral kingship. On death, one might descend into one of 18 hells; otherwise there is a form of paradise in the west, or an island in the East China Sea. Also there are various heavens culminating in the Jade Heaven. Where one goes has a lot to do with the carefully kept records by the bureaucrats in the sky. This is unique in that god is a bureaucratic official, and yet other aspects of it tie in with other cultures, including the fascination with jade.

What it does show is that God can so often and so easily be fashioned in our own image, as a larger-than-life version of the ideal person (or maybe not so ideal). Conversely we understand that mankind is fashioned in God's image, a sort of micro-god. There is an element of 'chicken and egg' in this. The paradox here is that both claims are true in their own way. On the one hand, God created humanity according to his design and expectations; on the other hand, humanity can only understand God in terms of our own experience and use of metaphor. It is very unusual for a myth to be lacking in some form of human or animal representation of God. Even the Jews, who were forbidden to make idols, still understood God as having all manner of traits in common with humanity and with animals.

A rare system comes from the Pericu Indians of California. They hold that Niparaya, their god, has no body and is invisible. Even so he has a wife and three sons. On coming down to earth the Indians managed to murder him. He is dead to this day and yet his blood flows continuously. There is a certain amount of inconsistency in this, as with most myths, and yet it shows the impossibility of understanding God in other than human terms. The paradox is a good one and is as deep as the paradox of life itself.

Multi-myth

It will now be instructive to outline four myths coming from the same area, namely Ancient Greece;[20] it will show the various thoughts on the matter without it resulting in accusations of heresy. There is also the implication that such myths were never taken completely literally.

The Pelasgian creation myth involves the goddess of all things, Eurynomede, rising naked from Chaos and dividing the sea from the sky. She produced the great serpent Ophion and became pregnant by him. Assuming the form of a dove, she laid the Universal Egg. Ophion coiled round it seven times until it hatched and let out created things, the heavenly bodies, earth, and everything in it. The first man was Pelasgus (analogous to Adam) who came from the soil of Arcadia and invented shelter, food and clothing.

The Orphic myth says that black-winged Night was courted by the Wind and laid a silver egg in the womb of Darkness. When it hatched, Eros emerged and set the universe in motion. He was double-sexed, roared like a bull, hissed like a snake, and bleated like a ram. Night was triadic, living in a cave with him. Eros created earth, sky and moon, but Wind ruled the universe until Uranus became king.

The Olympian myth says that Mother Earth emerged from Chaos at the beginning and she bore Uranus. He showered rain upon her body so that all living creatures could appear, including lakes and seas. The first people were three semi-human giants; then came the three wild Cyclopes, the blacksmiths.

The Homeric version, rather sketchy, says that all gods and living creatures originated in the stream of Oceanus which girdles the world, and Tethys was the mother of all his children.

Rather unusual, a fifth idea, is another scheme in which the earth bore men spontaneously. Here we see the five ages of man: the first was of gold, ruled by Cronus, when everything was idyllic; the silver race were also divinely created, inclined to quarrel but not make war; the bronze age had men falling from an ash tree, armed with brazen weapons and delighting in war; the fourth race was brazen too but begotten by the gods on mortal mothers, giving us the great Greek epics such as the Trojan War, and they became heroes and now dwell in the Elysian Fields; the fifth race, of iron, is descended from the fourth, but a degeneration of it, being mean, vicious and treacherous.

In this latter myth we see the emphasis on early human developments. This can be compared with the images in Daniel. There is the awareness of a Golden Age in the past with the implication that the future holds a resolution of this state. We can sense the attempt to grapple with the imponderables, how all things began, how the gods relate to humanity, and man's unworthiness. It is not done in high-flown philosophical language, and yet we can see how the Gnostics refined these crude ideas into something quite elaborate and intellectual. Again we can see the intertwining of myth with historical events such as the Trojan War.

The final resolution

It is not enough to relegate human mythology to the dustbin as a collection of idle superstition. These myths indicate something important in human instinct, that has to be addressed. A positive approach is by far the better way of understanding it: that approach is to say that the coming of Jesus the Messiah brings about the correction, completion and fulfilment of all these speculations. This is seen first and foremost in the way the early Genesis material is brought to fulfilment, but going further it takes in mythologies from all over the world. This does not have to mean that Jesus knew all these crude ideas from far and near: if the Incarnation was genuine, he probably did not know them; rather he was aware of the main essentials and provided an answer to them in his own way. The paradox here is that the archaic human speculation and guesswork of humanity came to a defining moment at a real point in history with a real person who had the authority to give the final answers.

The most obvious resolution is seen in St John's Gospel, 'In the beginning was the Word,' where the first few words of Genesis are evoked, with all those remarks about darkness and light. But the true light and real agent of creation is the pre-existent Son of God. It makes little difference whether St John took Genesis literally; he probably did. The contradictory and lurid mythologies of the rest of the world must have seemed crazy against the sanity of Genesis. Whatever their quality, they all find resolution in Jesus. He was not some sort of agent, or lesser god doing the actual work of creation, leaving the Supreme God to be disassociated with the realities. St John corrects this by saying, 'The Word was with God, and the Word was God. He was in the beginning with God: all things were made through him.'

The idea of the champion, great hero, super-man, who might be one of the offspring of the Supreme God also comes to resolution. Jesus, the true Son of God, comes into the world to do battle against the powers of evil. But it is a very different battle compared with the pagan ones which involve extreme violence, for Jesus was a man of peace and overcame the demons with his heavenly authority. The battle with the Devil is one of humility, acceptance of suffering, but final triumph. It is the corrective to all the crude and bloodthirsty pagan accounts.

As far as dualism is concerned, there is frequent mention of the Devil and evil spirits in the ministry of Jesus. It is saying in effect that evil is a force to be reckoned with, not diminished or underestimated. This does not mean that Satan is an alternative god: the Devil is never elevated to equality with God. Rather, Jesus ingeniously allows Satan to prepare the way for the final triumph of the cross; Judas Iscariot had one plan but God had another which made subtle use of evil for the purpose of good. What went wrong in the Garden of Eden is put right in the darkness of Gethsemane, and in the garden of the Resurrection. In death he spends time in the underworld redeeming souls in torment. This tells us that Jesus has defeated evil in all three zones of the universe, and there is no need to fear evil any more. This is not to say that evil is totally eradicated: that will be the task for the Messiah when he comes again.

The three-tier system is the main assumption made by Jesus; he could hardly have worked with any other mind-set if he were genuinely human. But in many places the way the Gospel writers quote him shows clearly that Jesus did more than just assume this system: he had personal experience of it and knew how to cope with it, but had difficulties in explaining it to us in meaningful language. 'In my Father's house there are many mansions,' puzzling to us now as then. In short, whatever the details of the reality of this world and the world of the spirit, the truth is that Jesus is supreme in all areas, up and down. He brings this whole mind-set to resolution with a touch of vagueness.

The connection between the three tiers is also resolved in Jesus. In one sense, according to the parable of Dives and Lazarus (Luke 16:19ff) there is an uncrossable chasm between heaven and hell. How literally we take this is not easy to answer, since Abraham and Dives are able to communicate with each other, and with Dives' brother who is still on earth. Jesus never mentions anything about bridges, ladders or any other devices. Instead he claims to be the Way, the Door, the Resurrection and the Life. He personally is the connection: it is not a theory, a gadget or a doctrine: it is a living person who is God himself. This is where the tree motif comes in. There are many trees in the Bible, some with great spiritual loading, but the final one is the cross (often termed thus in Christian poetry). It is stuck in the ground but reaches up to heaven; Jesus himself is attached to it. Christ crucified is the final connection between humanity and the Eternal Father.

Every myth tries to cope with the worrying matter of death. The survival instinct is strong in all of us and results in all manner of methods for extending life or indeed some form of resurrection. The Genesis myth implies that there need never have been any death (also procreation) if Adam and Eve had not disobeyed God, but now 'you are dust and to dust you shall return' (3:19), the fate of all mankind. With the coming of Jesus we see the reversal and resolution of this situation. The urge to defeat or sidestep death is brought to fulfilment in real terms. He raises people from the dead: Jairus's daughter and Lazarus. But these are only signs or indicators of what is to come: the final defeat of death on Easter Day. If this sounds a little like the pagan gods being raised again, this could well be intentional; he is in effect saying, 'here is the true and ultimate indestructible life.' It is not linked to the seasons, even if Easter happens to coincide with spring in the Northern Hemisphere. His claim to be the Resurrection and the Life is not just a piece of wishful thinking or mythical speculation. It is worked out in real terms in the life, death and resurrection of a real historical figure, Jesus.

The motif of promotion and demotion, seen in many permutations in the pagan myths, whether it be of gods or humans, also comes to conclusion. But the Incarnation of the Messiah (discussed in detail earlier) is of a different quality. It is not illusory as some tried to claim, but he was really human and paradoxically divine in the one person. He accepts 'demotion' (Philippians 2:6), 'emptied himself, taking the form of a servant' and then accepts 'promotion': 'God has highly exalted him, and bestowed on him the name which is above every name.' This means that all our speculations about moving from earth to heaven are fulfilled, but in real terms. It is not a ghost, a fiction, wishful thinking; it is a real person who provides the transition between two worlds. To those who accept the Wheel of Becoming, the answer is that Yama the god of the dead is defeated: the wheel stops spinning and we can all get off. Everyone can have release from Karma and the remorseless despair of life and death. Everyone, regardless of their race or religion, can have direct access to the Eternal Father through Jesus the living way.

Everlasting justice and the difference between right and wrong have always been included in some way in the myths. Jesus works on this right from the start with the two major sermons and in other places, taking the laws of Moses and working them up to an impossibly high ethic. The answer to this is that we realise our inadequacy and this shows up the importance of everlasting mercy and forgiveness. The pre-existent love of God is often conspicuous by its absence in most myths, but that is the crucial answer that Jesus gives: that there is everlasting mercy. For those who know they are submerged in guilt, he takes it away on his own shoulders by his sacrificial death. Eternal justice is brought to completion; eternal mercy is the bedrock of freedom with God. With this paradox all our worries about legalism and moral failure are balanced by loving mercy and release.

The need for purification is also brought to resolution, firstly with John the Baptist and then with Jesus. John brings people to baptism for spiritual cleansing but also speaks of baptism by fire. In the myths, water and fire are seen as cleansing agents. A telling remark in Luke 12:49: 'I have cast fire upon the earth: and would that it were already kindled. I have a baptism to be baptised with.' Baptism and spiritual cleansing is accomplished by both water and fire. St Luke records that the first Pentecost was with tongues of fire on the disciples. With this we see that the Christian purification is the genuine and everlasting release from the mire of moral failure and that we can face life with a clear conscience.

It is now noticeable that the resolution of mythology is not purely and simply confined to the Gospels. Other parts of the Bible bring these matters to fulfilment. One example is the flood motif (already discussed): if it ever were a historical reality it has acquired mythical overtones relating to the attitude of the gods and the condition of mankind. The Biblical answer to it is to turn it into the first basic covenant, which prefigures the New Testament. 1 Peter 3:20 takes up this theme: 'the ark, in which a few ... were saved through water. Baptism, which corresponds to this, now saves you, not as a removal of dirt from the body, but as an appeal to God for a clear conscience, through the resurrection of Jesus Christ.' Altogether there are various incidents involving water: the crossing of the Red Sea, the crossing of the River Jordan by Joshua and even Naaman's washing in the Jordan. It is a positive approach to mythology, not so much about destruction but salvation: out of loss of life comes new life. This is a paradox seen in many myths in different imagery.

The use of precious metals, jewels and a variety of semi-precious stones, though not universally seen in myth, are worked into Biblical thinking. Obviously they were associated with snobbery, power, royalty and eternal life. In Exodus, Moses is instructed to put jewels in the high priest's breastplate and in the *ephod* (Exodus 25:7 and 35:9). Onyx, another translucent stone like jade, was used and was also inscribable. At the climax of the Bible in Revelation comes the lavish use of every jewel imaginable, and the use of glass and crystal. It speaks of light, truth, indestructibility and fascination (Revelation 21:9 to 22:1). We come close to hearing about mirrors in Hebrews 1:3 where Jesus 'reflects the glory of God', and in James 1:23 we actually have mention of a mirror, though not in a context which would connect with mythology. All these things, which to the ancient mind would have stirred thoughts of fascination and eternal life, are now brought to resolution with regard to Jesus and the eternal life provided by him in the presence of God.

Associated with trees is the fruit, although many myths seem to ignore this idea. In China, the peach is a symbol of immortality. The nearest we come to fruit in the Gospels is the lack of it on the fig tree and in the vineyard, and this is symbolic of the lack of response from the Jewish leadership to the ministry of Jesus. In Genesis the fruit is forbidden as being the 'knowledge of good and evil'; it does not bring eternal life but rather the opposite. There is another tree (Genesis 3:22) which has to be guarded by a cherubim with a flaming sword. Mankind at this stage is prevented from gaining eternity. This theme is balanced and reversed in Revelation 22:2 where the tree of life is planted on each side of the river, producing 12 kinds of fruit, one for each month of the year, and the leaves are for the healing of the nations. In other words, the collapse of innocence brought about by Adam is reversed and in Jesus we are all given release from sin, pain and death, and qualify for eternal life.

The idea of the first man and woman is by no means confined to the Old Testament. Adam and Eve appear under different names in many myths; occasionally it is a collection of people, as in China: the Jade Emperor made them of clay and left them out in the rain which explains why the human race has failings. Usually the first people go wrong somehow, and even if they do not, there is a sense of unease that they have not lived up to the standards expected by the creating deity, either in ritual or in moral matters. The resolution of this, implicit in the Gospels, is actually spelt out by St Paul in 1 Corinthians 15:22: 'For as by man came death, by a man came also the resurrection of the dead: for as in Adam all die, so also in Christ shall all be made alive.'

It is beyond the New Testament that this motif receives a much more thorough treatment, with Ireneaus in particular. The point about it is that all our worries about failure, unworthiness and human deterioration are taken away and transformed by the triumph of Jesus. In being supreme he balances out all the negativity of mankind with his positive masterstroke.

Time itself or the passage of history has importance in myth, although with this we see the merging and interweaving of myth with historical realities. The Mayans especially had it all worked out in an extremely clever cyclical system, whereas the Jews had it working in epochs in a straight line. More attention to this will come in a later chapter. Often there is a 'Golden Age' in the past. The resolution for this is partly found in the eschatological material, Daniel and Revelation, but mainly found outside the Bible in the pseudepigraphal literature. It brings us to a futuristic golden age, the return of the Garden of Eden, with the assurance that all things will be restored. The minuses of history will all become plusses in God's new Jerusalem.

It would be possible to find many more minor examples of how the myths of mankind are balanced out and resolved in the Judaeo-Christian tradition. We need only think of the baby floating in the basket (Mesoamerica) to realise that Moses is the answer to that. It is highly unlikely that the one culture gave the idea to the other. The conclusion is that the mind of man is the same the world over and that the answer to all his speculations, worries and expectations are found in the true Messiah, Jesus. Following the same process of thought seen in Hebrews, whereby the sacrificial system is brought to a conclusion in the ministry of Jesus, so too human mythology, both within and outside of the Scriptures, is brought to completion and in some aspects to obsolescence. In this we see the true function and realisation of all mythology. Even so the memory of mythology still goes on in people's minds; its fascination, especially for Genesis, is still there even though we know, rationally, that there are problems with it. Mythology, in its world-view and moral hold on people, is just as real on the symbolic level as it ever was.

The modern demythologisation process: Bultmann and others

Under the influence of modern scientific knowledge we have seen a process known as demythologising[21] being applied to the New Testament message, perhaps less so with the Old Testament, and hardly at all with regard to non-Scriptural myths. Strangely the Buddhists and others are allowed to hold on to their myths whereas the Christians are not.

The process of demythologising is nothing new and the first stirrings of it can be seen in the New Testament itself. Consider this situation: Luke 4:2, 'tempted by the devil', but in Matthew 4:1, 'to be tempted by the devil ... and the tempter came to him', this time in human terms, the mythological element here being toned down a little. The passage ends with 'and angels came and ministered to him', but Luke does not mention that at all. This may indicate an uneasiness about expressing it in purely mythological terms. With regard to the event at Caesarea Philippi, Mark and Matthew record Jesus as saying to Peter, 'Get behind me, Satan, for you are not on the side of God, but of man,' (Mark 8:35). But Luke does not include this remark in spite of the same situation demanding it. Firstly, we can see that the 'devil' is not so much a spirit but a human outburst from one of Jesus' close associates; secondly, we see Luke omitting any reference to it, possibly because he did not like to see Peter as a front for an evil influence. Whichever way it is seen, there is some sort of ambivalence about mythology here. To compare two resurrection accounts we see the same process at work. Matthew 28:1ff gives Jesus the most dramatic and exciting version, as the guards fell down and 'an angel of the Lord descended from heaven and rolled back the stone and sat upon it. His appearance was like lightning and his raiment white as snow.' But St John is much more reserved, peaceful and sentimental. There is no angel, and Mary thinks the body has been stolen. Emphasis is laid on the grave-clothes; also that Jesus is not immediately recognisable. The tone of it is very different; one might say it is demythologised, except that it is not certain which of the two Gospels was written before the other. The other two Gospels take a moderate course, with men in white who might be taken for angels, but the whole tone is one of fear and bewilderment. From these four accounts we see that mythology has a differing influence on the way the resurrection is described. It is not a simple matter just to root out mythological features like angels and devils in the hopes that modern people will find the Gospel more acceptable.

The process of demythologising has gone on throughout the history of the Church in various ways. Every time an attempt is made to re-express the Gospel in terms of contemporary thought forms or philosophy, it is the same process. The early heresies are a case in point; also the hair-splitting of the Schoolmen; now we have the scientific upsurge of the last 200 years. Even so, mythology will not go away and is still the bedrock of religious thought. To look at the Lord's Prayer, which is universally used by Christians of all types, it begins, 'Our Father who art in heaven ... thy Kingdom come' and ends with another outburst of mythology, 'for thine is the Kingdom'.

Bultmann maintains that the New Testament mythical view of the world and many other aspects of it are now obsolete. He cannot believe in spirits, good or evil, the miracles have ceased to be miraculous, eschatology is wrong, the resurrection is quite incredible, the atonement unacceptable, the pre-existence of Christ, the Virgin Birth, the Ascension all fiction. It is clear from the way he writes that there is a degree of Gnostic influence, for he cannot see any of this as historical reality but as figurative, illusionary and beyond modern man to assimilate.

One wonders if he has ever acquainted himself with other mythologies; still less has he come to any serious understanding of how these systems of thought function and what they give to the spirituality of humanity. Trying to express faith purely in existentialist terms is not only impossible but deeply unwise. The wise and constructive approach is to acknowledge that myth is a deeply rooted reality in the human mind, even if it is not historically true, but the Bible has a way of bringing all these factors to a conclusion in real terms. It is not good enough to say that myth is brought to conclusion by another round of myth: that is meaningless. One fantasy follows upon another?

The New Testament writers are at pains to point out the historical reality of the coming of Jesus. St Luke particularly anchors the whole thing in real historical situations: 'in those days a decree went out from Caesar Augustus', and 'in the fifteenth year of the reign of Tiberius Caesar, Pontius Pilate being governor of Judea, Herod being tetrarch of Galilee ... Philip tetrarch of Ituraea', all accurate history from the Roman Empire. A lot of emphasis is laid on those who could vouch for the death and resurrection of Jesus: it was no fiction. John 19:35: 'he who saw it has borne witness ... his testimony is true and he knows he tells the truth,' and 'this is the disciple who is bearing witness to these things and who has written these things, and we know that his testimony is true,' Of course such matters are difficult for modern man; they were never meant to be easy for them 20 centuries ago, as for us now. This is because such things are not within our own experience; but we can recall that it was difficult for some people then, who were minded to label Jesus as a fraud and the whole thing a charade.

'Sir, we remember how that imposter said, while he was still alive, "After three days I will rise again." Therefore order that the sepulchre be made secure ... lest his disciples go and steal him away,' Matthew 27:63.

Bultmann, as with many doubters, is assuming that such wonders could never happen. That is a gratuitous assumption. We know from recent experience that spiritual healing is a reality, also that exorcism is practised by specialist priests. These are factors that have lain dormant in the Church for many centuries but are now re-emerging as an answer to the current wave of disbelief. It is impossible to judge, assess and undervalue Jesus of Nazareth. He stands as a unique figure in human history. Scientific analysis is nonsense in this situation. To do such an analysis would involve having other similar figures and making comparisons: that is proper analysis. But this cannot be done. If it is true that God came into the world as a human being, then we would expect amazing things to happen. It could be said that much of what Jesus did went against the 'laws of nature'. But what are the laws of nature? Laws made by God, many of which we do not yet fully understand. We would also expect all manner of paradoxes to emerge, which to the doubter seem like errors, inconsistencies and illogicalities. When two worlds coincide in one man, what else would one expect? But to the man of faith, these matters simply deepen the mystery of the Incarnation and provide fresh challenges to belief.

Bultmann fails to realise that using mythology, which involves picture language, is an excellent way of speaking to people of all grades of intelligence and experience. To express the message of the Gospel purely in philosophical terms, such as existentialism may seem very clever, but how many people can understand it? Everyone knows what heaven, hell, angels and devils mean, even if they are not on a literal level. If asked, Jesus might have said (Matthew 11:25): 'I thank thee Father, Lord of heaven and earth, that thou hast hidden these things from the wise and understanding and revealed them to babes.'

Indeed one of the qualifications for entering the kingdom of heaven is to accept it as a little child: 'Whoever does not receive the kingdom of God like a child shall not enter it,' Mark 10:15.

All the teachings, miracles and parables of Jesus, almost entirely based on mythological assumptions, may sound naive and ignorant, but they are basic to the human psyche and we ignore them at our peril. It is not possible to dismiss them without seriously undermining the message of the Gospel. This is something that Bultmann seems not to appreciate.

Myth in the making: the Apocryphal New Testament Gospels[22]

At this juncture, it could be appropriate to discuss the significance of the New Testament Apocryphal infancy Gospels. The chief one is the Infancy Gospel of Thomas, not to be confused with the Gospel of Thomas recently discovered at Nag Hammadi. It is believed that the Infancy Gospel of Thomas appeared early in the second century AD and probably just after the canonical Gospels began to enter circulation. It was known all through the Middle Ages and had some influence on Mediaeval art. There is a genuine difficulty for us now in assessing its validity, as indeed is true for all New Testament apocryphal work. There is always the awkward question of what happened between the birth and the appearance of Jesus in the Temple at the age of 12. There is no way we can verify any of this material except by subjective analysis. The early Church rejected it for inclusion in the canon; they probably had sound reasons. The suggestion here is that this material is not worthless. It may be problematic for a literal interpretation, but it does have ramifications from the point of view of mythology being fabricated after the event. It tells us something about how people felt about Jesus; that his childhood must have been just as amazing as his public ministry. Also there is the fact that across the spectrum of various infancy gospels (for Thomas is not the only one), there is a considerable degree of consistency. How much they copied each other is impossible to assess. Always there is that degree of exaggeration often seen in the New Testament teachings. These following remarks largely follow 'Thomas'.

At the age of five, Jesus was playing by the ford of a stream. He gathered the water into pools and purified them. He then took soft mud and made 12 sparrows from it; they flew away. This was done on the Sabbath. If we assess this from the point of view of myth (that is not to say it is completely untrue) there are several features here which coincide with the factors seen earlier. The esoteric use of the number 12, the tribes of Israel; the sparrows are formed from mud, just as mankind is formed from dust (Genesis 2:7). This means that the Jews have a common ancestry with the rest of humanity and yet a special breath of life has been given to them by the Lord. Ironically the Jews object to this because the Sabbath has been infringed. The sparrows chirped and flew away: does this mean that the Jews have lost the original inspiration? Purifying the pools of water is redolent of baptism and the need for us all to be purified. The account goes on as the son of Annas took a willow branch and scattered the pool. This annoyed Jesus and he withered the boy, not unlike the withering of the Fig Tree. Does this mean that Jesus was a vindictive child? Not necessarily: it could indicate that the legalists of Judaism were trying to undo his work but it backfired on them.

Always there is the underlying mythological hint of new life and purification. In chapters 4 and 5 a boy bumps into Jesus: he falls down dead. Those who accused him were blinded. This sounds dreadful until we read in chapter 8 that he healed them all. Again the hint of resurrection and enlightenment are there.

Jesus has an instructor called Zachaeus who was amazed at the remarks Jesus made. He tries to teach him the alphabet in Greek. Does that sound wrong somehow? The point is that Alpha has a set pattern 'so that it is divided into three equal parts, each of them fundamental and foundational, of equal length'. Here we see the use of three as basic in so many mythological systems, and coming to completion in the Holy Trinity. Zachaeus is completely floored and concludes that Jesus is 'a divine being or an angel'. His second teacher offers to teach him Greek and then Hebrew. Does that sound wrong somehow? He hits Jesus on the head, whereupon the teacher faints and falls dead. His third teacher fared rather better; he realised the intelligence of Jesus and praised him: 'He is filled with wisdom and grace.' Because of this the second teacher is healed. Again there is the hint of three with the number of teachers: third time lucky. There is also the hint that Jesus was receptive to a Gentile language in addition to his own, which was Aramaic. Hebrew seems to take second place here, which may be symbolic of his universal appeal.

A boy falls off a rooftop and dies; Jesus is accused of throwing him down; Jesus heals the boy. Zenon, which is a Greek name, rises up and says, 'You did not throw me down: but you have raised me up.' So resurrection is for the Gentiles as well as the Jews (chapter 9). Also we see the same ingredient in chapters 17 and 18. A man was building a house and fell down dead. Jesus raised him and said, 'Rise up and do your work.' Is this the house of Israel being told to take fresh inspiration, or is it the household of faith being given a fresh impetus?

A young man was splitting wood with an axe (chapter 10). He split open the sole of his foot and was bleeding to death. Jesus grabs his foot and heals him, saying, 'Rise now, split wood and remember me.' This is much more esoteric, as nothing like it appears in the New Testament. However it does recall a remark made in the Gospel of Thomas: 'Split the wood and I am there: lift the stone and I am there,' and 'I am the All: the All issues from me and reaches me.' Apart from the hint of pantheism, does this tell us that Jesus is to be found in all situations, even in the most secretive of places? The hidden Messiah?

James the son of Joseph went out to fetch wood; a snake bit his hand. As he lay dying, Jesus came and breathed on his hand; James was healed and the snake burst open. This tells us that Jesus cared for his brother (as well as his earthly family). On the mythological level, the serpent is defeated and actually dies: this is the ultimate defeat of the Devil. It is also a parallel to the incident when St Paul is bitten by a poisonous snake on Malta.

At the age of eight, Jesus is sowing wheat with Joseph. Jesus sowed one single grain which turned, when threshed, into 100 large bushels. He gave a lot away to the poor of the village. This reminds us of the parable of the Sower, with some exaggeration, but the message is the same: that from a very small beginning, the Kingdom of God grows mightily during the interim period. It is the same motif as the Mustard Seed parable, only there it is a tree, with all its mythological implications.

At the age of six, Jesus was sent out with a jug to fetch water. The crowd jostled him and the jug was shattered; he scooped up the water in his cloak and brought it back to his mother (chapter 11). We can suppose that the jug represents the Jewish faith: they smash it themselves by being careless, but Jesus rescues the essentials of faith and gives it to his mother, who represents the Church. So we see the basics of the Old Testament being preserved by Jesus, and the Church is the new recipient, in the New Testament, of the essentials of faith. Again, water as the medium of purification in baptism, is seen as provided by Jesus.

Joseph was making a bed for a rich man. The measurement for one of the crossbeams came out too short. Jesus pulled on the short piece of wood and made it longer (chapter 13). With the mention of wood we are immediately reminded of trees, which have much mythological significance. It also hints at the cross of Calvary, with a crossbeam which is too short, and Jesus stretched it out. He himself was stretched out on the cross. The hint here is that he widened his arms out to embrace all people.

Some of this must seem quite fantastic to modern minds and yet we must realise that in the ancient world people's minds worked in ways which we do not fully understand now. Jesus comes across as precocious, intellectually clever and vengeful. He is a child like others, inclined to lose his temper, and yet takes guidance from his parents. In some ways, these infancy gospels throw an interesting light on various features in the Gospels. This is not to say that we can just take them purely at face value. There is much of mythological substratum, metaphor and allegory at work here. It is mythology in the making, and paradoxically in the completing. But one thing comes a little clearer: if Jesus really was capable of performing miracles on this sort of level, as a child, it would explain why he imagined he could turn stones into bread at the Temptations. The Apocryphal Gospels remain a mystery, but there are various things that they are valid for, as evidence.

The Apocryphal material as a corpus of literature, whether recently discovered (the Gospel of Judas), or known right through the Christian era, can be divided into three main categories. Firstly, the material which is 'proto-orthodox' which is genuinely in line with New Testament theology. An example would be the Shepherd of Hermas, which nearly was included in the canon. Secondly, the material which takes Jesus and tries to turn him into a basis for some cranky theory, such as Gnosticism. Two examples would be the Gospel of Thomas and the Gospel of Judas. Thirdly, the material which tried to discredit Jesus altogether with some kind of smear campaign. A recent example of this would be the so-called Gospel of Jesus' Wife (Mary Magdalene?). We have the early Church to thank for discriminating between the genuine and the spurious in the early years. Even so, all this material, of whatever quality, has something to tell us in one way or another.

It is difficult to see into which category 'Thomas' falls, but since it was retained, not as canonical but on the fringe, it may be seen as 'proto-orthodox'. Allowing for the element of exaggeration, which is understandable if it were written over a century after the events it purports to describe, we may be seeing a genuinely difficult situation in Nazareth: that of a child with extraordinary abilities, and no one really knowing how to cope with it. Reading between the lines, we see a child of five performing deeds which to him might have seemed quite normal, not realising that other children could not do such things. He may not have realised his own potential, and only gradually came to understand his own spiritual strength. We see him almost accidentally causing people to die; and yet he is capable of rectifying the matter. He genuinely loves his parents and accepts their guidance.

We do not know what happened after the age of 12, which would have meant he was regarded as an adult and so responsible for his own actions. It may be a fair interpretation that, if the Incarnation were genuine, as an infant he had to learn the hard way, by bitter experience, just how far he could go when dealing with other people, especially children. How he coped with teachers is interesting: he is clearly better informed than any of them. No teacher likes to have an over-precocious pupil! But we see him coming to terms with them too. We see the villagers totally amazed and ready to dub him an angel or some kind of god. This was because his miracles were done publicly, not so much as public display but because he has yet to realise the effect it will have on people. By the time we reach his public ministry in later life, we see him being much more guarded and secretive about the miracles. He has realised that it will engender the wrong kind of loyalty. He has had to learn, the hard way, how to dispense his gifts in a manner appropriate to his being the servant of all. In this way we see him as genuinely human and yet paradoxically endowed with extraordinary abilities.

Modern mythology in the making

Another factor that Bultmann fails to address is the emergence of new mythology in the modern world. The reason for this may be because the ancient myths have been brought into question and regarded with scorn. A notable new one is the idea of the 'noble savage' fostered by Rousseau, which may be a permutation on the 'Golden Age' motif.[23] True or false it may have been a major factor in underpinning certain political theories. One such was the 'Age of Reason' which underpinned the blood-letting of the French Revolution (quite ironic). In the last century the Nazis contrived to justify their excesses by reference to a revival of ancient Nordic mythology, combined with evolutionism.

The current wave of science fiction produced by such writers as Arthur C. Clark, and TV serials such as *Star Trek* and *Quatermass*, is another example of modern myth-mongering. There is an obsession about discovering 'life' on other planets, on the assumption that if there were such living things, they would be similar in structure and outlook to the human race: they might even speak English! All this is sheer speculation. Once again human traits, usually failings, are projected into the skies. Vast sums of money are spent on trying to research such matters: every probe to another planet costs billions. Von Daniken's space visitors are another symptom of the same thing:[24] also UFOs have a massive hold on people's minds.

Another modern myth is the theory of evolution: it is the prevailing assumption in the modern world. Just as ancient man would probably have claimed the evidence of his eyes as proof of his myths, so too the scientists claim that modern discoveries and conjectures substantiate evolution. Many take it as a proven fact, but it may turn out to be just as much a mirage as any other theory. As an attempt to omit God from the picture, it fails: there still has to be the assumption that all things had to have a beginning somewhere; moreover there is no convincing explanation for how animal consciousness became human consciousness. There is the tacit assumption that biologically (and possibly morally) we shall continue to improve. Even if the 'Golden Age' in the past is missing, there is one waiting in the future. It is an interesting example of how the myths of the past have been transformed into the myths of the present and the future. So often religio-mythical assumptions are the substratum of scientific theorising.

With regard to deep space exploration, we have been assured that there was a 'Big Bang' and that the universe is expanding. The scientist who coined the phrase only offered it tentatively about 60 years ago, but the idea became popular and became standard doctrine. Now, it seems, there are doubts about it, and questions about what happened before this uncertain 'Big Bang'. All kinds of interesting and frightening prophecies are offered about the fate of mankind on this planet; even so we are not allowed to take Revelation seriously, and that is far less frightening. But since with all our clever techniques we are only glimpsing about 5 per cent of what goes on in deep space, it is impertinent of us to talk with such confidence about matters that we do not really understand. Such terms as 'black hole' and 'quasar' and the like are just as much metaphoric and are simply fodder for modern myth-making.

Another modern preoccupation which amounts to a mania is the myth of good prevailing over bad. This is seen in pantomimes, cowboy films, police thrillers, detection stories and even soap opera. With detection there is the added element of mystery, and of the amateur sleuth managing to find a solution which evaded the attention of the police. In real life, sometimes criminals do manage to evade the law, but the urge for eternal justice in people's minds ensures that the detectives seldom fail to get their man. We also see the champion element and also the resurrection motif when occasionally the detective is believed to have been defeated and yet manages to surprise everyone with a flash of genius. Sherlock Holmes actually did 'die', and later reappeared after his encounter with Moriarty at the Reichenbach Falls! This simply shows that the ancient myth ingredients are far from dead in people's minds, especially eternal justice. The difference is that the presentation of them and the rituals pertaining to it are noticeably different from ancient times. Bultmann never seems to address this matter. It is clear that myth will not go away: it is a fact of the human mentality and must be taken into account. Any attempt to restate the Gospel in a way relevant to modern times must reckon with these basic impulses.

The final resolution as with the ancient myths is to be found in the ministry of Jesus Christ, who is shown to be the ultimate judge and exposer of wickedness. With regard to all the scientific advances in recent times, the answer is found in Revelation 22:13: 'I am Alpha and Omega, the beginning and the end,' meaning that the whole of life, however it comes about, will come to resolution in the future and is in the hands of God. That means it is not chance, coincidence, mindless blundering that drives creation along, but the work of a personal, caring, infinite intelligence that causes all things to come about.

Teilhard de Chardin in relation to mythology

In contrast to Bultmann with his negative and unsympathetic attitude to mythology, Teilhard de Chardin presents a completely different aspect of modern thinking.[25] He has been very influential in recent times, but his thinking is already looking somewhat dated. If he were writing now, his general overview of human development might have been somewhat modified if not completely reconsidered. We have to remember that much of his thinking was conditioned by the political events of the mid-twentieth century, particularly the great dictators and the Second World War.

He takes an entirely optimistic view of the future for humanity, and this ties in neatly with his general understanding of human history: 'tendency towards unification is everywhere manifest and especially in the different branches of religion. We are looking for something that will draw us all together,' (p. 189). And p. 91: 'are we not steering towards the fulfilment of the world?'

He stands out as a thoroughly liberalistic, evolutionary thinker. In fact, his basic assumption is that of evolution in every respect, not just biologically. If evolution ever were to fall into disrespect, his whole theorisings would collapse into dust. On the liberalistic side, there is never any mention of evil as a spiritual force, and this is quite amazing as he has lived through times when there has been an unprecedented outpouring of evil. In fact, he is rather vague on the difference between Good and Evil. 'Who can say what is Good and what is Evil? Can we even maintain that Good and Evil exist?' (p. 90). A wonderful but totally unrealistic way out of the problem of Theodicy!

As a liberalistic evolutionary thinker it is quite paradoxical that his use of metaphor, when talking about origins and creation, is very often reminiscent of the imagery of ancient mythologies (not just Biblical). Whether he is doing this consciously or not is difficult to say, but the way it is phrased indicates that he has thought up these images for himself. If so, this is interesting because it indicates that ancient mythological assumptions are deeply embedded in the human mind at the instinctive level, and not just something superficial.

'At the beginning ... primordial chaos was excessively unstable ... coiled in more and more tightly ... in enormous clots ... this was the first stage of the birth of the galaxies,' (p. 102). How does he know this? The phrases 'coiling', and 'coilings of complexity' and 'cosmic coiling' and other similar images are significant. This is what a snake does, and as we have seen, the snake is an important symbol found everywhere.

Also an indirect reference to the Flood is interesting. 'We are faced with torrents of unapplied power ... it is no good trying to force back this outburst: the right action is to direct the flood along the slope it wants to go' (p. 105).

Admittedly this is talking about human research and scientific progress, but the metaphor is still just as apposite even if differently applied. Of course he fails to see that the Tower of Babel motif is juxtaposed with the Flood, and that is the problem we are now faced with, in which scientific research is actually tinkering with the building blocks of life and no one can foresee the long-term consequences of it, except that we are all frightened about the possible consequences.

De Chardin must be aware of modern space exploration and yet in various places his metaphors involve (not so much the three-tier universe) but the egg motif: 'the universe suddenly closing in over our heads like a dome ... the transition from expansion to compression,' (p. 1020).

In other places the metaphor is slightly different, 'a spindle shaped universe', also a 'cone' seems important to him. Very significant is his concept of the 'Tree of Life' which he actually renders into various diagrams. These are derived from biological evolutionary thinking, but for him it has more far-reaching significance. The main stem is the ascent of mankind, but he will not accept that our present situation is the full destination of human evolution. We know that the 'tree' is an important motif in mythology, making a connection between the underworld, the earth and heaven. Interestingly, the connection to heaven is understood: 'The impulse which urges us upwards,' (and here he refers to Jacob and the Angel which implies the ladder) (p.187ff).

Not surprisingly there is no mention of the impulse which urges us down, since in his view there is no hell. Most significant however is his assumption about the ages of man, not so much on a biological level, but more to do with spiritual awareness or consciousness. This involves inventing new words, such as the 'Noosphere', the meaning of which is not always totally clear.

But basically it is the same assumption as with the eschatologists of the ancient world, with the vital difference that they thought that mankind was going downhill; De Chardin thinks we are going uphill. 'Now we see mankind extending within the cone of time beyond the individual. It coils in collectively upon itself above our heads in the direction of some sort of higher mankind,' (p. 98). All very optimistic: we go through phases, culminating in Ultra-humanity. But is this realistic in the light of recent developments in world politics and scientific enquiry?

And finally, although we cannot have the Devil, we do have God. Not that God is the active personal God of Biblical times. He sounds much more like the Gnostic passive God who is a kind of eternal 'back-stop' rather than the day-to-day batsman. The phrase 'the problem of God' emerges, although this is not explained; 'the rise of a God', 'a universal focus, Omega' also surfaces, and yet the relationship to mankind is even more complex.

'Faith in Man does not exclude but must on the contrary include the worship of Another, one who is higher than Man ... faith in man must cast us into the arms of the One who is greater than ourselves. The one who is greater is in fact identical with ourselves. Why should Man look for God outside himself?' (p.187ff).

This could be taken as a kind of pantheism, but De Chardin

probably never intended it to be such. More likely it is the nearest we come to a liberalistic version of Messianism. Otherwise divine intervention never figures in his thinking.

De Chardin's writings are an interesting admixture of evolutionary speculation, neo- Gnosticism, watered-down pantheism and upgraded mythology. The optimism shown in relation to the future of the human race ignores the threats and horrors of recent events, to the extent that he now verges on the level of naivety. Even so, it demonstrates that for all our modernistic attempts to play down or regard as superstitious nonsense, the mythologies of the past, there is still the backdrop of ancient thinking and the tendency to work up new metaphors which are derived from the past.

It is only now that we can look back on his writings and see them in proportion. Fifty years ago they seemed to be the cutting edge of theology and philosophy. Now they seem decidedly jaded and fanciful. Now we see the importance of allowing the test of time to show us the true worth of all so-called 'new' ideas.

Von Daniken and the *Chariots of the Gods*

A book which appears to have been popular in the 1980s but now is beginning to look rather dated, it attempts to find explanations for the mysteries of the past and relate them to what can be described as the mythology of the future. One is struck by the mass of gratuitous assumptions and imaginative prognostications, intermingled with now solid information and now pure speculation. The nub of his thesis is that people came from outer space in remote prehistory, interbred with early humanity, and gave them all kinds of clever ideas. All kinds of interesting 'evidence' for this is adduced. One wonders how much this book has influenced popular thought. It would seem to be a contemporary mania that life on other planets, maybe millions of light years away, must be investigated just to assure ourselves that we are not alone in the universe. Although this line of argument has its implications for religious belief, so far we have seen no evidence of it undermining anyone's faith.

One of Von Daniken's basic assumptions is that early man was stupid (all of them?). Looking at the amazing achievements still surviving from the ancient world, it is true that we today find them very difficult to explain. The pyramids are one such case but there are many others, as Von Daniken describes. What he fails to see is that even today there are many of the human race who are also stupid, and yet we know there are some who are very clever, and occasionally we see a prodigy. An example of this was Mozart, a musical prodigy who could conceive an entire orchestral work in his head before writing it down. There are prodigies in many fields of knowledge, notably mathematics, technology and, yes, even prophecy. It is far simpler and more convincing to say that in proportion to the resources available to them, early man was far more intelligent and resourceful than we are now. If there is any doubt about this, refer to Chapter 14 on Calendars and take into account the amazing work done in this field of study, not just in Egypt but in Mesoamerica.

It is true that many features surviving from the ancient world are beyond easy explanation, both in terms of construction and of purpose. But this does not require space men coming from another planet, the intelligence of whom is assumed to be greater than ours. The assumption that they must have been biologically compatible with the human race is also a gratuitous one. Could they really have interbred with humans?[26]

Strangely, Von Daniken does not make much play over the issue of UFOs: he seems somewhat puzzled by them. Although this has become another mania with many people over the last 70 years, it is now becoming realised that this has nothing to do with outer space, and still less to do with so-called 'chariots of the gods'. Since it is now admitted that their first sightings were during Allied bombing raids over Germany in 1942, it may be that the Nazis had been developing some form of spherical or saucer-shaped vehicle which could defy gravity but was not much use as a weapon. The idea went to the USA after the war. The whole matter of UFOs is being kept under wraps for obvious reasons. But it has nothing to do with mythology or religion. Conversely, UFOs are ready fodder for the invention of modern mythology, as indeed Von Daniken's ideas about men from outer space.

Another aspect of the matter which Von Daniken picks up is the strange accounts of Viracocha in the Inca civilisation. Everywhere the Spaniards went they encountered recollections of Viracocha as an active person in Incan history. This must alert us to the fact that while Viracocha was understood to be the original creator God in Incan prehistory, also it would seem that he was present and active in recent times, to the effect that the Inca Emperor named himself after Viracocha (1438 AD). In certain respects the descriptions of Viracocha recall the activities of Jesus, before or after the resurrection. This has been referred to Chapter 7 on Incarnation and may be relevant to the problem of particularity. Are we seeing resurrection appearances of Jesus in the New World? This does not seem to have occurred to Von Daniken (nor anyone else, presumably).

Putting it in more general terms, Von Daniken admits to a belief in Almighty God, and yet, strangely, all the remarkable aspects of the ancient world are never seen as directly attributable to the intervention and inspiration of God. But rather than conjuring up intriguing accounts of space men intervening in remote prehistory, would it not be easier and more realistic to say that it was God who gave early man certain ideas through the medium of dreams, theophanies and direct encounters? In support of this bold assertion, it is to be noted that many of our human mythologies say as much in plain language. At the very least, the Viracocha situation is a prime example of how myth and historical reality are often very closely interwoven, and it is simplistic at the least the try to separate them in the hopes that religion will be more acceptable to modern minds.

Notes

1. Burridge, *Four Gospels, one Jesus?*
2. Littleton, *The Sacred East*, p. 107.
3. Littleton, op. cit., p. 26.
4. Rig Veda, R. Pandey, Sookta-wise translation, Diamond Books, 2010.
5. The concept of 'cartouche' is explained in Chapter 1.
6. Littleton, op. cit., pp. 51 and 75.
7. Yen Wang.
8. It is interesting that Karma worked its way into Platonic thought and the ideas of Origen. The term 'metempsychosis' is interesting.
9. The Koran makes the same assumption, Pelican, p. 146.
10. 'Sheol' was the earlier idea in the Old Testament but by New Testament times, hell is fiery and torturous, and termed 'Gehenna'.
11. *Basil and the Gregories.*
12. John Milton, *Paradise Lost.*
13. Herodotus, *The Histories.* His main theme is to explain the antagonism between Greece and Persia.
14. Josephus, *Antiquities and Jewish War.* He argues that the sane Jews never wanted a revolt against Rome in AD 66–70.

15. Tacitus, Severus, Dio Cassius, Suetonius, Pliny and Eusebius, for example.
16. Winston Churchill, *History of the English Speaking People*.
17. Ian Wilson, *The After Death Experience*.
18. Bultmann, *Kerygma and Myth*.
19. Drew, *The Lost Chronicles of the Mayan Kings*, the world tree (see illustration).
20. Robert Graves, *Greek Myths*.
21. Bultmann, op. cit.
22. Bart D. Ehrman, *Lost Scriptures*, pp. 57–62.
23. J.J. Rousseau, *Discourse on the Origin of Inequality*, 1755.
24. Von Daniken, *The Chariots of the Gods*.
25. Teilhard de Chardin, *The Future of Man* and *Man's Place in Nature*.
26. Von Daniken, op. cit.

12

Mysticism and Proofs for the Existence of God

Following on from mythology, proofs for the existence of God are a natural development. But mysticism is the opposite, for such people do not need proof; it is self-evident for them. Both matters have been touched on so far, but now it is appropriate to balance the two. I start with mysticism, which can now be viewed on a primary level as a major feature of religious experience, regardless of which religion is involved. The word 'mysticism' itself was coined about 1900 but the actual processes have been occurring from many centuries before. Bouquet's analysis is a useful starting point but does not cope with every aspect.[1]

Bouquet maintains that all mystics would agree on three criteria. Firstly, the unity of the universe: all division is unreal. Secondly, evil is illusory: it comes from seeing part of the universe as self-subsistent. Thirdly, time is unreal: reality is out of time. He maintains that there are two main streams of mysticism: the Christian and the non-Christian. The Christian one means communion with Christ as a living force in the life of the believer and also the community of believers. This is very much a this-worldly state of mind as well as of the world of the spirit. The paradox of this has already been seen from the thoughts of St Paul. Indeed, St Paul could be seen as the first Christian mystic (that is, apart from Jesus). It is interesting to see how these three criteria relate to Christian mysticism. It will be seen to work in a different way when considering non-Christian mysticism. The unity of the universe is obvious if God is one and Christ the Messiah of the One God is relevant to the whole universe, not just parts of it. Christ is seen as supreme in all things, and anyone 'in Christ' shares in this status. Point 2, 'evil being illusory', is important since Jesus is seen constantly to be battling with the powers of evil, and the assumption that certain forces are somehow opposed to God. And yet, when we view the climax of his ministry, good and bad are not necessarily always quite what they might appear to be. Good Friday is not termed Bad Friday: the treachery of Judas was not a mistake but a part of the scheme. Point 3, time as unreal, is of great importance for the problem of particularity, for Christ is not confined to chronology or geography. He reaches out into prehistory as well as the future, to other cultures in faraway lands as well as his own land. God's Messiah is not bounded by time: time and sequence is merely a derivative of his divine scheme of salvation for the entire universe.

The non-Christian form of mysticism, something on Neo-Platonist lines, has often been intermingled with the Christian mysticism, and many make the mistake of confusing the two. The non-Christian one can be traced back to the Upanishads and worked its way into the fourth-century Christian orbit through the works of Pseudo-Dionysius and from thence into the Mediaeval mystics and also the Sufis of the Muslim tradition. In the Protestant world there was George Fox (Quaker), and the Pietists. Today, Eastern ideas on mysticism are constantly being foisted on mainstream Christianity without much thought as to the inherent contradiction involved.

The contradiction is roughly as follows: for the Christian, the coming of Christ into one's spiritual life is not something that can be induced by a clever technique or philosophical argument. It is a gift from the divine which cannot be induced by human effort. It is not a 'work', it is a 'grace'. The sacraments are there on a physical level to confirm and stabilise this mystic relationship with the believer. But belief and faith cannot be manufactured by human effort; when it is given, it lifts one into a new relationship with the divine.

For the non-Christian, the assumption is that one can reach absorption with the divine by one's own efforts. This will involve strenuous mental exertion, use of gadgetry and self-inflicted hardship. It is analogous to the pagan sacrifice in that the more one puts into it the more the unseen divinity is supposed to respond; it is like a celestial slot-machine. It can be very reassuring to those who practise it but this may be pure self-delusion. It often involves an escape from the realities of life. In the East, this works on the assumption of Karma and the escape from it. In the West, the Karma element is normally absent, but the escapist element is certainly there, on the assumption that this world's hardships are there to be escaped from. This is the opposite of what Christ came to show us: that the way of the cross and the hardships of life are the true way forward and the genuine way of transforming pain and suffering into something glorious. This is the true paradox: that out of evil comes good, out of failure comes triumph.

Going back to ancient India, the Upanishads describe the theory behind pagan meditation.[2] There are three mental states: wakefulness, dreaming sleep and dreamless sleep. All three are defective in that they are tied up with the duality of self and non-self, the ego and the non-ego. But there is a fourth state, pure consciousness, which transcends the three: it is union with Brahman *turiya* in the purest being of soul. The self and the world are held together; there is no more distortion or illusion. One is united with Brahman-Atman and thus we obtain *moksha*, the final liberation from Karma.

In practical terms, the methods used might be thus. There is a mystical symbol, Om, which means the wholeness of the universe. It is the vibratory sound of Brahman which is chanted before or after a ceremony or before using one's mantra. With it one gains access to the powers of the universe: it is past, present, and future, and all that transcends time.[3] Here we see the use of a special sound and a key word (mantra) which has a stirring effect on the gods, rather like the key to a front door. There are various types of yoga, such as the Sutra (by Patanjali), outlined at the end of this chapter. Mental concentration leads to spiritual liberation. One removes oneself from worldly entanglements, which gives the power to escape from this world and from rebirth. We have seen how Mahavira and Nanak found what they thought was a way out of Karma: with Mahavira it was extreme asceticism, with Nanak it was abandonment of ritual and concentration on inner spiritual life.

This leads on naturally to the discovery by Siddhartha of the Middle Way, which involved meditation combined with an ethical code. The Noble Eightfold Path can be broken down into three elements: *shila* (morality); *samadhi* (concentration); and *prajna* (wisdom); a fourth element *dana* (giving) is an element of *shila*.[4] These matters are inseparably linked and intertwined. The meditational method is twofold. *Bhavana* requires *shamatha* (calm) which leads to *dhyana* (abstraction). This can be helped by gadgets which lead to different mental absorptions. The second element is *vispashyana* (insight) in order to acquire *prajna* (wisdom) by working on insight. The aim is to comprehend three characteristics of the phenomenal world: *anitya* (impermanence), *duhkha* (suffering) and *atman* (no-self). This technique combined with the Buddhist ethic is claimed to lead to Nirvana and an escape from Karma. It is noticeable that this is yet another system of mental effort and psychological speculation. It has worked its way into China and Japan and heavily influenced their religious procedures. The Taoist meditation, which probably came before all this, is much simpler and less speculative: that of simply admiring a beautiful view and allowing nature to speak to the heart.

With all these approaches there is the assumption that the eternal can be reached by human effort and self-discipline. There seems to be no mention of divine assistance in achieving these wonderful states of calm and insight. There is no certain equation between Nirvana and heaven: more likely they are complete opposites. Nirvana sounds as if it is some sort of nothing, with the soul floating with no self-consciousness or sense of meaning. Heaven, however, is about joy and fulfilment in the company of an active God. To be fair, the Eastern method has much to commend it on the therapeutic level, where the pressures of modern life lead to excesses of stress. Calmness and meditation can and do bring relief to those who are too tied up with the pace of modern living. But this must not be confused with a genuine positive relationship with the Living Christ which is essentially the Christian mysticism.

Thomas à Kempis, *The Imitation of Christ*

One of the most influential books on mysticism is this work of Thomas à Kempis. It is quite amazing that in a world of political strife and corruption in the Church, such a work of spiritual profundity could be produced, in the Late Middle Ages. Its influence has been worldwide and both Catholic and Protestant have gained much from it. The explanation for this may be that Thomas is not a churchmanship campaigner. His main focus is Christ as known from the Gospels, and that is a unifying factor for Christians of all shades of opinion. His work has the tone of the Old Testament wisdom literature, especially Proverbs, but this is seen through the filter of Christ. It is unfortunate that the Mediaeval Latin in which it is written is not always easy to render into modern English, and yet the simplicity of Thomas still shines through.[5]

Although superficially there are many points on which he would agree with Siddhartha and the Eastern yogis, essentially Thomas starts in a different place, God and the unity of life:

> From One Word proceed all things and all things tell of him. It is he the author of all things who speaks to us ... the man to whom all things are one, who refers everything to One and who sees everything as in One, is enabled to remain steadfast in heart, and abide at peace with God ... let all creation be still before you: do You O Lord, speak alone (p. 30).

This is in spite of his remarks about the Devil; he does not lay undue emphasis on any sort of dualism. He can see the positive side of temptation: 'for by them we are humbled, cleansed and instructed,' (p. 39). Those who try to avoid temptation will only be faced by more later on; temptation is to be overcome by God's help, not one's own efforts. 'The beginning of all evil temptation is an unstable mind and lack of trust in God ... temptation reveals our true nature,' (p. 40).

On the subject of 'desire' Thomas would probably have agreed with Siddhartha. It is the central problem in human nature: 'The greatest and indeed the whole obstacle to our advance is that we are not free from passions and lusts,' (p. 37). Worldly desires are the nub of the problem but we should fight against them. This can only be done with the active help of 'Our Lord from Heaven: he is ever ready to help all who fight trusting in his Grace'.

But with the Buddhists there is no active personal God or Christ who comes to one's aid: it is all one's own effort. In a way, Thomas makes a reply to the Four Noble Truths, 'Four things that bring Peace':

> Christ: 'My son: resolve to do the will of others rather than your own.
> Always choose to possess less rather than more.
> Always take the lowest place and regard yourself as less than others.
> Desire and pray always that God's will may be perfectly fulfilled in you,' (p. 122).

This is the way of freedom, peace of mind and tranquillity of soul. We notice that it is thoroughly Christ-centred and God-orientated.

Also it is a code achievable by any believing soul, not just those committed to monastic life or some pattern of discipline. This peace of mind is not dependent on man: no one can manufacture it by his own efforts (p. 131).

This is the answer to those who would inflict upon themselves all manner of hardships, mental exercises, techniques and gadgets. The way to peace is simple trust and asking for help. As an answer to the abstruse philosophical speculations of both East and West, Thomas has this answer: 'I am God . . . I teach in silence, without the clamour of controversy, without ambition for honours, without confusion of argument,' (p. 147).

Thomas is quite aware of the senseless wranglings of his day, which are no less than in the twenty-first century. Hair-splitting controversy and abstruse points and subtleties are as nothing against God, who grants his children a clearer understanding than man can impart (p. 147): 'I alone am the Teacher of Truth, the searcher of men's hearts.'

Thomas has a way of helping those who do not all think on the same level: 'To some I speak on everyday affairs: to others on particular matters. To some I graciously reveal myself in signs and symbols. To some who are enlightened I reveal my mysteries,' (p. 147).

This is an admission that not all can cope with just one approach to understanding God's words. We see something of this in the Gospels where Jesus speaks to different people on different levels. In the last remark there is just the hint of the Gnostic idea of some sort of esoteric mystery, and yet he does not really intend this. The deep truths about God are available to all who fully put their trust in him. The fundamental answer to all our uncertainties, questionings and speculations is not some clever theory or convincing argument: it is a relationship with a Living Lord, the Messiah of God, who holds all the answers.

One important aspect of Thomas as a mystic is his thorough reliance on and reverence for the Sacraments, especially Holy Communion. It is for him the way into the presence of God, but seen in normal physical commodities, bread and wine. 'I could not endure to gaze on you in the full glory of your divinity, nor could the whole world bear the splendour and glory of your majesty. Therefore you bear with my frailty and conceal yourself in this Holy Sacrament,' (p. 202).

This is not just for the mystic; it is for all believers. Anyone who can come to Communion, offering himself totally as a sacrifice, can come into God's presence. The basis of the sacrament is the sacrifice of Christ, and anyone who truly believes can become a part of it.

We notice that Eastern mysticism does not have the clear dependence on sacramental worship. Admittedly the Hindus have sacraments which are completely related to rites of passage. They do not, however, relate to yoga or methods of meditation, with the result that it all becomes increasingly vague and abstruse. The same is true in Buddhism where there are no ceremonies approaching sacramental worship. There is no sense of coming into the presence of the Living God. Sacramental worship with its use of basic commodities which are charged with spiritual power are the true focus of mysticism, not just for the individual but for the community of believers.

Thomas tells us how Christ speaks inwardly to the soul. But first one must exclude the desires of the senses and the entanglements of the world so that one can hear God speaking within one's soul: 'Blessed are those who enter deeply into inner things and daily prepare themselves to receive the secrets of heaven,' (p. 89).

Here is the hint of regular sacramental worship. It is not difficult or mind-teasing; it is a basic quietness and faith in the heart, and that is available to all living souls. To those who think that mysticism is escapism from the realities of life, Thomas would say: 'Why then do you seek any other road than this royal road of the Holy Cross?' (p. 85).

In this we see the configuration of life as a pilgrimage, a kind of procession towards the ultimate goal of heavenly bliss. The idea of a pilgrimage in not specifically a Christian one: it occurs in Islam, Hinduism, and the Sufis have term *tariqat* or 'journey of life' so as to attain union with God. The idea of the Way, the Road, the Highway is found in the Scriptures (Isaiah), and in many prehistoric patterns of worship. It has deep implications for the development of faith. Thomas warns that to shirk the cross is to risk being encumbered with an even heavier one; also that as one advances in the spiritual life, the 'heavier and more numerous he finds the crosses, for his ever-deepening love of God makes more bitter the sorrows of his earthly exile,' (p. 83).

Thomas would say that not all desires are bad, nor the root of the human problem. It is not wrong to have desires, just to have wrong desires. The way to sort out the good from the bad is to commit it to the Lord with a humble heart. 'Not every desire comes from the Holy Spirit, though it may seem right and good: for it is often hard to judge whether it arises from your own inclinations,' (p. 110).

But in contrast, Siddhartha would say that all desires are bad and need to be escaped from, if we are ever to have an escape from the miseries of this world. Thomas sees it differently: 'Grant me ... to rest in you, that my heart may find its peace in you alone, for you are the heart's true peace, its sole abiding place, and outside yourself all is hard and restless' (p. 111).

Biblical mysticism

There are many instances in which Biblical people have startling encounters with God: Abraham, Jacob, Moses, Elijah, to name a few. But this is not mysticism in the sense that Thomas à Kempis was talking about: theophanous encounters are unusual and normally overwhelming; normal unspectacular mysticism of the type that Thomas understands is something else. It too is traceable in the Scriptures. It is principally seen in the canonical prophets where the quickening of the eye perceives a message from God, which resonates with the prophet's soul. A prime case of this is Jeremiah, who in his primary encounter with God sees a rod of almond, *shaqed*, and this means that God is watching, *shoqed*, over his word to perform it. The pun in Hebrew is the key to it. Only the true mystic will make the mental connection and see the implications in it. With this inbuilt closeness to God, we find the so-called 'confessions of Jeremiah' to be revealing of his inner life. Jeremiah 7:14–18, 18:19–23 and 20:7–18 are the core of it. Sadly this is infiltrated with deep bitterness and despair, but it is a relationship to God hardly seen before.

This is reminiscent of much in the Psalms, where the inner life of the Psalmist (David?) reveals all manner of moods. Psalm 51 reveals a soul riddled with guilt but receiving forgiveness; there is depth and torment and yet release: 'Create in me a clean heart, O God, and put a new and right spirit within me.'

It is no surprise that monastic orders have made a thorough use of the Psalms because of their inner spirituality. There is nothing spectacular or theophanous in this; it is a day-to-day working relationship with a God who is present in the believer's heart.

The ultimate example of mysticism is seen in the ministry of Jesus.

While the Synoptic Gospels concentrate on the public ministry of Jesus, St John's emphasis is on the inner life of Jesus. Here is someone who is not trying to achieve union with God: he already has it. He is not trying to find Nirvana in some sort of escape method, he is doing the opposite. He is deliberately engaging with pain and misery in the knowledge that this is the ultimate way of bringing salvation to a broken world. In John 17 we see him including his disciples in the pattern of mysticism; it is not some sort of esoteric method of insulating oneself from the rest of humanity. 'I have manifested thy name to the men whom thou gavest me ... all mine are thine and thine are mine and I am glorified in them ... that they may be one, even as we are one.'

The contrast is between Christianity and Buddhism, but the paradox lies elsewhere: it is between genuine mysticism and the philosophical debate about the existence of God, a debate which is always sterile and inconclusive.

The first clock analogy

There was a clock, and at the critical part of the workings was a balance staff which operated the escapement by swaying to and fro regularly. A BBC interviewer asked the staff: 'What are you doing that for?' and the reply was, 'I've always been doing it: it makes that lever there go "click" and these wheels behind me move on little by little.'

But the balance staff could not see the spring and only dimly glimpsed the big wheels at the bottom: 'I don't know: all I know is these big wheels keep pushing me along.'

'You must have some idea of what makes you work.'

'There's a funny-looking person, not a machine, who opens up the clock now and then and puts oil on the right places. Also he takes out a key and winds something up down below. Other than that I don't really know what makes me keep on going.'

'But what's the point of it all?'

'I have no idea: I seem to see a shaft going off outside which seems to turn very slowly; it might be something to do with the way I'm twisting about, but I can't really see. I suppose there is some sort of purpose to it.'

The BBC man came all clever: 'Well let me tell you: that shaft turns two hands which tell people the time.'

'What are you talking about? People? Hands? Time? What are they?'

'There are people out there, like your clock-repairer, who like to tell the time for lunch, tea and bedtime and so forth. You are a very useful little chap.'

'Never, you're joking!' sneered the balance staff.

'No, I'm not, and what's more there are lots of chaps like you telling the time. Clocks are very useful, if not essential.'

'I just don't believe you,' came the reply. 'Anyway, what is a clock?' And so it went on.

The point being, humanity is a small but vital part of a much greater structure. We cannot even see properly what is going on inside the rest of the clock let alone realise what effect is occurring outside the clock, and even then whether there are any other clocks doing the same thing or something completely different. It is idle of us to discount, or reduce to our own limited terms, any ideas of what is going on outside our limited parameters.

But the importance of this analogy is that we cannot conceive of the total workings of things, nor do we have any language with which to discuss it. All our thought-forms are limited to our experience of our own world. The world of the balance staff, though a busy, restless and seemingly pointless world, was a very limited and confined experience, and when greater powers than himself did intervene, he really could make very little sense of it except in that it was usually beneficial. It is senseless to talk of proof or certainty beyond what we can actually experience in day-to-day living. We are all philosophers to some extent, and speculation on the meaning of life is a natural impulse, but since we are encased in our own sphere it is impossible to stand back from it and see it from the outside and realise the implications in full. Just occasionally, God provides us with a few helpful remarks; a common response is to disbelieve even that.

Proofs for the existence of God

This line of argument, which is the opposite of mysticism, has been going on for centuries. It is the attempt to show by logical process that God is not just an inner factor in the mind of humanity, but an external one which can have the decisive effect on atheism or agnosticism. Suffice to say that if any one of these lines of argument had been seen as 'proof', there would be no atheism. The truth is that 'proof' in these matters is not the same as proof in other areas of life such as scientific research.

When dealing with scientific experimentation, there are carefully established methods which involve comparisons, conclusions and generalisations. A battery of tests will be made so that conclusions can be made and 'laws' formulated: from that, technological advances can be made. Similar procedures have been established with the social sciences: experiments are done using people and animals, but a control group is important, otherwise the conclusions can be meaningless. From this it can be seen that scientific proof has got nothing whatsoever to do with religious faith or philosophical reasoning. To do something approaching a scientific analysis for 'proving' the existence of God would involve not just one person, but an assortment of people, who could stand back from the universe, compare it with another universe (if one could be found) and start making comparisons and generalisations. At the moment, we are only just scratching the surface of our own universe, not from the outside but from within. Even this planet is not fully explored and many features are not properly explained. It is arrogant of humanity to talk of proof or disproof of God.

Another difficulty is that for all our 'wisdom', all our thoughts on the matter are couched in metaphor, figurative terms, pejorative words and mythological assumptions. It is not possible to discuss the matter in purely neutral terms. All our language is dependant on predigested thought and assumptions. Though we may not realise it, every argument is in some respect circular.

The old adage, 'the chicken and the egg' situation, is a truism. No amount of proof will convince someone who does not wish to be convinced. The same is true in other areas of life. The basis of religious faith is partly the human soul trying to make sense of life, reaching out to God. Vice versa, it requires God to reach out to the human soul and become real in his life. Here we see another paradox: belief is a two-way situation but the final proof is the day-to-day relationship with the Almighty. Even so, it is instructive to review the traditional proofs for the existence of God. Certain aspects of them have changed since the first thoughts on them in Ancient Greece.

Aquinas presented it as Five Ways,[6] and more recent thinkers have expanded and adapted these ideas.

The teleological argument (design)

This is a very ancient one going back to Plato, at least. The best analogy for this is Paley's watch: supposing one found a pocket watch lying on the ground, and on inspecting it found that all its parts were intricately fashioned with the purpose of telling the time. It would be idle to say that the watch just occurred all by itself: all its works just came as a result of a string of coincidences, and can now tell us the time in terms of solar movements. So too it would be idle to say that the world, if not the universe, just occurred all by itself, complete with all its intricate workings. This line of reasoning has to gather more strength in our own times because of the immense amount of scientific data being produced, which tends to support the notion of design and planning in the natural world. It must have some sort of purpose, primary or secondary, and all things are cleverly related and interdependent. The more we see of it, the more it reminds one of Paley's watch. The idea of the natural world being a series of coincidences or accidents is becoming increasingly less realistic. The idea of design implies the designer. Even so, atheism is still a fact of life. The general comment can be: Paley's argument is only trying to use our own thought-forms to describe something which is outside of our world and our limited minds. It cannot be called 'proof' in the normal sense of the word. At best it can be called a strong indication which is gathering cogency at the moment, as our scientific enquiries become more sophisticated.

Since mankind has managed to investigate the moon and other planets are being investigated in our space programme, this has brought about a different aspect to Paley's argument. Looking back at Earth from another planet has shown us so many aspects of it of which we were not aware before. One such is the uniqueness of Earth with so many systems operating, interrelatedly and independently. It is becoming highly likely that there are no such other worlds in existence. Space exploration has so far shown worlds that are radically different from our own: to find another such world as ours may remain unproven for a very long time, if not for ever. Are we looking at a superb piece of design work not equalled anywhere else? It is a compelling argument, but even so an emotional one. For those who lack this emotion, the proof falls short.

An atheist is likely to say, 'If it is so wonderfully planned, why does the plan go wrong sometimes?' This brings us back to Theodicy, which has been examined before. A lot depends on what is meant by 'wrong': are we judging the plan by our own limited terms of reference? Supposing the plan only appears to go wrong? Here we go round in circular argument again, like Job's whirlwind.

The cosmological argument (prime cause)

This is where Aquinas contributes a lot, and his Five Ways subtly use this idea in various permutations. To put it simply, everything we know in life is caused by something else ('somethings' else). There is nothing that happens all by itself. We can trace things back historically; each act, object or circumstance having some form of cause, going back to the mists of pre-history. There has to be a point where a final cause, which is not caused by something else, starts everything off. It resembles a domino run, or even a chain reaction as with certain chemicals, any of which need someone or something independent of the run to kick-start the process. To quote Hick,[7] 'if reality is not to be ultimately inexplicable it must include a being whose existence is self-explanatory, in relation to which the existence of everything else can be understood.' Essentially the logic of it is: there must be a prime cause.

It is interesting that this sounds like a subtle version of Gnosticism: we are left with a God who is highly remote from daily life and is assumed to kick-start creation but leave it to its own devices thereafter. This theory has met with considerable favour since the popularisation of the theory of evolution, which involves one form of life causally developing into another in a kind of chain reaction. This does raise the question of how, who or what set the process in motion at the start. For many this is quite a convincing piece of reasoning; for others it means nothing. This is probably because the argument makes as many assumptions as any other. These assumptions are essentially mythological, or at least mythology is a major substratum in them all.

We have seen in all the mythologies across the world that there was a beginning of all things somewhere in the remote past. Even the

Hindus, who assume that life goes on eternally, still maintain that it had to start somehow with reference to Brahman-Atman (with Agni as the actual creator). In our own times, the 'Big Bang' theory is another permutation on the 'beginning of all things', but this is just as much a mythological assumption as anything else. Worth noting is the fact that cutting-edge thought is now beginning to throw doubt on the Big Bang and to question what was there beforehand. The truth is that we do not know what was going on millions of years ago in deep space: still less do we know what 'chaos' actually consists of: no one can conceive what utter darkness and nothingness really means. All this is, again, essentially emotional. We need to have a notion of all things having a start somewhere. Talking about facts in this context is utter nonsense: all our philosophical ideas are circular, emotional and ultimately based on mythological fundamentals. Perhaps the most helpful remark comes from Ecclesiastes, to the effect that God has left an impression of himself on our minds. But this again begs the question.

The moral argument

Although this idea in its modern form begins with Kant, the potential for it can be traced back through Aquinas to ancient Greece. To find the essentials of it: there is 'good' in the world but not perfection. Thinking firstly about moral values (but also involving aesthetic values), it is beyond us to arrive at perfection in this world. Even so, it is the underlying assumption that an absolute perfection or beauty exists somewhere, assumed to be in the next world. It is an urge in the mind of man to achieve perfection, or at least aim for the highest good. The presupposition goes further in that the highest good is an active (not passive) force which apportions happiness in response to moral attainment. Thus a creator or ruler that has the power to bring moral desert is important in this argument; so happiness coincides with morality. And since the reward of virtue is not always seen in this life, then it will be in the next life of eternity.

There are various permutations on this system but essentially it means that perfection is something existing above and beyond the capability of human effort. That 'something' is God. In support of this view, it has to be admitted that all of humanity, of whatever culture, has values, principally in ethics but also in aesthetics. It would be crass to say that every moral value is the same the world over; even so, we are coming much closer to this with increasing globalisation. But moral values have existed in every society since the dawn of time; the details of them may have been different but the essentials have been the same. They centre round three core values: the sanctity of life, the sanctity of property and the sanctity of the person. All three have their symbolisms in attendance as well as being interrelated. Life is symbolised by blood, property by gold; the person, which is a more diffuse area but including sexual values, clothing, gender, courtship and even rites of passage, might be symbolised by the fig leaf. We see evidence of this in the ethical assumptions of cultures all over the world: the Ten Commandments, the Noble Eightfold Path, Chairman Mao's *Little Red Book*, to name but a few. It is just a short step to assume that it is a divine impulse that has imprinted these basic values on the human mind from the start.

Difficulties with this idea would be that nobody can really say what 'goodness' actually consists of. We can in relative terms, by saying that one deed is 'better' than another, but the highest, ultimate perfection is beyond us to conceive; and yet people appear to assume it and strive for it.

It is also to be noted that Kant's argument comes close to the Old Testament configuration: 'if you do good, you will be rewarded: if you do bad, you will be punished.' As discussed earlier, this is a basic assumption in the human mind and is evidenced in many cultures in the world, possibly every one. For it to work, it requires a superior spiritual force of some kind. Without God it has no meaning or implementation. We are back to Theodicy again.

Certain aspects of this do carry some sort of conviction. Modern writers have taken up this idea, for instance Hastings Rashdall: 'A moral idea can exist nowhere and nohow but in a mind: an absolute moral ideal can exist only in a Mind from which Reality is derived.'[8] Tempting as this is, there are at least two assumptions at work here. How do we know that a moral idea can only exist in a mind? It might exist in some other form or dimension of which we are not aware. Also how do we know there is an 'absolute' moral ideal? This is an assumption probably derived from the Sermon on the Mount, but has no independent verification as some sort of 'fact'. We would all like to think that there is an absolute moral standard somewhere, but now we are in the realms of wishful thinking and emotion.

Another problem is that with increasing globalisation and the admixture of cultures comes also the denial of absolute moral values. They are becoming increasingly a matter of personal opinion. One man's virtue is another man's crime. It is paradoxical that absolute moral values have been rendered down to relative values. The moral argument has its persuasive aspects, but does not carry complete conviction, especially among those who are predisposed to deny any absolute perfection.

The ontological argument

This argument works in a different direction from those seen already. They argue backwards, from actual experience of life and relationships, to postulate a supreme being who is the ultimate reference point. The ontological argument works in the opposite direction, like a backspace on a typewriter: it is an 'a priori' argument, starting with the idea of God as infinite perfection to his existence. The potential for it can be traced back to Augustine and earlier, but it was Anselm who brought out the full workings of this idea: 'Above which there is no superior.' Augustine had said that our intelligence must recognise something superior to itself, namely wisdom and truth; and this is God, or if there be something superior to it, then that is God. Anselm phrases it slightly differently: 'Something than which nothing superior can be thought.'

This is no problem, even for the atheist, but the question now arises: if it is a concept in the mind, does it have to exist outside of the mind, in external reality? Anselm's answer is as follows: to exist in reality, as well as in the mind, is greater than to exist only in the mind; if a thing only exists in the mind it cannot be that than which no greater can be thought.

This all sounds very subtle, and yet there are all manner of assumptions in here, as with the other arguments. Does anything exist independently of the human mind? Why does 'greatness' have to be limited by the human mind? Behind it all is a certain degree of Neoplatonist thinking, another kind of sanitised mythology. The Good itself is the source both of being and of goodness in everything else: also they are identical in our finite world, which is an emanation of the One. Here we are brushing up against another modest form of Gnosticism again. As a 'proof' it either carries complete conviction or fails completely, and yet as an idea it keeps re-emerging, even in our times, and will not go away. There is more to it than just a piece of Mediaeval chop-logic.

An idea used by Clement of Alexandria, derived from Aristotelian philosophy, is that of 'first principle' or 'primary premise'. This is what one accepts as the ground of investigation which by definition is not subject to demonstration. If one can prove a 'first principle' it is then no longer a first principle.[9] Another principle, or assumption superior to it must then be found. Here we see the same process of the mind: we all have to make some kind of assumption or beg some kind of question before any process of logic can take place. This is the ontological argument in a secular setting, and yet it is the same. The same goes on with the scientific, astro-physical world: now that the 'Big Bang' is beginning to fade as a theory, it requires something before it, which no one can really quantify, but it is the same process of mind. Everyone has to assume something which is unprovable: atheists, scientists, believers, politicians, the list is unending. In the end, it all comes down to one kind of emotion or another: 'I happen to feel that . . .', 'I sense that . . .', 'I would like to imagine that . . .'. No one is exempt from this dilemma.

Another possible proof for God, based on balance and paradox

Contemporary scientific doctrine assures us that all matter is made up of tiny 'building blocks' called atoms. No one has actually seen an atom, but there is much circumstantial evidence for their existence. Going further, we are assured that every atom consists of tiny electrical impulses, positive and negative (and neutral). Each atom in itself is balanced between the nucleus and the outer rings, and yet, paradoxically, the outer rings vary in their content of electrons. This makes some atoms prone to attraction to other atoms: others less so. To take a simple example: sodium chloride (NaCl): sodium has only one electron in the outer shell and chlorine has seven electrons in the outer shell, but would like to have eight. When the two atoms come into contact they merge, becoming a sodium and a chlorine ion, the electrical charge holding the tiny crystal together. To separate them again requires a method or force stronger than the attraction, for example hydrolysis, an independent electrical force. Without that, the tiny salt crystal would stay in a state of electrical balance indefinitely.

The question arises: if this tension between plus and minus is the ongoing state of things in the material world, there must be some kind of power which sets up the tension in the first place. Tension such as we see between plus and minus is not the sort of thing that can happen all by itself. It requires a superior force to install the tension. Even if one were to say that that superior force had to be installed by something superior to itself, the same problem arises: that tension cannot just invent itself, any more than a light bulb can light itself up, providing its own plus and minus without the aid of a generator. If this sounds like the ontological argument in a different level of reasoning, so be it. It would be easy to slide into some kind of idolatry and make God out to be a gigantic power station in outer space. But it is not a simple as that. All these amazing ideas about atomic analysis cannot work if everything equals everything. There has to be an array of different atoms, of differing qualities, combinations, contrasts, paradoxes and balancing in the natural world. Without that, there would be no differences, qualities, growth and decay, achievement or completion.

Paradoxes cannot just invent themselves: it takes a poet such as Shakespeare or a mathematician such as Euclid to devise them or at least discover them. Balancing is achieved when the two contrary statements in a paradox are of equal force. Also looking at atomic theory, balancing with the atoms and across the molecules can be exceedingly subtle and ingenious. Can this really occur all by itself? It requires a superior agency to make the adjustments, as when one adjusts the weights on a pair of scales. Can we imagine a pair of scales with multiple dimensions, all needing to be fine-tuned simultaneously? It would now be easy to slide into another idolatry: that of God holding the scales and being the eternal judge (mind you, that image is used in the Bible). The adjustments of the scales are known to be very subtle and multifaceted. Can this really be the product of one accident after another, one coincidence after another? Highly unlikely!

These remarks can be seen as making a whole list of unprovable assumptions. Also it can be seen that the traditional 'proofs' for the existence of God keep sliding in regardless, in a different guise. In a way, scientific analysis of atomic theory has handed us a further possible 'proof', but like all the others it can only work if one's mind is ready to accept it. A mind which is not prepared to accept it will easily find fault with it. The problem is that when talking about God, we can only do it by using human language and analogies. This raises the basic problem of idolatry. As soon as we begin to conceptualise God it turns into a picture of God, and that is always misleading. It is also carte blanche for the atheist to find fault and dismiss the idea. We live in a universe of opposites and multiple and delicate balancing. If one can really imagine that such processes came about spontaneously, and continue to interplay and correct themselves in ways that we do not yet fully understand, then that is the atheist. If one accepts that the subtle processes of the universe are sustained, adjusted, modified and given meaning by an agency unseen, but nevertheless real, then one is aware of deity. The balance between belief and disbelief is just as much a paradox and a matter of balance as any of these other paradoxes.

The tension plays itself out at all manner of different levels in human life and nature. We recall the dualistic solution to the problem of Theodicy (Chapter 2). We see it in politics, where Left and Right are constantly in a tug of war. We recall Jacob and Esau: the one chosen by God and the other rejected. Now we see the sheep and goats in a fresh light: Jesus himself knew about the pluses and minuses of life. We recall the yin–yang sign in Taoism. There is a constant interplay of positive and negative in all of life. Can this really be the result of pure coincidence and accident? Can this tension really invent itself?

Two analogies may be helpful here. Imagine a coiled spring which has the potential of tension but will do nothing unless force is applied at each end, pulling away. Those forces have to be equal, otherwise the tension will not build and the spring will just pull away to one side. There has to be a balance of force across the ends of the spring for its springiness to come into action. Also, imagine a see-saw, two seats on the ends of a beam, placed over a fulcrum. The weight on each seat has to be the same for the see-saw to work. The ends can only go up and down when someone (who is independent of the see-saw) applies a little more force at one end and then pulls it up again. So the balance can be struck but it requires an external force independent of the see-saw to cause any alteration in the relative height of the seats on the ends. The weakness with any analogy is always that it is concocted to suit the idea being put over; however, this is the only way we can deal with these deep matters: by analogy. The atheist is welcome to attempt to concoct his own analogy, but that too will be subject to the same human limitations as any other analogy.

Always, when trying to talk about God, there is the limitation of human language and thought forms. We cannot conceive of God in anything but human terms; that is the root of idolatry.

General conclusions: mysticism and proofs for the existence of God

Both of these approaches have been with us since the first millennium BC and keep reappearing in different permutations to this day. With regard to the 'proofs', this is not proof in the normal use of the word; at best they are strong indications. They are circular arguments with some aspect of mythology as a substratum. That does not have to mean that they are wrong: but there is no certainty about them. With mysticism we are nearer to some sort of certainty, at least in the mind of the believer. Even so, it too has some kind of emotionalism at its base.

Looking at the 'proofs' we note that there is nothing like these philosophical discussions in the Scriptures; neither is there anything like it in the holy writings of other religions.[10] The reality of God is assumed; atheism is noted; doubt is dealt with in real terms but not by clever arguments. When Jesus was asked to provide proof, he refused to give it. Proof is not the answer in any of this: faith is the key, and that is only possible as the gift of God, not the invention of mankind.

Looking at mysticism, which is the opposite of proof, the Bible and other sacred writings do give us various insights into a close relationship with the deity. A misuse of this is to become far too intense and withdrawn from daily realities. This is where the sacraments are of value: for whatever one's flights of spiritual fancy, one is brought down to earth with the use of basic commodities such as bread and wine, oil and water. And this is the positive side of doubt: we are brought down to earth every time some difficult account of a miracle is related. It is a reminder from God that we are only human, frail and unable to cope with all his mysteries, and in particular his logic, which is not the same as human rationality. Living religion which relates to real situations in life is a challenge to and a stress on credibility; it is not a bland reassurance of certainties.

From the point of view of balance, mysticism and proof are opposites in more than one sense: the one springs from the Bible, the other springs from the Church trying to come to terms with current philosophical trends. It is not good enough to ignore the one in favour of the other: both balance each other out. It may be that we are seeing a subtle paradox between the two. Both are needed in their own way: people of different mentalities respond to them in different ways.

St Thomas Aquinas: the 'Five Ways', *quinque viae*

Thomas tried to prove the existence of God *a posteriori*. It will be seen that he covers virtually all of earlier and later thinking on the matter:

1. Motion implies a first mover.
2. A sequence of efficient causes and their effects implies a first cause (uncaused).
3. The existence of things which are not self-explanatory, and therefore might logically not exist, implies some necessary being (see the cosmological argument).
4. The comparisons we make about goodness, truth, beauty, and so on, imply a standard of comparison which is itself perfect (see the moral argument).
5. The fulfilment by inanimate or unintelligent objects of an end to which they are evidently designed to work implies a purposive intelligence in their creation and direction (see the teleological argument).

Behind it all is Aquinas's assumptions about Aristotelian philosophy, a mode which came to fascinate Mediaeval thinking. This is another example of the Church trying to express theology in terms of current philosophical thinking. It is worthwhile to make the attempt, as new metaphors are always helpful; but to allow one set of imagery to monopolise thinking can easily stop other possibilities.

B.K.S. Iyengar: yoga wisdom and practice

Yoga defined: there are four paths for the evolution of man:

1. Jnana (knowledge).

2. Bhakti (love or devotion).
3. Karma (action).
4. Yoga (control of the consciousness).

Each path came to be known as 'yoga': the fourth could hardly be called 'yoga yoga', so it was subdivided, bearing different names:

1. Mantra yoga (thoughtful prayer).
2. Laya yoga (love and dissolution in the object of devotion).
3. Hatha yoga (firmness and determined discipline).
4. Raja yoga (the royal path of yoga).

Patanjali codified yoga in a treatise. He did not call it the Raja yoga, but the eight-petalled yoga, Astanga yoga. Each petal has a name:

1. Yama (social discipline): the great commandments, non-violence, truth, non-stealing, continence, non-coveting.
2. Niyama (individual discipline): purity, contentment, arduous study of self, devotion to the Lord.
3. Asana (posture): physical health, mental steadiness and lightness.
4. Pranayama (control of breathing).
5. Pratyahara (control of senses by the mind).
6. Dharana (complete attention to a single point).
7. Dhyana (meditation, uninterrupted flow of concentration).
8. Samadhi (the body and senses are at rest as if in sleep, but the mind is alert as if awake).

Notes

1. Bouquet, *Comparative Religions.*
2. *The Upanishads*, Penguin Classics, 1965.
3. Littleton, *The Sacred East*, p. 31.
4. Littleton, op. cit., p. 77.
5. Thomas à Kempis, *The Imitation of Christ*, Penguin Classics, 1952.
6. Thomas Aquinas, *Summa Theologica*, I q. 2, art. 3.
7. John Hick, *The Arguments for the Existence of God.*
8. T. Hughes, *The Atonement*, 1949, p. 207ff.
9. C.E. Hill, *Who Chose the Gospels?* p. 242.
10. St Paul (Romans 1:20) as a passing remark points out that intuitively humanity is aware of God.

13

Miracles in Paradox

The miracles as recorded in the Bible stand out as virtually unique in religious thinking.[1] Certainly other sacred writings do not make such reference to such matters. Bultmann would say that it is all mythological and must be discounted so that the real proclamation of the Gospel can be seen. There may be an element of truth in this as far as the Old Testament is concerned, but we shall see that the New Testament miracles are closely interwoven with the parables and the *kerygma*; it is no easy matter to cross out the bits which are a strain on credibility. After all we are seeing it through the modern eyes of a sceptical materialistic world. In the ancient world they almost certainly saw the whole matter in a completely different light.

People have problems with the Virgin Birth. Interestingly enough, it is not the only case of a quasi-miraculous or 'special' birth situation. Siddhartha, Confucius and Zoroaster are noted as having special circumstances surrounding their births. It is difficult to see how authentic these claims are: were they later exaggerations under the influence of what they had heard about Jesus? With the birth of Isaac and Samuel we also see that the semi-miraculous circumstances of a great man's birth were of importance in the ancient world. It leant support to the authority of a great religious leader if there was something unusual about his conception or birth.

The ancient world was not without its wonder-workers. In Mesopotamia they were the magi, and Egypt had its magicians too. The materialism of the modern world finds this sort of thing very difficult to comprehend, and yet for those who practise shamanism in remote parts of the world it is probably not so difficult a matter. In New Testament times there was a well-documented account of one Simon Magus who did amazing stunts to impress the public; it worked well, until one day he was seen to be a fraud. In the modern world we are impressed with people like David Nixon and David Copperfield who do 'magic' tricks, but we all know it is cleverly devised prestidigitation. More serious is the 'brain teaser' Uri Geller who can bend nails and stop clocks just by mental exertion. In the ancient world he would have been a candidate for deification; the modern world is left dumbfounded. The question of fraud is a real one; it runs along parallel to the problem of true or false prophecy.

We notice with Jesus that he was often tempted to do a miraculous stunt in order to impress people and engender a kind of fantasy-loyalty. His use of miracles is always low-key, secretive, and often unobserved by the public. People are left puzzled, without an explanation. It is non-triumphalist, humble, and occasionally does not work because of people's lack of faith. We see him handing on his healing powers to his disciples to continue his work.

It is symptomatic of a materialistic world that the Biblical miracle material has been subjected to so much scepticism. This is somewhat ironic since nowadays we have so many ingenious processes in technology, produced by the modern equivalent of the magi, namely the scientists. Rationalisation has been the usual way out of the problem: people seem content with some sort of 'natural explanation' which really amounts to a modest form of demythologising. It does not altogether work. It is like the prophecies of Nostradamus: the vast majority of them could just be reasonably explained away, but there is a hard core that defy rationalisation. So too with the miracles. The plagues of Egypt are a case in point. Almost all of them can be seen as the primary and secondary effects of volcanic and seismic activity in the area: Mount Sinai was almost certainly a volcano which disturbed the workings of nature in the Nile Valley. But the final plague, the death of the firstborn (but not of the Israelite firstborn), takes a lot of ingenuity to explain: it is actually simpler to say that God did it using one of his angels. Colin Humphreys[2] tries to cope with it but he is not very convincing. It is worth quoting Sarna on 'the tenth plague ... for which no rational explanation can be given. It belongs entirely to the category of the supernatural.' It is fruitless to accept nine plagues but discount the final one; that was the last straw for Pharaoh which secured the release of the Israelites. The full and true miracle lies in the sequencing and the timing of the plagues.

As with many Biblical miracles there is a secondary agenda in the background. In the case of the Exodus, it is rather more in the foreground. Exodus 7:8–13 explains that Moses and Aaron were given miraculous powers which could overwhelm the magicians of

Egypt. They are seen to be attempting similar tricks by their arts, but Moses quickly outdoes them. When Aaron's serpent swallows up the magicians' serpent, what is this saying? It is saying that the God of Israel is far greater than the Egyptian gods. This is a message that Pharaoh did not want to hear, which is why he refused to accept the proof laid before his eyes.

A similar situation appears with Elijah in his confrontation with the prophets of Baal (1 Kings 18:20–38). A sacrificial contest to prove the reality of God as opposed to Baal culminates in Elijah's sacrifice going up in flames, much to the dismay of the prophets of Baal. This time there is no convenient volcanic activity available to help with an explanation: it is just a challenge for faith and an embarrassment for materialism. The secondary agenda is that Baal is powerless and the God of Israel is powerful. Again this comes at a time of crisis in the life of Israel: with Moses it was 'ethnic cleansing' and with Elijah it was absorption into Canaanite practice. Whatever one makes of this miracle, Elijah stands out as a pillar of spiritual power on the same level as Moses. It is no surprise that later generations were in expectation of his return and that Jesus was suspected of being such. Jesus would have had to have performed miracles of the same magnitude in order to be associated with or identified as one of these great figures. In the logic of completion, Jesus brought all their work to a fulfilment that even they would have marvelled at. It is no surprise that at the transfiguration Jesus is seen with both of them on the mountain. We can also see that although these accounts are intended by their writers to be historical, mythological elements are included. This does not turn them into myth but it does show how myth is brought to completion in the work of these major Biblical figures.

In both these situations Moses and Elijah were able to perform miracles to impress and silence the pagans. One would think that 'proof' on this level would induce them to turn to the God of Israel, but this seems not to have happened. In both cases, Pharaoh and Ahab responded with indignation and increased the persecution of the faithful; clearly they saw 'proof' in this situation as something that had to be ignored or argued against. This helps us towards an understanding of why Jesus always resisted the temptation to do a spectacular miracle to prove his identity. Even on the cross he was taunted with the idea of coming down from the cross so that everyone would (presumably) believe in him (Matthew 27:40–41).

From an early age he must have been aware of his exceptional powers. Some of the Apocryphal Gospels record him doing such things in his childhood,[3] but the early Church did not wish to allow such things to assume too much importance. They may be legendary exaggerations produced by Gnostic fantasists. In the normal course of his ministry, Jesus never performs a miracle as a public stunt to impress people: very much the opposite, following St Mark, it is low-key, private and recondite. The nearest we come to 'proof' is in John 2:11 where the disciples believed him after the miracle of turning the water into wine; it was not done to impress the public. Most of the people there had no idea of what had happened. His disciples were allowed to work out what had happened, but they were predisposed to believe in him anyway. So 'proof' in this case is a matter of confirming people in their inclination to faith, it is not about convincing hardened disbelievers. Always he refuses to misuse his powers; always his intention is to provide release and mercy to suffering humanity; never is it done solely for his own benefit.

It is important to realise that with the miracles there is always a secondary and even sometimes a tertiary agenda. The miracle itself might even be seen as secondary or even illustrative. They have this in common with the parables and the teachings: they are the substratum of the *kerygma*. Bultmann does not see it this way at all. He sees all the miracles as mythological. But myth is never far from the way these matters are recorded. To take an example in St Mark 1:22ff, Jesus, on the Sabbath, heals a man with an unclean spirit. This is followed by the healing of Peter's mother-in-law with her fever. What is this saying? In real or figurative terms, Jesus is supreme in both worlds at once: he is working on both levels concurrently, God and man at the same time. He has authority over the evil spirits with both mental and physical illnesses. The tertiary strand is that being performed on the Sabbath, Jesus is bringing Genesis chapter 1 to a conclusion: the Sabbath of God has arrived and the old regime is being transformed into the new. The completion of all things is taking place. The primary strand here is the identification of Jesus as the 'Holy One of God', which coming from someone who is possessed by a spirit, carries extra weight, and ties in with the first verse of St Mark, 'Jesus Christ, the Son of God'. This Gospel may appear to be rather crude and basic in some ways, but actually it is multifaceted and contains many subtleties which are easily missed. There is balance (the mental and the physical healing), there is completion (the Sabbath coming to fulfilment): and paradox (Jesus is human and divine at the same time): all this contained within a few verses of chapter 1. Very clever!

The healing miracles of Jesus: mostly in St Mark

Mark 1:40 to 2:12

Again two healings are juxtaposed, the leper and the paralytic. The primary strand here is the cleansing of the leper and the forgiveness of sins for the paralytic, both amounting to virtually the same thing. The secondary strand for the leper is that he should conform to the public health rules and be inspected by the priest and make an offering. Thirdly, there is the secrecy element, which is soon ignored. The secondary element with the paralytic is the faith required from the patient and his helpers who lowered him down through the roof. Thirdly, claiming to forgive sins raises the question of blasphemy, the old law interfering with the new, but also raising the question of the true identity of Jesus. The age-old assumption that illness is some kind of punishment for sin is at work here; it would be a mistake to say that every illness has this cause, yet we know that many conditions are, to this day, connected with guilt and fear.

Mark 5:1ff, the dramatic account of the Gaderene Swine

This is another multifaceted healing, a severe case of schizophrenia, in today's terms, but is still a puzzle to the so-called psychiatric experts of today. Jesus clearly understands the workings of the world of the evil spirits and has the spiritual strength to clear the man's affliction. Secondly, Jesus reaches out to the non-Jewish world, since this takes place in a Greek-speaking colony in the Decapolis. This area would have been taboo to the Jews and the fact that there were pigs involved would have been the last straw. But he bridges over racial and cultural divides. Thirdly, this time there is no secrecy element: the man is told to go and tell how God has had mercy on him. Is this the very first beginnings of the Gentile mission? Sadly the locals were so terrified of Jesus that they told him to depart. This is a feature seen today amongst people who can only see God (and Jesus) as some kind of threat. Again myth is brought into reality and resolved, but there are some who cannot let go of myth.

Mark 7:21–43, another double healing

A woman in the crowd touches his garment and is healed immediately. This clearly indicates that there was a numino-spiritual power in Jesus, which only operated when it came into contact with someone with a need for it. It must have been like a battery where the positive only activates when connected to something negative: plus has no meaning unless there is a minus. This brings us back the Theodicy. Secondly, as Jesus approaches Jairus's house, his prescience is seen in that he knows the girl is not dead. His advice is not to be obsessive about mourning: think of death in positive terms, take courage and believe. The clever juxtaposition of the two miracles, as the number 12 is involved, reminds us of the 12 disciples and the 12 tribes of Israel. The hint is that this one is for the people of Israel, in contrast to the one in the Decapolis. The element of faith required in the patient is also stressed in both accounts.

In Matthew and Luke we see the same factors at work. The healing of the Centurion's servant (Matthew 8:5ff) shows that Jesus could do healings at a distance; but secondarily, the Roman (Gentile) soldier, surprisingly, for all his authority submits in faith to Jesus. Even if he was pro-Jewish as St Luke points out (Luke 7:4), the idea of the Gentile mission is there. Matthew emphasises this more heavily by saying that the sons of the kingdom will be thrown out and people from far away will be sharing in the messianic banquet. Faith, which is needed for the miracles, is in short supply in Israel but abundant in the Gentiles. And for Matthew the tertiary agenda is fulfilment of prophecy, 'He took our infirmities and bore our diseases.'

Luke 7:11–17, the Raising of the Widow of Nain's Son

Jesus brings a man back to life, pointing us forward to the Resurrection. Secondly, he is the only son of a widow, and we can see the compassion heavily emphasised in the story, for this lady would probably be reduced to dire poverty and loneliness. We are all engaged in the sympathy. Thirdly, as she is a widow, Luke sees it as important to show how Jesus cared for the outcasts, the rejects and anyone who did not fit in too well with the excellence of Judaism. Fourthly, 'A great prophet has arisen among us' reminds us that Jesus was, for many, to be associated with people like Moses and Elijah.

Luke 10:17ff, the Return of the Seventy Evangelists

It is clear that Jesus hands on his healing gifts to his disciples: this is the first point. Secondly, we see mythology associated with illness, and the cure is the defeat of the powers of evil: 'I saw Satan fall like lightning from Heaven.' The Garden of Eden situation is reversed, where we tread on snakes and scorpions. This is hardly meant literally. But we can see that mythology is brought to a resolution and even obsolescence by the actual curing of illnesses both physical and spiritual. Thirdly, the mention of 70 evangelists recalls that Moses appointed 70 elders in the wilderness period, thus linking us back to the inception of the Covenant of Sinai.

Matthew 15:21–28, the Healing of the Canaanite Woman's Daughter

At first Jesus seems to ignore her entreaties and the disciples want her to go away. There is a sense in which Jesus knows he is meant to help the Jewish people first and foremost. However, paradoxically, he is drawn to helping a pagan woman and accepts her argument which clearly shows her faith. It shows that he is torn over his ministry; finding the Jews so difficult, he finds the Gentiles much more amenable. The solution is obvious: faith is to be found in all people, not just the people of the Old Covenant.

Another issue raised in the healing miracles is the true source of the spiritual power. Is it from God or the Devil? This emerges in Luke 11:15 where the actual healing is of minor interest. The secondary strand which draws in mythology, is 'he casts out demons by Beelzebul', and others wish for confirmation from God. It is typical of the confused thinking of those who cannot see that the Kingdom of God has arrived.

Jesus is prepared to admit that there are others who do healing miracles, even on a different basis to his God-orientated method. He is not going to stop them, except to say (Mark 9:40): 'He who is not against us is for us.' However, Luke 11:23 holds the paradoxical statement: 'He who is not with me is against me and he who does not gather with me, scatters.'

Contrasting statements which are true in their own way. Just because one has a different label does not invalidate one's caring. On the other hand there is the need to make one's mind up about the focus of one's loyalty. Back to mythology, the war going on between good and evil does not have any space for neutrals or ditherers. Truth is not some sort of happy average, compromise or even worse, trifling with the matter. This is pointed out forcefully in the next parable (11:24) and is a warning to those who interfere with the world of the spirit but cannot cope with it properly. It can make matters seven times worse. The answer is to join forces with the true and only source of spiritual power. It is interesting that in Matthew 12:43ff the same teaching comes in an altered context, one might almost say a demythologised application. Here, Jesus is talking about a generation that seeks a sign but will only receive the sign of Jonah, which is referring to the resurrection. The Jews are unable to see the greatness of Jesus, his wisdom being superior to that of Solomon. The ones who scatter are the legalists who are basically evil (v. 34). They must realise that they are going to land in seven times worse problems. 'So shall it be with this evil generation' (v. 46), words which came true in AD 70.

The natural-world miracles of Jesus

Many of the natural-world miracles of Jesus display the same characteristics as the healing ones. It is a false dichotomy to try to separate them off into a different category. It is more constructive to take the work of Jesus as a whole rather than to pigeonhole his works, as has been happening in scholarship in recent times. Again the secondary and tertiary elements keep emerging, very often the same message as with the healings. He was noted for exaggerated preaching; his parables and miracles bring clarity and reality to his words. The parables explain; the miracles demonstrate in real terms. It is all one message.

Mark 4:35, the Calming of the Storm

The primary strand here is that Jesus is in control of the elements. Secondly, he reassures his followers to put aside fear and have faith. Thirdly, they become aware of his eternal identity and significance. This is more heavily emphasised in St Matthew (14:22–33) where the disciples reach the conclusion, 'Truly you are the Son of God.' Again the miracle was not done to impress the crowd but rather at a time of crisis when the fledgling Church was about to be overwhelmed. God intervenes dramatically with his acute sense of timing, which is the core of the miracle. This was seen with Moses and Elijah.

Mark 6:35, the Feeding of the Five Thousand

This is an occurrence which may have been a normal procedure in his ministry. There is no way that such a feat can be supported by rational evidence, still less disproved by some kind of earthbound logic. The amazing thing is that Jesus did not overdo it as he was tempted to do by the Devil, to turn stones into bread just for his own convenience. The main message is that Jesus cares for people, just like a shepherd with his flock. The secondary element concerns the recollection of the manna in the wilderness: it is St John who relates the event to Passover time. Jesus brings the Exodus to a fulfilment. Thirdly, there is the hint again of esoteric use of numbers. This was very important to the people of that day, and still is with certain people now. The number 12 appears again, as with the two healing miracles, thus recalling the 12 tribes of Israel. The indication is that Jesus cares for his own people, the Jews. There were five loaves: this reminds us of the Pentateuch, which implies that the Jewish law was the main contributor to the new faith. But also there were two fish: fish as we see from John 21:11 were (in the ancient world) symbolic of the nations of the earth, 153 in total. This implies that there is a certain input from the Gentiles.[4]

Mark 8:1–10, the Feeding of the Four Thousand

There is no need to assume that this is a confused version of the Five Thousand. There was doubtless a reason for St Mark including this account as well as the other one. The primary message is the same as before: Jesus' compassion. The secondary one is also the same, even this time mentioning the 'desert', which locates it in the wilderness period. But the tertiary message, using esoteric numbers, is slightly different. This time there are seven baskets left over, a number which betokened the four corners of the earth and the three layers, heaven, earth and the underworld. In contrast to the 12 baskets, Jesus now sustains the whole cosmos. The miracle is for all people. But there has to be some sort of input from the people, seven loaves. The fish this time are left vague in number. This miracle is for the whole universe, not just the Jewish religion. In case one might think that this is pure speculation, Jesus actually teases the disciples later (Mark 8:19), 'Do you not yet understand?' In other words the 12 and the seven do have a subtle significance. Possibly a fourth strand here is the paradox that from a simple offering of basic foodstuffs, fetched by a little child (as in St John), Jesus can transform them into the sustenance for the entire universe. So the faith of a little child underpins the system of faith for us all, regardless of race or religion. Also we see that mythological assumptions are never very far beneath the surface in any of these accounts.

Mark 6:45–52, Walking on the Water

This miracle follows the Feeding of the Five Thousand and is clearly meant to relate to it. Somehow it is meant to underpin the previous miracle. There is the secondary element of how his followers were terrified out of their wits, and yet Jesus calms them down, and the wind too. Thirdly, 'their hearts were hardened' recalls part of Psalm 95:8: 'harden not your hearts.' It is in the context of the wilderness period at Meribah where Moses produced water from the rock. This was a bitter occasion when the Israelites wanted proof and failed to respond in faith to God. Because of this, God decided that they would not enter the promised land. After so many wonders they were still in denial over it. With the Jews demanding a sign as proof, this is probably the tipping point when Jesus decides that the Gentiles will be offered the Kingdom instead. The Exodus period comes to completion, and like history repeating itself the people of God show a serious lack of faith, which is the prerequisite of entering the

Kingdom. This explains why the next major feeding follows in 8:1–10 and again the Pharisees want proof from heaven.

St Matthew, with the same incident of walking on the water, alters the thrust of it to some extent, although it is in the same context of the Feeding of the Five Thousand. The secondary element here (14:28ff) is that Peter comes to Jesus walking on the water and has to be buoyed up by Jesus as Peter's faith slips a little. The primacy of Peter is shown here, as at the Rock at Caesarea Philippi. A tertiary strand is the conclusion over the identity of Jesus: 'Truly you are the Son of God.'

Matthew 21:18, the Withering of the Fig Tree

This enigmatic miracle is in contrast to the others for it is destructive as opposed to constructive. In the parables the motif of the fig tree, which is symbolic of Israel, is closely connected with the interim period between the start and the finish of Jesus' ministry. Here, in the last few days of his earthly life, he is forced to admit that the faith of Israel has not responded to his *kerygma* in the way that he had hoped. He now condemns it to wither and bear no fruit again. Being sentimental about the tree is irrelevant: the big moment of crisis has arrived. In the same context in Luke 13:6, that of the Jews refusing to repent, there is even a hint of his three-year ministry: 'Lo these three years I have come seeking fruit.' There is even mention of a temporary reprieve as the vine-dresser offers to give it extra attention, 'if not you can cut it down.' This is actually what happened in AD 70. In this way the parables and the miracles are interlaced, interlocked, interwoven and prophetic. Any artificial attempt to separate them in order to play down the miraculous simply betrays a failure to appreciate the integrity of the message conveyed by the Gospel writers. Again, with the mention of a tree, mythology is not very far beneath the surface.

General remarks on the miracles

It may be that St John had this issue in mind when he gave the parables much less prominence and used the miracles to convey the same messages. Essentially he selects a few miracles as signs of his glory. The dominant theme is the inability of the Jewish leadership, the people of the Old Testament, to cope with the emergence of the New Testament. This is in spite of him using all their imagery, mythology, thought-forms and prophecies in fulfilment. They react violently, leading on to the rejection of Good Friday. The paradox is that the ones who would have been expected to accept him, failed to do so; others who would have been expected to refuse his ministry, accepted him. This goes against all human common sense; it is another example of divine logic being the opposite of human rationality.

The miracles have been and always will be a stumbling-block for those who try to reduce them to a materialistic rationalisation. The fact that people try to rationalise them is evidence that they know there is some degree of reality in them, even though they cannot bring themselves to admit the full truth of them. We need to see them in the light of the greater paradoxes of life: the difference between this world and the next. If it is true that Almighty God did break into this world in real terms, then we would expect his time, the interim period, to be characterised by extraordinary happenings. He would hardly have come like Confucius to give us a nice humane list of precepts which had no relation to the realities of human nature; hardly like Siddhartha, who was deeply puzzled about the realities of life. He came with his eternal power and glory and yet, paradoxically, it was in one sense veiled and in another sense blatantly obvious. A case in point is the final miracle in St John 18:6: 'He said to them, "I am he" and they drew back and fell to the ground.' John does not mention the healing of Malchus's ear, as he might have done. The power of the Eternal God showed through for a moment and then was withdrawn, as he allowed himself to be taken away and put to death.

This paradox goes on all through the four Gospels: his eternal power in relation to his earthly humility: two irreconcilable factors and yet combined in one person, Jesus. As we have seen with the Incarnation, attempts at rationalising this, which amounts to tampering with the Gospels to produce something acceptable to human canons of reason, simply do not work. The gospels must be taken as a whole and allowed to speak for themselves and work in with each other. All their differences in emphasis are there for a purpose. The disagreements are not some sort of mistake made by ill-informed historians. They are bringing out the deep paradoxes in the life of

Jesus. It may be that at the time of writing they did not realise what they were doing, any more than Isaiah realised what he was saying in the messianic prophecies, and yet, miraculously, they bring forth so much of the deep truths about God and his Messiah. That may be the fundamental miracle of these writings: in that they managed to convey, in working-class Greek, the deep truths about life and death, something that the philosophers of many an age have attempted but failed to achieve.

Before discounting the miracles, it is as well to take note that only recently, in this age of materialism and scepticism, there has been a re-emergence of the healing ministry of the Church. Such names as Harry Edwards, Christopher Woodward and Russel Parker have shown that spiritual healing is a reality. We notice that once again, the community of faith is under pressure and in danger of absorption into the vagaries of a new paganism. The reappearance of the miraculous in the Church can be seen in the same light as at the Exodus and as with Elijah. The mysterious account of Linda Martel, excellently documented by Charles Graves, serves as a challenge to a materialistic and doubting age. This account will warrant a separate excursus at the end of this chapter.

An analogy from the Bouncing Bomb

During the Second World War an inventor-scientist called Barnes Wallis speculated that he could make a device bounce across water before coming to rest against a target such as a dam wall. The experts thought this was a crazy idea and were full of derision. Wallis asked to borrow a Wellington bomber so that he could test and perfect the idea. They refused, with the words, ‘Why should you be allowed to borrow a Wellington: they are in such short supply?’ His reply was to this effect, ‘How about, it was me that invented it in the first place?’ Reluctantly they supplied him with a bomber and a test pilot in order to experiment with this ‘impossible’ device. The impossible turned out to be a reality and the dams in Germany were breached. And still people find it difficult to comprehend how a bomb can bounce in a controlled fashion over water. But it did happen.

So too with God: it is impertinent of the human race to say that God cannot do as he wishes with his own creation. He makes the laws of science and we try to discover them. But we do not know all of them and probably never will. When God performs what seems to be a breach of his own laws, it may not be quite as simple as that. For him it may be just an accommodation to different circumstances. We see it as a miracle; he sees it as a temporary alteration in the normal course of things. Jesus never claimed to be the only one to heal the sick: he empowered his disciples to do it; in recent times his followers have rediscovered the healing ministry. It remains as a challenge to materialism, bureaucracy and 'common sense'. The logic of God is superior to that of all the experts.

The miracle of the Resurrection

In assessing the miracles of Jesus, the Resurrection stands out as the ultimate and conclusive miracle of them all. It is also the greatest challenge to faith, or conversely the most obvious starting-point for those inclined to disbelieve. Much ink has been spilled over this across the years but there is no final answer to it because it defies rational explanation. This is a problem early realised by the Apostolic Church, for they saw the need to bring together witnesses for the Resurrection; indeed the chief qualification for being a bishop was such at first. The best they could do was to assemble witnesses, which it was claimed amounted to over 500 people: 'Then he appeared to more than five hundred brethren at one time, most of whom are still alive,' 1 Corinthians 15:6.

Even so, it was still a problem, as Matthew 28:17 admits: 'Now the eleven ... went to Galilee ... and when they saw him they worshipped him: but some doubted.' Right from the start it has been a bone of contention, and always will be.

It is however the nub of the Christian faith: if there is no Resurrection, the whole thing falls apart. 'If Christ has not been raised, then our preaching is in vain and your faith is in vain,' 1 Corinthians 15:14.

Just as Theodicy is an unanswerable question and yet is still there in people's minds, demanding an explanation, so too is the Resurrection. It is the positive side of Theodicy. We have seen that all the attempts at coping with Theodicy have resorted to some sort of negative mentality; the Resurrection is the positive counterpart of Theodicy. This can even be seen in embryo in the Book of Job; the writer may not have realised the full ramifications of his remarks: 'For I know that my redeemer lives and at the last he will stand upon the earth ... then from my flesh shall I see God,' Job 19:25.

But the deepest paradox of all is that out of death, under the most horrific and humiliating circumstances, come not just ordinary life such as is lived by ordinary people, but triumphant, transformed and indestructible life. It is the new life that the Messiah provides for all the people in this world and the next. It is his way of breaking through the 'insulation' between two different worlds. The Eternal God comes into each human soul and the channel is the Living Christ. Also paradoxically, this life is there for all people, past, present and future, regardless of whether they know about it or accept it; in another sense Jesus has provided a way into God's presence which people need to know about.

The ultimate illogicality, that of a God who allowed himself to be put to death, coincided at a specific time and place in human history with the ultimate divine logicality of providing a new relationship between himself and humanity. How this worked is beyond us to explain. Even so, the Resurrection is the final assurance that God understands the problem and provides the answer in his own way, not some sort of human way.

We can see from the various mythologies of the world and the way various religions have addressed the problem of Theodicy, that the Resurrection is the answer. But it is not a theory or some sort of fantasy. It is a solid answer in real terms. The Gospel writers and St Paul are insistent that Jesus really rose again and it was not some sort of fiction. It is the fulfilment of all the hopes of new life, whether associated with sacral kingship or some form of peri-mythological assumption such as Karma. Virtually every faith on earth works on the assumption that death is not the end, but usually there is no real understanding of how this comes about. The Christian answer is that Christ has provided eternal life; in this way the Christian resurrection is the fulfilment, completion and clarification of every other religion on earth. Recollecting the thoughts on Theodicy in Chapter 2, we can see that the Resurrection provides a positive answer to each approach to the problem of evil.

To the pagan multi-god approach, the final problem was the fallibility of the ultimate God. The death and resurrection of Jesus show that there is suffering in the godhead: he allows himself to be injured and die but in order to be raised again. It is not like the pagan gods who appear to die and come back to life once a year to stimulate the harvest. Christ does it once, not in some sort of ritual or pretence, but really. He brings the pagan expectation to a fulfilment they would never have guessed at. This is not done by a lower god but by the eternal supreme God himself.

To the Gnostic modified pagan system, death and resurrection is shown in real terms. It is not a fantasy, charade or even a cinematic projection. Life is real; death is real; so is new life on an eternal basis. It is provided by Christ who is active in people's lives. The believer knows him as a real person, not just as some sort of abstract principle.

To the 'no-evil' theory (pantheism), in which God is the one and only pervading force, the Gospels have an answer. We see an unmatched outpouring of love and caring in Jesus and yet paradoxically this evoked the deepest outpourings of hatred, intolerance and cruelty coming from the very people who should have known better. Evil is a reality despite God being the only pervading force. The defeat of evil in a most dramatic and convincing way, as seen in the death and Resurrection, showed ultimate love in the face of ultimate hatred. The victory means that no human soul needs to be lost eternally.

To the dualist theory, we see many instances of Jesus encountering spiritual forces of evil, Satan, the Devil. He has to overcome them finally and convincingly. On the cross he was tempted to give in and decide the matter by a show of force. The victory of the cross is still at large in human affairs. But through the triumph of Jesus, no one need get involved with evil if they take Christ seriously and live the Christian life.

To the pure monotheist, which involves some kind of 'Fall' of mankind in the distant past, the answer is that God is indeed one, even if paradoxically he came as a human being at a certain time in history. This human was the 'second Adam' who brought the whole scheme of history to a fulfilment and conclusion and provided a way to attain perfection and a new relationship with the one eternal God. The Resurrection clinched the whole scheme.

To the 'no-god' theory, atheism in its many forms, the answer is that to expect humanity to save itself by its own 'goodwill' is a vain hope. For this world with all its problems to be straightened out, it requires intervention from some form of agency above and beyond the greed and stupidity of human nature. It is not realistic to expect mankind, the chief source of our problems anyway, to root out our problems. The 'perfect man' Jesus did not manage to be perfect by trying very hard to be good; it was a gift from God. So too, salvation is not something that we can conjure up by trying very hard to be virtuous. It requires divine assistance. One lesson we can learn from the collapse of Communism is that trying to 'save' mankind by materialistic means, leaving out the spiritual needs and realities in human nature, simply does not work. The ministry of Jesus, especially the Resurrection, shows that divine intervention which involves the miraculous is the only way forward for a broken world.

This brings us back to the finale of the Book of Job. When Elihu cuts in with a positive stance on the problem of suffering, he can see that it is God's method for saving people. It is a positive plan on the part of God, not a negative one or a terrible mistake. This will seem hard on those who were victims of the Holocaust; and yet, how many positive and helpful things have emerged from the horrors of the early 1940s?

'Whether it be for correction, or for his land, or for love, he causes it to happen . . . but man does not perceive it'; it is beyond us to know exactly how this works. Death and Resurrection are a mystery explicable only in God's terms, not ours. And yet, we can come to realise that through this process comes the salvation of the entire universe.

The Legend of Linda Martel, Charles Graves[5]

It is inappropriate to call this a legend: it is one of the best-documented and authenticated accounts of spiritual healing ever to surface. Linda Martel was born in 1956 to Roy and Eileen Martel, and died in 1961. She never survived beyond infancy and yet the people she helped were many. The people of Guernsey remember her well but her fame has spread abroad. The media locally and nationally made a lot of it at the time. Charles Graves, an established author and experienced investigator, worked on the written evidence, tapes, photographs and published a seminal work on the matter in 1968.

It is a severe stumbling-block to doubters, materialists and atheists. From a very early age, Linda was clearly aware of the presence of Jesus and the Virgin Mary: she was 'seeing' them. She was not being raised as a Roman Catholic; no Church at all in fact. And yet she had a deep spirituality and healing ability and also diagnostic powers. Healing by touch, knowing where the problem was located and healing at a distance all remind us of how Jesus worked. Sadly she only survived to the age of five. She was born with spina bifida and very little could be done to rectify the problem. Her brain was gradually filling up with fluid which made her head swell up; she could not hope to live to childhood. This was not helped by the scores of people coming for healing, which was sapping her strength. She was an amazing child, very mature for her age and yet desperately weak and ill. To this day, the Martels are sending off handkerchiefs and bits of clothing for people to use for healing.

The whole thing is beyond easy explanation. It is to be noted that from an infant wracked with pain, comes life and alleviation of suffering for others. This reminds us of the Suffering Servant in Isaiah. We can also see the same tendency in human nature to airbrush these matters away: it made quite a sensation in the mid-1960s but now it is almost completely forgotten. And the evidence is still there. People choose to ignore Linda Martel just as they try to ignore Jesus; it does not fit in with their cosy materialistic assumptions about life. Such is the hardness of heart that Jesus encountered and is still with us in spite of all God's miracles.

The Turin Shroud

To leave this artefact out of the debate would be a mistake, even if it is a forgery. At the very least, one can see that the same reactions from people are evinced as with the Resurrection and the broader canvas of Jesus' ministry. Some react with disbelief; others with complete acceptance. But whatever their reaction is, there is a strange fascination which will not allow people to ignore it. The same is true with Resurrection.

To summarise briefly, the Shroud purports to be the authentic burial shroud of Jesus, and has an image of his complete body, front and back mysteriously imprinted on the cloth. No one has yet been able to explain the cause of this impression; it is not paint. It is somehow photographic, but not of a plain two-dimensional picture. It is a negative, but responds to three-dimensional (3D) imaging, a process only recently devised by those involved in space exploration. As yet, no one can explain how, centuries before the advent of photography, such an image could have been faked. Moreover, the image is an accurate impression of a crucifixion victim, showing detail which could not have been possible for a Mediaeval forger to fake. Radio carbon tests have offered a date of 1260–1390, but this has been questioned since the sample may have been taken from a 'repaired' section of the cloth. The fact remains that until further technological advances are available and permission received from the Vatican, it is not possible to be certain of anything about the Shroud. No one has been able to replicate the nature of the image in spite of exhaustive attempts to show how it could have been done.

The Shroud remains a mystery and probably always will be. But what does it prove? Our scientific techniques have brought to light matters concerning it that had not been known before 1898, namely that it is some kind of photograph. In one sense it has been a help to faith: in another sense it has raised more uncertainties and puzzles. The controversy rages. If it is a genuine first-century relic, then it is really a Jewish crucifixion victim. At the most, it can prove that Jesus really did die and was buried. The Resurrection, like the other miracles, is beyond proof; also beyond disproof.

The effect on people, however, is certain: some react with disbelief, others with great faith. This has nothing to do with the pronouncements of the scientists, for when recently it was declared a Mediaeval forgery because of the carbon 14 testing, believers simply ignored it. It would seem that the fascination engendered by the Shroud has nothing to do with proof or evidence: it speaks directly to the soul of humanity. People know instinctively that this is the face of Jesus Christ; others simply cannot cope with it. It was the same problem then as it is now. Jesus brings a division in the world between those who react positively and those who react negatively. This seems to have little to do with the genuineness of the Shroud. It is a paradox deeply embedded in the human soul: the positive and negative reaction to the Messiah of God.[6]

Notes

1. The possible exception to this would be in Zoroastrianism in which Zoroaster is claimed to have performed miracles.
2. Colin Humphreys, *The Miracle of the Exodus*, p. 137.
3. James, *The Apocryphal Gospels*. The Koran refers to these matters and assumes them to be literally true.

4. C.K. Barrett, *Commentary on St John.*
5. Charles Graves, *The Legend of Linda Martel.*
6. Ian Wilson, *The Turin Shroud.*

14

Calendars, Era and Religious Significance

Mention in passing has already been made of times, seasons and dates. This is an area which seems largely to be ignored by the mainstream of theology and yet it does need some attention. We tend to take for granted the Gregorian calendar that is in use in virtually every country of the world. But it must be remembered that in the time of Jesus, no such easy assumption could be made.[1] People then had strong views on the calculation of time; it had deep religious significance for them, not least for Jesus himself. A moderately simplified review of the development of the Gregorian calendar is now appropriate, not least to clear away some of the facile assumptions that we make today.

The mathematical and astronomical skills involved in producing calendars have been in action from the very earliest times. China, Babylon, and Egypt are significant examples, but there are many others. It is amazing the degree of sophistication attained by peoples with the most rudimentary of resources.[2] This is why Von Daniken[3] thinks the inspiration came from outer space; but he fails to explain why these ancient people did not all have the same scheme, as one would expect if helpful little spacemen came along with a neatly worked out plan. The truth of the matter is that it took many centuries of empirical effort to achieve what we have nowadays. There are two major factors available for calendar construction: the sun and the moon. There were various attempts at working a system which took account of both factors together, but this never really worked. The results were decidedly clumsy and unworkable. We have now clearly based our workings on the movements of the sun; the moon only has influence on the timing of certain religious festivals.

The fact has always been, and will continue to be, that the solar year does not equate exactly to a discrete number of days; still less does the lunar year equate to an exact number of months; neither do the two systems coincide at all well. With the lunar month being 29.5 days and 13 moons per solar year, this does not fit comfortably with the solar year being at slightly less than 365.25 days. This explains why lunar calculation has been out of fashion since the reforms of Julius Caesar. To make matters worse, the solar year does not accord with any convenient multiple of days: the actual total of days in a year is 365.2421873 and is decreasing at the rate of about 0.46 seconds per century. There was some awareness of this problem in ancient times but they lacked the resources to pin the problem down. It was Sosigenes, an Egyptian, whom Julius Caesar brought to Rome for the express purpose of reforming the calendar.[4] The Julian calendar was a brilliant solution in its day, but they must have known that, in the long term, more adjustments would be needed. It was only after 1600 years that it became obvious that the seasons were becoming increasingly out of line with the actual dates. The Gregorian reform of 1582 was important, and to correct the discrepancy caused by taking the year as exactly 365.25 days, eleven days had to be removed from the calendar. It took a long time for other countries to follow suit, largely because the Protestants could not cope with the Papal initiative over the Gregorian calendar. Now, virtually every country in the world follows the Pope's calendar; even so, minor corrections have to be made, cutting out a few seconds from time to time. Even though the Gregorian calendar has its anomalies, it is acceptable for its relative simplicity, ease of operation and fair relationship with the residual lunar religious needs.

Calendar reform is never popular: it takes a major historical figure such as Julius Caesar or a major international council such as the Council of Nicea to enact it, and even then there will be disagreements and civil unrest accompanying such measures. This is not just because of the calendar's politico-economic implications but also because of the religious ones. Deeply held beliefs may seem threatened. Because of the anomalous situation over calendar calculation over the centuries, it would be very difficult, perhaps impossible, to determine exactly when Jesus was born and died. We like to imagine that we know exactly when Christmas and Easter occur, but this is only a calendar construct; even so, we seem to need something definite to orientate our lives around.

It is certainly a mathematical paradox that such things as leap years and intercalatory months have had to occur in order that the dates can be synchronised with the seasons. It is not, however, a theological paradox. The calendar is and always has been a human calculation in spite of people's assumptions about its divine status. Much scientific observation and deduction has gone into it, and all manner of permutations have been tried or suggested. The World Calendar of 1956 was the latest attempt, but it was rejected by the United Nations. The theological paradox lies in this: although God entered human history at a specific time and place, actually pinning it down to precise dates has not been possible; this is in terms of the Julian calendar and even the AUC[5] reckoning which preceded it. In a way, this adds to the mystery of the Incarnation. Should archaeological research ever manage to clarify this matter, then the paradox might possibly cease. The minor fact that Dennis Exiguus miscalculated the birth of Jesus so that he appears to have been born in 4 BC is not the point, for we can easily allow for that. Strangely, everyone celebrated the millennium in AD 2000, but of course the real millennium was in 1996! But the matter is deeper: with all the shifts in calendar science over the centuries, all dating in the ancient world has to be speculative and approximate.

The seven-day week is another aspect of the matter, and is essentially tied to religious beliefs. It is thought to have originated in ancient Babylon, as a ten-day span, with the awareness of certain unlucky days. Egypt, Mesoamerica, revolutionary France and Russia have also tried a ten-day system. This has never worked too well: seven days is now the basis of the working week all over the world. It would seem that it works reasonably well with the Gregorian system. The notion of the World Calendar would have meant that Sunday would have been tied to 1st January, April, June and October, which may have sounded like a useful idea, but with having to add an extra day before 1st January and the leap year day before 1st June would have confused the sequence of hebdomands.[6] This may explain its rejection in 1956. We can see in this not so much a paradox as a resolution, since now we are seeing the whole world following what is essentially an important provision in the Ten Commandments: the seven-day week is seen to underpin virtually every aspect of modern life, satisfying both religious and secular needs.

Another matter relevant to the hebdomadal cycle is the naming of the days of the week, also of the months. The naming of the days goes back to ancient Egypt, where the five extra days inserted before the autumnal equinox were named after their gods: Osiris, Horus, Set, Isis and Nephthys (twice if it were a leap year). This pattern worked its way into Babylon, Greece, Rome and Northern Europe, each culture simply applying the name of an equivalent god. After the time of Constantine, the Christian missionaries applied the names to all the days of the routine week and added Sunday and Monday to fill out the seven. Attempts at 'depaganising' this have never worked and now all the world has names for the days of the week loosely following the same idea, even if the actual names differ.

The same is largely true for the months of the year. Our naming of the months is derived from the Romans and vestiges of merely numbering the months are seen in September to December. But counting from the New Year, the vernal equinox, we have Martius, Aprilis, Maius, Iunius – all gods; and Quintilis became July, after Julius Caesar; Sextilis became August, after Augustus. It was Nero who had April renamed as Neroneus, May as Claudius, and June as Germanicus. Caligula had September renamed Germanicus, but these alterations did not last long.[7] Virtually every country in the world follows this pattern today, even if the actual names vary. The paradox is that the whole Judaeo-Christian system is underpinned by what is essentially a pagan scheme of days and months. Attempts at getting away from it have not worked, most notably the French revolutionary calendar which only lasted 12 years. In this we can see an intimation of resolution. In Genesis 37:6 we read that in Joseph's dream his sheaf stood upright while his brothers' sheaves bowed down; also the sun, moon and eleven stars bowed down to him. We can give an allegorical interpretation for this: the religions and calendars of the seasons and the heavenly bodies will all become subservient and secondary to the God of Israel. We can see further resolution of this idea, for at the birth of Christ, there was reported an unusual happening in the heavens (the star), and the visit of the Magi who themselves would have been astrologers and calendar experts. They all bowed down to him. Going further, when St Paul speaks of the 'elemental spirits' to which we have been slaves (Galatians 4:3 and 9), he is largely talking about the calendar and all the astral speculations that went with it in those days: 'You observe days and months and seasons of the years!'

These are the weak and beggarly elemental spirits. It is not that St Paul wishes to tear up the calendar; it is the superstitious, paganistic attitude to gods in relation to dates and heavenly bodies that concerns him. In other words, the triumph of Jesus has made him superior to all calculations, astronomy, astrology and associated matters. It is the theology of resolution. The pagan deities and heavenly powers are all subservient to the Christian week and year.

Jesus and calendar awareness

This in an area hardly ever addressed by scholarship, and yet there is much evidence that it was an important ingredient in his thinking. He had an acute sense of timing and occasion. This is most noticeable in St John but there are traces of it in the Synoptics too. There are two Greek words which are important in this matter: *kairos* and *hora*.[8] Both have much the same meaning, 'time' and 'hour'. They appear to have a certain pejorative loading, although they seem to be used as synonyms. Mark 13:22 and 33: 'But of that day or that hour no one knows ... for you do not know when the time will come ... in the evening, or at midnight or at cockcrow, or in the morning.'

Hora is time, as in 60 seconds per hour, but also fitting time, the appropriate moment, the time is ripe, even going further, the Horai were the keepers of the heavenly gate in Greek mythology. *Kairos* also means time, the critical moment, the right time, the right spot, even a season such as spring. Using them in parallel, as in St Mark, may mean the New Testament writers did not see much difference in meaning or pejorative loading. *Hora* does however evoke more mythological background.

Somehow, Jesus was aware that the critical moment in his ministry was looming and that it would be connected with one of the Jewish festivals. The Passover would be the most appropriate since he saw his ministry as the new Exodus. There seems to be no uncertainty in St Matthew 26:18, 'My time is at hand ... I will keep the Passover.' But in St John we have a kind of rising crisis and the festival in question might have turned out to be the Feast of Tabernacles. In chapter 7 we have a narrowly avoided messianic confrontation somehow related to the Tabernacles. Jesus himself was aware that his time had not yet 'fully come' (7:8). It is not clear whether the Tabernacles would have been the appropriate moment: after all, it did commemorate the Wilderness period when the Israelites had no fixed abode. With it also being one of the harvest festivals, the sense of 'season' and 'when it is ripe' would also be appropriate, as with *hora*.

Mostly St John uses *hora*, but *kairos* twice. There does not appear to be any significance in this. In 2:4 he tells his mother, in a way which seems quite out of context, 'My hour has not yet come', but later we learn that the Passover is looming. Instead of it being the critical moment in history that he is aware of, it turns out to be the Cleansing of the Temple. But the suspense builds up as he tells the Samaritan woman that God will be worshipped not in Jerusalem nor in Samaria, but in spirit and truth. This foreshadows the end of the era and the start of spiritual worship in the New Testament aegis. This is reinforced with the prophecy that the dead will hear the saving words of Jesus: looking forward to the Crucifixion and the three days in hell. But the right moment was to come (12:37) just after the triumphal entry (Palm Sunday).

Jesus was depressed at the thought of what was impending: 'Father save me from this hour.' He is aware that the critical moment has arrived, the big showdown between good and evil. Quite why it should have been this Passover as opposed to any other is not really explained. But the sense of it being a landmark in human history is clearly there. No one thinks to clarify this matter: it may be that the Gospel writers were assuming that the reader would not need to have it explained. It is John 19:31 which comes the nearest to shedding some light on this matter. He remarks that that Sabbath was a 'high day' (*megale hemera ekeinon*) though in what respect is left unstated. He emphasises that the Passover does coincide with the Sabbath, which in itself might have given it that degree of unusual importance. This situation would have occurred once in six years, if they were using the Julian calendar. Since Jesus saw the Sabbath as highly significant and the Passover too, the two of them coinciding would have been a highly appropriate moment for the decisive moment in history. Other than that we are unaware of any special significance in that particular Passover. From the point of view of resolution, the sacrificial death of Jesus brings to completion the Passover, not just for the Israelites but for us all; for the pagans, the hours that Jesus was aware of brings to resolution the Horai keeping guard on the gates of heaven. In this way, history and mythology are subtly worked in together. Another factor in the same context in St John (19:30) is when Jesus is offered the vinegar and says 'it is finished'. *Tetelestai* has been discussed earlier (page 154), but it can be rendered as 'it has been completed'. On the face of it this concerns the fulfilment of prophecies, which actually continues after he dies. On the other hand, *telos*, the root of this verb, carries various pejorative overtones: 'An end accomplished, completion, fulfilment, to have prayers answered, to be in possession of full powers, to receive consummation as in being accepted into a mystery religion.' It does mean that Jesus understood his death as the completion of all things, and that would, one would assume, involve the timing of the event.

Calendar awareness in the Acts and Epistles

The awareness of time and occasion seen with Jesus carries on into the thinking of the Apostolic Church. It is clear that they saw the timing of Jesus' ministry as important; also that it related to his Second Coming, even if they did not have any idea of how to anticipate it. This is clear from Acts 1:7 where the disciples are still thinking in terms of an earthly messianic revolution: 'It is not for you to know the times (*chronos*) or seasons (*kairos*) which the Father has fixed by his own authority.'

The appeal to this way of thinking appears to be offered to Jews and Greeks alike. In Acts 3:21 Peter is talking to the Jews, his brethren, and in Acts 17:26 Paul is preaching to the theological philosophers of Athens, using their own thought forms: 'He made from every nation ... having determined allotted periods (*kairos*) and boundaries of their habitation.'

The use of 'determined' is interesting here for it hints at God's planning and even predestination in relation to the course of history.[9] In many places in the Pauline Epistles the assumption of God's plan in relation to the correct timing for Christ's ministry surfaces. Usually it relates to the completion of Jesus' earthly ministry; sometimes it refers to the Second Coming which is equally carefully timed and planned. This is a mystery which will be revealed in God's good time.

It is no surprise to find that he writes to the Ephesians (3:9), 'to make all men see what is the plan of the mystery hidden for ages in God who created all things,' and also 1:10, 'as a plan for the fullness of time (*kairos*) to unite all things in him (Christ), things in heaven and things on earth.'

Here we see that timings and calendar awareness is seen as a cosmic matter and not just a side issue: the whole of creation comes to a new unity as everything converges on the triumph of Jesus. It is also interesting that the word *aiwn* (age) is worked into his thinking: this has ramifications for Zoroastrian and Mithraic thinking too (to be discussed later). There are various other allusions in the Pauline Epistles which indicate that Paul was acutely aware of the nexus in history upon which he stood. 1 Corinthians 10:11: 'and they were written down for our instruction, upon whom the ends (*tele*) of the ages (*aiwnwn*) has come.'

This is in the context of the Israelites in the Wilderness period, finding fault with God. It sounds as if Paul believes in an 'age' of history starting with Moses has come to completion with Jesus. The word *tele* is plural here which indicates that Paul is thinking beyond just the span of time from Moses to Jesus. To a Jewish audience that would have made a lot of sense: to a Greek audience in Corinth the use of *aiwnwn* would have appealed to their framework of thought. Their system too is being brought to completion at the same juncture. Whichever way one takes it, Jesus is seen here as standing at the pivotal point in history, Jewish and Greek alike.

That Paul was influenced by the intertestamental literature of the day is without question. Their emphasis on dividing history into periods or ages is well known; it will be discussed later. We have already seen that in one Greek system of mythology there is a scheme of 'ages' (*aiwnwn*), and this frame of thought had become current in Hellenistic culture. It may be that Zoroastrianism had worked its way into both Jewish and Greek thinking. Whichever way the influence worked, the apocalyptic notion of ages leading up to the end of the world was a common assumption. The difference was that with Jewish and Zoroastrian thought, there was a strong element of Messianism; with Greek thought, Messianism took a slightly transmuted form, that of the 'Divine Man' (*theios aner*). This concept refers to such exceptional people as Moses, Elijah and other significant religious leaders who were seen as exceptionally godly. It was normally someone in the past and not just one person. This, incidentally, is indirect evidence that the pagan world did take the Hebrew religious tradition seriously, at least to some extent. But the Greeks did not have a messianic expectation as such.

For the first Christians, this understanding of Christ as appearing as a completion of ages and eras on a kind of fulcrum of history seems to have been very important and stemming from his own understanding of himself; also his Second Coming was to be equally carefully determined and related to the subtle scheme of history. The futuristic application of this framework of thought surfaces in various references, not least 1 Timothy 6:15: 'until the appearing of our Lord ... and this will be made manifest at the proper time (*kairos idios*) by (God).'[10] Jesus is seen as bringing all these matters to a completion and pointing us forward into the future.

Calendar awareness in Daniel and the intertestamental literature

Although we cannot understand precisely what was going on in the mind of Jesus with regard to timing, it is almost certain that this kind of mentality was almost completely derived from the apocalyptic writings of Jewish tradition: perhaps a little from Greek and Persian thought. The Book of Daniel had a profound influence on him, not just for the notion of the heavenly Son of Man, but for the whole question of times, seasons and the 'right moment' for events to take place: 'until the time of the end, for it is yet for the time appointed,' Daniel 11:35.

'How long shall it be to the end of these wonders?' Daniel 12:6. The reply, couched in cryptic terms with (again) the esoteric use of numbers, is 3.5 days. This is normally taken to refer to the Abomination of Desolation of the Temple in 167 BC when for 3.5 years the Temple sacrifices were suspended because Antiochus IV Epiphanes had defiled the altar; indeed chapter 11 reads like a fairly accurate summary of the events surrounding that time. On the other hand, Jesus talks about the Abomination of Desolation in the future (Matthew 24:15) and the ruination of the Temple (Mark 13:1–3) also. In the latter context it is clearly meant to indicate his death, and its rebuilding his Resurrection. In the former case, it too could be seen as the Crucifixion. Even then, there is the prophecy which was seen to come true, when Jerusalem was defeated in AD 70. It is a double-sided prophecy, containing the paradox that it refers to Jesus himself but also to historical events at the destruction of the Jewish nation. In fact, one of the accusations at his trial was that he would destroy and rebuild the Temple in three days. They took it literally as blasphemy; the irony was that it was the truth: he himself was the true Temple that would be destroyed and rise again after three days.

From this we can deduce that 3.5 days is referring to more than one event in the future. We suspect that Jesus' ministry spanned approximately three years and also that he spent three days in death.

Could Daniel be hinting at one or either of those? More likely, did Jesus take these figures as a divine demarcation signalling the start and finish of his ministry? The mention of 1290 days and then of 3335, which no one has managed convincingly to explain, suggests that there is some sort of symbolism being used here which is not obvious to us now. It is possible that the 1290 days, which comes out as about 3.5 years, could be taken as Jesus' earthly ministry. The End is looming: the end of time? A fresh start in history? What about the 3335 days which is just over nine years? How can this relate to the ministry of Jesus? In I Enoch 93 we read that in week 9, righteousness will be revealed to all the world: does this refer to the coming of Christ who 'came to fulfil all righteousness' and the ministry of the Apostolic Church? More will be said about this later. It is a mistake to take these figures totally mathematically literally, any more than 70 years foretold by Jeremiah turned out to be exactly 70 years to the minute; and indeed three days in hell is not literally accurate, as Jesus died on the Friday afternoon and rose again on the Sunday morning. There is a certain amount of poetic approximation in all this. Even so, we have to appreciate that Jesus did read all these writings and almost certainly saw them as giving a demarcation for the span of his ministry.

A possible way forward for understanding these cryptic remarks may be found in chapters 3 and 4 of Hebrews. Admittedly, Paul may not have written this book, and yet it must have been contemporaneous with the other epistles and assumed the same ideas on periods of history. He talks about the Wilderness period and how it relates to the ministry of Jesus. He also relates it to the hebdomadal cycle of weekdays, especially the Sabbath; but 'today' is of much importance to him: 'So then there remains a Sabbath rest for the People of God: for whoever enters God's rest also ceases from his labours, as God did from his,' Hebrews 4:9.

So from the Creation to Moses there is a span of time ending in a refusal to enter into the 'rest', in this case the Promised Land. From Moses to Jesus there is another span of time ending in a new chance to enter another 'rest' at the culmination of the work of Jesus. Here we see a rudimentary division of history into major periods. More will be said about this later.

We can strengthen this idea by recalling that Jesus died on the Friday just before the Sabbath began. He entered into his 'rest' just as the Creator did after day number 6. The implication in this is that his works were completed just in time. It is now possible to see how and why Jesus selected a certain Passover which would coincide with a certain Friday evening. Paradoxically, he was resting in the tomb on the Sabbath; on the other hand he was rescuing souls in torment in the underworld. Another paradox appears in 4:3: 'although his works were finished from the foundation of the world'.

Even so the work of salvation is just coming to completion (4:7): 'In the days of his flesh, Jesus ... was heard for his godly fear ... and being made perfect he became the source of eternal salvation ... being designated by God a high priest.'

Moreover, God's work goes on, since he is the builder of all things (3:4). Paradoxically, he never rests, and yet there is the completion of all things in the Sabbath of God.

If it is true about the timing of the Passover in relation to the Crucifixion, it would lend indirect support to St John, who claims that the Passover was on the Friday evening. The Passover meal would have been eaten after 6 p.m. on the Friday, which in the Jewish reckoning is the start of the Sabbath. Whether they were using the Julian calendar or not at that time makes no difference. The inference is that Jesus saw the culmination of his ministry as the completion of God's work in creation: the ultimate act of salvation for the whole universe. The way that he relates it to the days of the week and the Passover calculation is an ingenious use of calendar awareness, and resolution not just of Jewish Passover theology but possibly also of the Julian system which can be traced back to Ancient Egypt (which incidentally was the scene of the first Exodus).

In addition to this, we have what appears to be an eclipse of the sun as Jesus is on the cross. We know that the ancients had very successful methods for predicting eclipses; there is no reason why Jesus could not have known in advance of this happening. In recent times, we have discovered the Antikithera Mechanism, a kind of calculator made of bronze, which was clearly used to predict eclipses and movements of the planets. People are amazed at the accuracy and brilliance of such a gadget. It all lends cogency to the matter of Jesus knowing the right moment for the final phase of his ministry.[11]

The fact that we do not really know when Daniel was written (see chapter 3) is of secondary importance; the first matter is the influence that it had on later Judaism, nascent Christianity and Jesus himself. I have argued for an early date (in a previous chapter); a late date around the Maccabean era would hardly allow it to gather the influence and authority that it did, resulting in its inclusion in the Old Testament canon. Clearly many apocryphal and pseudepigraphal books took their inspiration from Daniel. It is not easy to assemble them in any chronological order: they all claim to be inspired by worthies of the past such as Moses or Abraham in some attempt to give themselves a kind of latter-day authority. Many of them are only known by passing mention in other works, or fragments that have been unearthed. Most of them did not succeed in being taken seriously enough for inclusion in the canon, although some of the early Christians did appear to quote from them as authoritative. But none of them come anywhere near the vividness, inspiration and authority of Daniel. Of relevance to this argument, they all indulge in some form of manipulation of figures and anticipation of the 'end', including periods for the calculation of significant moments in the sequence leading up to the 'end'. Interpreting them is not always as straightforward as one might like to think: there is much ambiguity and opportunity for forced interpretation.

One example of this is the comment in Daniel 7:25 in a context which gives many hints of Antiochus IV Epiphanes: 'and shall think to change the times and law . . . for a time, two times and half a time.' Three and a half years here clearly associates it with the defilement of the Temple in 167 BC. However, it is not known whether Antiochus actually attempted to modify the calendar. We do know that Ptolemy III in 239 BC attempted a calendar alteration but the priests of Egypt raised objections which concerned the implementation of leap year. Calendar correction had to wait until Augustus (31 BC) enforced this; even Julius Caesar did not manage to carry all his ideas into practice. What this indicates is that calendar reform was in the air and becoming urgent at that time. As a general prophecy, Daniel is right on this point, but not as a specific prognostication.[12]

It is clear that people in those days believed that the calendar was God-given and could not be altered by human hand. In Jubilees 82 it is claimed that 364 days of the year are inscribed in heaven, which implies that any attempt to interfere with the calendar is contrary to God. There is no admission that another day and still less a quarter of a day is needed to keep the dates in line with the seasons. 1 Enoch, a book which came close to inclusion in the canon, is more reasonable about intercalatory days. He is aware of the problems with the solar and lunar year, but accepts a 364-day year; the correct calendar calculation is linked to righteousness (82:4–5). This fixed idea continued into the Qumran Community, the Essenes. This was a subset of Judaism with its own system of calendar and rituals in relation to it. The feeling that ritual acts had to be related to the correct times was important. Earthly liturgy was intended to be a replica of the observances in the heavenly Temple by choirs of angels. The Community rule laid it down that they could not depart from any command of God concerning their times, not being late or early for any observance. The two important moments of daily prayer, when the morning and evening sacrifice in the Temple would be performed, must be punctual. In other respects, the Essenes departed from the mainstream Jewish method for calculating festivals, which was based on lunar observations, thus producing a most clumsy calendar. They embarked on a solar system using 364 days per year, as seen in Jubilees and 1 Enoch, 52 weeks per year exactly. They saw it as the 'certain law from the mouth of God'. This meant that each festival fell on the same day of the week every year: Passover fell on a Wednesday, Pentecost on a Sunday, Yom Kippur always on a Friday. The rest of Judaism would be using the Julian Calendar (presumably) which meant that 14th Nisan would be moving around the weekdays rather like our Christmas Day. The Essenes made no mention of any intercalation in order to keep the calendar in line with the solar year. The result was that they were usually out of step with the rest of Judaism, so that while one Jew would be observing a festival, another would not be. This would be rather like the discrepancy between the Western and Eastern churches on the matter of Christmas and Easter.

The mentality of the age was to take seriously the timings for various festivals. The fact that there were different methods of calculation at work at the time of Jesus is interesting and one wonders if there is any significance in it. Was Jesus trying to find the 'right moment' in the sense of trying to bring to conclusion more than one system at once? Could it be that he was trying to observe the Essene Passover as well as the official Jerusalem one? For this to work it would mean that Tuesday was the Day of Preparation: 18 hours on Tuesday was the start of the Passover with the meal; then Jesus might have been arrested in the night, put on trial on Wednesday or Thursday; this would give much more time for all the proceedings before he was crucified on Friday. This could be a way of resolving the discrepancy between St John and the Synoptics: it is theoretically possible that there were two Passovers in the same week, the Essene one and the Jerusalem one. For a fuller discussion of this idea, it is worth inspecting Barrett's commentary on St John.[13]

One might wonder how or why Jesus might have any connection with the Essenes of Qumran. On the face of it, they are never mentioned in the New Testament, unless one sees the 'Scribes' as such people. Even so, John the Baptist has been thought to have had some kind of connection with the Essenes. There is also some suspicion that Judas Iscariot was an Essene, according to the so-called Gospel of Judas, recently discovered.[14] Also there may be a little extra significance in the remark made in Matthew 3:15 at the Baptism: 'For thus it is fitting for us to fulfil all righteousness.'

We have already seen that the correct calendar calculation is an important aspect of 'righteousness' (1 Enoch). The whole issue of times, seasons and the 'right moment' is clearly an important part of Jesus' thinking, derived not just from Daniel but from other apocalyptic writers too.

In Jubilees, the writer is obsessive about the division of days, relating it to the law; the history of the world from start to finish is schematised into weeks and jubilees: 'the first and the last, which shall come to pass in all the divisions of the days in the Law and the testimony and in the weeks and the jubilees unto eternity until I descend and dwell with them throughout eternity', Jubilees 1:26.

So for instance there are 49 jubilees from Adam to Moses, plus a week and two years, making 4950 years, presumably. All this is symbolic, figurative and unconvincing to the modern mind. Yet it is symptomatic of the tendency to schematise history into some kind of ground plan. Sadly Jubilees does not complete the scheme of jubilees up to the end, but there is the assumption that history is divided up into three major sections, the Age of Testimony, the Age of Law and the New Age.[15]

The notion of Jubilees is again seen in the Assumption of Moses but this time it is a 50-year span, not 49. World history consists of 85 jubilees: from Adam to Moses is 2500 years and from Moses to 'the end' is 1750 years. Added together this makes 4250 years or 85 jubilees.

In the finale of 1 Enoch, the Apocalypse of Weeks, we see a complete scheme from creation to the end and beyond, in chapter 93. The periods of time are not seen as exactly the same but are related more specifically to historical events. When we arrive at the tenth week, many more are envisaged (91:17): 'after that there will be many weeks without number for ever, and all shall be goodness.'

Interestingly for the Christians, week 9, in which righteousness will be revealed to all the world, could mean the coming of Christ and the Church's ministry. After the tenth there will be many more weeks, which must lead up to modern times. It is only a general impression about timings and periods: there is nothing too precise about it. The mention of 'nine' might be a subtle link-up with the last verses of Daniel, with 3335 days which equal about nine years.

2 Esdras is again a book which must have influenced Jesus considerably, and came close to inclusion in the canon. He thinks that from the creation to the Temple of Solomon was 3000 years; also from the Exile to the coming of the Messiah will be 400 years. No one likes to comment on this passage, but with our understanding of Nostradamus, it is not necessarily a problem: 'For my Son Jesus shall be revealed with those that be with him, and rejoice them that remain 400 years. After these years shall my Son Christ die and all that have breath of life,' 2 Esdras 7:28.

There are various references to the Son and also the Lion which is equated with the Messiah, and even an oblique reference to the Incarnation (13:52): 'Can no man upon earth see my Son or those that be with him but in the time of his day.'

The estimate of 400 years of the post-exilic period is not wildly wrong: it agrees with Daniel with his 490 years. But the important thing here is the time scheme, even if it is somewhat different from the others (13:58): 'For him governeth the time and such things as fall in their seasons.'

This means that God has the whole scheme of events under his control. The world is divided into 12 parts: 10.5 of them have already gone (at the end of the Exile?). The imminence of it, the precision and vividness, is quite striking. It is idle to attempt to explain it away as prophecy after the event; if so, why then did Esdras (Ezra) not get the details more accurate? There has to be some element of genuine prognostication in this literature even if much of it is completely wild and fanciful.

Even though the apocalyptists have differing ideas on their time schemes and calculations, the underlying truth is that they were trying to understand God's intervention in history as rationalised, calculatable and according to a definite plan (Acts 2:23). The difficulty was that because the world of eternity was breaking into human history, there was bound to be a degree of uncertainty and disagreement among men. This is evidenced by the profusion of symbolism and rather crude attempts at mathematics in relation to the calendar. But at least we can get some impression of what was in the minds of the New Testament writers when they talk of Jesus coming to draw together the ends of the ages and bring in the final Sabbath of God.

We can also now see an extra relevance in Matthew's version of the words of Jesus on this subject: 'And of that day and hour no one knows, not even the angels in heaven, nor the Son but the Father only ... the Son of Man is coming at an hour you do not expect,' Matthew 24:36–44. Against the backdrop of all these calendar manipulators, Matthew is saying, 'Don't even try to work it out'.

It could be an indication that Jewish apocalyptic writing, including 2 Esdras, had been produced well before the ministry of Jesus, was regarded as quotable in an authoritative way, and yet was almost a spent force. People were growing tired of all this clever and contradictory arithmetic. This may help to explain the upsurge in messianic activity around the time of Jesus: there was a panic because the 490 years stated by Daniel were seen to be slipping away and the Roman tyranny was tightening.

This can also help to explain why, in the New Testament Apocalypse, the Revelation, a different approach to number symbolism is beginning to emerge. We must remember that the ministry of Jesus is now in the past and St John is now talking about the Second Coming. There is no attempt at calculating dates and times. He is content to be vague: Revelation 1:1–3, 'what must soon take place ... for the time is near.' His use of numbers is there, but done in a different way, using much of the method seen in Daniel and Ezekiel. There is a strong hint that such matters should not be taken literally: 'This calls for wisdom: let him who has understanding reckon the number of the beast, for it is a human number. Its number is 666.'

This can be taken to mean that to try to make a precise literal application of these symbolic numbers is a failure to realise the true intention of the writer(s). St John plays down the calculatory aspect and plays up the wonder, splendour and eternal significance of Christ's ministry: that is the true purpose of apocalyptic literature.

A datum point for the calendar

All this speculation over the start and finish of the world does raise the question of what dates these would be. It is almost certain that the Zoroastrian interest in these matters raised the question of a datum point. In the prehistoric period, before the concept of the Christian era, the normal method was to date everything by the regnal years of the kings. This may seem reasonable enough, except that sometimes a king might not last more than a few months (think of Edward VIII), or there might be parallel dynasties in the same country, as in Egypt. Going back beyond the time of King David (presumably about 1000 BC) regnal reckonings are increasingly difficult and there is little in the way of a datum point available.[16]

It was the Zoroastrians who decided that the datum point ought to be the birth of Zoroaster, but since no one knew exactly when he had been born, it was a matter of discussion. In the end, they decided that he had been born 3000 years after the creation, and then the first saviour, Ukhshyat-ereta, would appear in year 4000; then a repeat of history in year 5000 as his brother Ukhshyat-Nemeh would appear. In the last millennium Astvat-ereta the third saviour would appear. Now we can see the relevance of Hebrews saying the Jesus Christ only came once and for all. The three saviours were all to be virgin-born and related to the 'world year', segments of 1000 years. However, there was no agreement on how many millennia would occur: was it six, or nine or 12? We can see how this ties in with Jewish apocalyptic speculation. It all lacked the real fact of a datum point.

With the Seleucid kings, however, we arrive at a real datum related to an observable historical character, namely Alexander the Great. So the year 312 BC became year 1 of the era of Alexander. We can see this method at work in 1 and 2 Maccabees. The concept of eras and epochs was basic thinking in that part of the world. The Arcacids followed suit (248 BC), trying to relate the Seleucid system to the Zoroastrian one. It may have been this thinking that induced the Romans to calculate their year one: the AUC reckoning was related to the foundation of Rome in 735 BC, but even this was subject to debate.

The Jews, probably prompted by this activity, attempted to calculate the years since the creation: there were various versions of this, none of which carried complete conviction. The most well-known attempt in the Christian era was Bishop Ussher's reckoning of 4004 BC! With modern scientific methods at work, none of this is taken seriously any longer. By the time that Christianity had matured enough to have its first major council at Nicea, the need was felt for a datum point and a clarification of the Christian era. Year 1 AD was delineated as the birth of Christ and all dating since has been orientated around that. Paradoxically, Dennis Exiguus is thought to have a made a mistake in his arithmetic which means that Jesus is now thought to have been born in 4 BC or possibly even earlier than that. Even so, as a datum point AD 1 holds good to this day, and all other datum points, some of which are rigorously retained by other religious groups, seem to be dependent on it. The Christian era seems to dominate calendar reckoning all over the world.

Time as deified

It is interesting that in Greek mythology time is deified as the first principle, Chronos. Whether this concept pre-dates Zoroastrianism is a good question, but not an essential one. It simply indicates that in that part of the ancient world time was understood to be of great importance. A later heresy of Zoroastrianism, the Zurvanite idea, actually conceived of Zurvan being the god of time.[17] It is interesting how the dualism of Ahura Mazda and Angra Mainya, seen as twins, raised the question of who was their father. Here is an example of mythology being forced to supply more mythology! The answer was that Zurvan, the god of time, was their father. But this was not and never became mainstream Zoroastrianism. Even so, the problem of Theodicy is seen to be the backdrop of this piece of theology.

Another 'heresy' of Zoroastrianism, Mithraism, appeared in the Roman Empire. It appealed specifically to soldiers and their retinue of slaves on campaign: otherwise it had many features which ran parallel to nascent Christianity. The chief difference was that it was certainly not 'catholic': it was more like the equivalent of Freemasonry in the Roman world and was an exclusive and secretive sect, even to the extent of wearing ceremonial aprons. So secretive was it that much of it is not really understood this day. But the relevance to this discussion is one trait which cannot escape our notice: they held time to be of great importance, a thread which clearly derived itself from Zoroastrian thinking. Time was deified. They had a god called Aion, who had a bunch of keys to open up the solsticial gates. He stands unmoved and unmoving over the entire universe. The silver key opens the Gate of Cancer which leads to the Way of the Ancestors and reincarnation; the golden key opens the Gate of Capricorn, the Way of the Gods, which leads to release from the round of birth and death. Here we see a Buddhist influence in the Roman world, something which the early Christian theologians rejected completely. The Buddhists would probably equate Aion with Shin-je, the judge of the dead who rotates the wheel of becoming. The Capricorn Gate is the way that Mithras and Jesus Christ descend to earth at the winter solstice. Aion is also shown with four wings and a serpent, symbolising the fourfold divisions of time and its cyclic motion. He has an open lion's mouth to devour his offspring (like Chronos) and four arms (like Shiva). Aion was also a god of the underworld. Also he is seen as superior to the Zodiac and is perched on top of the world (seen as a globe!). He is a creator, not of worlds, rather of gods and principles.

Even if Mithraism did emerge rather later than Christianity, the raw materials for it had been there for a long time. We can see that the work of Christ came very largely as a completion of these ideas but also, importantly, as a correction. Jesus is the true light of the world and the cosmic battle between good and evil was won by Jesus, not Mithras, who was in any case an imaginary figure.

Time as cyclic

It is understandable that mankind assumes, from observation of heavenly bodies, that time is cyclic, or that history repeats itself. Almost all sophisticated systems of calendar schemes have some version of cyclical motion. This varies greatly from one civilisation to another but there are points of agreement.

The most ingenious system must be accorded to the Mayans whose ideas worked their way into the Aztec method which the Spaniards found when they arrived. There was a feature called the calendar round which was 18,980 days which corresponds to about 52 tropical years. (Does this remind us of the jubilees?) There was another feature, the 'long count', which was a tally of days since the start of an era, the great cycle, in the remote past. They believed that time was cyclic and that at the end of a great cycle of 13 *baktuns*, the world would be destroyed, only to be recreated to begin the next great cycle. One element missing here is messianism; even so, there was an expectation of the reappearance of a god (Cortez quite cynically impersonated him). It is unfortunate that the Spaniards destroyed much of the Aztec codices which could have told us much more of their ideas. What we can see in this is the human trait that we attempt to relate the workings of our gods in history according to some form of calendar calculation or prediction.

Other civilisations which developed time cycles were China, India, Greece and the Zoroastrians. These can be studied in detail in Richards's book.[18] Of relevance to Christianity, the Jews had the jubilee system of 49 or 50 years; this still surfaces to this day in the 'Holy Year' idea, although it is not strictly tied to these numbers. The Metonic cycle, which was devised by Meton of Athens (432 BC), was a span of 19 years by which the motions of the sun and the moon came round to the same relationship. This clever system is now the basis upon which Easter is calculated for each year; another example of how a pagan realisation underpins a Christian feature. Incidentally, the Chinese also arrived at the Metonic cycle independently.

On a smaller scale, the working week as a cyclic movement is not just a Jewish idea. Some areas had a different span of days but the hebdomadal cycle now conditions virtually all activity in the world today.

Another cycle not normally discussed but basic to our calendar is the solar cycle, a Christian Julian idea. About the time of Nicea, it was first described ('invented' is the wrong word): since the first day of the year can fall on any of seven days of the week, added to which there is a leap day every four years, it follows that there is a complete cycle of 28 years before the coincidence of the same weekday falling on the first day of the year appears again. Although it was remarked upon at Nicea, they decided to work backwards and start the solar cycle at 9 BC, so that AD 1 (Christ's presumed birth) was deemed to be year 10 of the first solar cycle. Has this any relevance to the thinking of Jesus? If he had been following the Julian Calendar, which is quite possible since Augustus had forced it on the entire world, then it would have been an observable fact: if he had been following native Jewish calendars, then not. But the span of 28 years almost agrees with 'thirty years among us dwelling'!

Astrology and cyclic motion

Whatever one's views on astrology, it is a fact that it was a very strong influence on the mentality of the ancient world. The Jews were the exception; even so, later on in the fourth century AD, Zodiacs began to appear in synagogue mosaics.

With there being five observable planets in circulation of the earth at different distances and speeds, plus the sun and moon, it is a very rare occasion on which all seven are in conjunction. The Chinese seem to have been the first to remark on this; in theory this happens once in every 138,240 years. A further extension of this was 'the supreme grand origin' which began a world cycle of 23,639,040 years.[19]

It is only in the last few years that Molnar has managed to link this kind of thinking to the Star of Bethlehem. His workings can be followed in his book[20] which explains how the Magi would have calculated these matters; it would have given them much excitement. It would seem that 17th April in 6 BC gave rise to an alignment of all seven heavenly bodies in conjunction in Aries. The meaning of this would have been 'most important, the horoscope must be so incredibly portentous that it points unquestionably to a regal birth in Judea' (Molnar, p. 97). What would it have meant to the Persian Magi? That one of Zoroaster's saviours was about to arrive? But when they came to enquire of Herod, being Jewish, he had no idea what they were talking about. It may not have been unduly striking in the night sky: five planets in the same area of the sky at the same time. Other striking conjunctions would have been noted in the following weeks and months but not to the same intensity as on the 17th April, 6 BC. Are we looking at the actual birthday of Jesus, or his conception? The appearance of a star or a very unusual conjunction would bring to fulfilment the expectations of firstly the Gentiles who placed so much emphasis on astrology, but also of the Jews with the prophecy of Balaam, Numbers 24:17: 'A star shall come forth out of Jacob, and a sceptre shall rise out of Israel.'

On this basis it is no surprise to hear Peter referring to astral matters in Acts 2:19: 'I will show wonders in the heaven above (portents) and signs on the earth below.'

Normally there is no mention of astrological matters in the Old or New Testament. This can be explained by saying that being good Jews, they had no basis for understanding such matters: they were not magi. This is why such matters, when referred to, go unexplained. But a conjunction such as 7th April, 6 BC would have indicated to the Magi that a new era was beginning, an era which involved some sort of 'King of Judea'. What is slightly puzzling is that there was no evidence of the death and Resurrection being related to any astral configuration. It was the birth that was of significance to the ancients. We know that many of the leading names in the Roman world had their horoscopes examined carefully and much importance was attached to them: Augustus, Nero, Hadrian and Constantine, to name but a few. Much importance was attached to birth horoscopes: even today some people take this matter as significant. Very largely, however, modern minds find the whole matter trivial, superstitious and even comical. But even if we disagree with astrology, we have to see into the mind-set of the ancients. It cannot have been easy to think oneself out of it, any more than we today can think ourselves out of the assumptions we accept as normal. On that basis, it is quite significant that a Jew like Matthew can utilise astrological terminology. 'Went before' and 'stood above' only make sense as translations of astrological terms; one wonders if he actually knew what they meant himself.

What is the significance of these matters? Firstly, it sheds a little light on Jesus' own awareness of the right time and place for his ministry, an awareness taken up by the disciples but not fully understood and certainly not receiving any attempt at explanation. Secondly, we can see that the coming of the Messiah was seen as a fulfilment not just of the Jewish traditions, but also of Gentile expectations. The intellectuals of the Hellenistic world were made aware of a most significant birth; God spoke to people in their own language and thought-forms. Thirdly, thinking of the 'miracle of the star', just because it may not have been visually striking to ordinary people but 'seen' by the Magi, does not diminish the wonder of it. The wonder lies in the rare and highly portentous configuration noted for 17th April, 6 BC. The miracle of the star is just as real: another example of God's immaculate timing.

Notes

1. E.G. Richards, *Mapping Time*, 1998.
2. A. Thom, *Megalithic Stone Circles*. Evidence that Stone Age man was fascinated by celestial movements and calendar calculation.

3. Erich von Daniken, *Chariots of the Gods – was God an astronaut?* 1971.
4. Richards, p. 212; this is when lunar calculation was finally given up in favour of a solar 12-month calendar, p. 156.
5. Richards, pp. 205ff. 'AUC' is the initials of *ab urbi condita*, the presumed date of the foundation of Rome, but this was never completely agreed.
6. Richards, op. cit., p. 118, describes the 'World Calendar' of 1956.
7. See Tacitus, p. 374, Penguin edition. Also Suetonius, p. 156, Penguin edition.
8. *Kairos* and *hora* are most commonly used in the New Testament, *chronos* just occasionally
9. Acts 2:23, 'This Jesus delivered up according to the definite plan and foreknowledge of God.'
10. Other New Testament references relevant here are: Colossians 1:26, Ephesians 2:7 and 3:21, 1 Timothy 4:1, Titus 1:3 and 1 Peter 1:20.
11. The Antikithera Mechanism is a stunningly clever device for predicting eclipses, astral movements and so on, dating from just over 2000 years ago.
12. Richards, op. cit.
13. Barrett, *The Gospel According to St John*, pp. 48–51, the most up-to-date treatment of the Passover week; but still there is no final answer to the discrepancy between the Synoptics and St John.
14. Alan Jacobs, *The Gnostic Gospels*, p. 255.
15. Testuz, pp. 139ff.
16. Rohl, *A Test of Time*, 1995.
17. M. Boyce, *Zoroastrianism*, 2001.
18. Richards, op. cit.
19. Richards, op. cit.
20. M. Molnar, *The Star of Bethlehem*, 2000. Various references in that book.

15

Ritual, Symbolism, Sacramentalism and Rites of Passage

That plain language and theological statements are insufficient to satisfy the needs of human nature is fairly obvious: parable and allegory and also mythology are clearly necessary to convey religious truths; so too the use of actions and materials in worship are essential. Those who have sought to minimise ritual have had to resort to other methods to fill the gap, so to speak. Ritual and symbolism speak to the human soul on a different level and in a different language than mere words. The spiritual power of such things should not be underestimated: for those who consider it to be 'mumbo-jumbo', there is the caution that trivialisation of it can backfire and produce unexpected repercussions. Normally ritual and symbolism are related to deeply instinctive strains in human nature, many of which are the same the world over.

It is no surprise that given two different worlds, the physical and the spiritual, something other than just plain language is needed to seal belief and status in one's religion and community. We have seen how parables show eternal truths in words and picture language; also mythology reveals the basic assumptions in the soul of mankind. Now we see that deeper in the human soul than these is the use of symbols, using materials which appeal to all our five known senses. We are accustomed to thinking of five senses: sight, hearing, taste, smell and touch. In other creatures, we understand that there are other senses highly developed, which we do not possess. Sharks are thought to possess at least two senses that humans do not have. One possibility is that of vibration, as seen in some creatures that have whiskers. All of these senses are appealed to in the many methods at work in worship. It is an attempt to cope with the paradox of physical versus spiritual; good versus evil; faith in relation to works. The degree to which they succeed is very largely related to the amount of faith or acceptance the believer brings to the situation.

At this level, there is the most promising chance of understanding faith across different religions. The appeal to the various senses is much the same the world over. Everybody knows what black and white, green and red symbolise. At this level faith is a commodity shared by all people regardless of religious superstructure and doctrinaire.

This chapter will give some thought to such features as water, candles, clothing, foodstuffs, blood and gadgets. Also ceremonies such as rites of passage and festivals will need some attention. It is unnecessary here to go into too much detail on such matters as this can be read up from many worthwhile descriptions elsewhere. It is the underlying significance of these matters that is the main focus.

Water

Virtually every system in the world has water as some kind of cleansing agent in its spirituality. This has already been seen in mythology, and it is a good example of how myth has worked its way into ritual practice. The use of water is an important preparatory step for coming into the presence of the divine. This is particularly true for priests or other kinds of minister, as their offerings would be seen as ineffective without ritual cleansing. The flood motif, as already seen with mythology, is also important: a fresh start for a corrupt world is needed. The old world of fallenness cannot relate to the ultimate truth or everlasting justice; a clear conscience is needed. With regard to the insulation between two worlds, the washing is part of the process of trying to reduce the insulation. The efficacy of this act depends a lot on the extent to which the believer trusts in the action of the washing. There are some, like Lady Macbeth, who will never believe they are free from guilt no matter how hard they scrub themselves. Strangely, Naaman the Syrian was cleansed of his leprosy by bathing in the River Jordan despite his objections to Elisha's advice (2 Kings 5:14). Others will accept that a once and for all ritual at infant baptism will be sufficient to bring one into the right relationship with God, even if the child does not know what is happening. It is possible to become obsessive about washing rituals: in Mark 7:1ff it is pointed out that the Pharisees, the meticulous legalists, have all sorts of washing procedures. This is done not so much for the sake of kitchen cleanliness but rather as self-purification in a ritual sense. The symbolism of it is quickly lost if it becomes a complete mania, and other more weighty matters are understated.

Human impurity

Human impurity is very often related to or imagined to be caused by sexual activity or matters relating to it. Strangely, washing with water does not appear to be involved with this level of uncleanness. In spite of the assurance in Genesis 1 that God created male and female and told them to be fruitful and multiply, there is much in the Old Testament that encourages a feeling of disgust for these matters: Genesis 38:9, Ezekiel 18:6, Leviticus 18:19–22. These are examples of ancient attitudes to these matters, and many of them still surface to this day. Old reactions die hard; they are embedded in human nature at the instinctive level.

It is no surprise then to find that the Messiah is seen as above and beyond this level of activity. People have pondered the possibility of Jesus having been married; there is no mention of this in Christian tradition. There has even been a reluctance to admit that he had siblings, also that the disciples had wives. It begins with Isaiah 7:14, 'Behold a virgin shall conceive and bear a son, and shall call his name Immanuel'. It matters little whether the Hebrew should be rendered as 'virgin' or 'young woman'; the fact is that Mary the mother of Jesus was understood to be pure and Jesus was not the result of earthly progenitation. He was seen to be above human degradation. The subsequent veneration and quasi-apotheosis of Mary 'ever virgin' simply serves to underscore the importance of purity in the Messiah and his miraculous birth. Following on from this, many have embarked on a life of chastity or celibacy, sometimes as a monastic or priestly life-style, but also on a personal and private basis. Furthermore, such a life-style is not confined to Christianity. It indicates a special closeness to God or an enhanced spiritual awareness. Although the Protestants allowed their 'priests' and ministers to marry, there was a heavy onus upon them to observe the commitment of wedlock.

We have already noted that Siddhartha's birth was somehow special, miraculous:[1] his mother had a dream of a white elephant that entered her womb; Siddhartha was born in a beautiful garden and two streams of water came from heaven; he and his mother were bathed. A similar legendary background applies to Mahavira: a supernatural birth allowed him to grow up sinless. Zoroaster too had a miraculous birth: his mother was purified by Ahura Mazda, and she did not have any pain during the birth.[2] Confucius too is believed to have had a virgin birth.

All these legends, regardless of their level of truth, show the deep need in human nature for the religious leader to be pure, set apart from worldly corruption, with his mother somehow associated. In this way, the insulation between the two worlds is penetrated: the immaculate leader is on the other side of the insulation. It is unlikely that one religion borrowed such ideas from other religions. But it can be seen in this light: that Jesus Christ fulfilled all these human needs in his own birth, family and ministry. It is interesting that St Luke 2:24 records the purification of the Virgin Mary, not by washing, but by the sacrifice stipulated in Leviticus 12:2ff.

Value placed on life

The importance and symbolism of blood cannot be underestimated. In the ancient world, the blood was understood to be the life force in any living creature. Leviticus 17:14 puts it neatly: 'For the life of every creature is the blood in it.' Here it is only stating what was generally assumed. This meant that performing a sacrifice would bring about a change in the situation either with the gods or with other humans. The more valuable the creature the more effective the ritual. Extreme procedures have been derived from this assumption. The Jews and the Muslims will not eat any meat with blood in it; the meat has to be butchered by strict procedures. The Jehovah's Witnesses take the matter even further and will not accept a blood transfusion. Auto-sacrifice is also a feature of ritual. The prophets of Baal cut themselves to try to persuade their god to respond. The Aztecs[3] had special instruments for bleeding oneself: this was in addition to the wholesale offering of humans on their temples. The assumption behind it was that new life requires a life to be given: something has to die before there is rebirth.

This is of course a truism but the New Testament teaches us that taking such matters to such literal extremes is not just unnecessary but well and truly superceded. Our understanding of blood has moved on into the figurative mode: the blood of Christ, the final and eternal sacrifice, is now given to us in the form of wine at the Eucharist. This is a good example of the tension between literal and figurative. Difficulties with this still surface over the debate over transubstantiation, consubstantiation and no substantiation at all: a basic factor in Christian disunity. If it could be admitted that there is an important paradox involved here, that in a very real sense the life-energy of Christ is imparted to the believer at the Eucharist, also that the Eucharist is a memorial ritual for the recollection of Christ's ministry and sacrifice, both of these truisms could be held as paradoxical.

It is interesting that some of the mystery religions which are contemporaneous with nascent Christianity had rituals concerning blood. Some had a sort of 'communion' not unlike the Christian one: Serapis, Mithras and others. A very lurid procedure, found with the cult of Cybele and Attis, was the *taurobolium*. It was what might be called a 'baptism' in which the initiate stood in a pit[4] under a bull that was bled to death. The candidate was celebrated as 'eternally reborn': the bull's blood was issued in some sort of 'communion' and the flesh was eaten raw. It was believed that the physical strength of the bull would be transmuted into psychic energy for the benefit of the participant or vicariously for someone else. It was not just the physical energy but the sexual energy of the bull that was mystically transferred. For the most ardent of her adherents, Cybele demanded castration, following the example of Attis. This very often took place at a spring festival which had features in common with the Christian Palm Sunday, Good Friday and Easter Day. Whether there was ever any direct or indirect borrowing between these mystery cults is difficult to say. But the faith of Jesus stands as a fulfilment and a correction to such fantastic ideas.

Light and darkness in ritual

Candles and other forms of lights as substitutes are widely used in religious and quasi-religious ceremonies the world over. Lanterns, torches and lamps of many kinds are a well-established feature and lend a special ambience to any act of worship or festival. They tend to heighten the emotion and lift the soul out of the mundane world.

Light in Buddhism reminds one of Siddhartha's enlightenment; the Hindu festival of Divali is centred around light.[5] For the Christian the candle reminds one of Jesus being the light of the world: two candles on the altar are a reminder of Jesus' human and divine nature. There is also the historical connection when the Christians had to hide in the catacombs. Attempts at electrical imitations of candles remain unconvincing. Certain Christian denominations that fight shy of candle usage often overdo it in the other direction when it comes to something like a carol service.

In Old Testament tradition, the fiery pillar at the Exodus was also matched by the cloudy pillar, leading the people in God's presence. The cloud has clearly been represented by incense, a medium virtually universal in worship in the ancient world. For many today, incense or joss sticks is an integral part of religious expression. There is the underlying assumption that whether it be candles or incense, one's prayers continue to ascend on high long after the worshipper's attention has gravitated to something else. Incense also has the implication of sacrifice and, by extension, the presence of one's God.

It can be seen that usage of such things appeals to more of our senses than just hearing. If all five senses are appealed to, it gives a much more comprehensive aspect to worship. It lifts us out of the banality of this world. Also it accords well with the understanding that God's logic is not the same as ours: the realms of heaven are on a different plane and are pure light; paradoxically, God is in another sense hidden from us, 'a God that hidest thyself'. The cloud is an important feature in Biblical thought.

There has been a reaction, with the Protestants, to the over-ritualisation of worship. The danger is that in oversimplifying it and bringing it down to just basic matters, it becomes purely words and personalities, almost to the extent that it ceases to be worship at all. There is however an important balancing mechanism here: the elaborate against the simplified; both have their part to play.

Foodstuffs

The classic account of diet in relation to religious faith can be read up in the Pentateuch. One suspects that the dietary restrictions were related to the conditions of the time. It is entirely[6] possible that there was some problem with pork and shellfish in that milieu. It is worth remarking that the Hittites regarded the pig as unclean. That does not have to mean that the Israelites derived the idea from the Hittites: the opposite is just remotely possible. But the Jewish tradition has extended these prohibitions to all manner of diaspora situations and gone into vast elaborations on the matter with food inspectors and special kitchens. Diet and the whole issue of *kosher* is now a major strand which holds Judaism together across the world.

Judaism is not the only religion to have strictures on diet. Islam too, taking its cue from the Mosaic laws, has strict dietary prescriptions. The reasoning for the Hindu partial or complete vegetarianism makes sense if one believes that an animal may be a reborn human being,[7] or that eating meat is some sort of 'cannibalism'. Krishna is identified with a bull; this explains why this animal is regarded as sacred in India. Other than that, dietary strictures may appear to have little rationality; the purpose of it may be lost in the mists of time and tradition.

It is Christianity which stands out almost uniquely as the faith with an easy conscience over foodstuffs. This can be traced back to Peter's vision in Acts 10:9–18 in which God declares, 'What God has cleansed, you must not call common.' In other words, all foodstuffs are acceptable (barring poison), and this explains why the Christians at an early date jettisoned the dietary laws, including the removal of blood. This is quite consistent with the dictum of Jesus that it is 'not what goes into a person that defiles him but what comes out'. Even so, in recent times, dietary strictures have begun to re-emerge: vegetarianism in its various degrees of strictness is a reality. This only relies on medico-secular arguments intermingled with sentimentality about animals. There may be some mild form of Hindu influence here, but it is not stated openly.

There seems to be some need, based on religious presuppositions, to place a limit on what may be eaten and drunk, and when. Sometimes it emerges not so much as what, but when one should abstain from food. So fasting, which is by no means confined to Lent or Ramadan, is a well-established feature of penitential seasons or of preparation for important rituals. Self-denial can be clearly linked to sacrifice: conversely, the sacrificial meal in a holy place is seen as a way of communing with the deity.

Jesus himself was not against fasting as a way of coming closer to spiritual realities but he was critical of those who indulge in such practices simply to advertise their holiness. He emphasised the joy of the messianic banquet and he must surely have seen that as involving wine. There are many groups that find alcoholic drink as unacceptable: Islam, Buddhism, the Mormons, the Methodists and the Salvation Army. Total abstinence has never become an established feature of mainstream Christianity. It can be seen that a difficult conscience over food and drink belongs to the Old Testament thinking; New Testament thinking is the opposite: it means an easy conscience which uses moderation and common sense in the light of the joy of Christ's victory.

Clothing

That different clothing from ordinary everyday life is common in worship need hardly be emphasised. But the opposite is also true: that less clothing is also a factor. Something different is required when in the presence of one's God. This would have been normal in the ancient world, but the Sinai event epitomises it: that Moses was instructed to remove his shoes and cover his head. Further on in the Exodus, Aaron has special garments prepared for his task of priesthood. Special ceremonial robes are not confined to priesthood. Laity too often wear something special for a solemn occasion. Even the Sunday suit can be seen in this light. Mahavira and some of the shamans, however, operate completely naked.

Often there is some sort of symbolism involved in the special clothing. The Christian priest will wear garments clearly descended from the dress code of the Roman Empire; otherwise something similar to what the first Christians would have worn is normal. It is a matter of historical identification and recognition within the worshipping community. The recent trend in Western Christianity to conduct worship in plain clothes may be just an ephemeral phase. It has to do with supposed equality of leaders and followers, but this may be found not to carry conviction in the long run.

To assess the importance of different clothing, we may come back to the idea of insulation. There is a feeling of unworthiness and awe in approaching the deity, and the clothing acts as a sort of barrier between the power of the spirit world and the weakness of humanity. On the other hand the idea of nakedness suggests a removal of the insulation and an invitation to the spirits to come in and merge with the human. Such a procedure is probably well in the minority and yet it serves as a balance over against the elaborate costuming of other procedures.

A subset of this is the attitude towards hair: some will remove all or part of it as a mark of commitment to their faith; others will allow it to grow and never cut it. So there we have a balance between the Nazirites (John the Baptist) and the Buddhist monks, with various moderate versions in between.

Special clothing is not confined to religious observances: Freemasonry, courts of justice, theatre, royalty, degree ceremonies, are just a few. It acts as a communal and professional identification. For many it is still important that a nurse, a policeman, a priest can be easily recognisable in the community. This is not to detract from the spiritual importance of special apparel in religious observances; if anything, it serves to underscore it.

Music, dance and drama

This aspect of worship could well be seen as clothed in ambivalence. Although music, dance and movement have been associated with ritual since the dawn of time, there is a strain in human nature that regards such things as trivial and a distraction. A passage in 2 Samuel 6:14 might well sum up some people's feelings on the matter:

> And David danced before the Lord with all his might and David was girded with a linen ephod ... they brought the Ark of the Lord with shouting and with the sound of the horn ... But Michal ... saw King David leaping and dancing ... and she despised him with all her heart.

There are those who find it perfectly natural to go into a frenzy of excitement at a religious event; others find it difficult to take. The same situation is still with us to this day.

With regard to music, many religions display fixed attitudes towards it. So, for instance, Western Christianity has a fixation with organs. This is ironic since we understand that organs were playing in the amphitheatre when the Christians were fed to the lions. The idea of having an orchestra, which is what used to happen before organs were installed, is only just beginning to reappear. It is fair to say that organ music is deeply integrated with the spirituality of the

West, both Protestant and Roman Catholic. With Eastern Christianity it is the massed choir with deep rich harmonies that predominates, instrumentalism hardly having a chance. It is claimed that organs began to appear in the late Greek and then the Roman Empire. It has even been claimed that the Temple in Jerusalem had one. But its main use was in the Roman theatres and paganistic practices, especially of Dionysus. For this reason, the puritanical element in Christianity (and other religions) have held a prejudice against organs, and this still keeps surfacing to this day. There is no doubt, however, that the paganistic associations with music and dance were easily overcome by the Psalmist who wrote in Psalms 149 and 150: 'Praise him with the trumpet sound ... praise him with the timbrel and dance ... strings and pipe!'

The idea of a procession, as seen in 2 Samuel, is a very ancient one. The 'sacred way' is evidenced in many parts of the world: Mycene, Stonehenge, and even the King's Highway in the Wilderness. Isaiah makes much play on the theme of the 'Highway for our God'. Movement and procession towards one's God is an important instinct. It surfaces in modern worship in such things as the Stations of the Cross; in many countries there are processions around the town carrying effigies of the saints in fancy dress and dancing is included. Of course there is the reaction to this: certain Protestant groups feel they have to be rooted to the spot and design their churches in such a way that a procession cannot possibly take place.

When looking at drama, there was no difficulty in the ancient world, when it came to re-enacting the exploits of the gods or the kings. The New Year festival is a case in point. The Greeks, with their monumental theatres, were probably the first to formalise drama. It was not something facile: it was clearly an attempt, through a proper script, to delve deeply into human emotion and produce some sort of release or healing. The Romans followed suit. It may be the paganistic associations here that made drama a problem for the early Church. However, by the Middle Ages, we see the Mystery Plays as a well-established feature of spiritual life. Sadly repressed at the Reformation, we now see a resurgence of drama in worship: the York Mystery Plays, Oberammergau Passion Play, and drama in general in church as integrated into worship. Regardless of passing fashions in this matter, the drama of the Eucharist has always been a mainstay for those who need to see a 're-enactment' of the Last Supper.

An unusual case comes from the Aztec world. The archaeologists have uncovered a 'ballcourt' associated with a Temple. We are not certain of the extent to which this occurred.[8] But King 18-Rabbit played a ball game with a rubber ball in the court and then allowed himself to be sacrificed. The sporting game was clearly integrated to the pattern of worship. This may have been the general procedure. But it does raise the question of whether sport, in some shape or form, could not be worked in with religious ritual. The Greeks with their important sporting events certainly did include a religious element. It is interesting that in the modern world the whole matter of sport, including major events like the Olympic Games, is underpinned by a code of ethics which for many amounts to a form of religious commitment.

When assessing any particular approach in religion, it is worth noting the balance which occurs between those groups that encourage movement, drama, dance and other forms of rhythmic expression, and those that try to fight shy of it. There is no doubt that worship that involves sitting still and listening to a preparation of mere words certainly appeals to some but does not satisfy others. With worship that allows for all aspects of human expression to surface, we see the appeal to all the senses and instincts and less reliance on dogmas and personalities. The balance is there and it is interesting how it works out in practical terms. In today's world there is much more freedom and fluidity and interchange of ideas than was formerly so.

Artwork, pictorial representation, idolatry and iconography

A major feature of religions, not necessarily involved in rituals, is the matter of representation of God or gods. Even in the modern world, a linguistic philosopher like Hepburn sees the need for an 'ostensive definition of God'.[9] Such a thing is not possible for God is above the canons of human expression, whether it be artwork, language, philosophical expression or any other approach. Idolatry, though usually associated with some form of visual representation, is not confined to such vehicles. The modern use of the word 'idol' comes very close to the basic truth about this mental state: an obsession, a distraction, a fulfilment of yearnings by attachment to somebody or something famous, rich or influential. The pop star 'idol' typifies this situation, and indicates that idolatry can be a feature of a non-religion or secularised faith.

This serves to show the reason for the Second Commandment, Exodus 20:4: 'You shall not make for yourself a graven image.' A heavy emphasis is placed on this, and it is still a crucial element in the Jewish faith. The Muslims too and certain elements in Christianity have taken this completely literally: it has meant that their artwork and decorations of places of worship has centred on geometric patterns and interesting colours. Virtually every religion in the ancient world has made use of statuary, and the rituals surrounding them could be most elaborate. Only the Zoroastrians, in their early phases, did not indulge in temples and idols; this was all to change in the mid-Persian period. The absurdity of idolatry was brought out by later Jewish writers, Isaiah, Jeremiah and Daniel. In Bel and the Dragon, the priests of Babylon were exposed as being fraudulent over the offerings to the idol. But the deeper truth was, and still is, that the idol is only a projection of the human imagination: the god is clearly anthropomorphic. The problem is that it obscures the eternal and undefinable nature of God. God is dragged into this world and forced to pose as the lowest common denominator. Just because we are in a modern age where God appears to be of less relevance to people does not mean that this mind-set has disappeared: very much to the contrary. Idolatry does not have to be centred on some form of artwork. It can be any obsessional or mind-preoccupying notion that gets in the way of the deep and eternal truths about life and God.

The question now arises: it is possible to have a visual representation of God (or saints), without it becoming idolatrous? The strict adherence to the Second Commandment had its purpose in that day and age, and still does in many respects. But does it have to be taken totally literally? There is the need, in the human mind, for something to focus on, a picture, a paradigm. A Buddhist, if asked about the many statues of Siddhartha, would probably deny that this was idolatry. He would probably claim that it was an aid to meditation rather than a focus for worship. An Orthodox Christian, if asked about the many icons in their churches, would probably say that the icon is a picture specially prepared by an icon artist, and is not an idol, but gives some form of spiritual enhancement. Stained glass windows in the Western churches are not intended to be an object of worship but to display elements from the Scriptures and the lives of the Saints.[10, 11]

What can be learnt from the teachings of Jesus? Much of his teachings were in the medium of parables and allegories, in other words, picture language. Very often God is equated with the master, the landowner, the king or the employer. In this medium we are given a legitimate use of pictures and metaphors: enough to give the imagination much to ponder without it degenerating into some sort of human projection of God. The essential difference is that it is God-given, not a human concoction.

It was early recognised that Jesus himself was the true representation of God. Hebrews 1:3: 'He reflects the Glory of God and bears the very stamp of his nature.' Here we see the Christian answer to idolatry: we can have a picture of God, but it is God's artistry, not ours. Hence the Christian claim that the eternal God is fully, truly and unmitigatedly shown to mankind through the Messiah Jesus. It was Philip who asked, 'Lord show us the Father and we shall be satisfied,' (John 14:8). This is the deep yearning of the ages: that we all want to know what God is and to peer into his eternity. But Jesus is saying that in one sense you cannot but in another sense you can. This is where the paradox of the Incarnation comes into its own: 'He who has seen me has seen the Father.' John 1:18 comments on this quite clearly: 'No one has ever seen God: the only Son who is in the bosom of the Father, he has made him known.'

St John provides the balance and the paradox between the Burning Bush incident where God says 'I am that I am', and the completion of this thought with the 'I am' statements by Jesus. There is no attempt to define God in philosophical or metaphysical terms; even so, God can be understood in terms of his active intervention in this world. The seven statements which are usually associated with one of the miracles serve to show the nature of God in the actions of Jesus:

'I am the bread of life', 6:35.
'I am the light of the world', 8:1.
'I am the good shepherd', 10:11.
'I am the door of the sheep', 10:7.
'I am the resurrection and the life', 11:25.
'I am the way, the truth and the life', 14:6.
'I am the true vine', 15:1.[12]

There is nothing vague or speculative about these claims. They are the completion of the Old Testament expectation about God coming to his people in real terms. God is there in the life of every believing soul and Jesus is the catalyst. It is no surprise that the disciples did not understand what he was saying: it is one thing to have a picture, another to perceive what it is really saying. The fact that no one could comprehend what he was saying supports the claim that it was God-given, not of some sort of human devising. But his claims did strike home because they resonated with deep-down needs in human nature. We recall the violent reaction when he said (8:58), 'Before Abraham was, I am.' This indirect claim to be God was clearly blasphemy, which required him to be stoned. The irony of it was that he was telling the truth and they had misconstrued the whole thing.

We can sympathise with the Jewish authorities to some extent, in their aim to resist idolatry: in this case to allow Jesus to be taken as the true representation of God. Iconoclasm has appeared in various ways in history. The Puritans removed statues and parts of stained glass windows in their zeal to comply with the Second Commandment. The Confucianists went through a similar phase of removing all the statues, but this did not last very long. There is a Hindu sect called Brahmo Samaj, a modern syncretistic sect which tries to reach some kind of understanding between Christianity[13] and other faiths; they too have no idols. When we saw the statues of Lenin and Stalin being smashed in the 1990s, that was an example of people freeing themselves from some sort of false religion. While there is the urge to provide a pictorial representation of one's faith, there is also an urge to smash the idol and break free from its mastery.

It is ironic (and paradoxical) that for those who try to base their faith on 'no idols', something else has to creep in as a substitute. So, for instance, the Puritans and Bible fundamentalists allow the Bible to become a paper idol. But there are many other substitutes: the priest, the Pope, the Eucharistic elements, the church building itself, the King James Bible, to mention just a few. An extreme case would be the Sikh attitude to the Guru Granth: it has to have its own room, be put to bed each evening and got up each morning, just like a human child. It is so holy that attempts at publishing it are heavily resisted, which means that outsiders scarcely know what is contained within its pages.

All artwork or human artefact is a pale imitation, a human construct, a guess at the real glory of God and his Messiah. Even so there is a strong urge to provide it in spite of its feebleness. Perhaps there is a certain spiritual gain in portraying Jesus and the saints. We notice that Jesus almost always is shown according to the racial group that is depicting him: in England he is often seen as an Englishman. There is some resistance to him being shown as Jewish! But then the Turin Shroud comes in as a corrective to all our distorted ideas. This does not involve accepting the genuineness of the Shroud, it is simply a reminder that idolatry is faulted; God's provision of a visual aid is another matter entirely.

We can see that there is a balance between idolatry and non-idolatry: it is between idolatry in its many forms and the true depiction of the eternal as seen in Jesus. The danger lies in allowing one depiction of God to occupy the centre of one's devotions. We may never discover what Jesus looked like, visually. That is not important. More important is to understand that God is beyond human imagination and that Jesus is the final, reliable and clear representation of God given to the human race. To quote John 14:6: 'Jesus said ... "I am the way, the truth and the life: no one comes to the Father but by me."' A severe embarrassment to those who try to equalise religions, but a mainstay for those who have come to see the fundamental truth in it.

Sacramentalism

The word 'sacrament', coming from a Roman soldier's oath of loyalty, is a peculiarly Christian word. Words or synonyms concerning it do not appear in other religions and yet the thought pattern behind it does occur widely. A sacrament is a form of worship which involves the use of symbols and verbal formulae which bring the believer into a closer relationship with the deity than would normally be so. Within the Christian orbit there are widely differing attitudes and interpretations of the sacraments, their number, efficacy and importance in the total scheme of each group or denomination. There is the realisation that whatever sacraments they have, they are well rooted in the Scriptures, even the Old Testament, regardless of how the people of God saw them then.

The spiritual feeding of the believing community can be traced back to Abraham where Melchizedek brought forth bread and wine, the manna in the wilderness, and the many sacrificial meals which engendered a closeness to God. Sacrifice in its various forms and intentions can be seen as the Old Testament 'sacrament': the action of giving a life implied life given back to the community. The spiritual washing in baptism is traceable back to Noah's Flood, for that is how 1 Peter 3:21 interprets it, when the faithful were 'saved through water'. And more noticeably in Exodus 29:4 where the inauguration and ordination of the priests is laid down. By New Testament times, the Jewish rite of baptism was a well-established procedure; John the Baptist was not inventing a new ritual by any manner of means. Baptism still persists as an important element in the initiatory rites of the Jewish faith to this day. Another important rite, that of anointing, goes back to the appointment of Aaron and his sons (Exodus 18:41). It also concerns the inauguration of kings and sometimes prophets. This procedure was probably more recognisable as a 'sacrament' in those times than the others.

The Christian adaptation of these three elements is in line with New Testament awareness. Baptism became the basic initiatory rite, displacing circumcision which was seen as superfluous. It accords well with Jesus' injunction to make a firm decision about joining in the Kingdom and not wavering. Also it became symbolic of dying and rising with Christ: early baptisms were normally centred around Easter. Nearly all Christian groups still retain baptism as the basic initiatory rite. Those who do not practise it, Quakers and the Salvation Army, can be seen as a reaction against over-ritualisation, similar to the Buddhist reaction to Hinduism. Strange permutations on this theme have occurred: in the Patristic period, many people (Constantine) did not embark on baptism until they were on their death-bed, for fear of committing a sin after baptism. In Soviet Russia, people had to baptise themselves in a river to maintain secrecy. Infant baptism has always been practised, in spite of the child being unaware of what is taking place; this explains the use of Confirmation in many Churches.

With anointing, we see the adaptation of this ritual to the healing of the sick in mind and body. Mark 6:13 has the disciples using this as an important part of their first steps into ministry. So, anointing has remained as a special gift in Christian ministry, notably employed at special occasions such as coronations and ordinations; its general use for persons in danger of death or with severe health problems is now becoming more frequent. Anointing with this intention is probably now peculiar to Christianity.

The Lord's Supper is a crucial element in Christian worship. It is clearly an adaptation of the Jewish Passover meal, which was only sacramental in the sense that a lamb was sacrificed. The Eucharist, which is one of the few direct commands which Jesus gave to his disciples, has remained central to Christian practice in spite of attempts to minimise or omit it. It too has had its permutations: the 'sacrifice of the Mass'; also communion by 'extension'. The assumption here is that the words spoken by the 'president' at the Eucharist actually brings about some kind of change in the bread and wine. This has brought about varying attitudes and beliefs surrounding the elements. When Jesus said, 'This is my body,' what did he actually mean? Was it to be taken literally or metaphorically? It is unfortunate that this issue has probably more than anything else produced disunity, embittered argument and entrenched attitudes in the Christian world. It underlies many of the problems concerning schism and denominationalism. The literal versus the figurative in many ways mirrors the various treatments of the Scriptures, the Incarnation and the Trinity. That there is some kind of spiritual power in the Eucharist is not denied even by the lowest in churchmanship. Where this power is actually located – whether in the elements, or the minister, or in the assemblage of believers – is a matter for debate and personal conviction. But spiritual power is there, and Christians of all types would say that they feel inspired, enlivened, strengthened and especially blessed by partaking of the Eucharist.

The paradox lies particularly with the Eucharist, but also with the other sacraments, that while material objects like bread, wine, oil and water are used, through them a spiritual enhancement can and does take place. Some would say that this depends on the faith of the participant; others that it will make a spiritual alteration regardless of the recipient's attitude. In this there may be another paradox. The paradox of sacramentalism can be seen as a derivative of the paradox of Incarnation. It could be that if Christians could realise that there is truth in both ways of looking at it, this could be a major contributor to Christian unity and ecumenical outreach.

The Biblical basis for the remaining sacraments is rather more sketchy. This explains why at the Reformation the Protestants recognised only two sacraments, baptism and the Eucharist. This has held true largely to this day, even though some reformed groups have made use of more than two. The Roman and Orthodox Churches held on to seven sacraments. But however many are accepted, it is important to see that help from the other world should be obtained by a God-given procedure on a sacramental basis, rather than just trying to make direct contact via methods of our own devising.

Hindu Sacramentalism

Although the word 'sacrament' does not come into their vocabulary, it has been maintained that the Hindus have four stages in life which are punctuated with certain ceremonies. They are termed *sams-kara*.[14] This may not quite carry the same implication as the Christian sacrament; it is more clearly a system of rites of passage. While it would be fair to say that certain of the Christian sacraments have a rite-of-passage element in them, the Hindu framework is somewhat different.

The Brahacarin is the student level. This concerns a boy of 8 to 12 years: this is his first initiation, or *upanayana*. It is analogous to Bar Mizbah.

The Vivaha is the marriage sacrament. This is the start of keeping house and home and producing children. The wife is the partner in the Dharma. It involves elaborate rituals and preparations. It is worth commenting that virtually every religion has some form of marriage ritual (even atheistic materialism). Unusual is the fact that Buddhism has no wedding ceremony, since family life and commitment is not seen in the same light. In Japan, it is normal to be married as a Shintoist and buried as a Buddhist.

The Vanaprastha is when, as a grandparent, grey hairs appear, and one becomes a hermit or a forest-dweller. A detachment from the cares of parenthood and household means a simplification of life.

The Sanyasin, complete renunciation of previous attachments, means one can spend more time considering the nature of self and one's relationship to the universe. Many do not take this to extremes, but simplicity becomes a feature of later life.

It would be fair to add that sacramentalism in a form more recognisable to Western minds can be seen in the *yagya* ceremony as described in the Rig Veda. This includes the use of *soma*[15] an intoxicating and hallucinatory preparation from a certain plant, a ceremony which involves invocations to Agni and various other gods. In this session, there is a closeness and identification with the god, which engenders blessings and success in life. Although no blood sacrifice is involved, there are offerings and a sacrificial meal. This is strongly reminiscent of what is hinted at in the Old Testament with sacramento-sacrificial meals.

Rites of passage

Every culture has had and still does have rites of passage. These concern the various stages in life from birth to death, some of which have been already included under sacramentalism. However, a rite of passage is not necessarily a sacrament. Substantially there are four rites of passage common to almost all cultures:

1. Birth. This stage usually involves the mother and sometimes the father. It may require a period of seclusion or separation from the normal patterns of life. Ceremonies and festivities often take place when the child is brought into the community.
2. Puberty. One's graduation into full adulthood is often marked as some form of 'coming of age' or full acceptance into the responsibilities of manhood. In modern life this may be associated with the eighteenth birthday or the right to vote, or confirmation.
3. Marriage. In most societies one is not fully regarded as a mature member unless one is married and producing children. Elaborate ceremonies with giving of presents usually accompany such an arrangement and usually there are heavy legal overtones involved. The modern trend to dispense with marriage on a formal level may turn out to be a temporary phase; it certainly was when the French Revolutionaries tried it.
4. Death. Funerary customs and rites have always been of the first importance and still are even in the modern world where religious belief has been diminished. Death is seen as of considerable significance and a period of mourning is a necessary procedure. Burial is by far the most usual procedure, the implication being that one is being returned to the underworld. Cremation is not a new procedure but assumes that a bodily resurrection is not to be taken literally.

Although the rites involved with these stages of life vary across the world, usually a derivative of religious belief, there is a common thread holding them together. It is the mystery of life itself and the reality that new life requires death, and vice versa, that death implies new life. In this way it is connected with sacrifice. It is no surprise that such rites often involve 'sacrifice' in some shape or form. The feeling that life in its many phases is a gift from God is not just a Christian one; and it requires some form of response as celebration and thanksgiving. The life of Christ can be seen as a completion and fulfilment of all these rites of passage.

Notes

1. Littleton, *The Sacred East*, p.59.
2. M. Boyce, *Zoroastrianism*.
3. D. Drew, *The Lost Chronicles of the Mayan Kings*.
4. J. Godwin, *The Mystery Religions of the Ancients World*, p.24.
5. Littleton, op. cit., p.51.
6. O.R. Gurney, *The Hittites*, p.151.
7. Littleton, op. cit.
8. Drew, op. cit.
9. Hepburn, *Christianity and Paradox*.
10. Buddhist statuary; a Buddhist would probably maintain that the statues of Buddha are not idolatry but an aid to mediation; the statues are all different.
11. Zernov, *Eastern Christendom*, chapter 11. The icons are not idolatry; they are something approaching Sacramentalism.
12. The miracles in St John are carefully selected and largely related to the 'I am...' statements.
13. Bouquet, *Comparative Religions*, p.146.
14. Littleton, op. cit., p.27.
15. Rig Veda.

16

Unity, Diversity, Assimilation and Intolerance

That disunity and intolerance has been a noted feature within religions, as well as outside them, is a sad fact in world affairs. There are those who point out that many if not all wars are fought because of some religious disagreement. The example of Northern Ireland is often cited, with the implication that we should abandon religion altogether. However, it can be seen in another light: that virtually all wars are fought over some sort of territorial disagreement and that religion is dragged in to justify the cause, on either side. We notice that wars still occur when atheism is supposed to be the ruling factor, as with Russia and China.

But what are we to make of the vast range of religious beliefs and practices in the world today? If we consider a town like Birmingham where there are reckoned to be 184 different nationalities with their differing religious ideas, and virtually every major, minor and tiny sect of opinion to be found, what hope is there for any form of unity and community cohesion? Amazingly there is a certain unity of purpose, but it is not without its problems. In many ways the situation resembles that of the Roman Empire, especially the city of Rome itself, at the time of Jesus. There was just about every permutation of thought and practice available and yet the Empire held together. This was achieved not so much through democracy but through a contrived system of loyalty to the Emperor. He was usually elevated to the status of divinity and sacrificing to the Emperor was the normal method of determining loyalty. After that, there was an amazing tolerance for just about anything in the line of religious practice or non-practice. Notable exceptions to this were, firstly, the Jews, who had gained exemption from having to acknowledge 'the genius of the Emperor'; this was through the good offices of Herod the Great who had gone out of his way to befriend the early emperors. Secondly were the Christians, who refused to accept the Emperor's divinity and, being seen as a separate group from the Jews, came in for periodic persecutions. They were suspected of being a corroding influence on the Empire.

It is interesting to consider the so-called Mystery Religions and their effect on Roman culture and also as a background to nascent Christianity. The Romans were great syncretisers which helped in assimilating Greece and many other territories into their control. But the Mystery Religions came as something exotic and as a major contrast to their normal patterns. Roman state religion had become increasingly institutionalised, austere and personally undemanding for many rank-and-file Romans. Something eccentric from newly conquered territories easily captured their imaginations: Christianity must have seemed like that for many of them. Most of the Mystery Religions stemmed from Egypt or other parts of the Orient and were a transmuted or debased form of something very ancient; almost everything except for Judaism had undergone some sort of reinvention under the influence of the Hellenistic Empires. That, plus the mystery element, engendered fascination for the Romans. Because they guarded their procedures with much secrecy, still to this day we are unable to ascertain exactly what rituals and beliefs they held. Certain features can be deduced from their statuary; also the early Christian writers made reference to some of their ideas. This may seem strange to us today as we are used to religious groups being open about their procedures and willing to accept scrutiny. The Freemasons and the Scientologists would be the exception to this, and in many ways are the modern equivalents of the Mystery Religions.

Syncretism was the order of the day; the assumption was that one could choose a fancy religion to suit oneself. In many ways the Romans were spoilt for choice, and it was not really a matter of deep commitment: rather a dilettante experimentation. This was the opposite of Biblical teaching: that God had chosen his disciples and destined them for service and glory. It has been suggested that the Mystery Religions provided ideas for nascent Christianity. This is probably not true; the reverse is more likely, that they took ideas from Christianity. The reason for this is that the full flowering of the Mystery Religions is thought to have come in the second and third centuries AD, long after Christianity had settled into a basic routine of practice and theory. There was a time when Mithraism, with its

Zoroastrian background and very similar ideas, was a strong contender to rival Christianity. But this turned out not to be. Possibly the most dangerous set of ideas came from the Gnostics. This was more of theorising than of actual practice in ritual or everyday living. Greek philosophy had established itself in a thorough manner in the centuries even before the Greek expansion into the Orient, and was a powerful influence everywhere. The very word *logos* was a sort of catch-word with much pejorative overloading. It was at the heart of many philosophical approaches to God. Mithras was seen to be the divine *logos*. The concept was a gift for such rationalisers as Arius who tried to find a neat explanation for the Incarnation. In fact many of the early heresies were some form of adaptation of current philosophical thinking; possibly also some influence from the Mystery Religions.

One may wonder why the Christian Church succeeded in the face of this plethora of theories and exotic practices. After all, it was some achievement to start with a crucified leader and 300 years later to be the dominant force in the known world and beyond, and enjoy the patronage of the first Christian Emperor. Several factors may help here to understand it.

Firstly, the plethora of cults were never, internally or externally, united in their message. There was no single Gnostic message: each teacher had his own set of weird theories. The strange cults had all manner of strange ideas which were cloaked in secrecy. It was all mutually contradictory and confusing. It was great fun for anyone who wished to dabble, nonsense for anyone who wished to approach the deep matters of life and death on a basis of serious commitment.

Secondly, there had for some time been a general move towards monotheism, especially in the East. The Jews in particular had been proselytising far beyond their own home boundaries. This message was well received in many areas such as Asia Minor and Greece. For many it made sense to say that there was only one God. The Christians were saying this; in a way they reaped the harvest the Jews had been sowing.

Thirdly, the cults almost always appealed to specific groups in Roman society. Mithraism was for the soldiery and their slave retinues and had nothing to do with peaceful people at home. The Isis cult was relevant to sailors and related occupations. The Cybele cult appealed to ladies, housewives and those at home rather than on campaign. Gnosticism appealed to the intellectuals and probably meant little to the masses. The Christians, by contrast, had the 'catholic' Church, which meant that all sorts and conditions of people were accepted on an equal basis. It might at first have seemed to be associated with the slaves and lower classes, but this was not to last very long. It promised a different kind of unity as compared with the compulsory political unity demanded by the government.

Fourthly, the cults had varying attitudes to moral values: some a very high ethic, others less so. But then people realised that it was the Christians who rescued abandoned babies, took on orphans and widows, the sick and the dying; they made a point of giving people a decent funeral in spite of their poverty. It must have seemed like the love of God coming into harsh world and offering something akin to what we now call the welfare state.

Fifthly, coupled with this was the fact that the Christians were persecuted ferociously, not according to any clear logic, but according to the whims and neuroses of certain emperors. The various charges against them, notably disloyalty to the Empire, were ably dismissed by various apologists. After all, there were Christians fighting in the Roman army. The unfairness and sadism of it simply engendered a wave of sympathy for them. The paradox was that the more they were persecuted, the more they grew in number and influence. The same is true today where Christians are under persecution.

Sixthly, none of the cults, and particularly Gnosticism, claimed any kind of historical reality for their ideas. It was all mythology and speculation. Even a historical figure like Zoroaster seems not to have been worked into the scheme of Mithraism. But the Christians were insistent that Jesus was a real historical figure and that the amazing events surrounding his life were not fantasy or the work of overwrought imagination. It was true that the Gnostics attempted to water down the Incarnation by denying that Jesus actually suffered, and that there was some sort of 'appearance' of humanity about him. Valentinus tried to maintain that even though Jesus appeared to eat things, he never needed to go to the toilet! But the purpose of the Gospels and early Christian literature was to emphasise that Jesus was genuinely flesh, real on earth and real in heaven; he was the true *logos*. Add to that that his death was an appalling miscarriage of justice (as emphasised by St Luke), and the public could easily identify themselves with him.

Seventhly, to modern minds the fulfilment of prophecy does not carry much weight, but we must realise that in the ancient world it had a massive influence. The pagans as well as the Jews had their own prophets, and fulfilment was always at the back of their minds. To show that Jesus had completed the expectations of the Hebrew Scriptures would have a large influence in helping people to see God's hand in the life of Christ, and to see him as the genuine Messiah. After all there were plenty of false ones in the Graeco-Roman world.

Christian unity and diversity

In general in the early years, the Christian faith presented a very largely united message and pattern of worship to the world, and this must have been a major factor in its rapid success. There were of course minor schisms and heresies, but these were never allowed to take centre stage; never anything like the Reformation in the West. It was then that a massive splintering took place. Although the makings of it were already present beforehand, with the Hussites, the main break with Rome came after Martin Luther's outburst in 1517. Denominationalism as we now know it is the legacy of the upheaval in the sixteenth century, not that Martin Luther himself ever intended this to happen. It is only in our own times that the absurdity of it is beginning to occur to people, and the Ecumenical movement has been gathering strength by fits and starts over the last century. Does this mean that the sixteenth-century Reformation is now coming to its conclusion? A major impetus for this came as the Churches in India realised that the Hindus were genuinely perplexed as to which denomination to join: after all, minor differences (real or imagined) meant absolutely nothing to a non-Christian audience. It is a sad fact that Christians have managed to impose their differences of opinion on just about every mission field in the world. The fact that Jesus prayed that all his followers should be 'one' seemed to elude people. It is only now that this reality is beginning to exert some influence on Christian thinking. In spite of deeply entrenched attitudes still clouding the issue, there is a genuine urge to cooperate, minimise differences and work together.

In considering the causes of Christian disunity, this may be for various reasons but the core of the problem is one of authority. At the Reformation, Papal authority was seen to be faulted and its policies actually contrary to Biblical teachings. There was a strong urge to recover the original simplicity of the primitive Church and to make the Scriptures available to everybody in their own language. Unfortunately it was not as simple as it may have seemed. For one thing the primitive Church may not have been as simple as one would like to think. Granted, there would have been synagogue worship which was reflected in many a 'nonconformist' church: but there was also Temple worship, which was a lot more elaborate. Also, making the Scriptures available also had its own set of problems, for any translation inevitably allows the presuppositions of the translator to creep in and influence the reader. In fact what did happen was that each Protestant group can be seen as centring round a leader or founder, who in effect became a substitute 'Pope' and in so doing, the groups with their separate centres of authority simply cancelled each other out. Was it Calvin, or Knox, or Baxter or Wesley who was right? Who knows?

The question of authority is one main factor in this matter. It can often be noted that the more extreme a group is, the more authoritarian it tends to be. The authority may be claimed to be derived from 'scriptures', but such writings are not always the same as other groups use. Also they need a figure of authority to control the selection of and interpretation of such writings. It seems that we all need some kind of doctrine which provides a degree of certainty in the midst of an uncertain world. We all need to have our little certainties to hold on to. If we did not, we would be drifting, neurotic, purposeless robots; this is the true form of atheism. The fact that the Bible is unclear or silent on many matters arising in the modern world does not stop people who wish to dominate others from enforcing some sort of dogma and contriving support for their own position. This is particularly true for politicians. The truth is that the Bible has enough ideas, often contradictory, to encourage almost any theory or course of action. This is why we have this issue of contradiction and paradox.

The modern attitude to authority has been coloured by the antics of various recent dictatorships, where the authority of the state has clearly been abused and used as a tool for personal advancement and domination. Even though the Pope has moderated the authoritarianism of the Roman Church, many people find authority in religion to some extent suspicious. This would apply to many Roman Catholics in addition to the vast majority of Protestants. But authority in religion there has to be. How is it to be understood? 'Authority' can be seen in two ways: firstly, as the way to dominate people and reduce their freedom; secondly, it can mean being in possession of information not generally available but which is of some importance. It would be fair to say that with Jesus the latter would be very true: that he had inside knowledge of the intentions of the Eternal Father, and was quite confident to speak out and contradict those who were wrong on these matters. The other meaning, that of controlling people, arises in one of the Temptations, where he is tempted to rule the world by foul means; but he refuses to do it and proclaims himself as the servant of all, which is the true form of leadership. The only time he 'pulled rank' was when overcoming evil spirits when performing an exorcism. Many of his teachings end with a question mark, which implies the freedom to draw one's own conclusions. The issue of authority was alive in people's minds then as now. The Sadducees (Matthew 21:23) wanted to know by what authority Jesus did all these things. He avoided giving a direct answer and left them with a poser, 'a Morton's fork' to ponder over. A religious group that can cope with the matter of authority without abusing it is going to be acceptable in today's world of democracy. Protestantism has encouraged the fashion of 'self-appointed experts' and that does lead to much confusion and the need for careful leadership.

This now raises the question: how can unity be achieved, given that individual believers will almost certainly have differing opinions? The most recent attempt at solving this has been the World Council of Churches dictum 'Jesus is Lord' as a unifying factor for all Christendom. This dictum can be taken in all manner of ways and there is no need for the heresy-hunting that caused so many problems in the past. There is an underlying unity between Christian people of all shades of opinion and it is a mark of its resilience that out of so much diversity Christianity has got a basic unity.

Apart from the basic problem over authority, there are other factors which are at the root of denominationalism. There is the historical level: we can see how successive generations of idealists have produced yet another little band of hope: the Congregationalists, the Baptists, the Methodists (of varying types and labels) to mention just a few. The differences between them is often unclear or very slight, and people wonder what is the point of them being separate entities. Many groups have already united at a local level and yet there is still no major reconciliation at head office level. The exception to this is the Netherlands and Norway, where the Protestant churches have all decided to merge.

Another aspect of the historical level is the political dimension. At the Reformation it quickly became clear that this theological revolution was being hijacked by the politicians. Many rulers in Northern Europe saw it as their chance to cast off Papal authority and the financial entailment that went with it, and rule their own countries in their own way. In matters of religion, political issues are seldom very far below the surface. It is easy to see that a political agenda was very often tied in with the various schismatic groups. So for instance, the Methodists and Congregationalists were the spiritual side of the Liberal and later the Labour parties. The Church of England was seen as the 'Tory party at prayer'. National identity too has been a dominant ingredient: Welsh nonconformism underpinned proto-Welsh nationalism; Irish Catholicism relates to Irish independence; Greek Orthodox underpins Greek nationality and independence from Turkey. Lutheranism is the spiritual side of nationalism in many Northern European countries. It is perhaps inevitable that one's politics must find some justification in one's religious values.

For many the political aspect is of less importance now; more important is the aesthetic aspect of denominationalism. Everyone knows the difference between 'High Church' and 'Low Church', even if they have never actually given such matters a try. There are those who feel at home with a simple form of worship; others like something more elaborate. On that level it is a matter of taste. But a substratum of this is one's understanding of the sacraments. To some extent this has been discussed before, but the crux of the matter with churchmanship is the nature of the Eucharist and the importance of Baptism. This again relates to a figurative or a literal interpretation of them. If people could see that there is truth in both understandings of the sacraments, and accept that there is a paradox here which is an offspin from the Incarnation, it could be a key factor in Christian reconciliation.

Also related to denominational differences is the status or acceptance of the minister. While some groups will accept the validity of the ministry of other groups, some will not. This is on the official level: unofficially, there is much cooperation and acceptance between ministers of varying types. Again there is another paradox at work: on the one hand, there is the 'priesthood of all believers' as brought out at the Reformation; on the other hand most groups appoint 'priests' and other types of minister in positions of leadership. Again there is truth in both these positions: both are necessary in their own way. If and when people would accept that this paradox will not go away and we must learn to live with it, there may then be a chance of solid Christian reconciliation.

It is also ironic that as petty denominationalism seems to be diminishing, another element is creeping in which will provide the grounds for future rifts in Christianity. There is the move to modernise worship into something far less formal, more personal and allegedly more enjoyable. This trend cuts across all the old denominational barriers. Conversely there is a strong element of resistance to this trend. There is many a church where verbal battles are fought over the choice of hymns, traditional or trendy. So far this has not erupted into actual splits, it just varies from one church to another. One can understand the motives of the modernisers: it is important to make worship relevant and understandable to a public which has virtually lost contact with the Church. The traditionalists might well reply that dumbing-down worship to some sort of basic common denominator is not at all wise in the long run, and that worship is just being trivialised. What the outcome of this will be over the next few decades is difficult to calculate.

The substratum of this is that over the last two centuries there has been a rollercoaster of changes in just about every aspect of life. Scientific and technological developments have been the root cause. The theory of evolution, though not the only factor, has posed a severe challenge to Christian doctrine. Many people have taken a fatalistic view and assumed that faith would just collapse because the first chapters of Genesis have been questioned. Nothing could be further from the truth. What has happened has been threefold: a fresh crop of atheists has appeared on the assumption that science is correct; the appearance of the 'Bible fundamentalist' who takes the whole of the Scriptures literally; and a new position which could be called creation-evolutionist which is an array of varying grades of accommodation between Darwin and the Bible. Faith is certainly not dead, it has simply adapted itself to cope with different 'certainties'. Just as Christianity survived the Copernican shake-up, so too it has thrived on the Darwinian storm. It will continue to survive because essentially it does not matter by what processes life on this planet arrived at what it is now. Whichever way one sees it, it is the work of a designing eternal hand. That hand is not a machine: it is a person with whom a relationship can be formed. That is the whole point of talking about 'covenant'. It is a living relationship. It works on an eternal level for each and every believer and believing group and is above and beyond the level of earthly logic, scientific enquiry and even 'common sense'. In a way, Darwin has done us a favour: he has shown that being dogmatic on matters of biology and so on is simply folly and beyond any sort of religious certainty; the only certainty left is that God is the ultimate biologist, physicist, chemist and so on.

It would be wrong to assume that Christianity is the only religion that is having to adapt itself to the modern situation. It would be fair to say that each one has the tension between modernising tendencies and traditionalist retention. A brief look at each one will be instructive.

Judaism in the modern world

There seems to be no problem with Jews in relation to scientific progress. Many of the Jews are leading experts in the world. Some of the cleverest people we have are of Jewish background. There does not seem to be a neurosis over evolution or any other aspect of modern speculation. The crux of the matter is adherence to the Torah, the laws of Moses. This involves diet, Sabbath observance and the general way of life as handed down from the time of the Exodus. Even belief in God is not the crucial defining factor that one might have thought. So we see in the modern state of Israel a mature democracy with all manner of advanced agricultural, industrial and military development. The Jews are wealthy, confident, forward-looking and yet they have a deeply rooted anchorage in the legal system of the Pentateuch. It is a well-balanced faith and yet within it are differences of emphasis which lead to groupings such as strict Jews, liberal and purely nominal Jews. The racial factor used to be an important part of the definition of a Jew, but is far less so now. It is far easier to convert to Judaism than before. The final definition of a Jew is adherence to the Law.

Islam in the modern world

There was a time when Islam led the world in scientific progress but this slipped about the time of the Renaissance. For a long time, there was a refusal to assimilate with scientific advances being made in the Christian world. Now there is a kind of schizoid situation at work: for while many Muslims are successfully adapting their faith to the modern world, others are making an outright refusal and rejecting modern Western values in quite violent terms. The term recently coined, 'Islamic fundamentalist', means those who are trying forcibly to put the clock back. Forcing women to wear *burkas* is just a symptom of the underlying urge. For many Muslim countries some form of dictatorship or absolutist monarchy is the only thing that works; democracy seems to be difficult to achieve. And yet for those who have made the effort to integrate in countries where they are in a minority, there must be admiration, for they make excellent doctors, nurses, teachers and scientists.

Buddhism in the modern world

The Buddhists are notably attempting to adapt to contemporary circumstances. They are shaping their faith to make a valuable contribution to major world issues. The environmental issue is often high on their agenda; so too is world peace as a morally urgent policy. In the East many educational and health projects are inspired by Buddhists. The inner life of peace and finding the truth within oneself is an important corrective to greed and the self-interest of rampant materialism. There are many ways in which the Buddhists and the Christians could work together; the difference is that for the Buddhist, the ultimate truth is to be found within oneself; for the Christian, the ultimate truth is a gift from God and not a human invention. There are many areas, usually remote like Tibet, where Buddhism is still heavily involved with traditionalism, but even there they are having to face up to modern circumstances. If asked about such matters as evolution, a Buddhist might reply that we have a situation which we must face here and now. How it got like this, and the origins of human life, are not the point. Who knows how it all began? We must concentrate on each person's salvation, using Buddha's method. Although Buddhism has major groupings –

Theravada and Mahayana, with splinter groups in Japan – there seems to be no intolerance between them and no real need for an ecumenical campaign. One suspects that there is an awareness of the paradoxes in spiritual life which ought in theory to lead to a mutual acceptance of contrary opinions.

Hinduism in the modern world

As far as unity is concerned, this is probably a question that never arises in the Hindu world. There are all manner of groupings, splinter groups, different opinions, often actually contradictory. But since it is a very tolerant religion, almost anything goes. The central strand is still Karma, an assumption that is neither provable nor disprovable but which conditions every aspect of life. As for scientific and technological advances, there is in theory no problem for Hinduism: it can contain some of the most sophisticated contemporary ideas and also the most ancient and mythological ideas without some sort of clash. Evolution too is not a problem, for this is just another aspect in an eternal round of life which stretches back and forward in an indefinite series. As with Buddhism, the positive contribution to the world is ideas on meditation and calming of the mind, a matter which is of increasing relevance in a hectic and frenetic world. With regard to democracy and equality, the Hindus are hampered by inbuilt attitudes relating to Karma. Even if the 'outcaste' status has been legally abolished, these people still exist as a social reality. Modern India has democratic elections and the possibility of women being in the government, even up to prime minister, but it will be a long time before sexual and social equality works its way into the framework as it has done in the West.

In general, the picture is of some religions tenaciously holding on to traditional values and others making strenuous efforts to support and adapt to modern globalised values. We can see many contradictions emerging within and outside man's religions. The balance between old-fashioned and modernistic is becoming increasingly obvious. It may be possible to see some of these as paradoxes: there is a lot waiting to happen. An important factor in all this is that as we now have instant communications and global interchange of people and ideas, we now have what might be called a 'world morality'. This is essentially based on Judaeo-Christian values, but paradoxically facilitated by modern scientific and technological advances. These values centre round three major areas but are interconnected and interwoven: value of life, value of property, value of the person. Can we see in this a completion of the words of Isaiah (11:9), 'For the earth shall be full of the knowledge of the Lord, as the waters cover the sea'?

A paradigm about Nature in relation to religious agreement

One of the noted features in biology is the factor of 'recessiveness'. There are recessive species: while there are very common animals like cats and dogs, there also are very rare ones like the sloth and the king cobra. It seems to argue against the evolutionists, that is, 'the survival of the fittest'. Why do recessive creatures continue to appear against all the odds? The same is true of genes. It is also true of races. Why do minority races survive rather than become absorbed into dominant races? The same thing occurs in chemistry, for while there are vast amounts of carbon and hydrogen available, also there are tiny amounts of atoms forming trace elements, such as uranium and laurentium. But there is a purpose behind it: for the recessive or scarcer elements in nature do contribute something worthwhile in the general workings of things. Just because they are scarce and 'outvoted' does not mean they are of no importance. Sometimes their importance rests in their being scarce. The same applies in many areas of life.

When we apply the same paradigm to religious thought or theology, it then throws light on the vast array of differing ideas in that area. While there are major rafts of belief such as Mahayana Buddhism or Roman Catholic Christianity, which in appearance are a unified bloc, there are also smaller groupings and sects, sometimes within a recognised religion and sometimes floating free. They almost always have some sort of assumption or substratum of continuity at work beneath the surface. The same is true in chemistry with the make-up of atoms; the same also with genes, for they rely on basically the same building blocks of life. It has occurred to many people in the past to do a syncretistic job and try to merge different religions into one. The results are normally unconvincing. We can see the same happening with the attempt to produce a world language, namely

Esperanto: another scheme that lacked conviction. The fact is that differences of opinion, like recessive genes, are not going to disappear overnight. As in nature, these ideas only reappear again and again, usually with a different label or a different permutation. But they do not mysteriously vanish altogether; neither do rare atoms. The reason for this is that every idea, even contrary and fault-finding ideas, has its part to play in the general workings of theology.

In nature we see continuity and permutations on the same things: different combinations of these basic ingredients. So too with theology. There is continuity, which is an aspect of completion; also we see balance in all manner of ways. In theology we see an enormous array of balancing, sometimes really quite intricate. Why not say that all the groupings and splinter groups are there for a purpose? The contrasts between them and the questions they raise are there to stimulate deeper thought and bring us to a closer realisation of the intricate workings of the Almighty. Is it shocking to say that the atheist has a point? Not at all: it serves to make one reconsider and re-evaluate all our own beliefs, or lack of them. That does not mean that we all ought to embark on atheism: it would be absurd to say that all the carbon atoms ought to turn into uranium! But all things great and small have their part to play.

A paradigm for religious disunity and world peace

There was a stock-breeding farmer who had various cattle on his farm. There were cows which produced a lot of milk; others were noted for their meat; and a special one, a bull, that produced high-quality semen for breeding. The farmer had three sons who had a claim on his estate. It was going to be a problem writing his will; a common problem when farms have to be handed on to the next generation. The first son, Jim, had put a lot of work in and in effect became the manager of the farm. The second son, Fred, had done a lot of work and been very supportive, but not to the same extent as Jim. The third son, Charlie, had been a time-waster, done very little to help on the farm and had disagreed with his father on various matters. The father loved all three of them; it was difficult to write a will which did justice to the situation.

When the father died, imagine the puzzlement at these provisions in the will. There were 36 animals in the herd. Jim was to receive a half of the herd. Fred was to receive one third. Charlie was to receive one ninth, one of which was the special bull. A quick calculation showed that Jim would receive 18 beasts, Fred would receive 12 beasts, Charlie was to receive four beasts. That sounded fine until someone pointed out that there were two beasts left over: 18 + 12 + 4 = 34. That was when the family row broke out. It became embittered, with all sorts of infantile arguments, claims about how each one was his father's special boy. In the end they decided that an arbitrator should be called in, their solicitor.

In the first instance, the solicitor insisted that the will could not be set aside or rewritten: the father had been perfectly compos mentis when it had been written. Also the proportions of the estate did reflect fairly the contribution each son had made over the years; in the end the boys accepted that. But then there was the argument over the two extra beasts. Two into three does not go. Each son saw a reason for having an extra beast himself, but not for allowing the other two to have an extra beast. It was then that the solicitor suggested that none of them should receive an extra beast: there was a farmer over the hill who had lost all his herd to Foot and Mouth: how about giving him the two, one male and one female, to help him start all over again?

It was Charlie who needed most advice. The solicitor pointed out that the special bull was potentially a very valuable animal. He could, if he put his mind to it, make a fortune out of selling the semen; also he could do a deal with his brothers and all would be winners.

At last the solicitor made them all see sense: endless arguments and recriminations would lead nowhere, except to the office of the Official Receiver! Cooperation and a constructive deal between the lads could and would lead to an enrichment all round. There was no need to give up one's inheritance or compromise one's ownership. It could all be managed with goodwill on all sides. Also, generosity to the neighbour would ensure reciprocal help in the case of problems in the future.

In case one is wondering whether that mathematical trick is some sort of paradox: the answer is emphatically *no*! Any mathematician will tell us that the trick can be done with any number: it is only a matter of adding up fractions! But what does it mean?

The paradigm can be taken on at least two levels, if not three. Firstly, there is the issue of Christian unity. There are three main rafts in the Christian world: the Orthodox, the Roman Catholic and the Protestant; and of course a myriad of smaller groupings within and on the fringe. We can see that each has a degree of inheritance from God; none of them is totally disinherited. Some of the main groups would doubtless claim to be the true son and heir of the Father, but God probably sees it from a slightly different angle. There is no sense in having endless wrangles which almost always descend to the level of triviality. There is so much to be gained by finding ways of cooperating and finding common ground. From that, there is so much that the Christians can and do give to the world. Much of this is already happening; there is still a long way to go. This does not mean that we have to give up our various traditions and all follow the same patterns and methods. But the paradox in this is that it is in giving, in patience, in giving consideration to another point of view, that we receive: we come to understand and are enriched by just listening and, where necessary, helping out.

On the second level, there is the issue of spirituality which cuts across all denominations. There are the very keen practising churchmen, the not-so-keen background Christians who in general terms would be adherents but not fully active members. Then there are the Humanists, atheists, objectors, agnostics and the 'just not interested'. All of them are loved by God: they all have an inheritance of some kind. Often it is not fully realised. The non-believers have their part to play: they have so much potential. When they do realise their potential, it can take the form of a sudden conversion experience, and they turn out to be highly valued and resourceful for the faith. If they were prepared to think positively about spiritual matters instead of issuing carping criticism, so much would be gained.

On the third level, there is the 'inter-faith' situation. The world is now too small for senseless wrangles ending in violence. Whatever one's inheritance is from God, it is time to use it in constructive and cooperative ways. We have to accept that there are people with differing cultures and basic assumptions. This is not going to change overnight. But peace and the ability to listen are vital to the future. Also the referee, the 'solicitor', helps to calm people down, persuades them not to resort to court action, and points out the helpful and positive ways forward. That umpire is Christ himself.

The interaction of the two 'good' sons and the one wayward one is inevitable. It would be so cosy to think that the third lad would suddenly alter his temperament and harmonise himself with the others. But life is not as simple as that. But we can see a purpose in it: that the third son had something which could stimulate and strengthen the inheritance of the other two. It is in objecting, criticising and fault-finding that we find ways of justifying, strengthening and finding a deeper understanding of our own beliefs. It is easy just to repeat parrot-fashion our own assumptions and never really think about what they imply. It is the objector who forces us to think about these matters and discover new dimensions which we had not realised were there.

17

The Hard Sayings of Jesus

There are many difficult passages and ideas in the Bible. Some are difficult in the sense that we do not readily understand them because with our knowledge of twenty-first century life, we find it hard to see into the mind of the ancient world. It is sad to note that a person like Abraham is often judged by modern standards of ethics; in fact he was only following the normal code of his day and age and had to learn a higher ethic from God; this process is still happening with us today. Other passages are hard in the sense that they seem cruel or unforgiving. The term 'un-Christian' is often thrown around, but of course our understanding of 'Christian' is not always the same as theirs. This is particularly so with some of the sayings of Jesus, which sound harsh, uncompromising and unforgiving. Also we see contradictions at work in his sayings and this should alert us to the possibility of fresh paradoxes. Many of these hard sayings have already been discussed, particularly in Chapter 10 on Parables. It will be an interesting exercise to see if many more of his difficult teachings can have some light thrown on them. It could be said that Jesus was generous; for those who wished to find fault with his ministry, there is plenty of material to fuel the fires of atheism, objection and auto-rejection. It is interesting that a book such as the Hard Sayings of Jesus by F.F. Bruce[1] constantly brings up interesting ways of getting round the harshness of Christ's teachings. One clever device often used in modern liberalistic argument is to assert that 'Jesus never said that', or 'it was wrongly recorded by a scribe', and other 'bypass' methods. None of this is particularly honest; it is far better to accept that Jesus did hand out some really tough, soul-searching teachings. He did this on purpose: the way of the cross was never meant to be easy and faith in God does place a tremendous strain on human logic. All the time we are brushing up against divine logic which does not accord at all well with human rationality.

In the first place it is as well to remember the element of

exaggeration in Jesus' method of preaching. This is clearly something which was seen in Daniel and Ezekiel and had become his chosen method of arresting people's attention and heightening the emotion, as well as fostering the feeling of urgency. This feeling is particularly evident in St Mark, but it is St Matthew in the Sermon on the Mount who records some of the most hyperbolised ethical teachings. The problem has been that people have taken Jesus totally literally with the result that they have either damaged themselves physically or rejected the faith without even considering that these teachings can be taken symbolically or in moderation. 'You must be perfect as your heavenly Father is perfect' (Matthew 5:48) is hardly possible for any human soul. But it helps us to cope with a whole range of hard sayings which Bruce attempts to deal with and does not always quite succeed in. Examples of these would be: adultery in the heart (Matthew 5:28), forgiving one's brother (Matthew 18:35), turning the other cheek (Matthew 5:39), selling all that you have to give to the poor (10:21), being a eunuch for the sake of the Kingdom (Matthew 19:12), and many others. All these speak of exaggeration and of demands far beyond normal human capability. What is the effect? To augment guilt and point out to us the impossibility of manufacturing our own perfection. This is in contrast to the Jewish legalists who, assuming Old Testament ideas, had convinced themselves that they were in the right relationship with God by the proliferation of legalisms and having a superior attitude to those who could not cope with it. The message is that we are all in need of repentance, even the nicest person with an easy conscience. The need to admit to failure and ask God for forgiveness is paramount. There is condemnation: Jesus is the eternal Judge (as seen in Matthew), but paradoxically he is the one who comes in mercy to relieve the troubled conscience and bring healing to mind and body. Here again we see the theology of balance as seen in the parables: on the one hand Jesus rejects and condemns people; on the other hand he comes in mercy and forgiveness. This is beyond human analysis: only the logic of God understands this juxtaposition. There is also the theology of completion at work here, for the laws of Moses are not there to be ignored or abolished, they are there to be fulfilled and transformed. This leads on to a major strand in Jesus' teaching, that of the contrast between the Old and the New Covenant.

At this point it could be an act of bravery to consider the hardest of all his sayings. Quoting from Mark 3:28: 'For truly I say to you, all sins will be forgiven the sons of men and whatever blasphemies they utter: but whoever blasphemes against the Holy Spirit never has forgiveness, but is guilty of an eternal sin.'

This is recorded in much the same wording in Matthew and Luke. But the Mark context is probably the most relevant, in that the Scribes came down from Jerusalem and accused him of doing his miracles by resort to Beelzebul, the prince of devils. What an insult! No one has really satisfactorily managed to explain this saying, but here are a few ideas which might be helpful.

Firstly, there is the element of exaggeration: does he really mean 'never'? We can understand Jesus being furious at being insulted like this; and in a rage, which is only a natural human outburst, he may have said something hyperbolised like this. In a calmer mood he might have said something more moderate. Sadly we seldom have an indication of what tone of voice or mood he was in at any given moment.

Secondly, in Luke 12:10, in a slightly different context, Jesus says that if you speak a word against the Son of Man (that is, himself) you will be forgiven; but if you speak against the Holy Spirit you will not be forgiven. This does seem illogical from the human point of view, since Jesus and the Holy Spirit are later seen to be inseparable, although not identical. He does not mention speaking against the Father. Only the logic of God can really explain this.

Thirdly, there is the element of paradox to be considered. Jesus comes in judgement and condemnation; it is meant to worry people. The thought that there is something that is unforgiveable is a nagging fear, a neurosis for us all. Yet he comes in mercy: 'Father forgive them for they do not know what they are doing.' He makes allowances for our weaknesses and stupidities. Here we see balance and paradox on a massive exaggerated scale.

Fourthly, as Nineham points out,[2] the scribes have actually reversed black and white, good and bad, virtue and wickedness. Mistaking a good spirit for a bad spirit just shows how confused they are on a spiritual level. Why would this be unforgiveable? Something which is really so obvious as the difference between black and white shows that there must be something desperately twisted in their thinking. Is his remark an outburst of despair, that the legal purists from Jerusalem should make such a mess of their theology? It recalls something in Isaiah 5:20: 'Woe to those who call evil good and good evil: who put darkness for light and light for darkness ... woe to those who are wise in their own eyes and shrewd in their own sight.' It is important to recall that Jesus was steeped in the prophets.

As to them never being forgiven, verse 24 and onwards might give us a clue: 'Therefore as tongues of fire devours the stubble . . . so their root will be as rottenness . . . for they have rejected the law of the Lord of Hosts and despised the word of the Holy One of Israel.'

Even so, with all these ideas, we are still left with a saying which seems beyond human analysis. If we take it completely literally, it does not accord at all well with human rationality, but we are confronted here by divine logic, and this saying may remain an imponderable challenge for ever.

Returning to the contrast between the Old and the New Testament, something clearly alluded to in the changing of water into wine (John 2), and in various parables, it does seem hard to relegate John the Baptist to being the 'least in the Kingdom'. His ministry was of vital importance for summing up the laws of Moses and the prophets to prepare people's minds for the end of one era and the start of a new one. 'The law and the prophets were until John: since then the good news of the kingdom of God is preached,' Luke 16:16.

The best exposition of the contrast between the Old and the New comes in Mark 2:15 to 3:6. With wineskins and cloth it is clear that the two Covenants, though involving many of the same ingredients, are actually in total contrast. The New is a transformation of the Old. Jesus would never say that the Old is a mistake; the problem with it is the way that the contemporary exponents of it are missing the wood for the trees or, worse, reversing values to total confusion. Legalism has its validity as long as it does not become counterproductive, a thing we are now seeing with much of the modern health and safety legislation. This could be called the modern Phariseeism. This may help us partially to understand that cryptic remark in Mark 9:50, 'salt is good, but if it has lost its saltiness, how will you season it?' Many attempts have been made to unravel this motif and none have been completely convincing. The fact is that salt may be diluted or adulterated and yet can be crystallised back to its full strength; the ancients must have known that. Is Jesus talking about the Old Testament being perfectly good in itself, but if it is adulterated by petty legalism, it loses its force and cutting edge? That sharpness can be recovered: the essentials from Moses can be crystallised and become the basic building blocks of the New Testament.

Elsewhere the disciples are called the 'salt of the earth', that vital ingredient that brings in the sharp cutting edge of the Gospel.

We have already seen that there is a general assumption of an interim period from the Kingdom of God being at hand at the start of the ministry of Jesus, and yet it is still to come at the end. This is a major paradox: in one sense it has arrived; in another sense it is still to come. Bruce, p. 125, seems to sense this: 'the Kingdom of God is seen to be subject to temporary limitations until something happens to unleash its full power.' Many of the cryptic sayings can be seen in this light. So for instance, Matthew 10:23, 'you will not have gone through all the towns of Israel before the Son of Man comes.' Also Mark 9:1, Mark 13:30 and Matthew 10:5–6. With this last reference, we see what Jesus saw as the purpose of the interim period: that it was the last chance for the leadership of the Jewish faith to come to repentance. Seen in this light, a whole raft of difficult sayings now make sense: he wanted the people of Israel to have the first chance, and only when some of them hardened their hearts and rejected him did he broaden out his ministry to the Gentiles. The fig tree motif (it was symbolic of Israel) is crucial in this matter, as already discussed. Other sayings are Matthew 7:6, pearls before swine; Luke 18:8, finding faith on earth; Luke17:22ff, 'the day when the Son of Man is revealed'. In Mark 7:27, the motif is actually spelt out: 'let the children first be fed'. This sounds hard on the 'dogs' (the Gentiles) and yet he is realising that the Gentiles have more faith than his own people. How ironic!

Jesus clearly expected his earthly ministry to conclude (the end of the interim period) with a massive heavenly intervention, the coming of the Son of Man, as outlined in Daniel. This explains Mark 14:62, but of course the authorities take that as a blasphemous claim. Again ironic! It also goes some way to elucidating Mark 15:34, 'My God: why hast thou forsaken me?' Jesus may have thought that even at that final moment there would be a miraculous intervention to save him. Certainly the bystanders were expecting something of that sort to happen: they thought that someone like Elijah would appear to rescue him. Again ironic! The major theme stemming from this is that the Gospel intended for the faith of Israel turned out to be largely a non-starter; on the other hand, it was the beginnings of the faith of Israel proclaimed and adapted to the Gentile world.

It is interesting that the same thought about the interim period surfaces in St John, but expressed in different terms. Here it appears as almost literal language, in what may appear to be a rather clumsy contradiction. This in a way points up the importance of using figurative language when dealing with the deep paradoxes of faith. 'The hour is coming, and now is' seems awkward, but when we realise it is the paradox of the interim period, in different phrasing, it makes perfect sense. There are three contexts in which this occurs and they all throw much more light on the ramifications of the interim period.

'For salvation is of the Jews. But the hour is coming and now is, when the true worshippers will worship the Father in spirit and in truth,' John 4:24.

'The hour is coming, and now is, when the dead will hear the voice of the Son of God, and those who hear will live ... the hour is coming when all who are in the tombs will hear his voice and come forth ... those who have done good, to the resurrection of life ... those who have done evil to the resurrection of judgement,' John 5:25.

'The hour is coming, indeed it has come, when you will be scattered ... be of good cheer, I have overcome the world,' John 16:32.

With regard to the first quotation, that difficult saying about the Jews now comes clear. The old dispensation, the covenant of Moses, still holds good. It has not been abolished. All that went with it, the Laws, the Temple, the election of certain people, are still there and will remain. But paradoxically there is another disposition about to arrive. John does not phrase it the 'New Testament', but that is what it amounts to. The relationship between God and his people will rise to a new arrangement which takes no account of racial divisions or geographical locations. All those who are genuine seekers after God will relate to him regardless of time, place and circumstances. This, we assume, will be inaugurated at that great crisis at the end of his ministry; even so, it has already arrived at the start of his ministry, hence the relevance of the first miracle at the start of John's Gospel, the Water Turned into Wine.

The second quotation is looking more to the end of the ministry when Jesus is in death for three days. This was the time when he could appeal to those who had gone before and provide a rescue. The paradox here is that while he was physically dead, he was very much alive and active in the world of the spirit. This is also touched on by St Matthew and St Peter. The additional element here is that Jesus has been appointed as the eternal judge (John 5:22). This again raises the paradox that while there is judgement, there is also the love of God in mercy. This is beyond human analysis.

But we can see that Jesus thought, or expected, that at the end of his ministry there would be a divine intervention with judgement. From the human point of view, this did not happen; from the divine point of view, it did, as the whole of creation judged itself against the eternal yardstick of the Son of God.

The third quotation again concerns the end of Jesus' ministry and particularly the incident in the Garden of Gethsemane when the disciples all ran away. In a sense the desertion of his followers had already started, since Judas Iscariot had gone off to betray him. Also in one sense Jesus has overcome evil in the course of his ministry. In another sense there will be a decisive act of triumph at the end. It is difficult for us to understand that while evil had been overcome at the start of his ministry, even so the Devil had entered into Judas, and evil had still to be defeated at Calvary. This is a paradox beyond human analysis and yet an important truth nevertheless.

These remarks from St John show the interim period in a much fuller and more qualified light, and also help us to understand even more of the cryptic sayings in the fourth Gospel. It is not a simple matter of saying that John read the other gospels and simply enlarged on them; the opposite might be true for all we know. The relationship between John and the synoptics is much deeper and more subtle than that. In itself the tension between them provides another intriguing paradox.

Another important strand is that of making up one's mind: a full commitment with no dithering is what Jesus wants. Many hard sayings can be seen in this light. Mark 3:38 possibly sums it up, 'take up thy cross', accepting a complete commitment which will lead to humiliation and pain. Once on the road to a public execution, there was no turning back. This throws light on Luke 14:26, where one is advised to 'hate one's parents'. It is typical of the exaggeration used by Jesus. What he is saying is that hanging on to one's past life in the cosy home environment will not work if one is committed to the coming Kingdom. So, 'let the dead bury their dead,' (Luke 6:60). There is no need to boycott the family funeral; there is no need to take him completely literally. Matthew 6:24 says, 'you cannot serve God and mammon', for a commitment to the Kingdom cannot work if earthly values of greed and accumulation of wealth are at the centre of one's thinking. See also Luke 9:62 and Matthew 23:9. 'Entering the Kingdom violently', as seen in Luke 16:16 and Matthew 11:12, may also be seen in this light, namely that people are making a firm decision and sticking to it. On the face of it, many of these sayings sound strange if not harsh, but allowing for exaggeration in his preaching, it is possible to see them in this light.

This naturally leads on to a consideration of that strange dictum, 'many are called but few are chosen', for example Matthew 22:14 and others. As with many of the parables there is the element of separation and judgement. Sometimes the thought that one judges oneself creeps in, but still the paradox is there: that on the one hand Jesus appeals to all people to come to him, and yet there is also a sense in which many (or some) are rejected. This is difficult and defies human rationality. But this does throw light on several sayings which might appear to be difficult: 'I did not come to bring peace on earth, but a sword,' Matthew 10:34; and Luke 12:49, 'I came to cast fire upon the earth.' It is all about the separation between good and evil and the defeat of Satan, who is a very present reality in Jesus' spirituality. Mark 8:33, 'Get thee behind me Satan,' and 'I saw Satan fall like lightning from heaven.' The cosmic battle between good and evil is coming to a climax in the ministry of Jesus. He is in one sense the eternal judge; in another sense he tries to avoid condemning people and finds ways of bringing the fallen to rescue; in yet another sense he is judged and condemned by those who consider themselves to be super-righteous. This then leads on to the 'last shall be first and the first last', another of his favourite dicta, but it amounts to the same, as 'many are called but few are chosen.' It is all about the reversal of human values as seen in so many of the parables. What God values is not what we expect. This draws in the issue of wealth versus poverty, recalling that this works on two levels in the Gospels: the material level and the spiritual level. So it is no surprise to note that to some people he says, 'sell everything and give to the poor,' for example Mark 10:21, and Luke, the incident of the Widow's Mite (21:1ff.)

The hard sayings may now be seen in a modified light, and yet there is still an element of inexplicability about them. This brings us back to the paradox (already discussed) of the secrecy of the Kingdom juxtaposed with the fame. This actually receives a full treatment in Matthew, relating the matter to the ministry of Isaiah: 'You shall indeed hear but never understand ... see and never perceive, for this people's heart has grown dull ... lest they should perceive with their eyes ... and turn to me to heal them,' Matthew 13:13ff.

There is a sense in which the truths about God are plainly stated, often in parables and also in clear language, and yet there is some sort of blockage in people's souls. Somehow the teachings of Jesus resonate with them: either they react negatively and take offence, or they react positively and accept him. It is difficult for us to work out how this sort of judgement works and indeed why it is necessary at all. But in one sense the Gospel is a great uniter of mankind and in another sense it is a great divider. It is an important paradox; seen in that light, it ties in with all the other paradoxes already discussed, particularly Theodicy. And indeed, in Matthew the parable of the Sower immediately follows this quotation from Isaiah. The parable is the nearest we come, in the words of Jesus, to explaining the failure of faith or the success of it. Interestingly, the Sower parable is balanced in Luke 18:8 with the parable of the Unjust Judge, in which a widow keeps on pleading her case and eventually receives a favourable judgement. For all those who think it is unfair that their faith has gone wrong, as in the Sower, there is the other side of it, that if one persists in trying and appealing to God, it will come right. This leaves us with the searching question, 'When the Son of Man comes, will he find faith on earth?' In other words, at the great crisis when God intervenes at the end of Jesus' earthly ministry, will he find lots of believers? Or doubters? Indeed in Luke 23 we see the contrast between those who love him and those who despise him, at the climax of his ministry when he is the one who displays the supreme faith: 'Father into thy hands I commit my spirit.'

At this point we could discuss maybe the most cryptic remark Jesus ever made, in the context of the wailing women: 'For if they do this while the wood is green, what will happen when it is dry?' Luke 23:31. Strangely, Bruce declines to discuss this one. Other commentators are clearly confused by it and are groping around for an explanation. Plummer in the *International Critical Commentary*[3] has three ideas, none of which really find the core of the matter. We have already seen that the interim period, Jesus' three years of ministry, is the main chance for the Jews to repent and come to a realisation that he is the Messiah. But this period is coming to an end; like the fig tree which failed to give any fruit and was blasted, the Jewish nation has sealed its own fate. We all know what will happen to a dry (dead) tree: it will be cut down and burnt; so too the Jewish nation, as did happen in AD 70. Other passages are far less cryptic, as in Luke 19:41–44, where he even at this late stage holds out the possibility of them coming to their senses. The mention of the 'wood being green' is suggestive of the possibility of the problem being resolved, while there is still potential life in the nation, and him being accepted as the Messiah. But the last chance is going to slip away and they will seal their own doom.

One difficult collection of sayings concerns divorce and remarriage. This is a constant matter of concern in the modern world where divorce has become a commonplace procedure. We all know that family breakdown is a burgeoning social problem and will probably reach crisis levels unless somehow the pattern of easy divorce or desertion is stemmed. The whole matter hangs about on people's consciences and yet we have as yet no answer to the problem. Lack of commitment in the marriage bond is mirrored by a lack of commitment in many other areas of modern life. But the words of Jesus stand out as uncompromising and damning, even if the wording in Matthew is slightly ameliorated. It was clearly an issue in Jesus' day and rabbis gave differing rulings on it.

'Whoever divorces his wife and marries another, commits adultery against her (and vice versa),' Mark 10:2–10.

'It was also said, "Whoever divorces his wife, let him give her a certificate of divorce," but I say to you that everyone who divorces his wife, except on the grounds of unchastity makes her an adulteress: and whoever marries a divorced woman commits adultery,' Matthew 5:31–32.

This has been the Christian position right up to recent times, so much so that it has only been since 1947 that easy divorce has become available for the mass of people. However one may see this, it has been an important element in social and national cohesion over the centuries, something which is much diminished now. But on the theological level, what is Jesus saying? In common with most of the Sermon on the Mount, he is intensifying the laws of Moses and making them even more difficult to cope with. There is the element of exaggeration here and of completion. In common with many other of his sayings, are we to take this totally literally and at face value? This is at least debatable. But there is another level implied here. The relationship between God and his people is described in terms of the husband and wife situation. Hosea is just one writer but there are many others. Sometimes the two kingdoms are seen as sister wives of God (Ezekiel). This does not offer a justification for bigamy or incest! But it does talk of the closeness of the relationship between God and his people. This is based on the covenant metaphor in its various forms. It speaks of God's commitment to caring for the human race, and in a special way for his chosen people; that implies a loving and committed response from his people. Much of the Scriptures are concerned with the failure of humanity and in particular of the chosen people to respond to his love. So now we can understand Jesus (who saw himself as the bridegroom) placing the marriage commitment on such a high level. It is a relationship which transcends all other relationships, human or otherwise. The two become one flesh; so too God and the believing soul become closer than any other relationship. Now we understand the mystic who is so close to God that he does not need proofs of his existence. Also we can understand the doubter or the atheist who has some sort of awareness of God but cannot bring himself to admit it to himself or anyone else. God keeps his covenant; it is humanity that breaks the bond. As when a human marriage breaks down, there is damage done to the children, friends and relations; so too when the relationship with God goes wrong, there is spiritual damage to oneself and others who may be involved. We can understand how divorce has almost become a matter of routine: as the awareness of God has diminished in modern life, so too has the importance of unconditional love and deep commitment.

For this reason, it may be that in the case of marriage and divorce, Jesus may be taken much more literally than in other areas. It is a general understanding, reaching well beyond the Christian world, that when a couple marry they become one flesh, and previous family relationships now take second or third place. One's next of kin, for legal purposes, becomes one's spouse. This still applies in polygamous situations, such as in a Muslim country. Divorce simply serves to confuse and entangle family relationships. It implies the denial of the unconditionality of love and ongoing commitment.

One important New Testament strand which underpins the Christian Eucharist is the notion of eating and drinking Christ's flesh and blood. There were those who did take it totally literally at the time, and in the early years of the Church the fear of cannibalism did arise. But Christians have always held this motif to be figurative, even if on different levels of spiritual reality. For those who misunderstood it, it must have sounded particularly shocking and ghoulish. After all, the Jews were forbidden to imbibe the blood in animal meat, never mind human blood. But there is a deeper sense in which we go beyond the literal and the figurative sense and enter the mythological level. As we have seen in Chapter 13 on Miracles, the Feeding of the Five Thousand implies a deeper level than simply the miraculous feeding. We recall that it is St Mark who records two such events, combined with the esoteric use of numbers, in which the implication is that the whole of the Jewish system is underpinned by the life of the Messiah; also the whole world is also mysteriously given life by the Eternal Son of the Everlasting Father. His spiritual life-force (symbolised by the blood) permeates and invigorates all of life and every human system. On that basis the words of John 6:35 make perfect sense: 'unless you eat the flesh of the Son of Man and drink his blood, you have no life in you.'

From this it is but a short step to understand the Eucharist in terms of the Messiah underpinning the life of the Christian community and each individual believing soul. In one sense receiving the bread and wine is confirming what is already there in the believer; and paradoxically in another sense it strengthens and encourages each believer. This is nothing to do with magic or superstition. It all makes sense when we come to realise that the whole of creation is sustained by the all-pervading spirit of God. This is not some sort of pantheism but it is the realisation and true completion of that theology. God is at work in every aspect of his creation, and yet paradoxically he is completely other: he is not dependent on creation; creation is dependant on him. The words of Jesus may sound trivial or even ghoulish, but the deeper truth is that no one, or nothing, can avoid being dependent on him. This is a level of literality which is deeper even than the mythological. It comes down to the essential truths about life itself, and the Messiah of God is at the heart of it.

Difficult sayings in St Paul

With St Paul we are dealing with a noticeably different person as compared with Jesus. Even though he knows that the logic of God is different from the logic of humanity, he is nevertheless a much more logical person to read and less inclined to give way to exaggeration. Even so, he does give out some teachings which have posed and still do pose a problem for those who would try to explain his thoughts. Sometimes it can be simply our lack of knowledge about the world he lived in; sometimes it is clearly a matter of his thoughts clashing spectacularly with our modern liberalistic and humanistic mentality. At the very least we have to be aware that a different level of literality and figurativeness is at work here. In many ways, St Paul is more difficult to interpret than Jesus.

One notable passage is Romans 1:18–32, in which the 'wrath of God is revealed'. This is a very uncomfortable remark for the liberalistic mentality of today. People tend either to try to reinterpret 'wrath' as something rather less unpleasant or to say that St Paul was wrong, or just ignore it from their theological horizons. But if it is true that Theodicy is a reality and that there is guilt and moral failure in human nature, then condemnation makes sense. We have seen with Jesus that, paradoxically, he came to redeem the whole world and yet for some there is rejection. This is judgement: God is the eternal judge, also the eternal saviour. This is something we cannot explain. We can compare it with Romans 3:5 where Paul seems aware of the concern he is raising in people's minds: 'what shall we say? That God is unjust to inflict wrath on us? I speak in a human way.'

Did he have the liberals of his day voicing objections? Quite possibly! But the point is that it is God who is the final arbiter on all things; if he is not allowed to do any judging, it would be like a human court with the judge instructed by the public never to find anyone guilty.

It does seem very strange in a world which has seen two disastrous global conflicts, a Holocaust, various ethnic cleansings, and a horrific nuclear threat, that people cannot face up to a phrase like 'the wrath of God'. These problems are clearly a result of greed, aggression and the will to dominate others, all based on a determination to ignore God's standards of love and caring; what can we expect but difficulties in dealing with God? The only way out of it is through repentance.

The passage becomes more difficult (v. 20): 'ever since the Creation of the world his invisible nature has been clearly perceived.' This is the nearest we come, in the Bible, to reading about proofs for the existence of God. But the point he is making is that everybody knows there is a God, but they fail to honour him and it degenerates into paganism and idolatry. We have seen that shamanism and world mythology assume a supreme founding God, so Paul is right in that sense. But why idolatry should follow from not taking enough notice of God is perhaps a little strange. But that of course is what did happen: virtually every culture did and still does produce a plethora of lesser gods with their idols to go with them.

The difficulties increase when Paul says that idolatry leads on to immorality. It is assumed here that he is talking about homosexuality but it does not actually state it as such; it is however a reasonable assumption that he means this. Quite why it should be a result of idolatry is not clear. It is possible that he knew the realities of what was happening in the pagan temples and within the various priesthoods. So for him, such remarks would be entirely logical. But for us in the twenty-first century, there is no clear connection between idolatry and homosexuality. Nor is it clear why homosexuality should give way to all manner of crime and misbehaviour (v. 29). Again Paul may be thinking of the antics of the pagans of his day. In today's world these matters are very largely different.

Homosexuality has become in recent times a highly contentious issue, sharpened by the recent acceptance of such people for the ministry of the Church, and in particular admission to the office of bishop. Christians are deeply divided on the matter; attitudes differ greatly from one denomination to another; whatever one says, it is certain to be taken the wrong way by someone. A lot depends on how the Bible is interpreted, for this passage in Romans is not the only one to give some form of ruling on the matter. We have to remember that Paul was soaked in the laws of the Pentateuch; much of this is strong guidance for the Israelites not to imitate the worst and most horrific aspects of Canaanite religious practice. So, for instance, incest is forbidden along with many other sexually deviant behaviours, homosexuality being included. The situation was not much different in Paul's day, for all manner of paganistic practices were happening, especially in the Mystery Religions, much of which would not be tolerated today. We can understand how the condemnation of homosexuality has worked its way into Christian attitudes over the centuries. It is only today that a revised attitude has crept in under the influence of liberalistic thinking. There is a lot of confused and emotional thinking going on, some of it ill-informed, both for those who are inclined to favour it and those who are passionately against it.

The fact remains that any aspect of sexual behaviour always stirs up strong emotions in people. There is the fact that someone will feel threatened if another's practices are seen to be different or contradictory. It is not as simple as saying 'let's all do as we please without reference to anyone else': people's minds need to be at ease in their own milieu. Another aspect is that nobody really understands what causes homosexual attraction; it runs contrary to the normal expectation of the interrelation between male and female. It is not just the Bible that displays a negative attitude towards it, there is a gut feeling in people generally that there is a problem there, a threat, something indecent. Recent attempts to find a 'cure' by using drugs are evidence that people instinctively feel it is some sort of 'disease'. The modern sociological attempt to make homosexuality acceptable, if not a wonderful idea, may work up to a point but will come up against deeply rooted negative instincts.

It is not an easy passage for anyone today; we may be up against Paul in a specific ephemeral situation which hardly applies now. On a more general and positive note, one could say that assuming the two great commandments given by Jesus, one's love for God should rule out such things as idolatry and making undue claims to be wise when one is not. Failure in the first case can so easily lead on to failure in the second case: if one fails to love God, how long is it before love for one's neighbour falls apart and degenerates into crime and antisocial behaviour? Paul may be stating his case in strong terms but he may not be far from the truth after all.

Going further on the matter of sexual relationships, Paul has much to say on the subject of marriage and celibacy. The classic passage is 1 Corinthians 7:1–40. Much of this seems hard and negative on the subject: if one is not married, then he should stay that way; if one is married then he should also stay that way. There is concern over Satan tempting people through lack of self-control (v. 5): 'Because of the temptation to immorality each man should have his own wife (and vice versa).'

This can be seen as the basis for Christian monogamy which has prevailed up to the present day, with the exception of the Mormons. But what is Paul's real concern? After all, polygamy was widespread in the Roman world in spite of the Roman tendency towards a monogamous system for reasons of clarity over inheritance. Paul is concerned that we should be 'free from anxieties' (v. 32). This is because there is an 'impending distress' looming (v. 26). We must remember that he is convinced that the Second Coming is imminent. If we have entanglements with family matters and the care of children, this will make life more difficult when the Apocalypse comes (1 Thessalonians 4:13ff). In the light of this Paul is trying to be helpful;

perhaps he would have been more positive if he had not had the impression of 'the day of the Lord coming like a thief in the night' (1 Thessalonians 5:2). We have here another case of ephemeral thinking which has been taken by later generations of Christians as literal and immutable truth.

Perhaps not quite so difficult are Paul's remarks on family relationships as seen in Ephesians 5:21 and Colossians 3:18ff. 'Wives be subject to your husbands' may seem to some as outmoded, but of course many marriages still function quite successfully on this basis. In the Roman Empire it was quite the normal assumption. Even harder is 'slaves obey your masters'! In fairness these remarks must be seen against the backdrop of the normal Roman household. The man of the house was definitely in charge; a reasonable and lenient father might take into account the wishes of his wife and children but he did not have to. He had the power of life and death over his household. We must recall that the slaves would be counted as 'family' even if they were property. We cannot expect Paul to foresee the end of slavery as happened under Constantine. What Paul is advising is very much the caring, ideal and socially responsible family, which was very much an advance on what was happening in many households, not least the imperial family itself. Paul is not advocating slavery as an institution, he is just accepting it as a reality. This must be balanced by his remarks on Christian equality: 'There cannot be Greek and Jew, circumcised and uncircumcised, barbarian, Scythian, slave, free men but Christ is all and in all,' Colossians 3:11.

Astonishing words for those times: racial, sexual, religious and social equality, unheard of then but now seen as essential in today's democratic world. And who are we to judge, for slavery is still a reality today, albeit under different circumstances and labelling, not to mention family stresses and break-ups, and racial discrimination which is still a reality? In one sense Paul is again being ephemeral; in another sense he is being highly idealistic and futuristic.

Paradoxically, in another context, 1 Timothy 2:11ff, Paul displays a completely different attitude to women in the Church's ministry. A woman is to learn in silence, and is not allowed to teach and have authority over men: 'She is to keep silent.' In another context, 1 Corinthians 11:10, women have to cover their heads in church 'because of the angels'. No one has ever managed to explain this remark. Again we see the ephemeral nature of Paul's remarks. It accords well with the general assumption in the ancient world that women are secondary, of no importance and incapable of leadership. It is only with the modern world that women's liberation has challenged this assumption; Paul could hardly have foreseen that. Unfortunately his remarks have been taken as doctrinally binding which means that there is still a difficulty over the ordination of women as priests, and particularly as bishops. On a lower level, women have covered their heads often with a veil, up to comparatively recent times. This is something which almost certainly was a feature of Roman religious ceremonies which again indicates the ephemeral nature of some of his ideas.

Notes

1. F.F. Bruce, *The Hard Sayings of Jesus.*
2. D.Nineham, *The Gospel of St Mark*, Penguin.
3. Plummer, *The International Critical Commentary, on St Luke*, p. 529.

18

Belief, Doubt and Atheism

Just as religious belief contains all manner of differing ideas, some of which are contradictory, so the same is true with atheism. Atheism is not just one solid system of thought: there are many different variations on it, betraying all kinds of different motives. It is not easy to generalise about disbelief; it has many different facets. Very often it pertains to one specific religion or just certain aspects of it rather than a complete refusal to accept that there is a God.

A joke which used to circulate in Northern Ireland during the Troubles went like this. There was a motorist who inadvertently drove into a street riot in Belfast. He had no idea what was happening or who was threatening whom. A tough-guy wielding a petrol bomb came up to the car and demanded, 'Are ye a Protestant or a Catholic?' The motorist had no idea of what to say to please the tough-guy, so he managed to say, 'Neither: I'm an atheist.' To which the tough-guy replied, 'Are ye a Protestant atheist or a Catholic atheist?' History sayeth not the outcome of this encounter. Atheism almost always has some sort of relationship with one's background culture.

It will be instructive to look at various forms of atheism and doubt as experienced by people in different situations. Virtually everyone has some sort of mental framework, understanding of life, even some sort of idolatry to make life liveable. It is very unusual to find someone with absolutely no values or symbolic thought at work.

The atheism of revolutionary politics

Two violent revolutions have had a strong relationship with atheism: the French[1] and the Russian revolutions. In each case, the Church was seen as inextricably linked with the ideology of the monarchy, and when the monarchy was seen to be faulty and ready for destruction, the Church in that country came under the same condemnation. The atheism of the revolutionaries was almost certainly purely a political tactic to engender a new loyalty which was the opposite of monarchist combined with religionist. It is unlikely that it was an atheism on a purely philosophical basis. But it was a vicious form of atheism which deemed it necessary to administer ferocious persecution to anyone who held on to their beliefs and practices. This was because the need was seen to force loyalty to the new totalitarian government. Strangely, with the French situation, the process was inconsistent and confusing. At first, all religions were to be tolerated, which was good news for any non-Catholics. Then it swung to complete interdict so that all the churches were closed. At the same time, Papal properties were being appropriated. Eventually of course, under Napoleon, an accommodation had to be reached with the Pope. So it was the cynical atheism of political expediency and tactics. The Russian wave of persecution lasted much longer although varying in intensity. In legal terms there was supposed to be freedom of religion but the truth was very different indeed. All religious groups were under pressure and threat of punishment. It is interesting that in the crisis of 1941 when the Germans were within an ace of defeating Russia, churches were opened again! It was only with the fall of Communism that the persecution was finally lifted.

The atheism of disillusionment

There must be many who have started out with a simple faith as a child. This can also apply to adults. Taking the Bible completely literally, the miracles, the amazing events, the Genesis story of creation: all these become a strain on belief when something or someone comes along to suggest that these matters are impossible. Atheistic scientists and philosophers can be quite convincing when they set to work to destroy someone else's faith; it is somehow a bit different when one sets out to call into question their lack of faith! It is true that the Bible, more than any other sacred literature, does contain material that is a strain on people's credulity. It is also interesting that the Bible tries to cope with this fact about human nature: almost every account that contains a degree of incredulity, has someone expressing doubt. This begins in the Garden of Eden and reappears regularly, right through to Thomas who had problems with the Resurrection. Even those who must have seen the miracles being performed had problems with them. Matthew 28:17 puts the finger on it: 'And when they saw him they worshipped him, but some doubted.'

It would seem that faith and doubt are almost always carefully interwoven, which means that doubt is a part of the life of faith. This brings us back to balance and paradox. An unbalanced person is one who is totally credulous and accepts every fantastic claim regardless of its spiritual value. That is the sort of faith that can easily crash in disarray and disillusionment. The balanced person is one who can consider all these things, see the spiritual value in them and be prepared to accept that there may be an element of exaggeration or distortion somewhere. On that basis, belief in God can still be maintained regardless of the difficult passages in the Bible; belief does not necessarily have to be tied to the acceptance of the miraculous. Another unbalanced person is the categorical atheist who consigns the whole matter, including God, to rejection, and cannot even consider that there may be something worthwhile in it. The paradox comes in this way: that while we are inclined to believe what we read, especially if it is some form of authoritative scriptural writing, at the same time there should always be a degree of questioning in one's mind. St Mark 9:24 puts it very aptly: 'I believe: help my unbelief.'

So doubt goes hand in hand with faith. It is not a matter of finding proof or convincing people, for it all comes down to what a doubter will accept as evidence. Even so, such matters as Linda Martel,[2] St Bernardette and many other spiritual healers must be a severe embarrassment to those who cannot cope with miracles.

The atheism of convenience

There are many who claim to be atheist, but when it comes to discussing it, it becomes clear that such a thing as church attendance or admitting to having faith is a matter of embarrassment. They have sensed that it is not fashionable to support one's local church; also it does not fit in with the social climate to admit to having faith. Although there is no formal persecution as there was in Soviet Russia, there is much in the way of informal or social persecution active in Britain today. This may be less acute in other Western countries. It is suspected that people will not admit to a religious commitment for fear of discrimination.

Another aspect of this is that people's lives are so tied up with all manner of distractions that church attendance is very low on their list of priorities. It is probably not atheism in the theoretical sense, but in the sense of social convenience. A common excuse offered for keeping clear of any involvement with religious activities runs like this: 'I am far too busy these days: I simply could not find time for it.' It may be that the claim to be an atheist is not quite as sincere as one would have thought.

The root of the matter lies in the modern inclination to regard 'commitment' as out of fashion and favour. While it is still acceptable to make a commitment to preservationist and cultural groups such as the National Trust, the idea of a full commitment to a local place of worship is likely to attract scorn or failure to understand. A common assumption is that somebody else can keep the local church in existence so that when the family wedding or funeral becomes necessary, the church will still be there, willing and able to deal with the matter. The idea or suggestion that the local church may be closing down through lack of support generally produces consternation and anger, very often from the very people who seldom if ever patronise the place. It would seem that other people are expected to make a commitment on behalf of those who are busy making 'atheistic' excuses.

The atheism of scientific certainty

To quote, as a specimen, the type of remark often made: 'Science and religion do not agree: science has got to be right.' This is akin to the atheism of disillusionment but is not quite the same. It betrays the assumption that everything has to have a rational explanation in terms of human logic, and that the scientists have already found it, or will find it fairly soon. There is a thing called the 'God-gap' which means that things that used to be accredited to God have now been explained away in scientific terms, and eventually there will be no 'God-gap' left at all. The assumption goes further: that all our problems will be solved by one science or another: not just the physical sciences but the social sciences too. In this way, science can easily become some sort of idolatry. Scientists somehow get promoted to being 'gods', although this is now probably slightly less so than in recent times.

There is no doubt that scientific research has helped to produce many technological advances which have been beneficial to mankind; indeed scientific enquiry is nothing new in the modern world and it is inevitable that it will continue to probe the great mysteries of life. However, there is a tendency to forget that not every technological 'advance' has been helpful: some have actually been disastrous or potentially highly dangerous for the future of mankind. The nuclear bomb is a case in point: did anyone realise the harmful long-term consequences of this weapon before it was actually used in 1945? It is facile to assume that the scientists hold the answer to all our problems. To assume that humanity can save itself through its own clever devices is an optimism beyond all common sense. It is far healthier to apportion the scientists with a generous amount of scepticism; this will be in balance with the scepticism they often exhibit towards God. It is also a paradox that some scientists happen to be Bible fundamentalists. Others are practising believers with a more liberal view. This seldom percolates through to the public and is often ignored by those who imagine that science has disproved God. But there is one truism that no one can deny: that scientific experimentation has got to be limited by the moral and spiritual essentials of humanity. We have seen the depths of obscene cruelty performed by the perverted 'science' of the Third Reich. Such cruelty is not totally reserved by the Nazis. There is only one answer to this: that the sanctity of life as shown in the Scriptures must be respected. That is the one thing that protects us from gross exploitation and cruelty, and that brings us back to the moral authority of God.

The atheism of scientific certainty has been a 'creed' with much persuasive power in recent times, but we may be seeing its decline. People are becoming tired of the arrogance of those who speculate far too freely. It is another case of modern mythology in the making, in particular in the sphere of cosmology.[3]

The atheism of despair (Theodicy)

Every time there is a disaster we hear the phrase 'I can't believe in God: if there were a God he would not allow such dreadful things to happen.' This is of course the root of the question of Theodicy (see

Chapter 2): 'Why do we have to suffer?' It is a basic question in the human heart which is insoluable in terms of this world's logic. The nearest we have come to any understanding of it is to talk of paradox, and even then it is beyond us to cope with it.

But for the atheistic position of despair, it can be said that there are certain assumptions contained in this position. Firstly, it is assumed (gratuitously) that God, if he were a reality, is only concerned with 'good' things. Admittedly St John talks of God being good. But what does 'good' mean? Does it mean all things nice, pleasant and advantageous? But the ancients were realistic enough to see that all things, nice, nasty or anything else, stemmed from some form of spiritual power, whether it be a plurality of gods or just One God. It is a form of mental idolatry to see God as only concerned with the pleasant things in life and then, quite easily, to decide that he is non-existent when something nasty happens. As with everything else in the realms of theology and philosophy, it is essentially a circular argument: we start with an assumption and then make a doctrine out of it.

Secondly, there is the unspoken illogicality that God has to be a reality so that he can be blamed. If God does not exist, how can he be blamed for anything that goes wrong? Very often the assumption that God allows bad things to happen overwhelms the assumption that he allows good things to happen. The atheism of despair is real for many people; it is the opposite to the theism of fulfilment and rejoicing. It is a paradox that when God exerts a little pressure on people, one of two things happens: a mountain is thrust up or a chasm is thrust down. We can now see that atheism is not just an unfortunate mistake: it is the counterpart or paradox of belief. The one thing needs the other to make any sense of it. Belief would have no meaning unless there were unbelief: the opposite is true. The same is true with light and darkness: the one has no meaning without the other.

For those who do find suffering a difficult problem to cope with, there is the picture of God coming into this world and allowing himself to be damaged and put to death. Illogical, yes. But it does suggest that suffering has a positive purpose. It is not an easy matter to explain this but it is a reassurance to all those who live a life of despair that this is not the end game. There is resurrection and hope.

The atheism of spiritual collapse

This is similar to the atheism of disillusionment but somewhat more dramatic and disastrous. It usually concerns those who have had a very strong faith with a public profile, such as a parish priest or missionary. They work very hard, finding themselves becoming increasingly exhausted and frustrated at what appears to be severe lack of progress. This would apply especially to a very tough assignment such as a very difficult parish. In the end their spiritual life collapses, leaving them with nothing but a lack of trust in God. The phrase 'take not thy Holy Spirit from us' becomes of particular relevance. But it does happen.

He is left with three choices: either to carry on going through the motions and pretend that nothing has gone wrong; or he can decide to resign and embark on a new life doing something else; or he can plaster over the problem with alcohol or some other palliative. Whichever way it is, it is a sad sight and a reminder that we are all human. It is unlikely that this is total atheism, but a serious collapse of faith is usually at the root of it.

To help such a person, one could say that 'lack of progress' is not always quite what it might seem. In spiritual terms, the progress may not be measurable by human logic, but the presence of a believer in office does have its effect even in the most difficult of situations. It is as well to remember that Jesus himself had the ultimate difficult posting: that of having to contend with the hardened fault-finders of the Jewish leadership, who were determined to derail his mission. When it came to the Crucifixion, Jesus comes out with a phrase which could be taken as the atheist in the making: 'My God, my God, why have you forsaken me?'

Again this is not complete atheism but the deep-seated worry that at the crucial moment, God is not there to intervene. But it does suggest that, as with all those whose ministry has gone wrong, and find this difficult to admit, there is the feeling of dereliction and isolation. If anything the phrase indicates that Jesus was fully human and went through the same phases of spiritual difficulty as we all do. This was in spite of his closeness to the Father: he must have felt that that relationship had somehow come unravelled at the moment of crisis. This is something that we all have to face, believer or atheist alike, and there is no guaranteed immunity from it.

The atheism of philosophical subtlety

Perhaps the best example of this would be the thoughts of Paul Tillich on the existence of God. To quote him: 'God does not exist. He is being itself beyond essence and existence. Therefore to argue that God exists is to deny him.'[4]

Many people have understood this as atheism, but it is not. Elsewhere in his theological writings he talks of 'the ground of our being' and that to talk of God as existing would mean to drag him down to the same level of physical reality as we are on in this world. For him, God is beyond definition and yet can be said to be the factor underpinning all of existence. This reminds us of the Brahma of Hinduism or Buddhism, God as being so remote that he is a principle way beyond normal human understanding. Now we understand why Buddhism can be seen as 'atheistic', for God, if he is a reality, has no relationship with one's religious system. Also certain aspects of Tillich's thought remind us of the Gnostic frame of mind. But to read other parts of Tillich's writings there is a clear understanding of how the 'ground of our being' can come into our world of existence as a Messiah and his overwhelming power, namely the Spirit. He is not really an atheist; it is only that some of his remarks sound like it. He is denying the crude, idolatrous conceptions of God: not the reality of an eternal, all-pervading factor. A lot depends on what is meant by 'existence'.

Similar remarks could fairly be made about many a philosopher who has difficulties with the 'existence of God'. What they are really objecting to is the anthropomorphic idolatrous conception of God which can so easily lead to a collapse of personal faith. For any philosopher who is serious about exploring the 'truth' about life, existence and humanity, we can say: you have an understanding of God, even if he is some sort of abstract principle which the human mind can never quite locate. A philosopher who is not interested in the truth can hardly be termed a true philosopher. In this way, 'truth' becomes an abstract God. It is interesting that when Pilate wanted to know 'what is truth?' the answer was that he was staring truth right in the face, but failed to comprehend it.

This brings us to the important paradox about the nature of God. This is seen all through the Scriptures. On the one hand, God is an overwhelming Spirit that is beyond human cognisance; on the other hand, he is a personal presence in the heart of the believer (and sometimes the denier). If we take the textual analysis of the Pentateuch seriously,[5] the J source has God in anthropomorphic terms, often quite crude: the E source, less so, and the P source in much more transcendental terms. For many philosophers the P mentality is the answer and the others are simply a problem for faith. For others who are more down to earth, J and E are perfectly reasonable and real. In general terms, this is the paradox between Eastern and Western religion: the personal and the impersonal; the immediate and the distant. Both are true in their own way, but to deny one in favour of the other is to destroy the paradox.

But the resolution of this paradox comes in the provision of some form of 'Messiah'. Tillich can see this, others cannot. But even with the appearance of the true Messiah, Jesus of Nazareth, there is still the paradoxical tension between the divine and the human, which is inevitable in the Incarnation. It would be simplistic to say that the Synoptic Gospels give us the human side of Jesus, St John the divine side – but there is a strong element of truth in this. But it is not the total truth: Jesus was the final *logos* of God, as seen in all four Gospels. Other religions have some sort of 'messianism' which varies in intensity and realisation. These matters have been discussed under the headings of sacral kingship, prophecy and priesthood. For the Jews, who have none of these factors now, the Messiah is still a future hope. For the Christians, the Messiah is now a hope bound up with the Second Coming and the consummation of all things.

It is interesting that the atheism of philosophical subtlety is not just a feature of the modern world. If we consider Socrates we see the same factors at work. He had the courage to question[6] the existence of the Olympian gods and was branded as an atheist. Nothing could be further from the truth: he was trying to reach towards a transcendental notion of absolute virtue that could never be adequately conceived or expressed but could be sensed through various spiritual disciplines. It was quite clear that he had an inner spiritual life that related to the ultimate principle, the final wisdom. He could hardly be called an atheist, but must have appeared as such to many with a literalistic, anthropomorphic understanding of God. What it means is, 'What do you actually mean by atheism?'

It is often noted that the contrast between Greek and Hebrew thought is important; again an interesting paradox, for there is truth in both systems of thought. The Bible is almost completely based on the Hebrew assumption that the Eternal God is not just real but is a person with whom the believer can have a relationship. That is the whole basis of prayer: that God can speak to the believer and the believer can speak to God, an ongoing dialogue. For those who have never experienced this personal encounter, atheism is only to be expected, if not inevitable. But even so, the Hebrew frame of mind is a middle position between the high-flown philosophical attempts at reaching the ultimate truth (Greece) and the crudities of pagan idolatry (Canaanite and others). In the end it all comes down to what one means by 'God' and 'non-God'.

High-profile atheism: Richard Dawkins

Here is a case of a Fellow of New College, Oxford writing an influential book, *The Blind Watchmaker*,[7] on the subject of evolution, but also drawing conclusions on the theological level. It seems that evolutionism for him involves being an atheist. It is worth remarking that not all evolutionists, still less all biologists, are atheists. It is clear though that just as all theologians and philosophers have to make basic assumptions, which cannot be proven, the same is true for evolutionists, not least Dawkins himself. Evolution is his main assumption, and in places he makes it sound as if it is beyond doubt. It is worth saying that the idea that the world was flat was once thought to be beyond doubt: it turned out to be a complete mirage. Will the same happen to the assumption of evolution in times to come? One of Dawkins' assumptions, which appears several times in his book, is that almost certainly there are dozens of universes out there in space and that life is expected to exist on some remote planet (p. 164). This is the obsession of the modern age: quite an unsupported mania which may never be capable of proof or disproof. Still less does it have to have any relevance to alleged evolution on this planet.

It is interesting that Dawkins admits that there are various different versions of evolution in the world of scholarship. Accepting evolution is not such a simple matter as one might suppose. Since the times of Darwin, variant ideas have emerged and the pundits are not at all unanimous on how it was all supposed to have developed. It sounds at times a little like attempting to select the correct version of Christianity! But of course, Dawkins is scornful of all those who have 'the wrong theory'! What has changed since Darwin is the discovery that life in its various forms is far more complicated, interrelated and interdependent than we had realised, and this goes on getting deeper and deeper. The more we discover, the more there is to be discovered. There are still so many aspects of the natural world that have not been properly described, let alone explained.

This brings us back to the design theory as a proof for the existence of God, as developed by Paley with his watch. For most rational people, the image of Paley's watch is convincing, and becoming increasingly so.[8] Sadly this image has the opposite effect on Dawkins. He goes to great lengths to bring forth evidence that none of these wonderful things could possibly have been caused by something that might be termed 'God'. His arguments seem to become so fantastic in their attempt to avoid the obvious conclusion: if there is a design, that implies that there has to be a 'designer'.

Dawkins's argument is neatly summed up on page 5 of *The Blind Watchmaker*: 'The only watchmaker in nature is the blind forces of physics, albeit deployed in a very special way.' He continues: 'our modern hypothesis is that the job was done in gradual evolutionary stages by natural selection' (p. 37), and 'the watchmaker that is cumulative natural selection is blind to the future and has no long-term goal' (p. 50). This is his general assumption, but justifying it is not as simple as it would sound. It is easy if one cannot allow for any other alternative to evolution.

Dawkins lets slip a telling remark: 'This ... argument is frequently made ... because people want to believe its conclusion' (p. 80). How true! But in all these matters, theological, scientific or atheistic, what one wants to believe underlies virtually everything, and the conclusions are seen through the filter of one's own preconceived ideas. Evolutionists are no exception to this: belief or disbelief are the product of one's pre-existing inclinations. But the circularity of evolution may now be under a certain strain. There are people such as Michael Behe[9] who now maintain that certain features in the world of biology could not have been the result of gradual development over a long period: they had to have arrived with all their constituent parts fully functioning in the right order, otherwise they would not have functioned at all. This was something that Darwin himself wondered about, and thought that if it were true, evolution would be disproved: now it is coming home to roost! This matter usually begins with the complexity of the human eye, which Dawkins does discuss but will not admit to anything but a gradual development. But there are other factors in biology which follow the same pattern. Predictably the hardline atheist evolutionists will react with scorn on this matter, but well-balanced rational people will see it differently. They can see that it is possible that evolution is now on the brink of falling apart as a theory.

There have always been various problems with evolution. Dawkins himself admits to this. There is the fossil evidence, which is not consistent or continuous. Going back before life-forms would have (presumably) been capable of forming a fossil, there is so much conjecture as to what may or may not have happened. His book is punctuated with 'must-have-beens' and 'presumablies' and assumptions: in other words, unsupported guesswork. And because evolution has got to be true, we must all smile graciously and give him the benefit of the doubt. Even more disturbing is the reference to 'luck', 'good luck' and even 'bad luck', in this presumably scientific book! Also we have the mention of 'miracles' (see his Chapter 6)! How extraordinary! Surely these terms are a secularised version of 'God', 'the Devil' and 'Jesus' at work?! Also interesting is the 'missing ingredient of power' (p.153): would it not just be simpler to say that God is the power behind all these amazing processes? But Dawkins cannot see it.

Paradoxically, while the design theory is discounted here, the ontological theory almost breaks the surface: 'it leaves unexplained the origin of the Designer. You have to say something like, "God was always there" and if you allow yourself that kind of lazy way out ... you might as well say that "life was always there."' It may seem to him a lazy way out but to many it is the obvious and most honest way out. All the same, he is nearly there with the reality of God; all it requires is a slight rephrasing in theological terms.

Good and bad luck are somehow intermingled with extraordinary probabilities. We have monkeys playing with typewriters in the hopes of arriving at a phrase, 'methinks it is like a weasel', but not however getting as far as reproducing the works of Shakespeare. We have the intriguing image of a pile of scrap being thrust forth somehow to produce an airliner! We have amazing mathematical probabilities which render the development of life as needing more steps of development than the age of the earth would allow. We all know that probability is a mathematical construct and there is no 'fact' about it. The whole idea of these alleged coincidences is so fantastic as to elicit mirth. But these are the lengths that the evolutionists will go to, to avoid the admission of a guiding, creating hand. This is not to say that evolution is totally wrong: there may well be elements of truth in it in certain respects. But to dogmatise and say that it is the complete truth that can explain every aspect of things is asking too much of people's credibility. Also to say that evolution is blind and just goes ambling along with no sense of purpose or direction is a frightening thought. If that is true, then God help us!

But it may not be quite as simple as that. On page 72 we read this remark: 'It sounds as if evolution deals in distant targets as we have seen it never does. But if we think of our target as anything that would improve survival chances, the argument still works.'

One minute we cannot have a target, next minute we can. But the matter goes deeper than that. On the one hand we are told that evolution is blind, that there is no planning, foresight or direction. On the other hand we have things like luck, happenstance and odds at work. The substratum of this is the dilemma between free will and determinism, a paradox discussed earlier in this book. He admits to the dilemma between 'descent' and 'design' but does not develop the thought. We can: it is the paradox between free will and determinism.

Evolution has been the prevailing assumption for about 150 years, but it is high time that a different assumption took its place. There are various options available. What about balance in nature? What about circularity, as in the water cycle, the carbon cycle, and many others? Dawkins never mentions the possibility of animal intelligence, still less animal personality. A new major assumption is needed to occupy centre stage. This could be easier since it would not require endless gratuitous speculation over biological matters in the remote past. The fact remains that although we may think we know what happened many millions of years ago, we actually do not know, and may never be able to find out what happened for certain. It is time to resist the modern-day idolatry of allowing evolution to take centre-stage and rule all our thinking.

Dawkins will probably object to much of this book. Those who adduce analogies to illustrate their ideas are to be labelled as cranks. On the other hand, he does not hesitate to provide many interesting analogies, some of which are actually taken from the Bible! It is just possible that his atheism is that of misapprehension over the nature of God. For many people, God is somehow trapped in the mechanism of his own machine. It is the 'god of the gaps' mentality. When people have no explanation for a certain factor, it is then referred to God. But then, when an explanation does emerge, God is embarrassingly caught out yet again. To be fair to Dawkins, he does not appear to discuss this matter. Even so, there is the distinct feeling that behind it all is a 'power' activating all things. That is only a secularised scientific way of saying something about the creative impulse of God. God is not a part of his creation: he underpins the whole thing. Whether it is 'descent' or 'design' (using Dawkins' words) is of no importance, for God can use any method to achieve his works. God is entirely other than his creation and yet, paradoxically, he is nearer to every living soul, animal or human, than any of us can quantify. The mistake made by atheists is, so often, to allow God to become some sort of idol, a part of the created world, and a shrinking part at that. If anything, in our times he is an expanding part of life and reality. As we delve more deeply into the wonders of creation we can only be amazed at his brilliance.

Another avenue for future research is the notion that the world is a self-correcting mechanism. This implies that when something goes 'wrong', there are forces that bring about a rectification so that normality is achieved. This is not being done by humanity, normally, except that in recent times, with the environmental movement, we are seeing a greater awareness of the need to stop abusing or over-exploiting the natural world. This idea of self-rectification is just one aspect of the balance of nature, and it implies that there are forces at work to keep the world steady on its course. All of this should be reasonably easy to analyse since it is available to us now and is not locked up in the remote past. The theological implications of it could be interesting and relate well to the so-called proofs for the existence of God.

The second analogy from clockmaking

The title of Dawkins's book, *The Blind Watchmaker*, is a first-class contradiction, amounting to an oxymoron worthy of Shakespeare! Anyone who has experience of clock-mending or of watch repairs will know that there are certain requirements. Firstly, one's eyesight has to be first class: a magnifying glass or an eyeglass is commonly used to see the tiny intricate parts. Actually repairing a clock or watch is not too much of an ordeal. Even so, immense patience is the other requirement, for the clock may just refuse to work after all that time and fiddling about. Also experience is a valuable asset; one learns the hard way where the problems are likely to be found.

But actually making a clock is a whole different ball-game. Even if there is a pre-existent plan to follow with detailed dimensions set out, it is a tricky procedure. Without a plan and starting from scratch must be a much taller order: even so, it must envisage some sort of concept of the end product. Following a plan can be reasonably straightforward. It may take months to fashion all the parts. But then it does not work. This is where immense patience and determination come in, plus experience. The reason usually is because the distancing is faulty. This is the trickiest aspect of clockmaking. The teeth of the cogs and wheels must engage exactly right. Any slight inaccuracy will result in no result. The mistake will transmit itself right up the gear train to the escapement and mess things up.

We are talking about fractions of a millimetre. If the teeth are too far apart then they will miss or engage intermittently or clumsily. This is analogous to the atheist who does not really engage with God properly. If the teeth are too close together, the train is stiff and works in fits and starts, often jamming up altogether. This is analogous to the soul who is too close to God: the relationship is too intense and there is no let-up. He is the fanatic who throws common sense to the winds and embarks on all sorts of crazy ideas, often violent. But the teeth that are fairly spaced are not too close and not too distant. This allows the train to run freely in either direction. It can take endless patience and fiddling to achieve a well-balanced train. But this is the believer who engages with God in a fair relationship: not too tight and not too slack. It points up that we can be close to God, but there is a certain distance involved. The paradox is in the closeness versus the distance from God.

It is rubbish to talk about a 'blind watchmaker': a complete contradiction in terms! It was God who provided the plan and the components for the clock. But the fine-tuning of the distancing was achieved by the patience of the Messiah who came to adjust the cogs and make the train run smoothly.

In a way, Dawkins has provided us with a superb analogy from clockmaking. This image can only enhance and clarify faith, not destroy it. It is impossible to talk about the finely tuned mechanism of the world and indeed the universe without the implication of there being a plan and a 'clockmaker' of the highest order.

Humanism in relation to faith

Humanism is not necessarily atheism: Christianity and Humanism are not necessarily opposites. The relationship between Humanism and other systems of thought is not straightforward; in fact it is quite complicated. It would be fair to say that every Humanist has his own emphases and slant. It is not enough to say that Humanism is wrong: like all theological positions, it has its strengths and weaknesses. It also has its part to play in the balancing of things in the theological world.

Essentially, Humanism places faith in human nature. This does not necessarily rule out any part played by God, but in many cases it does. The modern liberalistic mind-set, coupled with varying degrees of materialism, certainly rules out evil either as a spiritual force or as a purely human trait. It also tends to reduce the influence of God; in some cases to rule out God altogether. For some it is linked to the theory of evolution, in that there is a (supposed) inevitable progression from crude, basic, illogical patterns of behaviour to more sophisticated, elevated and logical patterns. Some would say that eventually the human race will 'grow up' and will no longer need the guidance of God, as in earlier chapters of human history. Some would say that with scientific progress, all the answers to our problems will be found and there will be no 'gap' of unknowing which has to be filled in by the assumption of God.

Another strand in Humanism is the thought that morality does not need the assumption of God to give it motivation: one can practise 'Christian' ethics without reference to any divine guidance. For many this has become a neat excuse for avoiding any commitment to a religious group or Church.[10]

There are no easy, ready-made answers to this kind of thinking. It may be that every country or religious group will see these matters in a slightly different light. But to take it with the modern Western mind-set, whether Protestant or Roman Catholic, is perhaps the best starting point. It is probably true that much of the decline in church attendance and religious commitment can be explained by people's failure to see the relevance of God in modern life; also their view that morality (presumably) can function without the backing of religion. What people fail to appreciate is that the situation is markedly different in other parts of the world, where commitment is much stronger, and religions such as Christianity, Islam and Buddhism are making massive strides. It would be difficult to go into details about every differing situation. But for the Humanist who imagines that religion is on the decline, the answer is that it is not as simple as that: probably the opposite.

As far as the modern Western world is concerned, we are riding along on an unprecedented wave of material prosperity. This is all very comfortable for those enjoying it; there is a tendency to forget that not every part of the world is equally blessed. Even with aid organisations doing their best there is the will to airbrush these realities out of one's mind. The truth is that Western prosperity is very much at the expense of the Third World countries. It is only now that people are realising that there is no guarantee that this wave of prosperity will be sustained indefinitely. The waste situation coupled with emissions producing global warming are making responsible people consider the long-term consequences. If this modern world of prosperity did collapse, what would happen to all those wonderful ideas about evolutionary progress? The idea of an inevitable progress towards a lovely future is only wishful thinking; it is no more a fact than the mythological idea of a 'Golden Age' in the remote past.

It would not be the first time in history that complacency over material good fortune has tempted people to ignore God. 'Give us this day our daily bread' has ceased to mean anything for far too many people. The prophet Amos says (4:1): 'Hear this, you cows of Bashan ... who oppress the poor'. The northern kingdom of Israel went through a period of prosperity when they thought they could ignore God; so too the Roman Empire; so too the Communist Empire; what will happen to the American Empire? It all has to come to an end somewhere.

With regard to evolution, which figures large in modern thinking, most people take it as a proven fact. But there is no certainty about it at all. It is attractive as a biological theory because we have all been brainwashed with it. The truth may not be quite so simple: there may be aspects of it that are true at the biological level, but that does not have to mean it is true with regard to other areas, such as politics and religion. It is highly questionable to base one's social policy on it, and yet this has been done in the past, resulting in all manner of cruelties. Teilhard de Chardin[11] is being purely speculative when he says that humanity will evolve to something more wonderful in times to come. Time and again we have seen this assumption blown to smithereens by historical realities: the French Revolution, which was based on something called 'reason', degenerated into an unprecedented bloodbath; the optimism of the late nineteenth century descended into the carnage of the First World War. But these realities about the failures in human nature are regularly ignored in favour of some sort of optimistic speculation. The real answer is to apply humility, caring and fair play, and a willingness to repent: that is the Christian answer. The phrase, 'claiming to be wise they became fools' (Romans 1:22) comes to mind; it is important to beware of clever philosophical ideas which usually underpin humanistic ideas: they are usually faulty in some respect. With humility and a willingness to accept guidance from God, there is a far better chance of building a happier world.

It is interesting that St Paul was confronted by much the same dilemma as nowadays: perhaps there were not so many Humanists in the ancient world, and yet he says, 'Where is the wise man? Where is the scribe?'[12] (1 Corinthians 1:20). Jesus was confronted by the Scribes and Pharisees, the ones who thought they were very virtuous and clever. St Paul's answer is to say that God has made foolish the wisdom of the world. In short, the logic of God is not the same as the logic of humanity. Admittedly the Pharisees would claim to believe in God, and yet their approach to religion was to fabricate their own salvation by legal observances, which in effect removes the need for God in their system. For that reason, they can be seen as the equivalent of the Humanists in that age. Jesus criticised them for their hypocrisy and ostentatious religion that had no real basis; Paul criticised them for employing human logic and ignoring divine logic, that of the cross. The message of Jesus does sound infantile, naive and illogical to those who cannot see the deeper truth in it. Why else did he say that one has to accept the Kingdom of Heaven as a little child? It does not require clever arguments and philosophical analysis to know God, it just requires simple trust. For a Humanist to say that he can have morality without God means in effect that he trusts himself and does not need to trust God. That is a highly optimistic but basically foolish basis for life.

Relevant to this is the Christian doctrine of 'original sin'. Put in simple terms, this means that because Adam and Eve disobeyed God in the Garden of Eden, the human race has been infected with this failure right through history.[13]

Although the Bible does not actually spell out this line of thought, there are many references which do lend support to this kind of thinking: 'Behold, I was brought forth in iniquity and in sin did my mother conceive me,' (Psalm 51:5). This is the guilt-lament of one who has committed a serious misdemeanour, usually taken as David after the Bathsheba incident. But it does not necessarily spell out original sin. What it does spell out is the personal aspect of guilt and the need for release from it.

Much closer to this doctrine is 1 Corinthians 15:21: 'For as by man came death, by man came also the resurrection of the dead: for as in Adam, all die, so also in Christ shall all be made alive.' It must be stated that Paul in this passage is talking first and foremost about the importance of the Resurrection: without the reality of it, the Christian message is null and void. As a passing remark, this has supported the doctrine of original sin, but it is not a specific statement of it.[14]

This would have to wait until Augustine of Hippo spelt it out; he took the matter a lot further than the Bible: the sin of Adam condemned the whole of humanity to eternal damnation. Even though Christ had reversed the Fall, there was still 'evil concupiscence', the irrational desire to take pleasure in beings instead of God. Taking it even further, it was scarcely possible to have normal sexual relations without sinning. This is an assumption still current in Western thought, but it is not a Biblical notion, and has never been accepted by the Eastern churches. It is easy to condemn the extreme version of 'original sin' but of course the reality is that no human being is perfect: we all do something wrong somewhere along the line. This points up the need for the removal of guilt. Those who simply try to bury it or airbrush it out of their systems are not doing themselves any good: guilt will stack up and become a major problem especially if one has made a major error in one's life. If there is no God of mercy in one's life, offering release from these problems, then something else has to be found. Is the psychiatrist's couch a fully effective method?

To any Humanist who wishes to rule out God and ignore human moral failure, one should say, beware. Unresolved guilt can and does produce all manner of problems with health, social relationships, marital harmony, coping with religion, to name just a few areas. It is far simpler in the end to accept that there is a God of Mercy and that certain people, namely priests and ministers of various kinds, are empowered to dispense forgiveness. In this respect we see a serious weakness in Humanism in general terms, though it would be unfair to say that all Humanists are unable to cope with guilt.

In this we see another paradox emerging: it was the same dilemma as between Pelagius and Augustine, also between Erasmus and Luther. There are those who think humanity is essentially innocent and only goes wrong because of influence from evil in its various forms; there are those[15] who believe that humanity is essentially corrupt and needs to be influenced by the good. This dilemma is not confined to Christian theology: it is a bone of contention in the area of philosophy and other areas. It is very much allied to the dilemma over free will and predestination. In that case, we found that the solution is to say that both are true in their own way, and they form a paradox; why not say the same for innocence versus guilt?

It is interesting that the Gnostics thought that human nature is essentially corrupt. Also the Buddhists believe that desire is the root of all our problems. This reminds us of Augustine and 'evil concupiscence'.[16] It is not easy to discern what Jesus thought on the matter, since he never gave any direct indication. Perhaps the nearest we come to this would be the parable of the Wheat and the Tares (Matthew 13:24ff). If this can be taken to a certain degree of allegorisation, he is saying that at the start, the farmer sowed good seed on the land but it was spoiled by someone who played a filthy trick and sowed weeds (tares) later on. The implication is that if this is applied to human nature, we all began as innocent but evil was implanted later, but will eventually be removed, leaving the good as a residual quality. Whether Jesus was actually thinking like that or not is beyond us to say. The main thrust of the parable concerns the interim period and the moment of judgement at the end of time.
Another way of seeing this matter is to look at the parable of the Pharisee and the Publican (Luke 18:9ff). This does not actually talk about whether human nature is essentially good or evil. It concerns people's estimation of themselves, rather than some philosophical theory about human nature. Jesus begins with an example of one who is self-righteous and despises others whom he considers to be morally inferior. The Pharisee was praying 'with himself', which suggests that he was not actually praying to God, but to something

within himself, some sort of God-ego, perhaps. This is the one who thinks he can do without God's help in his life in the same way as the modern Humanists. Their righteousness is of their own fabrication. Jesus then contrasts this with the tax-collector 'standing afar off' who approached God with deep humility, not making a great parade of anything good he had done, and just begged for mercy, admitting his failures. But this one would receive forgiveness and be justified. It was not so much the details of one's conduct, rather it was the mental and spiritual attitude underpinning everything. To go through life with humility, and a willingness to admit to failure, is far healthier than boasting about how high one's morals are. Then comes a typical saying of Jesus, that if one exalts oneself, this will result in abasement; and the opposite if one is humble. This accords with 'the first will be last and the last first', and other sayings with slightly different wording. It is highly likely that to the modern Humanist, Jesus would say, 'you try to manufacture your own righteousness without reference to God: this is a fallacy and self-delusion. Seek rather to admit your failures and put your trust in God: that is the true and genuine righteousness.' Thus the paradox of 'the first and the last' is probably one of the easiest ones of Jesus to understand. Even so, those who think they are respectable and decent people will find it disconcerting. Those who have seriously failed in moral terms in life are the ones who really come to know the mercy of God.

But can humanity do without initiative and inventiveness? There is an important sense in that any kind of progress, discovery, improvement has to come from the ingenuity of mankind. It is surely instinctive that we have scientific enquiry, voyages of discovery and attempts at analysing just about every aspect of life. This is an important part of the human mentality and without it we would be all the worse off. But this must be tempered by the fact that to develop a new idea or technique is not easy: it may seem obvious after it is found, but actually finding it is a difficult process. It is important to remember that most of the great scientific discoveries were found purely by accident or coincidentally.[17] The same is true with most art-forms: it is not that easy to work up an entirely new idea. Most of the themes in drama now are a redevelopment of a pre-existing idea. The same is true with musical composition: virtually all the possibilities in that area have been worked into the repertoire of music already.

The answer is that in all these areas of discovery, whether scientific or artistic, there needs to be that important moment of inspiration, when a bright idea occurs and a new thing dawns on the inventive mind. This tells us that for all the cleverness and initiative in human nature there is also the need for inspiration which is not of our own inventing. This way we arrive at another paradox: that human progress depends on human curiosity and sometimes greed; on the other hand, it requires guidance and inspiration from the world of the spirit. The two sources converge into one.

There are those who assume that scientific enquiry and religious faith are in some sort of serious disagreement. This ignores the fact that many of our scientists have a commitment of faith in some sort of religion. It is unfortunate that the official line from certain Churches has been in contention with scientific enquiry. We recall how Copernicus and Galileo had problems with the dogmatism of the Roman Church. A similar problem has arisen today over the interference with the very building blocks of life, but this time is it not just the Roman Church, but the Protestants, the Jews and the Muslims who are showing concern. This time it is a moral issue; it is tied up with the Ten Commandments: 'Thou shalt not commit murder.' In other respects, however, the relationship between religion and science has been and still is a very positive one. It is easy to forget that in the era of the Enlightenment (in the seventeenth to eighteenth centuries) religion and science went very much hand in hand. In certain respects the same is true today. The paradox is that scientific enquiry reaches out to explain everything and remove the so-called 'God-gap'; conversely the 'God-gap' is enlarging all the time. The more we discover, the more there is to be discovered. God is not a shrinking explanation: he is an expanding reality underpinning the whole of life.

We need Humanism for that element of self-reliance and enquiry for any progress to be made in this world; on the other hand we need 'religionism' to place some sort of check on the morality of experimentation. In this way, the two 'isms' need each other to keep things in balance and proportion. Without this balance we either see science making free at the expense of humanity, or religion making free with far too much dogmatism, often in areas which have nothing to do with spiritual realities.

Certainty and doubt

To read Karen Armstrong's chapter on 'Unknowing',[18] one is struck by two things: firstly, that all the old certainties of the past are no longer certainties, and that includes so-called scientific facts; and secondly, that there is as yet nothing to take their place. Humanity is left in a sort of floating vacuum, at least the developed Western culture which is saturated with modern scientific and rationalistic assumptions.

There is an old saying: there are only two certainties in life, one is that you will die and the other is that you will pay tax! This is a populist way of saying something much more profound. It is absolutely true, but translated into more elevated jargon: one cannot avoid facing up to one's earthly ruler, and one cannot avoid facing up to eternity, one's heavenly ruler, one day. It is interesting that this now raises up the motif of sacral kingship, as seen in earlier chapters. Other than that there are no certainties in life, in spite of what the dogmatists tell us. This applies to science and religion just as much as to anything else. But of course we are left with two unavoidable factors: temporal rule and eternal rule. We are all subject to some sort of rule from somewhere, even the so-called free-thinkers.

Going beyond the basic certainties as mentioned, it is not possible to function without some sort of assumption or perhaps an entire collection of preconceived ideas. It is noticeable that almost always the liberalistic, humanistic framework of thought, varied as it may be, is some kind of reaction against a pre-existing dogma. Many examples of this could be adduced. One simple one can be discussed. If we look at the Enlightenment thinkers, who are the seedbed of modern Humanism, they were in reaction from the traditional thinking which seemed so hard. Their answer was to reduce God: remove him altogether or water him down to what they saw as something 'rational'. As we have seen, this is one of the methods of dealing with Theodicy; that is, remove God from the picture. Seldom, if ever, do we see a system of thought that has been conceived purely and simply out of 'thin air'. So often, possibly every time, there is some sort of substratum of Theodicy at work.[19] This is inevitable and only natural to human nature. After all, theologians and philosophers have been wrestling with the question since the dawn of time. It inevitably raises the question of God, however he may be conceived, and even attempts at not conceiving him. The question of everlasting 'right and wrong' rears up in the mind of every thinking person. But of course, there is no conclusive answer to it; neither can we stop thinking about it.

It is healthy that in the modern age there is so much debate, and searching in people's minds. The events of the Holocaust have done much to sharpen awareness of such matters. Complacency, which had become (and still is) a corroding influence on the human mind, has taken a sharp knock. What is rather odd is the failure of believing people and doubters to admit to the reality of evil and, going further, the personification of it in the Devil. Many can admit to 'God' in some framework of understanding, but little else. This is because they are in reaction against the overstated images of the Devil as in Mediaeval and later times. But this leaves us with no realistic explanation for the problems we face at the moment. It is easy to see how one situation led to another in history, on the physical side, and so we have the nuclear stalemate and the environmental problems of today. But few can see these developments and dangers as the result of adverse spiritual forces. Jesus probably would have seen it in such terms.

Religion as a bad thing

Some Humanists, but by no means all, see religion as a harmful factor in human life. They would like to see it expunged and life conducted on purely secular tenets. It is amazing that such a view still persists in the face of the evidence seen in the twentieth century. Several countries using a Marxist rationale have tried to remove religion and it has required extreme measures of persecution to make any kind of headway. The results are known to us all. Religion in Russia is now resurgent after many years of underground activity. The same is true in the former Eastern Bloc states. In China, in spite of extreme measures, religion persists in an underground capacity and the authorities are now having to face realities about it.

Some have argued that religion is the cause of all wars and that to remove it would ensure a peaceful future for the world. This is a deeply simplistic fallacy. The truth of the matter is that virtually every war is caused by some form of territorial claim or attempt to gain wealth, the two factors often closely related. The Second World War was a prime example of land-grabbing and attempts to secure resources contained in conquered lands.[20] Religion had hardly anything to do with it. Knowing that this amounts to greed and the guilt that emanates from it, religious ideas are worked into the rationale of it, to justify the aggression. Every belligerent nation likes to convince itself that 'God is on our side'. A reading of Homer's *Iliad* is a prime example of this thinking. The incident at Dunkirk was seen as divine intervention when the British and French armies escaped across the Channel in June 1940. People forget that the Germans had a similar experience in early 1945, when the River Elbe unfroze just in time to stop the Russians pouring straight into Germany. It is only natural to expect one's God to be on one's side. Again this is linked up with sacral kingship.

It is simplistic to say that religion is a bad thing. Like everything else in life, it can be used or misused, and this comes back to the urges and desires of human nature. There are strands of religious thought that advocate cruelty, violence and intolerance. There is no need to make a list here: we all know them. But how often do the anti-religionists admit that many strands of faith advocate peace, international cooperation, tolerance, helping the poor and underprivileged? What about the Christian teachers, doctors, technicians and many others who have given up a comfortable life in the First World to improve matters for the starving millions in the Third World? It is worth recalling that Jesus was deeply dissatisfied with many of the religionists of his day, for their hypocrisy and failure to see the wood for the trees. Essentially it is not about the outward appearances of religious activity: it is about the net results. 'By their fruits you shall know them' is the key to the whole thing. Never mind the labelling – atheist, Humanist, theist or whatever – if they can put love into practice, that is the clinching issue. For St John says, 'God is love, and he who abides in love abides in God and God abides in him,' (1 John 4:16). Can there be a higher and more helpful ethic than this? 'Let us love one another, for love is of God, and he who loves is born of God, and knows God,' (1 John 4:7). This cuts across all the 'isms' of humanity and unites all peoples of whatever creed or non-creed. All the philosophical arguments are as dross if they cannot have love, that deep caring, at the heart of their theories. Religion is only as good or bad as those who put it into practice.

Belief and disbelief in relation to space exploration

It is worth noting that when humans were first put into orbit round the world, there was a theological reaction. The Russian, Yuri Gagarin, remarked that when he orbited the earth he could see no sign of God. Was that what his political masters had instructed him to say? But the American astronaut, Alan Shepherd, came to the opposite conclusion: he could see God everywhere. It is very much a matter of what one expects to see and how one interprets what one sees.

There is no doubt that modern space exploration has had an enormous impact on theological thought. For those who think that God is an old man sitting on a chair up in the sky, there are now big problems. For those who do not wish to believe, it is easy to pour scorn on such anthropomorphic and literalistic beliefs. On the other hand, space exploration has made us aware of a great many factors not previously known about the universe. Out of the many examples that could be cited, one will suffice. The constellation with which we are so familiar, are stars which only appear to be related because of the angle at which we view them. In reality, not only are they stars of different qualities and magnitudes, but they are at different distances from us. This means that from somewhere else far out in space, they would not appear as related in a constellation. One could fairly say that a lot depends on what angle one is looking at things from, a truism valid in so many other aspects of life. Even so, it is difficult to escape the question: 'What does such a configuration of stars actually indicate?' The ancients turned these matters into various mythologies: even today when we identify new constellations, the same assumption creeps in.

The ancients gave them names; we do now. Also we have invented names like 'quasars' and 'black holes' and 'big bangs'. Always there is the inference that they hold significance for our existence and eternity. It is not possible to avoid the instinctive question, 'What does it signify?'

Going further, we are now aware of the vast distances in outer space, amounting to trillions of light years. It is difficult enough to comprehend one light year, the distance light travels in one earth year. These are quantities that the human mind simply cannot assimilate. The same is true for the many millions of stars: those that we see on a clear night are only a small fraction of what is really out there. The full complement of them is well beyond our imagination or calculation. Then we come to such phrases as 'the edge of the universe': does this actually have any meaning? We have to admit that trillions of light years away, we have absolutely no idea of what is there, or not there. But to contemplate all the features out in space, galaxies, circulatory motion, gravity, nebulae, has to raise the question: 'What does it all mean, why is it all there?' And more particularly, 'Why is our small planet a hive of activity, whereas others that we know of, are not?' This is not the same as asking by what processes did all these matters come to pass. That is the concern of the various sciences, and as yet they are only just beginning to scratch the surface.

But the question 'Why?' is for the theologian and the philosopher to tackle. The philosopher will try to work it out in terms of secular phraseology, trying to leave out religious assumptions. In this he will probably not succeed. This is because we all have some sort of mythological or religious assumptions at the back of our minds, even if they are negative ones. The theologian will attempt a solution with a mythological or religious backdrop, often attempting to work in current philosophical assumptions. This is nothing new: Christian exponents at various times in the history of the Church have used ancient Greek philosophies of varying kinds to support their theories. Whether it be secular or religious theorisings matters not: one will only ever make any progress in such matters when one comes to admit that the 'universe', or whatever it is that we are a part of, can only make sense in terms of purpose, beauty and reason. To put it another way, the universe has laws governing it, it is wonderful, awe-inspiring, and has some sort of meaning and destiny. If you think about it, that is a secularised version of the Trinity: Father (laws), Son (reason, that is, *logos*) and Holy Spirit (inspiration).

Once we admit to these matters, we are clearly on the way to reaching out to God. These matters are beyond our comprehension and yet there is still the opportunity at least to try to assimilate them and draw conclusions which are relevant to us here and now. For those who cannot see any purpose, reason, destiny, wonder, regulation, then the universe will remain meaningless; this is the ultimate form of atheism.

Now let us turn the argument completely around, like Hick with the ontological argument. If it were possible, can we see it from God's point of view? Not easily, but let us ask the question: 'What is God trying to tell us?'

The ancients thought that the world was a three-tiered arrangement; others thought it was egg-shaped. That does not matter. It was God's way of telling them, in their own thought-forms, that life is eternal, that there is the world of the spirit, and that there is eternal justice. The assumption that the world is the centre of the universe is now seen to be physically wrong; but spiritually, and paradoxically, human life on this planet is central to the life of the universe. To put it another way, the universe only has final meaning if it nurtures and protects the germ of life in one tiny corner. God is saying, 'Even though you are a tiny speck of life you are of great significance for the entire creation.'

We consider the constellations. Rationally we know that they are only points of light making interesting patterns. What is that telling us? It told the ancients, and us today, that outer space is not meaningless: it is there for us to interpret. At the very least they tell us of the magnificence and wonder of it all. There are those who take it a lot further and go in for astrology: some people regard this as nonsense: others take it very seriously in today's world. But let us remember that God speaks to us not just in our own language but in our own thought-forms too. A lot of this can be dubbed 'emotional', but then we are emotional people. Even Mr Spock in *Star Trek*, who was claimed to have no emotions, managed to form an attachment with a young lady! We are emotional people and it is impossible to side-step this matter.

Then to consider the planets, some of which were not known in ancient times, we have known about the effect the Moon has on matters on Earth. But now we are coming to realise the effect other planets are having in their respective orbits. A good example would be Jupiter with its massive gravitational pull: this has the effect of 'vacuuming up' all sorts of rubbish floating about in space, rubbish which could rain down on us and cause havoc. The same may well be true for the other gas and ice giants, Saturn, Neptune and Uranus. The more we investigate, the more amazing and purposeful it all becomes.

Turning to the Sun, this has always had immense theological significance in almost every culture, and still does. Investigation has simply underlined the importance of the Sun and Earth's relationship to it, essential to life. There are many aspects of the Sun that are at the moment beyond explanation but it is clear that it must have been 'born' and one day will 'die': but its life-span is expected to be millions of years. This can be worked out by studying other suns (stars) in their varying stages of life. All this serves to show us that we are dependent on factors way beyond our control, but it is reliable and consistent for the foreseeable future. But there is the inference that just as there was a beginning, there will be an end. Even if physically those two things are a long way apart, spiritually they are essentially balanced.

What is God saying to us in these matters? Firstly, he is saying, 'I planned it all very carefully, far more intricately than you may ever realise.' Also, 'Everything in the created universe has meaning and purpose and is there to tell you something.' And also, 'My glory and eternity are well beyond you to take in, but that does not mean you cannot keep on trying to explore and explain.' Just as God spoke to the ancients in their own thought-forms, in terms of mythology and even superstition, now he is speaking to us in the modern assumptions of rationality, explanation and purpose.

This is an interesting example of how the logic of God and the logic of humanity actually appear to converge and complement each other. God shows us reason and purpose in the workings of the creation; we are looking for the same things in all our attempts at understanding the universe. Virtually every religion on earth makes this fundamental assumption. The essential difference that Christianity brought was this: that the rationality of the Eternal is not just a mindless machine, it is a living person who also has emotions like us. That person is the eternal *logos*, Jesus the Messiah.

A paradigm on the apportionment of truth

There was a mansion with many rooms and doors. Some doors had one lock, some two, and some even three. There was a variety of locks: some were Yales, some five-lever, some padlocks and others cheap three-lever locks which could be fiddled with a hairgrip. All the doors were locked, but there were people outside who wanted to get in and explore this fascinating residence. The master of the house had various bunches of keys, none of them labelled. Some bunches had a lot of keys, other bunches had just a few. Some bunches had keys in common, but every bunch had at least one key that was different from all the others. The master gave the people various hints about opening the front door, but after that it was all going to be guesswork and trial and error. Nightmare!

Fred, who had the largest bunch, assumed that he had all the keys, and told the others to keep back and let him open all the doors. This soon proved to be a mistake, for although he managed to open the dining-room and drawing-rooms, there were many smaller rooms, the doors of which he could undo one lock but not the other one. When it was suggested that someone else's key would be needed, he felt threatened and went on the defensive.

Jim, who had a small bunch, assumed that he could only ever open a few doors. But since no one knew how many rooms there were, it was a puzzle as to how many keys would be needed in total. Even so, it soon became apparent that some of his keys were non-duplicates, and were essential for opening some doors.

Charles, who had another small bunch, flew into a rage, flung his keys down and stalked off to take up residence in the stables. He alleged himself to be quite happy with that, in spite of the residual smell left by the animals.

And then there was Pam, who could see that cooperation was the only way forward, as opposed to competition and loss of tempers. She picked up Charles's bunch of keys and suggested that they all went round together. In spite of the pique showed by Fred who still imagined he had a key for every door, it worked. They opened up many rooms until, mesmerised by the size and complexity of the mansion, they decided to go and relax in the dining-room, which had some superb pictures on the wall. It had become clear that they all needed each other in some way or other, and even then they were overwhelmed by the sheer size and magnificence of the mansion.

And so it is with God's truth, and indeed the basic truths about life. We can behave like Charles and give up; that is the person whose faith has gone and he simply crawls off into a corner to try not to think about things. Vain hope: the realities of life and death still press down on us. It is impossible to stop wondering what the deep truths of life and death really are. Having dumped his keys, the others who still did have faith soon found they could adapt what he had rejected and find some answers to certain questions.

Fred, who was really quite sure he had the answer to everything, a dogmatist who could not face the thought of discussing matters with someone of a different opinion, still less having to admit that they might have a partial answer, or could offer an alternative view of things, was quite happy to issue remarks about 'heresy' and 'the work of the Devil'! Even so, he had to admit that certain areas of truth could only be opened by the use of two keys or sometimes three, some of which he did not have.

Jim, however, was quite glad that someone else had a wide selection of keys, but was amused to find that occasionally he had one that was actually essential. He was less of a dogmatist and more of a listener. He was more aware than the others that the final truth about the mansion would hardly be uncovered even if collectively they did have enough keys.

There were some doors that needed all three of them, Pam, Fred and Jim, to insert a Yale key into three locks all together, otherwise the door would not open. It did not mean that one key was correct and the others wrong: it meant that each key was correct in its own way and could not be omitted. At last they all had to admit that they were unable to unlock every door even if they did have the right keys; they were mesmerised and totally confused.

So it is with the vast array of opinions on the subject of religion and God's truth. All of us are granted a portion of it initially; some more than others. There is the temptation to imagine that because one has a large portion, that this is the full amount of truth. There is the despair in thinking that because one has a small portion, that will never be enough. But in God's wisdom, all the keys are needed, and all those with a smattering of faith can contribute something somewhere. So we gain access to the front door and the main rooms. Many faithful people are content with just that and will sit back to admire the pictures, have something to eat in the dining-room, and feel glad that the owner allowed them on to his premises. But also there are many who cannot desist from speculating on the finer points of God's truths. The theologians, philosophers and theorists must probe into the deeper recesses. They have the keys to do it, but far too often they see it as some sort of competition rather than as constructive debate. Seldom does anybody see the situation as paradoxical, in that no one key, or bunch of keys, is the complete answer.

But God's truth is above and beyond us in this world. Some of the basic truths are shown to us as a starting point: various religions do have an array of factors in common. But after that, there are all kinds of permutations and fumblings with keys. Quite often an insight from another religion is of value. But the whole truth about

God is far too overwhelming for mortal man, and it gets to the point that even if we do have the right keys, we cannot cope with the sheer effort of finding and opening any more doors.

But the paradox is that we need all of these people, including the atheist. All their keys are needed to open up the great paradoxes of truth found in so many of the rooms in the mansion.

Notes

1. William Doyle, *The Oxford History of the French Revolution*, 1989.
2. Charles Graves, *The Legend of Linda Martel.*
3. Karen Armstrong, *The Case for God*, especially the chapter on 'Unknowing', pp. 252ff.
4. Op. cit., p. 270. Paul Tillich, *Theological Works.*
5. The sources of the Pentateuch, see H. H. Rowley, *The Growth of the Old Testament* for a full discussion of J, E, D & P.
6. Armstrong, pp. 64–70.
7. R. Dawkins, *The Blind Watchmaker.*
8. J. Hick, Arguments for the Existence of God, p.3ff
9. M. Behe, *Science and Evidence for Design in the Universe*, 1999, Ignatius Press.
10. Karen Armstrong, op. cit., chapter on 'Atheism', pp. 227ff.
11. Teilhard de Chardin, *Man's Place in Nature*, pp. 112 et al.
12. I Corinthians 1ff.
13. Bettenson, *Early Christian Fathers*, pp. 278, 151. Origen and Tertullian have a much more liberal approach to the question.
14. Bettenson, op. cit., p. 75: St Augustine and Pelagius.
15. Bettenson, op. cit., p. 295: Luther and Erasmus.
16. 'Evil concupiscence' is a phrase stemming from Augustine through to the Reformation: it is now out of favour.
17. A prime example of this is the discovery of America by Columbus: he was expecting to find India and it was a long time before the Spaniards realised that a new continent had been found.
18. Karen Armstrong, *The Case for God*, pp. 252ff.
19. Op. cit., pp. 231ff.
20. The Second World War was primarily about land-grabbing: the clash between Fascism and Communism was the excuse for aggression rather than the reason for Hitler's aggression.

19

Religion with Problems

It would be fair to say that there is no religion that is without its problems: the perfect system has not yet been found. The same is true with politics: Churchill would have said that there is no perfect political system; democracy is, however, the best of a bad bunch. But in pointing out the faults of each system there is the need to accept that there can easily arise a situation of the 'pot calling the kettle black'. We need to be clear on our criteria: judgement is not easy, and Jesus himself did not wish to issue easy judgements. It can so easily lead to arrant hypocrisy.

But what criteria can we employ fairly? Firstly, a religion ought to be faithful to its own basic and original tenets. If it has strayed a long way from its founder's original ideas or slid into something else which is contradictory to its own creed, then it clearly has a problem. Applying external criteria in judgement can raise difficulties but there are some basics which ought to be in place as applicable to all belief-systems. Questions that can fairly be asked could be: Is this religion in favour of peace? Is it in favour of fair treatment for people of different classes, races, cultures and ideas? Does it indulge in persecution? Is it a system that embarks on exploitation or some form of cruelty? Many of these remarks could be labelled as humanistic presuppositions: does this mean that Humanism is now 'playing God' in judging everything except itself? It will only be fair to judge all the 'isms'. A basic assumption here will be whether any given 'ism' is actually harmful to other people: 'harmful' means, I assume, destructive of life, property and health in its broadest sense and communal interests. Each person should be free to make his choice, but within this framework, what will be the effect on other people? It would be difficult to analyse every religious group in this chapter, but the main ones should be reviewed.

Christianity: strengths and weaknesses

A serious problem with Christianity (at least since the Reformation) has been its rampant disunity. This need not have been a problem if Christ had said 'you can all split up and have differing ideas and practices'. But he said the opposite: he wanted them all to be one. This only makes sense if there is one God, one Messiah, one baptism, one Church. We can trace disunity back to the very early heresies and schisms and we must ask the obvious question: why? It has been seen in the earlier chapters that there has been a serious failure to cope with the paradoxes implicit in Christian teaching. The fact that the word 'paradox' itself was not employed in this context fully until the twentieth century is significant. But even without the word itself, there could have been a more sympathetic approach to what must have been seen as the deep theological contradictions in the faith. But this failure to cope with paradox has resulted in a plethora of denominations, some large and some tiny, plus splinter groups, often cancelling each other out and making it difficult for a potential proselyte from another faith to make a sensible choice. It has been called the scandal of Christianity. It is only in recent times, over the last few decades, that there have been stirrings of conscience over Christian disunity. The ecumenical movement has made much progress in recent times but there is still a heavy legacy of distrust and misunderstanding blocking the process.

There is the disturbing tendency to say that some other group with a different opinion cannot be regarded as Christian. This is a neat way of skirting the problem of disunity, but not a very honest one: it verges on the idea of noticing a speck in one's brother's eye but failing to notice the log in one's own eye. It all depends on what one means by 'Christian'. The World Council of Churches (something which did not exist 100 years ago) has defined a Christian as one who accepts Jesus as Lord. This is a very wide definition and allows for all manner of permutations in belief. But it is a good umbrella statement for uniting such a varied collection of people as the Christians.

The Protestant tendency for splinterisation has sadly encouraged extremist splinter groups which regard themselves as the only Christians. Because of their peculiar views and attempts at avoiding compromises with other groups, they have actually caused damage to society and the faith in general terms. We have only to think of those groups that demand a separation from one's family and friends to realise that there are big problems latent in that. However, in spite of this, the general tendency in recent times has been a rapprochement between the Protestants and the Roman Catholics. The Eastern Orthodox seem not to have these problems, presumably because they do not have the difficult legacy of a Reformation situation in their history. This may be a disturbing thought for some, but it may be that the sixteenth-century Reformation is at last heading for closure and conclusion. There is now so much cooperation, renewed understanding and erosion of prejudice that the thought of one Church is just below the horizon of a lovely day of unity.

If the dicta of Jesus were to be taken seriously by those who reckon themselves to be Christian, we would have unity of purpose, a minimalisation of judgement and a willingness to love those who have a slightly different approach to things. This does not have to mean that all Christians will have to employ the same methods of worship; they probably never did, right from the start. But it does mean a willingness to listen to God and other people, rather than to tell God how right one's own opinion is and force it on to other people.

There is a feeling amongst Christian people that their religion is about peace and harmony. It does not seem like that to people of other faiths. We must recall that the Christians behaved rather badly over the Crusades, had an ongoing persecution of the Jews, and the Christian nations of Europe were the main instigators of three major world conflicts. All this is a difficult legacy and hangs over us like a toxic spider's web of guilt. Even so, we have learnt many lessons over this: Christian initiatives for world peace have been a major factor in the formation of the United Nations, and peacekeeping in general throughout the post-war years.

The question of guilt is also a difficult one. There are those who wish to give it far too much emphasis in relation to other matters. The result has been that going to church is, for many potential worshippers, a serious matter which requires a solemn face. The heart of the matter should be joy and triumph of the Resurrection, and while certain elements in the faith are prepared to make this a reality, many do not. Also, death is a major factor for many. This results in endless visits to the cemetery and elaborate formulae for funerary observances. All this would have made Jesus laugh, for the faith is essentially about life, and everlasting life at that.

More serious is the fundamental disagreement within the faith over the interpretation of the Bible. This cuts across denominational frontiers. The modern liberal approach has in effect meant that the Bible (literally and figuratively) can no longer be taken as authoritative in the way that it was before. With one's terms of reference very largely undermined, it is difficult for any Christian exponent to speak with confidence on any matter. Just going in for fundamentalism is not the answer: that too has its own set of problems. At the moment Christianity is swaying about with every contrary breeze that occurs. This is unsettling for those who do love their neighbour and embark on kind acts of mercy, and commitment to the poor, the needy, the sick and the dying. But the true worth of Christianity now lies not so much in its doctrinal lines, which at best are now somewhat wobbly, but in its kindly deeds in a world of turmoil and fear.

Judaism

In spite of all the vicissitudes of history, Judaism has survived and is now flourishing in its original homeland. Endless persecution from many quarters has given the Jews a resilience that people of many other faiths simply do not understand. Is Judaism faithful to its own terms of reference? The answer must be 'yes': the laws of Moses as given at Sinai are still paramount. Also the proliferation of legalisms continues. Jesus put a large question mark against the way that this was being done. Even so, within their own terms of reference, they are consistent and deeply committed. The Torah is everything. There are those who would deride their strict *kosher* practices, but this is only within their terms of reference. Another criticism would be over their readiness to take revenge. This conceals a basic unspoken assumption that 'one should love one's enemies'. But the Jews do not have such a stricture: they are not Christians and there is nothing in the Torah to forbid them from dealing harshly with anyone who attacks them.

Centuries of anti-Semitism have forced them to stick together, a kind of ghetto mentality and inward-looking stance. This has made them an easy target for persecution and discrimination. The Holocaust has awakened a new sympathy for them and also made them more outward-looking. It is now much easier to convert to Judaism than before. Israel, and its connections in many countries, is now becoming a major influence in world affairs even if the numbers of

Jews are relatively few. They are absolutely determined not to allow themselves to be humiliated as before. That is well within their terms of reference. Also the idea of them being a light to the Gentiles (Isaiah) is now becoming a reality.

Judaism, strictly speaking, is a messianic faith: the hope of the First Coming is still there (not the Second Coming). This is where many fail over their terms of reference, for many are lukewarm and even negative about this expectation. Also there are contradictory feelings about the Temple in Jerusalem. Both of these elements are in the Old Testament: the Temple law actually is in Deuteronomy; the messianic teaching is in the Prophets.

With regard to peace, fair treatment for people, and so on, it is difficult to address these matters with hooliganistic elements attacking one's country from within and without. Even so, the modern Jew, not under pressure, would surely be in favour of egalitarian principles and concord between nations.

Hinduism

This is a religion which is so diverse and varied that to assess it is difficult. Also it may not be everything that it superficially appears to be. It has been influenced by Christianity and Islam: this means that we do not have a clear starting point.

With all its variations, it is probably fair to say that Karma is at the heart of this faith, a prevailing common denominator. To Westerners and to Hindus themselves, the harshness and mechanistic remorselessness of it seem difficult. The result of it has been a strict caste system in India, with a substratum of outcastes. It was not possible to move from one caste to another or intermarry. Modern India has in legal terms moved away from this and yet even so there is still the legacy of this system. The unfairness of it has stimulated three other 'heresies', Jainism, Sikhism and Buddhism. This is a problem for Hinduism, even if 'caste' and Karma are within their terms of reference.

Also, in spite of frequent references to 'righteousness', there is no clear definition of what it consists of. There is nothing analogous to the Ten Commandments or any other clearly defined rules of conduct. There is no founding father of this faith to whom one can refer for definitive moral, ritual or spiritual guidance. There is much in the

Hindu scriptures, but nothing firm or generally accepted as a basis of belief and practice. To put it bluntly, you can believe what you like and include any other religions within the caste system, if you like.

Many have commented on the polytheistic nature of Hindu thought, a mind-set which seems absurd to the monotheists of the West. It is only fair to say that Hinduism is only being faithful to its own traditions. It is true that Hindus have Brahma as the supreme God, and some have seen this as a kind of 'monotheism'. But to do this would mean downgrading all the lesser gods to something equivalent to angels or devils. Hinduism can also be called idolatrous, but that is judging it by the tenets of other religions.

With regard to notions of peace, Hinduism has not been noted for an aggressive attitude. As regards fair treatment for less fortunate people, the assumption with Karma is that one has merited one's condition from one's conduct in a previous life. Consequently, Hinduism has not been noted for charitable giving or such things as international aid. Egalitarianism and democracy have been a blind spot in India, although in fairness, with the influence of the British, the position of women, especially widows, and of the lower classes, has significantly improved. Who would have expected the country to have a woman prime minister?

One is left with the impression that Hinduism is a very broad school of thought that can reasonably absorb new ideas which contradict traditional thinking. Perhaps this is a plus for Hindus, in that they can adapt to the modern world without it precipitating a crisis. A specific case of this would be Mahatma Gandhi. His was a non-violent campaign for equality and freedom, also for unity for all the peoples of the subcontinent of whatever religion. Sadly this did not all work out in fact. Even so, Gandhi's influence was immense and remains so. His remark, 'there is no God but Truth', is a valuable statement. Clearly there is Christian influence there.

Buddhism

With this system we see a clearly defined founder-member even though accounts of him can be legendary and blurred in the mists of antiquity. He gave up his royal status to become a mendicant and found an 'enlightenment' which would allow anyone to escape the pain and futility of life. In this respect, Buddhists are faithful to

Siddhartha in that they embark on a monastic pattern of life, some permanently and some just for a short time, and their technique is concerned with meditation in order to find or prepare oneself for Nirvana.

It is unlikely that Siddhartha ever expected his followers to split up into major or minor groupings, still less to develop something like Lama-ism as in Tibet. More likely he expected the Karma situation of Hinduism to be escaped from so that all could achieve Nirvana. As a break-away from Hinduism, Buddhism has not actually worked: it has simply produced a non-ritualistic version of the same thing. It is interesting that Siddhartha was not more radical and did not break away from the whole idea of Karma; Buddhism is essentially dependent on another faith even though it is a reaction to it. It is in fact very difficult to make a complete break with one's parent religion. The Protestants found this with regard to Roman Catholicism.

How far the Wheel of Becoming is original to Siddhartha's thinking is a good question. The basic idea of the cycle of rebirth is fair enough within its own terms of reference, and the idea that Buddha is present at all stages in mercy to offer release is a helpful thought; but it may be little more than that. There are all kinds of speculative notions about heavenly bodies and Bodhisattvas in the world of the spirit, but relating this to real events and historical people is a more speculative matter. There is a lot of high-flown thinking of a Gnostical tenor which is a problem for anyone who cannot cope with it. Salvation appears to be a gift for the mental gymnast.

It is to be noted that gods, mythical or otherwise, are very much a feature of Buddhism, even though Siddhartha managed to sideline them as irrelevant. Indeed Buddhism could be said to be essentially a non-theist faith, but this would be a case of the founder-member's intentions being somewhat distorted.

On a more mundane level, the monasticism of Buddhism has been accompanied by a lack of emphasis on family values and life. It is symptomatic that there is no marriage ceremony. People of other faiths find this difficult to take. Also the system of mendicant monks is questionable, even if it is consistent with the life of Siddhartha.

On the positive side, Buddhism has in recent times been a force for world peace, and it would be true that pacifism is an important factor in Buddhists' thinking. They have not started any major wars, although minor outbursts of violence have been noted.

Islam

Islam is claimed to be a united faith and indeed it is in comparison with many others. However there are deep disagreements at work which seem to erupt into violence. The Sunnis and the Shi'ites are the main groups and they disagree over who was to be the true successor to Mohammed; there are also smaller groups. One would suspect that Mohammed would not have been happy with this. He was not in favour of conversion by force, nor did he wish to clash with anyone who was a monotheist. But the course of Islam has sadly shown a departure from these criteria, not least in the deadlock between Judaism and Islam in the Middle East.

Islam's strict monotheism and ban on idolatry has been consistent to the present day; also its five pillars. In that sense Muslims are true to their original terms of reference. For many non-Muslims polygamy is a problem, but to be fair, this was seen as acceptable from the start. This is balanced by the fact that each wife and her children must be fairly treated and the marriage contract properly observed. Divorce may appear easy but the reality is that there is a strong sense of family unity and responsibility. For the Western world, female inequality is difficult to take, and yet this is spelt out in the Koran, which means Muslims are only being consistent with their own terms of reference. Even so, nothing is said about women's apparel in the Koran.

The original tenor of Islam was for equality between all believers. Symptomatic of this is the lack of any kind of sacral hierarchy. The result of this, putting it very crudely, is that every Muslim is his own 'vicar'. One might have expected this to result in some kind of egalitarian political system of democracy. Sadly this has not been the case: so many Muslim countries have either some kind of absolutist monarchy or a totalitarian dictatorship. One might expect Mohammed to have been unhappy with this. Still less would he have approved of the recent wave of terrorism perpetrated by Islamic extremists. The vast majority of Muslims fundamentally disagree with this.

All this is quite unfair on a faith which enjoins submission (the basic meaning of 'Islam') and doing acts of kindness to the poor and needy. Almsgiving is one of the five pillars of Islam.

Within its own terms of reference, Islam is probably one of the most consistent religions to be found. Even so, with the current problems it has a difficult reputation to cope with. People do not like violence, threats and heavy dogmatisms.

Confucianism

The founder member, Confucius, was a notable moralist and teacher and his tenets have probably done more than anything else to condition the mentality of the Chinese people down to the present day. His ideas were very much a this-worldly theory, very largely about respect. Underlying this is possibly a naive optimism about the goodness of human nature. As far as gods were concerned, he might be classed as an agnostic: they are not really of any relevance in day-to-day affairs, that is if they exist at all. He might have been in agreement with many a modern Humanist.

It would seem strange then that later generations sought to deify Confucius. He might have found that rather strange, if not amusing. He never made any grandiose claims for himself. Temples were built in his honour and rites performed.

Although there is not a clear idea of God in Chinese thought, Confucius believed that 'heaven' was in favour of his ideas. The phrase 'the Mandate of Heaven' is claimed to be important in Chinese thought. It refers to the right of a ruler to rule not because of heredity but because of moral worth. It is said that the Communists are concerned that the Chinese people will revoke 'the Mandate of Heaven' should the regime become over-oppressive or destructive of traditional values.

One of the main values in China is that of family respect and solidarity. Ancestor worship is one symptom of this. To Western ears this may sound superstitious but it may not amount to that in the Chinese mind-set. We have to remember that Confucianism is very much a this-worldly system of thought. It complemented Taoism quite well as that was far more interested in the spiritual side of things.

Difficulties arose in the twentieth century, well before the Communist upsurge. Many felt that Confucianism, with its tendency to hold back progress, should be marginalised if not stopped. Emphasis on family life meant that the elderly had to be cared for and obeyed; this meant that women were home-bound. Confucius' ideas of a Golden Age in the past, meant that people tended not to look forward. Under the Communists with their materialistic policy of rapid industrial development, there was no time for traditional values. China has been through a traumatic twentieth century, but even so the Confucianist mentality is still prevailing. In spite of all the violence and persecution, the Chinese are still essentially peaceful and respectful people.

One difficulty has been the Communist policy of population control, by which only one or two children may be had. The traditional view is that a son is needed to continue the family line and worship. People have gone to all kinds of subterfuges to obtain a son: a daughter is not the same. This is an example of a traditional value conflicting with a modern government policy. In spite of this, Confucianism could stand out as one of the faiths that is most faithful to its original tenets.

Taoism

Founded by Lao Zu in the distant past of China, this was principally a philosophy which taught the minimalisation of state control and the pursuit of individual happiness through meditation and reverence for nature. Strangely, the Tao, a profound metaphysical concept which guides and motivates the whole universe, is not styled as God: it is the Jade Emperor and his minions who are divine. One could see it as a kind of Gnosticism. But it did not remain as such for involvement with spirits, gods, the occult, spiritual healing and exorcism came in. As such it diverged very largely from the worldly, moralistic and bureaucratic elements of Confucianism and so formed a counterpart to that faith. Many will find the superstitious element, which is close to shamanism, difficult to take and yet it still survives in spite of all that the Communists have done to suppress Taoism. Now that persecution is easing off, Taoism is thought to be resurfacing in China.

There are splits and different groupings in Taoism but this matters little as there is no particular call for unity. Taoism has coexisted with Confucianism and Buddhism in China for hundreds of years with no particular friction.

A useful concept which may coincide with the Western approach to understanding God, is that the Tao ('way' or 'path') cannot be expressed in words: it is beyond definition. Even so, the Tao is the principle responsible for the creation of all things. There is much in Taoist philosophy which is useful and yet undogmatic. 'Nothing is softer than water and yet it is stronger than anything when it attacks hard and resistant things. Gentleness prevails over hardness: weakness conquers strength.' Profound. No less the yin–yang symbol, which is not confined to Taoism, with its thoughts on masculine and feminine attributes, as discussed earlier, is an example of the subtlety and depth in Taoist thinking and an approach to Theodicy. It is a pity that thoughts on morality and personal conduct have to be supplied by other faiths.

The attitude to prolongation of life in interesting. Again this is something which crept in later when Taoism developed into a religion. There were claims that meditation would prolong life. Also breathing exercises, sexual exercises, the eating of rare plants and the use of cinnabar were tried. Alchemy became a mania with certain people obsessive about lengthening their lives. Not that alchemy was confined to China: in the West it was seen as hocus-pocus and contradictory to the basics of faith. Even so, the alchemists, in their attempts at fabricating gold, made all kinds of useful chemical discoveries, quite incidentally. No one has managed to extend human life, but the urge is still there in today's world. For the Christian, life is a new life in this world as well as the next, and death is merely a transition.

With Taoism's reverence for nature we can see a possible agreement with the recent Western environmentalist interest. This is in itself basically a Biblical concept, even though many environmentalists would not necessarily claim to be Christian.

Shintoism

This indigenous religion of Japan does not have a founder-member. It is very close to shamanism and has had a strong element of sacral kingship until 1945. It is important to distinguish between State Shinto and Shrine Shinto, only two of many divisions and splinter groups in Japan. Since there is no particular reason for unity within this religion, its disunity cannot be cited as a criticism, any more than with Hinduism.

State Shinto is a feature augmenting from 1871 until its collapse in 1945. It involved an extreme form of nationalism with the Emperor as a sacral king, and with a world view which involved Japanese supremacy and the absorption of all other religions into Shinto. The horrific results of this are known to us from the course of the Second World War, with extremes of violence and cruelty to others and to themselves. Mercifully this all came to an end and the Emperor renounced his divine status. We are left with Shrine Shinto which is a much more moderate and gentle mentality, even if the Emperor is still associated with the Goddess Amateratsu.

As with Hinduism, there are many gods associated with every aspect of the natural world and human life. It is a personal faith, a family faith and a local community expression. On that level, its ceremonies and procedures give a strong bonding and identity to the Japanese people. On the other hand, Shinto has very little relevance to other races or nations. It would be fair to say that one needs to be born into Japanese culture to be a Shintoist.

Conversely, Shinto has shown itself capable of accommodating just about any other religion that has reached Japanese shores. The chief example of this has been Buddhism which has managed to intertwine itself with Shinto so that they complement each other quite happily. Many Japanese would claim to be both things at once and see no contradiction in it. Many are married as Shintoists and buried as Buddhists. Elements from other faiths such as Confucianism have also influenced Japanese culture. Religion does not seem to pose any problems with the modern scientific upsurge and Japan is at the forefront of technological advance. This is something that Westerners could give consideration to: how to retain the best elements of one's indigenous religion and yet learn from other cultures and make adaptations.

Obviously for the monotheists, the multiplicity of gods and spirits both good and bad is a problem, but one wonders how literally these matters are taken in Japan. It is very largely a cultural backdrop, analogous to what we in the West think on the subject of Santa Claus, fairies, goblins and 'bad luck'. There may be some spiritual value in the Japanese belief in *kami*. We are accustomed to a heavy dogmatism which results in heresy-hunting and sharp divisions of opinion; Japan does not seem to have this factor at work. Dogmas seem not to assume harsh proportions and there is an ease of conscience over belief.

One element that Christians do find difficult is the attitude towards suicide. *Harakiri* has traditionally been the accepted way of atoning for moral or procedural failure. This may be less so in recent times, but it is still a factor in Japanese culture.

Communism and Fascism

These ideologies are included on purpose, for they take the place of religion, inasmuch as it is a secular faith with overtones of divinity. They are more than just political ideas. They are exaggerations of genuine political aims. These aims have been nothing new: they can be evidenced from many situations in the past, before secular fanaticism had grown to the pitch seen in the twentieth century.

Starting with Communism, or extremist leftist theorising, the inspiration came from Karl Marx's book *Das Kapital*. The world had seen various working-class uprisings: the slave revolts in Ancient Rome, the Peasants' Revolt, the French Revolution; but none of this had the heavy ideological basis of Communism. It is clear that the industrial revolution, and the unfortunate effects on those being exploited on the working shop-floor, gave stimulus to Marx's political theory. On the face of it, religion and Communism need not necessarily be seen as clashing, but the fact was that Communists saw religion as supporting traditional capitalistic values, and this meant that religion would have to be expunged if the new system were ever to work. Strangely, it did not occur to them to notice what happened with the French Revolution, or even with the Roman persecution of the Christians: it simply did not work. Nevertheless, the implementation of the Revolution in Russia involved the policy of enforced atheism. One wonders if Marx ever intended it to assume the proportions it actually did.

In addition to this there was the notion that Communism ought to be spread to other countries by using the Red Army, namely by force. This did happen in the closing phases of the Second World War, in which many Eastern European countries were dragooned into accepting a Communist regime. In addition, there were all manner of infiltration initiatives to bring about conversion of other countries. The main catch was China and its satellites in the Far East. All manner of cruelties were inflicted on millions, sometimes on the basis of religion, but not always. Communism eventually earned itself a highly unacceptable reputation, something that it need not have had. The suspension of human rights and what could only be described as horrendous exploitation only ensured that Communism in its Stalinist form is now thoroughly out of favour. The Marxist theory behind it, however, is still alive and influential in many countries, albeit in a much moderated form.

What has become obvious is that a purely materialistic system which denies any kind of spirituality simply does not work. The Communists soon realised that they would have to provide some sort of substitute. This explains the adoration of Lenin and Stalin as they lay in state; also Chairman Mao as receiving some sort of apotheosis. Even a Communist Santa Claus was contrived to counter the Christian one. This did not work. The Christian dissidents in the Soviet Union were one of the main factors in the collapse of Communism in Russia and Eastern Europe. The world has yet to see what will happen in China, and more particularly in North Korea.

With regard to strengths and weaknesses, one can say that Communism was an all-out attempt to solve the wealth inequality problem, and also to even out the worst aspects of the capitalist pattern of boom and depression. Unfortunately the methods used were far from acceptable to those who value personal freedom. 'You cannot make omelettes without breaking eggs' may be a truism in cookery, but does not have to be the total truth in all other areas of life. Moreover Communism displayed itself as unable to understand or deal with certain basics in human nature: religion, family cohesion, personal security, greed, ambition. Always the resort to force and violence has spelt doom for this ideology in the long run.

With Fascism, we see a forceful reaction to Communism. As Churchill put it, 'Fascism is the ugly child of Communism.' This has been very largely true, except to say that the raw materials for this ideology have been with us since Roman times, at least, and have been in evidence every time some form of dictatorship has emerged. It would be anachronistic to call Machiavelli, or Oliver Cromwell, Fascists but their mentality gave much impetus to the twentieth-century dictatorships that have emerged. This is another totalitarian idea, hardly distinguishable from Communism. The methods used for its implementation were largely the same. One wonders what the difference could have been. Perhaps the difference was in this: that the Fascists were an extreme form of nationalist ideal, whereas Communism was more inclined to the international mentality – but this is a sweeping generalisation.

With regard to strengths and weaknesses, Fascism is not

necessarily always a bad thing. A country that is in chaos, or seriously threatened by an enemy, clearly needs a strong and single leader to bring it out of trouble. Churchill had to fulfil this role in the crisis of 1940. It is easy to see how Germany resorted to Nazism because of the political instability of the 1920s. The mistake occurs when that leader continues to grasp hold of power and abuse it, long after there is any need for any sort of dictatorship. That is when personal freedoms are withheld unreasonably. Another off-spin from extreme nationalism has been racism. This was less true in Mussolini's Italy, but Germany embarked on a nauseating policy of racial discrimination and 'ethnic cleansing' which has given Nazism an enduringly terrible reputation. The fanatical adherence to Hitler as the German Messiah is also a disturbing factor for all those who can see the lunacy and horror of the Third Reich. It has ensured that even milder forms of Fascism stand very little chance of becoming popular again in the foreseeable future.

With regard to religion, the antagonism seen in Communism does not seem to emerge. It is noticeable that many Roman Catholic countries have worked under a Fascist dictatorship without too much tension. But this is a hopeless generalisation. The Nazis were contemptuous of Christianity and tried to revive the old Norse mythology, but this only had limited success.

It is clear that for any country in a crisis, a strong leadership is a fair way of coping. When it comes to some sort of terror regime and the removal of personal freedoms, that is where problems begin. This applies to both Fascism and Communism.

Fanaticism

It can be seen from this short review of different religions and secular faiths that fanaticism is not confined to just one system of thought. In fact there are fanatics in just about every sphere of life. It is as well to consider what fanaticism consists of: it is a strong adherence to a particular idea to the exclusion of all else. As we all know, for virtually every question in life there is more than one solution: maybe several possible answers. An open-minded person will consider all the possible solutions to a problem and even then be open to reason if more information comes to light. He may be unable to make his mind up at all. The fanatic is one who fastens onto one solution to a problem and refuses to consider that there may be other answers available. He may take on an idea which to others seems crazy or extremist, and refuse to listen to an alternative argument, especially the opposite extremist view. This is where reasoned argument breaks down and it erupts into violence.

It may be that every 'ism' has had its outbursts of fanaticism; this is a wild generalisation but does contain a strong element of truth. The Jews had their hysterical element in the first century AD when Rome was exerting far too much pressure; the Zealots could not see that there was another way of coping with the matter, which Josephus advocated. In general the Jews have been a very peaceful group unless provoked by persecutors; now they do not wait for things to get out of hand as in the Holocaust. The Christians too have had their outbursts of crazy violence: the Crusades, the Civil War in Britain, two World Wars. In general terms the Christian nations have been a major factor in pacifying many troubled parts of the world. The Muslims are known, at times, to have spread their message by force of arms. We know that there have been Hindu, Shinto and Buddhist fanatics. It is unfortunate that the Sikhs began as a peaceful group, but when attacked they were forced to defend themselves. The same applied to the Mormons. We know about the fanaticism of Communism, and even more so, of the Nazis.

It is the Quakers, with another kind of fanaticism, who refuse to be involved in any kind of violence, to the extent that they will not even defend themselves if attacked. This requires an enormous amount of courage and fanatical adherence to achieve, but since their inception they have been consistent about it. The normal assumption in human nature is that if one is attacked, one is entitled to defend oneself, within reasonable limits. Even the Nazis tried to maintain that the Poles had begun the war by attacking Germany; no one believed them! But when Jesus said 'turn the other cheek' we must ask how much of this was exaggeration and high-powered preaching: do we take it totally literally?

In general terms we can see that across the broad spectrum of religious claims, and secular ones too, that there is just about every shade of opinion available. The fanatic is one who will fasten on to one or a few ideas and refuse to accept that any other ideas have any validity. The subtle balancing between varying shades of opinion mean nothing to him. The contradictions in the world of belief drive him to settle on one idea and ignore the opposite. The whole notion of paradox does not seem to occur to him. But as we have seen, there are so many paradoxes at work within each religion and across each divide. If people had been more aware of this and been capable of entertaining the alternative view, human history might have been very different. There could have been much more tolerance and a willingness to discuss matters without resort to loss of tempers.

But the essentials of balance, contradiction and paradox, as outlined in Chapter 1, are the crux of the matter. Also the assumption of fulfilment is the unspoken basic thought in all this, for the human mind tries to bring all these matters to some sort of resolution. The fanatical approach is to fix the mind on one idea, usually an extremist one, and try to ignore or destroy all the other ideas. This may work on a temporary basis but not on a long-term basis. For one thing, the mechanics of balance mean that someone takes the opposite extreme view and then a heavy contradiction emerges. When the contradiction cannot be resolved it then becomes a paradox. But as neither of them can understand a paradoxical situation, there is deadlock and that can lead to violence. When we realise that a paradox is insoluble and yet truth is to be found in both extremes, there may be a real opportunity for world peace. This does not have to mean that we never manage to make a decision on anything; still less that our problems can be solved by rendering everything down to some sort of compromising average. Of course, compromises have to be made in a world of realities. But truth is not a compromise, truth is almost always held in some sort of paradox.

A good example of this, already treated in detail, is the reality of Jesus of Nazareth. On the one hand he is claimed by himself and his followers to be God in human form with us on earth. On the other hand, the Koran says that God cannot 'beget': he is One, invisible, above and beyond the weakness of human nature. Both statements are the truth but are also irreconcilable by the canons of human logic. Rationalising attempts at some sort of compromise position or cheap explanation have always failed. It is beyond us to explain: only God can cope with the logic of it. Had people realised that we are dealing with a profound paradox, there need never have been any accusations of polytheism from the Muslims; and by the same token, counter-accusations from the Christians. It is fair enough for the Muslims to emphasise the unity and transcendence of God; fair enough for the Christians to emphasise the immediacy and messianic nature of God's interaction with humanity. Both sides of the argument are needed: to leave one out is to unbalance the whole matter and destroy the paradox. But then people regularly do that.

Christianity in relation to other faiths

There is a common assumption amongst people who have only a superficial knowledge of religions that all faiths are essentially the same. There is a sense in which there is some truth in this assumption. The truth lies in this respect: that the basic assumption of the human soul earning some form of merit with the unseen world is a deeply held belief. It is of course unprovable; nevertheless it persists in the face of all the evidence to the contrary. As we have seen in the chapter on Covenant (chapter 4), this is essentially the Old Testament mind-set. That is the instinctive assumption that to do good deeds will receive blessings in this life, and to do bad deeds will merit the opposite. It is not enough to say this is wrong: what we can say is that this is not the only covenant available for the human soul. The Old Testament is true as far as it goes: but it does not go the whole way.

With Western religions which have monotheism as axiomatic, the word 'covenant' frequently surfaces, even if it is not fully understood by its supporters. With Eastern religions, the metaphor of covenant is not stated in such terms and yet the assumption of it is still there in different thought-forms and metaphors. But the 'Old Testament' is traceable in every faith of whatever expression. It surfaces in such matters as sacrifice, cleansing, close relationship with one's God, fear of failure, promise of advancement. All this involves the human soul making some kind of advance on the world of divinity to gain some form of salvation. Does this really work? The answer is, for the most part, 'yes', but not always. We are confronted with the nagging question: 'Why does the innocent have to suffer?', the very basis of Theodicy. And this in itself points us forward to the other covenant, namely the New one.

The New Covenant is the completion, fulfilment and correction of the Old Testament. Without the Old one it would have no meaning, no basis, no rationale. The two covenants need each other to make sense of each other. But it is the coming of Jesus of Nazareth, God coming into our world in real terms, that we see the fulfilment not just of Judaism but of all the other 'Judaisms' in every part of the world. It would be unfair to say that all the others had no inkling of New Testament thinking. We can see traces of such thinking in the Hebrew Scriptures and in all kinds of other faiths under different phrasing. But the full revelation of God's love, forgiveness and cleansing for the human race is found in the ministry of Jesus. The Christian faith is the completion of every other incomplete faith in the world.

Does this mean that everyone claiming to be a Christian has got the right faith? Not necessarily! There are many who say they are glad to have the New Testament and yet do not really understand it. How many Christians do good works, pay out money to the Church and go in for elongated prayers on the assumption that they are buying favour with God? There is plenty of 'Judaism' going on in the Christian orbit. The real Christian is the one who knows he is forgiven, loved and accepted by God in advance of any good works. This is not easy to take in since it goes against deeply rooted instincts, but it means God first, humanity second the individual soul third.

This raises the thorny question of the relevance of Islam. Many have sensed that since Islam arrived six centuries after the ministry of Jesus, it might therefore be a superior revelation or development. We can see the underlying evolutionary assumption that anything that comes later has to be in some way superior; a fallacy of course! We must also remember that time sequences may mean something in human logic, but not necessarily in divine logic. We need to look at the Koran and see what kind of covenant is at work there. The answer is that the centre of gravity is plainly with Noah, Abraham, Moses and down to Ezekiel. Various mentions of covenant can be found but they are not explained in detail. Mention is made of Zechariah, and the Virgin Mary and various remarks about Jesus. There is much mention of merits and rewards for good deeds; the opposite for bad deeds. There is heavy emphasis on hell and damnation. It has been said that Islam is another Judaism, and that seems to be largely true. The Koran stands as a forceful and frightening restatement of the Old Testament mind-set, with no admission that the New Testament exists. Also there is no possibility of the paradox of the interplay of two Testaments as discussed earlier. The theological paradox then consists of this: that although Islam appeared after Christianity, its theology is very much pre-Christian.

It would be a major gain if Islam were simply a restatement of the real Judaism, but it is actually not. There is no real understanding or exposition of the Mosaic Covenant, still less of Abraham and of David. But it is tougher and less relenting. There is scant mention of love in the Koran: firstly, the love of God for mankind; and secondly, the injunction to love (not just believe) Almighty God. This is in spite of God being known as compassionate and merciful. There is not the closeness and personal knowledge and trust between God and the believing soul. The crucial problem with Islam is over the status of Jesus: although he is admitted to be the Messiah and the son of Mary, the very idea that he was the 'Son of God' is a problem. The Koran states that God cannot 'beget'; that applies to angels as well as the Messiah. We can understand the objection here, for 'beget' does imply a human biological function. But this is a good example of how a metaphor which was acceptable and current in one generation can become a problem for others in times to come. (The same problem was seen with Calvin on the Atonement and the modernist liberals.) There is a tendency for the Koran to take things literally, and indeed the Christians have made the same mistake. But 'beget' as applied to the relationship between God and the Messiah can only ever be taken as figurative, as indeed with many other metaphors used in Christian theology. Even so, there is a basic failure of understanding between Christianity and Islam. But it is only symptomatic of a deeper rift: the Muslims do not have a clear understanding of what the 'New Covenant' really means.

Paradox as a common denominator across religions

We have seen that Christian theology is thoroughly saturated with paradoxes of all magnitudes: major and minor ones naturally flowing from them. Many of the dilemmas in the Christian orbit can be seen in a completely different light on the basis of paradox. The amazing thing is that the concept itself is never actually mentioned or explored until now. The same is true with other religions. A few examples from varying sources will help to broaden the matter out.

Much mention of Gnosticism has been made earlier in this work. As a collection of religio-philosophical ideas in the decades following the birth of Christianity, it compares well with many features seen in Eastern religions, especially Buddhism and Taoism. Also we see outcroppings of neo-Gnosticism in many of the modern splinter groups which claim to be 'the real Christianity'. Gnosticism was labelled as heretical in the early years: the chief reason for this was that they rationalised the Incarnation away in such a fashion as to make Jesus as purely a fantasy and not really human flesh. But it is easy to forget that Gnosticism did have a few positive ideas to offer, not just on the subject of Theodicy but also on paradox.

A most intriguing work is called 'Thunder', a recently discovered work thought to be unique in that it talks about a female deity; it stresses the essential 'I-am-ness' or the 'Perfect mind'. It has parallels with ancient Indian literature. It also reminds us of Holy Wisdom who is pictured as feminine in Hebrew Wisdom literature. It describes the activities of this unnamed deity: almost all of it appears in some kind of paradox. We can take a sample of quotations, but the whole work is on the same lines:[1]

'I am knowledge and ignorance, I am embarrassment and effrontery, Shameless and ashamed. I am courage and fright.'

'I've been hated everywhere, but also adored. I am that which people call life and you call death. I am called the Law and lawlessness. I am the hunted and the captured. I am the dispersed and the collected.'

'I am ignorant yet I teach, I am despised, yet admired'.

'Those who are close don't know me. When you are near, I'm distant. On the day you're distant, I am close.'

It would be fair to say that many Gnostic writings from this era contain this type of paradoxical wisdom literature, and as such it has a certain spiritual value. It would be interesting to see how much of this is indirectly referring to Jesus. One example of this could be 'I am called the Law': that is, Jesus came to bring the Mosaic Law to fulfilment, and yet he is capable of ignoring many of the laws that the Pharisees thought were essential.

When considering the Tao Teh Ching, the scriptures of the Taoists, we find very much the same kind of thinking at work. Although Lao Tzu does not talk directly about God, he does say much about the Tao. This can be translated as the 'Way' but there is much more to it than that. It is the 'subtle essence of the universe' or the creative impulse beneath everything, and yet is beyond us to grasp, describe or quantify.

Much of his writings are couched in a string of paradoxes:[2]

'Confront it and you do not see its face: follow it and you do not see its back . . . There is nothing that can make this subtle essence of the universe distinct. When you try to make it clear to yourself, it evasively reverts to nothingness,' (Fourteen).

'The Tao appears to lack strength yet its power is inexhaustible. It has no sharpness yet it rounds off all sharp edges. It has no form yet it unties all tangles: it has no glare but it merges all lights. It seems so obscure yet it is the ultimate clarity.'

'The Tao is elusive and evasive: though it is evasive it unveils itself as indefinable substance. Shadowy and indistinct, it reveals itself as impalpable subtle essence. This essence is so subtle and yet so real. It is the subtle origin of the whole of creation and non-creation,' (Twenty-one).

And something that reminds us of Isaiah and St Luke: 'The yielding are preserved whole: the crooked become straight. The empty become filled. The depleted are renewed. What has little will gain: what has much will be confused.'

And to the person who follows the Tao: 'Because he does not flaunt his brightness he becomes enlightened. Because he is not self-important he becomes illustrious. Because he does not boast of his accomplishments he becomes successful. Because he is not self-assertive he becomes supreme,' (Twenty-two).

One paradox after another, all in line with New Testament thinking.

Something similar happens in the Upanishads. Brahman is described as imminent and transcendent, within all and outside of all:[3] 'He moves and he moves not. He is far and he is near. He is within all and he is outside of all,' (Isa Upanishad).

Wisdom is often defined in paradoxical statements: 'He is above the known and he is above the unknown.' And, 'What cannot be spoken with words, but that whereby words are spoken ... what cannot be thought by the mind, but that whereby the mind can think ... what cannot be seen with the eye but that whereby the eye can see.' This continues with 'the ear' and 'the breathing' (Kena Upanishad).

'Concealed in the heart of all beings is the Atman, the Atman, the Self: smaller than the smallest atom, greater than the vast spaces ... resting, he wanders far: sleeping he goes everywhere ... when the wise realise the omnipresent Spirit, who rests invisible in the visible and permanent in the impermanent, then they go beyond sorrow,' (Katha Upanishad).

With the Dammapada of Buddhism there appears to be less

emphasis on attempting to describe the Ultimate, although the 'Unmade' does receive a mention (v. 383). But minor paradoxes do occur in describing the Brahmin and the monk:[4]

'Whoever is united and free of distress, and for whom neither a 'beyond', a 'not-beyond', nor a 'both beyond-and-not-beyond' exist, I call a Brahmin,' (v. 385).

'Ashamed of what's not shameful and not ashamed of what is.'

'Seeing danger in what's not dangerous and not seeing danger in what is.'

'Finding fault in what's not at fault and seeing no fault in what is ... those who take up wrong views go to a bad rebirth,' (v. 315–18).

In this we see paradox associated with spiritual failure, in contrast to verse 385.

In the wisdom literature of the Old Testament there seems to be even less inclination to define wisdom in terms of paradox. In the classic accounts of the nature of wisdom, the description seems to be almost straightforward. The paradox appears in the Book of Ecclesiastes, which is credited to Solomon, and concerns the course of human life itself rather than God. The main theme is the futility of human life and this recurs in various places:

'So I gave my heart up to despair over all the toil of my labours ... because sometimes a man who has toiled with wisdom and knowledge and skill must leave all to be enjoyed by a man who did not toil for it. This also is a vanity and a great evil,' Ecclesiastes 2:20.

His favourite words 'vanity' and 'wind' are important and symptomatic of his view of life. The word *hebel* ('vanity') can be rendered as 'vapour, breath, worthless, to no purpose'. The word *ruah* has a very wide range of meaning. It is the same word used for the Spirit of God in Genesis 1; also it means animation, temper, disposition, vigour, impatience, impulse, trouble, sorrow and even overexcitement. Would it be possible to paraphrase 'this also is vanity and a striving after wind' as, 'the whole of life is worthless and getting worked up over nothing'? Would this be taking too much of a liberty?

But Solomon's answer to all this is the classic passage in 3:1–9: 'For everything there is a season and a time for every matter under heaven ... what gain has the worker from his toil?' In other words, one may as well just accept that life will run its course, inevitably, according to the deep paradoxes of God's world, 'a time to be born and a time to die', God has it all staked out and it works according to this list of paradoxes, no matter how much we allow ourselves to worry about it. One is almost tempted to translate 'vanity' as 'paradox' but that might be taking one too many liberties. The Greek philosophers may not by then have coined the term, if this is really the work of King Solomon. Here we may see him searching for a word, but all he can arrive at is 'futility' and possibly 'contradiction'. But we can see it as paradoxical that no matter how hard we strive in life, or the opposite, we all arrive at the same fate, namely death.

With regard to the nature of God, the Old Testament is never shy of discussing the matter in anthropomorphic terms. 'I am that I am' seems to be the substratum of the whole account and occasionally breaks the surface. So in Exodus 33:19: 'I will proclaim before you my name, "The Lord (YHWH)." '

It even begins to receive a partial definition – 'I will be gracious to whom I will be gracious and show mercy on whom I will show mercy' – but no one can see God's face. God puts his hand over Moses' face, only to allow him to see his back. Does this remind us of that passage in the Tao Teh Ching, 'confront it and you do not see its face'? The same paradox is seen so often across so many religions: God (or the Eternal) is transcendent and yet the human mind can have knowledge of him. This passage in Exodus is remarkable in that it is a subtle blend of anthropomorphic with the symbolic and the proto-philosophical. On this basis it can be seen that there is a substratum of basic understanding across the many religions. God is near and yet God is unapproachable. Even if the vocabulary and metaphors vary across the different cultures and religions, even so there is a basic sharing of thought. One could call it the Old Testament at work in the soul of humanity everywhere in the world.

When we come to the New Testament, this Exodus passage is clearly being referred to by St John 1:18: 'No one has ever seen God: the only Son, who is in the bosom of the Father, he has made him known.' Again, a transcendent approach to God with the inclusion of anthropomorphic metaphor ('in the bosom of the Father').

But this is where the New Testament radically departs from all the other 'isms' of this world. It is saying that the Eternal came in physical terms at a certain time and place and showed us really what God was all about. An amazing claim, which many find difficult to take on board, it is nevertheless the final truth about God and humanity. This is a paradox, namely of the Incarnation, which is beyond human comprehension. St Paul in 2 Corinthians is saying virtually the same thing but in different metaphor: 'For it is the God who said, "Let light shine out of darkness," who has shone in our hearts to give the light of the knowledge of the glory of God in the face of Christ (the Messiah).'

Even if it is a radical departure from all the other 'isms' of this world, it brings them all to fulfilment, completion and correction. This will help us to understand what Jesus meant at his baptism (Matthew 3:15): 'for thus it is fitting for us to fulfil all righteousness.'

To fulfil all righteousness

To say that the Christian faith is the completion of every other faith on earth is a massive claim and needs to be given some sort of substantiation. It is not as simple as taking each religion in turn and demonstrating how it relates to Christianity. We have seen that every religion is an amalgam of various ingredients and indeed the boundary line between them is often rather vague. The way forward is to use the basic components of religions and see how they relate to the ministry of Jesus.

Shamanism

The shaman as one who is in touch with the unseen world and can bring benefits to the people he serves is fulfilled in Jesus, especially in St Mark, for there we see him fully in touch with the unseen spiritual forces, both good and bad, and he has authority to control them. This is the ultimate shaman who can cure diseases and mental illnesses, control the weather and, going further, is in touch with the Eternal God. The corrective to the shaman is that Jesus the final shaman is always caring for all those who need help.

Sacral kingship

In many respects sacral kingship foreshadows the ministry of Jesus, but he comes as the ultimate and final king, the authority of the Eternal God in the affairs of mankind. This sums up and corrects all the versions of sacral kingship in both ancient or modern modes. His leadership was one of power but with humility, and readiness to give himself entirely to rescue humanity. Extending into the future, his kingship implies that he will be the eternal judge, the only one with the mandate to do so, since he committed no offence himself.

Prophecy

We have seen how prophecy is a strand seen in varying intensities in almost every system on earth. Jesus brings not only the Old Testament prophesies to completion but also those of every other prognostication. For the prophets who came later, he helps us to understand and moderate them, thus being the final corrective to some of the way-out ideas of some of them.

Priesthood

The need for someone to be some form of spokesman on behalf of mankind to God is understood in virtually every system of religion. But Jesus is the one who speaks to God directly and personally without any sort of hindrance. He was quickly seen as the eternal high priest: his representation of humanity to God goes on eternally in the very heart of God. In this way he is the ultimate completion of every human priesthood or transmuted version of it.

Sacrifice

The rationale of sacrifice has been discussed earlier. From God's or man's point of view, no sacrifice has ever been a completely satisfactory offering. The one exception is that of Jesus himself, God giving his very self to remove the barrier between himself and mankind. He is the ultimate and final sacrifice which causes a reinterpretation of all the others both in prehistory and in modern times.

Lawgiving

Clearly Jesus is portrayed as the final lawgiver who gives a far higher ethic than anything seen before or since. He brings to completion all the laws, conventions and ethics of every nation and gives us a standard which is unattainable for any human soul. The crystallisation of law into the two great commandments was also revolutionary: it was love that was the foundation of all ethical conduct.

Prayer and liturgy

Cognisant of the elaborate observances of religious expression in all their variety, Jesus gives us a simple short prayer which includes all the essential ingredients: the Lord's Prayer. With regard to liturgy, he gives us a very simple act which is capable of all manner of permutations: the Eucharist. Thus he brings to completion and correction all the religious observances of the entire world.

Theological paradoxes

Such issues as free will and predestination, grace and merit, and Theodicy are all given some degree of exposure in the ministry of Jesus. This does not mean that neat answers in terms of human rationality are reasoned out: they are given an airing in the parables, the healings and even the antics of Judas Iscariot. We are left with the feeling that the final answers are in the rationality of God, and yet Jesus works through these matters in terms of practical reality, bringing it all to a conclusion at the end of his ministry.

Philosophy

As an offspin and subset of theology, philosophy also comes to completion. Jesus is termed the *logos*, the ultimate wisdom, and as such all the speculative systems of humanity, including non-religious ones, are brought to a conclusion. He does not speculate: he knows the answers, and yet he is economical with the information. This leaves us with a wide degree of freedom to speculate on theological and philosophical matters, but the ultimate term of reference is the Word of God himself.

Mythology

As we have seen, Jesus has a subtle way of drawing mythological assumptions and historical realities into one integrated thought. This has the effect of leaving the way open for the mythologies of other nations and of the future, to be integrated into an appropriate pattern of thought for generations to come. To put it bluntly, the Christian understanding of life can be used to baptise just about anything in human thought and speculation.

Calendars and astral movements

We have seen that Jesus had an acute awareness of the timing of his ministry. For all those whose faith circulates around stargazing, horoscopes, zodiacs and related matters, Jesus is the last word: the Magi came to worship him, and the planetary movements heralded his coming. His ministry is not just an earthbound localised phenomenon: it is a universal sign for the whole of life in relation to the Eternal Creator.

Notes

1. Jacobs, *The Gnostic Gospels*, 2006.
2. Hua Ching Ni, *The Complete works of Lao Tzu, Tao Teh Ching*, 1979.
3. Upanishads, Penguin, 1979.
4. G. Fronsdal, *Dhammapada*, 2006.

20

The Theology of Continuity

We have already seen that tradition almost always plays an important part in theological thought. Even a new idea which has very little connection with events or personalities in the past usually tries to connect itself somehow with original terms of reference. This is inevitable since God is seen in terms of antiquity and originality; any religion relating to God has to reflect that aspect of things. This is seen in the tendency to use old-fashioned or obsolete language in scriptural material (as discussed earlier). Occasionally we see a complete break with the past. Such would be the case of Moses and the inception of the Covenant of Sinai and the giving of the Ten Commandments. It must have taken a massive force of personality and events to galvanise the Israelites into a cohesive force and a faith which has persisted to the present day regardless of all the vicissitudes of history. Even then, the Covenant of Sinai was not a totally fresh start coming out of nothing. The covenant notion was already there from the faith of Abraham, and before that, the faith of Noah.

Tradition plays an important part in religion and its adaptation into new forms takes much effort and force of personality. As we can see from the introduction of the first Prayer Book of Edward VI and of the latest modern Anglican prayer books in recent times, the only way to deal with people stuck in a rut is gently to adapt tradition in such a way that they hardly realise any drastic change has been foisted upon them.

These matters are particularly relevant to the 'historical' religions of the West. Starting with Judaism, we are constantly up against tradition and references to the past as some sort of trump card to convince people of what should be done. A notable example of this is the discovery of the Book of the Law in 2 Kings 22:8, which triggered off the Josianic reform. It does not matter which book or what portion of the Pentateuch was actually found: the fact is that they saw this document as authoritative because of its assumed antiquity.

Many have speculated that this was the Book of Deuteronomy and indeed this style of writing does pervade much of the historical material stemming from that era. But there is no complete certainty about this.

Looking further on to the era of Jeremiah, it is clear that much of the thinking of Deuteronomy can be evidenced in his style of writing. It looks very much as though Jeremiah was using this turn of phrase to make an impression on those who, at that time, did not wish to even contemplate his message. In a later era, we can see that much of what Ezekiel said was couched in terms of the phraseology of the Code of Holiness as seen in parts of Leviticus. With Ezra the reforming priest, we see an uncompromising and full-blooded return to the purity of the Mosaic legal system. With the late post-exilic literature of the apocalyptists, we see the attempt to give their writings some form of latter-day authority by claiming to be the inspiration of such people as Enoch, Abraham, Moses, and the Twelve Patriarchs. One wonders if people then were convinced by this?

With the ministry of Jesus we see a constant tension between the authority of the past and present, and the continuity which is assumed to be there, and often is not: 'observing the tradition of the elders', Mark 7:3. By this time, the Pharisees (and other groups) had managed to fabricate all manner of procedures as a sort of hedge round the Torah of Moses, and in so doing the hedge became increasingly inclined to obscure the basics of the original laws.

In many respects, the continuity which Jesus brought in was the completion of the Mosaic material as opposed to the destruction of it: 'think not that I have come to abolish the law and the prophets: I have come not to abolish them but to fulfil them,' Matthew 5:17. And in verse 20 there is the challenge that if you cannot exceed what the Pharisees achieve, you will not succeed. It means in effect that Jesus is giving us a colossally high standard which we cannot hope to cope with without the mercy of God in our lives and the guidance of the Holy Spirit.

The major disagreement between Jesus and the Jewish establishment appears to be over the issue of forgiving sins. It is never stated as such in the Pentateuch that only God can forgive sins, and indeed we have to turn to Daniel 9:9 for a remark that sounds like that: 'to the Lord our God belong mercy and forgiveness.' One might conclude that mankind could forgive, but this is never stated clearly. But by the time of Jesus, claiming to forgive sins was clearly taken as blasphemy, that is, claiming to be God. But since Jesus clearly did relieve people of guilt and the problems associated with it, namely illnesses, there was much evidence that his authority on the subject of forgiveness was hardly spurious but genuine.

Jesus' own comment on the issue of continuity might well have been on these lines, quoting John the Baptist: 'Do not presume to say to yourselves, "We have Abraham as our father," for I tell you that God is able from these stones to raise up children to Abraham,' Matthew 3:8. To put it in modern terms, 'it is no use quoting the past all the time as if that were some sort of nostrum: you need to be real yourselves and grasp the truths of God right in front of you.'

The whole issue of continuity surfaces in John 8:30–50. In short, Jesus throws doubt on the claim that the Jewish leadership are the children of Abraham: rather they are the Devil's brood with their murderous intentions. He himself is not just a child of Abraham, but his chief inspiration. And with that they concluded that he was deranged. To put it another way, the true Christian continuity runs through Noah, through Abraham and Moses and thence to Jesus; the bit in between had all manner of problems and Judaism had largely gone off the rails.

In most other respects, Jesus probably conformed to the Judaism of his day, in ritual and diet. It is with the primitive Church that we see a more serious divergence from Judaism. In Acts 10:15 we see Peter given carte blanche to eat anything, which meant that the dietary restrictions of Judaism were now obsolete. Also there was the issue of circumcision (Acts 15): should the Gentile converts be forced into this rite? By Acts 15:29 they had arrived at a formula for the new converts. We can see the new faith diverging from its parent religion but it takes the authority of Peter and other early Apostles to accomplish what must have been quite a serious break with 'tradition'. They must have seen it as quite a natural concomitant of the New Testament.

Continuity in the early Church was very largely connected with what became known as the Apostolic Succession. That meant that the succession of bishops from St Peter downwards through the ages was important. The same mentality prevailed in the Eastern churches. We can see in this the importance in people's minds, of the historical continuity. This still prevails to this day in the Roman and Anglican churches. One wonders how many contemporary bishops could display the same level of conviction and risk of martyrdom as Peter and his colleagues in the first century.

One wonders if the corruption in Rome at the time of the Borgia Popes would not have invalidated their system completely: certainly the early Protestants thought so. But Apostolic Succession is the same mentality as claiming to be descended from Abraham regardless of how far off the mark one has strayed.

It is interesting that the question of continuity must have been at the back of someone's mind when the Koran was written. Here was a new faith coming out of literally nowhere, not wishing to be simply a revival of Judaism or Christianity. How could it be validated? The answer lies in the Koran itself. There are many references to Noah, Abraham and Moses and the authority for the book rests very heavily on that era in theological history. Also there are many references to Mary and Jesus, but the chief divergence of thought is that God cannot 'beget' in the sense that a human can. The deduction from that is that Jesus cannot be 'begotten' of God or the 'only begotten Son of the Father'. Even so, the validation for this new faith is heavily dependent on references to the Old and New Testaments. This is a form of continuity but with certain important divergences.

One might have thought that with the so-called 'non-historical' religions of the East, the question of continuity would be much less of an issue. Very far from it! In Hinduism we find that the core value is the teaching on Karma. That is essentially all about continuity. That is not so much about teachings and leadership which enables interpretation of the scriptures to be done; it is about the continuity of each immortal soul. There is an impression of a beginning of creation which implies that souls are created. But then they continue eternally from one life to another. This could go on indefinitely, but there are some, it is claimed, that rise up to be absorbed into Brahma the Absolute and so cease to exist as such. Apart from this metaphor of continuity, there are many ritual and procedural traditions in Hinduism that add to the reality of continuity.

With Buddhism again we have the Karma situation and a short-cut available for those who follow the Noble Eightfold Path. It is interesting that continuity occurs in a different mode: not exactly historical, but in a sort of domino succession. There is an endless chain of Bodhisattvas, heavenly beings who have come into the world to offer suffering humanity a way of release from Karma.

Siddhartha himself was just one such person but there have been, and still are, many others. This is partly an answer to the problem of particularity but also to the issue of continuity. It is only fair that all people in the past and into the future could have the opportunity to gain Nirvana. We see continuity in the way the Dalai and the Panchen Lama are chosen, trained and deified. How this continuity of procedure can be perpetuated given the adverse situation over Chinese atheist domination is yet to be seen, but one hardly doubts that the Tibetan people will succeed in redeeming the situation somehow.

With the Chinese religions, Confucianism offers another kind of continuity, that of the family, heavily connected with ancestor worship. There is the sense that the family is connected on this side of the grave with those who are dead. Also there is the Mandate of Heaven frame of mind. This means that the temporal ruler is not there on the basis of genealogy (although in fact he might be) but on the basis of his acceptance of Confucianist values. These values have held the Chinese people together in a kind of continuity at least since the days of Confucius, and that, coupled with their interesting cultural traditions, has produced a mentality which the Communists may have dented but certainly have not destroyed.

It is with the coming of the Reformation and the sixteenth-century Protestant upsurge that we see an interesting use of continuity. The Anglicans sought to justify their departure from Rome by referring to the ancient Celtic Church. Indeed there is still this element of idealisation of Celtic Christian values at work in Anglicanism now, also to some extent with the Presbyterians. But the main thrust of Protestant theology was, following Luther's rediscovery of certain aspects of St Paul's theology, a full-blooded return to Biblical values and what was assumed to be the simplicity of the worship of the primitive Church. Just as Jesus took a short-cut back to Abraham, so the Protestant splinter groups took a short-cut back to the New Testament.

Enough has been said to evidence that continuity is an important aspect of virtually every religion or sect derived thereform. It is unusual if not highly unlikely for a 'new faith' to appear with completely new ideas without any kind of reference to any pre-existing system of thought. This underlying assumption of continuity can re-emerge in some strange ways. A noted example could be the British Israel theory which maintains that the lost ten tribes of Israel, as deported by the Assyrians, actually turned up in the British Isles and are in fact the British! Needless to say, no serious archaeologist or ethnologist has ever endorsed this idea. It is an idea clearly connected with British imperialism and we can see the belated attempt to justify it by reference to attachment to lost peoples of the Bible. On similar lines is the theory spelt out in the Book of Mormon. This time, a contingent from Jerusalem, in the last days before the Exile, went out into the desert to escape destruction and then managed to build a ship and cross the Atlantic Ocean. When Joseph Smith was given the plates of brass and a special pair of spectacles to translate them, in the 1820s, the 'new' faith of Mormonism was established. The Mormons will not admit that this is a new faith. They maintain that Adam was the first Mormon and that this faith was the original one. From this we see the unspoken element of continuity, even if the plates of brass did disappear for many centuries. Another permutation on continuity is seen with the Jehovah's Witnesses, for they cannot stomach any of the history of the Church, whether Roman Catholic or Protestant, but fasten on to certain Biblical strands with a fanatical literalism which was never intended in the first place.

It would be fair to say that most of the Protestant splinter-group sects attempt to justify their stance by some form of continuity with the Bible. It is usually a carefully selected part of the Bible, taken in a literal interpretation, and also the Authorised Version. Certain noted exceptions to this may now be reviewed. They tend to have some involvement with 'science' as their basis of justification. This might involve some form of rationality or philosophy underpinning this 'new' idea. This may be a generous degree of self-deception. As we know, there are no new ideas in theology: all we have is recycled and rephrased ideas.

To take the case of Emanuel Swedenborg, a scientist and mystical thinker: he tried to show by purely scientific methods that the universe had a fundamentally spiritual structure. Later he claimed to be in contact with angels and the spiritual world. It was not that he wanted to start a new Church, but to provide a certain influence in existing Churches. It was three ex-Wesleyan clergymen who later started the New Jerusalem Church. With this influence we see a minimum of continuity. The Swedenborgian tenets seem to be almost completely the bright ideas of the founder member. It does not appear to be dependent on the Bible as other splinter groups are. Its dependence on scientific insights probably carried conviction with some in his day, but now will appear decidedly cranky. This may help to explain why this system of thought is not very widespread; some would say it is almost non-existent.

A similar situation could be maintained for Christian Science. Mary Baker Eddy produced a personal theory of healing which entailed the denial of the reality of the physical world. Suffering and death are simply the result of false thinking, a mistaken belief in the existence of matter. Health is to be restored not by medical treatment but by dispelling the illusions of the patient. Although the worship of Christian Scientists does involve usage of the Bible, Eddy's writings are also seen as 'scriptural'. Although there is a degree of continuity here by reference to the Bible, this way-out theorising, which reminds one of aspects of Buddhist thinking, has little relationship to the rest of Christian tradition. None of the mainstream Churches will admit to the validity of this idea; moreover with the resurgence of spiritual healing within the Churches in recent times, Christian Science is increasingly being seen as irrelevant.

Spiritualism (whether Christian or not) is another modern American-inspired development. It is nothing new: necromancy as an aspect of shamanism has been with us since the Stone Age. But the modern version of it is not so much worship as various technical devices for allegedly making contact with the dead. Reference may be made to the Bible, but Spiritualists omit to take seriously the fact that the Bible specifically forbids this activity; all the mainstream Churches strongly advise against it. It is fraught with dangers to mental health, and wide open to possible fraud and exploitation. As far as continuity is concerned, necromancy is as old as the hills, but the modern commercialisation and sensationalism is a matter of concern for all people with any degree of integrity. The scientific aspect of it comes in the Society for Psychical Research, but this is not really a religion or theory.

With Scientology we see probably the latest 'new' idea concocted by a certain Mr Ron Hubbard. Unfortunately, since much of it is shrouded in secrecy, it looks very much like one of the Mystery Religions of Rome. Certainly it keeps a very tight rein and discipline on its membership. One is not free to depart should elements of doubt occur to one. From what little we do know of its teachings, it would seem that initiates work their way up a sort of ladder towards perfection. It sounds rather like a cross between Hindu Karma-ism and Gnosticism. If so, it is nothing 'new' at all: it has a degree of continuity simply re-expressed in different terms. How it relates to the Bible is not clear.

When we come to Quakerism, this appears to be an unusual, if not unique case. With the worship of Quakers being totally without ritual, music or established pattern, we see a complete reaction to the normal approach taken by both Roman Catholics and Protestants. Although the Bible is in use and quoted in their theorisings, it is only used selectively. In effect, the 'inner light', which is another way of saying that each person has the Holy Spirit, makes one superior to the Bible. At one time Quakers had a distinctive dress code and manner of speaking. In spite of them being at variance with civil procedures in most countries, they have gained a high reputation for honesty, truthfulness, industry and charity; they command a far greater influence than their numbers might suggest. In that sense there is an element of continuity from the teachings of the New Testament; in other respects their scheme seems to be about as 'new' as a religious idea can be. There is the added element of subjective thought; the early Quakers were mystics who went into spasms of ecstasy, not unlike the modern Elims. Continuity is not as clear or convincing as with most other groups. Possibly they are not too concerned about this. They would probably say that their faith validates itself without recourse to factors in the past.

The Communists, as a secular faith, made no attempt to justify their theories by reference to the Bible: on the contrary they felt that religion was an obstruction to their main aim, that of equality and fair dealings for all people. It was Rousseau and others of that era who provided the logic of it: the notion of the 'noble savage' in prehistory was a secularistic appeal to the 'Golden Age' mentality found in the mythology of many religions. How much historical truth there is in this idea is debatable, but the assumption was that once one freed the working classes from the tyranny of capitalists and imperialists, the world would return to some sort of Utopia. Although Rousseau may not have suggested it, violence was to become the short-cut method of the French and Russian Revolutions. In a way the socialist ideal was meant to be a complete break from monarchy, religion, capitalism and all associated 'evils'; the reality was that it had to validate itself by reference to some supposed 'truth' back in the remote past – continuity of a kind, even if tenuous.

Continuity between Judaeo-Christian and pagan practices

It is often interesting to note the attempt at continuity between paganism and the monotheistic faiths which came to replace them. In the early years of the Israelite nation, there was the urge to wipe out Canaanite practice completely. It may have begun like this, but soon the opposite was happening: Canaanite practice was infiltrating the 'pure' religion of the Hebrews. So by the time of King Ahab we see the vast majority of Israelites involved with traditions which were seriously at variance with the tenets of Moses at Sinai. Whether Ahab and his court honestly thought that they were embarking on some sort of accommodation in order to convert the Canaanites is not clear, but it soon became a compromise which all but cancelled out the truth of the One God. It became clearer later, when pressure from Assyria and Babylon compelled the Hebrews to accept pagan practices, that they were not exactly free to retain the absolute purity of their faith. From the Exile onwards we see the emergence of those who dug their heels in and would not compromise on any matter with the pagans, and those who felt that some sort of accommodation was only common sense and the way forward to adapt pagan practice to Hebrew thinking. This became acute in the Maccabean era.

With this kind of background, the early Christians were faced with the awkward question of how much continuity there needed to be with the parent religion, Judaism, and also pagan practice. Christianity was in many respects a complete break from Judaism but in other respects it relied heavily on Old Testament theology, as indeed it still does. This was how the New Covenant was to be validated: by reference to and development of the Old Covenant. This was an essential aspect of continuity, going back to Abraham and Noah.

At the same time, the Christians were aware that not everything in paganism was absolutely wrong, and to be expunged. We have already seen how the accumulated skills over calendar construction, devised by the pagans, were easily adapted into the Christian scheme. There was simply no point in tearing up the Julian calendar and starting afresh. It went further, as Christian festivals and Saints' Days became superimposed on pagan Roman festivals. The Saturnalia adapted into Christmas is a case in point. The Roman Emperor, the Pontifex Maximus, became the Pope. The dress code of the Romans, people and soldiers, became the regalia of the

Christian liturgy. Many other instances of this could be found. Was this a compromise which would contradict the essentials of the faith, as with Ahab, or was this a clever method of 'baptising' not just people but whole institutions and thought forms, another aspect of continuity?

As the Christian missionaries encountered the Men of the North, another kind of accommodation was seen to take place. How many of our modern-day ideas about Christmas (and other festivals) are actually a subtle adaptation of ancient Norse or druidic practices? Such carols as 'Deck the Halls', 'The Sans Day Carol', 'The Gloucestershire Wassail' and 'The Holly and the Ivy' are symptomatic of this process. Even the mistletoe has reappeared in recent times, as indeed the Christmas tree. The little red goblin of Norse tradition was easily transferred into Santa Claus. Some might say that this is compromising with paganism. A more realistic and constructive approach is to say that so many features of pagan religion and mythology can be given a Christian interpretation, in other words, 'baptised'. Of course there have been backlash reactions to this, sometimes an overreaction: Oliver Cromwell tried to cancel Christmas altogether. But in general terms, Christianity has been able to absorb and reinterpret a whole range of features from pagan religion, without undue compromise. Done in this way, the main features of the Christian year with their rituals appeal to something basic and instinctive in human nature. This explains why the purists and rigorists will not succeed in removing them.

In this sense, the theology of continuity is seen in the reinterpretation of bedrock spiritual needs in the pagan world. This helps to explain why Christianity has flourished in Europe and with the European peoples throughout the world. It also may help to explain why Christianity has had a difficult time making converts in the Eastern countries where Hinduism, Buddhism and others have been the prevalent force. Can we really say that there has been an attempt to reinterpret Eastern thought and symbolisms into Christian assumptions? Have we tried to 'baptise' the Bodhi tree, the Jade Emperor, or the Yantra of Hindu meditational methods?

The Muslims too have had the same situation to face. Even if the Koran was intended to be a clean break and a new start, in practice the Muslims retained various features from the Arabic pagan past. So for instance, the Kaaba in Mecca is still the focal point of their pilgrimage. While some are attempting to relate to the non-Muslim populations in many countries, others of a purist approach are reacting against any form of what they see as compromise with Western values. This, it would seem, is the theology of continuity in a markedly different permutation.

Continuity is an important element in the human mind, not least in the sphere of religious belief and practice. A faith which takes this into account and develops a fair relation to the values of the past, and yet offers something worthwhile for the present and the future, is likely to be of value to the people of the third millennium.

An interesting example of how Greek culture was grafted into Christian thinking came with the 'relocation of Delphi'. For centuries Delphi, with its whole mystique and culture, had been regarded as the centre of the world. By the time of Constantine, its influence had largely waned since the Christians were not interested in pagan priestesses issuing ambiguous prognostications. When Constantine relocated the capital of the Roman world to Constantinople, and built the Hagia Sophia Basilica, there was a blatant attempt at relocating the *omphalos* from Delphi to the actual spot on which the Byzantine emperors were crowned. This was a kind of continuity in which the authority of paganism and the centre of the world were relocated and reinterpreted to identify the centre of the Christian world.

Even more interesting is the situation over the Renaissance. As the Mediaeval age drew to a close, there was seen a need for a fresh questioning of everything. The dogmatism and yet corruption in the Roman Church left many people dissatisfied and ready to try new ideas. This came in the rediscovery of the ancient Greek culture, its art forms and philosophies. But going further, there was the rediscovery of the ancient Book of Thoth, the Trismegister, an ancient Egyptian text, albeit in a Greek translation. One may wonder how such a work of pagan origin would be a focus of attention: the answer must lie in its antiquity and the drive for continuity with the past, which is such an important strand in human thinking. The original work in hieroglyphics has not been found; there have been varying versions of the book 'concocted' up to the present day, and scholars are still trying to piece together bits of papyrus in an attempt to reconstruct it. The material in such documents is ambiguous, magical and mystical, and yet there is a fascination in it for those who find a straightforward Christian message difficult. This is a case of continuity from the past not directly relating to

Christianity, still less being 'baptised' by it. Yet it would seem that the wave of cultural revolt, as seen in the 1970s and 1980s, had to have some sort of justification rooted in the past, namely the Trismegister.

The Fascists, being a violent reaction to Communism, also had the question of self-validation through continuity with the past in mind. Being a secularised faith with no particular religious element, there was no clear appeal to the Bible or Christian tradition. Hitler himself was contemptuous of the Churches. The appeal to the past lay in dragging up various elements of Nordic mythology. Whether this was ever meant literally is debatable, but the appeal of the Teutonic knights, whose noble heroic exploits in the eastern territories had spread German culture right round the Baltic, was seen as literally true. Also seen as literally true was evolution and the survival of the fittest: it was easy to maintain from this that certain races (conveniently the Teutonic ones) were entitled to dominate and exploit so-called inferior races; some peoples were below the level of humanity and could be liquidated altogether. A sinister aspect of this, which was the obsession of Himmler, was the quest for *Germania*, a book written by Tacitus in AD 98. In it, he believed, the German peoples were lauded as blue-eyed, fair-haired and wonderful people, undefeated by the Romans, and therefore militarily brilliant. They were claimed to be the descendants of Atlantis and were the pinnacle of civilisation and racial purity. How much of this book Himmler actually read is debatable; also one wonders if he took note of Tacitus's remarks about the idleness, drunkenness and depravity of these people. But then the selective use of ancient literature is a feature not confined to Nazism. It was enough, however, to justify to Himmler the excesses of the Holocaust. This is a horror that Tacitus himself would hardly have advocated, but it goes to show how a few casual remarks in an ancient book can be turned into the justification for all manner of abuses.

Mussolini's version of Fascism did not involve such a sinister racialist agenda; however his expansionist policies, as with Hitler, did involve a certain rationale of justification from the past. Since the Roman Empire had been a wonderful thing, it was time to reinvent it and reclaim all those territories to the south. Even the word 'Fascist' was derived from the Roman word *fasces*, the bundle of sticks which symbolised strength through unity. Mussolini managed to ignore the fact that the Romans spent a lot of time and energy in fighting each other, also that the imperial family was riddled with vice and corruption. But then, as with Himmler, history has to be quoted selectively to validate one's propaganda. All this goes to illustrate the fact that continuity from the past is very important, especially for what might appear to be a new idea.

Two examples of continuity in action

A visit to Dresden reveals two buildings which have arisen from the destruction of February 1945: the Frauenkirche and the Synagogue; both in their own way exemplify continuity which implies completion.

The Frauenkirche remained as a ruin all through the Communist era but at the Fall of the Berlin Wall, a new initiative arose, connected with the peace movement, to rebuild and reproduce faithfully the original structure. This has been brilliantly done, albeit with a few concessions to modern ideas on safety. It is a subtle blend of the old and the new. Large portions of the original masonry, completely blackened, were used along with new material. The cross on the top of the dome is a gift from England, but the original one is preserved inside. One bell, dating from 1518, which escaped destruction, was rehung along with the seven new ones. The cross of nails, linking the church to Coventry Cathedral, is on the altar. Underneath in the crypt are rooms dedicated to prayer and memorials. It is a brilliant reproduction with careful use of certain original features worked in. The theology of continuity with the past is clearly the basis of it, and yet it points forward to completion and fulfilment, for the church has become a symbol for world peace and understanding. This is the very opposite of what the Third Reich stood for.

The Synagogue, which also had to wait for the fall of Communism, is another inspired but very different reconstruction. There was nothing left of the old Semper building. A larger plot of land which included the original Semper outline was obtained. Now it includes two modern buildings: a community hall with all amenities provided. The actual synagogue itself is an attempt at mimicking the Temple in Jerusalem: the base conforms to the plot of land but the top conforms to the line of the Semper building; this means that the building is skewed from top to bottom by about 10 degrees. There is much symbolism in this, even if it does look rather strange. Inside it is a 'veil', a massive curtain of interwoven metal wire which is partly translucent and very cleverly done, a masterpiece of art and inspiration. There are certain surviving items from the old synagogue: the star of David which was on one of the domes; the *ampel* which would hold a light; also the scrolls from the Genizah. In this wonderful example of resurgent Judaism, we see a new initiative and courageous realisation of the future combined with elements of continuity not just from the Semper era but relating to the roots of Judaism in the land of Israel. We cannot condone the antics of the Third Reich; all the same, the effect of the Holocaust has been to revitalise and stimulate the Jews into a new future and relevance to the world which might never have come about otherwise. Such is the paradox of persecution. From these two examples we can see the importance of continuity as an aspect of completion, in religious thinking, and theology in general.

The old and the new in paradox

The theology of continuity can now be seen as an important element in virtually every permutation of faith. It is an aspect of completion and fulfilment. It can be seen as completion from the past. The future has no meaning unless it is guided by the past. But the paradox now emerges that the past cannot always be the trump card in validating the present: there is a strong sense in which we need to face up to the present and the future with courage and determination to find new ways forward. It must be clear to most rational people that the vast array of religions and their associated splinter groups is some sort of lunacy. The trend now is for 'One World': the world needs unity. That unity needs to be on varying levels: political, cultural, moral. The world is too small for different sets of values to be in operation in different corners. The threats to our continuation are several: the nuclear threat; the threat of economic collapse; the threat from terrorism; climate change – these are just a sample. It is an urgent matter now for 'nation to speak peace unto nation'.

The relationship between 'old' and 'new' in theology is a subtle one. In one sense there are no new ideas in theology (or philosophy for that matter). My overview of the ancient mystery religions and of recent splinter group ideas simply underlines that. All we have is circulating ideas which reappear with slight alterations of phraseology. But what is the real difference between old and new? It is seen in the relationship between the Old and the New Testament, a relationship which is not confined to the Bible, but remains as a tension or dilemma seen in many religions. The 'old' is essentially about gaining merit, buying favour with someone, whether it be God or the government or just other people. The 'new' is essentially the opposite: God's free love for the human race. Even so it is a subtle adaptation of the 'old'. The two interrelate with one another: one is the seedbed, the other is the flower. One cannot be dispensed with without undermining the other. It is a profound paradox in the human soul. This was what the Messiah Jesus came to show to humanity; that does not mean that everyone fully understands it. Many do not. But we all know the dilemma going on between justice and mercy. On the one hand, things that have gone wrong must be put right; on the other hand humanity is incapable of righting all wrongs: it requires the loving intervention of mercy from the Eternal. This matter presupposes that there is a balance going on between the two. Also, implicit is the expectation that all will be corrected and resolved in the future and this is where completion, fulfilment, which includes continuity, become relevant.

There is no suggestion here that we should all embark on some sort of mean between extremes of religion, a sort of syncretistic mush which means nothing. It is a sound principle that every human should be allowed to believe what appears to him to be true. But at the same time, he must realise that another person is likely to have a different belief which he thinks is the truth. Time and again we have seen that the resort to violence or intolerance does not alter anything: it may appear so in the short term, but the theology of balance is an important one. Somehow, mysteriously, a reaction sets in and we are back to the original situation.

Still less is there any intention here of justifying or enlarging upon the vast array of differing ideas in theology. It would be quite easy to manufacture another theory or sect based on the theology of paradox, or even the theology of balance. We have no need for any fresh ideas on the theology of completion; we already have one major religion doing just that: it is called Christianity. There is no claim in this book to inventing any new theology. Very far from it. The theology of balance is only an offspin from what everyone assumes about nature: that there is balance at work – and that applies in other areas such as politics and religion. The theology of paradox has been with us as long as mankind has speculated on the teasing problem of Theodicy; what has been missing has been the actual use of the word 'paradox' itself. The word has been with us since ancient Greece, but its application to theology is a relatively recent realisation. It would be so tempting to invent a 'new' religion based on paradox, but that would be yet another nonsense.

The purpose of this work is to show that all theological ideas and religious practices can be seen from a certain angle which indicates a latent unity between faiths of all kinds. This is emphatically not saying that 'all religions are really the same' (as some might say): what it is saying is that the same basic, instinctual needs in human nature are the same, regardless of race, culture and historical developments. What are those needs? We can make a list and see how they relate to matters raised so far.

The nagging question for everyone is, 'What happens when we die?' All manner of theories, dogmas and speculations have emerged from this. In one sense we are all in denial of death; on the other hand we are fascinated by it. All manner of rituals, procedures and funerary rites have been developed but none of this takes away the fear and uncertainty of the final adventure. We all like to think we will never die: life continues in another dimension in another world. Life is precious, even if it is hard. It is an open house for wishful thinking.

By the same token, birth and the major stages of life also fascinate people. Rites of passage are noted in every known culture. Life has to have some sort of shape or meaning. And so often we note the unspoken assumption (sometimes explicit) that for life to be engendered there has to be death, and vice versa. From this we see the fundamental urge for sacrifice.

Coexisting with this is the assumption of justice: that life should be fair and things should be evenly balanced. When this balance is disturbed it raises the painful question of Theodicy: 'Why does the innocent have to suffer?' and vice versa. There are various attempts at answering this conundrum, none of them totally convincing; no one really has the answer in spite of all the philosophising over the history of humanity.

Another important urge is to be reassured of security. Will there be enough food to carry us through? What if the harvest fails? What if there is a natural disaster? What if I can't have children who will carry my memory forward into the future? Precautions have to be taken to reassure ourselves about the future; complacency is asking for trouble.

This brings us to considering the future. If there was a beginning, somewhere in the past, there must therefore be an end. This explains all the mythology and eschatology of the human speculation. Life is seen as shaped: this explains all the calendar calculations and the mathematics that flow from them. There is an element of predictability in life when we are aware of the cyclic nature of many aspects of life.

This inevitably raises the question of predestination and the antithesis of it, free will. This is another nagging problem ongoing from earliest times. Again, no one has the final answer to it and yet there is a fascination about this paradox. It is very much linked to mythology and eschatology; it is the same dilemma but in a slightly demythologised form.

And finally there is the overwhelming question: if there is a Great Spirit (called God by some people), what does he expect from us? Does he expect certain conduct, moral or ritual? How does one find out about his intentions? How do we contact him? How do we know what his intentions are towards us, if any?

An atheist might claim that all this is irrational fears, superstition decorated with wishful thinking. But for those who have an awareness of God in some shape or mode, the answer is again supplied by that telling quotation from Ecclesiastes: 'God has put eternity into man's mind and yet so that he cannot find out what God has done from the beginning to the end.' In other words, put in today's parlance, 'God placed certain instinctive reactions in the human mind, relating to life and its meaning: and yet we cannot define God or pin him down to anything certain'. Of course this is a circular argument: but then everything in these matters is a circular argument. What is required from the start is that basic 'chip' of faith. And that is the basic requirement for making a start on any religion of any kind, including the modern secular ones.

This book has attempted to explore all these matters raised above. It is not that a new dogma is about to emerge from it; on the contrary it has raised a number of questions which thinking people could consider. The world is tired of repetitious dogma; if the Nazis and the Communists achieved anything, they made us suspicious of cheap indoctrination. But the main question is: how does each religion tackle these matters fundamental to human nature? We have seen that in many ways they do just that. We have also seen in what ways they fall short. Whether this is in theory or in practice (which may be a distortion of theory) will vary enormously. But we can see that every theory, whether of the main religions or of the splinter groups with a private agenda, makes some sort of attempt at these basic questions. Is there an answer to all this? A solution?

The answer lies in understanding the ministry of Jesus the true Messiah. This work makes no apology for this claim. In many places, it has been shown that the real completion, fulfilment and the answer to life's deepest dilemmas is found in what Jesus came to teach and demonstrate. To take each element in order, Jesus himself accepted death but showed us that death is not the end: there is Resurrection, and a glorious one too. Speculations about the next world are idle: the truth is that life is precious but is also the gift of God and is in his hands. Jesus himself went through the rites of passage of a normal human life. In the end he gave his life for the salvation of the world, as a sacrifice which produced new life which is available for all. Jesus came over as the final lawgiver, bringing the assumption of justice to a climax. Paradoxically he is far more merciful than anyone would have expected. He loved everyone, even the sinners. With regard to Theodicy, he was the innocent who voluntarily suffered. But his suffering was not purposeless: it brought in a new relationship between the Eternal and humanity. And what of security? He was the one who told people to stop worrying about the future and what might go wrong. The future is very firmly in the hands of the Eternal. He showed that God feeds us in so many ways, but that does require a generous element of faith on our part.

Jesus completes the mythology of creation and human origins: also points forward to the end: 'I am Alpha and Omega,' the beginning and the end, is a massive claim, but for those who can understand it, it is obvious. He was also aware of timings and the appropriate moment for the plan of his life. He knew it was all mapped out by the Eternal: even so there was freedom of action, choices to be made between right and wrong. And the final question, 'Is there a God and how does he relate to us?' Jesus assures us that he is the final and ultimate channel of communication between two worlds. 'He who has seen me has seen the Father.' There is enough in the Gospels to offer us a deep faith which can cope with all the deep dilemmas and fears of life. The rest of the New Testament simply elaborates on it. At the heart of it is the cross, the way of Calvary. This is the bit that people find hard, if not unacceptable. But to quote Beethoven, 'difficult is closer to the truth'.

From this one might wonder why the whole world has not been scooped up into Christianity; it certainly looked as if it would be so in the early years. But wherein lies the problem? The mistake has been to subject the life of Jesus, the mystery of the Incarnation, the Trinity and the Atonement, to name but a few, to human canons of rationality, or human logic. People have been unable to cope with divine logic, and this is quite understandable, and have assumed that human logic can explain away all the aspects of Christ's ministry. This has been the big mistake: it has produced endless controversies, entrenched positions, deadlock, and has led to violence. The many divisions, sects and splinter groups in the Christian orbit have simply cancelled each other out and confused those who were considering making a commitment of faith. The true focus of the faith of Jesus is not some sort of rationality, theory or dogma: it is knowing him as a living person in one's own life. To know him is to love him; to love him removes all arguments, fears and vain rationalities. Sadly, all too often, the Churches have managed to lose sight of this. There has been wealth, power politics, exploitation, legalistic bureaucracy working its way in, even violence. None of this was on Jesus' agenda. In a sense the Jehovah's Witnesses are right in that the Churches have fallen short of Christ's example, but the hypocrisy comes in assuming that one can invent a Church free from corruption. Sadly, every little band of hope has some kind of human failing interwoven with the fabric.

But paradoxically, the whole world has come to the point where Christ's values have come to prominence worldwide. That does not mean that the majority of people are signed-up members of one Church or another. What it does mean is that the basics of what Jesus taught and demonstrated are understood and implemented by the vast majority of countries. We have only to consider that international travel has forced every country into a code of safety, courtesy and hospitality. It means that the sanctity of life, of property and of personal integrity are understood everywhere. But the main contributor of this has been the excesses of the Second World War. The foundation of the United Nations, which is essentially based on Christian values, was seen as urgent. Peace was seen as vital to the future of the world, but not peace at any price. Consideration for all people: international aid, caring for all people even if they might be seen as one's 'enemy'. Even the dominant calendar, which is Judeao-Christian in its fabrication, governs virtually every calculation in the world now. In a sense, the humble carpenter from Nazareth is calling the trumps everywhere. Violence is now right out of fashion: aggression is bad news. Human rights, democracy and consideration for the feelings of others is the dominant trend. Equality for gender, race and many other aspects is now in the ascendency. But what has it taken to bring us to this point after 2000 years? It took an evil crackpot called Adolf Hitler to force most reasonable people to see the lunacy of prejudice, discrimination and aggression. Are we seeing in our own times the words of Isaiah – 'for the earth shall be full of the knowledge of God as the waters cover the sea' – coming to fulfilment? One could say that there are still people like Saddam Hussein and Muammar Gaddafi who are only moderated versions of Hitler; even so, that sort of thing is generally out of favour and people are taking steps to resolve the matter. The world knows it is desperately in need of unity; that unity can and should be based on the values of Jesus Christ. It is certainly heading in that direction.

A difficulty with this is the modern phenomenon of international terrorism. It is unlikely that it will destroy or even check the resolution of the United Nations. In a sense, every time there is an outrage, it serves to remind us of the importance of pursuing world peace. The 9/11 outrage, horrific as it was, served as a catalyst for a root-and-branch policy of dispatching world terrorism. The world has grown tired of these crazy and iniquitous attempts at blackmailing reasonable people. Sadly, force has to be used to apprehend the culprits, but not gratuitous force, or unprincipled force. It may be that terrorism may be with us for a long time: in a sense there has to be violence in order that the importance of peace may be seen.

21

Concluding Remarks

It can now be seen that virtually every aspect of theological thought, of whatever religion, involves paradoxes of one kind or another. This is far from being an entirely new idea. The potential for seeing paradox in so many matters has been present all along. It is the realisation of paradox that has been sadly lacking. Many people have taken the contradictions in theology to be indications of confusion, vague faith. This need not happen, for many of the contradictions are in fact profound paradoxes. These occur at all levels: the major ones are creation out of nothing, the Incarnation, Trinity and Atonement. Free will and predestination seem never to have been seen as a paradox; now they can be. The minor paradoxes sometimes circulate within the major ones: sometimes they are part of the structure of the teachings of Jesus; sometimes they help us to cope with the difficult bits in the Scriptures. It is a mistake to take a negative view of paradox as Hepburn does (see chapter 1). He has not appreciated the positive side of it, the contribution it makes to our understanding of God.

A useful analogy could be as follows: in nature there is a thing called a vortex, a whirlpool. This is essential for heavier-than-air flight (powered or not). The wing of the aeroplane is so shaped that when the aeroplane is pulled along, the wind produces vortices. The purpose of this is to produce lift. But the vortex in itself is a self-contradictory thing: the wind goes round in circles, contradicting itself. The faster it goes, the more lift it produces. Without this fact, aeroplanes would never manage to take off. Now, to push the analogy further, if there were no paradoxes in theology, the whole subject would never get off the ground. It would be a matter-of-fact, mundane, list of trite remarks. Too many 'isms' work like that: all far too logical, obvious and banal. But theology is much more than that: it deals with another dimension, that of the divine, which is essentially a contradiction of human life. Because of this major paradox, and all the minor ones too, we are lifted from the obvious to the mysterious; from the purely physical and functional to the spiritual and inspirational; from the purely descriptive to the interpretative. Paradox is not just an inconvenience: it is essential for the soul of mankind.

To push the analogy even further, a whirlpool, which is a vortex going down in water, has the opposite effect: it drags one down. So too in the life of the Spirit: there are the possibilities of being sucked into wickedness, despair and loss of faith. This may be politically wrong in today's thinking! Even so, depression, despair and moral failure very often are some sort of vicious circle which is very difficult to break out of unless one is prepared to accept divine assistance.

The related matter of balance in theology is also important. It is a natural aspect of paradox, for two opposing ideas balance one another out across a fulcrum. So we see the contrast between plain, simple and basic religion as opposed to elaborate, fancy and highly theorised religion. This sort of contrast appears in all kinds of aspects of theology, not least in the ministry of Jesus himself: the Synoptic Gospels offer a basic, human and public view of Jesus: St John offers the exalted, heavenly, messianic view of him. Like all generalisations, this is very much an oversimplification, but the contrast between the two views produces a three-dimensional (3D) effect of Jesus. It is to no purpose to say that one view is right and the other wrong. Saying that destroys the sense of balance and loses the inherent paradoxes. On a larger scale we can see there is balance between the major religions of the world. For some, God is distant, unapproachable and transcendent: this would be Buddhism, Hinduism and much of Eastern thinking. For others, God is imminent, near to the believing soul and active in daily affairs: this would be Christianity, Judaism and Islam. It is to no purpose to condemn the one approach and applaud the other; both aspects of the matter are correct in their own way and form a stunning paradox. When we learn to see the truth on both sides of the balance, then we shall be coming close to understanding the deep realities of divine nature and the spiritual needs of humanity. The big mistake is to fasten on to just one or two aspects of theology, give them far too much emphasis, and ignore other aspects of these matters. This is the root cause of all the heresies of the past. Avoiding heresy involves taking all aspects of faith in due measure and balance. That is the way forward for understanding between peoples of all manner of religions. It is to no purpose to say that all religions are essentially the same (a view often expressed by those who have little experience of these matters): it is true that many of the same essential needs in human nature are served by different religions, but that is not saying the same thing at all.

One of the basic factors in all religions is the need for completion or fulfilment. It is not always expressed in the same way. But we notice that the factor of prophecy is very often found in human thinking, and even more noticeably is messianism in its various forms, some fairly mild and others quite acute. All this indicates the realisation that this life is in need of amendment, correction and purification. No system on earth assumes that this life is perfect and there is nothing to look forward to or hope for. Admittedly, the idea of completion does not take the same form in every system, but there is the general assumption that there has to be something better somewhere in the future, either in this life but more likely in the next. This brings us back to the paradox of Theodicy. The theology of completion implies that somewhere in the great workings of things there will be a resolution, the answering of all questions, and all the impossible contradictions – that is, paradoxes – will be settled. To put it another way, we shall all come to appreciate the wonderful workings of the divine. This is something that we can only glimpse in the logic of this mortal life. To quote St Paul, we can only see things through a glass, darkly, at the moment: but we live in hope that all will come clear, and that completion will involve not just the resolution of all imponderable questions but also the removal of all distress and failure.

It may seem shocking to some to have it said that all theological ideas have a certain validity in their own way. When we talk about the balance of nature, we assume that every feature in the natural world has its part to play in the great workings of things. This is becoming increasingly apparent as scientific investigation reveals ever more intriguing aspects of the natural world. It would seem that everything has its part to play in some shape or form. This is one reason why the 'design' theory as a proof for the existence of God ought to be receiving more credibility in today's world. But the challenge here is for all of us, of no matter what religious persuasion, to consider the matter of balance with regard to theology. Has it occurred to people to see that paganism, shamanism, Humanism and atheism, to name but a few, all have their part to play? There is no need for anyone to go into a panic: it is not being maintained here that atheism, for instance, is correct. What is being said is that atheism has its part to play in the total picture of belief and religious practice.

Just as, for instance, a thunderstorm, a venomous snake and an earthquake are liable to induce fear, if not panic, and yet all the unpleasant aspects of nature are there for a purpose. That does not mean we should fly kites in thunderstorms, interfere with venomous snakes and try to induce earthquakes! We do not have to seek out trouble just for the sake of it. The same is true with religious expression: some of it is distinctly unpleasant, threatening and even evil. That does not mean we should deliberately seek out trouble, but we need to admit that difficult ideas have always been there and will continue to form a balance with all the pleasant, helpful and positive aspects of religion. For this we have Biblical support: Job, the good man, was tempted to deny God. In this account we see God and the powers of evil actually in some sort of collusion over Job's fate. The negative aspects of spirituality are just as real as the positive ones, and from that progress is made with human salvation. That does not mean that we should all go in for Satanism: on the contrary, the Bible instructs us to refrain from such things. Even so we need to realise that the powers of evil are just as much a spiritual reality as the powers of good. At this point, the theology of resolution comes into play, for there is the assurance that this situation will not prevail for ever, that in God's good time he will intervene and bring all things to a conclusion. Again there is Biblical support for this claim. If we look at the parable of the Wheat and the Tares, we are assured that there will come a consummation: good and evil will continue to interplay until the decisive moment in history comes and all will be resolved.

There is nothing new in this work, it has simply reviewed existing theological ideas and added nothing, nor subtracted anything. What is a slightly different departure is to see everything in a slightly different light, or from a new angle. The idea of paradox has been available since Ancient Greece, but has not been applied in a thoroughgoing fashion until now. It is hoped that this can be helpful for all those who find religious ideas confusing, contradictory and plain difficult to accept. Once one accepts that there are two systems of logic at work, the human and the divine, and that the two do not coincide at all well on most points, that is a starting point for seeing so many things in terms of paradox. That is actually the first and deepest paradox: that humanity, and the world of physical reality, are on a different dimension to the other world of spiritual reality. All the other paradoxes in theology spring forth quite naturally from that.

For those who cannot accept or cope with the thought of another world of divinity, one can say this. That it is one thing to explain things in terms of scientific description and physical processes; this is fair enough as far as it goes. But to try to deny that all these wonders have no deeper significance, meaning or long-term purpose is not really worthy of the human soul. Theology works on a different level; gone are the days when theology and cosmology were somehow confused and the one tried to contradict the other. Theology works on a different level as compared with the physical sciences. Theology is concerned with interpretation, not merely description. We might quote Sherlock Holmes when he teased poor Watson: 'You *see* but you don't *perceive*!' The scientists are there to see and describe things; the theologian and the philosopher are there to 'perceive' what is the significance of these wonders. We can also recall the words of Genesis 1:26: 'Let us make man in our own image.' This means that humanity has the authority and freedom to adapt, control and generally interfere with the processes of this world. An extension of that is that humanity has the faculty of judgement, making decisions. This is an attribute of God which has been handed down but which can be used or abused. For those who have discernment in such matters as the meaning of life, wisdom, beauty, ultimate truth, perfection, these are factors which cannot be sidestepped. An understanding of God in some form or permutation is obvious. In that respect the wisdom literature of the Bible is an obvious pointer to the reality of God. But for those who cannot see beyond merely 'seeing' the facts of the physical world, they may be content with this on an ephemeral basis, but the deeper realities of life and death are unavoidable in the long run. Like Yama, the god of the dead, who holds up the 'Wheel of Becoming' like a mirror so that we see what we really are, there comes a point when closing one's eyes to it cannot be kept up for ever. We have the freedom of judgement: why not judge wisely and accept that life is a mystery that can only be resolved in terms of the divine.

For those who wish to accept the concept of paradox and all its ramifications, there is this caution. There is no intention here of starting up another 'ism'. Down with the crank who wishes to start up the 'Latter Day Church of Paradoxism' or some such nonsense. There are too many 'isms' on the go already: half of them could usefully do a merger and simplify matters for us all. One of the unintended disasters at the Reformation was that Luther, with his challenge to the Church of Rome, had no intention of starting up a rival Church, but sadly, the challenge to authority gave leeway for all manner of splinter-group churches, the legacy of which we are still encumbered with to this day. But with this work, there is no challenge to any authority; no denial of any traditional teaching; no refusal to come to terms with any doctrine. The intention is entirely constructive. So many matters can be seen in a different light: that of paradox. This means that issues that have been a bone of contention, and the cause of so many rifts in the household of faith, could be and should be healed.

It only takes understanding and a willingness to see the elements of truth in another's opinion and the ability to accept each other's differences. Obviously, certain persons of an extreme mentality will register a deep shock on reading such matters, but it is urgent, in the state of the world today, for the sake of world peace, that we all need to stop and think before flying to extremes of opinion and action. This is not to say that we should all abandon our ideas and wallow in some sort of confused average of syncretistic vagueness. We can retain our traditions and our differing understandings of God, but there is no need to come to blows over it. The matter is urgent: another conflict like the Second World War could spell doom for global civilisation or indeed life itself on this planet. The tools are to hand for achieving understanding. The key to it is to allow the concept of paradox to apply the bandage to all our wounds.

An attempt at a list of paradoxes: probably not exhaustive

It could be helpful to make a list of the paradoxes as discovered in this work. Some are major ones and others are subsidiary and dependent on the major ones. A few words as to their significance can also be offered, but as with every paradox there is that element of inexplicability and mystery. That goes a long way to assure us that it is of divine devising, not of human rationality.

1. Creation out of nothing: the world of the spirit produces something physical. This is impossible for the human mind to contemplate. It has to be seen through the metaphor of a Creator God.
2. The question of Theodicy: how can a perfect divine spirit produce or permit an imperfect world? The tension between these two statements produces all manner of rationalisations, none of which entirely answer the question.
3. The question of contact between the world of the spirit and of the flesh. The use of shaman, prophet, priest, king, sacred writings are all seen as attempts to bridge the gap, but none are totally convincing or all-embracing.
4. Free will and predestination is a dilemma which has always haunted the human soul. There is no answer to it unless we see it as a profound paradox.
5. Allied to this is the dilemma over the basic innocence of humanity, and basic corruption.
6. Allied to this is the tension over works righteousness and 'meritology' versus salvation by grace. This is essentially the difference between the Old and the New Testament. Both have their place in the spiritual needs of humanity.
7. The coming of the Messiah in terms of the Incarnation. The impossibility of the Eternal God coming as a human being: but without this, there is no final and conclusive representation of man to God or God to man.
8. The implication of Incarnation is that the Messiah was with God from eternity and always was, is and will be. How he came to earth and yet still remained with the Eternal God is a paradox well beyond human rationality.
9. How can a God suffer and die? Impossible: and yet this was an essential element in the Messiah's ministry.
10. How can a dead man be raised in the Resurrection? Again this is beyond our powers of comprehension, and yet the mystery of the death and Resurrection shows that love is stronger than hate, good will always prevail over evil. Out of complete failure comes absolute triumph.
11. The implication of the Ascension is that the Messiah being with the Eternal God means that within the godhead, there is an understanding of what it is like to be human, to suffer, to fail, to be rejected. God understands our weaknesses.

12. The problem of particularity points out that while the Messiah came at a particular time in history and place in geography, the ramifications of his ministry are relevant to all of the human race and, more than that, to the whole relationship between the Creator and his Creation. The Messiah's ministry brought about a 'sea change' in the whole universe: the change from the Old to the New Testament.
13. The Incarnation implies the Trinity. How can God be three as well as one? This cannot be explained in terms of mathematics or any other human discipline. But the spirit of God was active with the Eternal from the beginning, right through human history, all through the ministry of the Messiah, and then into the workings of the Church and world history into modern times. How the three elements interact or relate is beyond us to define, but it is a stunning three-way paradox, sadly one of the most badly understood of all.
14. But the understanding of God as Trinity implies that the work of the Messiah is not just confined to history and geography. It is of eternal significance: it extends forwards and backwards in time, and sideways, to include all peoples and aspects of the created universe.
15. The Atonement, with its three main theories, is also a three-way paradox. None of the three theories hold the complete truth in itself, and yet put together, gems of truth emerge and reassure us that there is ultimately divine forgiveness.
16. There is the tension between trying to define God and being unable to do so. The paradox is that on the one hand, idolatry is wrong and completely foolish; on the other hand, God provides us with an 'icon' of himself in the Messiah.
17. Following on from this, the Messiah provides us with the completion of the definition of God – 'I am that I am' – and talks about God's rule in terms of parables and allegories. God can be defined and yet he cannot. The definition is provided by him, not us. It has to be in our terms of vocabulary and metaphor.
18. The parables display various subsidiary paradoxes: the interim period, the tension between justice and mercy, the fact that the people of God rejected the Son of God, the issue of wealth versus poverty; on two different levels, the secrecy versus the fame of the Kingdom and others.

19. The issue of literalism versus imagery. This involves mythology and historical account, and how they are cleverly interwoven.
20. The miracles: how on the one hand there is the tendency to find a rational explanation, juxtaposed with the inexplicable element that God can, and does, apply different procedures as and when he decides.
21. There is the tension between mysticism and the philosophical mentality of proving God's existence. Both are essentially underpinned by some sort of emotional response and yet the two results are the exact opposite.
22. With calendars and any calculation of time, there is the implication that history is real. Even so we know that time and dates are only a human construct. God is above and beyond all human calculations; even so he allows himself to become enmeshed in it, in his appearance on earth.
23. Ritual, symbolism and sacramentalism provide another paradox, for eternal truths and spiritual enhancement can be provided through ordinary physical vehicles such as bread and wine.
24. The tension between belief and disbelief is also an important paradox. It would seem that the one requires the other and vice versa. It is only through the interplay and contradiction of the two that the depth of spiritual realities can be experienced.
25. Related to this is the tension between 'descent' and 'design' (to use Dawkins's phrasing). Although this is essentially a scientific dilemma, it is a subset of free will and predestination. It also serves to show that science is underpinned by theology.
26. In religion there is always the tension between the old and the new, not just in terms of patterns of worship but also in ways of expressing the basics of teaching. Continuity is important; innovation is important. It is a spin-off from the tension between the Old and the New Testaments.
27. The understanding of God as, firstly, transcendental and beyond the parameters of physical existence; and secondly, as imminent, closer to the human soul than anyone can understand, crosses the divide not just between elements in the Bible, but also between various major world religions.

Doubtless many more paradoxes could be found to add to this list. It is important to admit that life is a whole procession of paradoxes. For those who have faith and an awareness of spiritual values, this list will make a lot of sense. For those who claim to have no such awareness, life is still a paradox, and the exploits of the scientists simply underline this. They too have their dilemmas!

But the desperate truth is still unavoidable. While there is yet time to come to our senses in this world, regardless of whether we are believers or not, let us grasp the moment. The key to it is repentance: a willingness to admit to our inadequacies, follies and sometimes outright wickedness. The truth does not lie in force, intolerance, hatred and conflict; the truth does lie in humility, acceptance and caring for all. These are values that the Messiah came to show us. He showed us a supreme example of love, to the extent of giving his very self without reservation. It matters very little what theory of incarnation we hold, or what theology of God, or indeed any 'ism'. The truth is a real, living person who transcends all the crazy theorisings of neurotic humanity. He carries us over the turmoil of our broken world and offers us peace. Now is the time to take him seriously.

Subject Index

Index of Biblical References, Excluding the Gospels

Index of Gospel references